Capital Acquisitions Tax Consolidation Act 2003

&

Stamp Duties Consolidation Act 1999

Finance Act 2015

Capital Acquisitions Tax Consolidation Act 2003

&

Stamp Duties Consolidation Act 1999

Finance Act 2015

Editor Kimberley Rowan

General Editor Brian Keegan

Chartered Accountants Ireland

Published by
Chartered Accountants Ireland
Chartered Accountants House
47-49 Pearse Street
Dublin 2
www.charteredaccountants.ie

ISBN: 978-1-910374-49-8

Printed and bound by CPI Group (UK) Ltd, Croydon, CR0 4YY

TABLE OF CONTENTS

CAPITAL ACQUISITIONS TAX CONSOLIDATION ACT 2003

PART 1
PRELIMINARY

PART 2
GIFT TAX

PART 3
INHERITANCE TAX

CHAPTER 1
General

CHAPTER 2
Initial Levy on Discretionary Trusts

CHAPTER 3
Annual Levy on Discretionary Trusts

PART 4

VALUE OF PROPERTY FOR TAX

PART 5

PROVISIONS RELATING TO GIFTS AND INHERITANCES

PART 6

RETURNS AND ASSESSMENTS

PART 7

PAYMENT AND RECOVERY OF TAX, INTEREST AND PENALTIES

PART 8

APPEALS

PART 9

EXEMPTIONS

PART 10
RELIEFS

CHAPTER 1
Agricultural Relief

CHAPTER 2
Business Relief

CHAPTER 2A
Clawback of Agricultural Relief or Business Relief: Development Land

CHAPTER 3
Miscellaneous Reliefs

PART 11
MISCELLANEOUS

PART 12
REPEALS, ETC.

STAMP DUTIES CONSOLIDATION ACT 1999

PART 1
INTERPRETATION

PART 2
CHARGING AND STAMPING OF INSTRUMENTS

PART 3

VALUATION

PART 4

ADJUDICATION AND APPEALS

PART 5

PROVISIONS APPLICABLE TO PARTICULAR INSTRUMENTS

CHAPTER 1

Bills of Exchange and Promissory Notes

PART 7
EXEMPTIONS AND RELIEFS FROM STAMP DUTY

CHAPTER 1
Instruments Which must be Presented to the Commissioners for Adjudication in Order to Obtain Exemption or Relief

CHAPTER 2
Other Instruments

PART 8
COMPANIES CAPITAL DUTY

PART 9
LEVIES

PART 10
ENFORCEMENT

PART 11
MANAGEMENT PROVISIONS

CHAPTER 1
Interpretation, Application and Care and Management

CHAPTER 2
Mode of Recovering Money Received for Duty

CHAPTER 3
Offences

CHAPTER 4
SALE OF STAMPS

CHAPTER 5
ALLOWANCE FOR SPOILED OR MISUSED STAMPS

CHAPTER 6
MISCELLANEOUS

CHAPTER 7
TIME LIMIT FOR REPAYMENT OF STAMP DUTY, INTEREST ON REPAYMENT AND TIME LIMITS FOR ENQUIRIES AND ASSESSMENTS

CHAPTER 8
CALCULATION OF INTEREST ON UNPAID DUTY AND OTHER AMOUNTS

PART 12
REPEALS, ETC.

Capital Acquisitions Tax Consolidation Act 2003

Number 1 of 2003

CAPITAL ACQUISITIONS TAX CONSOLIDATION ACT 2003

AN ACT TO CONSOLIDATE ENACTMENTS RELATING TO CAPITAL ACQUISITIONS TAX.

[*21st February* 2003]

BE IT ENACTED BY THE OIREACHTAS AS FOLLOWS:

PART 1

Preliminary

1 Short title

This Act may be cited as the Capital Acquisitions Tax Consolidation Act 2003.

2 General interpretation

[CATA 1976 s2]

(1) In this Act, unless the context otherwise requires—

"*absolute interest*", in relation to property, includes the interest of a person who has a general power of appointment over the property;

"*accountable person*" means a person who is accountable for the payment of tax by virtue of *section 45* ;

"*benefit*" includes any estate, interest, income or right;

"*child*" includes—

(a) a stepchild;

[(b) a child who is adopted under an adoption order within the meaning of *section 3(1)* of the Adoption Act 2010 or the subject of an intercountry adoption effected outside the State and recognised under that Act;][1]

["*child of the civil partner*" in relation to an individual, means a child of the individual's civil partner who was born before the registration of their civil partnership or during their civil partnership;

"*civil partner*" means a civil partner within the meaning of the Civil Partnership and Certain Rights and Obligations of Cohabitants Act 2010;

"*civil partnership*" means—

(a) a civil partnership registration referred to in section 3(*a*) of the Civil Partnership and Certain Rights and Obligations of Cohabitants Act 2010, or

(b) a legal relationship referred to in section 3(*b*) of that Act;][2]

"*Collector*" means the Collector-General appointed under section 851 of the Taxes Consolidation Act 1997;

"*Commissioners*" means the Revenue Commissioners;

"*date of the disposition*" means—

(a) in the case of a will, the date of the testator's death,

(b) in the case of an intestacy or a partial intestacy, the date of death of the intestate,

(c) in the case of a benefit under Part IX or section 56 of the Succession Act 1965, the date of death of the relevant testator or other deceased person, and correspondingly in the case of an analogous benefit under the law of another territory,

(d) in the case of a disposition which consists of the failure to exercise a right or a power, the date of the latest time when the disponer could have exercised the right or the power if that disponer were *sui juris* and not under any physical disability, and

(e) in any other case, the date on which the act (or where more than one act is involved, the last act) of the disponer was done by which that disponer provided or bound that disponer to provide the property comprised in the disposition;

"*date of the gift*" means the date of the happening of the event on which the donee, or any person in right of the donee or on that donee's behalf, becomes beneficially entitled in possession to the benefit, and a reference to the time when a gift is taken is construed as a reference to the date of the gift;

"*date of the inheritance*" means—

(a) in the case where the successor or any person in right of the successor or on that successor's behalf becomes entitled in possession to the benefit on the happening of any such event as is referred to in *section 3(2)*, the date of the event,

(b) in the case of a gift which becomes an inheritance by reason of its being taken under a disposition where the date of the disposition is within 2 years prior to the death of the disponer, the date which would have been the date of the gift if the entitlement were a gift, and

(c) in any other case, the date of the latest death which had to occur for the successor, or any person in right of the successor or on that successor's behalf, to become beneficially entitled in possession to the benefit,

and a reference to the time when an inheritance is taken is construed as a reference to the date of the inheritance;

["*decree of dissolution*" means a decree under section 110 of the Civil Partnership and Certain Rights and Obligations of Cohabitants Act 2010;][3]

"*discretionary trust*" means any trust whereby, or by virtue or in consequence of which—

(a) property is held on trust to accumulate the income or part of the income of the property, or

(b) property (other than property to which for the time being a person is beneficially entitled for an interest in possession) is held on trust to apply, or with a power to apply, the income or capital or part of the income or capital of the property for the benefit of any person or persons or of any one or more of a number or of a class of persons whether at the discretion of trustees or any other person and notwithstanding that there may be a power to accumulate all or any part of the income;

"*disponer*", in relation to a disposition, means the person who, for the purpose of the disposition, directly or indirectly provided the property comprised in the disposition, and in any case where more than one person provided the property each is deemed to be the disponer to the extent that that disponer so provided the property; and for the purposes of this definition—

(a) the testator is the disponer in the case of a disposition referred to in *paragraph (k)* of the definition of "*disposition*",

(b) the intestate is the disponer in the case of a disposition referred to in *paragraph (l)* of that definition,

(c) the deceased person referred to in *paragraph (m)* of that definition is the disponer in the case of a disposition referred to in that paragraph, and

(d) a person who has made with any other person a reciprocal arrangement by which that other person provided property comprised in the disposition is deemed to have provided that property;

"*disposition*" includes—

(a) any act or omission by a person as a result of which the value of that person's estate immediately after the act or omission is less than it would be but for the act or omission,

(b) any trust, covenant, agreement or arrangement, whether made by a single operation or by associated operations,

(c) the creation of a debt or other right enforceable against the disponer personally or against any estate or interest that disponer may have in property,

(d) the payment of money,

(e) the allotment of shares in a company,

(f) the grant or the creation of any benefit,

(g) the grant or the creation of any lease, mortgage, charge, licence, option, power, partnership or joint tenancy or other estate or interest in or over any property,

(h) the release, forfeiture, surrender or abandonment of any debt or benefit, or the failure to exercise a right, and, for the purpose of this paragraph, a debt or benefit is deemed to have been released when it has become unenforceable by action through lapse of time (except to the extent that it is recovered subsequent to its becoming so unenforceable),

(i) the exercise of a general power of appointment in favour of any person other than the holder of the power,

(j) a *donatio mortis causa*,

(k) a will or other testamentary disposition,

(l) an intestacy, whether total or partial,

(m) [the payment of a share as a legal right under Part IX of the Succession Act 1965, to a deceased person's spouse or civil partner, or the making of provision for a widow, surviving civil partner or child of a deceased person under section 56 or section 117 of the Succession Act 1965, or an analogous share or provision paid or made on the death of a deceased person to or for the benefit of any person under the law of another territory,][4] and

(n) a resolution passed by a company which is deemed by *subsection (3)* to be a disposition;

"*donee*" means a person who takes a gift;

"*entitled in possession*" means having a present right to the enjoyment of property as opposed to having a future such right, and without prejudice to the generality of the foregoing a person is also, for the purposes of this Act, deemed to be entitled in possession to an interest or share in a partnership, joint tenancy or estate of a deceased person, in which that person is a partner, joint tenant or beneficiary, as the case may be, but that person is not deemed to be entitled in possession to an interest in expectancy until an event happens whereby this interest ceases to be an interest in expectancy;

"*general power of appointment*" includes every power, right, or authority whether exercisable only by will or otherwise which would enable the holder of such power, right, or authority to appoint or dispose of property to whoever the holder thinks fit or to obtain such power, right or authority, but exclusive of any power exercisable solely in a fiduciary capacity under a disposition not made by the holder, [...][5] or as mortgagee;

"*gift*" means a gift which a person is by this Act deemed to take;

["*the Income Tax Acts*" has the meaning assigned to it by section 2 of the Taxes Consolidation Act 1997;][6]

"*inheritance*" means an inheritance which a person is by this Act deemed to take;

"*interest in expectancy*" includes an estate in remainder or reversion and every other future interest, whether vested or contingent, but does not include a reversion expectant on the determination of a lease;

"*limited interest*" means—

(a) an interest (other than a leasehold interest) for the duration of a life or lives or for a period certain, or

(b) any other interest which is not an absolute interest;

['*local authority*' means a local authority for the purposes of the Local Government Act 2001 (as amended by the *Local Government Reform Act 2014*) and includes a body established under the Local Government Services (Corporate Bodies) Act 1971;][7]

"*market value*", in relation to property, means the market value of that property ascertained in accordance with *sections 26* and *27*;

"*minor child*" means a child who has not attained the age of 18 years and is not and has not been married;

"*personal property*" means any property other than real property;

"*personal representative*" means the executor or administrator for the time being of a deceased person and includes—

(a) any person who takes possession of or intermeddles with the property of a deceased person,

(b) any person having, in relation to the deceased person, under the law of another country, any functions corresponding to the functions, for administration purposes under the law of the State, of an executor or administrator;

"*property*" includes rights and interests of any description;

"*real property*" means real and chattel real property;

"*regulations*" means regulations made under *section 116*;

"*relative*" means a relative within the meaning of *subsection (4)*;

"*return*" means such a return as is referred to in *section 46*;

"*share*", in relation to a company, includes any interest whatever in the company which is analogous to a share in the company, and "shareholder" shall be construed accordingly;

"*special power of appointment*" means a power of appointment which is not a general power of appointment;

"*successor*" means a person who takes an inheritance;

["*surviving civil partner*", in relation to 2 individuals who were civil partners of each other until the death of one of them, means the civil partner other than the civil partner who died;][8]

"*tax*" means any tax chargeable under this Act;

["*the Tax Acts*" has the meaning assigned to it by [section 1(2)][9] of the Taxes Consolidation Act 1997;][10]

"*valuation date*" has the meaning assigned to it by *section 30*;

"*year of assessment*" has the meaning assigned to it by section 2 of the Taxes Consolidation Act 1997.

[(1A) For the purposes of the definition of '*discretionary trust*' in *subsection (1)*, any entity which is similar in its effect to a discretionary trust shall be treated as a discretionary trust irrespective of how it is described in the place where it is established.

(1B) Any reference in this Act to trustees in relation to a discretionary trust shall be deemed to include persons acting in a similar capacity to trustees in relation to an entity referred to in *subsection (1A)*.][11]

(2) For the purpose of the definition of "*general power of appointment*" contained in *subsection (1)*, a person is deemed to have a general power of appointment—

- (a) notwithstanding that the person is not *sui juris* or is under a physical disability,
- (b) over money which the person has a general power to charge on property, and
- (c) over property of which the person is tenant in tail in possession.

(3) For the purpose of the definition of "*disposition*" contained in *subsection (1)*, the passing by a company of a resolution which, by the extinguishment or alteration of the rights attaching to any share of the company, results, directly or indirectly, in the estate of any shareholder of the company being increased in value at the expense of the estate of any other shareholder, is deemed to be a disposition made by that other shareholder if that other shareholder could have prevented the passing of the resolution by voting against it or otherwise; and in this subsection, "*share*" includes a debenture and loan stock and "*shareholder*" includes a debenture holder and a holder of loan stock.

(4) For the purposes of this Act, the following persons and no other person are relatives of another person, that is—

- (a) the spouse of that other person,
- (b) the father, mother, and any child, uncle or aunt of that other person,
- (c) any child (other than that other person), and any child of a child, of any person who is by virtue of *paragraph (a)* or *(b)* a relative of that other person, and
- (d) the spouse of a person who is by virtue of *paragraph (b)* or *(c)* a relative of that other person,
- (e) the grandparent of that other person.

(5) For the purposes of this Act, the relationship between a child, adopted in the manner referred to in *paragraph (b)* of the definition of "*child*" contained in *subsection (1)*, and any other person, or between other persons, that would exist if such child had been born to the adoptor or adoptors in[...][12], is deemed to exist between such child and that other person or between those other persons, and the relationship of any such child and any person that existed prior to that child being so adopted is deemed to have ceased.

(6) For the purposes of this Act—

(a) a reference to a person being resident in the State on a particular date is construed as a reference to that person being resident in the State in the year of assessment in which that date falls (but, for those purposes, the provisions of Part 34 of the Taxes Consolidation Act 1997, relating to residence of individuals is not construed as requiring a year of assessment to have elapsed before a determination of whether or not a person is resident in the State on a date falling in that year may be made), and

(b) a reference to a person being ordinarily resident in the State on a particular date is construed as a reference to that person being ordinarily resident in the State in the year of assessment in which that date falls.

(7) In this Act, references to any enactment are, unless the context otherwise requires, construed as references to that enactment as amended or extended by any subsequent enactment.

(8) In this Act, a reference to a Part, Chapter, section or Schedule is a reference to a Part, Chapter, section of, or Schedule to, this Act, unless it is indicated that reference to some other enactment is intended.

(9) In this Act, a reference to a subsection, paragraph, subparagraph, clause or subclause is to the subsection, paragraph, subparagraph, clause or subclause of the provision (including a Schedule) in which the reference occurs, unless it is indicated that reference to some other provision is intended.

Amendments

[1] Substituted by FA12 s110(1). Applies as on and from 8 February 2012.

[2, 3, 8] Inserted by F(No.3)A11 sched3(1). Deemed to have come into operation as respects a gift or an inheritance taken on or after 1 January 2011.

[4] Inserted by F(No.3)A11 sched3(2). Deemed to have come into operation as respects a gift or an inheritance taken on or after 1 January 2011.

[5] Deleted by the Land and Conveyancing Law Reform Act 2009 sched 1. With effect from 1 December 2009 S.I. No. 356 of 2009.

[6] Inserted by FA04 sched3(2)(a)(i). Has effect as on and from 21 February 2003.

[7] Substituted by LGRA14 sched2(part5).

[9] Substituted by FA10 sched(4)(3)(a). Has effect as on and from 3 April 2010.

[10] Inserted by FA04 sched3(2)(a)(ii). Has effect as on and from 21 February 2003.

[11] Inserted by FA12 s111(1)(a). Applies on and from 8 February 2012.

[12] Deleted by FA04 s77.

Case Law

The word "issue" means the issue or descendants of a marriage, and for intestacy purposes, does not include adopted children. In the mater of John Stamp deceased, Patrick Stamp v Noel Redmond & Others IV ITR 415

'Stepchild' includes the child of a spouse from a former marriage even if the natural parent is still alive. IRC v Russell 1953 36 TC 83

The term "interest in possession" is not defined in CATCA 2003; however, this phrase was the subject of much judicial comment in the UK case of Pearsons v IRC 1981 AC 253

Revenue Information Notes

Pt 19.7 Revenue CAT Manual – Child of a stepchild

Cross References

From Section 2

Section 3 Meaning of "on a death".
Section 26 Market value of property.
Section 27 Market value of certain shares in private companies.
Section 30 Valuation date for tax purposes.
Section 45 Accountable persons.
Section 46 Delivery of returns.
Section 116 Regulations.

To Section 2

Section 27 Market value of certain shares in private companies.
Section 89 Provisions relating to agricultural property.
Schedule 2 Computation of tax

3 Meaning of "*on a death*"

[CATA 1976 s3]

(1) In this Act, "*on a death*", in relation to a person becoming beneficially entitled in possession, means—

(a) on the death of a person or at a time ascertainable only by reference to the death of a person,

(b) under a disposition where the date of the disposition is the date of the death of the disponer,

(c) under a disposition where the date of the disposition is on or after 1 April 1975 and within 2 years prior to the death of the disponer, or

(d) on the happening, after the cesser of an intervening life interest, of any such event as is referred to in *subsection (2)*.

(2) The events referred to in *subsection (1)(d)* are any of the following—

(a) the determination or failure of any charge, estate, interest or trust,

(b) the exercise of a special power of appointment,

(c) in the case where a benefit was given under a disposition in such terms that the amount or value of the benefit could only be ascertained from time to time by the actual payment or application of property for the purpose of giving effect to the benefit, the making of any payment or the application of the property, or

(d) any other event which, under a disposition, affects the right to property, or to the enjoyment of that property.

Cross References

To Section 3

Section 2 General interpretation.
Section 113 Tax, in relation to certain legislation.

PART 2

Gift Tax

4 Charge of gift tax

[CATA 1976 s4 (part)]

A capital acquisitions tax, to be called gift tax and to be computed in accordance with this Act, shall, subject to this Act and any regulations made under the Act, be charged, levied and paid on the taxable value of every taxable gift taken by a donee.

Revenue Information Notes
CAT 1 – Gift Tax

To Section 4
Section 102A Agricultural and business property: development land.

5 Gift deemed to be taken

[CATA 1976 s5; FA 1993 s121(1) (part); FA 1994 s147 (part)]

(1) For the purposes of this Act, a person is deemed to take a gift, where, under or in consequence of any disposition, a person becomes beneficially entitled in possession, otherwise than on a death, to any benefit (whether or not the person becoming so entitled already has any interest in the property in which such person takes such benefit), otherwise than for full consideration in money or money's worth paid by such person.

(2) A gift is deemed—

(a) to consist of the whole or the appropriate part, as the case may be, of the property in which the donee takes a benefit, or on which the benefit is charged or secured or on which the donee is entitled to have it charged or secured, and

(b) if the benefit is an annuity or other periodic payment which is not charged on or secured by any property and which the donee is not entitled to have so charged or secured, to consist of such sum as would, if invested on the date of the gift in the security of the Government which was issued last before that date for subscription in the State and is redeemable not less than 10 years after the date of issue, yield, on the basis of the current yield on the security, an annual income equivalent to the annual value of the annuity or of the other periodic payment receivable by the donee.

(3) For the purposes of *section 6(1)(c)* and *6(2)(d)*, the sum referred to in *subsection (2) (b)* is deemed not to be situate in the State at the date of the gift.

(4) Where a person makes a disposition [under which—

(a) a relative of the person,

(b) the civil partner of the person,

(c) a child of the civil partner of the person,

(d) any child of a child of the civil partner of the person,

(e) the civil partner of a person who is by virtue of *section 2(4)(b)* or *(c)* a relative of the person, or

(f) the civil partner of a child or the child of a child of the civil partner of a person, becomes][1] beneficially entitled in possession to any benefit, the creation or disposition in favour of the person of an annuity or other interest limited to cease on the death, or at a time ascertainable only by reference to the death, of the person, shall not be treated for the purposes of this section as consideration for the grant of such benefit or of any part of such benefit.

(5) For the purposes of this Act, "*appropriate part*", in relation to property referred to in *subsection (2)*, means that part of the entire property in which the benefit subsists, or on which the benefit is charged or secured, or on which the donee is entitled to have it so charged or secured, which bears the same proportion to the entire property as the gross annual value of the benefit bears to the gross annual value of the entire property, and the gift shall be deemed to consist of the appropriate part of each and every item of property comprised in the entire property.

(6) (a) Where a contract or agreement was entered into, under or as a consequence of which a person acquired the right, otherwise than for full consideration in money or money's worth, to have a benefit transferred to that person, or to another in that person's right or on that person's behalf, and an act or acts is or are done, on or after that date, in pursuance of, or in performance or satisfaction, whether in whole or in part, of such contract or agreement, then the gift or inheritance, as the case may be, taken by or in right or on behalf of that person, is deemed to have been taken, not when the right was acquired, but either—

(i) when the benefit was transferred to that person or to another in that person's right or on that person's behalf, or

(ii) when that person or another in that person's right or on that person's behalf became beneficially entitled in possession to the benefit,

whichever is the later.

(b) In this subsection, a reference to a contract or agreement does not include a reference to a contract or agreement—

(i) which is a complete grant, transfer, assignment or conveyance, or

(ii) which was enforceable by action.

(7) (a) In *paragraph (b)*, the expression "shares in a private company" shall be construed by reference to the meanings that "*share*" and "*private company*" have, respectively, in *section 27*.

(b) Where a person becomes beneficially entitled in possession to a benefit, and the property in which the benefit is taken consists wholly or partly of shares in a private company and where the consideration referred to in *subsection (1)*, being consideration in relation to a disposition, could not reasonably be regarded (taking into account the disponer's position prior to the disposition) as representing full consideration to the disponer for having made such a disposition, *subsection (1)* is deemed to apply as if "otherwise than for full consideration in money or money's worth paid by such person" were deleted in that subsection.

Amendments

[1] Substituted by FA13 s103(2)(a). Has effect as if it had come into operation as respects a gift (within the meaning of the Capital Acquisitions Tax Consolidation Act 2003) or an inheritance (within that meaning) taken on or after 1 January 2011.

[2] Substituted by F(No.3)A11 sched3(3). Shall apply to gifts and inheritances taken on or after 27 July 2011.

Case Law

In AG v Boden 1912 1 KB 539 goodwill of a partnership, which passed to a son on the death of his father, was regarded as having been taken for full consideration in money or money's worth.
AG v Kitchin 1941 AER 735 considered whether or not there had been full consideration in money or money's worth.
The term "interest in possession" is not defined in CATCA 2003; however, this phrase was the subject of much judicial comment in the UK case of Pearsons v IRC 1981 AC 253

Revenue Briefings

eBrief

eBrief No. 12/2013 – CAT and Debt Forgiveness Arrangements

Revenue Information Notes

IT 39 Gift/Inheritance Tax – A Guide to completing the Self Assessment Return – Pre Finance Act 2010, Appendix 8.1 – A benefit which consists of a Right, Annuity or other Periodic Payment

Cross References

From Section 5

Section 6 Taxable gift.
Section 27 Market value of certain shares in private companies.

To Section 5

Section 10 Inheritance deemed to be taken.
Section 28 Taxable value of a taxable gift or inheritance.
Section 37 Cesser of liabilities.
Section 76 Provisions relating to charities, etc.
Section 86 Exemption relating to certain dwellings.
Schedule 2 Computation of tax

6 Taxable gift

[CATA 1976 s6 (part)]

(1) In relation to a gift taken under a disposition, where the date of the disposition is before 1 December 1999, "*taxable gift*" in this Act means—

(a) in the case of a gift, other than a gift taken under a discretionary trust, where the disponer is domiciled in the State at the date of the disposition under which the donee takes the gift, the whole of the gift,

(b) in the case of a gift taken under a discretionary trust where the disponer is domiciled in the State at the date of the disposition under which the donee takes the gift or at the date of the gift or was (in the case of a gift taken after that [disponer's][1] death) so domiciled at the time of that [disponer's][2] death, the whole of the gift, and

(c) in any other case, so much of the property of which the gift consists as is situate in the State at the date of the gift.

(2) In relation to a gift taken under a disposition, where the date of the disposition is on or after 1 December 1999, "*taxable gift*" in this Act means—

(a) in the case of a gift, other than a gift taken under a discretionary trust, where the disponer is resident or ordinarily resident in the State at the date of the disposition under which the donee takes the gift, the whole of the gift,

(b) in the case of a gift taken under a discretionary trust where the disponer is resident or ordinarily resident in the State at the date of the disposition under which the donee takes the gift or at the date of the gift or was (in the case of a gift taken after the death of the disponer) so resident or ordinarily resident at the date of that death, the whole of the gift,

(c) in the case where the donee is resident or ordinarily resident in the State at the date of the gift, the whole of the gift, and

(d) in any other case, so much of the property of which the gift consists as is situate in the State at the date of the gift.

(3) For the purposes of *subsections (1)(c)* and *(2)(d)*, a right to the proceeds of sale of property is deemed to be situate in the State to the extent that such property is unsold and situate in the State.

(4) For the purposes of *subsection (2)*, a person who is not domiciled in the State on a particular date is treated as not resident and not ordinarily resident in the State on that date unless—

(a) that date occurs on or after 1 December 2004,

(b) that person has been resident in the State for the 5 consecutive years of assessment immediately preceding the year of assessment in which that date falls, and

(c) that person is either resident or ordinarily resident in the State on that date.

(5) (a) In this subsection—

"*company*" and "*share*" have the same meaning as they have in *section 27* ;

"*company controlled by the donee*" has the same meaning as is assigned to "*company controlled by the donee or successor*" by *section 27*.

[(b) For the purposes of *subsection (2)(d)*, so much of the market value of any share in a private company incorporated outside the State (which after taking the gift is a company controlled by the donee) as is attributable, directly or indirectly, to property situate in the State at the date of the gift shall be deemed to be a sum situate in the State.][3]

(c) *Paragraph (b)* shall not apply in a case where the disponer was domiciled outside the State at all times up to and including the date of the gift or, in the case of a gift taken after the death of the disponer, up to and including the date of that death or where the share in question is actually situate in the State at the date of the gift.

Amendments

[1, 2] Substituted by FA04 sched3(2)(b). Has effect as on and from 21 February 2003.

[3] Substituted by FA06 s113(1). This section shall apply to gifts taken on or after 2 February 2006.

Case Law

Goodwill is situate where the business is situate. IRC v Muller & Co's Margarine Ltd 1901 AC 217
If the share certificates and one of the duplicate or multiple registers are in Ireland and the transfer can be done in Ireland, then the shares will be regarded as Irish situs assets. Re Clark, McKechnie v Clark 1904 Ch 294
A credit balance at a bank is situate where the account is held. R v Lovitt 1912 AC 212

Cross References

From Section 6

Section 27 Market value of certain shares in private companies.

To Section 6

Section 5 Gift deemed to be taken.
Section 28 Taxable value of a taxable gift or inheritance.
Section 37 Cesser of liabilities.
Section 40 Free use of property, free loans, etc.
Section 46 Delivery of returns.

7 Liability to gift tax in respect of gift taken by joint tenants

[CATA 1976 s7]

The liability to gift tax in respect of a gift taken by persons as joint tenants is the same in all respects as if they took the gift as tenants in common in equal shares.

8 Disponer in certain connected dispositions

[CATA 1976 s8]

(1) Where a donee takes a gift under a disposition made by a disponer (in this section referred to as the original disponer) and, within the period commencing 3 years before and ending 3 years after the date of that gift, the donee makes a disposition under which a second donee takes a gift and whether or not the second donee makes a disposition within the same period under which a third donee takes a gift, and so on, each donee is deemed to take a gift from the original disponer (and not from the immediate disponer under whose disposition the gift was taken); and a gift so deemed to be taken is deemed to be an inheritance (and not a gift) taken by the donee, as successor, from the original disponer if—

(a) the original disponer dies within 2 years after the date of the disposition made by that original disponer, and

(b) the date of the disposition was on or after 1 April 1975.

(2) This section shall not apply in the case of any disposition (in this subsection referred to as the first-mentioned disposition) in so far as no other disposition, which was connected in the manner described in *subsection (1)* with such first-mentioned disposition, was made with a view to enabling or facilitating the making of the first-mentioned disposition or the recoupment in any manner of the cost of such first-mentioned disposition.

Revenue Information Notes

Pt 19.16 Revenue CAT Manual – Connected Gifts

PART 3

Inheritance Tax

CHAPTER 1

General

9 Charge of inheritance tax

[CATA 1976 s10 (part)]

A capital acquisitions tax, to be called inheritance tax and to be computed in accordance with this Act, shall, subject to this Act and any regulations made under the Act, be charged, levied and paid on the taxable value of every taxable inheritance taken by a successor.

Revenue Information Notes

IT41 – Bereavement – Tax Related Information
CAT 2 – Inheritance Tax

10 Inheritance deemed to be taken

[CATA 1976 s11; FA 1993 s123 (1) (part); FA 1994 s148 (part)]

(1) For the purposes of this Act a person is deemed to take an inheritance, where, under or in consequence of any disposition, a person becomes beneficially entitled in possession on a death to any benefit (whether or not the person becoming so entitled already has any interest in the property in which such person takes such benefit), otherwise than for full consideration in money or money's worth paid by such person.

(2) *Subsections (2)*, *(4)* and *(5)* of *section 5* shall apply, with any necessary modifications, in relation to an inheritance as they apply in relation to a gift.

(3) For the purposes of *section 11(1)(b)* and *11(2)(c)*, the sum referred to in *section 5(2)(b)* is deemed not to be situate in the State at the date of the inheritance.

(4) (a) In *paragraph (b)*, the expression "shares in a private company" is construed by reference to the meanings that "*share*" and "*private company*" have, respectively, in *section 27*.

(b) Where a person becomes beneficially entitled in possession to a benefit, and the property in which the benefit is taken consists wholly or partly of shares in a private company and where the consideration referred to in *subsection (1)*, being consideration in relation to a disposition, could not reasonably be regarded (taking into account the disponer's position prior to the disposition) as representing full consideration to the disponer for having made such a disposition, *subsection (1)* is deemed to apply as if "otherwise than for full consideration in money or money's worth paid by such person" were deleted in that subsection.

Revenue Information Notes

Pt 19.18 Revenue CAT Manual – Co-Directors and Business Partners Assurances – proceeds from such policies are exempt from Inheritance Tax in certain circumstances.

Cross References

From Section 10

Section 5 Gift deemed to be taken.
Section 11 Taxable inheritance.
Section 27 Market value of certain shares in private companies.

To Section 10

Section 76 Provisions relating to charities, etc.

11 Taxable inheritance

[CATA 1976 s12 (part)]

(1) In relation to an inheritance taken under a disposition, where the date of the disposition is before 1 December 1999, "*taxable inheritance*" in this Act means—

(a) in the case where the disponer is domiciled in the State at the date of the disposition under which the successor takes the inheritance, the whole of the inheritance, and

(b) in any case, other than the case referred to in *paragraph (a)*, where, at the date of the inheritance—

(i) the whole of the property—

(I) which was to be appropriated to the inheritance, or

(II) out of which property was to be appropriated to the inheritance,

was situate in the State, the whole of the inheritance;

(ii) a part or proportion of the property—

(I) which was to be appropriated to the inheritance, or

(II) out of which property was to be appropriated to the inheritance,

was situate in the State, that part or proportion of the inheritance.

(2) In relation to an inheritance taken under a disposition, where the date of the disposition is on or after 1 December 1999, "*taxable inheritance*" in the Act means—

(a) in the case where the disponer is resident or ordinarily resident in the State at the date of the disposition under which the successor takes the inheritance, the whole of the inheritance,

(b) in the case where the successor (not being a successor in relation to a charge for tax arising by virtue of *sections 15(1)* and *20(1)*) is resident or ordinarily resident in the State at the date of the inheritance, the whole of the inheritance, and

(c) in any case, other than a case referred to in *paragraph (a)* or *(b)*, where at the date of the inheritance—

(i) the whole of the property—

(I) which was to be appropriated to the inheritance, or

(II) out of which property was to be appropriated to the inheritance,

was situate in the State, the whole of the inheritance;

(ii) a part or proportion of the property—

(I) which was to be appropriated to the inheritance, or

(II) out of which property was to be appropriated to the inheritance,

was situate in the State, that part or proportion of the inheritance.

(3) For the purposes of *subsections (1)(b)* and *(2)(c)*—

(a) "property which was to be appropriated to the inheritance" and "property out of which property was to be appropriated to the inheritance" shall not include any property which was not applicable to satisfy the inheritance, and

(b) a right to the proceeds of sale of property is deemed to be situate in the State to the extent that such property is unsold and situate in the State.

(4) For the purposes of *subsection (2)*, a person who is not domiciled in the State on a particular date is treated as not resident and not ordinarily resident in the State on that date unless—

(a) that date occurs on or after 1 December 2004,

(b) that person has been resident in the State for the 5 consecutive years of assessment immediately preceding the year of assessment in which that date falls, and

(c) that person is either resident or ordinarily resident in the State on that date.

(5) (a) In this subsection—

"*company*" and "*share*" have the same meaning as they have in *section 27* ;

"*company controlled by the donee*" has the same meaning as is assigned to "*company controlled by the donee or successor*" by *section 27*.

[(b) For the purposes of *subsection (2)(c)*, so much of the market value of any share in a private company incorporated outside the State (which after taking the inheritance is a company controlled by the successor) as is attributable, directly or indirectly, to property situate in the State at the date of the inheritance shall be deemed to be a sum situate in the State.][1]

(c) *Paragraph (b)* shall not apply in a case where the disponer was not domiciled in the State at the date of the disposition under which the successor takes the inheritance or where the share in question is actually situate in the State at the date of the inheritance.

Amendments

[1] Substituted by FA06 s114(1). This section shall apply to inheritances taken on or after 2 February 2006.

Case Law

Goodwill is situate where the business is situate. IRC v Muller & Co's Margarine Ltd 1901 AC 217

If the share certificates, and one of the duplicate or multiple registers are in Ireland, and the transfer can be done in Ireland, then the shares will be regarded as Irish situs assets. Re Clark, McKechnie v Clark 1904 Ch 294

A credit balance at a bank is situate where the account is held. R v Lovitt 1912 AC 212

Cross References

From Section 11

Section 15 Acquisitions by discretionary trusts.

Section 20 Annual acquisitions by discretionary trusts.

Section 27 Market value of certain shares in private companies.

To Section 11

Section 10 Inheritance deemed to be taken.

Section 28 Taxable value of a taxable gift or inheritance.

Section 37 Cesser of liabilities.
Section 40 Free use of property, free loans, etc.
Section 45AA Liability of certain persons in respect of non-resident beneficiaries.
Section 46 Delivery of returns.
Section 77 Exemption of heritage property.

12 Disclaimer

[CATA 1976 s13]

(1) If—

(a) (i) a benefit under a will or an intestacy, or

(ii) an entitlement to an interest in settled property,

is disclaimed;

(b) a claim—

(i) under a purported will in respect of which a grant of representation (within the meaning of the Succession Act 1965) was not issued, or

(ii) under an alleged intestacy where a will exists in respect of which such a grant was issued,

is waived; or

(c) a right under Part IX of the Succession Act 1965, or any analogous right under the law of another territory, is renounced, disclaimed, elected against or lapses,

any liability to tax in respect of such benefit, entitlement, claim or right shall cease as if such benefit, entitlement, claim or right, as the case may be, had not existed.

(2) Notwithstanding anything contained in this Act—

(a) a disclaimer of a benefit under a will or intestacy or of an entitlement to an interest in settled property;

(b) the waiver of a claim—

(i) under a purported will in respect of which a grant of representation (within the meaning of the Succession Act 1965) was not issued, or

(ii) under an alleged intestacy where a will exists in respect of which such a grant issued; or

(c) (i) the renunciation or disclaimer of,

(ii) the election against, or

(iii) the lapse of,

a right under Part IX of the Succession Act 1965, or any analogous right under the law of another territory,

is not a disposition for the purposes of this Act.

(3) *Subsection (1)* shall not apply to the extent of the amount of any consideration in money or money's worth received for the disclaimer, renunciation, election or lapse or for the waiver of a claim; and the receipt of such consideration is deemed to be a gift or an inheritance, as the case may be, in respect of which no consideration was paid by the donee or successor and which was derived from the disponer who provided the property in relation to which the benefit, entitlement, claim or right referred to in *subsection (1)*, arose.

Case Law

Stratton v CIR 1958 1 Ch 42 confirmed that a disclaimer is a conveyance or transfer of an interest and the interest remains up until the date of disclaimer.

A disclaimer need not be in writing. Re Paradise Motor Co 1968 2 All ER 625

Revenue Information Notes

Pt 6 Revenue CAT Manual – Disclaimers of Benefits

13 Surviving joint tenant deemed to take an inheritance, etc

[CATA 1976 s14]

(1) On the death of one of several persons who are beneficially and absolutely entitled in possession as joint tenants, the surviving joint tenant or surviving joint tenants is or are deemed to take an inheritance of the share of the deceased joint tenant, as successor or successors from the deceased joint tenant as disponer.

(2) The liability to inheritance tax in respect of an inheritance taken by persons as joint tenants is the same in all respects as if they took the inheritance as tenants in common in equal shares.

CHAPTER 2

Initial Levy on Discretionary Trusts

14 Interpretation (Chapter 2)

[FA 1984 s104]

In this Chapter—

"*object*", in relation to a discretionary trust, means a person for whose benefit the income or capital, or any part of the income or capital, of the trust property is applied, or may be applied;

["*principal objects*", in relation to a discretionary trust, means such objects, if any, of the trust for the time being as are—

(a) the spouse or civil partner of the disponer,

(b) the children of the disponer,

(c) the children of the civil partner of the disponer,

(d) the children of a child of the disponer, where such child predeceased the disponer,

(e) the children of a child of the civil partner of the disponer, where such child predeceased the disponer,

(f) the children of the civil partner of a child of the disponer, where such child predeceased the disponer, or

(g) the children of the civil partner of a child of the civil partner of the disponer, where such child predeceased the disponer.][1]

Amendments

[1] Substituted by F(No.3)A11 sched3(4). Deemed to have come into operation as respects a gift or an inheritance taken on or after 1 January 2011.

Revenue Information Notes

Pt 5 Revenue CAT Manual – Discretionary Trust Tax

IT 41 – Bereavement – Tax Related Information

Cross References

To Section 14

Section 19 Interpretation (Chapter 3).

15 Acquisitions by discretionary trusts

[FA 1984 s106]

(1) Where, on or after 25 January 1984, under or in consequence of any disposition, property becomes subject to a discretionary trust, the trust is deemed, on—

(a) the date on which that property becomes or became subject to the discretionary trust,

(b) the date of death of the disponer, or

(c) where there are principal objects of the trust, the date on which there ceases to be a principal object of the trust who is—

(i) under the age of 25 years, where the property became subject to the trust on or after 25 January 1984 and before 31 January 1993, or

(ii) under the age of 21 years, where the property becomes or became subject to the trust on or after 31 January 1993,

whichever date is the latest, to become or to have become beneficially entitled in possession to an absolute interest in so much, if any, of that property or of property representing that property and of accumulations of income of that property or of property representing those accumulations as remains subject to the discretionary trust on that latest date, and to take or to have taken an inheritance accordingly as if the trust, and the trustees as such for the time being of the trust, were together a person for the purposes of this Act, and that latest date shall be the date of the inheritance.

[(1A) For the purposes of this section and *section 20*, where a discretionary trust is created under the will (including under a codicil to that will) of a deceased person property shall be deemed to be subject to the trust on the date of death of that person.][1]

(2) Property which, under or in consequence of any disposition, was subject to a discretionary trust on 25 January 1984 is, for the purposes of *subsection (1)*, deemed to have become subject to the trust on that date.

(3) Property which, under or in consequence of any disposition, was subject to a discretionary trust on 31 January 1993 is, for the purposes of *subsection (1)*, deemed to have become subject to the trust on that date.

(4) For the purposes of this section—

(a) an interest in expectancy is not property until an event happens whereby the interest ceases to be an interest in expectancy or is represented by property which is not an interest in expectancy,

(b) an interest in a policy of assurance on human life is not property until, and then only to the extent that, the interest becomes an interest in possession under *section 41* or is represented by property which is not an interest in expectancy.

(5) Where, apart from this subsection, property or property representing such property would be chargeable under this section, or under this section and the corresponding provisions of the repealed enactments, with tax more than once under the same disposition, such property is so chargeable with

tax once only, that is, on the earliest occasion on which such property would become so chargeable with tax.

Amendments

[1] Inserted by FA12 s111(1)(b). Applies on and from 8 February 2012.

Case Law

Sudeley v AG 1897 AC 11, Re Smyth 1891 1 Ch 89, and AG v Johnson 1907 2 KB 885 all illustrate the difficulty in determining when a 'settled residuary estate' becomes 'subject to the discretionary trust' for the purposes of s15(1)(a).

In Revenue Commissioners v Executors and Trustees of the Wills of Jeannie Hammet Irvine Deceased 2005 No 172 R HC it was argued that the date of ascertainment of residue was the date when the property in a will discretionary trust became 'subject to the discretionary trust'. As such, the 1% annual charge did not apply until this date.

Cross References

From Section 15

Section 41 When interest in assurance policy becomes interest in possession.

To Section 15

Section 11 Taxable inheritance.
Section 16 Application of this Act.
Section 17 Exemptions.
Section 18 Computation of tax.
Section 20 Annual acquisitions by discretionary trusts.
Section 44 Arrangements reducing value of company shares.
Section 46 Delivery of returns.
Section 55 Payment of tax on certain assets by instalments.
Section 91 Application (Chapter 2)

16 Application of this Act

[FA 1984 s107 (*a*) to (*d*) and (*g*)]

In relation to a charge for tax arising by reason of *section 15*—

(a) a reference in *section 27* to a company controlled by the successor and the definition in that section of "*group of shares*" is construed as if (for the purpose of that reference) the list of persons contained in *subsection (3)* of that section and (for the purpose of that definition) the list of persons contained in that definition included the following, that is, the trustees of the discretionary trust, the living objects of the discretionary trust, the relatives of those objects, nominees of those trustees or of those objects or of the relatives of those objects, and the trustees of a settlement whose objects include the living objects of the discretionary trust or relatives of those living objects,

(b) *section 30* shall apply, with the modification that the valuation date of the taxable inheritance is—

(i) the date of the inheritance, or

(ii) the valuation date ascertained in accordance with that section,

whichever is the later, and with any other necessary modifications;

(c) a person who is a trustee of the discretionary trust concerned for the time being at the date of the inheritance or at any date subsequent to that date is a person primarily accountable for the payment of the tax;

(d) an object of the discretionary trust concerned to whom or for whose benefit any of the property subject to the trust is applied or appointed is also accountable for the payment of tax the charge in respect of which has arisen prior to the date of the application or appointment of the property to that person or for that person's benefit[...][1]; and

(e) *section 45(1)*, *sections 50*, *56* and *81* and *Schedule 2* shall not apply.

Amendments

[1] Deleted by FA10 s(147)(1)(a). Has effect as on and from 3 April 2010.

Cross References

From Section 16

Section 15 Acquisitions by discretionary trusts.
Section 27 Market value of certain shares in private companies.
Section 30 Valuation date for tax purposes.
Section 45 Accountable persons.
Section 50 Computation of tax.
Section 56 Payment of inheritance tax by transfer of securities.
Section 81 Exemption of certain securities.
Schedule 2 Computation of tax

To Section 16

Section 46 Delivery of returns.
Section 90 Interpretation (Chapter 2).

17 Exemptions

[FA 1984 s108]

(1) *Section 15* shall not apply in relation to a discretionary trust which is shown to the satisfaction of the Commissioners to have been created exclusively—

[(a) for purposes which, in accordance with the law of the State, are public or charitable,][1]

(b) for the purposes of—

(i) any scheme for the provision of superannuation benefits on retirement established by or under any enactment or by or under an instrument made under any enactment, or

(ii) any sponsored superannuation scheme within the meaning of *subsection (1)* of section 783 of the Taxes Consolidation Act 1997 or a trust scheme or part of a trust scheme approved by the Commissioners under that section or section 785 of that Act, but shall not include a scheme or arrangement which relates to matters other than service in particular offices or employments;

(c) for the purposes of a registered unit trust scheme within the meaning of the Unit Trusts Act 1990;

(d) (i) for the benefit of one or more named individuals, and

(ii) for the reason that such individual, or all such individuals, is or are, because of age or improvidence, or of physical, mental or legal incapacity, incapable of managing that individual or those individuals' affairs;

or

(e) for the purpose of providing for the upkeep of a house or garden referred to in *section 77(6)*.

[(1A) For the purposes of *subsection (1)(a)* a discretionary trust that is at any time a party to any arrangements the main purpose (or one of the main purposes) of which is to secure a tax advantage for any person shall be regarded as not having been created exclusively for purposes which, in accordance with the law of the State, are public or charitable.

(1B) For the purposes of *subsection (1A)*—

'arrangements' includes any agreement, understanding, scheme, 35 transaction or series of transactions (whether or not legally enforceable);

'tax advantage' has the same meaning as in section 811 of the Taxes Consolidation Act 1997.][2]

(2) *Section 15* shall not apply—

(a) in relation to a discretionary trust in respect of the property subject to or becoming subject to the trust which, on the termination of the trust, is comprised in a gift or an inheritance taken by the State, or

(b) in respect of an inheritance which, apart from this subsection, would be deemed, by the combined effect of *section 15* and *section 40*, to be taken by a discretionary trust.

Amendments

[1] Substituted by FA14 s80(1)(a). Applies to inheritances taken on or after 23 December 2014.

[2] Inserted by FA14 s80(1)(b). Applies to inheritances taken on or after 23 December 2014.

Revenue Briefings

eBrief

eBrief No. 19/2012 – Capital Acquisitions Tax – Discretionary Trust Tax

Revenue Information Notes

Pt 5.4 Revenue CAT Manual – Exemptions

CHY 1 – Applying for Relief from Tax on the Income and Property of Charities

Cross References

From Section 17

Section 15 Acquisitions by discretionary trusts.

Section 40 Free use of property, free loans, etc.

Section 77 Exemption of heritage property.

To Section 17

Section 22 Exemptions.

18 Computation of tax

[FA 1984 s109]

(1) In this section—

['*appropriate trust*', in relation to a relevant inheritance, means the trust by which that inheritance was deemed to be taken;][1]

"*earlier relevant inheritance*" means a relevant inheritance deemed to be taken on the date of death of the disponer;

"*later relevant inheritance*" means a relevant inheritance which, after the date of death of the disponer, is deemed to be taken by a discretionary trust by virtue of there ceasing to be a principal object of that trust who is under the age of 21 years;

"*relevant inheritance*" means an inheritance which, by virtue of *section 15(1)*, is deemed to be taken by a discretionary trust;

["*relevant period*" means—

(a) in relation to an earlier relevant inheritance, the period of 5 years commencing on the date of death of the disponer,

(b) in relation to a settled relevant inheritance, the period of 5 years commencing on the date of death of the life tenant concerned, [and][2]

[…][3]

(d) in relation to a later relevant inheritance, the period of 5 years commencing on the latest date on which a later relevant inheritance was deemed to be taken from the disponer;][4]

"*settled relevent inheritance*" means a relevent inheritance taken on the death of a life tenant;

[…][5]

[…][6]

(2) Subject to *subsection (3)*, the tax chargeable on the taxable value of a taxable inheritance which is charged to tax by reason of *section 15* is computed at the rate of 6 per cent of such taxable value.

[(3) Where, in the case of each earlier relevant inheritance, each settled relevant inheritance or each later relevant inheritance, as the case may be, taken from the same disponer, one or more objects of the appropriate trust became beneficially entitled in possession before the expiration of the relevant period to an absolute interest in the entire of the property of which that inheritance consisted on and at all times after the date of that inheritance (other than property which ceased to be subject to the terms of the appropriate trust by virtue of a sale or exchange of an absolute interest in that property for full consideration in money or money's worth), then, in relation to all such earlier relevant inheritances, all such settled relevant inheritances or all such later relevant inheritances, as the case may be, the tax so chargeable is computed at the rate of 3 per cent.][7]

(4) Where 2 or more persons are together beneficially entitled in possession to an absolute interest in property, those persons shall not, by reason only that together they are beneficially so entitled in possession, be regarded for the purposes of *subsection (3)* as beneficially so entitled in possession.

[…][8]

Amendments

[1] Inserted by FA12 s111(1)(d). Applies on and from 8 February 2012.

[2] Inserted by FA12 s111(1)(c). Applies on and from 8 February 2012.

[3] Deleted by FA12 s111(1)(c). Applies on and from 8 February 2012.

[4] Substituted by FA07 s113(1)(a). This section applies to inheritances deemed to be taken on or after 1 February 2007.

[5] Deleted by FA12 s111(1)(d). Applies on and from 8 February 2012.

[6] Deleted by FA12 s111(1)(e). Applies on and from 8 February 2012.

[7] Substituted by FA12 s111(1)(f). Applies on and from 8 February 2012.

[8] Deleted by FA03 s145(1)(a). With effect from 1 November 2003 per SI 515 of 2003.

Revenue Briefings

eBrief

eBrief No. 19/2012 – Capital Acquisitions Tax – Discretionary Trust Tax

Cross References

From Section 18

Section 15 Acquisitions by discretionary trusts.

To Section 18

Section 50 Computation of tax.
Section 57 Overpayment of tax.

CHAPTER 3

Annual Levy on Discretionary Trusts

19 Interpretation (Chapter 3)

[FA 1986 s102]

In this Chapter—

["*chargeable date*", in relation to any year, means—

(a) in respect of the year 2006, 5 April and 31 December in that year, and

(b) in respect of the year 2007 and subsequent years, 31 December in the year concerned;][1]

"*chargeable discretionary trust*" means a discretionary trust in relation to which—

(a) the disponer is dead, and

(b) none of the principal objects of the trust, if any, is under the age of 21 years;

"*object*" and "*principal objects*", in relation to a discretionary trust, have the meanings respectively assigned to them by *section 14.*

Amendments

[1] Substituted by FA06 s116(1)(a). This section shall apply as respects the year 2006 and subsequent years.

Revenue Information Notes

Pt 5.3 Revenue CAT Manual – The annual 1% charge
IT 41 – Bereavement – Tax Related Information

Cross References

From Section 19
Section 14 Interpretation (Chapter 2).

20 Annual acquisitions by discretionary trusts

[FA 1986 s103]

(1) Where, in any year commencing with the year 2003, under or in consequence of any disposition, property is subject to a chargeable discretionary trust on the chargeable date, the trust is deemed on each such date to become beneficially entitled in possession to an absolute interest in that property, and to take on each such date an inheritance accordingly as if the trust, and the trustees as such for the time being of the trust, were together a person for the purposes of this Act, and each such chargeable date shall be the date of such inheritance.

(2) (a) In this subsection, "*property*" includes property representing such property.

(b) Where—

(i) under or in consequence of any disposition, property was subject to a discretionary trust prior to a chargeable date,

(ii) that property is not on that chargeable date subject to that discretionary trust (being on that date a chargeable discretionary trust) because such property is on that date property to which for the time being a person is beneficially entitled for an interest in possession, and

(iii) on that chargeable date that property is property which is limited to become subject again to that chargeable discretionary trust, or will do so by the exercise of a power of revocation,

that property is deemed to be subject to that chargeable discretionary trust on that chargeable date if that interest in possession is an interest which is revocable or which is limited to cease on an event other than—

(I) the death of that person, or

(II) the expiration of a specified period, where that interest is taken by that person under a power of appointment contained in that disposition and is, at the time of the appointment of that interest, an interest for a period certain of 5 years or more.

(3) For the purposes of this section—

(a) an interest in expectancy is not property until an event happens whereby the interest ceases to be an interest in expectancy or is represented by property which is not an interest in expectancy;

(b) an interest in a policy of assurance on human life is not property until, and then only to the extent that, the interest becomes an interest in possession under the provisions of *section 41* or is represented by property which is not an interest in expectancy.

(4) This section shall not apply in relation to property which is subject to a chargeable discretionary trust on a chargeable date if that property or property representing that property is subject to a charge for tax arising under or in consequence of the same disposition by reason of *section 15*, or that provision of the repealed enactments which corresponds with *section 15*, on that same date or within the year prior to that date.

Cross References

From Section 20

Section 15 Acquisitions by discretionary trusts.
Section 41 When interest in assurance policy becomes interest in possession.

To Section 20

Section 11 Taxable inheritance.
Section 21 Application of this Act.
Section 22 Exemptions.
Section 23 Computation of tax.
Section 24 Values agreed.
Section 46 Delivery of returns.
Section 54 Payment of tax by instalments.
Section 55 Payment of tax on certain assets by instalments.
Section 56 Payment of inheritance tax by transfer of securities.
Section 77 Exemption of heritage property.
Section 91 Application (Chapter 2)

21 Application of this Act

[FA 1986 s104 (*a*) to (*e*) and (*g*)]

In relation to a charge for tax arising by reason of *section 20*—

(a) a reference in *section 27* to a company controlled by the successor and the definition in that section of "group of shares" is construed as if (for the purpose of that reference) the list of persons contained in *subsection*

(3) of that section and (for the purpose of that definition) the list of persons contained in that definition included the following, that is, the trustees of the discretionary trust, the living objects of the discretionary trust, the relatives of those objects, nominees of those trustees or of those objects or of the relatives of those objects, and the trustees of a settlement whose objects include the living objects of the discretionary trust or relatives of those living objects;

[(b) (i) subject to *subparagraph (ii)*, the valuation date of the taxable inheritance is the relevant chargeable date,

(ii) where—

(I) a charge for tax arises on a particular date by reason of *section 15* or *section 118* (in so far as that section relates to a provision repealed by this Act that corresponds to *section 15*), giving rise to a taxable inheritance (in this subparagraph referred to as the 'first taxable inheritance'),

(II) on a later date, a charge for tax arises under or in consequence of the same disposition by reason of *section 20* giving rise to a taxable inheritance (in this subparagraph referred to as the 'second taxable inheritance') comprising the same property or property representing that property, and

(III) the valuation date of the first taxable inheritance is a date after the chargeable date of the second taxable inheritance,

then the valuation date of the second taxable inheritance is the same date as the valuation date of the first taxable inheritance.][1]

(c) a person who is a trustee of the discretionary trust concerned for the time being at the date of the inheritance or at any date subsequent to that date is a person primarily accountable for the payment of the tax;

(d) an object of the discretionary trust concerned to whom or for whose benefit any of the property subject to the trust is applied or appointed is also accountable for the payment of tax the charge in respect of which has arisen prior to the date of the application or appointment of the property to that object or for that object's benefit[...][2];

[...][3]

(f) *section 30*, *section 45(1)*, [*section 50* and *section 81* and *Schedule 2*][4] shall not apply.

Amendments

[1] Substituted by FA12 s111(1)(g). Applies on and from 8 February 2012.

[2] Deleted by FA10 s(147)(1)(a). Has effect as on and from 3 April 2010.

[3] Deleted by FA06 s117(1)(a)(i). This section shall apply as respects the year 2006 and subsequent years.

[4] Substituted by FA06 s117(1)(a)(ii). This section shall apply as respects the year 2006 and subsequent years.

Cross References

From Section 21

Section 20 Annual acquisitions by discretionary trusts.
Section 27 Market value of certain shares in private companies.
Section 30 Valuation date for tax purposes.
Section 45 Accountable persons.
Section 50 Computation of tax.

Section 81 Exemption of certain securities.
Schedule 2 Computation of tax

To Section 21
Section 46 Delivery of returns.

22 Exemptions

[FA 1986 s106]

Section 20 shall not apply in relation to a discretionary trust referred to in *section 17(1)* or in respect of the property or the inheritance referred to in *section 17(2)*.

Revenue Briefings

eBrief
eBrief No. 19/2012 – Capital Acquisitions Tax – Discretionary Trust Tax

Revenue Information Notes
CHY 1 – Applying for Relief from Tax on the Income and Property of Charities

Cross References

From Section 22
Section 17 Exemptions.
Section 20 Annual acquisitions by discretionary trusts.

23 Computation of tax

[(1) Subject to *subsection (2)*, the tax chargeable on the taxable value of a taxable inheritance which is charged to tax by reason of *section 20* is computed at the rate of one per cent of that taxable value.

(2) The tax chargeable on the chargeable date that is 31 December 2006 shall be an amount equal to 73.97 per cent of the tax chargeable by virtue of *subsection (1)*.][1]

Amendments

[1] Substituted by FA06 s116(1)(b). This section shall apply as respects the year 2006 and subsequent years.

Revenue Briefings

eBrief
eBrief No. 19/2012 – Capital Acquisitions Tax – Discretionary Trust Tax

Cross References

From Section 23
Section 20 Annual acquisitions by discretionary trusts.

To Section 23
Section 50 Computation of tax.

24 Values agreed

[FA 1986 s107]

(1) Where—

(a) under or in consequence of any disposition, a charge for tax arises by reason of *section 20* on a chargeable date (in this section called the first chargeable date),

(b) an accountable person has furnished all the information necessary to enable the Commissioners to ascertain the market value of—

(i) real property, or

(ii) shares which are not dealt in on a stock exchange,

comprised in the taxable inheritance so taken on the valuation date of that taxable inheritance,

(c) pursuant to an application in writing to the Commissioners on that behalf, the market value of such property on that valuation date is agreed on between that person and the Commissioners,

(d) under or in consequence of the same disposition, a charge for tax arises by reason of *section 20* on either or both of the 2 chargeable dates in the years next following the year in which the first chargeable date occurs (in this section called the subsequent chargeable dates), and

(e) the same property at *subparagraph (i)* or *(ii)* of *paragraph (b)* is comprised in the taxable inheritances so taken on the subsequent chargeable dates,

the value so agreed on is treated for the purposes of this Chapter as the market value of such property on that valuation date and on the valuation dates of the taxable inheritances so taken on the subsequent chargeable dates.

[(1A) Where the market value of property is on a valuation date determined in accordance with *subsection (1)* and that valuation date is 5 April 2006, then that market value as so determined shall be treated as the market value of the property on the valuation date that is 31 December 2006.][1]

(2) Notwithstanding *subsection (1)*, the market value so agreed is not binding—

(a) in any case where there is failure to disclose material facts in relation to any part of the property comprised in the taxable inheritances taken on the first chargeable date or on the subsequent chargeable dates, or

(b) where, at any time after the first chargeable date and before the third of those chargeable dates—

(i) in the case of real property, there is any alteration in the tenure under which the property is held or let, or

(ii) in the case of shares, there is any alteration in the capital or the ownership of the capital of the company concerned or of the rights of the shareholders *inter se*,

or

(c) where, at any time after the first chargeable date and before the third of those chargeable dates—

(i) in the case of real property, there is any change whatever, whether affecting that or any other property, which would materially increase or decrease the market value over and above any increase or decrease which might normally be expected if such a change had not occurred, or

(ii) in the case of shares, there has been any material change in the assets of the company or in their market value over and above any such change which might normally be expected,

and in such cases the market value of the real property, or of the shares, may be ascertained again by the Commissioners for each of the relevant valuation dates, but in the case of any change referred to in *paragraph (c)*, the market value may be ascertained again by the Commissioners only at the request of the person primarily accountable for the payment of the tax arising by reason of *section 20* on that relevant valuation date.

(3) Any agreement made under this section shall be binding only on the persons who as such are accountable for the payment of the tax arising by reason of *section 20* on the first chargeable date and on the subsequent chargeable dates.

Amendments

[1] Inserted by FA06 s116(1)(c). This section shall apply as respects the year 2006 and subsequent years.

Cross References

From Section 24

Section 20 Annual acquisitions by discretionary trusts.

25 Penalty [Deleted]

Deleted by F(No.2)A08 sched5(part4)(a). The enactments specified in Schedule 5 are amended or repealed to the extent and manner specified in that Schedule and, unless the contrary is stated, shall come into effect after 24 December 2008.

PART 4

Value of Property for Tax

26 Market value of property

[CATA 1976 s15]

(1) In *subsection (6)*, "*unquoted shares or securities*" means shares or securities which are not dealt in on a stock exchange.

(2) Subject to this Act, the market value of any property for the purposes of this Act is estimated to be the price which, in the opinion of the Commissioners, such property would fetch if sold in the open market on the date on which the property is to be valued in such manner and subject to such conditions as might reasonably be calculated to obtain for the vendor the best price for the property.

(3) In estimating the market value of any property, the Commissioners shall not make any reduction in the estimate on account of the estimate being made on the assumption that the whole property is to be placed on the market at one and the same time.

(4) The market value of any property shall be ascertained by the Commissioners in such manner and by such means as they think fit, and they may authorise a person to inspect any property and report to them the value of such property for the purposes of this Act, and the person having the custody or possession of that property shall permit the person so authorised to inspect it at such reasonable times as the Commissioners consider necessary.

(5) Where the Commissioners require a valuation to be made by a person named by them, the costs of such valuation shall be defrayed by the Commissioners.

(6) Subject to this Act, in estimating the price which unquoted shares or securities might be expected to fetch if sold in the open market, it shall be assumed that in that market there is available to any prospective purchaser of the shares or securities all the information which a prudent prospective purchaser might reasonably require if that prudent prospective purchaser were proposing to purchase them from a willing vendor by private treaty and at arm's length.

Case Law

Every possible purchaser must be taken into account in determining the open market value. IRC v Clay, IRC v Buchanan 1914 3 KB 466

In both Ellesmere v Commissioners of Inland Revenue 1918 2 KB 735 and AG of Ceylon v Mackie 1952 2 ALL ER 775, it was held that market value is determined based on the open market value of the property.

Cross References

To Section 26

Section 2 General interpretation.
Section 44 Arrangements reducing value of company shares.
Schedule 3 Consequential Amendments

27 Market value of certain shares in private companies

[CATA 1976 s16]

(1) In this section—

["*group of shares*", in relation to a private company, means the aggregate of the shares in the company of—

(a) the donee or successor,

(b) the relatives, civil partner, children, or children of the children of the civil partner, of the donee or successor,

(c) the civil partners of persons who are by virtue of *section 2(4)(b)* or *(c)* relatives of the donee or successor,

(d) the civil partners of any children or any children of the children of the civil partner of the donee or successor,

(e) nominees of the donee or successor,

(f) nominees of—

(i) relatives of the donee or successor,

(ii) the civil partner of the donee or successor,

(iii) children or children of the children of the civil partner of the donee or successor,

(iv) the civil partners of persons who are by virtue of *section 2(4)(b)* or *(c)* relatives of the donee or successor, or

(v) the civil partners of any childrenor any children of the children of the civil partner of the donee or successor,

and

(g) the trustees of a settlement whose objects include—

(i) the donee or successor,

(ii) relatives of the donee or successor,

(iii) the civil partner of the donee or successor,

(iv) the children or children of the children of the civil partner of the donee or successor,

(v) the civil partners of persons who are by virtue of *section 2(4)(b)* or *(c)* relatives of the donee or successor, or

(vi) the civil partners of any childrenor any children of the children of the civil partner of the donee or successor;][1]

"*nominee*" includes a person who may be required to exercise that person's voting power on the directions of, or who holds shares directly or indirectly on behalf of, another person;

"*private company*" means a body corporate (wherever incorporated) which—

(a) is under the control of not more than 5 persons, and

(b) is not a company which would fall within section 431 of the Taxes Consolidation Act 1997 if the words "*private company*" were substituted for the words "*close company*" in *subsection (3)* of that section, and if the words "are beneficially held by a company which is not a private company" were substituted for the words of *paragraph (a)* of *subsection (6)* of that section;

"*share*", in relation to a private company and in addition to the interpretation of "*share*" in *section 2(1)*, includes every debenture, or loan stock, issued otherwise than as part of a transaction which is wholly and exclusively a bona fide commercial transaction.

(2) (a) The market value of each share in a private company which (after the taking of the gift or of the inheritance) is, on the date of the gift or on the date of the inheritance, a company controlled by the donee or successor, shall be ascertained by the Commissioners, for the purposes of tax, as

if, on the date on which the market value is to be ascertained, it formed an apportioned part of the market value of a group of shares in that company, such apportionment, as between shares of a particular class, to be by reference to nominal amount, and, as between different classes of shares, to have due regard to the rights attaching to each of the different classes.

(b) For the purpose of ascertaining the market value of a share in a private company in the manner described in *paragraph (a)*, the benefit to any private company (in this paragraph referred to as "the first-mentioned company") by virtue of its ownership of an interest in shares in another private company (in this paragraph referred to as "the second-mentioned company") is, where each of the companies so connected is a company which (after the taking of the gift or of the inheritance) is, on the date of the gift or on the date of the inheritance, a company controlled by the donee or successor, deemed to be—

[(i) such benefit as would be appropriate to the ownership of that interest if the second-mentioned company were under the control of the first-mentioned company in the same manner as (on the date on which the market value is to be ascertained) the second-mentioned company is under the control of any of the following:][2]

[(I) the first-mentioned company;

(II) the donee or successor;

[(III) the—

(A) relatives, civil partner, children or children of the children of the civil partner,

(B) civil partners of persons who are by virtue of *section 2(4)(b)* or *(c)* relatives, or

(C) civil partners of the children or the children of the children of the civil partner,

of the donee or successor;][3]

(IV) nominees of the donee or successor;

[(V) any nominees of—

(A) the relatives, the civil partner, children or children of the children of the civil partner,

(B) the civil partners of persons who are by virtue of *section 2(4)(b)* or *(c)* relatives, or

(C) the civil partners of the children or the children of the children of the civil partner,

of the donee or successor;][4]

(VI) the trustees of a settlement whose objects include—

(A) the donee or successor, or

[(B) any—

(ai) relatives, civil partner, children or children of the children of the civil partner,

(aii) civil partners of persons who are by virtue of *section 2(4)(b)* or *(c)* relatives, or (aiii) civil partners of children or children of the children of the civil partner,

of the donee or successor,][5]

or][6]

(ii) the actual benefit appropriate to the ownership of that interest,

whichever is the greater.

[(3) In this section, a reference to a company controlled by the donee or successor is a reference to a company that is under the control of any one or more of the following:][7]

[(a) the donee or successor;

[(b) the—

(i) relatives, civil partner, children or children of the children of the civil partner,

(ii) civil partners of persons who are by virtue of *section 2(4)(b)* or *(c)* relatives, or

(iii) civil partners of the children or the children of the children of the civil partner,

of the donee or successor;][8]

(c) nominees of the donee or successor;

[(d) nominees of—

(i) the relatives, the civil partner, children or children of the children of the civil partner,

(ii) the civil partners of persons who are by virtue of *section 2(4)(b)* or *(c)* relatives, or

(iii) the civil partners of the children or the children of the children of the civil partner,

of the donee or successor;][9]

(e) the trustees of a settlement whose objects include—

(i) the donee or successor, or

[(ii) the—

(I) relatives, the civil partner, children or children of the children of the civil partner,

(II) civil partners of persons who are by virtue of *section 2(4)(b)* or *(c)* relatives, or

(III) civil partners of the children or the children of the children of the civil partner,

of the donee or successor,][10]

and for the purposes of this section, a company which is so controlled by the donee or successor shall be regarded as being itself a relative of the donee or successor.][11]

(4) For the purposes of this section—

(a) a company is deemed to be under the control of not more than 5 persons if any 5 or fewer persons together exercise, or are able to exercise, or are entitled to acquire control, whether direct or indirect, of the company and for this purpose—

[(i) persons who are—

(I) relatives of any other person,

(II) the civil partner of any other person,

(III) children or children of the children of the civil partner of any other person,

(IV) the civil partners of persons who are by virtue of *section 2(4)* (b)or *(c)* relatives of any other person, or

(V) the civil partners of the children or the children of the children of the civil partner of any other person,

together with that other person,][12]

(ii) persons who are nominees of any other person together with that other person,

(iii) persons in partnership, and

(iv) persons interested in any shares or obligations of the company which are subject to any trust or are part of the estate of a deceased person,

shall respectively be treated as a single person, and

(b) a person is deemed to have control of a company at any time if—

(i) that person then had control of the powers of voting on all questions, or on any particular question, affecting the company as a whole, which, if exercised, would have yielded a majority of the votes capable of being exercised on such questions or question, or could then have obtained such control by an exercise at that time of a power exercisable by that person or at that person's direction or with that person's consent,

(ii) that person then had the capacity, or could then by an exercise of a power exercisable by that person or at that person's direction or with that person's consent obtain the capacity, to exercise or to control the exercise of any of the following powers, that is:

(I) the powers of a board of directors of the company,

(II) powers of a governing director of the company,

(III) power to nominate a majority of the directors of the company or a governing director of the company,

(IV) the power to veto the appointment of a director of the company, or

(V) powers of a like nature;

(iii) that person then had a right to receive, or the receipt of, more than one-half of the total amount of the dividends of the company, whether declared or not, and for the purposes of this subparagraph, "*dividend*" is deemed to include interest on any debentures of the company, or

(iv) that person then had an interest in the shares of the company of an aggregate nominal value representing one-half or more of the aggregate nominal value of the shares of the company.

Amendments

[1] Substituted by FA13 s103(2)(b). Has effect as if it had come into operation as respects a gift (within the meaning of the Capital Acquisitions Tax Consolidation Act 2003) or an inheritance (within that meaning) taken on or after 1 January 2011.

[2, 6] Substituted by F(No.3)A11 sched3(6). Shall apply to gifts and inheritances taken on or after 27 July 2011.

[3] Substituted by FA13 s103(2)(c). Has effect as if it had come into operation as respects a gift (within the meaning of the Capital Acquisitions Tax Consolidation Act 2003) or an inheritance (within that meaning) taken on or after 1 January 2011.

[4] Substituted by FA13 s103(2)(d). Has effect as if it had come into operation as respects a gift (within the meaning of the Capital Acquisitions Tax Consolidation Act 2003) or an inheritance (within that meaning) taken on or after 1 January 2011.

[5] Substituted by FA13 s103(2)(e). Has effect as if it had come into operation as respects a gift (within the meaning of the Capital Acquisitions Tax Consolidation Act 2003) or an inheritance (within that meaning) taken on or after 1 January 2011.

[7, 11] Substituted by F(No.3)A11 sched3(7). Shall apply to gifts and inheritances taken on or after 27 July 2011.

[8] Substituted by FA13 s103(2)(f). Has effect as if it had come into operation as respects a gift (within the meaning of the Capital Acquisitions Tax Consolidation Act 2003) or an inheritance (within that meaning) taken on or after 1 January 2011.

[9] Substituted by FA13 s103(2)(g). Has effect as if it had come into operation as respects a gift (within the meaning of the Capital Acquisitions Tax Consolidation Act 2003) or an inheritance (within that meaning) taken on or after 1 January 2011.

[10] Substituted by FA13 s103(2)(h). Has effect as if it had come into operation as respects a gift (within the meaning of the Capital Acquisitions Tax Consolidation Act 2003) or an inheritance (within that meaning) taken on or after 1 January 2011.

[12] Substituted by FA13 s103(2)(i). Has effect as if it had come into operation as respects a gift (within the meaning of the Capital Acquisitions Tax Consolidation Act 2003) or an inheritance (within that meaning) taken on or after 1 January 2011.

Case Law

In Barclays Bank Ltd v IRC 1961 AC 509 the definition of control was held not to be exhaustive.

Cross References

From Section 27

Section 2 General interpretation.

To Section 27

Section 2 General interpretation.
Section 5 Gift deemed to be taken.
Section 6 Taxable gift.
Section 10 Inheritance deemed to be taken.
Section 11 Taxable inheritance.
Section 16 Application of this Act.
Section 21 Application of this Act.
Section 38 Disposition enlarging value of property.
Section 43 Disposition by or a company.
Section 44 Arrangements reducing value of company shares.
Section 78 Heritage property of companies.
Section 80 Payments relating to retirement, etc.
Section 83 Exemption where disposition was made by the donee or successor.
Section 93 Relevant business property.
Section 95 Replacements.
Schedule 2 Computation of tax
Schedule 3 Consequential Amendments

28 Taxable value of a taxable gift or inheritance

[CATA 1976 s18]

(1) In this section, "*incumbrance-free value*", in relation to a taxable gift or a taxable inheritance, means the market value at the valuation date of the property of which the taxable gift or taxable inheritance consists at that date, after deducting any liabilities, costs and expenses that are properly payable out of the taxable gift or taxable inheritance.

(2) Subject to this section (but except where provided in *section 89*), the taxable value of a taxable gift or a taxable inheritance (where the interest taken by the donee or successor is not a limited interest) is ascertained by deducting from the incumbrance-free value of such a taxable gift or a taxable inheritance the market value of any bona fide consideration in money or money's worth, paid by the donee or successor for the gift or inheritance, including—

(a) any liability of the disponer which the donee or successor undertakes to discharge as that [donee or successor's][1] own personal liability, and

(b) any other liability to which the gift or inheritance is subject under the terms of the disposition under which it is taken,

and the amount so ascertained is the taxable value, but no deduction shall be made under this subsection in respect of any liability which is to be deducted in ascertaining the incumbrance-free value.

(3) Where a liability (other than a liability within the meaning of *subsection (9)*) for which a deduction may be made under *subsection (1)* or *(2)* is to be discharged after the time when it is to be taken into account as a deduction under either of those subsections, it is valued for the purpose of making such a deduction at its current market value at the time when it is to be so taken into account.

(4) The taxable value of a taxable gift or a taxable inheritance, where the interest taken by the donee or the successor is a limited interest, is ascertained as follows—

(a) the value of the limited interest in a capital sum equal to the incumbrance-free value is ascertained in accordance with the Rules contained in *Schedule 1*, and

(b) from the value ascertained in accordance with *paragraph (a)* a deduction is made in respect of the market value of any bona fide consideration in money or money's worth paid by the donee or the successor for the gift or the inheritance and the amount remaining after such deduction is the taxable value, but no deduction is made under this paragraph in respect of any liability which is to be deducted in ascertaining the incumbrance-free value.

(5) A deduction shall not be made under this section—

(a) in respect of any liability the payment of which is contingent on the happening of some future event, but if the event on the happening of which the liability is contingent happens and the liability is paid, then, on a claim for relief being made to the Commissioners and subject to the other provisions of this section, a deduction is made in respect of the liability and such adjustment of tax as is appropriate is made; and such adjustment is made on the basis that the donee or successor had taken an interest in possession in the amount which is to be deducted for the liability, for a period certain which was equal to the actual duration of the postponement of the payment of the liability,

(b) in respect of any liability, costs or expenses in so far as the donee or successor has a right of reimbursement from any source, unless such reimbursement can not be obtained,

(c) in respect of any liability created by the donee or successor or any person claiming in right of the donee or successor or on that donee or successor's behalf,

(d) in respect of tax, interest or penalties chargeable under this Act in respect of the gift or inheritance, or of the costs, expenses or interest incurred in raising or paying the same,

(e) in respect of any liability in so far as such liability is an incumbrance on, or was created or incurred in acquiring, any property which is comprised in any gift or inheritance and which is exempt from tax under any provision of this Act or otherwise,

(f) in the case of any gift or inheritance referred to in *section 6(1)(c), 6(2)(d), 11(1)(b)* or *11(2)(c)* in respect of—

(i) any liability, costs or expenses due to a person resident outside the State (except in so far as such liability is required by contract to be paid in the State or is charged on the property which is situate in the State and which is comprised in the gift or inheritance), or

(ii) any liability, costs or expenses in so far as the same are charged on or secured by property which is comprised in the gift or inheritance and which is not situate in the State,

except to the extent that all the property situate outside the State and comprised in the gift or inheritance is insufficient for the payment of the liability, costs or expenses,

(g) for any tax in respect of which a credit is allowed under *section 106* or *107.*

[(5A) Notwithstanding section 57(3), relief shall be given under *subsection (5)(a)* on a claim which shall be made within 4 years after the liability referred to in that paragraph has been paid.][2]

(6) In the case of a gift or inheritance referred to in *subsection (5)(f)*, any deduction to be made under *subsection (2)* or *(4)(b)* is restricted to the proportion of the consideration which bears the same proportion to the whole of the consideration as the taxable gift or taxable inheritance bears to the whole of the gift or the whole of the inheritance.

(7) A deduction shall not be made under this section—

(a) more than once for the same liability, costs, expenses or consideration, in respect of all gifts and inheritances taken by the donee or successor from the disponer, or

(b) for any liability, costs, expenses or consideration, a proportion of which is to be allowed under *section 89(2)(ii)* or *(iii)* in respect of a gift or inheritance taken by the donee or successor from the disponer.

(8) Where a taxable gift or a taxable inheritance is subject to a liability within the meaning of *subsection (9)*, the deduction to be made in respect of that liability under this section shall be an amount equal to the market value of the whole or the appropriate part, as the case may be, of the property, within the meaning of *section 5(5)*.

(9) For the purpose of *subsection (8)*, "*liability*", in relation to a taxable gift or a taxable inheritance, means a liability which deprives the donee or successor, whether permanently or temporarily, of the use, enjoyment or income in whole or in part of the property, or of any part of the property, of which the taxable gift or taxable inheritance consists.

(10) Where—

(a) bona fide consideration in money or money's worth has been paid by a person for the granting to that person, by a disposition, of an interest in expectancy in property, and

(b) at the coming into possession of the interest in expectancy, that person takes a gift or an inheritance of that property under that disposition,

the deduction to be made under *subsection (2)* or *(4)(b)* for consideration paid by that person is a sum equal to the same proportion of the taxable value of the taxable gift or taxable inheritance (as if no deduction had been made for such consideration) as the amount of the consideration so paid bore to the market value of the interest in expectancy at the date of the payment of the consideration.

(11) Any deduction, under this section, in respect of a liability which is an incumbrance on any property, is, so far as possible, made against that property.

Amendments

[1] Substituted by F(No.2)A08 sched6(3). This paragraph is deemed to have come into force and have taken effect as on and from 21 February 2003.

[2] Inserted by FA08 sched6(2)(a). Applies as on and from 31 January 2008.

Case Law

Even if a deed states that certain consideration is due, this is only evidential and can be invalidated by evidence to the contrary. The Revenue Commissioners v Moroney V ITR 589

In AG v Wreford-Brown 1925 2 KB 429 it was held that the value of partial consideration paid should be allowed as a deduction from the incumbrance-free value of the taxable gift or the taxable inheritance.

Legal relationships in family matters are generally not accepted by law. Mackay v Jones 1959 93 ILTR 177

Also in Jones v Padavatton 1961 1 WLR 328 and Balfour v Balfour 1919 2 KB 571 there was a presumption against contractual relations within the family.

Revenue Information Notes

Pt 19.1 Revenue CAT Manual – Claim for Wages etc.

Pt 19.5 Revenue CAT Manual – Arrears of income tax etc. due to the British Revenue.

Pt 19.12 Revenue CAT Manual – The words "exempt from tax" in section 28(5)(e)

IT 39 Gift/Inheritance Tax – A Guide to completing the Self Assessment Return – Pre Finance Act 2010, Pt 7 – Taxable Value of Benefit

Cross References

From Section 28

Section 5 Gift deemed to be taken.

Section 6 Taxable gift.

Section 11 Taxable inheritance.

Section 57 Overpayment of tax.

Section 89 Provisions relating to agricultural property.

Section 106 Arrangements for relief from double taxation.

Section 107 Other relief from double taxation.

Schedule 1 Valuation of Limited Interests

To Section 28

Section 34 Settlement of an interest not in possession.
Section 35 Enlargement of interests.
Section 37 Cesser of liabilities.
Section 89 Provisions relating to agricultural property.
Schedule 1 Valuation of Limited Interests

29 Contingencies affecting gifts or inheritances

[CATA 1976 s20]

(1) Where, under a disposition, a person becomes beneficially entitled in possession to any benefit and, under the terms of the disposition, the entitlement, or any part of the entitlement, may cease on the happening of a contingency (other than the revocation of the entitlement on the exercise by the disponer of such a power as is referred to in *section 39*), the taxable value of any taxable gift or taxable inheritance taken by that person on becoming so entitled to that benefit is ascertained as if no part of the entitlement were so to cease; but, in the event and to the extent that the entitlement so ceases, the tax payable by that person is, to that extent, adjusted (if, by so doing, a lesser amount of tax would be payable by such person) on the basis that such person had taken an interest in possession for a period certain which was equal to the actual duration of such person's beneficial entitlement in possession.

[(1A) Notwithstanding section 57(3), relief shall be given under *subsection (1)* on a claim which shall be made within 4 years after the entitlement referred to in that subsection ceases.][1]

(2) Nothing in this section shall prejudice any charge for tax on the taking by such person of a substituted gift or inheritance on the happening of such a contingency.

Amendments

[1] Inserted by FA08 sched6(2)(b). Applies as on and from 31 January 2008.

Revenue Information Notes

Pt 16 Revenue CAT Manual – Contingencies Affecting Gifts or Inheritances.
IT 39 Gift/Inheritance Tax – A Guide to completing the Self Assessment Return – Pre Finance Act 2010, Appendix 8.6 – Contingencies

Cross References

From Section 29

Section 39 Gift subject to power of revocation.
Section 57 Overpayment of tax.

30 Valuation date for tax purposes

[CATA 1976 s21]

(1) Subject to *subsection (7)*, the valuation date of a taxable gift is the date of the gift.

(2) The valuation date of a taxable inheritance is the date of death of the deceased person on whose death the inheritance is taken if the successor or any person in right of the successor or on that successor's behalf takes the inheritance—

(a) as a *donatio mortis causa*, or

(b) by reason of the failure to exercise a power of revocation.

(3) If a gift becomes an inheritance by reason of its being taken under a disposition where the date of the disposition is within 2 years prior to the death of the disponer, the valuation date of the inheritance is determined as if it were a gift.

(4) The valuation date of a taxable inheritance, other than a taxable inheritance referred to in *subsection (2)* or *(3)*, is the earliest date of the following:

(a) the earliest date on which a personal representative or trustee or the successor or any other person is entitled to retain the subject matter of the inheritance for the benefit of the successor or of any person in right of the successor or on that successor's behalf,

(b) the date on which the subject matter of the inheritance is so retained, or

(c) the date of delivery, payment or other satisfaction or discharge of the subject matter of the inheritance to the successor or for that successor's benefit or to or for the benefit of any person in right of the successor or on that successor's behalf.

(5) If any part of a taxable inheritance referred to in *subsection (4)* may be retained, or is retained, delivered, paid or otherwise satisfied, whether by means of part payment, advancement, payment on account or in any manner whatever, before any other part or parts of such inheritance, the appropriate valuation date for each part of the inheritance is determined in accordance with that subsection as if each such part respectively were a separate inheritance.

(6) The Commissioners may give to an accountable person a notice in writing of the date determined by them to be the valuation date in respect of the whole or any part of an inheritance, and, subject to any decision on appeal pursuant to *subsection (9)*, the date so determined is deemed to be the valuation date.

(7) If a taxable inheritance referred to in *subsection (4)* or *(5)* is disposed of, ceases or comes to an end before the valuation date referred to in those subsections in such circumstances as to give rise to a taxable gift, the valuation date in respect of such taxable gift is the same date as the valuation date of the taxable inheritance.

(8) Notwithstanding anything contained in this section, the Commissioners may, in case of doubt, with the agreement in writing of the accountable person or that person's agent, determine the valuation date of the whole or any part of any taxable inheritance and the valuation date so determined is substituted for the valuation date which would otherwise be applicable by virtue of this section.

(9) An appeal shall lie against any determination made by the Commissioners under *subsection (6)* and *section 67* shall apply, with any necessary modifications, in relation to an appeal under this subsection as it applies in relation to an appeal against an assessment of tax.

Cross References

From Section 30

Section 67 Appeals in other cases.

To Section 30

Section 2 General interpretation.
Section 16 Application of this Act.
Section 21 Application of this Act.
Section 102A Agricultural and business property: development land.
Schedule 3 Consequential Amendments

PART 5

Provisions Relating to Gifts and Inheritances

31 Distributions from discretionary trusts

[CATA 1976 s22]

Where a person becomes beneficially entitled in possession to any benefit—

(a) under a discretionary trust, other than a discretionary trust referred to in *paragraph (b)*, otherwise than for full consideration in money or money's worth paid by the person, that person is deemed to have taken a gift,

(b) under a discretionary trust created—

(i) by will at any time,

(ii) by a disposition, where the date of the disposition is on or after 1 April 1975 and within 2 years prior to the death of the disponer, or

(iii) by a disposition *inter vivos* and limited to come into operation on a death occurring before, on or after the passing of this Act,

otherwise than for full consideration in money or money's worth paid by the person, that person is deemed to have taken an inheritance.

32 Dealings with future interests

[CATA 1976 s23]

(1) In *subsection (2)*, "*benefit*" includes the benefit of the cesser of a liability referred to in *section 37*.

(2) Where a benefit, to which a person (in this section referred to as the remainderman) is entitled under a disposition, devolves, or is disposed of, either in whole or in part, before it has become an interest in possession so that, at the time when the benefit comes into possession, it is taken, either in whole or in part, by a person (in this section referred to as the transferee) other than the remainderman to whom it was limited by the disposition, then tax is payable, in respect of a gift or inheritance, as the case may be, of the remainderman in all respects as if, at that time, the remainderman had become beneficially entitled in possession to the full extent of the benefit limited to that remainderman under the disposition, and the transferee is the person primarily accountable for the payment of tax to the extent that the benefit is taken by that transferee.

(3) *Subsection (2)* shall not prejudice any charge for tax in respect of any gift or inheritance affecting the same property or any part of it under any other disposition.

Cross References

From Section 32
Section 37 Cesser of liabilities.

To Section 32
Section 45 Accountable persons.
Section 46 Delivery of returns.
Section 54 Payment of tax by instalments.
Section 86 Exemption relating to certain dwellings.
Section 89 Provisions relating to agricultural property.

Section 90 Interpretation (Chapter 2).
Section 111 Liability to tax in respect of certain sales and mortgages.

33 Release of limited interests, etc

[CATA 1976 s24]

(1) In this section, "*event*" includes—

(a) a death, and

(b) the expiration of a specified period.

(2) Where an interest in property, which is limited by the disposition creating it to cease on an event, has come to an end (whether by another disposition, the taking of successive interests into one ownership, or by any means whatever other than the happening of another event on which the interest was limited by the first-mentioned disposition to cease) before the happening of such event, tax is payable under the first-mentioned disposition in all respects as if the event on which the interest was limited to cease under that disposition had happened immediately before the coming to an end of the interest.

(3) *Subsection (2)* shall not prejudice any charge for tax in respect of any gift or inheritance affecting the same property or any part of it under any disposition other than that first mentioned in *subsection (2)*.

(4) Notwithstanding anything contained in *subsection (3)*, if—

(a) an interest in property which was limited to cease on an event was limited to the disponer by the disposition creating that interest, and

(b) on the coming to an end of that interest, *subsection (2)* has effect in relation to a gift or inheritance which was taken by a donee or successor under that disposition and which consists of the property in which that interest subsisted, then—

a further gift or inheritance taken by the same donee or successor under another disposition made by the same disponer (being the disposition by which that interest has come to an end) is not a taxable gift or a taxable inheritance in so far as it consists of the whole or any part of the same property.

Revenue Information Notes

Pt 7 Revenue CAT Manual – Break-up of Settlements and Trusts and Payment for future Interest

Cross References

To Section 33

Section 34 Settlement of an interest not in possession.

34 Settlement of an interest not in possession

[CATA 1976 s25]

(1) In this section, "*event*" has the same meaning as it has in *section 33(1)*.

(2) Where any donee or successor takes a gift or an inheritance under a disposition made by such donee or successor then, if at the date of such disposition such donee or successor was entitled to the property comprised in the disposition, either expectantly on the happening of an event, or subject to a liability within the meaning of *section 28(9)*, and such event happens or such liability ceases during the continuance of the disposition, tax is charged on the taxable value of the taxable gift or taxable inheritance which such donee or successor would have taken on the

happening of such event, or on the cesser of such liability, if no such disposition had been made.

(3) *Subsection (2)* shall not prejudice any charge for tax in respect of any gift or inheritance affecting the same property or any part of it under the disposition referred to in that subsection.

Cross References

From Section 34

Section 28 Taxable value of a taxable gift or inheritance.
Section 33 Release of limited interests, etc.

To Section 34

Section 113 Tax, in relation to certain legislation.

35 Enlargement of interests

[CATA 1976 s26]

(1) Where a person, having a limited interest in possession in property (in this section referred to as the first-mentioned interest), takes a further interest (in this section referred to as the second-mentioned interest) in the same property, as a taxable gift or a taxable inheritance, in consequence of which that person becomes the absolute owner of the property, the taxable value of the taxable gift or taxable inheritance of the second-mentioned interest at the valuation date is reduced by the value at that date of the first-mentioned interest, taking such value to be the value, ascertained in accordance with the Rules contained in *Schedule 1*, of a limited interest which—

(a) is a limited interest in a capital sum equal to the value of the property,

(b) commences on that date, and

(c) is to continue for the unexpired balance of the term of the first-mentioned interest.

(2) For the purposes of *subsection (1)(a)*, "*value*" means such amount as would be the incumbrance-free value, within the meaning of *section 28(1)*, if the limited interest were taken, at the date referred to in *subsection (1)*, as a taxable gift or taxable inheritance.

(3) This section shall not apply where the second-mentioned interest is taken under the disposition under which the first-mentioned interest was created.

Case Law

The case of BKJ v The Revenue Commissioners 1983 III ITR 104 considered the difference between a contingent interest and an interest subject to defeasance.

Cross References

From Section 35

Section 28 Taxable value of a taxable gift or inheritance.
Schedule 1 Valuation of Limited Interests

To Section 35

Schedule 1 Valuation of Limited Interests

36 Dispositions involving powers of appointment

[CATA 1976 s27]

(1) Where, by virtue of or in consequence of the exercise of, or the failure to exercise, or the release of, a general power of appointment by any person having such a power, a person becomes beneficially entitled in possession to any benefit, then, for the purposes of this Act, the disposition is the exercise of, or the failure to exercise, or the release of, the power and not the disposition under which the power was created, and the person exercising, or failing to exercise, or releasing, the power is the disponer.

[(1A) In *subsections (1B)* and *(1C)* 'arrangement' includes any agreement, understanding, scheme, transaction or series of transactions (whether or not legally enforceable).

(1B) Notwithstanding *subsection (1)*, where the exercise of, failure to exercise, or release of, a general power of appointment form part of an arrangement the main purpose or one of the main purposes of which is the avoidance of tax, tax shall be chargeable as if the disposition were the disposition under which the power was created and the person who created the power were the disponer.

(1C) Where the grant of a general power of appointment in or over property to any person forms part of an arrangement the main purpose or one of the main purposes of which is the avoidance of a charge to tax arising under *sections 15(1)* or *20(1)*, the grant of that general power of appointment shall not prejudice any such charge to tax.][1]

(2) Where, by virtue of or in consequence of the exercise of, or the failure to exercise, or the release of, a special power of appointment by any person having such a power, a person becomes beneficially entitled in possession to any benefit, then, for the purposes of this Act, the disposition is the disposition under which the power was created and the person who created the power is the disponer.

Amendments

[1] Inserted by FA12 s112(1). Applies to gifts and inheritances (including inheritances referred to in sections 15(1) and 20(1)) taken on or after 8 February 2012.

Revenue Information Notes

Pt 9 Revenue CAT Manual – Powers of Appointment

37 Cesser of liabilities

[CATA 1976 s28]

(1) In this section, "*appropriate part*" has the meaning assigned to it by *section 5(5)*.

(2) The benefit of the cesser of—

(a) a liability within the meaning of *section 28(9)*, or

(b) any liability similar to that referred to in *paragraph (a)* to which the taking of a benefit which was a gift or inheritance was subject,

is deemed to be a gift or an inheritance, as the case may be, which is deemed—

(i) to the extent that the liability is charged on or secured by any property at the time of its cesser, to consist of the whole or the appropriate part, as the case may be, of that property, and

(ii) to the extent that the liability is not charged on or secured by any property at the time of its cesser, to consist of such sum as would, under *section 5(2)(b)*, be the sum the annual income of which would be equal to the annual value of the liability.

(3) For the purposes of *sections 6(1)(c)*, *6(2)(d)*, *11(1)(b)* and *11(2)(c)*, the sum referred to in *subparagraph (ii)* of *subsection (2)* is deemed not to be situate in the State at the date of the gift or at the date of the inheritance.

Cross References

From Section 37

Section 5 Gift deemed to be taken.
Section 6 Taxable gift.
Section 11 Taxable inheritance.
Section 28 Taxable value of a taxable gift or inheritance.

To Section 37

Section 32 Dealings with future interests.

38 Disposition enlarging value of property

[CATA 1976 s29]

(1) In *subsection (4)*, "*company*" means a private company within the meaning of *section 27*.

(2) In this section, "*property*" does not include any property to which a donee or successor became beneficially entitled in possession prior to 28 February 1969.

(3) Where the taking by any person of a beneficial interest in any property (in this section referred to as additional property) under any disposition made by a disponer has the effect of increasing the value of any other property (in this section referred to as original property) to which that person is beneficially entitled in possession, and which had been derived from the same disponer, the following provisions shall apply—

(a) the increase in value so effected is deemed to be a gift or an inheritance, as the case may be, arising under that disposition and taken by that person, as donee or successor, from that disponer, at the time that donee or successor took the beneficial interest in the additional property,

(b) the original property is treated as having been increased in value if the market value of that property at the time referred to in *paragraph (a)* would be greater if it was sold as part of an aggregate of the original property and the additional property rather than as a single item of property, and the increase in value for the purposes of this section is the amount by which the market value of the original property if sold at that time as part of such aggregate would be greater than the amount of the market value of that property if sold at that time as a single item of property,

(c) the additional property is, for the purpose of determining its market value, deemed to be part of an aggregate of the original property and the additional property, and

(d) the market value of any property which is to be valued as part of an aggregate of property is ascertained as being so much of the market value of such aggregate as may reasonably be ascribed to that part.

(4) For the purpose of this section, the donee or successor is deemed to be beneficially entitled in possession to any property notwithstanding that within 5 years prior to such a disposition as is referred to in *subsection (3)* that donee or successor has divested such donee or successor of such property, or any part of such property, otherwise than for full consideration in money or money's worth or has disposed

of it to a company of which such donee or successor is, at any time within that period of 5 years, deemed to have control within the meaning of *section 27(4)(b)*.

Revenue Information Notes

IT 39 Gift/Inheritance Tax – A Guide to completing the Self Assessment Return – Pre Finance Act 2010, Appendix 8.8 – Disposition enlarging the value of property

Cross References

From Section 38

Section 27 Market value of certain shares in private companies.

39 Gift subject to power of revocation

[CATA 1976 s30]

Where, under any disposition, a person becomes beneficially entitled in possession to any benefit and, under the terms of the disposition, the disponer has reserved to such disponer the power to revoke the benefit, such person is, for the purposes of this Act, deemed not to be beneficially entitled in possession to the benefit unless and until the power of revocation is released by the disponer, or otherwise ceases to be exercisable.

Revenue Information Notes

IT 39 Gift/Inheritance Tax – A Guide to completing the Self Assessment Return – Pre Finance Act 2010, Appendix 8.5 – Power of Revocation

Cross References

To Section 39

Section 29 Contingencies affecting gifts or inheritances.

40 Free use of property, free loans, etc

[CATA 1976 s31]

(1) In *subsections (2)* and *(4)*, "*relevant period*", in relation to any use, occupation or enjoyment of property, means the period of 12 months ending on 31 December in each year.

(2) A person is deemed to take a gift in each relevant period during the whole or part of which that person is allowed to have the use, occupation or enjoyment of any property (to which property that person is not beneficially entitled in possession) otherwise than for full consideration in money or money's worth.

(3) A gift referred to in *subsection (2)* is deemed to consist of a sum equal to the difference between the amount of any consideration in money or money's worth, given by the person referred to in *subsection (2)* for such use, occupation or enjoyment, and the best price obtainable in the open market for such use, occupation or enjoyment.

(4) A gift referred to in *subsection (2)* is treated as being taken at the end of the relevant period or, if earlier, immediately prior to the time when the use, occupation or enjoyment referred to in *subsection (2)* comes to an end.

(5) In any case where the use, occupation or enjoyment of property is allowed to a person, not being beneficially entitled in possession to that property, under a disposition—

(a) made by will,

(b) where the date of the disposition is on or after 1 April 1975 and within 2 years prior to the death of the disponer, or

(c) which is a disposition *inter vivos* and the use, occupation or enjoyment is had by that person after the cesser of another person's life interest,

subsections (2), *(3)* and *(4)* shall apply in relation to that property as if a reference to an inheritance were substituted for the reference to a gift wherever it occurs in those subsections, and for the purpose of this subsection "relevant period" in *subsections (2)* and *(4)*, in relation to the use, occupation or enjoyment of property, means the period of 12 months ending on 31 December in any year.

(6) For the purposes of *sections 6(1)(c)*, *6(2)(d)*, *11(1)(b)* and *11(2)(c)*, the sum referred to in *subsection (3)* is deemed not to be situate in the State at the date of the gift or at the date of the inheritance.

Revenue Information Notes

Pt 19.14 Revenue CAT Manual – Free Loans

IT 39 Gift/Inheritance Tax – A Guide to completing the Self Assessment Return – Pre Finance Act 2010, Appendix 8.4 – Free Use of Property

Cross References

From Section 40

Section 6 Taxable gift.

Section 11 Taxable inheritance.

To Section 40

Section 17 Exemptions.

41 When interest in assurance policy becomes interest in possession

[CATA 1976 s32]

(1) For the purposes of this Act, an interest in a policy of assurance on human life is deemed to become an interest in possession when either—

(a) the policy matures, or

(b) prior to the maturing of the policy, the policy is surrendered to the insurer for a consideration in money or money's worth,

but if during the currency of the policy the insurer makes a payment of money or money's worth, in full or partial discharge of the policy, the interest is deemed to have come into possession to the extent of such payment.

(2) This section has effect in relation to a contract for a deferred annuity, and for the purposes of this section such a contract is deemed to mature on the date when the first instalment of the annuity is due.

Cross References

To Section 41

Section 15 Acquisitions by discretionary trusts.

Section 20 Annual acquisitions by discretionary trusts.

42 Provisions to apply where section 98 of Succession Act 1965 has effect

[CATA 1976 s33]

(1) If, on the death of a testator and by virtue of section 98 of the Succession Act 1965, or otherwise, a disposition takes effect as if a person, who had predeceased the testator, had survived the testator, the benefit taken by the estate of that person is not deemed to be an inheritance.

(2) Where a person survives a testator, and—

(a) such person becomes beneficially entitled, under a disposition made by a person who predeceased the testator, to any benefit in relation to any property devised or bequeathed by the testator, and

(b) section 33 of the Wills Act 1837, or section 98 of the Succession Act 1965, or any analogous provision of the law of another territory has effect in relation to the devise or bequest,

such person is deemed for the purposes of inheritance tax to derive the benefit from the testator, as disponer.

43 Disposition by or to a company

[CATA 1976 s34]

(1) In this section—

"*company*" means a private company within the meaning of *section 27*;

"*market value*" means—

(a) in the case of a person's beneficial interest in shares and entitlements, the market value of that interest on the date of the payment, disposition, gift or inheritance, as the case may be, ascertained by reference to the market value on that date of the shares and entitlements in which the interest subsists, and

(b) in the case of a share in which a beneficial interest subsists, the market value of that share ascertained in the manner described in *section 27* as if, on the date on which the market value is to be ascertained, it formed an apportioned part of the market value of a group of shares consisting of all the shares in the company issued and outstanding at that date;

"*share*" has the same meaning as it has in *section 27*;

"*specified amount*", in relation to a person's beneficial interest in shares and entitlements, means—

(a) in the case of consideration paid, or a disposition made, by the company, a nil amount or, if greater, the amount by which the market value of the beneficial interest was decreased as a result of the payment of the consideration or the making of the disposition, and

(b) in the case of consideration, or a gift, or an inheritance taken by the company, a nil amount or, if greater, the amount by which the market value of the beneficial interest was increased as a result of the taking of the consideration, gift or inheritance.

(2) For the purposes of this Act—

(a) consideration paid by, or a disposition made by, a company is deemed to be consideration, or a disposition, as the case may be, paid or made, and

(b) consideration, or a gift, or an inheritance taken by a company is deemed to be consideration, or a gift or an inheritance, as the case may be, taken,

by the beneficial owners of the shares in the company and the beneficial owners of the entitlements under any liability incurred by the company (otherwise than for the purposes of the business of the company, wholly and exclusively) in the same proportions as the specified amounts relating to their respective beneficial interests in the shares and entitlements bear to each other.

(3) For the purposes of *subsection (2)* all acts, omissions and receipts of the company are deemed to be those of the beneficial owners of the shares and entitlements, referred to in *subsection (2)*, in the company, in the proportions mentioned in that subsection.

(4) Where the beneficial owner of any shares in a company or of any entitlement of the kind referred to in *subsection (2)*, is itself a company, the beneficial owners of the shares and entitlements, referred to in *subsection (2)*, in the latter company, are deemed to be the beneficial owners of the latter company's shares and entitlements in the former company, in the proportions in which they are the beneficial owners of the shares and entitlements in the latter company.

(5) So far as the shares and entitlements referred to in *subsection (2)* are held in trust and have no ascertainable beneficial owners, consideration paid, or a disposition made, by the company are deemed to be paid or made by the disponer who made the disposition under which the shares and entitlements are so held in trust.

Cross References

From Section 43

Section 27 Market value of certain shares in private companies.

To Section 43

Section 83 Exemption where disposition was made by the donee or successor.

44 Arrangements reducing value of company shares

[FA 1989 s90(1) to (10) and (12)]

(1) In this section—

"*arrangement*" means an arrangement which is made on or after 25 January 1989, and includes—

(a) any act or omission by a person or by the trustees of a disposition,

(b) any act or omission by any person having an interest in shares in a company,

(c) the passing by any company of a resolution, or

(d) any combination of acts, omissions or resolutions referred to in *paragraphs (a)*, *(b)* and *(c)* ;

"*company*" means a private company within the meaning of *section 27*;

"*event*" includes—

(a) a death, and

(b) the expiration of a specified period;

"*related shares*" means the shares in a company, the market value of which shares is increased by any arrangement;

"*related trust*" has the meaning assigned to it by *subsections (3)* and *(5)* ;

"*specified amount*" means an amount equal to the difference between—

(a) the market value of shares in a company immediately before an arrangement is made, and ascertained under *section 27* as if each share were a share in a company controlled at that time by the disponer concerned and that share was the absolute property of that disponer at that time, and

(b) the market value of those shares, or of property representing those shares, immediately after the arrangement is made, and ascertained under *section 26*, and such specified amount is deemed to be situate where the company is incorporated.

(2) In this section, a reference to a company controlled by the disponer concerned is a reference to a company that is under the control of any one or more of the following, that is, that disponer, the relatives of that disponer, nominees of relatives of that disponer, and the trustees of a settlement whose objects include that disponer or relatives of that disponer, and for the purposes of this section, a company which is so controlled by that disponer is regarded as being itself a relative of that disponer.

(3) Where—

(a) a person has an absolute interest in possession in shares in a company, and

(b) any arrangement results in the market value of those shares, or of property representing those shares, immediately after that arrangement is made, being less than it would be but for that arrangement,

then, tax is payable in all respects as if a specified amount which relates to that arrangement were a benefit taken, immediately after that arrangement is made, from that person, as disponer, by—

(i) the beneficial owners of the related shares in that company, and

(ii) so far as the related shares in that company are held in trust (in this section referred to as the "related trust") and have no ascertainable beneficial owners, by the disponer in relation to that related trust as if, immediately after that arrangement is made, that disponer was the absolute beneficial owner of those related shares,

in the same proportions as the market value of the related shares, which are beneficially owned by them or are deemed to be so beneficially owned, is increased by that arrangement.

(4) Where—

(a) an interest in property is limited by the disposition creating it to cease on an event,

(b) immediately before the making of an arrangement to which *paragraph (c)* relates, the property includes shares in a company, and

(c) the arrangement results in the market value of those shares, or of property representing those shares, immediately after that arrangement is made, being less than it would be but for that arrangement,

then, tax is payable under that disposition in all respects—

(i) where the interest in property is an interest in possession, as if such property included a specified amount which relates to that arrangement,

(ii) where the interest in property is not an interest in possession, as if it were an interest in possession and such property included a specified amount which relates to that arrangement, and

(iii) as if the event on which the interest was limited to cease under that disposition had happened, to the extent of the specified amount, immediately before that arrangement is made.

(5) Where—

(a) shares in a company are, immediately before the making of an arrangement to which *paragraph (b)* relates, subject to a discretionary trust under or in consequence of any disposition, and

(b) the arrangement results in those shares, or property representing those shares, remaining subject to that discretionary trust but, immediately after that arrangement is made, the market value of those shares, or of property representing those shares, is less than it would be but for that arrangement,

then, tax shall be payable under that disposition in all respects as if a specified amount, which relates to that arrangement, were a benefit taken immediately after that arrangement is made—

(i) by the beneficial owners of the related shares in that company, and

(ii) so far as the related shares in that company are held in trust (in this section referred to as the "related trust") and have no ascertainable beneficial owners, by the disponer in relation to that related trust as if, immediately after that arrangement is made, that disponer was the absolute beneficial owner of those related shares,

in the same proportions as the market value of the related shares, which are beneficially owned by them or are deemed to be so beneficially owned, is increased by that arrangement.

(6) *Subsections (3)*, *(4)* and *(5)* shall not prejudice any charge for tax in respect of any gift or inheritance taken under any disposition on or after the making of an arrangement referred to in those subsections and comprising shares in a company, or property representing such shares.

(7) Where shares in a company, which are held in trust under a disposition made by any disponer, are related shares by reason of any arrangement referred to in this section, any gift or inheritance taken under the disposition on or after the arrangement is made and comprising those related shares, or property representing those related shares, are deemed to be taken from that disponer.

(8) In relation to the tax due and payable in respect of any gift or inheritance taken under *paragraph (ii)* of *subsection (3)* or *paragraph (ii)* of *subsection (5)*, and notwithstanding any other provision of this Act—

(a) the disponer in relation to the related trust is not a person primarily accountable for the payment of such tax, and

(b) a person who is a trustee of the related trust concerned for the time being at the date of the gift or at the date of the inheritance, or at any date subsequent to that date, is so primarily accountable.

(9) A person who is accountable for the payment of tax in respect of any specified amount, or part of a specified amount, taken as a gift or an inheritance under this section shall, for the purpose of paying the tax, or raising the amount of the tax when already paid, have power, whether the related shares are or are not vested in that person, to raise the amount of such tax and any interest and expenses properly paid or incurred by that person in respect of such tax, by the sale or mortgage of, or a terminable charge on, the related shares in the relevant company.

(10) Tax due and payable in respect of a taxable gift or a taxable inheritance taken under this section shall be and remain a charge on the related shares in the relevant company.

(11) Where related shares are subject to a discretionary trust immediately after an arrangement is made in accordance with the provisions of this section, the amount by which the market value of such shares is increased by such

arrangement is property for the purposes of a charge for tax arising by reason of *section 15*.

(12) Where, immediately after and as a result of an arrangement, shares in a company have been redeemed, the redeemed shares are, for the purpose of the references to property representing shares in *subsection (1)* and *subsection (3)*, *(4)* or *(5)*, except a reference in relation to which the redeemed shares are actually represented by property, deemed, immediately after the arrangement, being an arrangement made on or after 6 May 1993, to be represented by property, and the market value of the property so deemed to represent the redeemed shares is deemed to be nil.

Cross References

From Section 44

Section 15 Acquisitions by discretionary trusts.
Section 26 Market value of property.
Section 27 Market value of certain shares in private companies.

PART 6

Returns and Assessments

45 Accountable persons

[(1) The person accountable for the payment of tax is—

(a) the donee or successor, and

(b) in the case referred to in *section 32(2)*, the transferee referred to in that subsection, to the extent referred to in that subsection.

(2) The tax shall be recoverable from the person referred to in *subsection (1)* and the personal representative of such person, where that person has died, on whom the Commissioners have served notice in writing of the assessment of tax in accordance with *section 49(4)*.

(3) The person referred to in *subsection (1)* and the personal representative of such person shall, for the purposes of paying the tax, or raising the amount of the tax when already paid, have power, whether the property is or is not vested in that person, to raise the amount of such tax and any expenses properly paid or incurred by that person in respect of raising the amount of such tax, by the sale or mortgage of, or a terminable charge on, that property or any part of that property.

(4) Every public officer having in such person's custody—

(a) any rolls, books, records, papers, documents or proceedings, or

(b) any other data maintained in electronic, photographic or other process,

the inspection of which may tend to secure the tax, or to prove or lead to the discovery of any fraud or omission in relation to the tax, shall at all reasonable times permit any person authorised by the Commissioners to inspect those rolls, books, records, papers, documents or proceedings or that other data so maintained, and to copy by any means, take notes and extracts as that person may deem necessary.][1]

Amendments

[1] Substituted by FA10 s(147)(1)(b). Has effect as on and from 3 April 2010.

Revenue Briefings

eBrief

eBrief No. 47/2011 – Revised Pay and File date for Capital Acquisitions Tax 2011

Cross References

From Section 45

Section 32 Dealings with future interests.
Section 49 Assessment of tax.

To Section 45

Section 2 General interpretation.
Section 16 Application of this Act.
Section 21 Application of this Act.
Section 49 Assessment of tax.
Section 68 Conditions before appeal may be made.
Section 111 Liability to tax in respect of certain sales and mortgages.

45A Obligation to retain certain records

[(1) In this section—

"*records*" includes books, accounts, documents, and any other data maintained manually or by any electronic, photographic or other process, relating to—

(a) property, of any description, which under or in consequence of any disposition, a person becomes beneficially entitled in possession to, otherwise than for full consideration in money or money's worth paid by that person,

(b) liabilities, costs and expenses properly payable out of that property,

(c) consideration given in good faith, in money or money's worth, paid by a person for that property,

(d) a relief or an exemption claimed under any provision of this Act, and

(e) the valuation, on the valuation date or other date, as the case may be, of property the subject of the disposition.

(2) Every person who is an accountable person shall retain, or cause to be retained on his or her behalf, records of the type referred to in *subsection (1)* as are required to enable—

(i) a true return, additional return or statement to be made for the purposes of this Act, or

(ii) a claim to a relief or an exemption under any provision of this Act to be substantiated.

(3) Records required to be retained by virtue of this section shall be retained—

(a) in written form in an official language of the State, or

(b) subject to section 887(2) of the Taxes Consolidation Act 1997, by means of any electronic, photographic or other process.

(4) Records retained for the purposes of *subsections (2)* and *(3)* shall be retained by the person required to retain the records—

[(a) where the requirements of *section 46(2)*, requiring the delivery of a return on or before the dates mentioned in *section 46(2A)*, are met, for the period of 6 years commencing on the valuation date of the gift or inheritance, or][1]

(b) notwithstanding *paragraph (a)*, where an accountable person fails to comply with the requirements of the provisions referred to in *paragraph (a)* in the manner so specified, or, where any person is required to deliver a return, additional return or statement under this Act other than the provisions referred to in *paragraph (a)*, for the period of 6 years commencing on the date that the return, additional return or statement is received by the Commissioners.

(5) Any person who fails to comply with *subsection (2)*, *(3)* or *(4)* in respect of the retention of any records relating to a gift or inheritance is liable to a penalty of [€3,000][2]; but a penalty shall not be imposed under this section on any person who is not liable to tax in respect of that gift or inheritance.][3]

Amendments

[1] Substituted by FA10 s(147)(1)(c). Has effect as on and from 3 April 2010.

[2] Substituted by FA10 sched(4)(3)(b). Has effect as on and from 3 April 2010.

[3] Inserted by FA03 s146(1)(b). With effect from 1 October 2003 per SI 466 of 2003.

Cross References

From Section 45A

Section 46 Delivery of returns.

45AA Liability of certain persons in respect of non-resident beneficiaries

[(1) Where—

(a) property passing under a deceased person's will or intestacy or under Part IX or section 56 of the Succession Act 1965, or otherwise as a result of the death of that person, is taken by a person or persons who is or are not resident in the State,

(b) the personal representative or one or more of the personal representatives, where there is more than one personal representative, of the deceased person's estate is or are resident in the State, and

(c) the person or persons referred to in *paragraph (a)* do not deliver a return and make a payment of tax in accordance with *section 46(2)*,

then, the personal representative or one or more of the personal representatives, as the case may be [...][1] shall be assessable and chargeable for the tax payable by the person or persons referred to in *paragraph (a)* to the same extent that those persons are chargeable to tax under *section 11*.

[(1A) The solicitor referred to in *section 48(10)* shall be assessable and chargeable for the tax payable by the person or persons referred to in *paragraph (a)* of that subsection to the same extent that those persons are chargeable to tax under *section 11*.][2]

(2) *Subsection (1)* [and *subsection (1A)*][3] shall not apply where a liability to inheritance tax arises by virtue of the fact that a person referred to in *paragraph (a)* of that subsection has not disclosed that he or she has received a taxable gift or a taxable inheritance prior to the taxable inheritance or taxable inheritances, as the case may be, consisting of property referred to in *subsection (1)(a)* [and *subsection (10)(a)* of *section 48*][4] and the personal representative or solicitor referred to in *section 48(10)*, as the case may be, has made reasonable enquiries regarding such gifts or inheritances and has acted in good faith.

(3) The personal representative or one or more of the personal representatives and the solicitor referred to in *section 48(10)* shall be liable only to the extent that that person or those persons, as the case may be, have control of the property referred to in *subsection (1)(a)* [and *subsection (10)(a)* of *section 48*][5] or which that person or those persons would, but for that person's or those persons' own neglect or default, have control of such property.

(4) The persons referred to in *subsection (3)*—

(a) shall be entitled to retain so much of the property referred to in *subsection (1)(a)* [and *subsection (10)(a)* of *subsection 48*][6] as may be required to pay the tax in respect of the person or persons referred to in [*paragraph (b)* of that subsection and *subsection (10)(a)* of *section 48*][7], and

(b) shall have power, whether the property is or is not vested in that person, to raise the amount of such tax and any expenses properly paid or incurred by that person in respect of raising the amount of such tax, by the sale or mortgage of, or a terminable charge on, that property or any part of that property.][8]

Amendments

[1] Deleted by FA12 s115(1)(a). Applies on and from 8 February 2012.

[2] Inserted by FA12 s115(1)(b). Applies on and from 8 February 2012.

[3] Inserted by FA12 s115(1)(c). Applies on and from 8 February 2012.

[4, 5, 6] Inserted by FA12 s115(1)(d). Applies on and from 8 February 2012.

[7] Substituted by FA12 s115(1)(e). Applies on and from 8 February 2012.

[8] Inserted by FA10 s(147)(1)(d). Has effect as on and from 3 April 2010.

Cross References

From Section 45AA

Section 11 Taxable inheritance.
Section 46 Delivery of returns.
Section 48 Affidavits and accounts.

46 Delivery of returns

[CATA 1976 s36]

(1) In this section—

(a) notwithstanding anything contained in *sections 6* and *11* reference, other than in *subsection (13)* or *(14)*, to a or a taxable gift includes a reference to an inheritance a taxable inheritance, as the case may be, and

(b) a reference to a donee includes a reference to a successor.

(2) [Any person who is primarily accountable for the payment of tax by virtue of *paragraph (c)* of *section 16*, *paragraph (c)* of *section 21*][1][, or who is accountable by virtue of [section 45(1), shall][2]][3][...][4]—

(a) deliver to the Commissioners a full and true return of—

(i) every gift in respect of which that person is so [...][5] accountable,

(ii) all the property comprised in such gift on the valuation date,

(iii) an estimate of the market value of such property on the valuation date, and

(iv) such particulars as may be relevant to the assessment of tax in respect of such gift;

(b) notwithstanding *section 49*, make on that return an assessment of such amount of tax as, to the best of that person's knowledge, information and belief, ought to be charged, levied and paid on that valuation date, and

(c) duly pay the amount of such tax.

[(2A) For the purposes of *subsection (2)* (other than in the case of an inheritance to which *section 15* or *20* applies), where the relevant date occurs—

(a) in the period from 1 January to 31 August in any year, tax shall be paid and a return shall be delivered on or before [31 October][6] in that year, and

(b) in the period from 1 September to 31 December in any year, tax shall be paid and a return shall be delivered on or before [31 October][7] in the following year.

(2B) *Subsection (2A)* shall only apply as respects tax to be paid and returns to be delivered as respects valuation dates arising on or after such day as may be appointed by order of the Commissioners.][8]

[(2C) In the case of inheritances referred to in *sections 15(1)* and *20(1)*, returns shall be delivered and tax shall be paid within 4 months of the valuation date of such inheritances.][9]

[(3) *Subsection (2)(c)* (other than in respect of tax arising by reason of *section 20*) shall be complied with, where the tax due and payable is inheritance tax which is being paid wholly or partly by the transfer of securities to the Minister for Finance under *section 56*, by—

(a) making an application to the Commissioners to pay all or part of the tax by such transfer,

(b) completing the transfer of the securities to the Minister for Finance within such time, not being less than 30 days, as may be specified by the Commissioners by notice in writing, and

(c) duly paying the excess, if any, of the amount of tax referred to in *subsection (2)(b)* over the nominal face value of the securities tendered in payment of the tax in accordance with *paragraph (a)*.

(3A) A return to be delivered in accordance with *subsection (2A)* shall only be delivered in accordance with the provisions of Chapter 6 of Part 38 of the Taxes Consolidation Act 1997 except where a relief or an exemption (other than the exemption referred to in *section 69*) is not being claimed by a person under this Act and the interest taken by a person in property is an absolute interest which is not subject to any conditions or restrictions.][10]

(4) *Subsection (2)* applies to a charge for tax arising by reason of [*section 15* or *20*][11] and to any other gift where—

(a) the aggregate of the taxable values of all taxable gifts taken by the donee on or after 5 December 1991, which have the same group threshold (as defined in *Schedule 2*) as that other gift, exceeds an amount which is 80 per cent of the threshold amount (as defined in *Schedule 2*) which applies in the computation of tax on that aggregate, or

(b) the donee or, in a case to which *section 32(2)* applies, the transferee (within the meaning of, and to the extent provided for by, that section) is required by notice in writing by the Commissioners to deliver a return,

and for the purposes of this subsection, a reference to a gift includes a reference to a part of a gift or to a part of a taxable gift, as the case may be.

(5) For the purposes of this section, the relevant date shall be—

(a) the valuation date, or

(b) where the donee or, in a case to which *section 32(2)* applies, the transferee (within the meaning of, and to the extent provided for by, that section) is required by notice in writing by the Commissioners to deliver a return, the date of the notice.

[…][12]

(7) (a) Any accountable person shall, if that person is so required by the Commissioners by notice in writing, deliver and verify to the Commissioners within such time, not being less than 30 days, as may be specified in the notice—

(i) a statement (where appropriate, on a form provided, or approved of, by them) of such particulars relating to any property, and

(ii) such evidence as they require,

as may, in their opinion, be relevant to the assessment of tax in respect of the gift.

(b) The Commissioners may authorise a person to inspect—

(i) any property comprised in a gift, or

(ii) any books, records, accounts or other documents, in whatever form they are stored, maintained or preserved, relating to any property as may in their opinion be relevant to the assessment of tax in respect of a gift,

and the person having the custody or possession of that property, or of those books, records, accounts or documents, shall permit the person so authorised to make that inspection at such reasonable times as the Commissioners consider necessary.

[(7A) The making of enquiries by the Commissioners for the purposes of *subsection (7)(a)* or the authorising of inspections by the Commissioners under *subsection (7)(b)* in connection with or in relation to a relevant return (within the meaning given in *section 49(6A)(b)*) may not be initiated after the expiry of 4 years commencing on the date that the relevant return is received by the Commissioners.

(7B) (a) The time limit referred to in *subsection (7A)* shall not apply where the Commissioners have reasonable grounds for believing that any form of fraud or neglect has been committed by or on behalf of any accountable person in connection with or in relation to any relevant return which is the subject of any enquiries or inspections.

(b) In this subsection "*neglect*" means negligence or a failure to deliver a correct relevant return (within the meaning given in *section 49(6A)(b)*).][13]

(8) The Commissioners may by notice in writing require any accountable person to—

(a) deliver to them within such time, not being less than 30 days, as may be specified in the notice, an additional return, if it appears to the Commissioners that a return made by that accountable person is defective in a material respect by reason of anything contained in or omitted from it,

(b) notwithstanding *section 49*, make on that additional return an assessment of such amended amount of tax as, to the best of that person's knowledge, information and belief, ought to be charged, levied and paid on the relevant gift, and

(c) duly pay the outstanding tax, if any, for which that person is accountable in respect of that gift,

and

(i) the requirements of *subparagraphs (ii)*, *(iii)* and *(iv)* of *subsection (2)(a)* shall apply to such additional return required by virtue of *paragraph (a)*, and

(ii) *subsection (3)* shall, with any necessary modifications, apply to any payment required by virtue of *paragraph (c)*.

(9) Where any accountable person who has delivered a return or an additional return is aware or becomes aware at any time that the return or additional return is defective in a material respect by reason of anything contained in or omitted

from it, that person shall, without application from the Commissioners and within 3 months of so becoming aware—

(a) deliver to them an additional return,

(b) notwithstanding *section 49*, make on that additional return an assessment of such amended amount of tax as, to the best of that person's knowledge, information and belief, ought to be charged, levied and paid on the relevant gift, and

(c) duly pay the outstanding tax, if any, for which that person is accountable in respect of that gift,

and

(i) the requirements of *subparagraphs (ii)*, *(iii)* and *(iv)* of *subsection (2)(a)* shall apply to such additional return required by virtue of *paragraph (a)*, and

(ii) *subsection (3)* shall, with any necessary modifications, apply to any payment required by virtue of *paragraph (c)*.

(10) Any amount of tax payable by an accountable person in respect of an assessment of tax made by that accountable person on a return delivered by that accountable person (other than an amount of that tax payable by the transfer of securities to the Minister for Finance under *section 56*) shall accompany the return and be paid to the Collector.

(11) Any assessment or payment of tax made under this section shall include interest on tax payable in accordance with *section 51*.

(12) The Commissioners may by notice in writing require any person to deliver to them within such time, not being less than 30 days, as may be specified in the notice, a full and true return showing details of every taxable gift (including the property comprised in such gift) taken by that person during the period specified in the notice or, as the case may be, indicating that that person has taken no taxable gift during that period.

(13) As respects a taxable gift to which this subsection applies, [the Commissioners may by notice in writing require a disponer to deliver to them within such time, not being less than 30 days, as may be specified in the notice,][14] a full and true return—

(a) of all the property comprised in such gift on the valuation date,

(b) of an estimate of the market value of such property on the valuation date, and

(c) of such particulars as may be relevant to the assessment of tax in respect of the gift.

(14) *Subsection (13)* applies to a taxable gift, in the case where—

(a) the taxable value of the taxable gift exceeds an amount which is 80 per cent of the group threshold (as defined in *Schedule 2*) which applies in relation to that gift for the purposes of the computation of the tax on that gift,

(b) the taxable value of the taxable gift taken by the donee from the disponer increases the total taxable value of all taxable gifts and taxable inheritances taken on or after 5 December 1991 by the donee from the disponer from an amount less than or equal to the amount specified in *paragraph (a)* to an amount which exceeds the amount so specified, or

(c) the total taxable value of all taxable gifts and taxable inheritances taken on or after 5 December 1991 by the donee from the disponer exceeds the amount specified in *paragraph (a)* and the donee takes a further taxable gift from the disponer.

(15) Where, under or in consequence of any disposition made by [a person who is resident or ordinarily resident in the State][15] at the date of the disposition, property becomes subject to a discretionary trust, the disponer shall within 4 months of the date of the disposition deliver to the Commissioners a full and true return of—

(a) the terms of the discretionary trust,

(b) the names and addresses of the trustees and objects of the discretionary trust, and

(c) an estimate of the market value at the date of the disposition of the property becoming subject to the discretionary trust.

[(16) For the purposes of *subsection (15)*, a person who is not domiciled in the State at the date of the disposition is treated as not resident and not ordinarily resident in the State on that date unless—

(a) that person has been resident in the State for the 5 consecutive years of assessment immediately preceding the year of assessment in which that date falls, and

(b) that person is either resident or ordinarily resident in the State on that date.][16]

Amendments

[1] Substituted by FA06 s117(1)(b). This section shall apply as respects the year 2006 and subsequent years.

[2] Substituted by FA11 sched3(2)(a). Applies to valuation dates arising on or after 14 June 2010.

[3] Substituted by FA10 s(147)(1)(e)(i). Has effect as on and from 3 April 2010.

[4] Deleted by FA10 s(147)(1)(e)(ii). Applies on and from the date the Revenue Commissioners make the order referred to in section 46(2B).

[5] Deleted by FA10 s(147)(1)(e)(iii). Has effect as on and from 3 April 2010.

[6, 7] Substituted by FA12 s116(1)(a). Applies on and from 8 February 2012.

[8] Inserted by FA10 s(147)(1)(f). S.I. No. 282 of 2010 appoints 14 June 2010 as the day section 46(2A) applies.

[9] Inserted by FA12 s115(2). Applies on and from 8 February 2012.

[10] Substituted by FA10 s(147)(1)(g). Has effect as on and from 3 April 2010.

[11] Substituted by FA06 s117(1)(d). This section shall apply as respects the year 2006 and subsequent years.

[12] Deleted by FA10 s(147)(1)(h). Has effect as on and from 3 April 2010.

[13] Inserted by FA03 s145(1)(b). With effect from 1 January 2005 per SI 515 of 2003.

[14] Substituted by FA10 s(147)(1)(i). Has effect as on and from 3 April 2010.

[15] Substituted by FA06 s117(1)(e). This section shall apply as respects the year 2006 and subsequent years.

[16] Inserted by FA06 s117(1)(f). This section shall apply as respects the year 2006 and subsequent years.

Revenue Briefings

eBrief

eBrief No. 37/2010 – Changes to Capital Acquisitions Tax and Probate Administration
eBrief No. 38/2010 – Changes to Capital Acquisitions Tax and Probate - New Forms
eBrief No. 42/2010 – Capital Acquisitions Tax Consolidation Act 2003 (Section 46(2B)) (Appointed Day) Order 2010 (S.I. 282 of 2010)
eBrief No. 65/2010 – Finance Act 2010 – Changes to Probate & Capital Acquisition Tax

Revenue Information Notes

IT 39 – Guide to Completing the IT38 Return (Pay and File)
IT 39 Gift/Inheritance Tax – A Guide to completing the Self Assessment Return – Pre Finance Act 2010
Notice on the Changes to CAT & Probate Finance Act 2010 – Changes to Probate & Capital Acquisition Tax

Statements of Practice

Revenue Powers – SP Gen 1/94 (Revised February 2006); SP Gen 1/99

Cross References

From Section 46

Section 6 Taxable gift.
Section 11 Taxable inheritance.
Section 15 Acquisitions by discretionary trusts.
Section 16 Application of this Act.
Section 20 Annual acquisitions by discretionary trusts.
Section 21 Application of this Act.
Section 32 Dealings with future interests.
Section 49 Assessment of tax.
Section 51 Payment of tax and interest on tax.
Section 56 Payment of inheritance tax by transfer of securities.
Schedule 2 Computation of tax

To Section 46

Section 2 General interpretation.
Section 45A Obligation to retain certain records.
Section 45AA Liability of certain persons in respect of non-resident beneficiaries.
Section 48 Affidavits and accounts.
Section 49 Assessment of tax.
Section 51 Payment of tax and interest on tax.
Section 53A Surcharge for late returns.
Section 58 Penalties.
Section 63 Recovery of tax and penalties.
Section 68 Conditions before appeal may be made.
Schedule 2 Computation of tax

46A Expression of doubt

[(1) Where an accountable person is in doubt as to the correct application of law to, or the treatment for tax purposes of, any matter to be included in a return or additional return to be delivered by such person under this Act, then that person may deliver the return or additional return to the best of that person's belief but that person shall draw the Commissioners' attention to the matter in question in the return or additional return by specifying the doubt and, if that person does so, that person shall be treated as making a full and true disclosure with regard to that matter.

(2) Subject to *subsection (3)*, where a return or additional return, which includes an expression of doubt as to the correct application of law to, or the treatment for tax purposes of, any matter contained in the return or additional return, is delivered by an accountable person to the Commissioners in accordance with this section, then *section 51(2)* does not apply to any additional liability arising from a notification to that person by the Commissioners of the correct application of the law to, or the treatment for tax purposes of, the matter contained in the return or additional return the subject of the expression of doubt, on condition that such additional liability is accounted for and remitted to the Commissioners within 30 days of the date on which that notification is issued.

(3) *Subsection (2)* does not apply where the Commissioners do not accept as genuine an expression of doubt as to the correct application of law to, or the treatment for tax purposes of, any matter contained in the return or additional return and an expression of doubt shall not be accepted as genuine where the Commissioners are of the opinion that the person was acting with a view to the evasion or avoidance of tax.

(4) Where the Commissioners do not accept an expression of doubt as genuine they shall notify the accountable person accordingly within the period of 30 days after the date that the expression of doubt is received by the Commissioners, and the accountable person shall account for any tax, which was not correctly accounted for in the return or additional return referred to in *subsection (1)* and *section 51(2)* applies accordingly.

(5) An accountable person who is aggrieved by a decision of the Commissioners that that person's expression of doubt is not genuine may, by giving notice in writing to the Commissioners within the period of 30 days after the notification of the said decision, require the matter to be referred to the Appeal Commissioners.][1]

Amendments

[1] Inserted by FA03 s146(1)(c). With effect from 1 October 2003 per SI 466 of 2003.

Cross References

From Section 46A

Section 51 Payment of tax and interest on tax.

47 Signing of returns, etc

[CATA 1976 s37]

(1) A return or an additional return required to be delivered under this Act shall be signed by the accountable person who delivers the return or the additional return and shall include a declaration by the person signing it that the return or additional return is, to the best of that person's knowledge, information and belief, correct and complete.

(2) The Commissioners may require a return or an additional return to be made on oath.

(3) The Commissioners may, if they so think fit, accept a return or an additional return under this Act that has not been signed in accordance with this section and such return or additional return is deemed to be duly delivered to the Commissioners under this Act.

(4) [(a) A return or additional return delivered under this Act shall be made on a form provided, or approved of, by the Commissioners.][1]

(b) An affidavit, additional affidavit, account or additional account, delivered under this Act, shall be made on a form provided, or approved of, by the Commissioners.

(5) Any oath or affidavit to be made for the purposes of this Act may be made—

(a) before the Commissioners,

(b) before any officer or person authorised by the Commissioners in that behalf,

(c) before any Commissioner for Oaths or any Peace Commissioner or Notary Public in the State, or

(d) at any place outside the State, before any person duly authorised to administer oaths in that place.

[(6) For the purposes of this section, references to an oath shall be construed as including references to an affirmation and references in this section to the administration or making of an oath shall be construed accordingly.][2]

Amendments

[1] Substituted by FA12 sched6(2)(a). Has effect as on and from 31 March 2012.

[2] Inserted by FA03 s147.

Revenue Briefings

eBrief

eBrief No. 65/2010 – Finance Act 2010 – Changes to Probate & Capital Acquisition Tax

48 Affidavits and accounts

[CATA 1976 s38]

[(1) In this section—

"*Inland Revenue Affidavit*" means the document, completed by or on behalf of the intended applicant or intended applicants for probate or letters of administration and sworn by them before a commissioner for oaths, a practicing solicitor or a court clerk, as the case may be;

"*Probate Office*" includes a district probate registry.][1]

(2) The Inland Revenue affidavit required for an application for probate or letters of administration shall extend to the verification of a statement of the following particulars:

[(a) details of all property in respect of which the grant of probate or administration is required and, in the case of a deceased person who on the date of his or her death was—

(i) resident or ordinarily resident and domiciled in the State, or

(ii) resident or ordinarily resident and not domiciled in the State and who had been resident in the State for the 5 consecutive years of assessment immediately preceding the year of assessment in which the date of death falls,

details of all property, wherever situate, the beneficial ownership of which, on that person's death, is affected—

(I) by that person's will,

(II) by the rules for distribution on intestacy, or

(III) by Part IX or section 56 of the Succession Act 1965, or under the analogous law of another territory;][2]

(b) details of any property which was the subject matter of a disposition *inter vivos* made by the deceased person where the date of the disposition was within 2 years prior to that person's death or of a *donatio mortis causa*;

(c) details of the inheritances arising under the will or intestacy of the deceased person or under Part IX or section 56 of the Succession Act 1965, or under the analogous law of another territory, together with a copy of any such will;

(d) particulars of the inheritances (including the property comprised in such inheritances) other than those referred to in *paragraphs (b)* and *(c)*, arising on the death of the deceased person;

(e) the name and address of each person who takes an inheritance on the death of the deceased person and that person's relationship to the disponer; and

(f) such other particulars as the Commissioners may require for the purposes of this Act.

(3) Where the interest of the deceased person was a limited interest and that person died on or after the date of the passing of this Act, the trustee of the property in which the limited interest subsisted shall deliver an account which shall contain the following particulars—

(a) details of each inheritance arising on the death of the deceased person under the disposition under which the limited interest of the deceased person arose, including the name and address of each person taking such inheritance and that person's relationship to the disponer, and

(b) such other particulars as the Commissioners may require for the purposes of this Act.

(4) If at any time it shall appear that any material error or omission was made in an affidavit or account referred to in this section, the persons liable to deliver an affidavit or account shall be liable to deliver an additional affidavit or an additional account, correcting the error or omission.

[(5) Except where submitted in accordance with regulations made under *subsection (8)*, the Inland Revenue Affidavit and the statements, accounts and additional affidavits referred to in *subsections (2)* to *(4)* shall be submitted to the Probate Office in duplicate.

(6) As soon as practicable after probate or letters of administration has or have been issued, the Probate Office shall transmit to the Commissioners such information as is held in electronic form by the Probate Office and which is relevant for the purposes of this Act.

(7) Except where submitted in accordance with regulations made under *subsection (8)*, the Probate Office shall send one copy of the Inland Revenue Affidavit referred to in *subsection (5)* together with a copy of the will (if any) to the Commissioners as soon as practicable after probate or letters of administration has or have been issued.

(8) (a) Subject to *paragraph (b)*, the Commissioners shall make regulations permitting the submission to the Probate Office of the Inland Revenue Affidavit, and the other documents referred to in *subsections (2)* to *(4)*, by simultaneous transmission of these documents in electronic form to that Office and to the Commissioners.

(b) Regulations under this subsection shall only be made by the Commissioners where they are satisfied that both the Probate Office and the Commissioners have the technical competence and ability to continue to perform their respective functions concerned if the regulations are made.

(c) Regulations under this subsection may contain such incidental and supplementary matters as appears necessary or appropriate to the Commissioners for the purpose of giving effect to this subsection.

(9) The Commissioners and the Probate Office shall both have access to the affidavits and documents that have been transmitted electronically under *subsection (8)*.

(10) Where—

(a) property passing under the deceased person's will or intestacy or Part IX or section 56 of the Succession Act 1965, or otherwise as a result of the death of that person, is taken by a person or persons who is or are not resident in the State,

(b) the market value of the property referred to in *paragraph (a)* taken by any person referred to in that paragraph exceeds €20,000,

(c) the intended applicant or all the intended applicants, where there is more than one intended applicant, for probate or letters of administration is or are resident outside the State, and

(d) a return would be required to be delivered to the Commissioners in respect of such property in accordance with *section 46(2)* if the valuation date in respect of that property were the date of death of that person,

then, the intended applicant or the intended applicants, as the case may be, for probate or letters of administration shall appoint a solicitor who is lawfully practicing in the State to act in connection with the administration of the deceased person's estate.

(11) The Probate Office shall not issue probate or letters of administration in respect of a deceased person's estate in any case to which *subsection (10)* applies unless a solicitor lawfully practicing in the State has been appointed by the intended applicant or the intended applicants to act in connection with the administration of the deceased person's estate.][3]

Amendments

[1] Substituted by FA10 s(147)(1)(k). With effect by Ministerial Order S.I. No. 282 of 2010, which appoints 14 June 2010 as the date from which FA10 s147 comes into effect.

[2] Substituted by FA05 s131(1). Has effect in relation to Inland Revenue affidavits in respect of estates of deceased persons where those persons died on or after 1 December 2004.

[3] Inserted by FA10 s(147)(1)(l). With effect by Ministerial Order S.I. No. 282 of 2010, which appoints 14 June 2010 as the date from which FA10 s147 comes into effect.

Revenue Briefings

eBrief

eBrief No. 37/2010 – Changes to Capital Acquisitions Tax and Probate Administration
eBrief No. 65/2010 – Finance Act 2010 – Changes to Probate & Capital Acquisition Tax

Revenue Information Notes

Pt 2 Revenue CAT Manual – The Inland Revenue Affidavit.
CA25 – A Guide to completing the Inland Revenue Affidavit (Form CA 24)
CAT 3 – Probate Tax
Notice on the Changes to CAT & Probate Finance Act 2010 – Changes to Probate & Capital Acquisition Tax

Cross References

From Section 48

Section 46 Delivery of returns.

To Section 48

Section 45AA Liability of certain persons in respect of non-resident beneficiaries.
Schedule 3 Consequential Amendments

49 Assessment of tax

[CATA 1976 s39; FA 1989 s75]

(1) Subject to *section 46*, assessments of tax under this Act shall be made by the Commissioners.

[(1A) The Commissioners may issue an assessment to a person referred to in *section 45(1)* where a return has not been delivered to them under *section 46(2)*.][1]

(2) If at any time it appears that for any reason an assessment was incorrect, the Commissioners may make a correcting assessment, which shall be substituted for the first-mentioned assessment.

(3) If at any time it appears that for any reason too little tax was assessed, the Commissioners may make an additional assessment.

(4) The Commissioners may serve notice in writing of the assessment of tax on any accountable person or, at the request of an accountable person, on that accountable person's agent, or on the personal representative of an accountable person if that person is dead.

(5) Where the place of residence of the accountable person or of that accountable person's personal representative is not known to the Commissioners they may publish in *Iris Oifigiúil* a notice of the making of the assessment with such particulars of that assessment as they shall think proper and on the publication of the notice in *Iris Oifigiúil* the accountable person or that accountable person's personal representative, as the case may be, is deemed to have been served with the notice of the assessment on the date of such publication.

(6) Any assessment, correcting assessment or additional assessment under this section may be made by the Commissioners from any return or additional return delivered under *section 46* or from any other information in the possession of the Commissioners or from any one or more of these sources.

[(6A) (a) For the purposes of *subsection (6)* an assessment, a correcting assessment or an additional assessment made in connection with or in relation to a relevant return may not be made after the expiry of 4 years from the date that the relevant return is received by the Commissioners.

(b) In this subsection "*relevant return*" means a return within the meaning of[...][2] a return or an additional return within the meaning of *section 46*.

(6B) The time limit referred to in *subsection (6A)* shall not apply where the Commissioners have reasonable grounds for believing that any form of fraud or neglect (within the meaning given in *section 46(7B)(b)*) has been committed by or on behalf of any accountable person in connection with or in relation to any relevant return (within the meaning given in *subsection (6A)*) which is the subject of assessment.][3]

(7) The Commissioners, in making any assessment, correcting assessment or additional assessment, otherwise than from a return or an additional return which is satisfactory to them, shall make an assessment of such amount of tax as, to the best of their knowledge, information (including information received from a member of the Garda Síochána) and belief, ought to be charged, levied and paid.

(8) Nothing in *section 46* shall preclude the Commissioners from making an assessment of tax, a correcting assessment of tax, or an additional assessment of tax, under the provisions of this section.

Amendments

[1] Inserted by FA10 s(147)(1)(m). Has effect as on and from 3 April 2010.

[2] Deleted by FA07 sched4(2)(c).

[3] Inserted by FA03 s145(1)(c). With effect from 1 January 2005 per SI 515 of 2003.

Statements of Practice

Revenue Powers – SP Gen 1/94 (Revised February 2006); SP Gen 1/99

Cross References

From Section 49

Section 45 Accountable persons.
Section 46 Delivery of returns.

To Section 49

Section 45 Accountable persons.
Section 46 Delivery of returns.
Section 51 Payment of tax and interest on tax.

50 Computation of tax

[CATA 1976 s40 (part)]

Subject to *sections 18* and *23*, the amount of tax payable shall be computed in accordance with *Schedule 2*.

Cross References

From Section 50

Section 18 Computation of tax.
Section 23 Computation of tax.
Schedule 2 Computation of tax

To Section 50

Section 16 Application of this Act.
Section 21 Application of this Act.
Schedule 2 Computation of tax

PART 7

Payment and Recovery of Tax, Interest and Penalties

51 Payment of tax and interest on tax

[CATA 1976 s41(1), (2), (2A) and (3) to (6) and (8); FA 1989 s76(2)]

(1) Tax shall be due and payable on the valuation date.

[(1A) (a) Simple interest is payable, without deduction of income tax, on the tax arising by reason of *section 15(1)* or *20(1)* from the valuation date to the date of payment of that tax, and the amount of that interest shall be determined in accordance with *paragraph (c)* of *subsection (2)*.

(b) Interest payable in accordance with *paragraph (a)* is chargeable and recoverable in the same manner as if it were part of the tax.][1]

[(2)

[(a) Simple interest is payable, without deduction of income tax, on the tax where the relevant date (within the meaning of *section 46(5)*) occurs—

(i) in the period from 1 January to 31 August in any year, from [1 November][2] in that year to the date of payment of that tax, and

(ii) in the period 1 September to 31 December in any year, from [1 November][3] in the following year to the date of payment of that tax,

and the amount of that interest shall be determined in accordance with *paragraph (c)*.][4]

(b) Interest payable in accordance with *paragraph (a)* is chargeable and recoverable in the same manner as if it were part of the tax.

(c) (i) In this paragraph—

"*period of delay*", in relation to any tax due and payable, means the period during which that tax remains unpaid;

"*relevant period*", in relation to a period of delay which falls into more than one of the periods specified in column (1) of *Part 1* of the Table, means any part of the period of delay which falls into, or is the same as, a period specified in that column;

"Table" means the Table to this subsection.

(ii) The interest payable in accordance with [*paragraph (a)* of this subsection and *paragraph (a)* of *subsection (1A)*][5], shall be—

(I) where one of the periods specified in column (1) of *Part 1* of the Table includes or is the same as the period of delay, the amount determined by the formula—

$$T \times D \times P$$

where—

T is the tax due and payable which remains unpaid,

D is the number of days (including part of a day) forming the period of delay, and

P is the appropriate percentage in column (2) of the Table opposite the period specified in column (1) of *Part 1* of the

Table within which the period of delay falls or which is the same as the period of delay,

and

(II) where a continuous period formed by 2 or more of the periods specified in column (1) of *Part 1* of the Table, but not (as in clause (I)) only one such period, includes or is the same as the period of delay, the aggregate of the amounts due in respect of each relevant period which forms part of the period of delay, and the amount due in respect of each such relevant period shall be determined by the formula—

$$T \times D \times P$$

where—

T is the tax due and payable which remains unpaid,

D is the number of days (including part of a day) forming the relevant period, and

P is the appropriate percentage in column (2) of *Part 1* of the Table opposite the period specified in column (1) of *Part 1* of the Table into which the relevant period falls or which is the same as the relevant period.

[Table

Part 1

(Period) (1)	(Percentage) (2)
From 31 March 1976 to 31 July 1978	0.0492%
From 1 August 1978 to 31 March 1998	0.0410%
From 1 April 1998 to 31 March 2005	0.0322%
From 1 April 2005 to 30 June 2009	0.0273%
From 1 July 2009 to the date of payment	0.0219%

Part 2

(1)	(2)
From 8 February 1995 to 31 March 1998	0.0307%
From 1 April 1998 to 31 March 2005	0.0241%
From 1 April 2005 to 30 June 2009	0.0204%
From 1 July 2009 to the date of payment	0.0164%][6]

(2A) For the purposes of calculating interest on the whole or the part of the tax to which *section 55* applies, *subsection (2)* shall apply as if references in that subsection to *Part 1* of the Table were references to *Part 2* of the Table.][7]

(3) Notwithstanding *subsection (2)*, interest is not payable on the tax—

(a) to the extent to which *section 89(4)(a)* applies, for the duration of the peiod from the valuation date to the date the agricultural value ceases to be applicable,

(b) to the extent to which *section 77(3)* and *(4)* applies, for the duration of the period from the valuation date to the date the exemption ceases to apply,

(c) to the extent to which *section 101(2)* applies, for the duration of the period from the valuation date to the date the reduction which would otherwise fall to be made under *section 92* ceases to be applicable,

(d) to the extent to which *section 78(6)* applies, for the duration of the period from the valuation date to the date the exemption ceases to apply,

[(e) to the extent to which *section 86(6)* or *(7)* applies, for the duration of the period from the valuation date to the date the exemption ceases to apply,

(f) to the extent to which *section 102A(2)* applies, for the duration of the period from the valuation date to the date the development land is disposed of.][8]

[(4) Where tax and interest, if any, on that tax is paid within 30 days of an assessment of tax made by the Commissioners in accordance with *section 49*, interest shall not run on that tax for the period of 30 days from the date of that assessment or for any part of that period.][9]

[(5) A payment of tax by an accountable person is treated as a payment on account of tax for the purposes of this section, notwithstanding that the payment may be conditional or that the assessment of tax is incorrect.][10]

(6) Subject to *subsections (2)*, *(4)* and *(5)*, payments on account may be made at any time, and when a payment on account is made, interest is not chargeable in respect of any period subsequent to the date of such payment on so much of the payment on account as is to be applied in discharge of the tax.

(7) In the case of a gift which becomes an inheritance by reason of its being taken under a disposition where the date of the disposition is within 2 years prior to the death of the disponer, this section has effect as if the references to the valuation date in *subsections (1)*, *(2)*, *(3)* and *(4)* were references to the date of death of the disponer.

(8) Where the value of a limited interest is to be ascertained in accordance with *rule 8* of *Schedule 1* as if it were a series of absolute interests, this section has effect, in relation to each of those absolute interests, as if the references to the valuation date in *subsections (1)*, *(2)*, *(3)* and *(4)* were references to the date of the taking of that absolute interest.

Amendments

[1] Inserted by FA13 s86(1)(a). Applies to inheritances taken by a discretionary trust by virtue of section 15(1) or 20(1) on or after 27 March 2013.

[2, 3] Substituted by FA12 s116(1)(b). Applies on and from 8 February 2012.

[4] Substituted by FA10 s(147)(1)(n). With effect by Ministerial Order S.I. No. 282 of 2010, which appoints 14 June 2010 as the date from which FA10 s147 comes into effect.

[5] Substituted by FA13 s86(1)(b). Applies to inheritances taken by a discretionary trust by virtue of section 15(1) or 20(1) on or after 27 March 2013.

[6] Substituted by FA09 s29(3). Applies as respects any unpaid tax or duty, as the case may be, that has not been paid before 1 July 2009 regardless of whether that tax or duty became due and payable before, on or after that date.

[7] Substituted by FA05 s145(4)(a).

[8] Substituted by FA07 s115(1). This section applies where the event that causes the exemption to cease to apply or the tax to be re-computed, as the case may be, occurs on or after 1 February 2007.

[9] Substituted by FA10 s(147)(1)(o). With effect by Ministerial Order S.I. No. 282 of 2010, which appoints 14 June 2010 as the date from which FA10 s147 comes into effect.

[10] Substituted by FA12 s115(3). Applies on and from 8 February 2012.

Revenue Briefings

eBrief

eBrief No. 37/2010 – Changes to Capital Acquisitions Tax and Probate Administration

Statements of Practice

Postponement of Tax and Registration of Charge – SP-CAT/1/90
Revenue Powers – SP Gen 1/94 (Revised February 2006); SP Gen 1/99

Cross References

From Section 51

Section 46 Delivery of returns.
Section 49 Assessment of tax.
Section 55 Payment of tax on certain assets by instalments.
Section 77 Exemption of heritage property.
Section 78 Heritage property of companies.
Section 86 Exemption relating to certain dwellings.
Section 89 Provisions relating to agricultural property.
Section 92 Business relief.
Section 101 Withdrawal of relief.
Section 102A Agricultural and business property: development land.
Schedule 1 Valuation of Limited Interests

To Section 51

Section 46 Delivery of returns.
Section 46A Expression of doubt.
Section 53 Surcharge for undervaluation of property.
Section 54 Payment of tax by instalments.
Section 55 Payment of tax on certain assets by instalments.
Schedule 1 Valuation of Limited Interests
Schedule 3 Consequential Amendments

52 Set-off of gift tax paid in respect of an inheritance

[CATA 1976 s42]

Where an amount has been paid in respect of gift tax (or interest on such gift tax) on a gift which, by reason of the death of the disponer within 2 years after the date of the disposition under which the gift was taken, becomes an inheritance in respect of which inheritance tax is payable, the amount so paid is treated as a payment on account of the inheritance tax.

53 Surcharge for undervaluation of property

[FA 1989 s79]

(1) In this section "*ascertained value*" means the market value subject to the right of appeal under *section 66* or *section 67*.

(2) Where—

(a) an accountable person delivers a return, and

(b) the estimate of the market value of any asset comprised in a gift or inheritance and included in that return, when expressed as a percentage of the ascertained value of that asset, is within any of the percentages specified in *column (1)* of the Table to this section,

then the amount of tax attributable to the property which is that asset is increased by a sum (in this section referred to as the "*surcharge*") equal to the corresponding percentage, set out in *column (2)* of that Table opposite the relevant percentage in *column (1)*, of that amount of tax.

(3) Interest is payable under *section 51* on any surcharge as if the surcharge were tax, and the surcharge and any interest on that surcharge is chargeable and recoverable as if the surcharge and that interest were part of the tax.

(4) Any person aggrieved by the imposition on that person of a surcharge under this section in respect of any asset may, within 30 days of the notification to that person of the amount of such surcharge, appeal to the Appeal Commissioners against the imposition of such surcharge on the grounds that, having regard to all the circumstances, there were sufficient grounds on which that person might reasonably have based that person's estimate of the market value of the asset.

(5) The Appeal Commissioners shall hear and determine an appeal to them under *subsection (4)* as if it were an appeal to them against an assessment to tax, and the provisions of *section 67* relating to an appeal or to the rehearing of an appeal or to the statement of a case for the opinion of the High Court on a point of law shall, with any necessary modifications, apply accordingly.

TABLE

Estimate of the market value of the asset in the return, expressed as a percentage of the ascertained value of that asset (1)	Surcharge (2)
Equal to or greater than 0 per cent but less than 40 per cent	30 per cent
Equal to or greater than 40 per cent but less than 50 per cent	20 per cent
Equal to or greater than 50 per cent but less than 67 per cent	10 per cent

Cross References

From Section 53

Section 51 Payment of tax and interest on tax.
Section 66 Appeals regarding value of real property.
Section 67 Appeals in other cases.

53A Surcharge for late returns

[(1) In this section "*specified return date*" means—

(a) in relation to a valuation date occurring in the period 1 January to 31 August in any year, [31 October][1] in that year, and

(b) in relation to a valuation date occurring in the period 1 September to 31 December in any year, [31 October][2] in the following year.

(2) For the purposes of this section—

(a) where a person fraudulently or negligently delivers an incorrect return on or before the specified return date, that person shall be deemed to have failed to have delivered the return on or before that date unless the error in the return is remedied on or before that date,

(b) where a person delivers an incorrect return on or before the specified return date, but does so neither fraudulently nor negligently and it comes to that person's notice (or, if he or she has died, to the notice of his or her personal representative) that it is incorrect, the person shall be deemed to have failed to have delivered the return on or before the specified return date unless the error in the return is remedied without unreasonable delay, and

(c) where a person delivers a return on or before the specified return date, but the Commissioners, by reason of being dissatisfied with any information contained in the return, require that person, by notice in writing served on him or her under *section 46(7)*, to deliver such statement or evidence as may be required by them, the person shall be deemed not to have delivered the return on or before the specified return date unless the person delivers the statement or evidence within the time specified in the notice.

(3) Where a person fails to deliver a return on or before the specified return date, any amount of tax which would have been payable if such a return had been delivered shall be increased by an amount (in this section referred to as "*the surcharge*") equal to—

(a) 5 per cent of the amount of tax, subject to a maximum increased amount of €12,695, where the return is delivered before the expiry of 2 months from the specified return date, and

(b) 10 per cent of the amount of tax, subject to a maximum increased amount of €63,485, where the return is not delivered before the expiry of 2 months from the specified return date.

(4) If the assessment to tax made on a return is not the amount of tax as increased in accordance with *subsection (3)*, then, the provisions of this Act and Part 42 of the Taxes Consolidation Act 1997 shall apply as if the tax contained in the assessment were the amount of tax as so increased.][3]

Amendments

[1, 2] Substituted by FA12 s116(1)(c). Applies on and from 8 February 2012.

[3] Inserted by FA10 s(147)(1)(p). Deemed to have applied on and from 14 June 2010 (FA12 s115(6)).

Cross References

From Section 53A
Section 46 Delivery of returns.

54 Payment of tax by instalments

[CATA 1976 s43]

(1) Subject to the payment of interest in accordance with *section 51* and to the provisions of this section, the [the tax due and payable (other than tax arising by reason of *section 20*)][1] in respect of a taxable gift or a taxable inheritance may, at the option of the person delivering the return or additional return, be paid by [monthly instalments over a period not exceeding 5 years in such manner as may be determined by the Commissioners, the first of which is due on 31 October immediately following the valuation date][2] and the interest on the unpaid tax shall be added to each instalment and shall be paid at the same time as such instalment.

(2) An instalment not due may be paid at any time before it is due.

(3) In any case where and to the extent that the property of which the taxable gift or taxable inheritance consists is sold or compulsorily acquired, all unpaid instalments shall, unless the interest of the donee or successor is a limited interest, be paid on completion of the sale or compulsory acquisition and, if not so paid, shall be tax in arrear.

(4) This section shall not apply in any case where and to the extent to which a taxable gift or a taxable inheritance consists of personal property in which the donee, or the

successor, or the transferee referred to in *section 32(2)*, as the case may be, takes an absolute interest.

(5) In any case where the interest taken by a donee or a successor is an interest limited to cease on that person's death, and that person's death occurs before all the instalments of the tax in respect of the taxable gift or taxable inheritance would have fallen due if such tax were being paid by instalments, any instalment of such tax which would not have fallen due prior to the date of the death of that donee or successor shall cease to be payable, and the payment, if made, of any such last-mentioned instalment is treated as an over-payment of tax for the purposes of *section 57*.

Amendments

[1] Substituted by FA06 s117(1)(g). This section shall apply as respects the year 2006 and subsequent years.

[2] Substituted by FA10 s(147)(1)(q). Has effect as on and from 3 April 2010.

Revenue Information Notes

Pt 17.1 Revenue CAT Manual – Payment by Statutory Installments.
Pt 17.2 Revenue CAT Manual – Payment by Non-Statutory Installments.
IT 39 Gift/Inheritance Tax – A Guide to completing the Self Assessment Return – Pre Finance Act 2010, Pt 8.10 – Are you paying by statutory installments

Cross References

From Section 54

Section 20 Annual acquisitions by discretionary trusts.
Section 32 Dealings with future interests.
Section 51 Payment of tax and interest on tax.
Section 57 Overpayment of tax.

To Section 54

Section 55 Payment of tax on certain assets by instalments.

55 Payment of tax on certain assets by instalments

[FA 1995 s164]

(1) In this section—

"*agricultural property*" has the meaning assigned to it by *section 89* ;

"*relevant business property*" has the same meaning as it has in *section 93*, other than shares in or securities of a company (being shares or securities quoted on a recognised stock exchange) and without regard to *sections 94* and *100(4)*.

(2) Where the whole or part of the tax which is due and payable in respect of a taxable gift or taxable inheritance is attributable to either or both agricultural property and relevant business property—

(a) *section 54* shall apply to that whole or part of the tax notwithstanding *subsection (3)* or *(4)* of that section but where all or any part of that agricultural property or relevant business property, or any property which directly or indirectly replaces such property, is sold or compulsorily acquired and, by virtue of *subsection (4)* of *section 89* or *section 101*, that sale or compulsory acquisition causes the taxable value of such a taxable gift or taxable inheritance to be increased, or would cause such increase if *subsection (2)* of *section 89* or *section 92* applied, all unpaid instalments referable to the property sold or compulsorily acquired shall, unless the interest of the donee or successor is a limited interest, be paid on completion of that sale or compulsory acquisition and, if not so paid, shall be tax in arrear, and [(b) notwithstanding *subsection (2)* of *section 51*, the interest payable on that whole or part of the tax shall be determined—

(i) in accordance with that subsection as modified by *subsection (2A)* of that section, or

(ii) in such other manner as may be prescribed by the Minister for Finance by regulations,

instead of in accordance with *subsection (2)* of that section, and that section shall apply as regards that whole or part of the tax as if the interest so payable were determined under that section, but the interest payable on any overdue instalment of that whole or part of that tax, or on such part of the tax as would represent any such overdue instalment if that whole or part of the tax were being paid by instalments, shall continue to be determined in accordance with *subsection (2)* of *section 51*.][1]

(3) For the purposes of this section reference to an overdue instalment in *paragraph (b)* of *subsection (2)* is a reference to an instalment which is overdue for the purposes of *section 54* (as it applies to this section) or for the purposes of *paragraph (a)* of *subsection (2)*.

(4) For the purposes of this section the value of a business or of an interest in a business shall be taken to be its net value ascertained in accordance with *section 98*.

(5) This section shall not apply in relation to an inheritance taken by a discretionary trust by virtue of *section 15(1)* or *section 20(1)*.

(6) Every regulation made under this section shall be laid before Dáil Éireann as soon as may be after it is made and, if a resolution annulling the regulation is passed by Dáil Éireann within the next 21 days on which Dáil Éireann has sat after the regulation is laid before it, the regulation shall be annulled accordingly, but without prejudice to the validity of anything previously done under that regulation.

Amendments

[1] Substituted by FA05 s145(4)(b).

Cross References

From Section 55

Section 15 Acquisitions by discretionary trusts.
Section 20 Annual acquisitions by discretionary trusts.
Section 51 Payment of tax and interest on tax.
Section 54 Payment of tax by instalments.
Section 89 Provisions relating to agricultural property.
Section 92 Business relief.
Section 93 Relevant business property.
Section 94 Minimum period of ownership.
Section 98 Value of business.
Section 100 Exclusion of value of excepted assets.
Section 101 Withdrawal of relief.

To Section 55

Section 51 Payment of tax and interest on tax.
Schedule 3 Consequential Amendments

56 Payment of inheritance tax by transfer of securities

[CATA 1976 s45]

Section 22 of the Finance Act 1954 (which relates to the payment of death duties by the transfer of securities to the Minister for Finance) and the regulations made under that Act shall apply, with any necessary modifications, to the payment of [inheritance tax (other than tax arising by reason of *section 20*)][1] by the transfer of securities to the Minister for Finance, as they apply to the payment of death duties by the transfer of securities to the Minister for Finance.

Amendments

[1] Substituted by FA06 s117(1)(h). This section shall apply as respects the year 2006 and subsequent years.

Revenue Information Notes

IT 39 Gift/Inheritance Tax – A Guide to completing the Self Assessment Return – Pre Finance Act 2010, Pt 8 – Alternative payment methods

Cross References

From Section 56

Section 20 Annual acquisitions by discretionary trusts.

To Section 56

Section 16 Application of this Act.
Section 46 Delivery of returns.

57 Overpayment of tax

[(1) In this section—

"*relevant date*", in relation to a repayment of tax means—

(a) the date which is [93 days][1] after the date on which a valid claim in respect of the repayment is made to the Commissioners, or

(b) where the repayment is due to a mistaken assumption in the operation of the tax on the part of the Commissioners, the date which is the date of the payment of the tax which has given rise to that repayment;

"*repayment*" means a repayment of tax including a repayment of—

(a) any interest charged,

(b) any surcharge imposed,

(c) any penalty incurred,

under any provision of this Act in relation to tax;

["*tax*" includes probate tax, payment on account of tax, interest charged, a surcharge imposed or a penalty incurred under any provision of this Act.][2]

(2) Where, a claim for repayment of tax made to the Commissioners, is a valid claim, the Commissioners shall, subject to the provisions of this section, give relief by means of repayment of the excess or otherwise as is reasonable and just.

[(3) Notwithstanding *subsection (2)*, no tax shall be repaid to an accountable person in respect of a valid claim unless that valid claim is made within the period of 4 years commencing on—

(a) 31 October in the year in which that tax was due to be paid in accordance with *section 46(2A)*, or

(b) the valuation date or the date of the payment of the tax concerned (where the tax has been paid within 4 months of the valuation date) in respect of inheritances to which *sections 15(1)* and *20(1)* apply.][3]

(4) *Subsection (3)* shall not apply to a claim for repayment of tax arising by virtue of *section 18(3)*, Article VI of the First Schedule to the Finance Act 1950, or Article 9 of the Schedule to the Double Taxation Relief (Taxes on Estates of Deceased Persons and Inheritances and on Gifts) (United Kingdom) Order 1978 (S.I. No. 279 of 1978).

(5) *Subsection (3)* shall not apply to a claim for repayment of tax arising on or before the date of the passing of the Finance Act 2003, where a valid claim is made on or before 31 December 2004.

(6) Subject to the provisions of this section, where a person is entitled to a repayment, the amount of the repayment shall, subject to a valid claim in respect of the repayment being made to the Commissioners and subject to [section 960H(4)][4] of the Taxes Consolidation Act 1997, carry simple interest at the rate of 0.011 per cent, or such other rate (if any) prescribed by the Minister for Finance by order under *subsection (11)*, for each day or part of a day for the period commencing on the relevant date and ending on the date upon which the repayment is made.

(7) A claim for repayment under this section shall only be treated as a valid claim when—

(a) it has been made in accordance with the provisions of the law (if any) relating to tax under which such claim is made, and

(b) all information which the Commissioners may reasonably require to enable them determine if and to what extent a repayment is due, has been furnished to them.

(8) Interest shall not be payable under this section if it amounts to €10 or less.

[(9) Except as provided for by this Act or by *section 941* of the Taxes Consolidation Act 1997 as it applies for the purposes of capital acquisitions tax, the Commissioners shall not repay an amount of tax paid to them or pay interest in respect of an amount of tax paid to them.][5]

(10) Income tax shall not be deductible on any payment of interest under this section and such interest shall not be reckoned in computing income for the purposes of the Tax Acts.

(11) (a) The Minister for Finance may, from time to time, make an order prescribing a rate for the purposes of *subsection (6)*.

(b) Every order made by the Minister for Finance under *paragraph (a)* shall be laid before Dáil Éireann as soon as may be after it is made and, if a resolution annulling the order is passed by Dáil Éireann within the next 21 days on which Dáil Éireann has sat after the order is laid before it, the order shall be annulled accordingly, but without prejudice to the validity of anything previously done under it.

(12) The Commissioners may make regulations as they deem necessary in relation to the operation of this section.][6]

Amendments

[1] Substituted by FA07 s121(4). Applies as on or after 2 April 2007

[2] Substituted by FA13 s87(1)(a). Applies as respects any claim for repayment made on or after 27 March 2013.

[3] Substituted by FA13 s87(1)(b). Applies as respects any claim for repayment made on or after 27 March 2013.

[4] Substituted by FA12 sched6(2)(b). Has effect as on and from 31 March 2012.

[5] Substituted by FA12 s128(3). Shall apply as respects any tax (within the meaning of section 865B (inserted by subsection (1)(d)) of the Taxes Consolidation Act 1997) paid or remitted to the Revenue Commissioners or the Collector-General, as the case may be, whether before, on or after 31 March 2012.

[6] Substituted by FA03 s145(1)(d). With effect from 31 October 2003 per S.I. 515 of 2003 insofar as it relates to subsections (2) to (5) and otherwise as respects repayments of capital acquisitions tax made on or after 1 November 2003.

Cross References

From Section 57

Section 18 Computation of tax.

To Section 57

Section 28 Taxable value of a taxable gift or inheritance.
Section 29 Contingencies affecting gifts or inheritances.
Section 54 Payment of tax by instalments.

58 Penalties

[CATA 1976 s63]

(1) (a) Any person who contravenes or fails to comply with any requirement or provision under *section 46* shall be liable to a penalty of [€3,000][1].

(b) Where the contravention or failure referred to in *paragraph (a)* continues after judgment has been given by the court before which proceedings for the penalty have been commenced, the person concerned shall be liable to a further penalty of €30 for each day on which the contravention or failure so continues.

[(1A) Where a person [deliberately or carelessly][2] fails to comply with a requirement to deliver a return or additional return under *subsection (2), (6)* or *(8)* of *section 46*[...][3] that person is liable to a penalty of—

(a) [€3,000][4], and

(b) the amount[...][5] of the difference specified in *subsection (5A).*][6]

(2) Where, under, or for the purposes of, any of the provisions of this Act, a person is authorised to inspect any property for the purpose of reporting to the Commissioners the market value of that property and the person having custody or possession of that property prevents such inspection or obstructs the person so authorised in the performance of that person's functions in relation to the inspection, the person so having custody or possession is liable to a penalty of [€3,000][7].

(3) Where an accountable person [deliberately or carelessly][8]—

(a) delivers any incorrect return or additional return,

(b) makes or furnishes any incorrect statement, declaration, evidence or valuation in connection with any property comprised in any disposition,

(c) makes or furnishes any incorrect statement, declaration, evidence or valuation in connection with any claim for any allowance, deduction, exemption or relief, or

(d) makes or furnishes any incorrect statement, declaration, evidence or valuation in connection with any other matter,

on the basis of which the amount of tax assessable in respect of a taxable gift or taxable inheritance would be less than it would have been if the correct return, additional return, statement, declaration, evidence or valuation had been delivered, made or furnished, that person is liable to a penalty of—

(i) €6,345, and

(ii) the amount[…][9] of the difference specified in *subsection (5)*.

(4) Where any such return, additional return, statement, declaration, evidence or valuation as is mentioned in *subsection (3)* was delivered, made or furnished neither [deliberately nor carelessly][10] by a person and it comes to that person's notice that it was incorrect, then, unless the error is remedied without unreasonable delay, such matter is treated, for the purposes of this section, as having been [carelessly][11] done by that person.

(5) The difference referred to in *subsection (3)* is the difference between—

(a) the amount of tax payable in respect of the taxable gift or taxable inheritance to which the return, additional return, statement, declaration, evidence or valuation relates, and

(b) the amount which would have been the amount so payable if the return, additional return, statement, declaration, evidence or valuation as made or submitted had been correct.

[(5A) The difference referred to in *paragraph (b)* of *subsection (1A)* is the difference between—

(a) the amount of tax paid by that person in respect of the taxable gift or taxable inheritance to which the return or additional return relates, and

(b) the amount of tax which would have been payable if the return or additional return had been delivered by that person and that return or additional return had been correct.][12]

(6) For the purpose of *subsection (3)*, where anything referred to in that subsection is delivered, made or furnished on behalf of a person, it is deemed to have been delivered, made or furnished by that person unless that person proves that it was done without that person's knowledge or consent.

(7) Any person who assists in or induces the delivery, making or furnishing for any purposes of the tax of any return, additional return, statement, declaration, evidence or valuation which that person knows to be incorrect shall be liable to a penalty of [€3,000][13].

(8) This section shall not affect any criminal proceedings.

[(9) Subject to this section—

(a) sections 987(4), 1062, 1063, 1064, [...][14] 1066 and 1068 of the Taxes Consolidation Act 1997 shall, with any necessary modifications, apply to a penalty under this Act as if the penalty were a penalty under the Income Tax Acts, and

(b) section 1077E (inserted by the *Finance (No.2) Act 2008*) of the Taxes Consolidation Act 1997 shall, with any necessary modifications, apply to a penalty under this Act as if the penalty were a penalty relating to income tax, corporation tax or capital gains tax, as the case may be.][15]

Amendments

[1, 4] Substituted by F(No.2)A08 sched5(part4)(b)(i). The enactments specified in Schedule 5 are amended or repealed to the extent and manner specified in that Schedule and, unless the contrary is stated, shall come into effect after 24 December 2008.

[2] Inserted by F(No.2)A08 sched5(part4)(b)(iii). The enactments specified in Schedule 5 are amended or repealed to the extent and manner specified in that Schedule and, unless the contrary is stated, shall come into effect after 24 December 2008.

[3] Deleted by F(No.2)A08 sched5(part4)(b)(iii). The enactments specified in Schedule 5 are amended or repealed to the extent and manner specified in that Schedule and, unless the contrary is stated, shall come into effect after 24 December 2008.

[5] Deleted by FA05 s132(1)(a). Applies to returns, additional returns, statements, declarations, evidence or valuations delivered, made or, as the case may be, furnished on or after 25 March 2005.

[6] Inserted by FA03 s146(1)(d)(i). With effect from 1 October 2003 per S.I. No. 466 of 2003.

[7] Substituted by F(No.2)A08 sched5(part4)(b)(ii). The enactments specified in Schedule 5 are amended or repealed to the extent and manner specified in that Schedule and, unless the contrary is stated, shall come into effect after 24 December 2008.

[8] Substituted by F(No.2)A08 sched5(part4)(b)(iv). The enactments specified in Schedule 5 are amended or repealed to the extent and manner specified in that Schedule and, unless the contrary is stated, shall come into effect after 24 December 2008.

[9] Deleted by FA05 s132(1)(b). Applies to returns, additional returns, statements, declarations, evidence or valuations delivered, made or, as the case may be, furnished on or after 25 March 2005.

[10, 11] Substituted by F(No.2)A08 sched5(part4)(b)(v). The enactments specified in Schedule 5 are amended or repealed to the extent and manner specified in that Schedule and, unless the contrary is stated, shall come into effect after 24 December 2008.

[12] Inserted by FA03 s146(1)(d)(ii). With effect from 1 October 2003 per S.I. No. 466 of 2003.

[13] Substituted by F(No.2)A08 sched5(part4)(b)(vi). The enactments specified in Schedule 5 are amended or repealed to the extent and manner specified in that Schedule and, unless the contrary is stated, shall come into effect after 24 December 2008.

[14] Deleted by F(No.2)A13 s78(3).

[15] Substituted by F(No.2)A08 sched5(part4)(b)(vii). The enactments specified in Schedule 5 are amended or repealed to the extent and manner specified in that Schedule and, unless the contrary is stated, shall come into effect after 24 December 2008.

Case Law

A criminal sanction cannot be imposed on a deceased person. Bendenoun v France 1994 12547/86

Revenue Information Notes

Code of Practice for Revenue Audit and other compliance interventions 2014

Cross References

From Section 58

Section 46 Delivery of returns.

59 Postponement, remission and compounding of tax

[CATA 1976 s44]

(1) Where the Commissioners are satisfied that tax leviable in respect of any gift or inheritance can not without excessive hardship be raised at once, they may allow payment to be postponed for such period, to such extent and on such terms (including the waiver of interest) as they think fit.

(2) If, after the expiration of the relevant period immediately following the date on which any tax became due and payable, the tax or any part of that tax remains

unpaid, the Commissioners may, if they think fit, remit the payment of any interest accruing after such expiration on the unpaid tax; and in this subsection, "*relevant period*" means the period at the end of which the interest on an amount payable in respect of tax would, at the rate from time to time chargeable during that period in respect of interest on tax, equal the amount of such tax.

(3) If, after the expiration of 20 years from the date on which any tax became due and payable, the tax or any part of that tax remains unpaid, the Commissioners may, if they think fit, remit the payment of such tax or any part of that tax and all or any interest on that tax.

(4) Where, in the opinion of the Commissioners, the complication of circumstances affecting a gift or inheritance or the value of that gift or inheritance or the assessment or recovery of tax on that gift or inheritance are such as to justify them in doing so, they may compound the tax payable on the gift or inheritance on such terms as they shall think fit, and may give a discharge to the person or persons accountable for the tax on payment of the tax according to such composition.

Revenue Information Notes

Pt 17.3 Revenue CAT Manual – Registration of the debt as a Voluntary Judgment Mortgage
Pt 19.9 Revenue CAT Manual – Common law spouses

Statements of Practice

Postponement of Tax and Registration of Charge – SP CAT/1/90

60 Tax to be a charge [Deleted]

Deleted by FA10 s(147)(1)(r). Has effect as on and from 3 April 2010.

61 Receipts and certificates [Deleted]

Deleted by FA10 s(147)(1)(r). Has effect as on and from 3 April 2010.

62 Certificate relating to registration of title based on possession

[FA 1994 s146]

(1) In this section—

["*Act of 1964*" means the Registration of Title Act 1964, as amended by the Registration of Deeds and Title Act 2006;][1]

["*Authority*" means the Property Registration Authority established by section 9 of the Registration of Deeds and Title Act 2006;][2]

[...][3]

"*relevant period*", in relation to a person's application to be registered as owner of property, means the period commencing on 28 February 1974 and ending on the date as of which the registration was made, but—

(a) where the certificate referred to in *subsection (2)* is a certificate for a period ending prior to the date of the registration, the period covered by the certificate shall be deemed to be the relevant period if, at the time of the registration, the [Authority][4] had no reason to believe that a death relevant to the application for registration occurred after the expiration of the period covered by the certificate, and

(b) where the registration of the person (if any) who, at the date of that application, was the registered owner of the property had been made as of a date after 28 February 1974, the relevant period shall commence on the date as of which that registration was made;

"*the Rules of 1972*" means the Land Registration Rules 1972 (S.I. No. 230 of 1972).

(2) A person shall not be registered as owner of property in a register of ownership maintained under the Act of 1964 on foot of an application made to the [Authority][5] on or after the date of the passing of this Act which is—

(a) based on possession, and

(b) made under the Rules of 1972, or any other rule made for carrying into effect the objects of the Act of 1964,

unless the applicant produces to the [Authority][6] a certificate issued by the Commissioners to the effect that the Commissioners are satisfied—

(i) that the property did not become charged with gift tax or inheritance tax during the relevant period, or

(ii) that any charge for gift tax or inheritance tax to which the property became subject during that period has been discharged, or will (to the extent that it has not been discharged) be discharged within a time considered by the Commissioners to be reasonable.

(3) In the case of an application for registration in relation to which a solicitor's certificate is produced for the purpose of rule 19(3), 19(4) or 35 of the Rules of 1972, the [Authority][7] may accept that the application is not based on possession if the solicitor makes to the [Authority][8] a declaration in writing to that effect.

(4) Where, on application to them by the applicant for registration, the Commissioners are satisfied that they may issue a certificate for the purpose of *subsection (2)*, they shall issue a certificate for that purpose, and the certificate and the application for that certificate shall be on a form provided by the Commissioners.

(5) A certificate issued by the Commissioners for the purpose of *subsection (2)* shall be in such terms and subject to such qualifications as the Commissioners think fit, and shall not be a certificate for any other purpose.

(6) In *subsection (2)*, the reference to a certificate issued by the Commissioners shall be construed as including a reference to a certificate to which *subsection (7)* relates, and *subsection (2)* shall be construed accordingly.

(7) (a) In this subsection—

"*the relevant particulars*" means the particulars of title to the relevant property which are required to be produced to the [Authority][9] for the purposes of paragraph 2 of Form 5 of the Schedule of Forms referred to in the definition of "*Forms*" contained in rule 2(1) of the Rules of 1972;

"*the relevant property*" means the property in respect of which the application for registration is being made.

(b) A certificate to which this subsection relates is a certificate by the solicitor for the applicant for registration in which it is certified, on a form provided by the Commissioners, that the solicitor—

(i) is satisfied—

(I) in a case where the applicant is a statutory authority within the definition of "*statutory authority*" contained in section

3(1) of the Act of 1964, that the market value of the relevant property at the time of the application does not exceed €127,000, or

(II) in any other case, that—

(A) the area of the relevant property does not exceed 5 hectares, and

(B) the market value of the relevant property at the time of the application does not exceed €19,050,

and

(ii) having investigated the title to the relevant property, has no reason to believe that the relevant particulars, in so far as relating to the relevant property at any time during the relevant period, are particulars which related at that time to significant other real property, that is, real property which, if combined with the relevant property for the purposes of *subparagraph (i)*, would cause a limit which applies to the relevant property by virtue of that subparagraph to be exceeded.

(8) Notwithstanding *subsection (7)*, a certificate by the solicitor for the applicant for registration shall be a certificate to which *subsection (7)* relates if it certifies, on a form provided by the Commissioners, that the solicitor is satisfied that—

(a) the area of the property in respect of which the application for registration is being made does not exceed 500 square metres,

(b) the market value of that property at the time of the application does not exceed €2,540, and

(c) the application is not part of a series of related applications covering a single piece of property the total area of which exceeds 500 square metres or the market value of which at the time of the application exceeds €2,540.

Amendments

[1] Substituted by FA08 s128(1)(a)(i). This section applies to applications to register property made on or after 4 November 2006.

[2] Inserted by FA08 s128(1)(a)(iii). This section applies to applications to register property made on or after 4 November 2006.

[3] Deleted by FA08 s128(1)(a)(ii). This section applies to applications to register property made on or after 4 November 2006.

[4] Substituted by FA08 s128(1)(a)(iv). This section applies to applications to register property made on or after 4 November 2006.

[5, 6, 7, 8, 9] Substituted by FA08 s128(1)(b). This section applies to applications to register property made on or after 4 November 2006.

Revenue Information Notes

Pt 4.5 Revenue CAT Manual – Registration of title based on possession

63 Recovery of tax and penalties

[CATA 1976 s49]

[…][1]

(3) If any accountable person is liable under *section 46* to deliver to the Commissioners a return or an additional return and makes default in so doing, […][2] the Commissioners may sue by action or other appropriate proceeding in the Circuit

Court for an order directing the person so making default to deliver such return or additional return or to show cause to the contrary; and the Circuit Court may by order direct such accountable person to deliver such return or additional return within such time as may be specified in the order.

[...][3]

Amendments

[1, 2] Deleted by F(No.2)A08 sched4(part1). Applies as respects any tax that becomes due and payable on or after 1 March 2009.

[3] Deleted by FA10 s(147)(1)(r). Has effect as on and from 3 April 2010.

Cross References

From Section 63

Section 46 Delivery of returns.

64 Application of certain income tax provisions in relation to the collection and recovery of capital acquisitions tax, etc [Deleted]

Deleted by F(No.2)A08 sched4(part1). Applies as respects any tax that becomes due and payable on or after 1 March 2009.

65 Evidence in proceedings for recovery of tax [Deleted]

Deleted by F(No.2)A08 sched4(part1). Applies as respects any tax that becomes due and payable on or after 1 March 2009.

PART 8

Appeals

66 Appeals regarding value of real property

[CATA 1976 s51]

(1) If a person is aggrieved by the decision of the Commissioners as to the market value of any real property, that person may appeal against the decision in the manner prescribed by section 33 of the Finance (1909-10) Act 1910, and the provisions as to appeals under that section of that Act shall apply accordingly with any necessary modifications.

(2) The particulars of any transfer or lease which are presented to or obtained by the Commissioners under section 12(2) of the Stamp Duties Consolidation Act 1999 shall, in any appeal under this section, be received as *prima facie* evidence of all matters and things stated in such particulars.

Cross References

To Section 66

Section 53 Surcharge for undervaluation of property.
Section 68 Conditions before appeal may be made.
Section 114 Delivery, service and evidence of notices and forms, etc.

67 Appeals in other cases

[CATA 1976 s52]

(1) In this section—

"*Appeal Commissioners*" has the meaning assigned to it by section 850 of the Taxes Consolidation Act 1997;

"*appellant*" means a person who appeals to the Appeal Commissioners under *subsection (2).*

(2) Subject to the other provisions of this Act, a person who is called on by the Commissioners to pay an assessment of tax in respect of any property and who is aggrieved by the assessment may, in accordance with this section, appeal to the Appeal Commissioners against the assessment and the appeal shall be heard and determined by the Appeal Commissioners whose determination shall be final and conclusive unless the appeal is required to be reheard by a judge of the Circuit Court or a case is required to be stated in relation to it for the opinion of the High Court on a point of law.

(3) An appeal shall not lie under this section in relation to the market value of real property.

(4) A person who intends to appeal under this section against an assessment shall, within 30 days after the date of the assessment, give notice in writing to the Commissioners of that person's intention to appeal against the assessment.

(5) (a) Subject to this section, the provisions of the Income Tax Acts relating to—

(i) the appointment of times and places for the hearing of appeals,

(ii) the giving of notice to each person who has given notice of appeal of the time and place appointed for the hearing of that person's appeal,

(iii) the determination of an appeal by agreement between the appellant and an officer appointed by the Commissioners in that behalf,

(iv) the determination of an appeal by the appellant giving notice of that appellant's intention not to proceed with the appeal,

(v) the hearing and determination of an appeal by the Appeal Commissioners, including the hearing and determination of an appeal by one Appeal Commissioner,

(vi) the publication of reports of determinations of the Appeal Commissioners,

(vii) the determination of an appeal through the neglect or refusal of a person who has given notice of appeal to attend before the Appeal Commissioners at the time and place appointed,

(viii) the extension of the time for giving notice of appeal and the readmission of appeals by the Appeal Commissioners and the provisions which apply where action by means of court proceedings has been taken,

(ix) the rehearing of an appeal by a judge of the Circuit Court and the statement of a case for the opinion of the High Court on a point of law,

(x) the payment of tax in accordance with the determination of the Appeal Commissioners notwithstanding that an appeal is required to be reheard by a judge of the Circuit Court or that a case for the opinion of the High Court on a point of law has been required to be stated or is pending,

(xi) the procedures for appeal,

(xii) the refusal of an application for an appeal hearing,

shall, with any necessary modifications, apply to an appeal under this section as if the appeal were an appeal against an assessment to income tax.

(b) The Commissioners shall, subject to their giving notice in writing in that behalf to the appellant within 10 days after the determination of an appeal by the Appeal Commissioners, have the same right as the appellant to have the appeal reheard by a judge of the Circuit Court.

(c) The rehearing of an appeal under this section by a judge of the Circuit Court shall be by a judge of the Circuit Court in whose circuit the appellant or one of the appellants resides or (in the case of a body corporate) has its principal place of business, but—

(i) in any case where no appellant is resident in or (in the case of a body corporate) has a place of business in the State, or

(ii) in any case where there is a doubt or a dispute as to the circuit,

the appeal shall be reheard by a judge of the Circuit Court assigned to the Dublin Circuit.

(6) (a) Where a notice or other document which is required or authorised to be served by this section is to be served on a body corporate, such notice shall be served on the secretary or other officer of the body corporate.

(b) Any notice or other document which is required or authorised by this section to be served by the Commissioners or by an appellant may be served by post and in the case of a notice or other document addressed to the Commissioners, shall be sent to the Secretaries, Revenue Commissioners, Dublin Castle, Dublin 2.

(c) Any notice or other document which is required or authorised to be served by the Commissioners on an appellant under this section may be sent to the solicitor, accountant or other agent of the appellant and a notice thus served shall be deemed to have been served on the appellant unless the appellant proves to the satisfaction of the Appeal Commissioners, or the Circuit Court, as the case may be, that that appellant had, before the notice or other document was served, withdrawn the authority of such solicitor, accountant or other agent to act on that appellant's behalf.

(7) Prima facie evidence of any notice given under this section by the Commissioners or by an officer of the Commissioners may be given in any proceedings by the production of a document purporting—

(a) to be a copy of the notice, or

(b) if the details specified in the notice are contained in an electronic, photographic or other record maintained by the Commissioners, to reproduce those details in so far as they relate to that notice,

and it shall not be necessary to prove the official position of the person by whom the notice purports to be given or, if it is signed, the signature, or that the person signing and giving it was authorised to do so.

(8) (a) The Commissioners may serve notice in writing, referring expressly to this subsection, on any person whom they have reason to believe to be accountable for the payment of tax, of any decision they have made which is relevant to such tax.

(b) Any person who is informed of a decision in accordance with *paragraph (a)* may appeal to the Appeal Commissioners against the decision.

(c) The Appeal Commissioners shall hear and determine an appeal to them under this subsection as if it were an appeal to them against an assessment to tax, and the provisions of this section relating to an appeal or to the rehearing of an appeal or to the statement of a case for the opinion of the High Court on a point of law shall, with any necessary modifications, apply accordingly.

Case Law

Battle v Irish Art Promotion Centre Ltd 1968 IR 252 discussed the right of audience in the Circuit Court and held that a director cannot appear on behalf of a company, as the company is a separate legal entity. In The Revenue Commissioners v Arida IV ITR 401 it was held that a Circuit Court judge has the power to award costs when hearing an appeal from the Appeal Commissioners to the successful party.

Cross References

To Section 67

Section 30 Valuation date for tax purposes.
Section 53 Surcharge for undervaluation of property.
Section 68 Conditions before appeal may be made.
Section 80 Payments relating to retirement, etc.

68 Conditions before appeal may be made

[CATA 1976 s52A]

No appeal shall lie under *section 66* or *67* until such time as the person aggrieved by the decision or assessment (as the case may be) complies with *section 46(2)* in respect of the gift or inheritance in relation to which the decision or assessment is made, as if there were no time-limit for complying with *section 46(2)* and that person were a person primarily accountable for the payment of tax by virtue of *section 45(1)* and required by notice in writing by the Commissioners to deliver a return.

Cross References

From Section 68

Section 45 Accountable persons.
Section 46 Delivery of returns.
Section 66 Appeals regarding value of real property.
Section 67 Appeals in other cases.

PART 9

Exemptions

69 Exemption of small gifts

[CATA 1976 s53(1), (2) and (4)]

(1) In this section, "*relevant period*" means the period of 12 months ending on 31 December in each year.

(2) The first [€3,000][1] of the total taxable value of all taxable gifts taken by a donee from any one disponer in any relevant period is exempt from tax and is not taken into account in computing tax.

(3) In the case of a gift which becomes an inheritance by reason of its being taken under a disposition where the date of the disposition is within 2 years prior to the death of the disponer, the same relief is granted in respect of that inheritance under *subsection (2)* as if it were a gift.

Amendments

[1] Substituted by FA03 s149. Applies as respects relevant periods ending after 31 December 2002.

Revenue Information Notes

IT 39 Gift/Inheritance Tax – A Guide to completing the Self Assessment Return – Pre Finance Act 2010, Pt 7 – Taxable Value of Benefit

Cross References

To Section 69

Schedule 2 Computation of tax

70 Exemption for spouses (gifts)

[FA 1990 s127(1)]

Notwithstanding any other provisions of this Act, a gift taken by a donee, who is at the date of the gift the [spouse or civil partner][1] of the disponer, is exempt from tax and is not taken into account in computing tax.

Amendments

[1] Substituted by F(No.3)A11 sched3(9). Deemed to have come into operation as respects a gift or an inheritance taken on or after 1 January 2011.

Revenue Information Notes

Pt 19.8 Revenue CAT Manual – Spouse of Disponer

Cross References

To Section 70

Section 73 Relief in respect of certain policies of insurance relating to tax payable on gifts.

71 Exemption for spouses (inheritances)

[FA 1985 s59(1)]

Notwithstanding any other provisions of this Act, an inheritance taken by a successor, who is at the date of the inheritance the [spouse or civil partner][1] of the disponer, is exempt from tax and is not taken into account in computing tax.

Amendments

[1] Substituted by F(No.3)A11 sched3(10). Deemed to have come into operation as respects a gift or an inheritance taken on or after 1 January 2011.

Revenue Information Notes

Pt 19.8 Revenue CAT Manual – Spouse of Disponer
IT41 – Bereavement – Tax Related Information

72 Relief in respect of certain policies of insurance

[FA 1985 s60(1), (1A) and (2); FA 1990 s130; FA 1991 s118; FA 1996 s124]

(1) In this section—

["*approved retirement fund tax*" means tax which a qualifying fund manager is obliged to deduct in accordance with the provisions of section 784A(4)(c) of the Taxes Consolidation Act 1997;][1]

"*insured*" means an individual or, in relation to a qualifying insurance policy where—

(a) the insured is an individual and the [spouse or civil partner][2] of that individual at the date the policy is effected,

(b) annual premiums are paid by either or both of them during their joint lives, and by the survivor of them during the life of such survivor, and

(c) the proceeds of the policy are payable on the death of such survivor, or on the simultaneous deaths of both such [spouses or civil partners][3],

means—

(i) where the proceeds of the policy are so payable on the death of such survivor, that survivor, and the proceeds of the policy [are deemed][4] to have been provided by such survivor, as disponer, or

(ii) where the proceeds of the policy are so payable on the simultaneous deaths of both such [spouses or civil partners][5], each of the [spouses or civil partners][6], and each such [spouse or civil partner][7] is deemed to have provided the proceeds of the policy—

(I) to the extent that such proceeds are applied in paying the relevant tax of the insured who is that [spouse or civil partner][8], and

(II) where the proceeds of the policy are not applied in paying relevant tax, to the extent that the proceeds not so applied are comprised in an inheritance taken under a disposition made by that [spouse or civil partner][9];

"*qualifying insurance policy*" means a policy of insurance—

(a) which is in a form approved by the Commissioners for the purposes of this section,

(b) in respect of which annual premiums are paid by the insured during the insured's life, and

(c) which is expressly effected under this section for the purpose of paying relevant tax;

"*relevant tax*" [means approved retirement fund tax and inheritance tax][10] payable in respect of an inheritance (excluding, in the computation of such tax, an interest in a qualifying insurance policy) taken—

(a) on the death of the insured,

(b) under a disposition made by the insured, where the inheritance is taken on or after the date of death of the insured and not later than one year after that [death, or][11]

(c) under a disposition made by the [spouse or civil partner][12] of the insured where the inheritance is taken only in the event of the insured not surviving the [spouse or civil partner][13] by a period of up to 31 days,

and the relevant qualifying insurance policy is—

(i) a policy of insurance within the meaning of *paragraphs (a)*, *(b)* and *(c)* of the definition of "*insured*" in this subsection, or

(ii) a policy of insurance where the insured is an individual and the proceeds of the policy are payable only on the contingency of the insured surviving that [spouse or civil partner][14].

(2) (a) An interest in a qualifying insurance policy which is comprised in an inheritance taken under a disposition made by the insured is, to the extent that the proceeds of the policy are applied in paying relevant tax, exempt from tax in relation to that inheritance and is not taken into account in computing tax.

(b) An interest in a qualifying insurance policy which is comprised in an inheritance taken under a disposition made by the insured is, to the extent that the proceeds of the policy are not applied in paying relevant tax, and notwithstanding the provisions of this Act, deemed to be taken on a day immediately after—

(i) the date of the death of the insured, or

(ii) the latest date (if any) on which an inheritance is taken in respect of which that relevant tax is payable,

whichever is the later.

[(c) For the purposes of this section, an amount of the proceeds of a qualifying insurance policy equal to the amount of approved retirement fund tax shall be treated as applied in paying relevant tax of that amount.][15]

Amendments

[1] Inserted by FA05 s133(1)(a)(i). Has effect in relation to relevant tax payable in respect of inheritances taken on or after 3 February 2005.

[2, 7, 8, 9, 12, 13, 14] Substituted by F(No.3)A11 sched3(11). Deemed to have come into operation as respects a gift or an inheritance taken on or after 1 January 2011.

[3, 5, 6] Substituted by F(No.3)A11 sched3(12). Deemed to have come into operation as respects a gift or an inheritance taken on or after 1 January 2011.

[4] Substituted by FA04 sched3(2)(d)(i). Has effect as on and from 21 February 2003.

[10] Substituted by FA05 s133(1)(a)(ii). Has effect in relation to relevant tax payable in respect of inheritances taken on or after 3 February 2005.

[11] Substituted by FA04 sched3(2)(d)(ii). Has effect as on and from 21 February 2003.

[15] Inserted by FA05 s133(1)(b). Has effect in relation to relevant tax payable in respect of inheritances taken on or after 3 February 2005.

Revenue Information Notes

Pt 15 Revenue CAT Manual – Insurance Policies.
IT 39 Gift/Inheritance Tax – A Guide to completing the Self Assessment Return – Pre Finance Act 2010, Pt 4 – Other Relevant Information

Statements of Practice

Section 60 Policies; Section 119 Policies – SP CAT/1/04.

Cross References

To Section 72

Section 73 Relief in respect of certain policies of insurance relating to tax payable on gifts.

73 Relief in respect of certain policies of insurance relating to tax payable on gifts

[FA 1991 s119(1) to (5)]

(1) In this section—

"*appointed date*" means—

(a) a date occurring not earlier than 8 years after the date on which a relevant insurance policy is effected, or

(b) a date on which the proceeds of a relevant insurance policy become payable either on the critical illness or the death of the insured, or one of the insured in a case to which *paragraph (b)* of the definition of "*insured*" relates, being a date prior to the date to which *paragraph (a)* of this definition relates;

"*insured*" means—

(a) where the insured is an individual, that individual, or

(b) where the insured is an individual and the [spouse or civil partner][1] of that individual at the date the policy is effected, that individual and the [spouse or civil partner][2] of that individual, jointly or separately, or the survivor of them, as the case may be;

"*relevant insurance policy*" means a policy of insurance—

(a) which is in a form approved by the Commissioners for the purposes of this section,

(b) in respect of which annual premiums are paid by the insured,

(c) the proceeds of which are payable on the appointed date, and

(d) which is expressly effected under this section for the purpose of paying relevant tax;

"*relevant tax*" means gift tax or inheritance tax, payable in connection with an *inter vivos* disposition made by the insured within one year after the appointed date, excluding gift tax or inheritance tax payable on an appointment out of an *inter vivos* discretionary trust set up by the insured.

(2) The proceeds of a relevant insurance policy are, to the extent that such proceeds are used to pay relevant tax, exempt from tax and are not taken into account in computing such tax.

(3) Subject to *sections 70* and *76*, where the insured makes an *inter vivos* disposition of the proceeds, or any part of the proceeds, of a relevant insurance policy other than in paying relevant tax, such proceeds are not exempt from tax.

(4) A relevant insurance policy is a qualifying insurance policy for the purposes of *section 72* where the proceeds of such relevant insurance policy become payable on the death of the insured or one of the insured in a case to which *paragraph (b)* of the definition of "*insured*" relates, if such relevant insurance policy would have been a qualifying insurance policy if it had been expressly effected under that section.

(5) A qualifying insurance policy for the purposes of *section 72* is a relevant insurance policy where the proceeds of such qualifying insurance policy are used to pay relevant tax arising under an *inter vivos* disposition made by the insured within one year after the appointed date.

Amendments

[1, 2] Substituted by F(No.3)A11 sched3(13). Deemed to have come into operation as respects a gift or an inheritance taken on or after 1 January 2011.

Revenue Information Notes

Pt 15 Revenue CAT Manual – Insurance Policies.
IT 39 Gift/Inheritance Tax – A Guide to completing the Self Assessment Return – Pre Finance Act 2010, Pt 4 – Other Relevant Information.

Statements of Practice

Section 60 Policies; Section 119 Policies – SP CAT/1/04.

Cross References

From Section 73

Section 70 Exemption for spouses (gifts).
Section 72 Relief in respect of certain policies of insurance.
Section 76 Provisions relating to charities, etc.

74 Exemption of certain policies of assurance

[FA 1993 s133]

(1) In this section—

"*assurance company*" has the meaning assigned to it by section 706 of the Taxes Consolidation Act 1997;

["*new policy*" means—

(a) a policy of assurance on the life of any person issued, or

(b) a contract within the meaning of Article 2(2)(b) of Directive 2002/83/EC of the European Parliament and of the Council of 5 November 2002* entered into,

on or after 1 January 2001 by an assurance company in the course of carrying on the business of life assurance;][1]

*OJ No. L345, 19.12.2002, p.1

"*old policy*" means a contract entered into by an assurance company in the course of carrying on a foreign life assurance business within the meaning of section 451 of the Taxes Consolidation Act 1997 and issued on or after 1 December 1992 and before 1 January 2001.

(2) Where any interest in a new policy or in an old policy is comprised in a gift or an inheritance, then any such interest—

(a) is exempt from tax, and

(b) is not taken into account in computing tax on any gift or inheritance taken by a donee or successor,

if it is shown to the satisfaction of the Commissioners that—

(i) such interest is comprised in the gift or inheritance at the date of the gift or at the date of the inheritance,

(ii) at the date of the disposition, the disponer is neither domiciled nor ordinarily resident in the State, and

(iii) at the date of the gift or at the date of the inheritance, the donee or successor is neither domiciled nor ordinarily resident in the State.

(3) Where—

(a) an interest in a new policy or in an old policy, as the case may be, which is comprised in a gift or inheritance came into the beneficial ownership of the disponer or became subject to the disposition prior to 15 February 2001, and

(b) the conditions at [*paragraphs*][2] *(i)* and *(iii)* of *subsection (2)* are complied with,

then that subsection shall apply to that interest in a new policy or in an old policy, as the case may be, if, at the date of the disposition, the proper law of the disposition was not the law of the State.

Amendments

[1] Substituted by FA13 s88.

[2] Substituted by FA03 s151(a).

Revenue Information Notes

IT 39 Gift/Inheritance Tax – A Guide to completing the Self Assessment Return Pre Finance Act 2010, Appendix 6.10 – Exemption of Certain Policies of Assurance

75 Exemption of specified collective investment undertakings

[(1) In this section—

"*collective investment scheme*" means a *bona fide* scheme for the purpose, or having the effect, solely or mainly, of providing facilities for the participation by the public or other investors in profits or income arising from the acquisition, holding, management or disposal of securities or any other property;

"*common contractual fund*" has the meaning assigned to it by section 739I of the Taxes Consolidation Act 1997;

"*investment undertaking*" has the meaning assigned to it by section 739B of the Taxes Consolidation Act 1997;

["*investment limited partnership*" has the meaning assigned to it by *section 739J* of the Taxes Consolidation Act 1997;

"*unit*", in relation to an investment limited partnership, has the meaning assigned to it by *section 739J* of the Taxes Consolidation Act 1997;][1]

"*unit*", in relation to a collective investment scheme, includes shares, members' interests, limited partnership interests and any other instruments granting an entitlement to the income or investments from the scheme;

"*unit*", in relation to a common contractual fund, has the meaning assigned to it by section 739I of the Taxes Consolidation Act 1997;

"*unit*", in relation to an investment undertaking, has the meaning assigned to it by section 739B of the Taxes Consolidation Act 1997.

(2) Where any unit of a collective investment scheme which is incorporated or otherwise formed under the law of a territory outside the State, [a common contractual fund, an investment limited partnership or an investment undertaking][2] is comprised in a gift or an inheritance, then, such unit—

(a) is exempt from tax, and

(b) is not taken into account in computing tax on any gift or inheritance taken by the donee or successor,

if it is shown to the satisfaction of the Commissioners that—

(i) the unit is comprised in the gift or inheritance—

(I) at the date of the gift or the date of the inheritance, and

(II) at the valuation date,

(ii) at the date of the disposition, the disponer is neither domiciled nor ordinarily resident in the State, and

(iii) at the date of the gift or at the date of the inheritance, the donee or successor is neither domiciled nor ordinarily resident in the State.

(3) Where—

(a) any unit of an investment undertaking which is comprised in a gift or an inheritance came into the beneficial ownership of the disponer or became subject to the disposition prior to 15 February 2001, and

(b) the conditions of *subparagraphs (i)* and *(iii)* of *subsection (2)* are complied with,

then, that subsection shall apply to that unit of an investment undertaking comprised in a gift or an inheritance, if at the date of the disposition, the proper law of the disposition was not the law of the State.][3]

Amendments

[1] Inserted by FA13 s89(1)(a). Applies to gifts and inheritances taken on or after 27 March 2013.

[2] Substituted by FA13 s89(1)(b). Applies to gifts and inheritances taken on or after 27 March 2013.

[3] Substituted by FA10 s(144)(1). This section applies to gifts and inheritances taken on or after 4 February 2010.

Revenue Information Notes

IT 39 Gift/Inheritance Tax – A Guide to completing the Self Assessment Return – Pre Finance Act 2010, Appendix 6.11 – Exemption of Specified Collective Investment Undertakings

76 Provisions relating to charities, etc.

[CATA 1976 s54(1), (2) and (4)]

(1) Where any person takes a benefit for public or charitable purposes that person is deemed—

(a) for the purposes of *sections 5(1)* and *10(1)*, to have taken that benefit beneficially, and

(b) for the purposes of *Schedule 2*, to have taken a gift or an inheritance accordingly to which the group threshold [referred to in *subparagraph (c)* of the definition of '*group threshold*' in *paragraph 1* of *Part 1* of *Schedule 2*][1] applies.

(2) A gift or an inheritance which is taken for public or charitable purposes is exempt from tax and is not taken into account in computing tax, to the extent that the Commissioners are satisfied that it has been, or will be, applied to purposes which, in accordance with the law of the State, are public or charitable.

(3) Except where provided in *section 80(5)*, a gift or inheritance which a person takes on becoming entitled to any benefit on the application to public or charitable purposes of property (including moneys provided by the Oireachtas or a local

authority) held for such purposes is exempt from tax and is not taken into account in computing tax.

Amendments

[1] Substituted by FA11 s69(1)(a). Applies to gifts and inheritances taken on or after 21 January 2011.

Case Law

In Blair v Duncan 1902 AC 37 and Houston v Lord Advocate 1917 55 SLR 208 it was held that a benefit for a political party was for public purposes.

National Anti-Vivisection v IRC 1948 AC 31 considered the terms 'public purposes', 'public benefit' and 'charitable purposes'

Revenue Information Notes

Pt 19.6 Revenue CAT Manual – Exemption for Charities.

IT 39 Gift/Inheritance Tax – A Guide to completing the Self Assessment Return – Pre Finance Act 2010, Appendix 6.08 – Exemption for Charities.

Statements of Practice

Tax Treatment of Political Donations – SP CAT/1/02

Cross References

From Section 76

Section 5 Gift deemed to be taken.
Section 10 Inheritance deemed to be taken.
Section 80 Payments relating to retirement, etc.
Schedule 2 Computation of tax

To Section 76

Section 73 Relief in respect of certain policies of insurance relating to tax payable on gifts.
Schedule 2 Computation of tax

77 Exemption of heritage property

[CATA 1976 s55; FA 1978 s39(1) and (1A)]

(1) This section applies to the following objects, that is, any pictures, prints, books, manuscripts, works of art, jewellery, scientific collections or other things not held for the purposes of trading—

(a) which, on a claim being made to the Commissioners, appear to them to be of national, scientific, historic or artistic interest,

(b) which are kept permanently in the State except for such temporary absences outside the State as are approved by the Commissioners, and

(c) in respect of which reasonable facilities for viewing are allowed to members of the public or to recognised bodies or to associations of persons.

(2) (a) Any object to which this section applies and which, at the date of the gift or at the date of inheritance, and at the valuation date, is comprised in a gift or an inheritance taken by a person is exempt from tax in relation to that gift or inheritance, and the value of that gift or inheritance is not taken into account in computing tax on any gift or inheritance taken by that person unless the exemption ceases to apply under *subsection (3)* or *(4)*.

(b) *Section 89(5)* shall apply, for the purposes of this subsection, as it applies in relation to agricultural property.

(3) If an object exempted from tax by virtue of *subsection (2)* is sold within 6 years after the valuation date, and before the death of the donee or successor, the exemption referred to in *subsection (2)* shall cease to apply to such object, but if the sale of such object is a sale by private treaty to [the Chester Beatty Library,

the Crawford Art Gallery Cork, the Irish Museum of Modern Art, the National Archives, the National Concert Hall, the National Gallery of Ireland, the National Library of Ireland, the National Museum of Ireland,][1] [the Commissioners of Public Works in Ireland,][2] [the Trust (within the meaning of section 1003A of the Taxes Consolidation Act 1997),][3] any university in the State or any constituent college of such university, a local authority or the Friends of the National Collections of Ireland, the exemption referred to in *subsection (2)* shall continue to apply.

(4) The exemption referred to in *subsection (2)* shall cease to apply to an object, if at any time after the valuation date and—

(a) before the sale of the object,

(b) before the death of the donee or successor, and

(c) before such object again forms part of the property comprised in a gift or an inheritance (other than an inheritance arising by virtue of *section 20*) in respect of which gift or inheritance an absolute interest is taken by a person other than the [spouse or civil partner][4] of that donee or successor,

there has been a breach of any condition specified in *paragraph (b)* or *(c)* of *subsection (1)*.

(5) Any work of art normally kept outside the State which is comprised in an inheritance which is charged to tax by virtue of *section 11(1)(b)* or *11(2)(c)* is exempt from tax and is not taken into account in computing tax, to the extent that the Commissioners are satisfied that it was brought into the State solely for public exhibition, cleaning or restoration.

(6) *Subsections (2)* to *(4)* shall apply, as they apply to the objects specified in *subsection (1)*, to a house or garden that is situated in the State and is not held for the purpose of trading and—

(a) which, on a claim being made to the Commissioners, appears to them to be of national, scientific, historic or artistic interest,

(b) in respect of which reasonable facilities for viewing were allowed to members of the public during the 3 years immediately before the date of the gift or the date of the inheritance, and

(c) in respect of which reasonable facilities for viewing are allowed to members of the public,

with the modification that the reference in *subsection (4)* to *subsection (1)(b)* or *(c)* shall be construed as a reference to *paragraph (c)* of this subsection and with any other necessary modifications.

(7) Without prejudice to the generality of *subsection (6)*, the provision of facilities for the viewing by members of the public of a house or garden is not regarded as reasonable in relation to any year which is taken into account for the purposes of *paragraphs (b)* and *(c)* of *subsection (1)*, unless—

(a) [the National Tourism Development Authority][5] has, on or before 1 January in that year, been provided with particulars of—

(i) the name, if any, and address of the house or garden, and

(ii) the days and times during the year when access to the house or garden is afforded to the public and the price, if any, payable for such access,

and

(b) in the opinion of the Commissioners—

(i) subject to such temporary closure necessary for the purpose of the repair, maintenance or restoration of the house or garden as is reasonable, access to the house or garden is afforded for not less than 60 days (including not less than 40 days during the period commencing on 1 May and ending on 30 September of which not less than 10 of the days during that period shall fall on a Saturday or a Sunday or both) in that year,

(ii) on each day on which access to the house or garden is afforded, the access is afforded in a reasonable manner and at reasonable times for a period, or periods in the aggregate, of not less than 4 hours,

(iii) access to the whole or to a substantial part of the house or garden is afforded at the same time, and

(iv) the price, if any, paid by members of the public in return for that access is reasonable in amount and does not operate to preclude members of the public from seeking access to the house or garden.

Amendments

[1] Substituted by FA12 s113(1). Applies to sales occurring on or after 8 February 2012.

[2] Inserted by FA04 s81(1). Applies as respects sales on or after 1 August 1994.

[3] Inserted by FA06 s115, with effect from 31 March 2006.

[4] Substituted by F(No.3)A11 sched3(14). Shall apply to gifts and inheritances taken on or after 27 July 2011.

[5] Substituted by FA06 sched2(2). Applies and have taken effect as on and from 28 May 2003.

Revenue Information Notes

CAT 8 – Heritage Property Relief

Cross References

From Section 77

Section 11 Taxable inheritance.
Section 20 Annual acquisitions by discretionary trusts.
Section 89 Provisions relating to agricultural property.

To Section 77

Section 17 Exemptions.
Section 51 Payment of tax and interest on tax.
Section 78 Heritage property of companies.
Schedule 3 Consequential Amendments

78 Heritage property of companies

[FA 1995 s166(1) to (7)]

(1) In this section—

"*relevant heritage property*" means any one or more of the following—

(a) objects to which *section 77(1)* applies,

(b) a house or garden referred to in *section 77(6)*;

"*private company*" has the meaning assigned to it by *section 27*;

"*subsidiary*" has the meaning assigned to it by section 155 of the Companies Act 1963.

(2) Where a gift or inheritance consists in whole or in part—

(a) at the date of the gift or at the date of the inheritance, and

(b) at the valuation date,

of one or more shares in a private company which (after the taking of the gift or inheritance) is, on the date of the gift or on the date of the inheritance, a company controlled by the donee or successor within the meaning of *section 27*, then each such share is, to the extent that its market value for tax purposes is, at the valuation date, attributable to relevant heritage property, exempt from tax and the value of such relevant heritage property is, to that extent, not to be taken into account in computing tax on any gift or inheritance taken by that person unless the exemption ceases to apply under *subsection (5)* or *(6)*, subject to the condition that the relevant heritage property was in the beneficial ownership of the company on 12 April 1995, or in the beneficial ownership on that date of another company which was on that date a subsidiary of the first-mentioned company.

(3) *Section 89(5)* shall apply, for the purposes of *subsection (2)*, as it applies in relation to agricultural property.

(4) Where in relation to a gift or inheritance—

(a) a part of a share in a private company is exempt from tax by virtue of *subsection (2)*, and

(b) such share is relevant business property within the meaning of *Chapter 2* of *Part 10*,

then the relevant heritage property to which the market value of such share is partly attributable is disregarded in determining for the purposes of that Chapter what part of the taxable value of that gift or inheritance is attributable to such share; but the amount of the reduction (if any) which would but for *subsection (2)* fall to be made under that Chapter in respect of such share shall not otherwise be restricted notwithstanding *subsection (2)*.

(5) If a share in a private company which is exempted in whole or in part from tax by virtue of *subsection (2)* is sold within 6 years after the valuation date, and before the death of the donee or successor, the exemption referred to in *subsection (2)* shall, subject to *subsection (7)*, cease to apply to such share.

(6) Where the whole or part of the market value of a share in a private company which is comprised in a gift or inheritance is on the valuation date attributable to an item of relevant heritage property and—

(a) that item of relevant heritage property is sold within 6 years after the valuation date, and before the death of the donee or successor, or

(b) at any time after the valuation date and—

(i) before the sale of such share or such item of relevant heritage property,

(ii) before the death of the donee or successor, and

(iii) before such share or such item of relevant heritage property forms part of the property comprised in a subsequent gift or inheritance in respect of which gift or inheritance an absolute interest is taken by a person other than the [spouse or civil partner][1] of that donee or successor, there has been a breach of any condition specified in *section 77(1)(b)* or *(c)* or *section 77(6)(c)*,

then the exemption referred to in *subsection (2)* shall, subject to *subsection (7)*, cease to apply to such share to the extent that that market value is attributable to such item of relevant heritage property.

(7) Notwithstanding *subsections (5)* and *(6)*, the exemption referred to in *subsection (2)* shall continue to apply if the sale of the share referred to in *subsection (5)*, or the sale of the item of relevant heritage property referred to in *subsection (6)*, is a sale by private treaty to [the Chester Beatty Library, the Crawford Art Gallery Cork, the Irish Museum of Modern Art, the National Archives, the National Concert Hall, the National Gallery of Ireland, the National Library of Ireland, the National Museum of Ireland,][2] any university in the State or any constituent college of such university, a local authority or the Friends of the National Collections of Ireland.

Amendments

[1] Substituted by F(No.3)A11 sched3(15). Shall apply to gifts and inheritances taken on or after 27 July 2011.

[2] Substituted by FA12 s113(2). Applies to sales occurring on or after 8 February 2012.

Revenue Information Notes

CAT 8 – Heritage Property Relief

Cross References

From Section 78

Section 27 Market value of certain shares in private companies.
Section 77 Exemption of heritage property.
Section 89 Provisions relating to agricultural property.

To Section 78

Section 51 Payment of tax and interest on tax.

79 Exemption of certain inheritances taken by parents

[FA 1995 s165]

Notwithstanding any other provision of this Act, an inheritance taken by a person from a disponer is, where—

(a) that person is a parent of that disponer, and

(b) the date of the inheritance is the date of death of that disponer,

exempt from tax and is not taken into account in computing tax if that disponer took a non-exempt gift or inheritance from either or both of that disponer's parents within the period of 5 years immediately prior to the date of death of that disponer.

Revenue Information Notes

IT 39 Gift/Inheritance Tax – A Guide to completing the Self Assessment Return – Pre Finance Act 2010, Appendix 6.09 – Inheritance taken by Parent from Child

80 Payments relating to retirement, etc

[CATA 1976 s56]

(1) In this section—

"*superannuation scheme*" includes any arrangement in connection with employment for the provision of a benefit on or in connection with the retirement or death of an employee;

"*employment*" includes employment as a director of a body corporate and cognate words shall be construed accordingly.

(2) Subject to *subsection (3)*, any payment to an employee or former employee by, or out of funds provided by, that employee's or former employee's employer or any other person, bona fide by means of retirement benefit, redundancy payment or pension is not a gift or an inheritance.

(3) *Subsection (2)* shall not apply in relation to a payment referred to in that subsection, and any such payment is deemed to be a gift or an inheritance where—

(a) (i) the employee is a relative of the employer or other disponer, or

(ii) the employer is a private company within the meaning of *section 27*, and of which private company the employee is deemed to have control within the meaning of that section;

(b) the payment is not made under a scheme (relating to superannuation, retirement or redundancy) approved by the Commissioners under the Income Tax Acts; and

(c) the Commissioners decide that in the circumstances of the case the payment is excessive.

(4) The Commissioners shall serve on an accountable person a notice in writing of their decision referred to in *subsection (3)* and the accountable person concerned may appeal against such decision and *section 67* shall apply with any necessary modifications in relation to such appeal as it applies in relation to an appeal against an assessment of tax.

(5) Any benefit taken by a person other than the person in respect of whose service the benefit arises, under the provisions of any superannuation fund, or under any superannuation scheme, established solely or mainly for persons employed in a profession, trade, undertaking or employment, and their dependants, is (whether or not any person had a right enforceable at law to the benefit) deemed to be a gift or an inheritance, as the case may be, derived under a disposition made by the person in respect of whose service the benefit arises and not by any other person.

Revenue Information Notes

IT 39 Gift/Inheritance Tax – A Guide to completing the Self Assessment Return – Pre Finance Act 2010, Appendix 6.03 – Exemption of payments relating to retirement

Cross References

From Section 80

Section 27 Market value of certain shares in private companies.
Section 67 Appeals in other cases.

To Section 80

Section 76 Provisions relating to charities, etc.

81 Exemption of certain securities

[CATA 1976 s57(1) and (2); FA 1997 s135(2) (part); FA 2001 s219 (part)]

(1) In this section—

"*security*" means any security, stock, share, debenture, debenture stock, certificate of charge or other form of security issued, whether before, on or after the passing of this Act, and which by virtue of any enactment or by virtue of the exercise of any power conferred by any enactment is exempt from taxation when in the beneficial ownership of a person neither domiciled nor ordinarily resident in the State;

"*unit trust scheme*" means an authorised unit trust scheme within the meaning of the Unit Trusts Act 1990, whose deed expressing the trusts of the scheme restricts the property subject to those trusts to securities.

(2) Securities, or units (within the meaning of the Unit Trusts Act 1990) of a unit trust scheme, comprised in a gift or an inheritance are exempt from tax (and are not taken into account in computing tax on any gift or inheritance taken by the donee or successor) if it is shown to the satisfaction of the Commissioners that—

(a) the securities or units were comprised in the disposition continuously for a period of [15 years][1] immediately before the date of the gift or the date of the inheritance, and any period immediately before the date of the disposition during which the securities or units were continuously in the beneficial ownership of the disponer is deemed, for the purpose of this paragraph, to be a period or part of a period immediately before the date of the gift or the date of the inheritance during which they were continuously comprised in the disposition;

(b) the securities or units were comprised in the gift or inheritance—

(i) at the date of the gift or the date of the inheritance, and

(ii) at the valuation date;

and

(c) the donee or successor is at the date of the gift or the date of the inheritance neither domiciled nor ordinarily resident in the State,

and *section 89(5)* shall apply, for the purposes of this subsection, as it applies in relation to agricultural property.

(3) *Subsection (2)(a)* shall not apply where—

(a) the disponer was neither domiciled nor ordinarily resident in the State at the date of the disposition, or

(b) the securities or units concerned came into the beneficial ownership of the disponer before 26 March 1997, or became subject to the disposition before that date, and the disponer was neither domiciled nor ordinarily resident in the State at the date of the gift or the date of the inheritance.

(4) Where the securities or units concerned came into the beneficial ownership of the disponer, or became subject to the disposition prior to 15 February 2001, then *subsection (2)* shall apply as if the reference to the period of [15 years][2] in that subsection were construed as a reference to a period of 3 years.

Amendments

[1] Substituted by FA03 s150(1)(a). Has effect in relation to securities or units comprised in a gift or an inheritance where the date of the gift or the date of the inheritance is on or after 24 February 2003.

[2] Substituted by FA03 s150(1)(b). Has effect as on and from 24 February 2003.

Revenue Information Notes

IT 39 Gift/Inheritance Tax – A Guide to Completing the Self Assessment Return Pre Finance Act 2010, Appendix 6.01 – Exemption of certain securities

Cross References

From Section 81

Section 89 Provisions relating to agricultural property.

To Section 81

Section 16 Application of this Act.
Section 21 Application of this Act.

82 Exemption of certain receipts

[CATA 1976 s58]

(1) The following are not gifts or inheritances:

(a) the receipt by a person of any sum bona fide by means of compensation or damages for any wrong or injury suffered by that person in that person's person, property, reputation or means of livelihood;

(b) the receipt by a person of any sum bona fide by means of compensation or damages for any wrong or injury resulting in the death of any other person;

[(ba) any payment to which section 205A of the Taxes Consolidation Act 1997 applies;][1]

(c) the receipt by a person of any sum bona fide by means of winnings from betting (including pool betting) or from any lottery, sweepstake or game with prizes;

[(ca) the receipt by a person of an award from the competition 'Your Country, Your Call' which was launched by the President on 17 February 2010,][2]

[(cb) any benefit arising out of the discharge of a debt under a Debt Relief Notice (within the meaning of *section 25* of the Personal Insolvency Act 2012) or arising out of the discharge or reduction in the amount of a debt under a Debt Settlement Arrangement or a Personal Insolvency Arrangement (both within the meaning of *section 2* of that Act) other than by reason of payment of that debt;][3]

(d) any benefit arising out of—

(i) the payment to the Official Assignee in Bankruptcy of money which has been provided by, or which represents property provided by, friends of a bankrupt, or

(ii) a remission or abatement of debts by the creditors of a bankrupt,

to enable the bankrupt to fulfil an offer of composition after bankruptcy in accordance with section 39 of the Bankruptcy Act 1988; and

(e) any benefit arising out of—

(i) the payment to the Official Assignee in Bankruptcy of money which has been provided by, or which represents property provided by, friends of an arranging debtor, or

(ii) a remission or abatement of debts by the creditors of an arranging debtor,

to enable the debtor to carry out the terms of a proposal made by that debtor under section 87 of the Bankruptcy Act 1988, which has been accepted by that debtor's creditors and approved and confirmed by the High Court.

(2) Notwithstanding anything contained in this Act, the receipt in the lifetime of the disponer of money or money's worth—

[(a) by—

(i) a minor child of the disponer or of the civil partner of the disponer, or

(ii) a child of the disponer, or of the civil partner of the disponer, who is more than 18 years of age but not more than 25 years of age and is receiving full-time education or instruction at any university, college, school or other educational establishment, or who, regardless of age, is permanently incapacitated by reason of physical or mental infirmity from maintaining himself or herself, or

(iii) a person in relation to whom the disponer stands in *loco parentis*,

for support, maintenance or education, or][4]

(b) by a person who is in relation to the disponer a dependent relative under section 466 of the Taxes Consolidation Act 1997, for support or maintenance,

is not a gift or an inheritance, where the provision of such support, maintenance or education, or such support or maintenance—

(i) is such as would be part of the normal expenditure of a person in the circumstances of the disponer, and

(ii) is reasonable having regard to the financial circumstances of the disponer.

(3) (a) In this subsection "*incapacitated individual*", "*trust funds*" and "*qualifying trust*" have the meanings assigned to them, respectively, by section 189A (inserted by the Finance Act 1999) of the Taxes Consolidation Act 1997.

(b) The receipt by an incapacitated individual of the whole or any part of trust funds which are held on a qualifying trust, or of the income from such a qualifying trust, is not a gift or an inheritance.

[(4) The receipt by—

(a) a minor child of the disponer or of the civil partner of the disponer, or

(b) a child of the disponer, or of the civil partner of the disponer, who is more than 18 years of age but not more than 25 years of age and is receiving full-time education or instruction at any university, college, school or other educational establishment, or who, regardless of age, is permanently incapacitated by reason of physical or mental infirmity from maintaining himself or herself,

of money or money's worth for support, maintenance or education, at a time when the disponer and the other parent of any such minor child or child of the disponer are dead or, in the case of any such minor child or child of the civil partner of the disponer, when the disponer and the civil partner are dead, is not a gift or an inheritance where the provision of such support, maintenance or education—

(i) is such as would be part of the normal expenditure of a person in the circumstances of the disponer immediately before the death of the disponer, and

(ii) is reasonable having regard to the financial circumstances of the disponer immediately before the death of the disponer.][5]

[(5) The references in *subsections (2)* and *(4)* to a child receiving full-time education or instruction at an educational establishment shall include references to a child undergoing training by any person (in *subsection (6)* referred to as 'the employer') for any trade or profession in such circumstances that the child is required to devote the whole of his or her time to such training for a period of not less than 2 years.

(6) For the purposes of this section, in the case of a child undergoing training, the Commissioners may require the employer to furnish such particulars as they may

reasonably require with respect to the training of the child in such form as may be prescribed by the 15 Commissioners.][6]

Amendments

[1] Inserted by F(No.2)A13 s77(2). Applies to payments to which section 205A of the Taxes Consolidation Act 1997 applies made on or after 1 August 2013.

[2] Inserted by FA10 s(145)(1). This section applies to gifts taken on or after 17 February 2010.

[3] Inserted by FA13 s100(2). Applies to gifts and inheritances (both within the meaning of the Capital Acquisitions Tax Consolidation Act 2003) taken on or after 27 March 2013.

[4] Substituted by FA14 s81(1)(a). Applies on and from 23 December 2014.

[5] Substituted by FA14 s81(1)(b). Applies on and from 23 December 2014.

[6] Inserted by FA14 s81(1)(c). Applies on and from 23 December 2014.

Case Law

AG for Northern Ireland v Heron 1959 TR 1; 38 ATC 3 (CA) looked at the definition of 'normal' and 'reasonable' as taken from estate duty.
In Bennett v IRC 1995 STC 54 the judge's view was that the term normal "connotes expenditure which at the time it took place accorded with the settled pattern of expenditure adopted by the transferor."

Revenue Briefings

eBrief

eBrief No. 109/2014 – Guide to the CAT Treatment of Receipts by Children from their Parents for their Support, Maintenance or Education

Revenue Information Notes

IT 39 Gift/Inheritance Tax – A Guide to completing the Self Assessment Return – Pre Finance Act 2010, Appendix 6.04 – Exemption of certain receipts

83 Exemption where disposition was made by the donee or successor

[CATA 1976 s59]

(1) In this section, "*company*" means a body corporate (wherever incorporated), other than a private company within the meaning of *section 27*.

(2) Tax is not chargeable on a gift or an inheritance taken by the donee or successor under a disposition made by that donee or successor.

(3) Where, at the date of the gift, 2 companies are associated in the manner described in *subsection (4)*, a gift taken by one of them under a disposition made by the other is deemed to be a gift to which *subsection (2)* applies.

(4) For the purposes of *subsection (3)*, 2 companies shall be regarded as associated if—

(a) one company would be beneficially entitled to not less than 90 per cent of any assets of the other company available for distribution to the owners of its shares and entitlements of the kind referred to in *section 43(1)* on a winding up, or

(b) a third company would be beneficially entitled to not less than 90 per cent of any assets of each of them available as in *paragraph (a)*.

Revenue Information Notes

IT 39 Gift/Inheritance Tax – A Guide to completing the Self Assessment Return – Pre Finance Act 2010, Appendix 6.05 – Exemption of dispositions made by the Donee or Successor

Cross References

From Section 83

Section 27 Market value of certain shares in private companies.
Section 43 Disposition by or a company.

84 Exemption relating to qualifying expenses of incapacitated persons

[CATA 1976 s59A]

(1) In this section, "*qualifying expenses*" means expenses relating to medical care including the cost of maintenance in connection with such medical care.

(2) A gift or inheritance which is taken exclusively for the purpose of discharging qualifying expenses of an individual who is permanently incapacitated by reason of physical or mental infirmity is, to the extent that the Commissioners are satisfied that it has been or will be applied to such purpose, exempt from tax and is not taken into account in computing tax.

Revenue Briefings

eBrief

eBrief No. 73/2011 – Exemption relating to Qualifying Expenses of Incapacitated Persons

85 Exemption relating to retirement benefits

[CATA 1976 s59B]

[(1) In this section "*retirement fund*", in relation to an inheritance taken on death of a disponer, means—

(a) an approved retirement fund or an approved minimum retirement fund, within the meaning of *section 784A* or *784C* of the Taxes Consolidation Act 1997, or

(b) a Personal Retirement Savings Account, within the meaning of *section 787A* of the Taxes Consolidation Act 1997, where assets of the Personal Retirement Savings Account are treated under *section 787G(4)* of that Act as having been made available to an individual,

being a fund which is wholly comprised of all or any of the following, that is—

(i) property which represents in wholeor in part the accrued rights of the disponer, or of a predeceased spouse or civil partner of the disponer, under—

(I) an annuity contract or retirement benefits scheme approved by the Commissioners for the purposes of *Chapter 1* or *Chapter 2* of *Part 30* of the Taxes Consolidation Act 1997, or

(II) a Personal Retirement Savings Account being a PRSA product approved by the Commissioners for the purposes of *Chapter 2A* of *Part 30* of the Taxes Consolidation Act 1997,

(ii) any accumulations of income of such property, or

(iii) property which represents in whole or in part these accumulations.][1]

(2) The whole or any part of a retirement fund which is comprised in an inheritance which is taken on the death of a disponer is exempt from tax in relation to that inheritance and the value of that inheritance is not taken into account in computing tax, where—

(a) the disposition under which the inheritance is taken is the will or intestacy of the disponer, and

(b) the successor is a [child of the disponer or of the civil partner of the disponer][2] and had attained 21 years of age at the date of that disposition.

Amendments

[1] Substituted by FA13 s90(1). Applies to inheritances taken on or after 27 March 2013.

[2] Substituted by F(No.3)A11 sched3(20). Deemed to have come into operation as respects a gift or an inheritance taken on or after 1 January 2011.

Revenue Information Notes

IT 39 Gift/Inheritance Tax – A Guide to completing the Self Assessment Return – Pre Finance Act 2010, Appendix 6.06 – Exemption in relation to retirement benefits

86 Exemption relating to certain dwellings

[CATA 1976 s59C]

(1) In this section—

"*dwelling-house*" means—

(a) a building or part (including an appropriate part within the meaning of *section 5(5)*) of a building which was used or was suitable for use as a dwelling, and

(b) the curtilage of the dwelling-house up to an area (exclusive of the site of the dwelling-house) of one acre but if the area of the curtilage (exclusive of the site of the dwelling-house) exceeds one acre then the part which comes within this definition is the part which, if the remainder were separately occupied, would be the most suitable for occupation and enjoyment with the dwelling-house;

"*relevant period*", in relation to a dwelling-house comprised in a gift or inheritance, means the period of 6 years commencing on the date of the gift or the date of the inheritance.

(2) In this section any reference to a donee or successor is construed as including a reference to the transferee referred to in *section 32(2)*.

(3) Subject to *subsections (4)*, *(5)*, *(6)* and *(7)*, a dwelling-house comprised in a gift or inheritance which is taken by a donee or successor who—

(a) has continuously occupied as that donee or successor's only or main residence—

(i) that dwelling-house throughout the period of 3 years immediately preceding the date of the gift or the date of the inheritance, or

(ii) where that dwelling-house has directly or indirectly replaced other property, that dwelling-house and that other property for periods which together comprised at least 3 years falling within the period of 4 years immediately preceding the date of the gift or the date of the inheritance,

(b) is not, at the date of the gift or at the date of the inheritance, beneficially entitled to any other dwelling-house or to any interest in any other dwelling-house, and

(c) continues to occupy that dwelling-house as that donee or successor's only or main residence throughout the relevant period,

is exempt from tax in relation to that gift or inheritance, and the value of that dwelling-house is not to be taken into account in computing tax on any gift or inheritance taken by that person unless the exemption ceases to apply under *subsection (6)* or *(7)*.

[(3A) For the purposes of *subsection (3)(a)*, in the case of a gift—

(a) any period during which a donee occupied a dwelling house that was, during that period, the disponer's only or main residence, shall be treated as not being a period during which the donee occupied the dwelling house unless the disponer is compelled, by reason of old age or infirmity, to depend on the services of the donee for that period,

(b) where *paragraph (a)(i)* of *subsection (3)* applies, the dwelling house referred to in that paragraph is required to be owned by the disponer during the 3 year period referred to in that paragraph, and

(c) where *paragraph (a)(ii)* of *subsection (3)* applies, either the dwelling house or the other property referred to in that paragraph is required to be owned by the disponer during the 3 year period referred to in that paragraph.][1]

(4) The condition in *paragraph (c)* of *subsection (3)* shall not apply where the donee or successor has attained the age of 55 years at the date of the gift or at the date of the inheritance.

(5) For the purpose of *paragraph (c)* of *subsection (3)*, the donee or successor is deemed to occupy the dwelling-house concerned as that donee or successor's only or main residence throughout any period of absence during which that donee or successor worked in an employment or office all the duties of which were performed outside the State.

(6) If a dwelling-house exempted from tax by virtue of *subsection (3)* is sold or disposed of, either in whole or in part, within the relevant period, and before the death of the donee or successor (not being a donee or successor who had attained the age of 55 years at the date of the gift or inheritance), the exemption referred to in that subsection shall cease to apply to such dwelling-house unless the sale or disposal occurs in consequence of the donee or successor requiring long-term medical care in a hospital, nursing home or convalescent home.

(7) The exemption referred to in *subsection (3)* shall cease to apply to a dwelling-house, if at any time during the relevant period and—

(a) before the dwelling-house is sold or disposed of, and

(b) before the death of the donee or successor,

the condition specified in *paragraph (c)* of *subsection (3)* has not been complied with unless that non-compliance occurs in consequence of the donee or successor requiring long-term medical care in a hospital, nursing home or convalescent home, or in consequence of any condition imposed by the employer of the donee or successor requiring the donee or successor to reside elsewhere.

(8) Where a dwelling-house exempted from tax by virtue of *subsection (3)* (in this section referred to as the "*first-mentioned dwelling-house*") is replaced within the relevant period by another dwelling-house, the condition specified in *paragraph (c)* of *subsection (3)* is treated as satisfied if the donee or successor has occupied as that donee or successor's only or main residence the first-mentioned dwelling-house, that other dwelling-house and any dwelling-house which has within the relevant period directly or indirectly replaced that other dwelling-house for periods which together comprised at least 6 years falling within the period of 7 years commencing on the date of the gift or the date of the inheritance.

(9) Any period of absence which would satisfy the condition specified in *paragraph (c)* of *subsection (3)* in relation to the first-mentioned dwelling-house shall, if it occurs in relation to any dwelling-house which has directly or indirectly replaced

that dwelling-house, likewise satisfy that condition as it has effect by virtue of *subsection (8)*.

(10) *Subsection (6)* shall not apply to a case falling within *subsection (8)*, but the extent of the exemption under this section in such a case shall, where the donee or successor had not attained the age of 55 years at the date of the gift or at the date of the inheritance, not exceed what it would have been had the replacement of one dwelling-house by another referred to in *subsection (8)*, or any one or more of such replacements, taken place immediately prior to that date.

Amendments

[1] Inserted by FA07 s116(1). This section applies to gifts taken on or after 20 February 2007.

Case Law

In Leedale v Lewis 1982 STC 835 it was established that a potential beneficiary of a discretionary trust can have an 'interest' for tax purposes.

In Danaher v Revenue Commissioners 2005 Circuit Court No. 8 RA it was held that the words "other property" mean other property owned by the disponer.

Revenue Briefings

Tax Briefing

Tax Briefing June 2000 – Issue 40 page 32 – Feature of Finance Act 2000 introduced at Committee Stage – Dwelling-House Exemption

Revenue Information Notes

Pt 19.15 Revenue CAT Manual – Exemption relating to Certain Dwellings – Section 86 CATCA 2003

CAT 10 – Gift/Inheritance Tax Exemption for Dwelling House

Cross References

From Section 86

Section 5 Gift deemed to be taken.

Section 32 Dealings with future interests.

To Section 86

Section 51 Payment of tax and interest on tax.

87 Exemption of certain benefits

[FA 1982 s98]

Where a gift or an inheritance is taken, by direction of the disponer, free of tax, the benefit taken is deemed to include the amount of tax chargeable on such gift or inheritance but not the amount of tax chargeable on such tax.

Revenue Information Notes

Pt 14 Revenue CAT Manual – Freedom from Tax.

IT 39 Gift/Inheritance Tax – A Guide to completing the Self Assessment Return – Pre Finance Act 2010, Appendix 8.07 – Tax "Free" Benefits

88 Exemption of certain transfers from capital acquisitions tax following dissolution of marriage or civil partnership

[(1) Notwithstanding any other provision of this Act, a gift or inheritance taken by virtue or in consequence of an order to which this subsection applies by an individual who was a party to the marriage concerned, or to the civil partnership concerned, is exempt from tax and is not taken into account in computing tax.

(2) *Subsection (1)* applies—

(a) to a relief order or an order under section 25 of the Family Law Act 1995, made, following the dissolution of a marriage,

(b) to a maintenance pending relief order made, following the granting of leave under section 23(3) of the Family Law Act 1995, to a spouse whose marriage has been dissolved,

(c) to an order referred to in section 41(*a*) of the Family Law Act 1995, or an order under section 42(1) of that Act made in addition to or instead of an order under section 41(*a*) of that Act, in favour of a spouse whose marriage has been dissolved,

(d) to an order under Part III of the Family Law (Divorce) Act 1996,

(e) to an order under Part 12 of the Civil Partnership and Certain Rights and Obligations of Cohabitants Act 2010, and

(f) to an order or other determination to like effect, made on or after 10 February 2000, which is analogous to an order referred to in *paragraph (a), (b), (c), (d)* or *(e)* of a court under the law of another territory made under or in consequence of the dissolution of a marriage or civil partnership, being a dissolution that is entitled to be recognised as valid in the State.][1]

Amendments

[1] Substituted by F(No.3)A11 sched3(21). Deemed to have come into operation as respects a gift or an inheritance taken on or after 1 January 2011.

88A Certain transfers by qualified cohabitants

[Notwithstanding any other provision of this Act, a gift or inheritance taken by virtue or in consequence of an order under Part 15 of the Civil Partnership and Certain Rights and Obligations of Cohabitants Act 2010 by a qualified cohabitant, within the meaning of that Act, is exempt from tax and is not taken into account in computing tax.][1]

Amendments

[1] Inserted by F(No.3)A11 sched3(21). Deemed to have come into operation as respects a gift or an inheritance taken on or after 1 January 2011.

PART 10

Reliefs

CHAPTER 1

Agricultural Relief

89 Provisions relating to agricultural property

[CATA 1976 s19]

(1) In this section—

["*agricultural property*" means—

(a) agricultural land, pasture and woodland situate [in a Member State][1] and crops, trees and underwood growing on such land and also includes such farm buildings, farm houses and mansion houses (together with the lands occupied with such farm buildings, farm houses and mansion houses) as are of a character appropriate to the property, and farm machinery, livestock and blood-stock on such property, and

(b) a payment entitlement (within the meaning of [Regulation (EU) No. 1307/2013 of the European Parliament and of the Council of 17 December 2013*][2]);][3]

* OJ No. L347, 20.12.2013, p.608

"*agricultural value*" means the market value of agricultural property reduced by 90 per cent of that value;

[*'farmer'*, in relation to a donee or successor, means an individual in respect of whom not less than 80 per cent of the market value of the property to which the individual is beneficially entitled in possession is represented by the market value of property in a Member State which consists of agricultural property, and, for the purposes of this definition—

(a) no deduction is made from the market value of property for any debts or encumbrances (except debts or encumbrances in respect of a dwelling-house that is the only or main residence of the donee or successor and that is not agricultural property), and

(b) an individual is deemed to be beneficially entitled in possession to—

(i) an interest in expectancy, notwithstanding the definition of 'entitled in possession' in section 2, and

(ii) property that is subject to a discretionary trust under or in consequence of a disposition made by the individual where the individual is an object of the trust,

and who—

(i) is the holder of any of the qualifications set out in *Schedule 2*, *2A* or *2B* to the Stamp Duties Consolidation Act 1999, or who achieves such a qualification within a period of 4 years commencing on the date of the gift or inheritance, and who for a period of not less than 6 years commencing on the valuation date of the gift or inheritance farms agricultural property (including the agricultural property comprised in the gift or inheritance) on a commercial basis and with a view to the realisation of profits from that agricultural property,

(ii) for a period of not less than 6 years commencing on the valuation date of the gift or inheritance spends not less than 50 per cent of that individual's normal working time farming agricultural property (including the agricultural property comprised in the gift or inheritance) on a commercial basis and with a view to the realisation of profits from that agricultural property, or

(iii) leases the whole or substantially the whole of the agricultural property, comprised in the gift or inheritance for a period of not less than 6 years commencing on the valuation date of the gift or inheritance, to an individual who satisfies the conditions in *paragraph (i)* or *(ii)*.][4]

[(1A) For the purpose of *paragraph (a)* of the definition of 'farmer' in *subsection (1)*, a loan secured on the dwelling-house referred to in that paragraph which is not used to purchase, repair or improve that dwelling-house will not be treated as a debt or an encumbrance.][5]

(2) Except where provided in *subsection (6)*, in so far as any gift or inheritance consists of agricultural property—

(a) at the date of the gift or at the date of the inheritance, and

(b) at the valuation date,

and is taken by a donee or successor who is, on the valuation date and after taking the gift or inheritance, a farmer, *section 28* (other than *subsection (7)(b)* of that section) shall apply in relation to agricultural property as it applies in relation to other property subject to the following modifications—

(i) in *subsection (1)* of that section, the reference to market value shall be construed as a reference to agricultural value,

(ii) where a deduction is to be made for any liability, costs or expenses in accordance with *subsection (1)* of that section only a proportion of such liability, costs or expenses is deducted and that proportion is the proportion that the agricultural value of the agricultural property bears to the market value of that property, and

(iii) where a deduction is to be made for any consideration under *subsection (2)* or *(4)(b)* of that section, only a proportion of such consideration is deducted and that proportion is the proportion that the agricultural value of the agricultural property bears to the market value of that property.

(3) Where a taxable gift or a taxable inheritance is taken by a donee or successor subject to the condition that the whole or part of that taxable gift or taxable inheritance will be invested in agricultural property and such condition is complied with within 2 years after the date of the gift or the date of the inheritance, then the gift or inheritance is deemed, for the purposes of this section, to have consisted—

(a) at the date of the gift or at the date of the inheritance, and

(b) at the valuation date,

of agricultural property to the extent to which the gift or inheritance is subject to such condition and has been so invested.

[(4) (a) Where—

(i) all or any part of the agricultural property (other than crops, trees or underwood) comprised in a gift or inheritance is disposed of or compulsorily acquired within the period of 6 years [commencing on][6] the date of the gift or inheritance, and

(ii) the proceeds from such disposal or compulsory acquisition are not fully expended in acquiring other agricultural property within a year of the disposal or within 6 years of the compulsory acquisition,

then, except where the donee or successor dies before the property is disposed of or compulsorily acquired, all or, as the case may be, part of the agricultural property shall, for the purposes of *subsection (2)* and in accordance with *paragraph (aa)*, be treated as property comprised in the gift or inheritance which is not agricultural property, and the taxable value of the gift or inheritance shall be determined accordingly (without regard to whether the donee or successor has ceased to be a farmer by virtue of the disposal or compulsory acquisition) and tax shall be payable accordingly.

(aa) For the purposes of *paragraph (a)*—

(i) the market value of agricultural property which is treated under *paragraph (a)* as not being agricultural property is determined by the following formula—

$$V1 \times \frac{N}{V2}$$

where—

V1 is the market value of all of the agricultural property on the valuation date without regard to *paragraph (a)*,

V2 is the market value of that agricultural property immediately before the disposal or compulsory acquisition of all or, as the case may be, a part thereof, and

N is the amount of proceeds from the disposal or compulsory acquisition of all the agricultural property or, as the case may be, a part thereof, that was not expended in acquiring other agricultural property,

and

(ii) the proceeds from a disposal include an amount equal to the market value of the consideration (not being cash) received for the disposal.][7]

(b) If an arrangement is made, in the administration of property subject to a disposition, for the appropriation of property in or towards the satisfaction of a benefit under the disposition, such arrangement is deemed not to be a [disposal][8] or a compulsory acquisition for the purposes of *paragraph (a)*.

[...][9]

[(4A) Where the proceeds referred to in *subparagraph (ii)* of *subsection (4)(a)* are expended in acquiring agricultural property which has been transferred by the donee or successor to his or her [spouse or civil partner][10], such property shall not be treated as other agricultural property for the purposes of that subparagraph.][11]

[(4B) Where a donee, successor or lessee ceases to qualify as a farmer under *subsection (1)* within the period of 6 years commencing on the valuation date of the gift or inheritance, all or, as the case may be, part of the agricultural property shall for the purposes of *subsection (2)*, otherwise than on the death of the donee, successor or lessee, be treated as property comprised in the gift or inheritance that is not agricultural property, and the taxable value of the gift or inheritance shall be determined accordingly and tax shall be payable accordingly.][12]

(5) For the purposes of *subsection (2)*, if, in the administration of property subject to a disposition, property is appropriated in or towards the satisfaction of a benefit in respect of which a person is deemed to take a gift or an inheritance under the disposition, the property so appropriated, if it was subject to the disposition at the date of the gift or at the date of the inheritance, is deemed to have been comprised in that gift or inheritance at the date of the gift or at the date of the inheritance.

(6) *Subsection (2)* shall apply in relation to agricultural property which consists of trees or underwood as if the words "and is taken by a donee or successor who is, on the valuation date and after taking the gift or inheritance, a farmer," were omitted from that subsection.

(7) In this section, any reference to a donee or successor includes a reference to the transferee referred to in *section 32(2)*.

Amendments

[1] Substituted by F(No.2)A08 s89(1). Applies to gifts and inheritances taken on or after 20 November 2008.

[2] Substituted by FA14 sched3(3). Has effect as respects gifts and inheritances taken on or after 1 January 2015.

[3] Substituted by FA06 s118(1)(a)(i). This section is deemed to have applied as regards gifts and inheritances of agricultural property taken on or after 1 January 2005.

[4] Substituted by FA14 s82(1)(a). Has effect in relation to gifts or inheritances taken on or after 1 January 2015.

[5] Inserted by FA12 s114(1)(a). Applies to gifts and inheritances taken on or after 8 February 2012.

[6] Substituted by FA11 s68(1)(a). Applies to gifts and inheritances taken on or after 21 January 2011.

[7] Substituted by FA05 s135(1)(a). This section has effect in relation to disposals or compulsory acquisitions of agricultural property occurring on or after 3 February 2005.

[8] Substituted by FA05 s135(1)(b). Has effect in relation to disposals or compulsory acquisitions of agricultural property occurring on or after 3 February 2005.

[9] Deleted by FA12 s114(1)(b). Applies to gifts and inheritances taken on or after 8 February 2012.

[10] Substituted by F(No.3)A11 sched3(22). Shall apply to gifts and inheritances taken on or after 27 July 2011.

[11] Inserted by FA10 s(146)(1). This section applies to transfers executed on or after 4 February 2010.

[12] Inserted by FA14 s82(1)(b). Has effect in relation to gifts or inheritances taken on or after 1 January 2015.

Case Law

In Faulks v Faulks 1992 15 EG 82 it was held that a milk quota is not an asset separate from the land.

Starke (executors of Brown deceased) v IRC CA 1995 STC 689 considered what constituted 'agricultural property' and held that a 2.5 acre site, containing a house and outbuildings, was not 'agricultural property'.

A barn with 2 acres was eligible for agricultural relief while the house on the land was not a farmhouse and therefore was not eligible for the relief. Rosser v IRC 2003 SpC 368

Revenue Briefings

eBrief

eBrief No. 51/2012 – Capital Acquisitions Tax – Agricultural Relief

eBrief No. 068/2015 – Capital Acquisitions Tax – Agricultural Relief – Finance Act 2014 changes – Frequently Asked Questions

Revenue Information Notes

Pt 11 Revenue CAT Manual – Agricultural Relief

Pt 19.13 Revenue CAT Manual – Agricultural relief

CAT 5 – Agricultural Relief

Cross References

From Section 89

Section 2 General interpretation.
Section 28 Taxable value of a taxable gift or inheritance.
Section 32 Dealings with future interests.

To Section 89

Section 28 Taxable value of a taxable gift or inheritance.
Section 51 Payment of tax and interest on tax.
Section 55 Payment of tax on certain assets by instalments.
Section 77 Exemption of heritage property.
Section 78 Heritage property of companies.
Section 81 Exemption of certain securities.
Section 90 Interpretation (Chapter 2).
Section 102 Avoidance of double relief.
Section 102A Agricultural and business property: development land.

CHAPTER 2

Business Relief

90 Interpretation (Chapter 2)

[FA 1994 s124]

(1) In this Chapter—

"*agricultural property*" has the meaning assigned to it by *section 89;*

"*associated company*" has the meaning assigned to it by section 16(1)(*b*) of the Companies (Amendment) Act 1986;

"*business*" includes a business carried on in the exercise of a profession or vocation, but does not include a business carried on otherwise than for gain;

"*excepted asset*" shall be construed in accordance with *section 100*;

"*full-time working officer or employee*", in relation to one or more companies, means any officer or employee who devotes substantially the whole of such officer's or employee's time to the service of that company, or those companies taken together, in a managerial or technical capacity;

"*holding company*" and "*subsidiary*" have the meanings assigned to them, respectively, by section 155 of the Companies Act 1963;

"*quoted*", in relation to any shares or securities, means quoted on a recognised stock exchange and "*unquoted*", in relation to any shares or securities, means not so quoted;

"*relevant business property*" shall be construed in accordance with *section 93*.

(2) In this Chapter a reference to a gift shall be construed as a reference to a taxable gift and a reference to an inheritance shall be construed as a reference to a taxable inheritance.

(3) For the purposes of this Chapter a company and all its subsidiaries and any associated company of that company or of any of those subsidiaries and any subsidiary of such an associated company are members of a group.

(4) In this Chapter any reference to a donee or successor is construed as including a reference to the transferee referred to in *section 32(2)*.

Revenue Information Notes

Pt 12 Revenue CAT Manual – Business Relief.
CAT 4 – Business Relief

Cross References

From Section 90

Section 16 Application of this Act.
Section 32 Dealings with future interests.
Section 89 Provisions relating to agricultural property.
Section 93 Relevant business property.
Section 100 Exclusion of value of excepted assets.

91 Application (Chapter 2)

[FA 1994 s125]

This Chapter shall apply in relation to gifts and inheritances, but shall not apply in relation to an inheritance taken by a discretionary trust by virtue of *sections 15(1)* or *20(1)*.

Cross References

From Section 91

Section 15 Acquisitions by discretionary trusts.
Section 20 Annual acquisitions by discretionary trusts.

92 Business relief

[FA 1994 s126]

Where the whole or part of the taxable value of any taxable gift or taxable inheritance is attributable to the value of any relevant business property, the whole or that part of the taxable value is, subject to the other provisions of this Chapter, treated as being reduced by 90 per cent.

Revenue Briefings

eBrief

eBrief No. 14/2014 – Capital Acquisitions Tax – Business Relief

Cross References

To Section 92

Section 51 Payment of tax and interest on tax.
Section 55 Payment of tax on certain assets by instalments.
Section 101 Withdrawal of relief.
Section 102A Agricultural and business property: development land.

93 Relevant business property

[FA 1994 s127(1), (2) and (4) to (8)]

(1) In this Chapter and subject to the following provisions of this section and to *sections 94, 96* and *100(4)* "*relevant business property*" means, in relation to a gift or inheritance, any one or more of the following, that is:

(a) property consisting of a business or interest in a business,

(b) unquoted shares in or securities of a company whether incorporated in the State or otherwise to which *paragraph (c)* does not relate, and which on the valuation date (either by themselves alone or together with other shares or securities in that company in the absolute beneficial ownership of the donee or successor on that date) give control of powers of voting on all questions affecting the company as a whole which if exercised would yield more than 25 per cent of the votes capable of being exercised on [all such questions][1],

(c) unquoted shares in or securities of a company whether incorporated in the State or [otherwise][2] which is, on the valuation date (after the taking of the gift or inheritance), a company controlled by the donee or successor within the meaning of *section 27*,

(d) unquoted shares in or securities of a company whether incorporated in the State or otherwise which do not fall within *paragraph (b)* or *(c)* and which on the valuation date (either by themselves alone or together with other shares or securities in that company in the absolute beneficial ownership of the donee or successor on that date) have an aggregate nominal value which represents 10 per cent or more of the aggregate nominal value of the entire share capital and securities of the company on condition that the donee or successor has been a full-time working officer or employee of the company, or if that company is a member of a group, of one or more companies which are members of the group, throughout the period of 5 years ending on the date of the gift or inheritance,

(e) any land or building, machinery or plant which, immediately before the gift or inheritance, was used wholly or mainly for the purposes of a business carried on by a company of which the disponer then had control or by a partnership of which the disponer then was a partner and for the purposes of this paragraph a person is deemed to have control of a company at any time if that person [, or that person and his or her spouse or civil partner,][3] then had control of powers of voting on all questions affecting the company as a whole which if exercised would have yielded a majority of the votes capable of being exercised on all such questions,

(f) quoted shares in or securities of a company which, but for the fact that they are quoted, would be shares or securities to which *paragraph (b)*, *(c)* or *(d)* would relate on condition that such shares or securities, or other shares in or securities of the same company which are represented by those shares or securities, were in the beneficial ownership of the disponer immediately prior to the disposition and were unquoted at the date of the commencement of that beneficial ownership or at 23 May 1994, whichever is the later date.

(2) Where a company has shares or securities of any class giving powers of voting limited to either or both—

(a) the question of winding-up the company, and

(b) any question primarily affecting shares or securities of that class,

the reference in *subsection (1)* to all questions affecting the company as a whole has effect as a reference to all such questions except any in relation to which those powers are capable of being exercised.

(3) A business or interest in a business, or shares in or securities of a company, is not relevant business property if the business or, as the case may be, the business carried on by the company consists wholly or mainly of one or more of the following, that is, dealing in currencies, securities, stocks or shares, land or buildings, or making or holding investments.

[(4) *Subsection (3)* shall not apply to shares in or securities of a company if—

(a) the business of the company consists wholly or mainly in being a holding company of one or more companies whose business does not fall within that subsection, or

(b) the value of those shares or securities, without having regard to the provisions of *section 99*, is wholly or mainly attributable, directly or indirectly, to businesses that do not fall within that subsection.][4]

(5) Any land, building, machinery or plant used wholly or mainly for the purposes of a business carried on as mentioned in *subsection (1)(e)* is not relevant business property in relation to a gift or inheritance, unless the disponer's interest in the business is, or shares in or securities of the company carrying on the business immediately before the gift or inheritance are, relevant business property in relation to the gift or inheritance or in relation to a simultaneous gift or inheritance taken by the same donee or successor.

(6) The references to a disponer in *subsections (1)(e)* and *(5)* include a reference to a person in whom the land, building, machinery or plant concerned is vested for a beneficial interest in possession immediately before the gift or inheritance.

(7) Where shares or securities are vested in the trustees of a settlement, any powers of voting which they give to the trustees of the settlement are, for the purposes of *subsection (1)(e)*, deemed to be given to the person beneficially entitled in possession to the shares or securities except in a case where no individual is so entitled.

Amendments

[1] Substituted by FA04 sched3(2)(f)(i). Has effect as on and from 21 February 2003.

[2] Substituted by FA04 sched3(2)(f)(ii). Has effect as on and from 21 February 2003.

[3] Inserted by FA14 s83(1). Applies on and from 23 October 2014.

[4] Substituted by FA04 s78(1). This section has effect in relation to gifts or inheritances taken on or after 25 March 2004.

Case Law

The Revenue CAT Manual at Pt 12.5 considers the definition of "business" and quotes definitions made by the courts over the years:

"it denotes the carrying on of a serious occupation". Town Investments v DOE 1977 1 All ER

"Anything which occupies the time and attention and labour of a man for the purpose of a profit". Smith v Anderson 1880 15 Ch D

"a serious undertaking earnestly pursued". Rael Brook Ltd v Minister of Housing and Local Government 1967 1 All ER

"any occupation or function actively pursued with reasonable or recognisable continuity". Morrison's Academy 1978 STC

The definition of a "business" was considered in the Irish case of A.E. v Revenue Commissioners 1994 V ITR 686. In this case land was let on conacre and the question was whether this was a business. It was held that it was a business although not a very successful one. However, in the Northern Ireland case; McCall and Keenan (as Personal Representatives of Eileen McLean deceased) v HMRC 2009 SpC 678 it was held that land let on conacre was not a business.

Council case of American Leaf Co. v Director-General 1979 AC 675 considered the definition of "business" in relation to rented property.

In Farmer (Farmers Executors) v IRC 1999 STC (SCD) 321 the UK Special Commissioners held that the net profit was not the only test to be applied when determining whether a business consists wholly or mainly of making or holding investments for business relief purpose. The approach taken by Revenue in applying the 'wholly or mainly' test accords mainly with the approach taken in this case.

Gittos v Barkley (Inspector of Taxes) 1982 STC 390 and Griffiths (Inspector of Taxes) v Jackson/Pearman 1983 STC 184 held that the letting of furnished accommodation, whether on a long or short-term basis, and whether for holiday or other purposes, should generally be treated as "investment".

Revenue and Customs v George 2004 STC 147 (CA) held that a 85% holding in a company owning and operating a caravan park site qualified for the relief.

Revenue Briefings

Tax Briefing

Tax Briefing April 2004 – Issue 55 pg 15 – Business Relief and Caravan Parks

Revenue Information Notes

Pt 12.5 Revenue CAT Manual for definition of "Relevant Business Property" and the meaning of "wholly or mainly", "dealing" and "investment".

Appendix II Revenue CAT Manual – Response to certain Business Relief Queries.

Appendix II Revenue CAT Manual – Summary of other Revenue opinions given on Business Relief in response to Queries

Cross References

From Section 93

Section 27 Market value of certain shares in private companies.
Section 94 Minimum period of ownership.
Section 96 Succession.
Section 99 Value of certain shares and securities.
Section 100 Exclusion of value of excepted assets.

To Section 93

Section 55 Payment of tax on certain assets by instalments.
Section 90 Interpretation (Chapter 2).
Section 99 Value of certain shares and securities.
Section 100 Exclusion of value of excepted assets.
Section 101 Withdrawal of relief.
Section 102A Agricultural and business property: development land.

94 Minimum period of ownership

[FA 1994 s128]

In relation to a gift or an inheritance, property shall not be relevant business property unless it was comprised in the disposition continuously—

(a) in the case of an inheritance, which is taken on the date of death of the disponer, for a period of 2 years immediately prior to the date of the inheritance, or

(b) in any other case, for a period of 5 years immediately prior to the date of the gift or inheritance,

and any period immediately before the date of the disposition during which the property was continuously in the beneficial ownership of the disponer, or of the [spouse or civil partner][1] of the disponer, is deemed, for the purposes of this Chapter, to be a period or part of a period immediately before the date of the gift or inheritance during which it was continuously comprised in the disposition.

Amendments

[1] Substituted by F(No.3)A11 sched3(23). Deemed to have come into operation as respects a gift or an inheritance taken on or after 1 January 2011.

Revenue Information Notes

Appendix II Revenue CAT Manual – Summary of other Revenue opinions given on Business Relief in response to Queries

Cross References

To Section 94

Section 55 Payment of tax on certain assets by instalments.
Section 93 Relevant business property.
Section 95 Replacements.
Section 96 Succession.
Section 97 Successive benefits.
Section 100 Exclusion of value of excepted assets.
Section 101 Withdrawal of relief.

95 Replacements

[FA 1994 s129]

(1) Property shall be treated as complying with *section 94* if—

(a) the property replaced other property and that property, that other property and any property directly or indirectly replaced by that other property were comprised in the disposition for periods which together comprised—

(i) in a case referred to at *paragraph (a)* of *section 94*, at least 2 years falling within the 3 years immediately preceding the date of the inheritance, or

(ii) in a case referred to at *paragraph (b)* of *section 94*, at least 5 years falling within the 6 years immediately preceding the date of the gift or inheritance,

and

(b) any other property concerned was such that, had the gift or inheritance been taken immediately before it was replaced, it would, apart from *section 94*, have been relevant business property in relation to the gift or inheritance.

(2) In a case to which *subsection (1)* relates, relief under this Chapter shall not exceed what it would have been had the replacement or any one or more of the replacements not been made.

(3) For the purposes of *subsection (2)* changes resulting from the formation, alteration or dissolution of a partnership, or from the acquisition of a business by a company controlled (within the meaning of *section 27)* by the former owner of the business, are disregarded.

Revenue Information Notes

Appendix II Revenue CAT Manual – Summary of other Revenue opinions given on Business Relief in response to Queries

Pt 12.5 Revenue CAT Manual for description of "Replacement Property"

Cross References

From Section 95

Section 27 Market value of certain shares in private companies.
Section 94 Minimum period of ownership.

To Section 95

Section 96 Succession.
Section 97 Successive benefits.
Section 100 Exclusion of value of excepted assets.

96 Succession

[FA 1994 s130]

For the purposes of *sections 94* and *95*, where a disponer became beneficially entitled to any property on the death of another person the disponer is deemed to have been beneficially entitled to it from the date of that death.

Cross References

From Section 96

Section 94 Minimum period of ownership.
Section 95 Replacements.

To Section 96

Section 93 Relevant business property.

97 Successive benefits

[FA 1994 s131]

(1) Where—

(a) a gift or inheritance (in this section referred to as "*the earlier benefit*") was eligible for relief under this Chapter or would have been so eligible if such relief had been capable of being given in respect of gifts and inheritances taken at that time, and

(b) the whole or part of the property which, in relation to the earlier benefit was relevant business property became, through the earlier benefit, the property of the person or of the [spouse or civil partner][1] of the person who is the disponer in relation to a subsequent gift or inheritance (in this section referred to as "*the subsequent benefit*"), and

(c) that property, or part, or any property directly or indirectly replacing it, would, apart from *section 94*, have been relevant business property in relation to the subsequent benefit, and

(d) the subsequent benefit is an inheritance taken on the death of the disponer,

then the property which would have been relevant business property but for *section 94* is relevant business property notwithstanding that section.

(2) Where the property which, by virtue of *subsection (1)*, is relevant business property replaced the property or part referred to in *subsection (1)(c)*, relief under this Chapter shall not exceed what it would have been had the replacement or any one or more of the replacements not been made, and *section 95(3)* shall apply with the necessary modifications for the purposes of this subsection.

(3) Where, in relation to the earlier benefit, the amount of the taxable value of the gift or inheritance which was attributable to the property or part referred to in *subsection (1)(c)* was part only of its value, a like part only of the value which, apart from this subsection, would fall to be reduced under this Chapter by virtue of this section is so reduced.

Amendments

[1] Substituted by F(No.3)A11 sched3(24). Deemed to have come into operation as respects a gift or an inheritance taken on or after 1 January 2011.

Revenue Information Notes

Pt 12.5 Revenue CAT Manual for description of "Successive Benefits"

Cross References

From Section 97

Section 94 Minimum period of ownership.
Section 95 Replacements.

To Section 97

Section 100 Exclusion of value of excepted assets.

98 Value of business

[FA 1994 s132]

For the purposes of this Chapter—

(a) the value of a business or of an interest in a business is taken to be its net value,

(b) subject to *paragraph (c)*, the net value of a business shall be taken to be the market value of the assets used in the business (including goodwill) reduced by the aggregate market value of any liabilities incurred for the purposes of the business,

(c) in ascertaining the net value of an interest in a business, no regard is had to assets or liabilities other than those by reference to which the net value of the entire business would fall to be ascertained.

Case Law

Ordinary liabilities incurred in the day to day running of the business would not be taken into account for business relief purpose. Hardcastle v IRC 2000 STC (SCD) 532

Revenue Information Notes

Appendix II Revenue CAT Manual – Response to certain Business Relief Queries, query dated 15 August 1997

Cross References

To Section 98

Section 55 Payment of tax on certain assets by instalments.

99 Value of certain shares and securities

[FA 1994 s133]

(1) Where a company is a member of a group and the business of any other company which is a member of the group falls within *section 93(3)*, then, unless that business consists wholly or mainly in the holding of land or buildings wholly or mainly occupied by members of the group whose business does not fall within *section 93(3)*, the value of shares in or securities of the company is taken for the purposes of this Chapter to be what it would be if that other company were not a member of the group.

(2) (a) In this subsection "*shares*" include securities and "*shares in a company*" include other shares in the same company which are represented by those shares.

(b) Where unquoted shares in a company which is a member of a group are comprised in a gift or inheritance and shares in another company which is also a member of the group are quoted on the valuation date, the value of the first-mentioned shares is taken, for the purpose of this Chapter, to be what it would be if that other company were not a member of the group, unless those unquoted shares were in the beneficial ownership of the disponer immediately prior to the disposition and those quoted shares were unquoted—

(i) at some time prior to the gift or inheritance when they were in the beneficial ownership of the disponer or a member of that group, while being a member of such group, or

(ii) at 23 May 1994,

whichever is the later date.

Revenue Information Notes

Appendix II Revenue CAT Manual – Response to certain Business Relief Queries, query dated 12 August 1994

Cross References

From Section 99

Section 93 Relevant business property.

To Section 99

Section 93 Relevant business property.
Section 100 Exclusion of value of excepted assets.
Section 101 Withdrawal of relief.

100 Exclusion of value of excepted assets

[FA 1994 s134]

(1) In determining for the purposes of this Chapter what part of the taxable value of a gift or inheritance is attributable to the value of relevant business property, so much of the last-mentioned value as is attributable to—

(a) any excepted assets within the meaning of *subsection (2)*, or

(b) any excluded property within the meaning of *[subsection (8)]1*,

is disregarded.

(2) An asset is an excepted asset in relation to any relevant business property if it was not used wholly or mainly for the purposes of the business concerned throughout the whole or the last 2 years of the relevant period; but where the business concerned is carried on by a company which is a member of a group, the use of an asset for the purposes of a business carried on by another company which at the time of the use and immediately prior to the gift or inheritance was also a member of that group is treated as use for the purposes of the business concerned, unless that other company's membership of the group is to be disregarded under *section 99*.

(3) The use of an asset for the purposes of a business to which *section 93(3)* relates is not treated as use for the purposes of the business concerned.

(4) *Subsection (2)* shall not apply in relation to an asset which is relevant business property by virtue only of *section 93(1)(e)*, and an asset is not relevant business property by virtue only of that provision unless either—

(a) it was used in the manner referred to in that provision—

(i) in the case where the disponer's interest in the business or the shares in or securities of the company carrying on the business are comprised in an inheritance taken on the date of death of the disponer, throughout the 2 years immediately preceding the date of the inheritance, or

(ii) in any other case, throughout the 5 years immediately preceding the date of the gift or inheritance,

or

(b) it replaced another asset so used and it and the other asset and any asset directly or indirectly replaced by that other asset were so used for periods which together comprised—

(i) in the case referred to at *paragraph (a)(i)*, at least 2 years falling within the 3 years immediately preceding the date of the inheritance, or

(ii) in any other case, at least 5 years falling within the 6 years immediately preceding the date of the gift or inheritance,

but where *section 97* applies *paragraphs (a)* and *(b)* are deemed to be complied with if the asset, or that asset and the asset or assets replaced by it, was or were so used throughout the period between the earlier and the subsequent benefit mentioned in that section, or throughout the part of that period during which it or they were in the beneficial ownership of the disponer or the disponer's [spouse or civil partner][2].

(5) Where part but not the whole of any land or building is used exclusively for the purposes of any business and the land or building would, but for this subsection, be an excepted asset, or, as the case may be, prevented by *subsection (4)* from being relevant business property, the part so used and the remainder are for the purposes of this section treated as separate assets, and the value of the part so used shall (if it would otherwise be less) be taken to be such proportion of the value of the whole as may be just.

(6) For the purposes of this section the relevant period, in relation to any asset, is the period immediately preceding the gift or inheritance during which the asset or, if the relevant business property is an interest in a business, a corresponding interest in the asset, was comprised in the disposition (within the meaning of *section 94*) or, if the business concerned is that of a company, was beneficially owned by that company or any other company which immediately before the gift or inheritance was a member of the same group.

(7) For the purposes of this section an asset is deemed not to have been used wholly or mainly for the purposes of the business concerned at any time when it was used wholly or mainly for the personal benefit of the disponer or of a relative of the disponer.

(8) Where, in relation to a gift or an inheritance—

(a) relevant business property consisting of shares in or securities of a company are comprised in the gift or inheritance on the valuation date, and

(b) property consisting of a business, or interest in a business, not falling within *section 93(3)* (in this section referred to as "*company business property*") is on that date beneficially owned by that company or, where that company is a holding company of one or more companies within the same group, by any company within that group,

that company business property shall, for the purposes of *subsection (1)*, be excluded property in relation to those shares or securities unless it would have been relevant business property if—

(i) it had been the subject matter of that gift or inheritance, and

(ii) it had been comprised in the disposition for the periods during which it was in the beneficial ownership of that first-mentioned company or of any member of that group, while being such a member, or actually comprised in the disposition.

(9) In ascertaining whether or not company business property complies with *paragraphs (i)* and *(ii)* of *[subsection (8)]3*, *section 95* shall, with any necessary modifications, apply to that company business property as to a case to which *subsection (1)* of *section 95* relates.

Amendments

[1] Substituted by FA03 s152(a).

[2] Substituted by F(No.3)A11 sched3(25). Deemed to have come into operation as respects a gift or an inheritance taken on or after 1 January 2011.

[3] Substituted by FA03 s152(b).

Revenue Briefings

Tax Briefing

Tax Briefing September 1998 – Issue 33 pg 27 – CAT – Business Relief – Treatment of Debts where there are Excepted Assets

Revenue Information Notes

Appendix II Revenue CAT Manual – Summary of other Revenue opinions given on Business Relief in response to Queries.
CAT 4 – Business Relief

Cross References

From Section 100

Section 93 Relevant business property.
Section 94 Minimum period of ownership.
Section 95 Replacements.
Section 97 Successive benefits.
Section 99 Value of certain shares and securities.

To Section 100

Section 55 Payment of tax on certain assets by instalments.
Section 90 Interpretation (Chapter 2).
Section 93 Relevant business property.

101 Withdrawal of relief

[FA 1994 s135]

(1) In this section "*relevant period*", in relation to relevant business property comprised in a gift or inheritance, means the period of 6 years commencing on the date of the gift or inheritance.

(2) The reduction which would fall to be made under *section 92* in respect of relevant business property comprised in a gift or inheritance shall cease to be applicable if and to the extent that the property, or any property which directly or indirectly replaces it—

(a) would not be relevant business property (apart from *section 94* and the conditions attached to *paragraphs (d)* and *(f)* of *subsection (1)* of *section 93* and other than by reason of bankruptcy or a bona fide winding-up on grounds of insolvency) in relation to a notional gift of such property taken by the same donee or successor from the same disponer at any time within the relevant period, unless it would be relevant business property (apart from *section 94* and the conditions attached to *paragraphs (d)* and *(f)* of *subsection (1)* of *section 93*) in relation to another such notional gift taken within a year after the first-mentioned notional gift,

(b) is sold, redeemed or compulsorily acquired within the relevant period and is not replaced, within a year of the sale, redemption or compulsory acquisition, by other property (other than quoted shares or securities or unquoted shares or securities to which *section 99(2)(b)* relates) which would be relevant business property (apart from *section 94* and the condition attached to *section 93(1)(d)*) in relation to a notional gift of that other property taken by the same donee or successor from the same disponer on the date of the replacement,

and tax is chargeable in respect of the gift or inheritance as if the property were not relevant business property, but—

(i) any land, building, machinery or plant which are comprised in the gift or inheritance and which qualify as relevant business property by virtue of *section 93(1)(e)* shall, together with any similar property which has replaced such property, continue to be relevant business property for the purposes of this section for so long as they are used for the purposes of the business concerned,

(ii) this section shall not have effect where the donee or successor dies before the event which would otherwise cause the reduction to cease to be applicable.

[(3) Notwithstanding *subsection (2)*, where relevant business property (in this section referred to as "*original property*") comprised in a gift or inheritance has been replaced directly or indirectly by other property and the market value of the original property is greater than the market value of that other property, then the reduction which would fall to be made under *section 92* in respect of the original property shall be reduced in the same proportion as the market value of the other property bears to the market value of the original property.][1]

Amendments

[1] Inserted by FA05 s136(1). Has effect in relation to relevant business property which has been replaced by other property on or after 3 February 2005.

Revenue Information Notes

Appendix II Revenue CAT Manual – Summary of other Revenue opinions given on Business Relief in response to Queries

Cross References

From Section 101

Section 92 Business relief.
Section 93 Relevant business property.
Section 94 Minimum period of ownership.
Section 99 Value of certain shares and securities.

To Section 101

Section 51 Payment of tax and interest on tax.
Section 55 Payment of tax on certain assets by instalments.

102 Avoidance of double relief

[FA 1994 s135A]

Where the whole or part of the taxable value of any taxable gift or taxable inheritance is attributable to agricultural property to which *section 89(2)* applies, such whole or part of the taxable value is not reduced under this Chapter.

Cross References

From Section 102

Section 89 Provisions relating to agricultural property.

CHAPTER 2A

Clawback of Agricultural Relief or Business Relief: Development Land

102A Agricultural and business property: development land

[(1) In this section—

"*agricultural property*" has the meaning assigned to it by *section 89*;

"*current use value*"—

(a) in relation to land at any particular time, means the amount which would be the market value of the land at that time if the market value were calculated on the assumption that it was at that time and would remain unlawful to carry out any development (within the meaning of section 3 of the Planning and Development Act 2000) in relation to the land other than development of a minor nature, and

(b) in relation to shares in a company at any particular time, means the amount which would be the value of the shares at that time if the market value were calculated on the same assumption, in relation to the land from which the shares derive all or part of their value, as is mentioned in *paragraph (a)*;

"*development land*" means land in the State, the market value of which at the date of a gift or inheritance exceeds the current use value of that land at that date, and includes shares deriving their value in whole or in part from such land;

"development of a minor nature" means development (not being development by a local authority or statutory undertaker within the meaning of section 2 of the Planning and Development Act 2000) which, under or by virtue of section 4 of that Act, is exempted development for the purposes of that Act;

"*relevant business property*" shall be construed in accordance with *section 93*;

"*valuation date*" shall be construed in accordance with *section 30*.

(2) Where—

(a) relief has been granted by virtue of *section 89(2)* or *section 92* in respect of a gift or inheritance of agricultural property or, as the case may be, relevant business property,

(b) the property is comprised, in whole or in part, of development land, and

(c) the development land is disposed of in whole or in part by the donee or successor at any time in the period [commencing on the sixth anniversary of the date of the gift or inheritance and ending 4 years after that date][1],

then tax shall be re-computed at the valuation date of the gift or inheritance as if the amount by which the market value of the land disposed of exceeds its current use value at that date was the value of property which was not—

(i) agricultural property, or

(ii) relevant business property,

as the case may be, and tax shall be payable accordingly.][2]

Amendments

[1] Substituted by FA11 s68(1)(b). Applies to gifts and inheritances taken on or after 21 January 2011.

[2] Inserted by FA06 s118(1)(b). Applies to gifts and inheritances taken on or after 2 February 2006.

Cross References

From Section 102A

Section 4 Charge of gift tax.
Section 30 Valuation date for tax purposes.
Section 89 Provisions relating to agricultural property.
Section 92 Business relief.
Section 93 Relevant business property.

To Section 102A

Section 51 Payment of tax and interest on tax.

CHAPTER 3

Miscellaneous Reliefs

103 Relief from double aggregation

[FA 1985 s61(1) and (2)]

(1) Property in respect of which tax is chargeable more than once on the same event is not included more than once in relation to that event in any aggregate referred to in *Schedule 2*.

(2) *Paragraph 5* of *Part 1* of *Schedule 2* shall not have effect in ascertaining the tax payable in respect of property which is chargeable to tax as being taken more than once on the same day.

Cross References

From Section 103

Schedule 2 Computation of tax

104 Allowance for capital gains tax on the same event

[FA 1985 s63]

(1) Where gift tax or inheritance tax is charged in respect of property on an event happening on or after the date of the passing of this Act, and the same event constitutes for capital gains tax purposes a disposal of an asset (being the same property or any part of the same property), the capital gains tax, if any, chargeable on the disposal is not deducted in ascertaining the taxable value for the purposes of the gift tax or inheritance tax but, in so far as it has been paid, is deducted from the net gift tax or inheritance tax as a credit against the same; but, in relation to each asset, or to a part of each asset, so disposed of, the amount deducted is the lesser of—

(a) an amount equal to the amount of the capital gains tax attributable to such asset, or to the part of such asset, or

(b) an amount equal to the amount of the gift tax or inheritance tax attributable to the property which is that asset, or that part of that asset.

(2) For the purposes of any computation of the amount of capital gains tax to be deducted under this section, any necessary apportionments are made of any reliefs or expenditure and the method of apportionment adopted is such method as appears to the Commissioners, or on appeal to the Appeal Commissioners, to be just and reasonable.

[(3) The deduction by virtue of *subsection (1)* of capital gains tax chargeable on the disposal of an asset against gift tax or inheritance tax shall cease to apply to the extent that the asset is disposed of within 2 years [commencing on][1] the date of the gift or, as the case may be, the date of the inheritance.][2]

Amendments

[1] Substituted by FA11 s68(1)(c). Applies to gifts and inheritances taken on or after 21 January 2011.

[2] Inserted by FA06 s119(1). This section shall apply to gifts and inheritances taken on or after 21 February 2006.

Revenue Information Notes

Pt 13 Revenue CAT Manual – Credit for Capital Gains Tax.

IT 39 Gift/Inheritance Tax – A Guide to completing the Self Assessment Return – Pre Finance Act 2010, Appendix 9.2 Capital Gains Tax

Cross References

To Section 104

Schedule 3 Consequential Amendments

105 Allowance for prior tax on the same event

[CATA 1976 s34A]

Where tax is charged more than once in respect of the same property on the same event, the net tax payable which is earlier in priority is not deducted in ascertaining the taxable value for the purposes of the tax which is later in priority, but is deducted from the tax which is later in priority as a credit against the same, up to the net amount of the same.

Revenue Information Notes

IT 39 Gift/Inheritance Tax – A Guide to completing the Self Assessment Return – Pre Finance Act 2010, Appendix 9.3 Prior Capital Acquisitions Tax on same event

106 Arrangements for relief from double taxation

[CATA 1976 s66]

[(1) If the Government by order declare that arrangements specified in the order have been made with the government of any territory outside the State in relation to—

(a) affording relief from double taxation in respect of gift tax or inheritance tax payable under the laws of the State and any tax imposed under the laws of that territory which is of a similar character or is chargeable by reference to death or to gifts inter vivos, or

(b) exchanging information for the purposes of the prevention and detection of tax evasion in respect of the taxes specified in *paragraph (a)*,][1]

[and that it is expedient that those arrangements should have the force of law and the order so made is referred to in the Table to this section, the arrangements shall, notwithstanding anything in any enactment, have the force of law as if each such order were an Act of the Oireachtas on and from the date of—

(i) the insertion of the Table, or

(ii) the insertion of a reference to the order in the Table,

whichever is the later.][2]

(2) Any arrangements to which the force of law is given under this section may include provision for relief from tax charged before the making of the arrangements and provisions as to property which is not itself subject to double tax, and the provisions of this section shall apply accordingly.

(3) For the purposes of *subsection (1)*, arrangements made with the head of a foreign state are regarded as made with the government of that foreign state.

(4) Where any arrangements have the force of law by virtue of this section, the obligation as to secrecy imposed by any enactment shall not prevent the Commissioners from disclosing to any authorised officer of the government with which the arrangements are made such information as is required to be disclosed under the arrangements.

(5) (a) Any order made under this section may be revoked by a subsequent order and any such revoking order may contain such transitional provisions as appear to the Government to be necessary or expedient.

(b) Where an order is proposed to be made under this section, a draft of such order shall be laid before Dáil Éireann and the order shall not be made until a resolution approving of the draft has been passed by Dáil Éireann.

[TABLE

Part 1

ARRANGEMENTS MADE BY THE GOVERNMENT WITH THE GOVERNMENT OF ANY TERRITORY OUTSIDE THE STATE IN RELATION TO AFFORDING RELIEF FROM DOUBLE TAXATION AND EXCHANGING INFORMATION IN RELATION TO TAX

1. The Double Taxation Relief (Taxes on Estates of Deceased Persons and Inheritances and on Gifts) (United Kingdom) Order 1978 (S.I. No. 279 of 1978).

Part 2

ARRANGEMENTS IN RELATION TO THE EXCHANGE OF INFORMATION RELATING TO TAX AND IN RELATION TO OTHER MATTERS RELATING TO TAX][3]

Amendments

[1] Substituted by FA04 s79, with effect from 25 March 2004.

[2] Substituted by FA08 s129(1)(a). This section has effect from 31 January 2008.

[3] Inserted by FA08 s129(1)(b). This section has effect from 31 January 2008.

Revenue Information Notes

IT 39 Gift/Inheritance Tax – A Guide to completing the Self Assessment Return – Pre Finance Act 2010, Appendix 9.1 Double Taxation

Cross References

To Section 106

Section 28 Taxable value of a taxable gift or inheritance.
Section 107 Other relief from double taxation.

107 Other relief from double taxation

[CATA 1976 s67(1) to (3) and (5)]

(1) (a) In this section—

"*foreign tax*" means any tax which is chargeable under the laws of any territory outside the State and is of a character similar to estate duty, gift tax or inheritance tax;

"*event*" means—

(i) a death, or

(ii) any other event,

by reference to which the date of the gift or the date of the inheritance is determined.

(b) For the purposes of this section, a reference to property situate in a territory outside the State is a reference to property situate in that territory at the date of the gift or the date of the inheritance, as the case may be, or to property representing such property.

[(2) Where the Commissioners are satisfied that a taxable gift or taxable inheritance, taken under a disposition by a donee or successor on the happening of any event, is reduced by the payment of foreign tax which is chargeable in connection with the same event under the same disposition in respect of property which is situate in any territory outside the State, they shall allow a credit in respect of that foreign tax against the gift tax or inheritance tax payable by that donee or successor on that taxable gift or taxable inheritance; but such credit shall not exceed—

(a) the amount of the gift tax or inheritance tax payable in respect of the same property by reason of such property being comprised in any taxable gift or taxable inheritance taken under that disposition on the happening of that event, or

(b) in so far as it has been paid, the amount of that foreign tax,

whichever is the lesser.][1]

(3) This section is subject to any arrangement to which the force of law is given under *section 106* and, if any such arrangement provides for the allowance of the amount of a tax payable in a territory outside the State as a credit against gift tax or inheritance tax, the provisions of the arrangement shall apply in relation to the tax payable in that territory in lieu of the provisions of *subsection (2)*.

(4) Where the foreign tax in respect of property comprised in a taxable gift or a taxable inheritance taken under a disposition on the happening of an event is, under the terms of the disposition, directed to be paid out of a taxable gift or a taxable inheritance (taken under that disposition on the happening of the same event) other than the taxable gift or taxable inheritance out of which it would be payable in the absence of such a direction, then, for the purposes of *subsection (2)*, the taxable gift or taxable inheritance out of which the foreign tax would be payable in the absence of such a direction, and no other taxable gift or taxable inheritance, is treated as reduced by the payment of the foreign tax.

Amendments

[1] Substituted by FA05 s137(1). Has effect in relation to gifts or inheritances taken on or after 1 December 2004.

Revenue Information Notes

IT 39 Gift/Inheritance Tax – A Guide to completing the Self Assessment Return – Pre Finance Act 2010, Appendix 9.1 Double Taxation

Cross References

From Section 107

Section 106 Arrangements for relief from double taxation.

To Section 107

Section 28 Taxable value of a taxable gift or inheritance.

PART 11

Miscellaneous

108 Certificates for probate [Deleted]

Deleted by FA10 s(147)(1)(r). Has effect as on and from 3 April 2010.

109 Payment of money standing in names of 2 or more persons

[CATA 1976 s61(1) to (5) and (7) and (8)]

(1) In this section—

"*banker*" means a person who carries on banking business in the State and includes a friendly society, an industrial and provident society, a building society, the Post Office Savings Bank, a trustee savings bank and any person with whom money is lodged or deposited;

"*pay*" includes transfer in the books of a banker and any dealings with any moneys which were lodged or deposited in the name of a person who died after the time of the lodgment or deposit and any other person or persons;

"*current account*" means an account which is customarily operated on by means of a cheque or banker's order;

"*banking business*" has the meaning assigned to it by section 2 of the Central Bank Act 1971;

references to moneys lodged or deposited include references to shares of a building society, friendly society or industrial and provident society.

(2) Where, either before or after the passing of this Act, a sum of money exceeding [€50,000][1] is lodged or deposited (otherwise than on a current account) in the State with a banker, in the joint names of 2 or more persons, and one of such persons (in this section referred to as the deceased) dies on or after the date of the passing of this Act, the banker shall not pay such money or any part of such money to the survivor or all or any of the survivors of such persons, or to any other person, unless or until there is furnished to such banker a certificate by the Commissioners certifying that there is no outstanding claim for inheritance tax in connection with the death of the deceased in respect of such money or any part of such money or a consent in writing by the Commissioners to such payment pending the ascertainment and payment of such tax.

(3) Notwithstanding anything contained in this Act, tax chargeable on the death of the deceased is deemed for the purposes of this section to become due on the day of the death of the deceased.

(4) A banker who, after the passing of this Act, pays money in contravention of this section is liable to a penalty of [€4,000][2].

(5) Where a penalty is demanded of a banker under this section, the onus of proving that such certificate or such consent as is mentioned in this section was furnished to such banker before that banker paid such money shall lie on such banker.

(6) Where a penalty is demanded of a banker under this section, it shall be a good defence to prove that, at the time when such banker paid such money, that banker had reasonable ground for believing that none of the persons in whose joint names such money was lodged or deposited with that banker was dead.

(7) This section shall not apply where the sum of money referred to in *subsection (2)* is lodged or deposited in the joint names of 2 persons, one of whom dies on or

after the date of the passing of this Act and is at the time of that person's death the [spouse or civil partner][3] of that other person.

Amendments

[1] Substituted by FA10 s(147)(1)(s). Has effect as on and from 3 April 2010.

[2] Substituted by FA10 sched(4)(3)(c). Has effect as on and from 3 April 2010.

[3] Substituted by F(No.3)A11 sched3(26). Deemed to have come into operation as respects a gift or an inheritance taken on or after 1 January 2011.

Revenue Information Notes

Pt 4.2 Revenue CAT Manual – Letters of Clearance

110 Court to provide for payment of tax

[CATA 1976 s62]

Where any suit is pending in any court for the administration of any property chargeable with tax under this Act, such court shall provide, out of any such property which may be in the possession or control of the court, for the payment to the Commissioners of any of the tax or the interest on that tax which remains unpaid.

111 Liability to tax in respect of certain sales and mortgages

[CATA 1976 s64]

(1) In this section—

"*death duties*" has the meaning assigned to it by section 30 of the Finance Act 1971; and

"*purchaser or mortgagee*" includes a person deriving title from or under a purchaser or mortgagee in the case of such a sale or mortgage as is referred to in this section.

(2) Where an interest in expectancy has, prior to 1 April 1975, been bona fide sold or mortgaged for full consideration in money or money's worth, and that interest comes into possession on a death occurring on or after the date of the passing of this Act, the following provisions shall apply, that is—

(a) the purchaser or mortgagee shall not be liable in respect of inheritance tax on the inheritance referred to in *paragraph (b)* for an amount greater than that referred to in *paragraph (c)* ;

(b) the inheritance referred to in *paragraph (a)* is the inheritance of property in which the interest so sold or mortgaged subsists and which arises in respect of the interest of the remainderman referred to in *section 32* so coming into possession;

(c) the amount referred to in *paragraph (a)* shall be the amount that would then have been payable by the purchaser or mortgagee in respect of death duties on the property in which the interest subsists as property passing under the same disposition as that under which the inheritance is taken, if the property, on so coming into possession, had been chargeable to death duties—

(i) under the law in force, and

(ii) at the rate or rates having effect,

at the date of the sale or mortgage;

(d) where such an interest is so mortgaged, any amount of inheritance tax payable in respect of the inheritance referred to in *paragraph (b)*, and from the payment of which the mortgagee is relieved under this section, shall, [...][1] rank, in relation to property charged with such tax under that section, as a charge subsequent to the mortgage;

(e) any person, other than the purchaser or mortgagee, who is accountable for the payment of so much of the inheritance tax as is not the liability of the purchaser or mortgagee by virtue of the relief given by this section, shall not be liable for the payment of any amount in respect of such inheritance tax in excess of the amount which is available to that person for such payment by reason of there being, at the time when the interest comes into possession, other property, or an equity of redemption, or both, subject to the same trusts, under the disposition referred to in *paragraph (c)*, as the property in which the interest in expectancy subsists; and

(f) nothing in [*section 45(3)*][2] shall be construed as derogating from the relief given by this section to a purchaser or mortgagee.

Amendments

[1] Deleted by FA11 sched3(2)(b)(i). Applies as on and from 3 April 2010.

[2] Substituted by FA11 sched3(2)(b)(ii). Applies as on and from 3 April 2010.

Cross References

From Section 111

Section 32 Dealings with future interests.
Section 45 Accountable persons.

112 References in deeds and wills, etc. to death duties

[CATA 1976 s65]

In so far as a provision in a document refers (in whatever terms) to any death duty to arise on any death occurring on or after the date of the passing of this Act, it shall apply, as far as may be, as if the reference included a reference to inheritance tax—

(a) if that document was executed prior to 31 March 1976, and the reference is to legacy duty and succession duty or either of them,

(b) if that document was so executed, and the reference is to estate duty, and it may reasonably be inferred from all the circumstances (including any similarity of the incidence of inheritance tax to that of estate duty) that the inclusion of the reference to inheritance tax would be just, and

(c) whether the document was executed prior to, on or after 31 March 1976, if the reference is to death duties, without referring to any particular death duty.

113 Tax, in relation to certain legislation

[CATA 1976 s68]

(1) Inheritance tax shall not be a duty or a death duty for the purposes of section 9 of the Succession Act 1965, but it shall be a death duty for the purposes of—

(a) section 34(3) of that Act,

(b) the definition of pecuniary legacy in section 3(1) of that Act, and

(c) paragraph 8 of Part II of the First Schedule to that Act.

(2) Section 72 of the Registration of Title Act 1964 shall apply as if gift tax and inheritance tax were mentioned in that Act as well as estate duty and succession duty.

Cross References

From Section 113

Section 3 Meaning of "on a death".

Section 34 Settlement of an interest not in possession.

114 Delivery, service and evidence of notices and forms, etc

[CATA 1976 s70]

(1) Any notice which under this Act is authorised or required to be given by the Commissioners may be served by post.

(2) A notice or form which is to be served on a person may be either delivered to that person or left at that person's usual or last known place of abode.

(3) Prima facie evidence of any notice given under this Act by the Commissioners or by an officer of the Commissioners may be given in any proceedings by production of a document purporting—

  (a) to be a copy of that notice, or

  (b) if the details specified in that notice are contained in an electronic, photographic or other record maintained by the Commissioners, to reproduce those details in so far as they relate to that notice,

and it shall not be necessary to prove the official position of the person by whom the notice purports to be given or, if it is signed, the signature, or that the person signing and giving it was authorised so to do.

(4) In any case where a time limit is specified by or under this Act, other than *Part 8* of this Act, for the doing of any act required by or under this Act, other than *Part 8* of this Act, to be done by any person other than the Commissioners, the Commissioners may, in their discretion, extend such time limit.

Cross References

From Section 114

Section 66 Appeals regarding value of real property.

115 Extension of certain Acts

[CATA 1976 s69]

(1) Section 1 of the Provisional Collection of Taxes Act 1927 is hereby amended by the insertion of "*and gift tax and inheritance tax*" before "*but no other tax or duty*".

(2) Section 39 of the Inland Revenue Regulation Act 1890, is hereby amended by the insertion of "*gift tax and inheritance tax,*" before "*stamp duties*".

116 Regulations

[CATA 1976 s71]

(1) The Commissioners shall make such regulations as seem to them to be necessary for the purpose of giving effect to this Act and of enabling them to discharge their functions under the Act.

(2) Every regulation made under this section shall be laid before Dáil Éireann as soon as may be after it is made and, if a resolution annulling the regulation is passed by Dáil Éireann within the next 21 days on which Dáil Éireann has sat after the regulation is laid before it, the regulation shall be annulled accordingly, but without prejudice to the validity of anything previously done under that regulation.

Cross References

To Section 116

Section 2 General interpretation.

117 Care and management

[CATA 1976 s72]

(1) Tax is hereby placed under the care and management of the Commissioners.

(2) Subject to the direction and control of the Commissioners, any power, function or duty conferred or imposed on the Commissioners by this Act may be exercised or performed on their behalf by an officer of the Commissioners.

PART 12

Repeals, etc.

118 Repeals

(1) Subject to *subsection (2),* the Capital Acquisitions Tax Act 1976 [and any enactment amending or extending that Act are][1] hereby repealed.

(2) This Act shall not apply in relation to gifts and inheritances taken before the date of the passing of this Act, and the repealed enactments shall continue to apply in relation to such gifts and inheritances to the same extent that they would have applied if this Act had not been enacted.

(3) Notwithstanding *subsection (1)*, any provision of the repealed enactments which imposes a fine, forfeiture, penalty or punishment for any act or omission shall, in relation to any act or omission which took place or began before the date of the passing of this Act, continue to apply in substitution for the provision of this Act to which it corresponds.

(4) Anything done under or in connection with the provisions of the repealed enactments which correspond to the provisions of this Act shall be deemed to have been done under or in connection with the provisions of this Act to which those provisions of the repealed enactments correspond; but nothing in this subsection shall affect the operation of *section 120(3) and (4)*.

Amendments

[1] Substituted by FA12 sched6(2)(c). Has effect as on and from 31 March 2012.

Cross References

From Section 118
Section 120 Transitional provisions.

119 Consequential amendments to other enactments

Schedule 3, which provides for amendments to other enactments consequential on the passing of this Act, shall apply for the purposes of this Act.

Cross References

From Section 119
Schedule 3 Consequential Amendments

120 Transitional provisions

(1) The Commissioners shall have all the jurisdictions, powers and duties in relation to capital acquisitions tax under this Act which they had before the passing of this Act.

(2) The continuity of the operation of the law relating to capital acquisitions tax shall not be affected by the substitution of this Act for the repealed enactments.

(3) Any reference, whether express or implied, in any enactment or document (including this Act and any Act amended by this Act)—

(a) to any provision of this Act, or

(b) to things done or to be done under or for the purposes of any provisions of this Act, shall, if and in so far as the nature of the reference permits, be construed as including, in relation to the times, years or periods, circumstances or purposes in relation to which the corresponding provision in the repealed enactments applied or had applied, a reference to, or, as the case may be, to things done or to be done under or for the purposes of, that corresponding provision.

(4) Any reference, whether express or implied, in any enactment (including the repealed enactments and enactments passed after the passing of this Act)—

(a) to any provision of the repealed enactments, or

(b) to things done or to be done under or for the purposes of any provisions of the repealed enactments,

shall, if and in so far as the nature of the reference permits, be construed as including, in relation to the times, years or periods, circumstances or purposes in relation to which the corresponding provision of this Act applies, a reference to, or as the case may be, to things done or to be done under, or for the purposes of, that corresponding provision.

Cross References

To Section 120

Section 118 Repeals.

SCHEDULE 1

Valuation of Limited Interests

Sections 28, 35 and *51.*

[CATA 1976 First Sch.]

PART 1

Rules Relating to the Valuation of Limited Interests Utilising Tables A and B in Parts 2 and 3 of this Schedule

1. The value of an interest for a single life in a capital sum shall be that sum multiplied by the factor, contained in *column (3)* or *(4)* respectively of *Table A*, which is appropriate to the age and sex of the person in respect of the duration of whose life the interest is to be valued.
2. The value of an interest in a capital sum for the joint continuance of 2 lives shall be the value of an interest in that sum for the older life, ascertained in accordance with *rule 1*, multiplied by the joint factor in *column (2)* of *Table A* which is appropriate to the younger life.
3. The value of an interest in a capital sum for the joint continuance of 3 or more lives shall be the value of an interest in that sum for the joint continuance of the 2 oldest of those lives, ascertained in accordance with *rule 2,* multiplied by the joint factor of the youngest of those lives.
4. The value of an interest in a capital sum for the longer of 2 lives shall be ascertained by deducting from the total of the values of an interest in that sum for each of those lives, ascertained in accordance with *rule 1*, the value of an interest in the capital sum for the joint continuance of the same 2 lives, ascertained in accordance with *rule 2.*
5. Where an interest is given for the longest of more than 2 lives, it shall be valued, in accordance with *rule 4*, as if it were for the longer of the 2 youngest of those lives.
6. The value of an interest in a capital sum for a period certain shall be the aggregate of—
   (a) the value of the capital sum, multiplied by the factor in *Table B* which is appropriate to the number of whole years in that period (or zero if that period is less than a whole year); and
   (b) where the period is not an integral number of years, a fraction (of which the numerator is the number of days in excess of the number of whole years, if any, in that period and the denominator is 365) of the difference between—
      (i) the value of an interest in the capital sum for one year longer than the number of whole years, if any, in the period; and
      (ii) the value ascertained under the provisions of *paragraph (a)* (or zero, where so provided in that paragraph).
7. In the case of a limited interest where the interest is for a life or lives, but is guaranteed for a period certain, the value shall be the higher of—

(a) the value of an interest for such life or lives, ascertained in accordance with the appropriate rule in this Part of this Schedule; and

(b) the value of an interest for the period certain, ascertained in accordance with *rule 6*.

8. The value of a limited interest for which the other rules in this Part of this Schedule provide no method of valuing shall be ascertained as if the interest taken were a series of absolute interests in the property applied in satisfaction of the interest from time to time, taken as separate gifts or inheritances as the case may be.

PART 2

TABLE A

Years of age (1)	Joint Factor (2)	Value of an interest in a capital of €1 for a male life aged as in column 1 (3)	Value of an interest in a capital of €1 for a female life aged as in column 1 (4)
0	.99	.9519	.9624
1	.99	.9767	.9817
2	.99	.9767	.9819
3	.99	.9762	.9817
4	.99	.9753	.9811
5	.99	.9742	.9805
6	.99	.9730	.9797
7	.99	.9717	.9787
8	.99	.9703	.9777
9	.99	.9688	.9765
10	.99	.9671	.9753
11	.98	.9653	.9740
12	.98	.9634	.9726
13	.98	.9614	.9710
14	.98	.9592	.9693
15	.98	.9569	.9676
16	.98	.9546	.9657
17	.98	.9522	.9638
18	.98	.9497	.9617
19	.98	.9471	.9596
20	.97	.9444	.9572
21	.97	.9416	.9547
22	.97	.9387	.9521
23	.97	.9356	.9493
24	.97	.9323	.9464
25	.97	.9288	.9432
26	.97	.9250	.9399
27	.97	.9209	.9364
28	.97	.9165	.9328
29	.97	.9119	.9289
30	.96	.9068	.9248
31	.96	.9015	.9205
32	.96	.8958	.9159
33	.96	.8899	.9111
34	.96	.8836	.9059

PART 2

TABLE A

Years of age (1)	Joint Factor (2)	Value of an interest in a capital of €1 for a male life aged as in column 1 (3)	Value of an interest in a capital of €1 for a female life aged as in column 1 (4)
35	.96	.8770	.9005
36	.96	.8699	.8947
37	.96	.8626	.8886
38	.95	.8549	.8821
39	.95	.8469	.8753
40	.95	.8384	.8683
41	.95	.8296	.8610
42	.95	.8204	.8534
43	.95	.8107	.8454
44	.94	.8005	.8370
45	.94	.7897	.8283
46	.94	.7783	.8192
47	.94	.7663	.8096
48	.93	.7541	.7997
49	.93	.7415	.7896
50	.92	.7287	.7791
51	.91	.7156	.7683
52	.90	.7024	.7572
53	.89	.6887	.7456
54	.89	.6745	.7335
55	.88	.6598	.7206
56	.88	.6445	.7069
57	.88	.6288	.6926
58	.87	.6129	.6778
59	.86	.5969	.6628
60	.86	.5809	.6475
61	.86	.5650	.6320
62	.86	.5492	.6162
63	.85	.5332	.6000
64	.85	.5171	.5830
65	.85	.5007	.5650
66	.85	.4841	.5462
67	.84	.4673	.5266
68	.84	.4506	.5070
69	.84	.4339	.4873
70	.83	.4173	.4679
71	.83	.4009	.4488
72	.82	.3846	.4301
73	.82	.3683	.4114
74	.81	.3519	.3928
75	.80	.3352	.3743
76	.79	.3181	.3559
77	.78	.3009	.3377
78	.76	.2838	.3198
79	.74	.2671	.3023
80	.72	.2509	.2855
81	.71	.2353	.2693

PART 2

TABLE A

Years of age (1)	Joint Factor (2)	Value of an interest in a capital of €1 for a male life aged as in column 1 (3)	Value of an interest in a capital of €1 for a female life aged as in column 1 (4)
82	.70	.2203	.2538
83	.69	.2057	.2387
84	.68	.1916	.2242
85	.67	.1783	.2104
86	.66	.1657	.1973
87	.65	.1537	.1849
88	.64	.1423	.1730
89	.62	.1315	.1616
90	.60	.1212	.1509
91	.58	.1116	.1407
92	.56	.1025	.1310
93	.54	.0939	.1218
94	.52	.0858	.1132
95	.50	.0781	.1050
96	.49	.0710	.0972
97	.48	.0642	.0898
98	.47	.0578	.0828
99	.45	.0517	.0762
100 or over	.43	.0458	.0698

PART 3

TABLE B

(Column (2) shows the value of an interest in a capital of €1 for the number of years shown in column (1))

Number of years (1)	Value (2)	Number of years (1)	Value (2)
1	.0654	26	.8263
2	.1265	27	.8375
3	.1836	28	.8480
4	.2370	29	.8578
5	.2869	30	.8669
6	.3335	31	.8754
7	.3770	32	.8834
8	.4177	33	.8908
9	.4557	34	.8978
10	.4913	35	.9043
11	.5245	36	.9100
12	.5555	37	.9165
13	.5845	38	.9230
14	.6116	39	.9295
15	.6369	40	.9360
16	.6605	41	.9425
17	.6826	42	.9490
18	.7032	43	.9555

PART 2

TABLE A

Years of age (1)	Joint Factor (2)	Value of an interest in a capital of €1 for a male life aged as in column 1 (3)	Value of an interest in a capital of €1 for a female life aged as in column 1 (4)
19	.7225	44	.9620
20	.7405	45	.9685
21	.7574	46	.9750
22	.7731	47	.9815
23	.7878	48	.9880
24	.8015	49	.9945
25	.8144	50 and over	1.0000

Cross References

From Schedule 1

Section 28 Taxable value of a taxable gift or inheritance.
Section 35 Enlargement of interests.
Section 51 Payment of tax and interest on tax.

To Schedule 1

Section 28 Taxable value of a taxable gift or inheritance.
Section 35 Enlargement of interests.
Section 51 Payment of tax and interest on tax.

SCHEDULE 2

Computation of Tax

Sections 46, 50, 69 and *76.*

[CATA 1976 Second Sch., Pt.I, paras. 1 to 5 and 8 to 11 and Pt.II; FA 2001 ss. 221 and 222]

PART 1

Preliminary

1. In this Schedule—

["*group threshold*", in relation to a taxable gift or a taxable inheritance taken on a particular day, means—

(a) [€280,000][1], where—

(i) the donee or successor is on that day—

(I) the child, or the minor child of a deceased child, of the disponer,

(II) the child of the civil partner of the disponer, or minor child of a deceased child of the civil partner of the disponer,

(III) the minor child of the civil partner of a deceased child of the disponer, or

(IV) the minor child of the civil partner of a deceased child of the civil partner of the disponer,

or

(ii) the successor is on that day a parent of the disponer and—

(I) the interest taken is not a limited interest, and

(II) the inheritance is taken on the death of the disponer;

(b) [€30,150][2], where the donee or successor is on that day—

(i) a lineal ancestor of the disponer,

(ii) a lineal descendant (other than a person referred to in any of clauses (I) to (IV) of *paragraph (a)(i)*) of the disponer,

(iii) a brother or a sister of the disponer,

(iv) a child of a brother or of a sister of the disponer, or

(v) a child of the civil partner of a brother or of a sister of the disponer;

(c) [€15,075][3], where the donee or successor (who is not a spouse or civil partner of the disponer) does not, on that day, stand to the disponer in a relationship referred to in *subparagraph (a) or (b)*;][4]

"*the consumer price index number*", in relation to a year, means the All Items Consumer Price Index Number for that year as compiled by the Central Statistics Office and expressed on the basis that the consumer price index number at mid-November 1996 is 100;

"*Table*" means the Table contained in *Part 2* of this Schedule;

['*threshold amount*', in relation to the computation of tax on any aggregate of taxable values under *paragraph 3*, means the group threshold that applies in relation to all of the taxable gifts and taxable inheritances included in that aggregate.][5]

2. In the Table "*Value*" means the appropriate aggregate referred to in *paragraph 3*.

3. The tax chargeable on the taxable value of a taxable gift or a taxable inheritance (in this Schedule referred to as the first-mentioned gift or inheritance) taken by a donee or successor shall be of an amount equal to the amount by which the tax computed on aggregate A exceeds the tax computed on aggregate B, where—

   (a) aggregate A is the aggregate of the following:

      (i) the taxable value of the first-mentioned gift or inheritance, and

      (ii) the taxable value of each taxable gift and taxable inheritance taken previously by that donee or successor on or after 5 December 1991, which has the same group threshold as the first-mentioned gift or inheritance,

   (b) aggregate B is the aggregate of the taxable values of all such taxable gifts and taxable inheritances so previously taken which have the same group threshold as the first-mentioned gift or inheritance, and

   (c) the tax on an aggregate is computed at the rate or rates of tax applicable under the Table to that aggregate, but where—

      (i) in a case where no such taxable gift or taxable inheritance was so previously taken, the amount of the tax computed on aggregate B shall be deemed to be nil, and

      (ii) the amount of an aggregate that comprises only a single taxable value shall be equal to that value.

4. In the Table any rate of tax shown in the second column is that applicable to such portion of the value (within the meaning of *paragraph 2*) as is shown in the first column.

[...][6]

[(6) Where any donee or successor is, at the date of the gift or at the date of the inheritance—

   (a) the surviving spouse of a deceased person, or

   (b) the surviving civil partner of a deceased person,

and, at the time of the death of the deceased person, that deceased person was of nearer relationship than such donee or successor to the disponer, then such donee or successor is, in the computation of the tax payable on such taxable gift or taxable inheritance, deemed to bear to the disponer the relationship of that deceased person.][7]

7.

(1) In this paragraph—

"*company*" means a private company which, for the relevant period—

   (a) is a private company controlled by the disponer and of which the disponer is a director, and

   (b) is not a private non-trading company;

"*control*", in relation to a company, is construed in accordance with *section 27(4)(b)*;

"*investment income*", in relation to a private company, means income which, if the company were an individual, would not be earned income within the meaning of section 3 of the Taxes Consolidation Act 1997;

"*nominee*" has the same meaning as it has in *section 27*;

"*private company*" has the meaning assigned to it by *section 27*;

"*private company controlled by the disponer*" means a private company that is under the control of any one or more of the following, that is—

(a) the disponer,

(b) nominees of the disponer,

(c) the trustees of a settlement made by the disponer;

"*private non-trading company*" means a private company—

(a) whose income (if any) in the 12 months preceding the date at which a share in that company is to be valued consisted wholly or mainly of investment income; and

(b) whose property, on the date referred to in *paragraph (a)*, consisted wholly or mainly of property from which investment income is derived;

"*relevant period*" means—

(a) the period of 5 years ending on the date of the disposition; or

(b) where, at the date of the disposition,

(i) an interest in possession in—

(I) the property referred to in *subparagraph (2)(a)*, or

(II) the shares referred to in *subparagraph (2)(b)*,

as the case may be, is limited to the disponer under the disposition, and

(ii) such property is not, or such shares are not, property consisting of the appropriate part of property, within the meaning of *section 5(5)*, on which is charged or secured an annuity or other annual right limited to cease on the death of the disponer,

the period of 5 years ending on the coming to an end of that interest,

subject, in relation to work, to the exclusion of reasonable periods of annual or sick leave from that period of 5 years.

[(2) For the purpose of computing the tax payable on a gift or inheritance made by a disponer to a donee or successor who is—

(a) a child of the disponer's brother or sister, or

(b) a child of the civil partner of the disponer's brother or sister,

the same rules apply as where the gift or inheritance is made to the disponer's child if—

(i) the donee or successor has worked substantially on a full-time basis for the disponer for the relevant period in carrying on, or in assisting in carrying on, the trade, business or profession of the disponer, and the gift or inheritance consists of property which was used in connection with that business, trade or profession, or

(ii) the donee or successor has worked substantially on a full-time basis for a company for the relevant period in carrying on, or in assisting in carrying on, the trade, business or profession of the company, and the gift or inheritance consists of shares in that company.][8]

(3) Without prejudice to the generality of *subparagraph (2)*, a donee or successor is not deemed to be working substantially on a full-time basis for a disponer or a company unless—

(a) where the gift or inheritance consists of property which was used in connection with the business, trade or profession of the disponer, the donee or successor works—

(i) more than 24 hours a week for the disponer, at a place where that business, trade or profession, is carried on, or

(ii) more than 15 hours a week for the disponer, at a place where that business, trade or profession is carried on, and such business, trade or profession is carried on exclusively by the disponer, [any spouse or civil partner of the disponer],[9] and the donee or successor,

or

(b) where the gift or inheritance consists of shares in the company, the donee or successor works –

(i) more than 24 hours a week for the company, at a place where the business, trade or profession of the company is carried on, or

(ii) more than 15 hours a week for the company, at a place where the business, trade or profession of the company is carried on, and such business, trade or profession is carried on exclusively by the disponer, [any spouse or civil partner of the disponer],[10] and the donee or successor.

(4) This paragraph shall not apply to a gift or inheritance taken by a donee or successor under a discretionary trust.

8. (a) In this paragraph "*specified disposition*" means a disposition—

(i) the date of which is a date prior to 1 April 1975,

(ii) in relation to which the disponer is a grandparent of the donee or successor, and

(iii) in which the marriage of the parents of the donee or successor was, at the date of the disposition, expressed to be the consideration.

(b) Where, on the cesser of a limited interest to which a parent of the donee or successor was entitled in possession, the donee or successor takes a gift or an inheritance under a specified disposition, then, for the purpose of computing the tax payable on the gift or inheritance, the donee or successor is deemed to bear to the disponer the relationship of a child.

9.

(1) In this paragraph—

"*the appropriate period*" means periods which together comprised at least 5 years falling within the 18 years immediately following the birth of the donee or successor.

(2) Where, on a claim being made to them in that behalf, the Commissioners are, subject to *subparagraph (3)*, satisfied—

(a) where the inheritance is taken by a successor on the date of death of the disponer, that the successor had, prior to the date of the inheritance, been placed in the foster care of the disponer under the Child Care (Placement of Children in Foster Care) Regulations 1995 (S.I. No. 260 of 1995), or the Child Care (Placement of Children with Relatives) Regulations 1995 (S.I. No. 261 of 1995), or

(b) that throughout the appropriate period the donee or successor—

(i) has resided with the disponer, and

(ii) was under the care of and maintained by the disponer at the disponer's own expense,

then, subject to *subparagraph (3)*, for the purposes of computing the tax payable on that gift or inheritance, that donee or successor is deemed to bear to that disponer the relationship of a child.

(3) Relief under *subparagraph (2)* shall not apply where the claim for such relief is based on the uncorroborated testimony of one witness.

10. Where, on a claim being made to them in that behalf, the Commissioners are satisfied that—

(a) the donee or successor had at the date of the gift or the date of the inheritance been adopted in the manner referred to in *paragraph (b)* of the definition of "*child*" contained in *section 2(1)*, and

(b) the disponer is the natural mother or the natural father of the donee or successor,

then, notwithstanding *section 2(5)*, for the purpose of computing the tax payable on that gift or inheritance, that donee or successor is deemed to bear to that disponer the relationship of a child.

11. For the purposes of this Schedule, a reference to a gift or an inheritance, or to a taxable gift or a taxable inheritance, includes a reference to a part of a gift or an inheritance, or to a part of a taxable gift or a taxable inheritance, as the case may be.

PART 2

TABLE

Portion of Value	Rate of tax Per cent
The threshold amount	Nil
The balance	[33][11]

Amendments

[1] Substituted by FA15 s67(1). Applies to gifts and inheritances taken on or after 14 October 2015.

[2] Substituted by FA13 s85(1)(a)(ii). Applies to gifts and inheritances taken on or after 6 December 2012.

[3] Substituted by FA13 s85(1)(a)(iii). Applies to gifts and inheritances taken on or after 6 December 2012.

[4] Substituted by F(No.3)A11 sched3(27).

[5] Substituted by FA12 s109(2)(a). Applies to gifts and inheritances taken on or after 7 December 2011.

[6] Deleted by FA12 s115(5). Applies on and from 8 February 2012.

[7] Substituted by F(No.3)A11 sched3(28). Deemed to have come into operation as respects a gift or an inheritance taken on or after 1 January 2011.

[8] Substituted by F(No.3)A11 sched3(29). Deemed to have come into operation as respects a gift or an inheritance taken on or after 1 January 2011.

[9] Substituted by FA12 s134(2)(a). Has effect as if it had come into operation as respects a gift (within the meaning of the Capital Acquisitions Tax Consolidation Act 2003) or an inheritance (within that meaning) taken on or after 1 January 2011.

[10] Substituted by FA12 s134(2)(b). Has effect as if it had come into operation as respects a gift (within the meaning of the Capital Acquisitions Tax Consolidation Act 2003) or an inheritance (within that meaning) taken on or after 1 January 2011.

[11] Substituted by FA13 s85(1)(b). Applies to gifts and inheritances taken on or after 6 December 2012.

Case Law

AE v Revenue Commissioners 1994 V ITR 686 defined the phrases 'full-time' and 'substantially'. The case also looked at whether herding of cattle under a letting agreement constituted a business.

Revenue Briefings

eBrief

eBrief No. 02/2010 – Capital Acquisitions Tax – 2010 Group Thresholds

Revenue Information Notes

Pt 1.2 Revenue CAT Manual – Gift and Inheritance Tax
Pt 10 Revenue CAT Manual – Favourite Nephew Relief.
Pt 19.10 Revenue CAT Manual – Donee or Successor a surviving spouse of a closer relation of the Disponer
IT 39 Gift/Inheritance Tax – A Guide to completing the Self Assessment Return – Pre Finance Act 2010, Appendix 1 – Favourite Nephew/Niece Relief – Notes & Examples

Cross References

From Schedule 2

Section 2 General interpretation.
Section 5 Gift deemed to be taken.
Section 27 Market value of certain shares in private companies.
Section 46 Delivery of returns.
Section 50 Computation of tax.
Section 69 Exemption of small gifts.
Section 76 Provisions relating to charities, etc.

To Schedule 2

Section 16 Application of this Act.
Section 21 Application of this Act.
Section 46 Delivery of returns.
Section 50 Computation of tax.
Section 76 Provisions relating to charities, etc.
Section 103 Relief from double aggregation.

SCHEDULE 3

Consequential Amendments

In the enactments specified in *column (1)* of the following Table for the words set out or referred to in *column (2)*, there shall be substituted the words set out in the corresponding entry in *column (3)*.

Enactment Amended (1)	Words to be replaced (2)	Words to be substituted (3)
Value-Added Tax Act 1972:		
section 30(5)(*b*)(i)	section 38 of the Capital Acquisitions Tax Act 1976	*section 48* of the *Capital Acquisitions Tax Consolidation Act 2003*
section 30(5)(*b*)(ii)	section 38	*section 48*
The Rules of the Superior Courts (S.I. No. 15 of 1986) :		
Order 79, rule 84	Capital Acquisitions Tax Act 1976	*Capital Acquisitions Tax Consolidation Act 2003*
Order 80, rule 85	Capital Acquisitions Tax Act 1976	*Capital Acquisitions Tax Consolidation Act 2003*
Ethics in Public Office Act 1995:		
section 2(4)	Capital Acquisitions Tax Act 1976	*Capital Acquisitions Tax Consolidation Act 2003*
Taxes Consolidation Act 1997:		
section 8(1)(*c*)	Capital Acquisitions Tax Act 1976	*Capital Acquisitions Tax Consolidation Act 2003*
section 176(1)(*b*)(i)(I)	section 21 of the Capital Acquisitions Tax Act 1976	*section 30* of the *Capital Acquisitions Tax Consolidation Act 2003*
section 577(5)(*a*)(ii)(I)	Capital Acquisitions Tax Act 1976	*Capital Acquisitions Tax Consolidation Act 2003*
section 577(5)(*a*)(ii)(II)	section 55	*section 77*
	section 39 of the Finance Act 1978	*section 77(6)* and *(7)* of the *Capital Acquisitions Tax Consolidation Act 2003*
section 730GB	section 63 of the Finance Act 1985	*section 104* of the *Capital Acquisitions Tax Act 2003*
section 739G(5)	section 63 of the Finance Act 1985	*section 104* of the *Capital Acquisitions Tax Consolidation Act 2003*
section 747E(5)(a)	section 63 of the Finance Act 1985	*section 104* of the *Capital Acquisitions Tax Consolidation Act 2003*
section 811(1)(*a*), in *paragraph (iv)* of the definition of "*the Acts*"	Capital Acquisitions Tax Act 1976	*Capital Acquisitions Tax Consolidation Act 2003*
section 818(*c*)	Capital Acquisitions Tax Act 1976	*Capital Acquisitions Tax Consolidation Act 2003*
section 825(1)(*c*)	Capital Acquisitions Tax Act 1976	*Capital Acquisitions Tax Consolidation Act 2003*
section 858(1)(*a*), in *paragraph (vi)* of the definition of "*the Acts*"	Capital Acquisitions Tax Act 1976	*Capital Acquisitions Tax Consolidation Act 2003*

Enactment Amended (1)	Words to be replaced (2)	Words to be substituted (3)
section 859(1), in *paragraph (f)* of the definition of "*the Revenue Acts*"	Capital Acquisitions Tax Act 1976	*Capital Acquisitions Tax Consolidation Act 2003*
section 887(1), in *paragraph (d)* of the definition of "*the Acts*"	Capital Acquisitions Tax Act 1976	*Capital Acquisitions Tax Consolidation Act 2003*
section 912(1), in *paragraph (f)* of the definition of "*the Acts*"	Capital Acquisitions Tax Act 1976	*Capital Acquisitions Tax Consolidation Act 2003*
section 917D(1), in *paragraph (e)* of the definition of "*the Acts*"	Capital Acquisitions Tax Act 1976	*Capital Acquisitions Tax Consolidation Act 2003*
section 1002(1)(*a*), in *paragraph (vi)* of the definition of "*the Acts*"	Capital Acquisitions Tax Act 1976	*Capital Acquisitions Tax Consolidation Act 2003*
section 1003(1)(*a*), in *paragraph (iii)* of the definition of "*the Acts*"	Capital Acquisitions Tax Act 1976	*Capital Acquisitons Tax Consolidation Act 2003*
section 1006(1), in *paragraph (d)* of the definition of "*the Acts*"	Capital Acquisitions Tax Act 1976	*Capital Acquisitions Tax Consolidation Act 2003*
section 1006A(1), in *paragraph (e)* of the definition of "*the Acts*"	Capital Acquisitions Tax Act 1976	*Capital Acquisitions Tax Consolidation Act 2003*
section 1078(1), in *paragraph (f)* of the definition of "*the Acts*"	Capital Acquisitions Tax Act 1976	*Capital Acquisitions Tax Consolidation Act 2003*
section 1079(1), in *paragraph (f)* of the definition of "*the Acts*"	Capital Acquisitions Tax Act 1976	*Capital Acquisitions Tax Consolidation Act 2003*
section 1086(1), in *paragraph (d)* of the definition of "*the Acts*"	Capital Acquisitions Tax Act 1976	*Capital Acquisitions Tax Consolidation Act 2003*
section 1089(2)	section 41 of the Capital Acquisitions Tax Act 1976	*section 51* of the *Capital Acquisitions Tax Consolidation Act 2003*
section 1104(5)	Capital Acquisitions Tax Act 1976	*Capital Acquisitions Tax Consolidation Act 2003*
Stamp Duties Consolidation Act 1999:		
section 19	section 15 of the Capital Acquisitions Tax Act 1976	*section 26* of the *Capital Acquisitions Tax Consolidation Act 2003*
section 91(2)(*b*)(ii)	section 16 of the Capital Acquisitions Tax Act 1976	*section 27* of the *Capital Acquisitions Tax Consolidation Act 2003*
section 92(1)(*b*)(ii)	section 16 of the Capital Acquisitions Tax Act 1976	*section 27* of the *Capital Acquisitions Tax Consolidation Act 2003*
section 92B(3)(*b*)(ii)	section 16 of the Capital Acquisitions Tax Act 1976	*section 27* of the *Capital Acquisitions Tax Consolidation Act 2003*
Finance (No. 2) Act 2000:		
section 5(1), definition of "*Act of 1976*"	"*Act of 1976*" means the Capital Acquisitions Tax Act 1976	"*Act of 2003*" means the *Capital Acquisitions Tax Consolidation Act 2003*
section 5(1), in the definition of "*date of the disposition*"	section 2 of the Act of 1976	*section 2* of the *Act of 2003*
section 5(1), in the definition of "*discretionary trust*"	section 2 of the Act of 1976	*section 2* of the *Act of 2003*

Enactment Amended (1)	Words to be replaced (2)	Words to be substituted (3)
section 5(1), in the definition of "*disponer*"	section 2 of the Act of 1976	*section 2* of the *Act of 2003*
section 5(1), in the definition of "*disposition*"	section 2 of the Act of 1976	*section 2* of the *Act of 2003*
section 5(1), in the definition of "*donee*"	section 2 of the Act of 1976	*section 2* of the *Act of 2003*
section 5(1), in the definition of "*entitled in possession*"	section 2 of the Act of 1976	*section 2* of the *Act of 2003*
section 5(1), in the definition of "*gift*"	section 2 of the Act of 1976	*section 2* of the *Act of 2003*
section 5(1), in the definition of "*interest in expectancy*"	section 2 of the Act of 1976	*section 2* of the *Act of 2003*
section 5(1), in the definition of "*limited interest*"	section 2 of the Act of 1976	*section 2* of the *Act of 2003*
section 5(1), in the definition of "*on a death*"	section 3 of the Act of 1976	*section 3* of the *Act of 2003*

Cross References

From Schedule 3

Section 26 Market value of property.
Section 27 Market value of certain shares in private companies.
Section 30 Valuation date for tax purposes.
Section 48 Affidavits and accounts.
Section 51 Payment of tax and interest on tax.
Section 55 Payment of tax on certain assets by instalments.
Section 77 Exemption of heritage property.
Section 104 Allowance for capital gains tax on the same event.

To Schedule 3

Section 119 Consequential amendments to other enactments.

TABLE OF CASES

Capital Acquisitions Tax Consolidation Act 2003

All references to sections or schedules in Capital Acquisitions Tax Consolidation Act 2003

ABBREVIATIONS

AC = Law Reports Appeal Cases
All ER = All England Law Reports
Ch = Chancery
ITR = Irish Tax Reports
IR = Irish Reports
KB = King's Bench
QB = Queen's Bench
STC = Simon's Tax Cases
SpC = UK Special Commissioner
WLR = Weekly Law Reports

Case	Case Reference	Section
A.E. v Revenue Commissioners	1994 V ITR 686	s93, sch2
AG for Northern Ireland v Heron	1959 TR 1; 38 ATC 3 (CA)	s82
AG of Ceylon v Mackie	1952 2 ALL ER 775	s26
AG v Boden	1912 1 KB 539	s5
AG v Johnson	1907 2 KB 885	s15
AG v Kitchin	1941 AER 735	s5
AG v Wreford-Brown	1925 2 KB 429	s28
American Leaf Co. v Director-General	1979 AC 675	s93
Balfour v Balfour	1919 2 KB 571	s28
Barclays Bank Ltd v IRC	1961 AC 509	s27
Battle v Irish Art Promotion Centre Ltd	1968 IR 252	s67
Bendenoun v France	1994 12547/86	s58
Bennett v IRC	1995 STC 54	s82
BKJ v The Revenue Commissioners	1983 III ITR 104	s35
Blair v Duncan	1902 AC 37	s76
Danaher v Revenue Commissioners	2005 Circuit Court No. 8 RA	s86
Ellesmere v Commissioners of Inland Revenue	1918 2 KB 735	s26
Farmer (Farmers Executors) v IRC	1999 STC 321	s93
Faulks v Faulks	1992 EG 82	s89
Gittos v Barkley (Inspector of Taxes)	1982 STC 390	s93
Griffiths (Inspector of Taxes) v Jackson/Pearman	1983 STC 184	s93
Hardcastle v IRC	2000 STC 532	s98
Houston v Lord Advocate	1917 55 SLR 208	s76
IRC v Clay, IRC v Buchanan	1914 3 KB 466	s26
IRC v Muller & Co's Margarine Ltd	1901 AC 217	s6, s11

Case	Case Reference	Section
IRC v Russell	1953 36 TC 83	s2
John Stamp deceased, Patrick Stamp v Noel Redmond & Others	IV ITR 415	s2
Jones v Padavatton	1961 1 WLR 328	s28
Leedale v Lewis	1982 STC 835	s86
Mackay v Jones	1959 93 ILTR 177	s28
McCall and Keenan (as Personal Representatives of Eileen McLean deceased) v HMRC	2009 SpC 678	s93
Morrison's Academy	1978 STC	s93
National Anti-Vivisection v IRC	1948 AC 31	s76
Paradise Motor Co	1968 2 All ER 625	s12
Pearsons v IRC	1981 AC 253	s2, s5
R v Lovitt	1912 AC 212	s6, s11
Rael Brook Ltd v Minister of Housing and Local Government	1967 1 All ER	s93
Re Clark, McKechnie v Clark	1904 Ch 294	s6, s11
Re Smyth	1891 1 Ch 89	s15
Revenue and Customs v George	2004 STC 147 (CA)	s93
Revenue Commissioners v Arida	1995 IV ITR 401	s67
Revenue Commissioners v Executors and Trustees of the Wills of Jeannie Hammet Irvine Deceased	2005 No 172 R HC	s15
Revenue Commissioners v Moroney	1971 V ITR 589	s28
Rosser v IRC	2003 SpC 368	s89
Smith v Anderson	1880 15 Ch D	s93
Starke (executors of Brown deceased) v IRC	CA 1995 STC 689	s89
Stratton v CIR	1958 1 Ch 42	s12
Sudeley v AG	1897 AC 11	s15
Town Investments v DOE	1977 1 All ER	s93

SUBJECT INDEX

Capital Acquisitions Tax Consolidation Act 2003

B

J

L

Q

R

S

T

Stamp Duties Consolidation Act 1999

Number 31 of 1999

STAMP DUTIES CONSOLIDATION ACT, 1999

AN ACT TO CONSOLIDATE CERTAIN ENACTMENTS RELATING TO STAMP DUTIES AND THE MANAGEMENT OF THOSE DUTIES.

[15*th December*, 1999]

BE IT ENACTED BY THE OIREACHTAS AS FOLLOWS:

PART 1

Interpretation

1 Interpretation

[SDMA1891 s27 (part); SA1891 s32, s33(1), s54, s86, s91, s98(1), s108 and s122(1); FA1898 s6 (part); FA1997 s115 and s118]

(1) In this Act, unless the context otherwise requires—

"*accountable person*" means [(subject to *subsection (1A)*)][1]—

(a) the person referred to in *column (2)* of the Table to this definition in respect of the corresponding instruments set out in *column (1)* of that Table by reference to the appropriate heading in *Schedule 1*,

(b) in the case of an instrument which operates, or is deemed to operate, as a voluntary disposition inter vivos under *section 30* or *54*, the parties to such instrument,

(c) in the case of any other instrument, the parties to that instrument,

(d) notwithstanding *paragraphs (a)*, *(b)* and *(c)*, in the case of any person who would be an accountable person if alive, the accountable person shall be the personal representative of such person:

TABLE

Instrument Heading specified in *Schedule 1* (1)	Accountable person (2)
CONVEYANCE or TRANSFER on sale of any stocks or marketable securities.	The purchaser or transferee.
CONVEYANCE or TRANSFER on sale of any property other than stocks or marketable securities or a policy of insurance or a policy of life insurance.	The purchaser or transferee.
DUPLICATE or COUNTERPART of any instrument chargeable with any duty.	Any of the persons specified in this column, as appropriate.
LEASE.	The lessee.
[...][2]	[...][3]

["*approved person*" and "*authorised person*" shall each be construed in accordance with section 917G of the Taxes Consolidation Act 1997;][4]

["*bill of exchange*" means a draft, an order or a cheque;][5]

["*child*", in relation to a claim for relief from duty made under this Act, includes a person, being a transferee or lessee, who, prior to the date of execution of the instrument in respect of which relief from duty is claimed, has resided with, was under the care of, and was maintained at the expense of the transferor or lessor throughout—

(a) a period of 5 years, or

(b) periods which together comprised at least 5 years,

before such person attains the age of 18 years, but only if such claim is not based on the uncorroborated testimony of only one witness;][6]

["*civil partner*" means a civil partner within the meaning of the Civil Partnership and Certain Rights and Obligations of Cohabitants Act 2010;

"*civil partnership*" means—

(a) a civil partnership registration referred to in section 3(*a*) of the Civil Partnership and Certain Rights and Obligations of Cohabitants Act 2010, or

(b) a legal relationship referred to in section 3(*b*) of that Act;][7]

"*Commissioners*" means Revenue Commissioners;

"*conveyance on sale*" includes every instrument, and every decree or order [...][8] of any court or of any commissioners, whereby any property, or any estate or interest in any property, on the sale or compulsory acquisition of that property or that estate or that interest is transferred to or vested in a purchaser, or any other person on such purchaser's behalf or by such purchaser's direction;

"*die*" includes any plate, type, tool, implement, apparatus, appliance, device, process and any other means, used by or under the direction of the Commissioners for expressing or denoting any duty, or rate of duty or the fact that any duty or rate of duty [or interest or penalty][9] has been paid or that an instrument is duly stamped or is not chargeable with any duty or for denoting any fee, and also any part or combination of any such plate, type, tool, implement, apparatus, appliance, device, process and any such other means;

["*electronic return*" means a return that is required to be made to the Commissioners by means of the e-stamping system;

"*e-stamping system*" means the electronic system established by the Commissioners by means of which electronic returns can be made to, and stamp certificates can be issued by, the Commissioners;][10]

[...][11]

"*executed*" and "*execution*", in relation to instruments not under seal, mean signed and signature;

["*filer*", in relation to an instrument in respect of which a paper return is delivered to the Commissioners, means the person who would be the approved person or, as the case may be, the authorised person had the paper return been an electronic return;][12]

"*forge*" includes counterfeit and "*forged*" shall be construed accordingly;

"*impressed*" includes any method of applying, producing or indicating a stamp on instruments or material by means of a die;

"*instrument*" includes every written document;

["*lineal descendant*", in relation to a conveyance or transfer (whether on sale or as a voluntary disposition inter vivos), includes a person who, as transferee, is a child of the transferor; ".][13]

"*marketable security*" means a security of such a description as to be capable of being sold in any stock market in the State;

"*material*" includes every sort of material on which words or figures can be expressed;

"*Minister*" means the Minister for Finance;

"*money*" includes all sums expressed in the currency of the State or in any foreign currency;

["*paper return*" means a return in paper form that satisfies the requirements of an electronic return and is processed by the Commissioners through the e-stamping system;][14]

[...][15]

"*policy of insurance*" includes every writing whereby any contract of insurance is made or agreed to be made, or is evidenced, and "*insurance*" includes assurance;

"*policy of life insurance*" means a policy of insurance on any life or lives or on any event or contingency relating to or depending on any life or lives except a policy of insurance for any payment agreed to be made on the death of any person only from accident or violence or otherwise than from a natural cause;

[...][16]

"*residential property*", in relation to a sale or lease, means—

(a) a building or part of a building which, at the date of the instrument of conveyance or lease—

(i) was used or was suitable for use as a dwelling,

(ii) was in the course of being constructed or adapted for use as a dwelling, or

(iii) had been constructed or adapted for use as a dwelling and had not since such construction or adaptation been adapted for any other use,

and

(b) the curtilage of the residential property up to an area (exclusive of the site of the residential property) of one acre;

but where—

[(I) in the year ending on 31 December immediately prior to the date of that instrument of conveyance or lease a rating authority—

(A) has made a rate or has not made a rate in respect of any particular property falling within Schedule 3 to the Valuation Act 2001, or

(B) has not made a rate in respect of any particular property falling within Schedule 4 to the Valuation Act 2001,

then the whole or an appropriate part of that property as is referable to ordinary use other than as a dwelling at the date of that instrument of conveyance or lease or, where appropriate, when last ordinarily used, shall not be residential property, in relation to that sale or lease, or.][17]

(II) the area of the curtilage (exclusive of the site of the residential property) exceeds one acre, then the part which shall be residential property shall be taken to be the part which, if the remainder were separately occupied, would be the most suitable for occupation and enjoyment with the residential property;

"*stamp*" means—

(a) any stamp, image, type, mark, seal, impression, imprint or perforation impressed by means of a die,

[(b) any receipt in whatever form issued by or under the direction of the Commissioners,

(c) an adhesive stamp issued by or under the direction of the Commissioners, or

(d) a stamp certificate,][18]

for denoting any duty or fee;

["*stamp certificate*" means—

(a) a certificate issued electronically by the Commissioners by means of the e-stamping system, or

(b) a certificate processed electronically by the Commissioners through the e-stamping system and issued by them in paper form;

"*stamped*", in relation to an instrument and material, applies as well to an instrument to which is attached a stamp certificate issued in respect of the instrument as to an instrument and material impressed with a stamp by means of a die and an instrument and material having an adhesive stamp affixed to it;][19]

['*stock*' includes any share in any stocks or funds transferable at the Bank of England or at the Bank of Ireland and any share in the stocks or funds of any foreign state or government, or in the capital stock or funded debt of any county council, corporation, company, or society in the State, or of any foreign corporation, company, or society and includes any option over any share in such stocks or funds;][20]

"*stock certificate to bearer*" includes every stock certificate to bearer issued under any Act authorising the creation of debenture stock, county stock, corporation stock, municipal stock, or funded debt, [by whatever name known;][21]

["*Teagasc*" means Teagasc — The Agricultural and Food Development Authority.][22]

[(1A) The following persons shall not be accountable persons for the purposes of this Act:

(a) the National Treasury Management Agency;

(b) the Minister in relation to a function exercised by the Minister 15 which is capable of being delegated to the National Treasury Management Agency under *section 5* of the National Treasury Management Agency Act 1990.][23]

(2) References in this Act to any enactment shall, except where the context otherwise requires, be construed as references to that enactment as amended or extended by any subsequent enactment.

(3) In this Act a reference to a Part, Chapter, section or Schedule is to a Part, Chapter or section of, or Schedule to, this Act, unless it is indicated that reference to some other enactment is intended.

(4) In this Act a reference to a subsection, paragraph, subparagraph, clause or subclause is to the subsection, paragraph, subparagraph, clause or subclause of the provision (including a Schedule) in which the reference occurs, unless it is indicated that reference to some other provision is intended.

Amendments

[1] Inserted by FA14 s73(a)(i).

[2] Deleted by FA07 s100(1)(a)(i)(I). This section applies to instruments executed on or after 7 December 2006.

[3] Deleted by FA07 s100(1)(a)(i)(II). This section applies to instruments executed on or after 7 December 2006.

[4] Inserted by F(No.2)A08 s79(1)(a)(i). With effect from 26 November 2009 as per S.I. No. 484 of 2009.

[5] Substituted by FA07 s101(1)(a)(i). This section applies to instruments drawn, made or executed on or after 2 April 2007.

[6] Inserted by FA06 s103(1)(a). Applies as respects instruments executed on or after 31 March 2006.

[7] Inserted by F(No.3)A11 sched2(1). Deemed to have come into operation in relation to stamp duty, as respects an instrument executed on or after 1 January 2011.

[8] Deleted by the the Land and Conveyancing Law Reform Act 2009 Sched 1. With effect from 1 December 2009 per S.I. 356 of 2009.

[9] Substituted by F(No.2)A08 sched5(part5)(chap2)(1)(a).

[10] Inserted by FA08 s111(1)(a)(i). With effect from 26 November 2009 as per S.I. No. 485 of 2009.

[11, 15] Deleted by FA07 s100(1)(a)(ii). This section applies to instruments executed on or after 7 December 2006.

[12] Inserted by F(No.2)A08 s79(1)(a)(ii). With effect from 26 November 2009 as per S.I. No. 484 of 2009.

[13] Inserted by FA06 s103(1)(b). Applies as respects instruments executed on or after 31 March 2006.

[14] Inserted by F(No.2)A08 s79(1)(a)(iii). With effect from 26 November 2009 as per S.I. No. 484 of 2009.

[16] Deleted by FA07 s101(1)(a)(ii). This section applies to instruments drawn, made or executed on or after 2 April 2007.

[17] Substituted by FA03 s133(1). This section has effect in relation to instruments executed on or after 28 March 2003.

[18] Substituted by FA08 s111(1)(a)(ii). With effect from 26 November 2009 as per S.I. No. 485 of 2009.

[19] Substituted by FA08 s111(1)(a)(iii). With effect from 26 November 2009 as per S.I. No. 485 of 2009.

[20] Substituted by FA12 s100(1)(a).

[21] Substituted by FA06 sched2(3)(a). Has effect as on and from 31 March 2006.

[22] Inserted by FA06 sched2(3)(b). Has effect as on and from 31 March 2006.

[23] Inserted by FA14 s73(a)(ii).

Case Law

In Fitch Lovell Ltd v IRC 1962 3 All ER 685 share transfers which omitted the consideration, the name of the transferee and the date were held to be conveyances or transfers on sale.

In Waterford Glass (Group Services) Ltd v Revenue Commissioners 1989 IV ITR 187 the Court was entitled to look at the substance of a transaction in deciding what constitutes a conveyance on sale.

The transaction will be taxed based on its result rather than the form. Viek Investments Ltd v Revenue Commissioners 1991 IV ITR 367

Following the court's approach in Waterford Glass (Group Services) Ltd v Revenue Commissioners, the judge in the case Cherry Court v Revenue Commissioners 1995 V ITR 180 held that the court was bound to look at the nature of the transaction and was not obliged to follow the intention of the parties involved.

Revenue Commissioners v Glenkerrin Homes Ltd 2007 ITR 119 considered what amount was due on date of conveyance.

A lease may be treated as a conveyance for certain purposes. Littlewoods Mail Order Stores Ltd v IRC 1961 Ch 210, 1961 1 All ER 195, 1961 2 WLR 25, 1961 TR 321

Where the benefit is a contract for property, an assignment of that benefit for consideration is liable to ad valorem conveyance on sale duty. Western Abyssinian Mining Syndicate Ltd v IRC 1935 14 ATC 286

A document worded as a receipt for consideration may in certain circumstances operate as a conveyance on sale of an equitable interest in property or as an agreement for sale. Fleetwood-Hesketh v IRC 1936 1 KB 351

An agreement creating an option to purchase land was chargeable to ad valorem as a conveyance on sale, in respect of the consideration paid for the grant of the option. Wimpey (George) & Co Ltd v IRC 1974 2 All ER 602

Cross References

From Section 1

Section 30 Voluntary dispositions inter vivos chargeable as conveyances or transfers on sale.
Section 54 Leases deemed to operate as voluntary dispositions inter vivos.
Schedule 1 Stamp Duties on Instruments

To Section 1

Section 14 Penalty on stamping instruments after execution.
Section 71 Application and adaptation of other Parts of this Act.

PART 2

Charging and Stamping of Instruments

2 Charging of, liability for, and recovery of stamp duty

[SA1891 s1(1) to (4)]

(1) Any instrument which—

(a) is specified in *Schedule 1*, and

(b) is executed in the State or, wherever executed, relates to any property situated in the State or any matter or thing done or to be done in the State,

shall be chargeable with stamp duty.

(2) The stamp duties to be charged for the benefit of the Central Fund on the several instruments specified in *Schedule 1* shall be the several duties specified in that Schedule, which duties shall be subject to the exemptions contained in this Act and in any other enactment for the time being in force.

[(3) Any instrument chargeable with stamp duty shall, unless it is written on duty stamped material, be duly stamped with the proper stamp duty before the expiration of 30 days after it is first executed.][1]

(4) Where any instrument chargeable with stamp duty is not stamped or is insufficiently stamped—

(a) the accountable person shall be liable, and

(b) where there is more than one such accountable person they shall be liable jointly and severally,

for the payment of the stamp duty or, where the instrument is insufficiently stamped, the additional stamp duty [...][2] [, any interest and penalty][3] relating to any such duty [...][4].

Amendments

[1] Substituted by FA12 sched3(2). In effect for all instruments that are executed on or after 7 July 2012 per S.I. No. 228 of 2012.

[2, 4] Deleted by F(No.2)A08 sched4(part1). Applies as respects any tax that becomes due and payable on or after 1 March 2009.

[3] Substituted by F(No.2)A08 sched5(part5)(chap2)(1)(b).

Case Law

In the case of IRC v Maples 1908 AC 22, the consideration passing for French land was shares in a UK registered company. As the document involved something to be done in the UK, the document was liable to UK stamp duty.

Specialty debts are located where the document is located. Re Deane (Deceased) 1936 IR 556

The location of the Register of Shareholders determines the location of the shares. Re Ferguson (Deceased) 1935 IR 21

Under a deed of covenant executed in Canada an engineer working in the UK, in consideration for the issue of shares and debentures agreed to pay an annuity to a Canadian company. It was held that the deed related to a matter or thing done in the UK and therefore liable to UK stamp duty. Faber v IRC 1936 1 All ER 617

Cross References

From Section 2

Schedule 1 Stamp Duties on Instruments

To Section 2

Section 14 Penalty on stamping instruments after execution.
Section 71 Application and adaptation of other Parts of this Act.
Section 116 Charge of stamp duty.
Schedule 1 Stamp Duties on Instruments

3 Variation of certain rates of duty by order

[FA1991 s95]

(1) Subject to this section, the Minister may—

(a) by order vary the rate of duty chargeable on any instrument specified in *Schedule 1* or may exempt such instrument from duty, and

(b) make such order in respect of any particular class of instrument,

but no order shall be made under this section for the purpose of increasing any of the rates of duty.

(2) No order shall be made under this section for the purpose of varying the duty on any instrument or class of instrument where—

(a) such instrument or class of instrument relates to—

(i) any immovable property situated in the State or any rights or interest in such property,

(ii) any stock or share of a company having a register in the State, or

(iii) any risk situated in the State in relation to the heading "INSURANCE" in *Schedule 1*,

or

(b) such instrument or class of instrument is a bill of exchange [...][1].

(3) Notwithstanding anything to the contrary contained in *subsection (2)*, the Minister may make an order in respect of an instrument which is executed for the purposes of debt factoring.

(4) The Minister may by order amend or revoke an order under this section, including an order under this subsection.

(5) An order under this section shall be laid before Dáil Éireann as soon as may be after it has been made and, if a resolution annulling the order is passed by Dáil Éireann within the next 21 days on which Dáil Éireann has sat after the order is laid before it, the order shall be annulled accordingly, but without prejudice to the validity of anything previously done under that order.

(6) Every order under this section shall have statutory effect on the making of that order and, subject to *subsection (5)*, unless the order either is confirmed by Act of the Oireachtas passed not later than the end of the year following that in which the order is made, or, is an order merely revoking wholly an order previously made under that subsection, the order shall cease to have statutory effect at the expiration of that period but without prejudice to the validity of anything previously done under that order.

Amendments

[1] Deleted by FA07 s101(1)(b). This section applies to instruments drawn, made or executed on or after 2 April 2007.

Cross References

From Section 3

Schedule 1 Stamp Duties on Instruments

To Section 3

Section 31B Licence agreements.
Section 50A Agreements for more than 35 years charged as leases.

4 How duties are to be paid

[SA1891 s2]

All stamp duties for the time being chargeable by law on any instruments are to be paid and denoted according to this Act and except where express provision is made to the contrary are to be denoted by [impressed stamps or by attaching to the instrument the stamp certificate issued in respect of that instrument][1].

Amendments

[1] Substituted by FA08 s111(1)(b). With effect from 26 November 2009 as per S.I. No. 485 of 2009.

Cross References

To Section 4

Section 71 Application and adaptation of other Parts of this Act.

5 Agreement as to payment of stamp duty on instruments

[FA1990 s113(1) to (4)]

(1) Where in the opinion of the Commissioners it is inexpedient or impractical for any person carrying on a business and who—

(a) in the course of that business, is a party to instruments liable to stamp duty under *Schedule 1*, or

(b) acts as agent for any such party,

to pay stamp duty in respect of each such instrument, then the Commissioners may enter into an agreement with that person for the delivery to them of accounts for specified periods giving such particulars as may be required of such instruments.

(2) The agreement shall be in such form and shall contain such terms and conditions as the Commissioners consider proper.

(3) Where an agreement has been entered into under this section between the Commissioners and any person, and any instrument to which the agreement relates—

[(a) (i) is issued during the period the agreement is in force, where the agreement is one that relates to the issue of such instrument, or

(ii) is processed during the period the agreement is in force, where the agreement is one that relates to the processing of such instrument, and][1]

(b) contains a statement that the appropriate stamp duty has been or will be paid to the Commissioners in accordance with this section,

then that instrument shall not be chargeable with any stamp duty but in lieu of such stamp duty, and by means of composition, there shall be charged, in respect of the instruments to which the agreement relates which [were issued or processed, as the case may be,][2] during each period of account under that agreement a stamp duty of an amount equal to the aggregate of the amounts of stamp duty which, but for this section, would have been chargeable on each of the instruments concerned, and the stamp duty chargeable under this subsection (by means of such composition) shall be paid by the person to the Commissioners on the delivery of the account.

[(3A) For the purposes of subsection (3) "processed", in relation to an instrument that is a bill of exchange, means a bill of exchange that has been presented for payment and has been paid.][3]

(4) Where a person makes default in delivering any account required by any agreement under this section or in paying the duty payable on the delivery of any such account, the person shall be liable to a penalty not exceeding [€125][4] for every day during which the default continues and shall also be liable to pay, in addition to the duty, [interest on the duty [...][5], calculated in accordance with section 159D,][6] from the date when the default begins.

(5) Section 126B (inserted by the *Finance Act 2008*) shall, with any necessary modifications, apply to an account relating to a specified period within the meaning of this section as it applies to a statement within the meaning of that section.

Amendments

[1] Substituted by F(No.2)A08 s80(1)(a). Applies as respects agreements (being agreements to which section 5 relates) entered into on or after 1 January 2009.

[2] Substituted by F(No.2)A08 s80(1)(b). Applies as respects agreements (being agreements to which section 5 relates) entered into on or after 1 January 2009.

[3] Inserted by F(No.2)A08 s80(1)(c). Applies as respects agreements (being agreements to which section 5 relates) entered into on or after 1 January 2009.

[4] Substituted by FA01 sched5.

[5] Deleted by F(No.2)A08 sched4(part1). Applies as respects any tax that becomes due and payable on or after 1 March 2009.

[6] Substituted by FA05 sched5, Part 2, with effect from 1 April 2005.

Cross References

From Section 5

Section 126B Assessment of duty charged on statements.
Schedule 1 Stamp Duties on Instruments

To Section 5

Section 159C Time limits for making enquiries etc. and assessments by the Commissioners.

6 How instruments are to be written and stamped

[SA1891 s3]

(1) Every instrument—

(a) written on stamped material shall be written in such manner, and

(b) partly or wholly written before being stamped shall be so stamped,

so as to have the stamp appear on the face of the instrument, and to prevent it being used for or applied to any other instrument written on the same piece of material.

(2) If more than one instrument is written on the same piece of material, every one of the instruments shall be separately and distinctly stamped with the duty with which it is chargeable.

Cross References

To Section 6

Section 71 Application and adaptation of other Parts of this Act.

7 Instruments to be separately charged with duty in certain cases

[SA1891 s4]

Except where express provision to the contrary is made by this or any other Act—

(a) an instrument containing or relating to several distinct matters shall be separately and distinctly charged, as if it were a separate instrument, with duty in respect of each of the matters;

(b) an instrument made for any consideration in respect of which it is chargeable with ad valorem duty, and also for any further or other valuable consideration or considerations, shall be separately and distinctly charged, as if it were a separate instrument, with duty in respect of each of the considerations;

(c) without prejudice to the generality of *paragraphs (a)* and *(b)*, where the consideration (other than rent) for the sale or lease of any property is partly attributable to residential property and partly attributable to property which is not residential property the instrument of conveyance or transfer or lease shall be chargeable to ad valorem stamp duty on the basis that it is a separate conveyance or transfer or lease of residential property to the extent that that consideration is attributable to residential property and also a separate conveyance or transfer or lease of property which is not residential property to the extent that that consideration is attributable to property which is not residential property.

Cross References

To Section 7

Section 52 Charging of duty on leases, etc.

8 Facts and circumstances affecting duty to be set forth in instruments, etc.

[SA1891 s5]

(1) Except as provided for in this section, all the facts and circumstances affecting the liability of any instrument to duty, or the amount of the duty with which any instrument is chargeable, are to be fully and truly set forth in the instrument.

(2) Where it is not practicable to set out all the facts and circumstances, to which *subsection (1)* refers, in an instrument, additional facts and circumstances which—

(a) affect the liability of such instrument to duty,

(b) affect the amount of the duty with which such instrument is chargeable, or

(c) may be required from time to time by the Commissioners,

are to be fully and truly set forth in a statement which shall be delivered to the Commissioners together with such instrument and the form of any such statement may from time to time be ["prescribed by the Commissioners; but where the instrument is stamped by means of the e-stamping system and subject to the Commissioners making regulations under section 17A in relation to when a statement is required to be delivered to them, then such statement [...][1] is not required to be delivered but only if the evidence in relation to all the facts and circumstances, affecting the chargeability of the instrument to duty, are retained for a period of 6 years from the date the instrument is stamped and are made available to the Commissioners on request][2].

(3) [Any person who before the passing of the *Finance (No. 2) Act 2008*][3]—

(a) fraudulently or negligently executes any instrument, or

(b) being employed or concerned in or about the preparation of any instrument, fraudulently or negligently prepares any such instrument,

in which all the facts and circumstances affecting the liability of such instrument to duty, or the amount of the duty with which such instrument is chargeable, are not fully and truly set forth in the instrument or in any statement to which *subsection (2)* relates, shall incur a penalty of—

(i) [€1,265][4], and

(ii) the amount[...][5] of the difference between—

(I) the amount of duty payable in respect of the instrument based on the facts and circumstances set forth and delivered, and

(II) the amount of duty which would have been the amount so payable if the instrument and any accompanying statement had fully and truly set forth all the facts and circumstances referred to in *subsections (1)* and *(2)*.

(4) Where any instrument was executed neither fraudulently nor negligently by a person and it comes to such person's notice, or it would have come to such person's notice, if such person had taken reasonable care, that such instrument or any statement to which *subsection (2)* relates does not fully and truly set forth all those facts and circumstances then, unless the Commissioners are informed of the error without unreasonable delay, such matter shall be treated, for the purposes of *subsection (3)*, as having been negligently done by such person.

[(4A) Any person who, on or after the passing of the *Finance (No. 2) Act 2008*, being employed or concerned in or about the preparation of any instrument, prepares any such instrument in which all the facts and circumstances, of which the person is aware, affecting the liability of such instrument to duty, or the amount of the duty with which such instrument is chargeable, are not fully and truly set forth in the instrument or in any statement to which subsection (2) relates, shall incur a penalty of €3,000.][6]

[(5) Where an instrument operates, or is deemed to operate, as a voluntary disposition inter vivos under *section 30* or *54* such fact shall be brought to the attention of the Commissioners in the electronic return or the paper return to be delivered in relation to an instrument required to be stamped and where the requirement of this subsection is not complied with an accountable person shall, for the purposes of *subsection (3)* of this section or *section 134A(2)(a)*, as the case may be, be presumed, until the contrary is proven, to have acted negligently or deliberately, as the case may be.][7]

[...][8]

Amendments

[1] Deleted by FA12 sched3(3)(a). In effect for all instruments that are executed on or after 7 July 2012 per S.I. No. 228 of 2012.

[2] Substituted by FA08 s111(1)(c). With effect from 26 November 2009 as per S.I. 485 of 2009.

[3] Substituted by F(No.2)A08 sched5(part5)(chap1)(5)(a)(i). The enactments specified in Schedule 5 are amended or repealed to the extent and manner specified in that Schedule and, unless the contrary is stated, shall come into effect after 24 December 2008.

[4] Substituted by FA01 sched5.

[5] Deleted by FA05 s115(1). This section has effect in relation to instruments executed or statements delivered to the Commissioners on or after 25 March 2005.

[6] Inserted by F(No.2)A08 sched5(part5)(chap1)(5)(a)(ii). The enactments specified in Schedule 5 are amended or repealed to the extent and manner specified in that Schedule and, unless the contrary is stated, shall come into effect after 24 December 2008.

[7] Substituted by FA12 sched3(3)(b). In effect for all instruments that are executed on or after 7 July 2012 per S.I. No. 228 of 2012.

[8] Deleted by FA12 sched3(3)(c). In effect for all instruments that are executed on or after 7 July 2012 per S.I. No. 228 of 2012.

Revenue Briefings

Tax Briefing

Tax Briefing June 2001 – Issue 44 (part 2) pg 30 – Revenue Certificates in Deeds

Cross References

From Section 8

Section 17A E-stamping regulations.
Section 30 Voluntary dispositions inter vivos chargeable as conveyances or transfers on sale.
Section 54 Leases deemed to operate as voluntary dispositions inter vivos.
Section 134A Penalties.

To Section 8

Section 15 Surcharges for undervaluation in case of voluntary dispositions inter vivos.
Section 16 Surcharges to apply when apportionment is not just and reasonable.
Section 71 Application and adaptation of other Parts of this Act.
Section 134A Penalties.
Section 159C Time limits for making enquiries etc. and assessments by the Commissioners.

8A Penalties: returns

[Where, in relation to an instrument, an approved person, authorised person or a filer, as the case may be, delivers an electronic return or a paper return, to the Commissioners which does not reflect the facts and circumstances of which the person is aware, affecting the liability of such instrument to duty or the amount of the duty with which such instrument is chargeable that are required by the Commissioners to be disclosed on such return, then such person shall incur a penalty of €3,000.][1]

Amendments

[1] Inserted by F(No.2)A08 s79(1)(b). With effect from 26 November 2009 as per S.I. No. 484 of 2009.

8B Penalties: failure to deliver returns

[Where an accountable person fails to cause an electronic return or a paper return to be delivered in relation to an instrument within the time specified in *section 2(3)*, the accountable person or, where there is more than one accountable person, each accountable person shall incur a penalty of €3,000.][1]

Amendments

[1] Inserted by FA12 sched3(4). In effect for all instruments that are executed on or after 7 July 2012 per S.I. No. 228 of 2012.

8C Expression of doubt

[(1) In this section—

'*the law*' has the meaning assigned to it by *subsection (2)*;

'*letter of expression of doubt*' means a communication received in legible form which—

(a) sets out full details of the facts and circumstances affecting the liability of an instrument to stamp duty, and makes reference to the provisions of the law giving rise to the doubt,

(b) identifies the amount of stamp duty in doubt in respect of the instrument to which the expression of doubt relates,

(c) is accompanied by supporting documentation as relevant, and

(d) is clearly identified as a letter of expression of doubt for the purposes of this section,

and reference to '*an expression of doubt*' shall be construed accordingly.

(2) (a) Subject to *paragraph (b)*, where, in relation to an instrument, an account able person is in doubt as to the correct application of any enactment relating to stamp duty (in this section referred to as '*the law*') to an instrument which could—

(i) give rise to a liability to stamp duty by that person, or

(ii) affects that person's liability to stamp duty or entitlement to an exemption or a relief from stamp duty,

then the accountable person may lodge a letter of expression of doubt with the Commissioners in such manner as the Commissioners may require.

(b) This subsection shall apply only if both—

(i) the electronic return or the paper return, and

(ii) the expression of doubt referred to in *paragraph (a)*,

are delivered to the Commissioners before the expiration of 30 days after the instrument is first executed.

(3) Subject to *subsection (4)*, where an accountable person causes an electronic return or a paper return to be delivered to the Commissioners and lodges an expression of doubt relating to the instrument in accordance with this section, then interest calculated in accordance with *section 159D* shall not apply to any additional stamp duty arising where the Commissioners notify the person of the correct application of the law to that instrument and the return will not be deemed to be an incorrect return if an amended return, which includes an assessment to be substituted for an earlier assessment, is delivered and the additional duty is paid within 30 days of the date on which that notification is issued.

(4) *Subsection (3)* does not apply where the Commissioners do not accept as genuine an expression of doubt in relation to the correct application of the law to an instrument, and an expression of doubt shall not be accepted as genuine in particular where the Commissioners—

(a) have issued general guidelines concerning the application of the law in similar circumstances,

(b) are of the opinion that the matter is otherwise sufficiently free from doubt as not to warrant an expression of doubt, or

(c) are of the opinion that the accountable person was acting with a view to the evasion or avoidance of duty.

(5) Where the Commissioners do not accept an expression of doubt as genuine, they shall notify the accountable person accordingly and the accountable person shall, on receipt of the notification, cause an amended return that includes

an assessment to be substituted for an earlier assessment to be delivered and the additional duty to be paid together with any interest payable calculated in accordance with *section 159D*.

(6) Where an accountable person is aggrieved by a decision of the Commissioners under *subsection (5)* he or she may appeal to the Appeal Commissioners in accordance with *section 21(9)*.][1]

Amendments

[1] Inserted by FA12 sched3(4). In effect for all instruments that are executed on or after 7 July 2012 per S.I. No. 228 of 2012.

9 Mode of calculating ad valorem duty in certain cases

[FA1933 s40]

Where an instrument is chargeable with ad valorem duty in respect of money in any currency other than the currency of the State, such duty shall be calculated on the value of that money in the currency of the State according to the rate of exchange current at the date of execution of such instrument.

10 Adhesive stamps

[SA1891 s7, s8 and s9(1)]

(1) Any stamp duties on instruments which are permitted by law to be denoted by adhesive stamps shall, if denoted by adhesive stamps, be denoted by adhesive stamps issued by the Commissioners.

(2) An instrument, the duty on which is required or permitted by law to be denoted by an adhesive stamp, shall not be deemed duly stamped with an adhesive stamp, unless the person required by law to cancel the adhesive stamp cancels the same by writing on or across the stamp his or her name or initials, or the name or initials of his or her firm, together with the true date of his or her so writing, or otherwise effectively cancels the stamp and renders the same incapable of being used for any other instrument or unless it is otherwise proved that the stamp appearing on the instrument was affixed to the instrument at the proper time.

(3) Where 2 or more adhesive stamps are used to denote the stamp duty on an instrument, each or every stamp shall be cancelled in the manner set out in *subsection (2)*.

(4) Every person who, being required by law to cancel an adhesive stamp, neglects or refuses duly and effectually to do so in the manner set out in *subsection (2)*, shall incur a penalty of [€630][1].

(5) If any person—

(a) fraudulently removes or causes to be removed from any instrument any adhesive stamp, or affixes to any other instrument any adhesive stamp which has been so removed, with intent that the stamp may be used again, or

(b) sells or offers for sale, or utters, any adhesive stamp which has been so removed, or utters any instrument, having any adhesive stamp on it which has to such person's knowledge been removed in the manner specified in *paragraph (a)*,

such person shall, without prejudice to any other fine or penalty to which that person may be liable, be guilty of an offence and section 1078 (which relates to revenue offences) of the Taxes Consolidation Act, 1997, shall for the purposes of such offence be construed in all respects as if such offence were an offence under subsection (2) of that section.

Amendments

[1] Substituted by FA01 sched5.

Cross References

To Section 10

Section 83C Exchange of houses.
Schedule 4 Consequential Amendments

11 Denoting stamps

[SA1891 s11]

Where the duty with which an instrument is chargeable depends in any manner on the duty paid on another instrument, the payment of the last-mentioned duty shall, on application to the Commissioners and production of both the instruments, be denoted on the first-mentioned instrument in such manner as the Commissioners think fit.

Cross References

To Section 11

Section 71 Application and adaptation of other Parts of this Act.

12 Particulars delivered stamps

[FA1994 s107(1) to (3) and (6)]

(1) In this section "*fee simple*", "*interest*", "*land*" and "*lease*" have the same meanings, respectively, as in section 41 of the Finance (1909-10) Act, 1910, and references to a "*transferee*" or a "*lessee*" include the personal representatives of any transferee or lessee.

(2) It shall be the duty of the transferee or lessee, on the occasion of any transfer of the fee simple of any land or of any interest in land or on the grant of any lease of any land for a term exceeding 14 years (whether the transfer or lease is on sale or operates as a voluntary disposition inter vivos), to present to the Commissioners such particulars in relation to such class or category of transfer or lease as they may prescribe by regulations and, without prejudice to the generality of the foregoing, the regulations may make provision in relation to all or any of the following matters:

(a) the form in which the particulars are to be delivered;

(b) the time limits within which the particulars are to be delivered;

(c) the manner in which the land is to be described or classified;

(d) the furnishing of tax reference numbers of the parties to the instrument.

(3) Notwithstanding anything in *section 20* or *127*, [any transfer or lease (not being a duplicate or counterpart of a transfer or lease)][1] to which regulations made pursuant to *subsection (2)* apply shall not, other than in criminal proceedings or in civil proceedings by the Commissioners to recover stamp duty, be given in evidence, or be available for any purpose unless it is stamped with a stamp denoting that all particulars prescribed by the Commissioners have been delivered.

(4) If the transferee or lessee fails to comply with this provision, such person shall be guilty of an offence and section 1078 (which relates to revenue offences) of the Taxes Consolidation Act, 1997, shall for the purposes of such offence be construed in all respects as if such offence were an offence under subsection (2) of that section.

[(5) Subsection (2) does not apply where the transfer or lease concerned is effected by an instrument which [has been stamped, or is not required under Regulations made pursuant to section 17A to be stamped,][2] by means of the e-stamping system.][3]

Amendments

[1] Substituted by FA07 s101(1)(c). This section applies to instruments drawn, made or executed on or after 2 April 2007

[2] Substituted by FA10 sched(4)(2)(b). Applies as on and from 30 December 2009.

[3] Inserted by FA08 s111(1)(d). With effect from 26 November 2009 as per S.I. No. 485 of 2009.

Cross References

From Section 12

Section 20 Assessment of duty by the Commissioners.
Section 127 Terms on which instruments not duly stamped may be received in evidence.

To Section 12

Section 21 Right of appeal of persons dissatisfied with assessment.
Schedule 4 Consequential Amendments

13 Duplicates and counterparts

[SA1891 s72]

The duplicate or counterpart of an instrument chargeable with duty (except the counterpart of an instrument chargeable as a lease, such counterpart not being executed by or on behalf of any lessor or grantor,) shall not be deemed duly stamped unless—

(a) it is stamped as an original instrument, or

(b) it appears by some stamp impressed on it that the full and proper duty has been paid on the original instrument of which it is the duplicate or counterpart.

14 Penalty on stamping instruments after execution

[SA1891 s15(1) to (5)]

(1) Except where express provision is in this Act made, any instrument which is unstamped or insufficiently stamped may be stamped after the expiration of the time for stamping provided for in *subsection (3)* of *section 2*, on payment of the unpaid duty and on payment [...][1] [...][2], where the unpaid duty [exceeds €30][3], of [interest on such duty, calculated in accordance with section 159D,][4] on which that instrument was first executed to the day of payment of the unpaid duty.

[...][5]

(4) The payment of any [interest [...][6]][7] payable on stamping shall be denoted on the instrument by a [particular stamp or by way of inclusion in a stamp certificate issued in respect of that instrument][8].

[...][9]

Amendments

1 Deleted by F(No.2)A08 sched5(part5)(chap2)(7)(c)(i)(I). Has effect as respects penalties incurred in respect of instruments executed on or after 24 December 2008.

[2] Deleted by F(No.2)A08 sched5(part5)(chap2)(7)(c)(i)(II).

[3] Substituted by FA01 sched5.

[4] Substituted by FA05 sched5.

[5] Deleted by FA12 sched3(5)(a). In effect for all instruments that are executed on or after 7 July 2012 per S.I. No. 228 of 2012.

[6] Deleted by FA12 sched3(5)(b). In effect for all instruments that are executed on or after 7 July 2012 per S.I. No. 228 of 2012.

[7] Substituted by F(No.2)A08 sched5(part5)(chap2)(7)(c)(iv).

[8] Substituted by FA08 s111(1)(e). With effect from 26 November 2009 as per S.I. No. 485 of 2009.

---

[9] Deleted by F(No.2)A08 sched4(part1). Applies as respects any tax that becomes due and payable on or after 1 March 2009.

Note:

F(No.2)A08 sched5 (part5)(chap 2)(7)

As respects paragraph 7 of this Schedule subparagraphs (a) to (aa) (other than subparagraph (c)(i)(I)) of that paragraph have effect as on and from the passing of this Act and to the extent that Chapter 3A (being inserted into Part 47 of the Taxes Consolidation Act 1997 by Part 1 of this Schedule) applies to penalties incurred under the Stamp Duties Consolidation Act 1999 before the passing of this Act which on the passing of this Act have not been paid, it shall not apply to such penalties which are in the form of interest accrued under any provisions of the said Act.

Revenue Briefings

eBrief

e-Brief No. 05/2009 – Stamp Duty: Late Stamping of Instruments

Statements of Practice

Revenue Internal Review Procedures – SP-GEN/2/99 (Revised January 2005)

Cross References

From Section 14

Section 1 Interpretation.
Section 2 Charging of, liability for, and recovery of stamp duty.

To Section 14

Section 27 Stamping of certain foreign bills of exchange.
Section 71 Application and adaptation of other Parts of this Act.
Schedule 4 Consequential Amendments

14A Late filing of return

[(1) In this section '*specified return date*' means the thirtieth day after the date of the first execution of an instrument chargeable with duty.

(2) For the purposes of this section—

(a) where an accountable person deliberately or carelessly causes the delivery of an incorrect electronic return or a paper return on or before the specified return date, that person shall be deemed to have failed to have delivered the return on or before that date unless the error in the return is remedied by the delivery of a correct return on or before that date,

(b) where an accountable person causes the delivery of an incorrect electronic return or a paper return on or before the specified return date, but does so neither deliberately nor carelessly and it comes to that person's notice (or, if he or she has died, to the notice of his or her personal representative) that it is incorrect, the person shall be deemed to have failed to have delivered the return on or before the specified return date unless the error in the return is remedied by the delivery of a correct return without unreasonable delay, and

(c) where an accountable person causes the delivery of an electronic return or a paper return on or before the specified return date, but the Commissioners, by reason of being dissatisfied with any information contained in the return, require that person, by notice in writing served on him or her, to deliver a statement or evidence, or further statement or evidence, as may be required by them, the person shall be deemed not to have delivered the return on or before the specified return date unless the person delivers the statement or evidence, or further statement or evidence, within the time specified in any notice.

(3) Where an accountable person fails to cause the delivery of an electronic return or a paper return in relation to an instrument on or before the specified return date, the stamp duty chargeable on such instrument shall be increased by an amount (in this section referred to as a '*surcharge*') equal to—

(a) 5 per cent of the amount of duty, subject to a maximum surcharge of €12,695, where the return is delivered before the expiry of 2 months from the specified return date, and

(b) 10 per cent of the amount of duty, subject to a maximum surcharge of €63,485, where the return is not delivered before the expiry of 2 months from the specified return date.][1]

Amendments

[1] Inserted by FA12 sched3(6). In effect for all instruments that are executed on or after 7 July 2012 per S.I. No. 228 of 2012.

15 Surcharges for undervaluation in case of voluntary dispositions inter vivos [Deleted]

Deleted by FA12 sched3(7). In effect for all instruments that are executed on or after 7 July 2012 per S.I. No. 228 of 2012.

16 Surcharges to apply when apportionment is not just and reasonable [Deleted]

Deleted by FA12 sched3(7). In effect for all instruments that are executed on or after 7 July 2012 per S.I. No. 228 of 2012.

17 Furnishing of an incorrect certificate [Deleted]

Deleted by FA12 sched3(7). In effect for all instruments that are executed on or after 7 July 2012 per S.I. No. 228 of 2012.

17A E-stamping regulations

[The Commissioners may make regulations with respect to the operation of the e-stamping system and those regulations may in particular, but without prejudice to the generality of the foregoing, include provision—

(a) for the commencement of the operation of the e-stamping system,

(b) for requiring instruments, or a specified class, or specified classes, of instruments, chargeable with stamp duty, to be stamped by means of the e-stamping system,

(c) for requiring delivery of information and the manner of its delivery in relation to the facts and circumstances affecting the chargeability of an instrument to duty,

(d) as to the making of an electronic return or a paper return and the information that is required to be included in the return, including the manner in which the information is to be entered into the e-stamping system,

(e) as to how stamp duty is to be paid to the Commissioners in respect of an instrument which is to be stamped by means of the e-stamping system,

(f) as to the issue of stamp certificates denoting in respect of an instrument—
  (i) that the stamp duty chargeable on the instrument (including any interest [...][1]) has been paid in accordance with the electronic return or paper return,

  [...][2]

  (iii) that the instrument is not chargeable with any stamp duty,
  (iv) that the instrument is a duplicate or counterpart of an original instrument, or
  (v) that the stamp duty with which the instrument is chargeable depends in any manner on the duty paid on another instrument,

(g) as to the issue, amendment or withdrawal of authorisations in relation to the use of the e-stamping system, and

(h) as to measures to protect the integrity of the e-stamping system.][3]

Amendments

[1] Deleted by FA12 sched3(8)(a). In effect for all instruments that are executed on or after 7 July 2012 per S.I. No. 228 of 2012.

[2] Deleted by FA12 sched3(8)(b). In effect for all instruments that are executed on or after 7 July 2012 per S.I. No. 228 of 2012.

[3] Inserted by FA08 s111(1)(f). By virtue of Stamp Duty (E-stamping of Instruments) Regulations 2009 (S.I. 476 of 2009) this section came into operation on 30 December 2009.

Revenue Briefings

eBrief

eBrief No. 82/2009 – New e-Stamping Regulations
eBrief No. 33/2011 – Stamp Duty - Mandatory Electronic Filing and Payment
eBrief No. 31/2012 – Stamp Duty and Self Assessment

Cross References

To Section 17A

Section 8 Facts and circumstances affecting duty to be set forth in instruments, etc.

PART 3

Valuation

18 Mode of valuing property

[FA1978 s34(5)]

For the purposes of *sections 30* and *33(1)*, the value of property conveyed or transferred by an instrument chargeable with duty in accordance with either of those sections shall be determined without regard to—

(a) any power (whether or not contained in the instrument) on the exercise of which the property, or any part of or any interest in, the property, may be revested in the person from whom it was conveyed or transferred or in any person on his or her behalf,

(b) any annuity or other periodic payment reserved out of the property or any part of it, or any life or other interest so reserved, being an interest which is subject to forfeiture, or

(c) any right of residence, support, maintenance, or other right of a similar nature which the property is subject to or charged with, except where such rights are reserved in favour of the transferor or the [spouse or civil partner][1] of the transferor and in any such case regard shall be had to such rights only to the extent that their value does not exceed 10 per cent of the unencumbered value of the property,

but if on a claim made to the Commissioners not later than [4 years from the date the instrument was stamped by the Commissioners][2] it is shown to their satisfaction that any such power as is mentioned in *paragraph (a)* has been exercised in relation to the property and the property or any property representing it has been reconveyed or retransferred in the whole or in part in consequence of that exercise, the Commissioners shall repay the stamp duty paid by virtue of this section, in a case where the whole of such property has been so reconveyed or retransferred, so far as it exceeds the stamp duty which would have been payable apart from this section and, in any other case, so far as it exceeds the stamp duty which would have been payable if the instrument had operated to convey or transfer only such property as is not so reconveyed or retransferred.

Amendments

[1] Substituted by F(No.3)A11 sched2(2). Deemed to have come into operation in relation to stamp duty, as respects an instrument executed on or after 1 January 2011

[2] Substituted by FA12 sched3(9). In effect for all instruments that are executed on or after 7 July 2012 per S.I. No. 228 of 2012.

Cross References

From Section 18

Section 30 Voluntary dispositions inter vivos chargeable as conveyances or transfers on sale.
Section 33 Conveyance or transfer in contemplation of sale.

19 Valuation of property chargeable with stamp duty

[FA1991 s105(1)]

The Commissioners shall ascertain the value of property the subject of an instrument chargeable with stamp duty in the same manner, subject to any necessary modification, as is provided for in [section 26 of the Capital Acquisitions Tax Consolidation Act 2003][1].

Amendments

[1] Substituted by CATCA03 sched3 and s119.

PART 4

Adjudication and Appeals

20 Assessment of duty by the Commissioners

[SA1891 s12]

[(1) Notwithstanding *subsection (2)*, where an electronic return or a paper return is delivered in relation to an instrument required to be stamped by means of the e-stamping system, there shall be included on that return an assessment of such amount of stamp duty that, to the best of the accountable person's knowledge, information and belief, ought to be charged, levied and paid on the instrument and the accountable person shall pay, or cause to be paid, the stamp duty so assessed together with interest calculated in accordance with *section 159D* unless the Commissioners make another assessment to be substituted for such assessment.

(2) Where an accountable person fails to cause an electronic return or a paper return to be delivered in relation to an instrument required to be stamped by means of the e-stamping system, the Commissioners shall make an assessment of such amount of stamp duty as, to the best of their knowledge, information (including information received from a member of the Garda Síochána) and belief, ought to be charged, levied and paid on the instrument and an accountable person shall be liable for the payment of the stamp duty so assessed together with interest calculated in accordance with *section 159D* unless the Commissioners make another assessment to be substituted for such assessment.

[(2A) If at any time it appears for any reason an assessment is incorrect the Commissioners shall make such other assessment as they consider appropriate and any such assessment shall be substituted for the first-mentioned assessment.][1]

(3) Where the Commissioners make an assessment to be substituted for another assessment, an accountable person shall be liable for the payment of the stamp duty so assessed together with interest calculated in accordance with *section 159D*.

(4) The Commissioners may require to be furnished with a copy of the instrument, together with such evidence as they may deem necessary, in order to show to their satisfaction that the instrument has been or will be correctly stamped.

(5) Every instrument stamped in conformity with an assessment made under this section shall be admissible in evidence and available for all purposes notwithstanding any objection relating to duty.

(6) An instrument which is chargeable with duty shall not, if it is unstamped or insufficiently stamped, be stamped otherwise than in accordance with an assessment.

(7) Nothing in this section shall authorise the stamping after its execution of any instrument which by law cannot be stamped after execution.

(8) The Commissioners may make such enquiries or take such actions as they consider necessary to satisfy themselves as to the accuracy of an electronic return or a paper return delivered in relation to an instrument required to be stamped.

(9) Where an amended electronic return or an amended paper return is delivered in relation to an instrument required to be stamped by means of the e-stamping system, there shall be included on that amended return an assessment to be substituted for an earlier assessment.][2]

Amendments

[1] Inserted by FA13 s77(a).

[2] Substituted by FA12 sched3(10). In effect for all instruments that are executed on or after 7 July 2012 per S.I. No. 228 of 2012.

21 Right of appeal of persons dissatisfied with assessment or decision

[(1) In this section—

'*Appeal Commissioners*' has the meaning assigned to it by *section 850* of the Taxes Consolidation Act 1997;

["*time for bringing an appeal*" means 30 days after the date of the assessment.][1]

[(2) An accountable person who is dissatisfied with an assessment of the Commissioners in relation to an instrument may appeal to the Appeal Commissioners against the assessment on giving, within the time for bringing an appeal, notice in writing to the Commissioners and the appeal shall be heard and determined by the Appeal Commissioners whose determination shall be final and conclusive unless the appeal is required to be reheard by a judge of the Circuit Court or a case is required to be stated in relation to it for the opinion of the High Court on a point of law.][2]

[(3) No appeal may be made against—

(a) an assessment made by an accountable person, or

(b) an assessment made on an accountable person by the Commissioners, where the duty had been agreed between the Commissioners and the accountable person, or any person authorised by the accountable person in that behalf, before the making of the assessment.][3]

[4 (a) Where—

(i) an accountable person fails to cause an electronic return or a paper return to be delivered in relation to an instrument, or

(ii) the Commissioners are not satisfied with the electronic return or the paper return which has been delivered, or have received any information as to its insufficiency,

and the Commissioners make an assessment in accordance with *section 20*, no appeal may be made against that assessment unless within the time for bringing an appeal—

(I) in a case to which *subparagraph (i)* applies, an electronic return or a paper return is delivered to the Commissioners, and

(II) in a case to which either *subparagraph (i)* or *(ii)* applies, the accountable person pays or has paid an amount of duty on foot of the assessment which is not less than the duty which would be payable on foot of the assessment if the assessment were made in all respects by reference to the return delivered to the Commissioners.][4]

(b) References in this subsection to an amount of duty shall be construed as including a surcharge under *section 14A(3)* and any amount of interest which would be due and payable on that duty, calculated in accordance with *section 159D*, at the date of payment of the duty, together with any costs incurred or other amounts which may be charged or levied in pursuing the collection of the duty contained in the assessment.

(5) Where an appeal is brought against an assessment made on an accountable person in relation to an instrument required to be stamped by means of the e-stamping system, the accountable person shall specify in the notice of appeal—

(a) each amount or matter in the assessment with which the accountable person is aggrieved, and

(b) the grounds in detail of the accountable person's appeal as respects each such amount or matter.

(6) Where, as respects an amount or matter to which a notice of appeal relates, the notice does not comply with *subsection (5)*, the notice shall, in so far as it relates to that amount or matter, be invalid and the appeal concerned shall, in so far as it relates to that amount or matter, be deemed not to have been brought.

(7) The accountable person shall not be entitled to rely on any ground of appeal that is not specified in the notice of appeal unless the Appeal Commissioners, or the Judge of the Circuit Court, as the case may be, are or is satisfied that the ground could not reasonably have been stated in the notice.

(8) Notwithstanding *subsection (2)*—

(a) any person dissatisfied with any decision of the Commissioners as to the value of any land for the purpose of an assessment under this Act may appeal against such decision in the manner prescribed by *section 33* (as amended by the Property Values (Arbitrations and Appeals) Act 1960) of the Finance (1909-10) Act 1910, and so much of Part I of that Act as relates to appeals shall apply to an appeal under this subsection;

(b) an appeal shall not lie under *subsection (2)* on any question relating to the value of any land.

(9) An accountable person who is aggrieved by a decision of the Commissioners under *section 8C(5)* that an expression of doubt is not genuine may, by giving notice in writing to the Commissioners within the period of 30 days after the notification of the said decision, require the matter to be referred to the Appeal Commissioners and on the hearing of an appeal under this subsection, the Appeal Commissioners shall have regard only to whether the expression of doubt is genuine.

(10) Subject to this section, *Chapter 1* of *Part 40* (which relates to appeals) of the Taxes Consoli dation Act 1997 shall, with any necessary modifications, apply as they apply for the purpose of income tax.][5]

Amendments

[1] Substituted by FA13 s77(b).

[2] Substituted by FA13 s77(c).

[3] Substituted by FA13 s77(d).

[4] Substituted by FA13 s77(e).

[5] Substituted by FA12 sched3(11). In effect for all instruments that are executed on or after 7 July 2012 per S.I. No. 228 of 2012.

PART 5

Provisions Applicable to Particular Instruments

CHAPTER 1

Bills of Exchange and Promissory Notes

22 Bills and notes purporting to be drawn outside the State [Deleted]

Deleted by FA07 s101(1)(d). This section applies to instruments drawn, made or executed on or after 2 April 2007.

23 Restriction on stamping after execution

[SA1891 s37(2)]

No bill of exchange […][1] shall be stamped with an impressed stamp after its execution.

Amendments

[1] Deleted by FA07 s101(1)(e). This section applies to instruments drawn, made or executed on or after 2 April 2007

24 One bill only of a set need be stamped [Deleted]

Deleted by FA07 s101(1)(d). This section applies to instruments drawn, made or executed on or after 2 April 2007

25 Denotion of duty by adhesive stamps

[FA1970 s41(2) and (3)]

(1) The duty on a bill of exchange […][1] may be denoted by an adhesive stamp which shall be cancelled by the person by whom the bill or note is signed before such person delivers it out of his or her hands, custody or power.

(2) Every person who issues, endorses, transfers, negotiates, presents for payment, or pays any bill of exchange […][2] liable to duty and not being duly stamped shall incur a penalty of [€630][3], and the person who takes or receives from any other person any such bill […][4] either in payment or as a security, or by purchase or otherwise, shall not be entitled to recover on such bill […][5], or to make the same available for any purpose.

(3) Notwithstanding *subsection (2)*, if any bill of exchange is presented for payment unstamped, the person to whom it is presented may affix to it an adhesive stamp of the amount of duty chargeable under this Act in respect of that bill, and cancel the same, as if he or she had been the drawer of that bill, and may, having affixed the stamp and cancelled it, pay the sum in that bill mentioned, and charge the duty in account against the person by whom that bill was drawn, or deduct the duty from that sum, and that bill shall, so far as respects the duty, be deemed valid and available.

(4) The affixing of an adhesive stamp to a bill of exchange in accordance with *subsection (3)* shall not relieve any person from any penalty incurred by such person in relation to such bill.

Amendments

[1] Deleted by FA07 s101(1)(f)(i). This section applies to instruments drawn, made or executed on or after 2 April 2007

[2] Deleted by FA07 s101(1)(f)(ii)(I). This section applies to instruments drawn, made or executed on or after 2 April 2007

[3] Substituted by FA01 sched5.

[4, 5] Deleted by FA07 s101(1)(f)(ii)(II). This section applies to instruments drawn, made or executed on or after 2 April 2007

26 Certain bills issued by local authorities to be chargeable as promissory notes [Deleted]

Deleted by FA07 s101(1)(d). This section applies to instruments drawn, made or executed on or after 2 April 2007

27 Stamping of certain foreign bills of exchange

[FA1936 s25]

Notwithstanding any enactment to the contrary, a bill of exchange which is presented for acceptance or is accepted or payable outside the State shall not be invalid in the State by reason only that it is not stamped in accordance with the law for the time being in force in the State in relation to stamp duties, and *sections 14(1)* and *127* shall apply to every such bill of exchange which is unstamped or insufficiently or not properly stamped as if it were an instrument which may legally be stamped after it has been executed within the meaning of *sections 14(1)* and *127*.

Cross References

From Section 27

Section 14 Penalty on stamping instruments after execution.
Section 127 Terms on which instruments not duly stamped may be received in evidence.

28 Notes promising the payment of sum of money out of a particular fund, etc. [Deleted]

Deleted by FA07 s101(1)(d). This section applies to instruments drawn, made or executed on or after 2 April 2007

CHAPTER 2

Conveyances on Sale

29 Conveyance on sale combined with building agreement for dwellinghouse or apartment

[FA1990 s112(1) to (8) (part)]

(1) (a) In this section—

"*building*" includes any improvement of any land, and any alteration to the character of any land, preliminary to the erection on that land of a dwellinghouse or apartment;

"*land*" includes any interest in any land but does not include the result of any act of building.

(b) For the purposes of this section, references to the repayment of stamp duty to a person who paid it include reference to any other person who satisfies the Commissioners that he or she is entitled to recover moneys owing to the person.

(2) Notwithstanding *section 43*, where, in connection with, or as part of any arrangement involving, a sale of any land, a dwellinghouse or apartment has been built, or is in the course of being built, or is to be built, on that land, any instrument whereby such sale is effected shall be chargeable to stamp duty under the heading "CONVEYANCE or TRANSFER on sale of any property other than stocks or marketable securities or a policy of insurance or a policy of life insurance" in *Schedule 1*, as if the property concerned were residential property on an amount equal to the aggregate of—

(a) any consideration paid in respect of the sale of that land, and

(b) any consideration paid, or to be paid, in respect of the building of the dwellinghouse or apartment on that land.

(3) Without prejudice to the generality of *subsection (2)*, a dwellinghouse or apartment shall be regarded as having been built or being in the course of being built or to be built in connection with, or as part of any arrangement involving, a sale of any land where building has commenced prior to the execution of any instrument effecting the sale.

(4) (a) Where in the case of any instrument of sale to which this section applies, the aggregate consideration to which *subsection (2)* relates cannot [...][1] be ascertained at the date on which the instrument is presented for stamping, then the instrument shall be chargeable to stamp duty as if the amount of the aggregate consideration which is chargeable under *subsection (2)* was equal to 10 times the unencumbered open market value of the land at the date of the instrument of sale [...][2].

(b) Where it is shown to the satisfaction of the Commissioners that the amount of the stamp duty paid under this subsection exceeded the stamp duty with which the instrument would have been charged under *subsection (2)* had the aggregate consideration paid or to be paid in respect of the dwellinghouse or apartment been ascertainable at the date of stamping of the instrument, then the amount of such excess stamp duty shall, on an application to the Commissioners within 3 years after the date of stamping of the instrument, be repaid to the person or persons by whom the stamp duty was paid and such repayment shall bear simple interest at the rate of [0.0161 per cent, or such other rate (if any) as stands prescribed by the Minister by regulations, for each day or part of a day][3] from the date of payment of the excess duty up until the date of such repayment and income tax shall not be deductible on payment of interest under this subsection and such interest shall not be reckoned in computing income for the purposes of the Tax Acts.

(5) For the purpose of determining whether this section shall apply to any instrument, the Commissioners may require the delivery to them, in such form as they may specify, of a statement or a statutory declaration by—

(a) any person directly or indirectly concerned with the sale of the land or with the building of a dwellinghouse or apartment on the land, and

(b) any solicitor acting on behalf of any person to whom *paragraph (a)* relates, of any facts which the Commissioners consider relevant in making any such determination.

[...][4].

(7) Where stamp duty has been charged on any instrument by reference to this section and, within 2 years after the date of stamping of the instrument, building has not commenced, then this section shall be deemed not to have applied to the instrument and, accordingly, the Commissioners shall, on application to them within 3 years after the date of stamping of the instrument by the person or persons by whom the stamp duty was paid, repay to such person or persons the amount of the stamp duty paid by such person or persons which, but for the other provisions of this section, would not have been chargeable and such repayment shall bear simple interest at the rate of [0.0161 per cent, or such other rate (if any) as stands prescribed by the Minister by regulations, for each day or part of a day][5] from the date of payment of the excess duty up until the date of such repayment and income tax shall not be deductible on payment of interest under this subsection and such interest shall not be reckoned in computing income for the purposes of the Tax Acts.

(8) Every regulation made under this section shall be laid before Dáil Éireann as soon as may be after it is made and, if a resolution annulling the regulation is passed by Dáil Éireann within the next 21 days on which Dáil Éireann has sat after the regulation is laid before it, the regulation shall be annulled accordingly, but without prejudice to the validity of anything previously done under that regulation.

Amendments

[1, 2] Deleted by FA12 sched3(12)(a). In effect for all instruments that are executed on or after 7 July 2012 per S.I. No. 228 of 2012.

[3, 5] Substituted by FA02 s129(6)(c).

[4] Deleted by FA12 sched3(12)(b). In effect for all instruments that are executed on or after 7 July 2012 per S.I. No. 228 of 2012.

Revenue Briefings

Tax Briefing

Tax Briefing June 2001 – Issue 44 (part 2) pg 30 – Revenue Certificates in Deeds

Revenue Information Notes

SD10A – Revenue Certificates Required In Deeds (for deeds prior to 8 December 2010)

Cross References

From Section 29

Section 43 Further consideration in respect of substantial improvements not chargeable.
Schedule 1 Stamp Duties on Instruments

To Section 29

Section 44 Procedure to apply where consideration, etc., cannot be ascertained.
Section 92 New dwellinghouses and apartments with no floor area certificate.
Section 92B Residential property first time purchaser relief.

30 Voluntary dispositions inter vivos chargeable as conveyances or transfers on sale

[F(1909-10)A1910 s74(1), (2), (5) and (6)]

(1) Any conveyance or transfer operating as a voluntary disposition inter vivos shall be chargeable with the same stamp duty as if it were a conveyance or transfer on sale, with the substitution in each case of the value of the property conveyed or transferred for the amount or value of the consideration for the sale.

(2) Notwithstanding *subsection (1)*, this section shall not apply to a conveyance or transfer operating as a voluntary disposition of property to a body of persons incorporated by a special Act, if that body is by its Act precluded from dividing any profit among its members and the property conveyed is to be held for the purposes of an open space or for the purposes of its preservation for the benefit of the nation.

[...][1]

(4) Any conveyance or transfer (not being a disposition made in favour of a purchaser or incumbrancer or other person in good faith and for valuable consideration) shall, for the purposes of this section, be deemed to be a conveyance or transfer operating as a voluntary disposition inter vivos, and the consideration for any conveyance or transfer shall not for this purpose be deemed to be valuable consideration where marriage is the consideration, or part of the consideration, or where the Commissioners are of opinion that by reason of the inadequacy of the sum paid as consideration or other circumstances the conveyance or transfer confers a substantial benefit on the person to whom the property is conveyed or transferred.

(5) *Subsections (1)* to *(4)* shall not apply in relation to conveyances or transfers coming within any of the following classes (whether the circumstances by virtue of which the conveyance or transfer comes within any such class are or are not stated in the conveyance or transfer), that is, a conveyance or transfer—

(a) made for nominal consideration for the purpose of securing the repayment of an advance or loan,

(b) made for effectuating the appointment of a new trustee or the retirement of a trustee (whether the trust is expressed or implied),

(c) under which no beneficial interest passes in the property conveyed or transferred,

(d) made to a beneficiary by a trustee or other person in a fiduciary capacity under any trust whether expressed or implied, or

(e) which is a disentailing assurance not limiting any new estate other than an estate in fee simple in the person disentailing the property.

Amendments

[1] Deleted by FA12 sched3(13). In effect for all instruments that are executed on or after 7 July 2012 per S.I. No. 228 of 2012.

Cross References

From Section 30

Section 20 Assessment of duty by the Commissioners.

Section 127 Terms on which instruments not duly stamped may be received in evidence.

To Section 30

Section 1 Interpretation.

Section 8 Facts and circumstances affecting duty to be set forth in instruments, etc.

Section 15 Surcharges for undervaluation in case of voluntary dispositions inter vivos.
Section 18 Mode of valuing property.
Section 33 Conveyance or transfer in contemplation of sale.
Section 46 Directions as to sub-sales.
Section 54 Leases deemed to operate as voluntary dispositions inter vivos.
Section 71 Application and adaptation of other Parts of this Act.
Section 92B Residential property first time purchaser relief.
Section 96 Transfers between spouses.
Section 97 Certain transfers following the dissolution of a marriage.
Schedule 4 Consequential Amendments

31 Certain contracts to be chargeable as conveyances on sale

[SA1891 s59(1) to (3), (6) and (7)]

(1) Any contract or agreement—

(a) for the sale of any equitable estate or interest in any property, or

(b) for the sale of any estate or interest in any property except lands, tenements, hereditaments, or heritages, or property locally situated outside the State, or goods, wares or merchandise, or stock or marketable securities (being stock or marketable securities other than any share warrant issued in accordance with section 88 of the Companies Act, 1963), or any ship or vessel or aircraft, or part interest, share, or property of or in any ship or vessel or aircraft,

shall be charged with the same ad valorem duty, to be paid by the purchaser, as if it were an actual conveyance on sale of the estate, interest, or property contracted or agreed to be sold.

(2) Where the purchaser has paid the ad valorem duty in accordance with *subsection (1)* and before having obtained a conveyance or transfer of the property enters into a contract or agreement for the sale of the same, the contract or agreement shall be charged, if the consideration for that sale is in excess of the consideration for the original sale, with the ad valorem duty payable in respect of such excess consideration, but shall not otherwise be chargeable with duty.

(3) Where duty has been duly paid in conformity with *subsections (1)* and *(2)*, the conveyance or transfer made to the purchaser or sub-purchaser, or any other person on his or her behalf or by his or her direction, shall not be chargeable with any duty, and the Commissioners, on application, either shall denote the payment of the ad valorem duty on the conveyance or transfer, or shall transfer the ad valorem duty to the conveyance or transfer on production of the contract or agreement, or contracts or agreements, duly stamped.

(4) The ad valorem duty paid on any contract or agreement to which this section applies shall be returned by the Commissioners in case the contract or agreement be afterwards rescinded or annulled, or for any other reason be not substantially performed or carried into effect, so as to operate as or be followed by a conveyance or transfer.

Case Law

The Act does not distinguish between the terms 'contract' and 'agreement'. Corey v IRC 1965 2 All ER 45

Revenue Briefings

Tax Briefing

Tax Briefing April 2010 – Issue 05 – Stamp Duty and the Land and Conveyancing Law Reform Act 2009

Cross References

To Section 31

Schedule 4 Consequential Amendments

31A Resting in contract

[(1) Where—

(a) the holder of an estate or interest in land in the State enters into a contract or agreement with another person for the sale of the estate or interest to that other person or to a nominee of that other person, and

(b) a payment which amounts to, or as the case may be payments which together amount to, 25 per cent or more of the consideration for the sale has been paid to, or at the direction of, the holder of the estate or interest at any time pursuant to the contract or agreement,

then the contract or agreement shall be chargeable with the same stamp duty, to be paid by the other person, as if it were a conveyance or transfer of the estate or interest in the land.

(2) *Subsection (1)* does not apply where, within 30 days of the date on which a payment which amounts to, or as the case may be payments which together amount to, 25 per cent or more of the consideration for the sale referred to in *subsection (1)* has been paid—

(a) an electronic return or paper return has been delivered to the Commissioners in relation to a conveyance or transfer made in conformity with the contract or agreement referred to in *subsection (1)*, and

(b) the stamp duty chargeable on the conveyance or transfer has been paid to the Commissioners.

(3) Where stamp duty has been paid, in respect of a contract or agreement, in accordance with *subsection (1)*, a conveyance or transfer made in conformity with the contract or agreement shall not be chargeable with any duty, and the Commissioners, where an electronic return or paper return has been delivered to them in relation to the conveyance or transfer, shall either denote the payment of the duty on the conveyance or transfer or transfer the duty to the conveyance or transfer on production to them of the contract or agreement, duly stamped.

(4) The stamp duty paid on any contract or agreement, in accordance with *subsection (1)*, shall be returned where it is shown to the satisfaction of the Commissioners that the contract or agreement has been rescinded or annulled.][1]

Amendments

[1] Inserted by FA13 s78(1)(a). Applies as respects instruments executed on or after 13 February 2013 other than instruments executed solely in pursuance of a binding contract or agreement entered into before 13 February 2013.

Note FA13 s78(2)

Section 82 (other than subsection (2) of that section) of Finance (No. 2) Act 2008 is repealed.

Cross References

From Section 31A
Section 843A

31B Licence agreements

[(1) In this section "*development*", in relation to any land, means—

(a) the construction, demolition, extension, alteration or reconstruction of any building on the land, or

(b) any engineering or other operation in, on, over or under the land to adapt it for materially altered use.

(2) Where—

(a) the holder of an estate or interest in land in the State enters into an agreement with another person under which that other person, or a nominee of that other person, is entitled to enter onto the land to carry out development on that land, and

(b) by virtue of the agreement, otherwise than as consideration for the sale of all or part of the estate or interest in the land, the holder of the estate or interest in the land receives at any time a payment which amounts to, or as the case may be payments which together amount to, 25 per cent or more of the market value of the land concerned,

which together amount to, 25 per cent or more of the market value of the land concerned,

then within 30 days of the first such time, the agreement shall be chargeable with the same stamp duty, to be paid by that other person, as if it were a conveyance or transfer of the estate or interest in the land.

(3) The stamp duty paid on any agreement, in accordance with *subsection (2)*, shall be returned where it is shown to the satisfaction of the Commissioners that the agreement has been rescinded or annulled.][1]

Amendments

[1] Inserted by FA13 s78(1)(a). Applies as respects instruments executed on or after 13 February 2013 other than instruments executed solely in pursuance of a binding contract or agreement entered into before 13 February 2013.

Note FA13 s78(2)

Section 82 (other than subsection (2) of that section) of Finance (No. 2) Act 2008 is repealed.

Cross References

From Section 31B

Section 3 Variation of certain rates of duty by order.

32 As to sale of an annuity or right not before in existence

[SA1891 s60]

Where on the sale of any annuity or other right not previously in existence such annuity or other right is not created by actual grant or conveyance, but is only secured by bond, warrant of attorney, covenant, contract, or otherwise, the bond or other instrument, or some one of such instruments, if there be more than one, is to be charged with the same duty as an actual grant or conveyance, and is for the purposes of this Act to be deemed an instrument of conveyance on sale.

33 Conveyance or transfer in contemplation of sale

[FA1978 s34(1) to (4)]

(1) Subject to this section, any instrument whereby property is conveyed or transferred to any person in contemplation of a sale of that property shall be treated for the purposes of this Act as a conveyance or transfer on sale of that property for a consideration equal to the value of that property.

(2) [In relation to an instrument chargeable with duty in accordance with *subsection (1)*, if on a claim made to the Commissioners not later than 4 years from the date the instrument was stamped by the Commissioners,][1] it is shown to their satisfaction—

(a) that the sale in contemplation of which the instrument was made or executed has not taken place and the property has been reconveyed or retransferred to the person from whom it was conveyed or transferred or to a person to whom his or her rights have been transmitted on death or bankruptcy, or

(b) that the sale has taken place for a consideration which is less than the value in respect of which duty was paid on the instrument by virtue of this section,

the Commissioners shall repay the duty paid by virtue of this section, in a case falling under *paragraph (a)*, so far as it exceeds the stamp duty which would have been payable apart from this section and, in a case falling under *paragraph (b)*, so far as it exceeds the stamp duty which would have been payable if the instrument had been stamped in accordance with *subsection (1)* in respect of a value equal to the consideration in question.

(3) In a case to which *subsection (2)(b)* relates, duty shall not be repayable if it appears to the Commissioners that the circumstances are such that a conveyance or transfer on the sale in question would have been chargeable with duty under *section 30* by virtue of *subsection (4)* of that section.

[...][2]

(5) This section shall apply whether or not an instrument conveys or transfers other property in addition to the property in contemplation of the sale of which it is made or executed, but this section shall not affect the stamp duty chargeable on the instrument in respect of that other property.

Amendments

[1] Substituted by FA12 sched3(14). In effect for all instruments that are executed on or after 7 July 2012 per S.I. No. 228 of 2012.

[2] Deleted by FA12 sched3(15). In effect for all instruments that are executed on or after 7 July 2012 per S.I. No. 228 of 2012.

Cross References

From Section 33

Section 20 Assessment of duty by the Commissioners.

Section 30 Voluntary dispositions inter vivos chargeable as conveyances or transfers on sale.

To Section 33

Section 18 Mode of valuing property.

34 Agreements in connection with, or in contemplation of, sale

[FA1986 s96(1)]

[Notwithstanding section 37, where,][1] in connection with, or in contemplation of, [a sale of property, or an exchange of property within the meaning of section 37, as the case may be,][2] [the vendor, or the transferor, as the case may be,][3] enters into—

(a) an agreement for the grant of a lease of the property for a term exceeding 35 years, or

(b) an agreement (other than a contract for the sale of the property) under which [the vendor, or the transferor, as the case may be,][4] grants any other rights in relation to the property,

any conveyance or transfer, subject to the agreement, of the property by [the vendor, or the transferor, as the case may be,][5] shall be charged to stamp duty as a conveyance or transfer on sale of the property for a consideration equal to the value of the property and the value shall be determined without regard to the agreement.

Amendments

[1] Substituted by F(No.2)A08 s83(1)(a). Applies as respects conveyances or transfers executed on or after 20 November 2008.

[2] Substituted by F(No.2)A08 s83(1)(b). Applies as respects conveyances or transfers executed on or after 20 November 2008.

[3, 4, 5] Substituted by F(No.2)A08 s83(1)(c). Applies as respects conveyances or transfers executed on or after 20 November 2008.

35 Deeds of enlargement

[FA1986 s96(2) and (3)]

(1) A declaration by deed under section 65(2) of the Conveyancing Act, 1881, to the effect that, from and after the execution of the deed, a term subsisting in land shall be enlarged, shall, where the term was created by an instrument executed within 6 years of the date of the execution of the deed, be charged to stamp duty as a conveyance or transfer on sale of that land for a consideration equal to the value of the land and that value shall be determined without regard to that term or any part of that term.

(2) *Section 82* shall not apply to a deed which is chargeable to stamp duty under *subsection (1)*.

Cross References

From Section 35

Section 82 Charities.

36 Certain contracts for sale of leasehold interests to be chargeable as conveyances on sale [Deleted]

Deleted by FA13 s78(1)(b). Applies as respects instruments executed on or after 13 February 2013 other than instruments executed solely in pursuance of a binding contract or agreement entered into before 13 February 2013.

Note FA13 s78(2)

Section 82 (other than subsection (2) of that section) of Finance (No. 2) Act 2008 is repealed. Section 82(1)(b) of that Act deleted section 36 but was subject to Commencement Order.

37 Exchanges

[FA1993 s104(2)]

Any instrument effecting a conveyance or transfer of any immovable property in exchange for any other property, wherever situated, whether movable or immovable and with or without the payment of any consideration, shall be chargeable in respect of such conveyance or transfer under the heading "CONVEYANCE or TRANSFER on sale of any property other than stocks or marketable securities or a policy of insurance or a policy of life insurance" in *Schedule 1*, with the substitution of the value of immovable property situated in the State thereby conveyed or transferred for the amount or value of the consideration for the sale.

Cross References

From Section 37

Schedule 1 Stamp Duties on Instruments

To Section 37

Section 81B Farm consolidation relief.
Schedule 1 Stamp Duties on Instruments

38 Partitions or divisions

[SA1891 s73]

(1) Where on the partition or division of any real or heritable property any consideration exceeding in amount or value [€130][1] is paid or given, or agreed to be paid or given, for equality, the principal or only instrument whereby the partition or division is effected shall be charged with the same ad valorem duty as a conveyance on sale for the consideration, and with that duty only.

(2) Where, in a case to which *subsection (1)* applies, there are several instruments for completing the title of either party, the principal instrument is to be ascertained, and the other instruments are to be charged with duty in the manner provided for in this Act in the case of several instruments of conveyance.

Amendments

[1] Substituted by FA01 sched5 and s240 with effect from 1 January 2002.

Cross References

To Section 38

Schedule 1 Stamp Duties on Instruments

39 Decree or order for foreclosure, etc., and stamp duty

[FA1898 s6 (part)]

(1) In relation to a conveyance on sale, ad valorem stamp duty on a decree or order for, or having the effect of an order for, foreclosure, shall not exceed the duty on a sum equal to the value of the property to which the decree or order relates, and where the decree or order states that value that statement shall be conclusive for the purpose of determining the amount of the duty.

(2) Where ad valorem stamp duty is paid on a decree or order for, or having the effect of an order for, foreclosure, any conveyance following on such decree or order shall be exempt from the ad valorem stamp duty.

40 Calculation of ad valorem duty on stock and securities

[SA1891 s55]

(1) Where the consideration, or any part of the consideration, for a conveyance on sale consists of any stock or marketable security, the conveyance shall be charged with ad valorem duty [in respect of the value of that stock or security on the date of execution of the conveyance.][1]

[(2) Where the consideration, or any part of the consideration, for a conveyance on sale of any property, consists of any security not being a marketable security, the conveyance shall be charged with ad valorem duty as a conveyance on sale of that property for a consideration equal to the value of that property on the date of execution of the conveyance.

(3) For the purposes of subsection (2) "*property*" includes any estate or interest in property.][2]

Amendments

[1] Substituted by FA04 sched3(3). Has effect as on and from 25 March 2004

[2] Substituted by FA05 s116(1). This section applies as respects instruments executed on or after 2 March 2005.

41 Conveyance in consideration of debt

[(1) Where any property is conveyed to any person in consideration, wholly or in part, of any debt due to such person, or subject either certainly or contingently to the payment or transfer of any money or stock, whether being or constituting a charge or incumbrance on the property or not, the debt, money or stock shall be deemed the whole or part, as the case may be, of the consideration in respect of which the conveyance is charged with ad valorem duty.

(2) Where, in connection with or as part of any arrangement involving any conveyance referred to in *subsection (1)* of stock of a company, the transferee procures, either directly or indirectly, the discharge of any indebtedness of the company (in this subsection referred to as the "*first-mentioned company*") or of any other company which is connected with the first-mentioned company within the meaning of section 10 of the Taxes Consolidation Act 1997, and the main or one of the main purposes of the arrangement is to secure a tax advantage, then the conveyance shall, in addition to any other payment of money or transfer of stock to which it is subject (if any), be deemed to be subject to the payment of an amount equal to the amount of such indebtedness.

(3) In *subsection (2)*—

"*arrangement*" includes any agreement, understanding, scheme, transaction or series of transactions (whether or not legally enforceable);

"*tax advantage*" means the avoidance or reduction of a charge to stamp duty.][1]

Amendments

[1] Substituted by FA10 s(136)(1). Applies as respects instruments executed on or after 4 February 2010.

42 Charging of consideration consisting of periodical payments

[SA1891 s56]

(1) Where the consideration, or any part of the consideration, for a conveyance on sale consists of money payable periodically for a definite period not exceeding 20 years, so that the total amount to be paid can be previously ascertained, the conveyance shall be charged in respect of that consideration with ad valorem duty on such total amount.

(2) Where the consideration, or any part of the consideration, for a conveyance on sale consists of money payable periodically for a definite period exceeding 20 years, the conveyance shall be charged in respect of that consideration with ad valorem duty on the total amount which will or may, according to the terms of sale, be payable during the period of 20 years next after the day of the date of the instrument.

(3) Notwithstanding *subsections (1)* and *(2)*, a conveyance on sale chargeable with ad valorem duty in respect of any periodical payments which contains a provision for securing the payments shall not be charged with any duty in respect of such provision, and any separate instrument made in such case for securing the payments shall not be charged with any higher duty than [€12.50][1].

Amendments

[1] Substituted by FA01 sched5.

Cross References

To Section 42

Section 46 Directions as to sub-sales.

43 Further consideration in respect of substantial improvements not chargeable

[FA1900 s10]

A conveyance on sale made for any consideration in respect of which it is chargeable with ad valorem duty and in further consideration of a covenant—

(a) by the purchaser to make, or of the purchaser's having previously made, any substantial improvement of or addition to the property conveyed to such purchaser, or

(b) relating to the subject matter of the conveyance,

shall not be chargeable with any duty in respect of such further consideration.

Cross References

To Section 43

Section 29 Conveyance on sale combined with building agreement for dwellinghouse or apartment.
Section 92 New dwellinghouses and apartments with no floor area certificate.

44 Procedure to apply where consideration, etc., cannot be ascertained

[FA1991 s104 (part)]

(1) Where the consideration for a sale cannot be ascertained at the date of execution of a conveyance and such consideration would, if ascertainable, be chargeable with ad valorem duty in respect of such sale, then stamp duty shall be charged on such sale based on the amount or value of the consideration that could be obtained from a purchaser paying full consideration for such sale.

(2) This section shall not apply to any instrument in relation to which *subsection (4)(a)* of *section 29* applies.

Cross References

From Section 44

Section 29 Conveyance on sale combined with building agreement for dwellinghouse or apartment.

45 Directions as to apportionment of consideration

[SA1891 s58(1) to (3)]

(1) Where property contracted to be sold for one consideration for the whole of it is conveyed to the purchaser in separate parts or parcels by different instruments, then the consideration shall be apportioned in such manner, as the parties think fit, so that a distinct consideration for each separate part or parcel is set forth in the conveyance relating to such separate part or parcel, and such conveyance shall be charged with ad valorem duty in respect of such distinct consideration.

(2) Where—

(a) any property which consists partly of an interest in residential property is sold to any person and the sale (in this subsection referred to as "*the first-mentioned sale*") does not form part of a larger transaction or of a series of transactions, or

(b) the sale to any person of property consisting in whole or in part of such an interest forms part of a larger transaction or of a series of transactions,

then the consideration attributable to the first-mentioned sale and the aggregate consideration (other than rent) attributable to that larger transaction or series of transactions, as the case may be, shall be apportioned, on such basis as is just and reasonable, as between that interest in residential property and the other property or part concerned, and that aggregate consideration shall likewise be apportioned as between each other such interest (if any) comprised in that larger transaction or series of transactions and the other property or parts concerned, and notwithstanding the amount or value of the consideration set forth in any instrument—

(i) the consideration so apportioned to that interest shall be deemed to be the amount or the value of the consideration for the sale which is attributable to that interest and the consideration so apportioned to the aggregate of all such interests comprised in that larger transaction or series of transactions shall be deemed to be the amount or value of that aggregate consideration which is attributable to residential property, and

(ii) the consideration so apportioned to the other property or part or parts concerned shall be deemed to be the amount or value of the consideration for the sale, or of that aggregate consideration, as the case may be, which is attributable to property which is not residential property.

(3) Where property contracted to be purchased for one consideration for the whole of it by 2 or more persons jointly, or by any person for such person and others, or wholly for others, is conveyed in parts or parcels by separate instruments to the persons by or for whom the same was purchased for distinct parts of the consideration, then the conveyance of each separate part or parcel shall be charged with ad valorem duty in respect of the distinct part of the consideration specified in the conveyance.

(4) Where there are several instruments of conveyance for completing the purchaser's title to property sold, the principal instrument of conveyance only shall be charged with ad valorem duty, and the other instruments shall be respectively charged with such other duty as they may be liable to, but the last-mentioned duty shall not exceed the ad valorem duty payable in respect of the principal instrument.

Cross References

To Section 45

Section 16 Surcharges to apply when apportionment is not just and reasonable.
Section 90A Greenhouse gas emissions allowance.
Section 101 Intellectual property.
Section 101A Single farm payment entitlement.

45A Aggregation of transactions

[(1) In this section "*dwellinghouse*" includes apartment.

(2) Where an existing interest or, as the case may be, existing interests, in a dwellinghouse are conveyed or transferred by more than one instrument, executed within a period of 12 months, *subsection (3)* shall apply to each of those instruments which operate as a conveyance or transfer, whether on sale or as a voluntary disposition inter vivos.

(3) An instrument to which this subsection applies shall be deemed for the purposes of the Heading "CONVEYANCE or TRANSFER on sale of any property other than stocks or marketable securities or a policy of insurance or a policy of life insurance" in *Schedule 1* to form part of a larger transaction or of a series of transactions in respect of which the amount or value, or the aggregate amount or value, of the consideration which is attributable to residential property[is equal to the value of the dwellinghouse.][1]

(4) Where a conveyance or transfer (referred to in this section as the "*first transfer*") of an interest in a dwellinghouse is effected by one instrument and—

(a) before 1 March 2005 without regard to *subsection (3)*, and

(b) on or after 1 March 2005 with or without regard to *subsection (3)*,

the duty chargeable (if any) in respect of the instrument has been accounted for to the Commissioners, and one or more conveyances or transfers (referred to in this section as "*subsequent transfers*") of other interests in the same dwellinghouse are effected within the subsequent 12 month period, the transferee or where there is more than one transferee, each such transferee, being a party to the first transfer, jointly and severally, shall become liable to pay to the Commissioners [an amount (in this subsection referred to as a "*clawback*")][2] equal to the amount of the difference between—

(i) the amount of duty chargeable if the first transfer was one to which *subsection (3)* applied, and

(ii) any duty paid on that first transfer together with the amount of any [clawback][3] previously paid in respect of that first transfer under this subsection,

together with interest charged on that amount at a rate of 0.0322 per cent for each day or part of a day from the date when the instrument was executed to the date when the [clawback is remitted][4].

[...][5]][6]

Amendments

[1] Substituted by FA08 s113(1). Applies as respects instruments executed on or after 5 November 2007.

[2] Substituted by F(No.2)A08 sched5(part5)(chap2)(7)(d)(i).

[3] Substituted by F(No.2)A08 sched5(part5)(chap2)(7)(d)(ii).

[4] Substituted by F(No.2)A08 sched5(part5)(chap2)(7)(d)(iii).

[5] Deleted by FA11 s63(1)(a). Shall not apply as respects any instrument executed before 1 July 2011 where—(a) the effect of the application of that subsection would be to increase the duty otherwise chargeable on the instrument, and (b) the instrument contains a statement, in such form as the Revenue Commissioners may specify, certifying that the instrument was executed solely in pursuance of a binding contract entered into before 8 December 2010.

[6] Inserted by FA05 s117(1). Applies as respects instruments executed on or after 3 February 2005.

Note:

F(No.2)A08 sched5 (part5)(chap 2)(7)

As respects paragraph 7 of this Schedule subparagraphs (a) to (aa) (other than subparagraph (c)(i)(I)) of that paragraph have effect as on and from the passing of this Act and to the extent that Chapter 3A (being inserted into Part 47 of the Taxes Consolidation Act 1997 by Part 1 of this Schedule) applies to penalties incurred under the Stamp Duties Consolidation Act 1999 before the passing of this Act which on the passing of this Act have not been paid, it shall not apply to such penalties which are in the form of interest accrued under any provisions of the said Act.

Cross References

From Section 45A

Schedule 1 Stamp Duties on Instruments

46 Directions as to sub-sales

[SA1891 s58(4) to (9)]

(1) Where—

(a) a person having contracted for the purchase of any property, but not having obtained a conveyance of that property, contracts to sell the same to any other person, and

(b) the property is in consequence conveyed immediately to the sub-purchaser,

then the conveyance shall be charged with ad valorem duty in respect of the consideration moving from the sub-purchaser.

(2) Where—

(a) a person having contracted for the purchase of any property but not having obtained a conveyance contracts to sell the whole, or any part or parts of that property, to any other person or persons, and

(b) the property is in consequence conveyed by the original seller to different persons in parts or parcels,

then the conveyance of each part or parcel shall be charged with ad valorem duty in respect only of the consideration moving from the sub-purchaser of such part or parcel, without regard to the amount or value of the original consideration.

(3) Where—

(a) a sub-purchaser takes an actual conveyance of the interest of the person immediately selling to such sub-purchaser, which is chargeable with ad valorem duty in respect of the consideration moving from such sub-purchaser, and

(b) such conveyance is duly stamped accordingly,

then any conveyance to be afterwards made to such sub-purchaser of the same property by the original seller shall be chargeable only with such other duty as it may be liable to, but the last-mentioned duty shall not exceed the ad valorem duty.

(4) (a) In paragraph *(b)* "*the original seller*" means, in relation to a case to which *subsection (1)* applies, the person from whom the property is conveyed to the sub-purchaser and, in relation to a case to which *subsection (2)* or *(3)* applies, the original seller referred to in *subsection (2)* or *(3)*, as the case may be.

(b) The consideration moving from the sub-purchaser shall, in a case to which *subsection (1)*, *(2)* or *(3)* applies, be ascertained without regard to the value of any covenant, power, condition or arrangement relating to the subject matter of the conveyance which was not in the contract for sale entered into by the original seller and also without regard to any consideration the duty on which or on any part of which would be charged in accordance with *subsection (2)* of *section 42*.

(5) [Paragraph (5)][1] of the heading "CONVEYANCE or TRANSFER on sale of any property other than stocks or marketable securities or a policy of insurance or a policy of life insurance" in *Schedule 1* shall not apply to determine the stamp duty to be charged on any conveyance referred to in *subsection (1)*, *(2)* or *(3)*.

(6) A conveyance in respect of which *subsection (4)* applies shall be deemed to be a conveyance operating as a voluntary disposition inter vivos for the purposes of *section 30*.

Amendments

[1] Substituted by FA13 sched2(2)(a).

Cross References

From Section 46

Section 30 Voluntary dispositions inter vivos chargeable as conveyances or transfers on sale.
Section 42 Charging of consideration consisting of periodical payments.
Schedule 1 Stamp Duties on Instruments

To Section 46

Section 96 Transfers between spouses.
Schedule 4 Consequential Amendments

47 Principal instrument, how to be ascertained

[SA1891 s61(2)]

The parties may determine for themselves which of several instruments is to be deemed the principal instrument, and may pay the ad valorem duty on the principal instrument accordingly.

Cross References

To Section 47

Section 123B Cash, combined and debit cards.

48 Stamp duty and value-added tax

[FA1994 s108(1) (part)]

The consideration chargeable under the heading "CONVEYANCE or TRANSFER on sale of any property other than stocks or marketable securities or a policy of insurance or a policy of life insurance" in *Schedule 1* shall exclude any value-added tax chargeable under section 3 of the Value-Added Tax Consolidation Act 2010, on such sale.

Cross References

From Section 48

Schedule 1 Stamp Duties on Instruments

CHAPTER 3

Conveyances on Any Occasion Except Sale or Mortgage

49 Certain transfers, etc., not sales or mortgages, deemed to be conveyances [Deleted]

Deleted by F(No.2)A08 sched6(2)(a). Has effect as on and from 24 December 2008.

CHAPTER 4

Leases

50 Agreements for not more than 35 years charged as leases

[SA1891 s75(1)]

An agreement for a lease or with respect to the letting of any lands, tenements, or heritable subjects for any term not exceeding 35 years, or for any indefinite term, shall be charged with the same duty as if it were an actual lease made for the term and consideration mentioned in the agreement.

Cross References

To Section 50

Schedule 1 Stamp Duties on Instruments

50A Agreements for more than 35 years charged as leases

[(1) An agreement for a lease or with respect to the letting of any lands, tenements, or heritable subjects for any term exceeding 35 years, shall be charged with the same stamp duty as if it were an actual lease made for the term and consideration mentioned in the agreement where 25 per cent or more of that consideration has been paid.

(2) The stamp duty paid on any agreement for a lease, in accordance with *subsection (1)*, shall be returned where it is shown to the satisfaction of the Commissioners that the agreement for a lease has been rescinded or annulled.][1]

Amendments

[1] Inserted by FA13 s78(1)(c). Applies as respects instruments executed on or after 13 February 2013 other than instruments executed solely in pursuance of a binding contract or agreement entered into before 13 February 2013.

Note FA13 s78(2)

Section 82 (other than subsection (2) of that section) of Finance (No. 2) Act 2008 is repealed.

Cross References

From Section 50A

Section 3 Variation of certain rates of duty by order.

To Section 50A

Schedule 1 Stamp Duties on Instruments

51 Leases how to be charged in respect of produce, etc.

[SA1891 s76]

(1) Where the consideration, or any part of the consideration, for which a lease is granted or agreed to be granted, consists of any produce or other goods, the value of the produce or goods shall be deemed a consideration in respect of which the lease or agreement is chargeable with ad valorem duty.

(2) Where it is stipulated that the value of the produce or goods is to amount at least to, or is not to exceed, a given sum, or where the lessee is specially charged with, or has the option of paying after any permanent rate of conversion, the value of the produce or goods shall, for the purpose of assessing the ad valorem duty, be estimated at the given sum, or according to the permanent rate.

(3) If a lease or agreement for a lease made either wholly or partially for any consideration to which *subsection (1)* relates—

(a) contains a statement of the value of such consideration, and

(b) is stamped in accordance with the statement,

it shall, in respect of the subject matter of the statement, be deemed duly stamped, unless or until it is otherwise shown that the statement is incorrect, and that the lease or agreement is in fact not duly stamped.

52 Charging of duty on leases, etc.

[SA1891 s77(1), (2), (5) and (6); RA1909 s8]

(1) A lease, or agreement for a lease, or with respect to any letting, shall not be charged with any duty in respect of any penal rent, or increased rent in the nature of a penal

rent, thereby reserved or agreed to be reserved or made payable, or by reason of being made in consideration of the surrender or abandonment of any existing lease, or agreement, of or relating to the same subject matter.

(2) A lease made for any consideration in respect of which it is chargeable with ad valorem duty, and in further consideration either of a covenant by the lessee to make, or of such lessee having previously made, any substantial improvement of or addition to the property demised to such lessee, or of any covenant relating to the matter of the lease, shall not be charged with any duty in respect of such further consideration.

(3) *Subsection (2)* shall not apply as respects any further consideration in the lease consisting of a covenant which if it were contained in a separate deed would be chargeable with ad valorem stamp duty and, accordingly, the lease shall in any such case be charged with duty in respect of any such further consideration under *section 7*.

(4) An instrument whereby the rent reserved by any other instrument chargeable with duty and duly stamped as a lease is increased shall not be charged with duty otherwise than as a lease in consideration of the additional rent thereby made payable.

(5) Where—

(a) any property which consists partly of an interest in residential property is leased to any person and that lease (in this subsection referred to as "*the first-mentioned lease*") does not form part of a larger transaction or of a series of transactions, or

(b) the lease to any person of property consisting in whole or in part of such an interest forms part of a larger transaction or of a series of transactions,

then the consideration (other than rent) attributable to the first-mentioned lease and the aggregate consideration (other than rent) attributable to that larger transaction or series of transactions, as the case may be, shall be apportioned, on such basis as is just and reasonable, as between that interest in residential property and the other property or part concerned, and that aggregate consideration shall likewise be apportioned as between each other such interest (if any) comprised in that larger transaction or series of transactions and the other property or parts concerned, and notwithstanding the amount or value of the consideration set forth in any instrument—

(i) the consideration so apportioned to that interest shall be deemed to be the amount or the value of the consideration for the lease which is attributable to that interest and the consideration so apportioned to the aggregate of all such interests comprised in that larger transaction or series of transactions shall be deemed to be the amount or value of that aggregate consideration which is attributable to residential property, and

(ii) the consideration so apportioned to the other property or part or parts concerned shall be deemed to be the amount or value of the consideration for the lease, or of that aggregate consideration, as the case may be, which is attributable to property which is not residential property.

Cross References

From Section 52

Section 7 Instruments to be separately charged with duty in certain cases.

To Section 52

Section 16 Surcharges to apply when apportionment is not just and reasonable.

Section 53 Lease combined with building agreement for dwellinghouse or apartment.

Section 92 New dwellinghouses and apartments with no floor area certificate.

53 Lease combined with building agreement for dwellinghouse or apartment

[FA1990 s112(1) to (8) (part)]

(1) (a) In this section—

"*building*" includes any improvement of any land, and any alteration to the character of any land, preliminary to the erection on that land of a dwellinghouse or apartment;

"*land*" includes any interest in any land but does not include the result of any act of building.

(b) For the purposes of this section, references to the repayment of stamp duty to a person who paid it include reference to any other person who satisfies the Commissioners that such person is entitled to recover moneys owing to the person.

(2) Notwithstanding *subsection (2)* of *section 52,* where, in connection with, or as part of any arrangement involving, a lease of any land, a dwellinghouse or apartment has been built, or is in the course of being built, or is to be built, on that land, any instrument whereby such lease is effected shall be chargeable to stamp duty under *subparagraph (a)* of *paragraph (3)* of the heading "*LEASE*" in *Schedule 1*, as if the property concerned were residential property on an amount equal to the aggregate of—

(a) any consideration (other than rent) paid in respect of the lease of that land, and

(b) any consideration paid, or to be paid, in respect of the building of the dwellinghouse or apartment on that land.

(3) Without prejudice to the generality of *subsection (2)*, a dwellinghouse or apartment shall be regarded as having been built or being in the course of being built or to be built in connection with, or as part of any arrangement involving, a lease of any land where building has commenced prior to the execution of any instrument effecting the lease.

(4) (a) Where in the case of any instrument of lease to which this section applies, the aggregate consideration to which *subsection (2)* relates cannot [...][1] be ascertained at the date on which the instrument is presented for stamping, then the instrument shall be chargeable to stamp duty as if the amount of the aggregate consideration which is chargeable under *subsection (2)* was equal to 10 times the unencumbered open market value of the land at the date of the instrument of lease [...][2]

(b) Where it is shown to the satisfaction of the Commissioners that the amount of the stamp duty paid under this subsection exceeded the stamp duty with which the instrument would have been charged under *subsection (2)* had the aggregate consideration paid or to be paid in respect of the dwellinghouse or apartment been ascertainable at the date of stamping of the instrument, then the amount of such excess stamp duty shall, on an application to the Commissioners within 3 years after the date of stamping of the instrument, be repaid to the person or persons by whom the stamp duty was paid and such repayment shall bear simple interest at the rate of [0.0161 per cent, or such other rate (if any) as stands prescribed by the Minister by regulations, for each day or part of a day][3] from the date of payment of the excess duty up until the date of such repayment and income tax shall not be deductible on payment of interest under this subsection and such interest shall not be reckoned in computing income for the purposes of the Tax Acts.

(5) For the purpose of determining whether this section shall apply to any instrument, the Commissioners may require the delivery to them, in such form as they may specify, of a statement or a statutory declaration by—

(a) any person directly or indirectly concerned with the lease of the land or with the building of a dwellinghouse or apartment on the land, and

(b) any solicitor acting on behalf of any person to whom *paragraph (a)* relates,

of any facts which the Commissioners consider relevant in making any such determination.

[...][4]

(7) Where stamp duty has been charged on any instrument by reference to this section and, within 2 years after the date of stamping of the instrument, building has not commenced, then this section shall be deemed not to have applied to the instrument and, accordingly, the Commissioners shall, on application to them within 3 years after the date of stamping of the instrument by the person or persons by whom the stamp duty was paid, repay to such person or persons the amount of the stamp duty paid by such person or persons which, but for the other provisions of this section, would not have been chargeable and such repayment shall bear simple interest at the rate of [0.0161 per cent, or such other rate (if any) as stands prescribed by the Minister by regulations, for each day or part of a day][5] from the date of payment of the excess duty up until the date of such repayment and income tax shall not be deductible on payment of interest under this subsection and such interest shall not be reckoned in computing income for the purposes of the Tax Acts.

(8) Every regulation made under this section shall be laid before Dáil Éireann as soon as may be after it is made and, if a resolution annulling the regulation is passed by Dáil Éireann within the next 21 days on which Dáil Éireann has sat after the regulation is laid before it, the regulation shall be annulled accordingly, but without prejudice to the validity of anything previously done under that regulation.

Amendments

[1, 2] Deleted by FA12 sched3(16)(a). In effect for all instruments that are executed on or after 7 July 2012 per S.I. No. 228 of 2012.

[3, 5] Substituted by FA02 s129(6)(c).

[4] Deleted by FA12 sched3(16)(b). In effect for all instruments that are executed on or after 7 July 2012 per S.I. No. 228 of 2012.

Revenue Briefings

Tax Briefing

Tax Briefing June 2001 – Issue 44 (part 2) pg 30 – Revenue Certificates in Deeds

Revenue Information Notes

SD10A – Revenue Certificates Required In Deeds (for deeds prior to 8 December 2010)

Cross References

From Section 53

Section 52 Charging of duty on leases, etc.
Schedule 1 Stamp Duties on Instruments

To Section 53

Section 55 Procedure to apply where consideration, etc., cannot be ascertained.
Section 92 New dwellinghouses and apartments with no floor area certificate.
Section 92B Residential property first time purchaser relief.

54 Leases deemed to operate as voluntary dispositions inter vivos

[FA1949 s24]

(1) Any lease, not being executed in good faith and for valuable consideration, shall, for the purposes of this section, be deemed to be a lease operating as a voluntary disposition inter vivos, and the consideration for any lease shall not, for this purpose, be deemed to be valuable consideration where the Commissioners are of opinion that, by reason of the inadequacy of consideration or other circumstances, the lease confers a substantial benefit on the lessee.

(2) Where by operation of this section any lease is deemed to operate as a voluntary disposition inter vivos the reference to consideration (other than rent) in the heading "*LEASE*" in *Schedule 1* shall be construed in relation to duty chargeable on such lease as a reference to the minimum amount or value that would be necessary in order that the lease, any rent under the lease remaining unchanged, would not be a lease operating as a voluntary disposition inter vivos.

[...][1]

Amendments

[1] Deleted by FA12 sched3(17). In effect for all instruments that are executed on or after 7 July 2012 per S.I. No. 228 of 2012.

Cross References

From Section 54

Section 30 Voluntary dispositions inter vivos chargeable as conveyances or transfers on sale.
Schedule 1 Stamp Duties on Instruments

To Section 54

Section 1 Interpretation.
Section 8 Facts and circumstances affecting duty to be set forth in instruments, etc.
Section 15 Surcharges for undervaluation in case of voluntary dispositions inter vivos.

55 Procedure to apply where consideration, etc., cannot be ascertained

[FA1991 s104 (part)]

(1) Where the average annual rent or consideration other than rent for a lease cannot be ascertained at the date of execution of a lease and such consideration or rent would, if ascertainable, be chargeable with ad valorem duty in respect of such lease, then stamp duty shall be charged on such lease based on the amount or value of the consideration or rent that could be obtained from a tenant paying full consideration or rent for such lease.

(2) Where, in the case of a lease to which *subsection (1)* would apply but for the fact that both the rent and the consideration other than rent payable cannot be ascertained, then stamp duty shall be charged on such lease based on the amount or value of the consideration other than rent that could be obtained from a tenant paying full consideration for such lease if the rent reserved in the lease was a nil amount.

(3) This section shall not apply to any instrument in relation to which *subsection (4)(a)* of *section 53* applies.

Cross References

From Section 55

Section 53 Lease combined with building agreement for dwellinghouse or apartment.

56 Stamp duty and value-added tax

[FA1994 s108(1) (part)]

The consideration or rent chargeable under the heading "*LEASE*" in *Schedule 1* shall exclude any value-added tax chargeable under section 3 of the Value-Added Tax Consolidation Act 2010, on such lease.

Cross References

From Section 56

Schedule 1 Stamp Duties on Instruments

CHAPTER 5

Mortgages, etc.

57 Charging of duty on mortgages, etc. [Deleted]

Deleted by FA07 s100(1)(c). This section applies to instruments executed on or after 7 December 2006.

58 Security for future advances, how to be charged [Deleted]

Deleted by FA07 s100(1)(c). This section applies to instruments executed on or after 7 December 2006.

CHAPTER 6

Policies of Insurance

59 Penalty for policy of insurance not duly stamped

[SA1891 s100; FA1959 s75(4)]

(1) Every person who—

(a) receives, or takes credit for, any premium or consideration for any insurance, and does not, within one month after receiving, or taking credit for, the premium or consideration, make out and execute a duly stamped policy of insurance, or

(b) makes, executes, or delivers out, or pays or allows in account, or agrees to pay or allow in account, any money on or in respect of any policy which is not duly stamped,

shall incur a penalty of [€630][1].

(2) *Subsection (1)* shall not apply in relation to an insurance or a policy effecting an insurance if the insurance is such that a policy effecting it is exempt from all stamp duties.

Amendments

[1] Substituted by FA01 sched5 and s240 with effect from 1 January 2002.

60 Short-term life insurance policies [Repealed]

Repealed by FA01 s203(1). Applies and has effect in relation to instruments executed and policies of life insurance varied on or after 1 January 2001.

61 Location of insurance risk for stamp duty purposes

[FA1992 s208]

(1) In *paragraph (d)* of *subsection (2)* "*branch*" means an agency or branch of a policyholder or any permanent presence of a policyholder in the State even if that presence does not take the form of an agency or branch but consists merely of an office managed by the policyholder's own staff or by a person who is independent but has permanent authority to act for the policyholder in the same way as an agency.

(2) For the purpose of charging stamp duty, the risk to which a policy of insurance or a policy of life insurance relates shall be deemed to be located in the State—

- (a) where the insurance relates either to buildings or to buildings and their contents, in so far as the contents are covered by the same insurance policy, if the property is situated in the State;
- (b) where the insurance relates to vehicles of any kind, if such vehicles are registered in the State;
- (c) in the case of policies of a duration of 4 months or less covering travel or holiday risks, if the policyholder took out the policy in the State;
- (d) in any other case, if the policyholder has his or her habitual residence in the State, or where the policyholder is a legal person other than an individual, if the policyholder's head office or branch to which the policy relates is situated in the State.

Cross References

To Section 61

Section 124B Certain premiums of life assurance.
Section 125 Certain premiums of insurance.

62 Limitation of stamp duty on certain instruments relating to 2 or more distinct matters

[FA1982 s94(4)(*b*)(ii)]

An instrument shall not be charged with duty exceeding [€1][1] by reason only that it contains or relates to 2 or more distinct matters each falling within the heading "POLICY OF INSURANCE other than Life Insurance where the risk to which the policy relates is located in the State" in *Schedule 1*.

Amendments

[1] Substituted by FA01 sched5 and s240 with effect from 1 January 2002.

Cross References

From Section 62

Schedule 1 Stamp Duties on Instruments

CHAPTER 7

Releases or Renunciations of Any Property, or of Any Right or Interest in Any Property

63 Letters of renunciation

[FA1986 s95(1) and (2)]

(1) In this section—

"*share*" includes stock;

"*unquoted company*" means a company none of whose shares, stocks or debentures are listed in the official list of a recognised stock exchange or dealt in on an unlisted securities market recognised by such a stock exchange.

(2) Any instrument which releases or renounces or has the effect of releasing or renouncing a right under a letter of allotment, or under any other document having the effect of a letter of allotment, to any share in an unquoted company shall be chargeable to stamp duty as if it were a release or renunciation of property consisting of stocks or marketable securities by reference to the heading "RELEASE or RENUNCIATION of any property, or of any right or interest in any property" in *Schedule 1* and that schedule shall be construed accordingly.

Cross References

From Section 63

Schedule 1 Stamp Duties on Instruments

CHAPTER 8

Share Warrants and Stock Certificates to Bearer, etc.

64 Instruments passing by delivery in pursuance of usage

[FA1899 s6]

For the purposes of this Chapter, an instrument used for the purpose of assigning, transferring, or in any manner negotiating the right to any share or stock shall, if delivery of such share or stock is by usage treated as sufficient for the purpose of a sale on the market, whether that delivery constitutes a legal assignment, transfer, or negotiation or not, be deemed an instrument to bearer and the delivery of such share or stock an assignment, transfer, or negotiation.

65 Penalty for issuing share warrant not duly stamped

[SA1891 s107; FA1899 s5(2) (part)]

If a share warrant which is chargeable to stamp duty, or any instrument to bearer having a like effect as such a share warrant, is issued without being duly stamped, the company issuing the same, and also every person who, at the time when it is issued, is the managing director or secretary or other principal officer of the company, shall incur a penalty of [€630][1].

Amendments

[1] Substituted by FA01 sched5 and s240 with effect from 1 January 2002.

66 Penalty for issuing stock certificate not duly stamped, etc

[SA1891 s109; FA1899 s5(2) (part)]

(1) Where the holder of a stock certificate to bearer, or any instrument to bearer having a like effect as such stock certificate to bearer, has been entered on the register of the local authority, or company or body of persons, as the case may be, as the owner of the share of stock described in the certificate, the certificate shall be forthwith cancelled so as to be incapable of being re-issued to any person.

(2) Every person by whom a stock certificate to bearer which is chargeable to stamp duty, or any instrument to bearer having a like effect as such stock certificate to bearer, is issued without being duly stamped shall incur a penalty of [€630][1].

Amendments

[1] Substituted by FA01 sched5 and s240 with effect from 1 January 2002.

CHAPTER 9

Surrenders of Any Property, or of Any Right or Interest in Any Property

67 Surrender and merger of leasehold interests

[FA1986 s99(2)]

An instrument bearing witness to, or acknowledging—

(a) the surrender, by parol or otherwise, of a leasehold interest in immovable property, or

(b) the merger of such an interest in a superior interest,

shall be charged to the same stamp duty as if it were a surrender of that leasehold interest.

PART 6

Special Provisions Relating to Uncertificated Securities

68 Interpretation (Part 6)

[FA1996 s101(1)]

(1) In this Part—

"*certificated securities*" means securities other than uncertificated securities;

[...][1]

[...][2]

[...][3]

"*securities*" means any stocks or marketable securities;

"*uncertificated securities*" means any securities, title to which is, by virtue of the Companies Act, 1990 (Uncertificated Securities) Regulations, 1996 (S.I. No. 68 of 1996), transferable by means of a relevant system.

(2) In this Part, "*generate*", "*instruction*", "*operator*", "*operator-instruction*", "*relevant system*" and "*system-member*" have the same meanings, respectively, as in the Companies Act, 1990 (Uncertificated Securities) Regulations, 1996.

(3) In this Part, references to title to securities include any legal or equitable interest in securities.

Amendments

[1, 2, 3] Deleted by FA07 s109(1)(a). With effect from 1 October 2007 per SI 649 of 2007.

Cross References

To Section 68

Section 134A Penalties.

Section 159C Time limits for making enquiries etc. and assessments by the Commissioners.

69 Operator-instruction deemed to be an instrument of conveyance or transfer

[FA1996 s102]

(1) Where a transfer of title to securities through a relevant system is effected by an operator-instruction, that operator-instruction shall, for all purposes of this Act, be deemed to be an executed instrument of conveyance or transfer of such securities and the date of execution shall be taken to be the date the operator-instruction is generated.

(2) Where an operator-instruction is generated in connection with the transfer through a relevant system of an equitable interest in securities, that transfer shall be deemed for the purposes of *subsection (1)* to have been effected by that operator-instruction.

(3) Where no operator-instruction is generated in connection with the transfer through a relevant system of an equitable interest in securities, that transfer shall, for the purposes of this Part, be deemed to have been effected by an operator-instruction generated on the date of the transfer.

[(4) Where a transfer of title to securities through a relevant system is effected by an operator-instruction relating to a single netted settlement in a relevant system of two or more contracts for sale of the same type of securities of a company that operator-instruction shall not be treated as an operator-instruction falling within subsection (1) and shall, instead, be deemed to be a separate operator-instruction generated in respect of each contract for sale included in that single netted settlement and each such operator-instruction shall be deemed to be an executed instrument of conveyance or transfer of the securities which are the subject of the contract for sale concerned and the date of execution of each such conveyance or transfer shall be taken to be the date the operator-instruction relating to the single netted settlement is generated.

(5) Where no operator-instruction is generated in connection with a single netted settlement in a relevant system of two or more contracts for sale of the same type of securities of a company, a separate operator-instruction shall be deemed to have been generated on the date of the single netted settlement in respect of each contract for sale included in that single netted settlement and each such operator-instruction shall be deemed to be an executed instrument of conveyance or transfer of the securities which are the subject of the contract for sale concerned and the date of execution of each such conveyance or transfer shall be taken to be the date the deemed operator-instruction is generated.][1]

Amendments

[1] Inserted by FA03 s135(1). Has effect in relation to instruments executed on or after 28 March 2003.

Cross References

To Section 69

Section 70 Rate of duty.
Section 71 Application and adaptation of other Parts of this Act.
Section 73 Exemptions.
Section 77 Overpayment of duty.
Section 159A Time limits for claiming a repayment of stamp duty.
Section 159B Interest on repayments of stamp duty.

70 Rate of duty

[FA1996 s103]

(1) Where an operator-instruction is, by virtue of *section 69*, chargeable with stamp duty under or by reference to the heading "CONVEYANCE or TRANSFER on sale of any stocks or marketable securities" in *Schedule 1*, the rate at which the duty is charged under that heading shall be the rate of 1 per cent of the consideration for the sale to which that operator-instruction gives effect.

(2) Notwithstanding *subsection (1)*—

(a) where the transfer operates as a voluntary disposition inter vivos, the reference in *subsection (1)* to the amount or value of the consideration for the sale shall, in relation to the duty so chargeable, be construed as a reference to the value of the securities transferred,

(b) where the calculation results in an amount which is not a multiple of one [cent][1], the amount so calculated shall be rounded to the nearest [cent][2], and any half of a [cent][3] shall be rounded up to the next whole [cent][4].

Amendments

[1, 2, 3, 4] Substituted by FA01 sched5 and s240 with effect from 1 January 2002.

Cross References

From Section 70

Section 69 Operator-instruction deemed to be an instrument of conveyance or transfer.

Schedule 1 Stamp Duties on Instruments

71 Application and adaptation of other Parts of this Act

[FA1996 s104]

In relation to a charge for stamp duty arising by virtue of *section 69*—

(a) the definition of "*accountable person*" in *subsection (1)* of *section 1* shall be construed as if the reference, in the Table to that definition, to the purchaser or transferee were a reference to the transferee,

(b) notwithstanding *section 2(3)*, the operator-instruction which is charged to stamp duty by virtue of *section 69* shall not be required to be stamped and, accordingly—

  (i) any duty so charged shall be due and payable and shall be paid to the Commissioners on the date on which that operator-instruction is generated, and

  (ii) that operator-instruction shall for the purposes of *section 2(4)* [...][1] be deemed to be duly stamped with the proper stamp duty when such duty and any [interest [...][2]][3] relating to such duty has been paid to the Commissioners,

(c) notwithstanding *paragraph (b)*, where an agreement referred to in *section 72* is in force between the Commissioners and an operator, any duty paid in respect of that operator-instruction in accordance with such agreement shall be deemed to have been paid to the Commissioners on the date on which it became due and payable,

(d) subject to *paragraph (e)*, *section 14* shall apply with the modification that the [interest [...][4]][5] imposed for not duly stamping the operator-instruction, which is charged to stamp duty by virtue of *section 69* within a particular period of the date of first execution, shall be imposed for non-payment of the stamp duty within that period, and with any other necessary modifications,

(e) *sections 4, 6, 8, 11, 14(4), 20, 127* and *129(1)* shall not apply,

(f) (i) if at any time it appears that for any reason no duty, or insufficient duty, has been paid to the Commissioners, they shall make an assessment of such amount of duty or additional duty as, to the best of their knowledge, information and belief, ought to be charged, levied and paid and the accountable person shall be liable for the payment of the duty so assessed,

  (ii) if at any time it appears that for any reason an assessment is incorrect, the Commissioners shall make such other assessment as they consider appropriate, which assessment shall be substituted for the first-mentioned assessment,

  (iii) *section 21* shall apply to an assessment under this paragraph as if it were an assessment mentioned in that section,

[...][6]

Amendments

[1] Deleted by FA13 sched2(b)(i)(I).

[2] Deleted by FA13 sched2(b)(i)(II).

[3] Substituted by F(No.2)A08 sched5(part5)(chap2)(7)(e)(i).

[4] Deleted by FA13 sched2(b)(ii).

[5] Substituted by F(No.2)A08 sched5(part5)(chap2)(7)(e)(ii).

[6] Deleted by FA12 sched3(18). In effect for all instruments that are executed on or after 7 July 2012 per S.I. No. 228 of 2012.

Note:

F(No.2)A08 sched5 (part5)(chap 2)(7)

As respects paragraph 7 of this Schedule subparagraphs (a) to (aa) (other than subparagraph (c)(i)(I)) of that paragraph have effect as on and from the passing of this Act and to the extent that Chapter 3A (being inserted into Part 47 of the Taxes Consolidation Act 1997 by Part 1 of this Schedule) applies to penalties incurred under the Stamp Duties Consolidation Act 1999 before the passing of this Act which on the passing of this Act have not been paid, it shall not apply to such penalties which are in the form of interest accrued under any provisions of the said Act.

Cross References

From Section 71

Section 1 Interpretation.
Section 2 Charging of, liability for, and recovery of stamp duty.
Section 4 How duties are to be paid.
Section 6 How instruments are to be written and stamped.
Section 8 Facts and circumstances affecting duty to be set forth in instruments, etc.
Section 11 Denoting stamps.
Section 14 Penalty on stamping instruments after execution.
Section 20 Assessment of duty by the Commissioners.
Section 21 Right of appeal of persons dissatisfied with assessment.
Section 30 Voluntary dispositions inter vivos chargeable as conveyances or transfers on sale.
Section 69 Operator-instruction deemed to be an instrument of conveyance or transfer.
Section 72 Collection and payment of duty.
Section 127 Terms on which instruments not duly stamped may be received in evidence.
Section 129 Penalty for enrolling, etc., instrument not duly stamped, etc.

72 Collection and payment of duty

[FA1996 s105]

The Commissioners may enter into an agreement with an operator, in such form and on such terms and conditions as they think fit, in relation to the collection of stamp duty and the payment of such duty to the Commissioners.

Cross References

To Section 72

Section 71 Application and adaptation of other Parts of this Act.

73 Exemptions

[FA1996 s106(1) and (2)]

(1) *Section 69* shall not apply—

[...][1]

[...][2]

[(c) in respect of an operator-instruction effecting a transfer of rights to securities, in a company which is not an unquoted company within the meaning of section 63, where that transfer is a renunciation of those rights under a letter of allotment.][3]

(2) Stamp duty shall not be chargeable under or by reference to any heading in *Schedule 1* other than the heading "CONVEYANCE or TRANSFER on sale of any stocks

or marketable securities" on an instrument effecting a transfer of securities if the transferee is a system-member and the instrument is in a form which will, in accordance with the rules of the system, enable certificated securities to be converted into uncertificated securities so that title to them may become transferable by means of the relevant system.

Amendments

[1] Deleted by FA07 s101(1)(g). This section applies to instruments drawn, made or executed on or after 2 April 2007

[2] Deleted by FA07 s109(1)(b). With effect from 1 October 2007 per SI 649 of 2007.

[3] Inserted by FA00 s67(1)(b). This section has effect in relation to instruments executed on or after 1 March 2003.

Cross References

From Section 73

Section 69 Operator-instruction deemed to be an instrument of conveyance or transfer.
Schedule 1 Stamp Duties on Instruments

To Section 73

Section 77 Overpayment of duty.
Section 96 Transfers between spouses.

74 Exemption for market makers [Deleted]

Deleted by FA07 s109(1)(c). With effect from 1 October 2007 per SI 649 of 2007.

75 Relief for intermediaries

[(1) In this section—

["*competent authority*" has the meaning assigned to it by the Directive;

"*Directive*" means Directive 2004/39/EC of the European Parliament and of the Council of 21 April 2004* on markets in financial instruments, as amended from time to time;][1]

* OJ No. L145, 30 April 2004, p.1

"*excluded business*" means any of the following:

(a) any business which consists in the making or managing of investments;

(b) any business which consists in, or is carried on for the purpose of, providing services to persons who are connected with the person carrying on the business; and the question of whether a person is connected with another person shall be determined in accordance with the provisions of section 10 of the Taxes Consolidation Act 1997;

(c) any business which consists in insurance business, or assurance business within the meaning of section 3 of the Insurance Act 1936;

(d) any business which consists in administering, managing or acting as trustee in relation to, a pension scheme, or which is carried on by the administrator, manager or trustee of such a scheme, in connection with or for the purposes of the scheme;

(e) any business which consists in operating, or acting as trustee in relation to, a collective investment scheme (within the meaning of *section 88*), or is carried on by the operator or trustee of such a scheme in connection with or for the purposes of the scheme;

"*intermediary*" means a person who carries on a *bona fide* business of dealing in securities and, for the purpose of this definition, the entering into derivative agreements referenced directly or indirectly to securities shall be treated as carrying on a business of dealing in securities;

"*member firm*" means a member of—

(a) the Irish Stock Exchange Limited,

(b) the London Stock Exchange plc, or

(c) any other exchange or market which is designated for the purposes of this section in regulations made by the Commissioners;

"*operator*", in relation to a collective investment scheme, means an administrator, manager or other such person who is authorised to act on behalf of, or in connection with, or for the purposes of, the scheme and habitually so acts in that capacity;

"*recognised intermediary*", in relation to an exchange or market, means a member of the exchange or market who is an intermediary and who is approved by the Commissioners as a recognised intermediary in accordance with arrangements made by the Commissioners with the exchange or market.

(2) For the purposes of this section, a transfer of securities is effected on an exchange or market if—

(a) it is subject to the rules of the exchange or, as the case may be, the market, and

(b) it is reported to the exchange or, as the case may be, the market, in accordance with the rules of the exchange or market concerned.

[(2A) For the purposes of subsection (2), a transfer of securities shall be deemed to be effected on an exchange or market, where the transfer of securities gives effect to a transaction that is required by a competent authority, in accordance with the Directive, to be reported directly or indirectly to the competent authority and is so reported in accordance with that requirement.][2]

(3) Stamp duty shall not be chargeable on an instrument of transfer whereby any securities are on the sale of such securities transferred to a person or a nominee of such person, where—

(a) the person is a member firm of an exchange or market,

(b) the person is a recognised intermediary in relation to the exchange or market,

(c) the transfer of securities is effected—

(i) on the exchange or, as the case may be, the market,

(ii) on any exchange or market operated by the Irish Stock Exchange Limited or the London Stock Exchange plc, or

(iii) on any other exchange or market designated by the Commissioners for the purposes of this section,

and

(d) the transfer of securities is not effected in connection with an excluded business.

(4) (a) The Commissioners may, from time to time, make arrangements with an exchange or a market setting out how a member firm is to be approved by the Commissioners as a recognised intermediary.

(b) Every recognised intermediary shall, whenever and wherever required to do so, make available for inspection by an officer of the Commissioners authorised for that purpose, all books, documents and other records in the possession of or under the control of, the recognised intermediary, as are relevant for the purposes of the Commissioners ensuring compliance by the intermediary with this section.

(5) (a) The Commissioners may, from time to time, make regulations to designate an exchange or market for the purposes of this section.

(b) Every regulation made under this section shall be laid before Dáil Éireann as soon as may be after it is made and, if a resolution annulling the regulation is passed by Dáil Éireann within the next 21 days on which Dáil Éireann has sat after the regulation is laid before it, the regulation shall be annulled accordingly, but without prejudice to the validity of anything previously done thereunder.][3]

Amendments

[1] Inserted by FA08 s114(1)(a). Applies to instruments executed on or after 1 November 2007.

[2] Inserted by FA08 s114(1)(b). Applies to instruments executed on or after 1 November 2007.

[3] Substituted by FA07 s109(1)(d). With effect from 1 October 2007 per SI 649 of 2007.

Revenue Briefings

eBrief

eBrief No. 47/2007 – Stamp Duty on transfers of Irish securities – New reliefs for certain market participants

Cross References

From Section 75

Section 88 Certain stocks and marketable securities.

75A Relief for clearing houses

[(1) In this section—

"*clearing house*" means a body or association which provides services related to the clearing and settlement of transactions and payments and the management of risks associated with the resulting contracts and which is regulated or supervised in the provision of those services (in this section referred to as "*clearing services*") by a regulatory body, or an agency of government, of a Member State of the European Communities;

"*clearing participant*" means a member of a recognised clearing house who is permitted by the clearing house to provide clearing services in connection with a transfer of securities;

"*client*" means a person who gives instructions for securities to be sold;

"*nominee*" means a person whose business is or includes holding securities as a nominee for a recognised clearing house acting in its capacity as a provider of clearing services or, as the case may be, a nominee for a clearing participant or a non-clearing participant;

"*non-clearing participant*" means a member of an exchange or market when not acting as a clearing participant;

"*recognised clearing house*" means—

(a) Eurex Clearing AG,

(b) LCH.Clearnet Limited,

[(c) SIX x-clear AG, or][1]

(d) any other clearing house designated as a recognised clearing house for the purposes of this section by regulations made by the Commissioners.

(2) Stamp duty shall not be chargeable on an instrument of transfer whereby any securities are on the sale of such securities transferred in the circumstances referred to in subsection (3) where the conditions referred to in subsection (4) are satisfied.

(3) The circumstances referred to in this subsection are that the transfer of securities is—

(a) from a clearing participant or a nominee of a clearing participant, to another clearing participant or a nominee of that other clearing participant,

(b) from a client or a non-clearing participant or a nominee of a non-clearing participant, to a clearing participant or a nominee of a clearing participant,

(c) from a non-clearing participant or a nominee of a non-clearing participant or a clearing participant or a nominee of a clearing participant, to a recognised clearing house or a nominee of a recognised clearing house,

(d) from a person other than a clearing participant, to a recognised clearing house or a nominee of a recognised clearing house, as a result of a failure by a clearing participant to fulfil that clearing participant"s obligations in respect of the transfer of securities to the recognised clearing house or a nominee of the recognised clearing house,

[(da) from a recognised clearing house or a nominee of a recognised clearing house, to another recognised clearing house or a nominee of that 10 recognised clearing house][2].

(e) from a recognised clearing house or a nominee of a recognised clearing house, to a clearing participant or a nominee of a clearing participant or a non-clearing participant or a nominee of a non-clearing participant, or

(f) from a clearing participant, or a nominee of a clearing participant to a non-clearing participant or a nominee of a non-clearing participant.

(4) The conditions referred to in this subsection are that the person to whom the securities are transferred under a transfer of securities referred to in paragraphs *(a)* to *(f)* of subsection (3) (in this section referred to as the "*relevant transfer*") is required on receipt of those securities to transfer securities under a matching transfer to another person, or in the case of a relevant transfer falling within paragraph *(d)*, would have been so required if the failure referred to in that paragraph had not occurred.

(5) For the purposes of subsection (4), a "*matching transfer*" means a transfer of securities under which—

(a) the securities transferred are of the same kind as the securities transferred under the relevant transfer, and

(b) the number of and consideration paid for, the securities transferred are identical to the number of and consideration paid for, the securities transferred under the relevant transfer.

(6) (a) The Commissioners may, from time to time, make regulations to designate a clearing house as a recognised clearing house for the purposes of this section.

(b) Every regulation made under this section shall be laid before Dáil Éireann as soon as may be after it is made and, if a resolution annulling the regulation is passed by Dáil Éireann within the next 21 days on which Dáil Éireann has sat after the regulation is laid before it, the regulation shall be annulled accordingly, but without prejudice to the validity of anything previously done thereunder.][3]

Amendments

[1] Substituted by FA12 s98(a).

[2] Inserted by FA12 s98(b).

[3] Substituted by FA07 s109(1)(d). With effect from 1 October 2007 per SI 649 of 2007.

Revenue Briefings

eBrief

eBrief No. 47/2007 – Stamp Duty on transfers of Irish securities – New reliefs for certain market participants

76 Obligations of system-members

[FA1996 s108]

(1) Where an instruction is entered or is caused to be entered in a relevant system by a system-member, and the effect of that instruction is that no stamp duty is calculated by the relevant system, that system-member shall retain evidence in legible written form, or readily convertible into such a form, for a period of [6 years][1] from the date of such instruction, in sufficient detail to establish that the related operator-instruction is not chargeable with stamp duty, and the system-member shall make any such evidence available to the Commissioners on request.

(2) A system-member who fails to comply with *subsection (1)* shall be liable to a penalty of [€1,265][2].

(3) [Where a system-member, before the passing of the *Finance (No. 2) Act 2008*,][3] fraudulently or negligently enters or causes to be entered an incorrect instruction in a relevant system and such incorrect instruction gives rise to an underpayment of stamp duty, or results in a claim for exemption from duty to which there is no entitlement, that system-member shall incur a penalty of [€1,265][4] together with the amount[...][5] of the difference between the duty so paid (if any) and the duty which would have been payable if the instruction had been entered correctly.

(4) A system-member shall be deemed to have acted negligently for the purposes of *subsection (3)* if it comes to the system-member's notice, or it would have come to the system-member's notice if the system-member had taken reasonable care, that an incorrect instruction has resulted in an underpayment of stamp duty, unless the system-member notifies the Commissioners accordingly, in writing, without unreasonable delay.

(5) An incorrect instruction to which [subsection (3) of this section or section 134A(2)(*b*), as the case may be,][6] applies shall be deemed to be the production of an incorrect document for the purposes of section 1078(2)(*d*) of the Taxes Consolidation Act, 1997.

Amendments

[1] Substituted by FA02 s112(1). Has effect in relation to instructions entered or caused to be entered in a relevant system by a system-member on or after 25 March 2002

[2, 4] Substituted by FA01 sched5 and s240 with effect from 1 January 2002.

[3] Substituted by F(No.2)A08 sched5(part5)(chap1)(5)(c)(i). The enactments specified in Schedule 5 are amended or repealed to the extent and manner specified in that Schedule and, unless the contrary is stated, shall come into effect after 24 December 2008.

[5] Deleted by FA05 s118(1). This section has effect in relation to instructions entered or caused to be entered in a relevant system (for the purpose of Part 6) by a system-member (for that purpose) on or after 25 March 2005.

[6] Substituted by F(No.2)A08 sched5(part5)(chap1)(5)(c)(ii). Has effect as respects penalties incurred on or after 24 December 2008.

Cross References

From Section 76

Section 134A Penalties.

To Section 76

Section 159C Time limits for making enquiries etc. and assessments by the Commissioners.

77 Overpayment of duty

[FA1996 s109]

(1) Where on a claim it is proved to the satisfaction of the Commissioners that there has been an overpayment of duty in relation to a charge to duty by virtue of *section 69*, the overpayment shall be repaid.

(2) A claim under this section shall—

[(a) was made within the period of 4 years from the date the operator-instruction referred to in section 69 was made,][1]

(b) set out the grounds on which the repayment is claimed,

(c) contain a computation of the amount of the repayment claimed,

(d) if so required by the Commissioners, be supported by such documentation as may be necessary to prove the entitlement to a repayment of the amount claimed, and

(e) if the claim arises by virtue of the operation of *section 73(1)(b)*—

(i) it shall be made on a form prescribed by the Commissioners, and

(ii) it shall not be made to the Commissioners before the 21st day of the month following the month in which the overpayment of duty arose.

(3) Where the claimant is not resident in the State and has no branch or agency in the State the Commissioners may require the claimant, as a condition for obtaining a repayment, to appoint and maintain a tax representative in the State who shall be personally liable to the Commissioners for any loss of duty arising out of an incorrect claim.

(4) A person shall not be a tax representative under this section unless that person—

(a) has a business establishment in the State, and

(b) is approved by the Commissioners.

Amendments

[1] Substituted by FA12 sched3(19). In effect for all instruments that are executed on or after 7 July 2012 per S.I. No. 228 of 2012.

Cross References

From Section 77

Section 69 Operator-instruction deemed to be an instrument of conveyance or transfer.

Section 73 Exemptions.

78 Regulations

[FA1996 s110]

(1) The Commissioners may make such regulations as seem to them to be necessary for the purpose of giving effect to this Part and of enabling them to discharge their functions in relation to administration, assessment, collection, recovery and repayment under this Part.

(2) Every regulation made under this section shall be laid before Dáil Éireann as soon as may be after it is made and, if a resolution annulling the regulation is passed by Dáil Éireann within the next 21 days on which Dáil Éireann has sat after the regulation is laid before it, the regulation shall be annulled accordingly, but without prejudice to the validity of anything previously done under the regulation.

PART 7

Exemptions and Reliefs from Stamp Duty

CHAPTER 1

Instruments Which must be Presented to the Commissioners for Adjudication in Order to Obtain Exemption or Relief

79 Conveyances and transfers of property between certain bodies corporate

[FA1952 s19]

(1) Stamp duty shall not be chargeable under or by reference to the following headings in *Schedule 1*—

(a) "CONVEYANCE or TRANSFER on sale of any stocks or marketable securities",

(b) "CONVEYANCE or TRANSFER on sale of a policy of insurance or a policy of life insurance where the risk to which the policy relates is located in the State", or

(c) "CONVEYANCE or TRANSFER on sale of any property other than stocks or marketable securities or a policy of insurance or a policy of life insurance",

on any instrument to which this section applies.

[...][1]

(3) This section applies to any instrument as respects which [...][2] the effect of the instrument was to convey or transfer a beneficial interest in property from one body corporate to another, and that at the time of the execution of the instrument the bodies in question were associated, that is, one was the beneficial owner of not less than 90 per cent of the [ordinary share capital][3] of the other, or a third such body was the beneficial owner of not less than 90 per cent of the [ordinary share capital][4] of each and that this ownership was ownership either directly or through another body corporate or other bodies corporate, or partly directly and partly through another body corporate or other bodies corporate, and subsections (5) to (10) of section 9 of the Taxes Consolidation Act, 1997, shall apply for the purposes of this section as if—

[(a) references to company were references to body corporate, and

(b) references to companies were references to bodies corporate.][5]

[(3A) For the purposes of subsection (3) "*ordinary share capital*", in relation to a body corporate, means all the issued share capital (by whatever name called) of the body corporate, other than capital the holders of which have a right to a dividend at a fixed rate, but have no other right to share in the profits of the body corporate.][6]

(4) Notwithstanding that at the time of execution of any instrument the bodies corporate between which the beneficial interest in the property was conveyed or transferred were associated within the meaning of *subsection (3)*, they shall not be treated as having been so associated unless, additionally, at that time—

(a) one such body was beneficially entitled to not less than 90 per cent of any profits available for distribution to the shareholders of the other such body or a third such body was beneficially entitled to not less than 90 per cent of any profits available for distribution to the shareholders of each, and

(b) one such body would be beneficially entitled to not less than 90 per cent of any assets of the other such body available for distribution to its shareholders on a winding-up or a third such body would be beneficially entitled to not less than 90 per cent of any assets available for distribution to the shareholders of each on a winding-up,

and, for the purposes of this section—

(i) the percentage to which one body corporate is beneficially entitled of any profits available for distribution to the shareholders of another body corporate, and

(ii) the percentage to which one body corporate would be beneficially entitled of any assets of another body corporate on a winding-up,

means the percentage to which the first body corporate is, or would be, so entitled either directly or through another body corporate or other bodies corporate or partly directly and partly through another body corporate or other bodies corporate.

(5) This section shall not apply to an instrument unless [...][7] the instrument was not executed in pursuance of or in connection with an arrangement under which—

(a) the consideration, or any part of the consideration, for the conveyance or transfer was to be provided or received, directly or indirectly by a person, other than a body corporate which at the time of the execution of the instrument was associated within the meaning of [*subsections (3) and (4)*][8] with either the transferor or the transferee (being, respectively, the body from whom and the body to whom the beneficial interest was conveyed or transferred),

(b) that interest was previously conveyed or transferred, directly or indirectly, by such a person, or

(c) the transferor and the transferee were to cease to be associated within the meaning of *subsections (3)* and *(4)*,

and, without prejudice to the generality of *paragraph (a)*, an arrangement shall be treated as within that paragraph if it is one under which the transferor or the transferee, or a body corporate associated with either as there mentioned, was to be enabled to provide any of the consideration, or was to part with any of it, by or in consequence of the carrying out of a transaction or transactions involving, or any of them involving, a payment or other disposition by a person other than a body corporate so associated.

[...][9]

[...][10]

(7) If—

(a) where any claim for exemption from duty under this section has been allowed, it is subsequently found that [the exemption was not properly due][11], or

(b) the transferor and transferee cease to be associated within the meaning of [*subsections (3) and (4)*][12] within a period of 2 years from the date of the conveyance or transfer, then the exemption shall cease to be applicable and stamp duty shall be chargeable in respect of the conveyance or transfer as if *subsection (1)* had not been enacted together with [interest on the duty, [...][13] calculated in accordance with section 159D,][14] on which the duty is paid, in a case to which *paragraph (a)* applies, from the date of the conveyance or transfer or, in a case to which *paragraph (b)* applies, from the date the transferor and transferee ceased to be so associated.

(8) For the purposes of *subsection (4)*—

(a) the percentage to which one body is beneficially entitled of any profits available for distribution to shareholders of another company has, subject to any necessary modifications, the meaning assigned to it by section 414 of the Taxes Consolidation Act, 1997, and

(b) the percentage to which one body is beneficially entitled of any assets of another body available for distribution on a winding-up has, subject to any necessary modifications, the meaning assigned to it by section 415 of the Taxes Consolidation Act, 1997.

[(9) This section shall apply notwithstanding that a body corporate, referred to in this section, is incorporated outside the State, and such body corporate, corresponds, under the law of the place where it is incorporated, to a body corporate which has an ordinary share capital within the meaning given in subsection (3A) and subject to any necessary modifications for the purpose of so corresponding, all the other provisions of this section are met.][15]

[(10) Subsection (1) shall not apply to an instrument conveying or transferring stocks or marketable securities (in this subsection referred to as the "*second transfer*") to the extent of the consideration for the sale that is attributable to those of the stocks or marketable securities being conveyed or transferred that were conveyed or transferred immediately prior to the second transfer by an instrument or instruments, as the case may be, to which section 75, as inserted by the Finance Act 2007, applied.][16]

Amendments

[1] Deleted by FA12 sched3(20)(a). In effect for all instruments that are executed on or after 7 July 2012 per S.I. No. 228 of 2012.

[2] Deleted by FA12 sched3(20)(b). In effect for all instruments that are executed on or after 7 July 2012 per S.I. No. 228 of 2012.

[3, 4] Substituted by FA03 s136(1)(a)(i). Has effect in relation to instruments executed on or after 6 February 2003.

[5] Substituted by FA03 s136(1)(a)(ii). Has effect in relation to instruments executed on or after 6 February 2003.

[6] Inserted by FA03 s136(1)(b). Has effect in relation to instruments executed on or after 6 February 2003.

[7] Deleted by FA12 sched3(20)(c). In effect for all instruments that are executed on or after 7 July 2012 per S.I. No. 228 of 2012.

[8] Substituted by FA01 s204(1)(b). Applies and has effect in relation to instruments executed on or after 6 March 2001.

[9] Deleted by FA13 s77(f).

[10] Deleted by FA12 sched3(20)(d). In effect for all instruments that are executed on or after 7 July 2012 per S.I. No. 228 of 2012.

[11] Substituted by FA12 sched3(20)(e). In effect for all instruments that are executed on or after 7 July 2012 per S.I. No. 228 of 2012.

[12] Substituted by FA01 s204(1)(a). Applies and has effect in relation to instruments executed on or after 15 February 2001.

[13] Deleted by F(No.2)A08 sched5(part5)(chap2)(7)(f).

[14] Substituted by FA05 sched5.

[15] Inserted by FA03 s136(1)(c). Has effect in relation to instruments executed on or after 6 February 2003.

[16] Inserted by FA08 s115(1). Applies as respects instruments executed on or after 31 January 2008.

Note:

F(No.2)A08 sched5 (part5)(chap 2)(7)

As respects paragraph 7 of this Schedule subparagraphs (a) to (aa) (other than subparagraph (c)(i)(I)) of that paragraph have effect as on and from the passing of this Act and to the extent that Chapter 3A (being inserted into Part 47 of the Taxes Consolidation Act 1997 by Part 1 of this Schedule) applies to penalties incurred under the Stamp Duties Consolidation Act 1999 before the passing of this Act which on the passing of this Act have not been paid, it shall not apply to such penalties which are in the form of interest accrued under any provisions of the said Act.

Case Law

National Westminster Bank plc v IRC 1994 3 All ER 1 considered the meaning of the issue of shares.
The percentage shareholding refers to the nominal value and not the real value of the shares. Canada Safeway Ltd v IRC 1972 1 All ER 666
In Central and District Properties Ltd v IRC 1996 2 All ER 433 options given over shares were deemed to form part of the consideration and consequently relief was not available as less than 90% of the consideration was in the form of shares.
In Brooklands Selangor Holdings Ltd v IRC 1970 1 All ER 76 a company could not deal as it pleased with its shares in another company, but was bound to transfer them to another. It was held that the company was not the beneficial owner of those shares.

Revenue Briefings

Tax Briefing

Tax Briefing June 2001 – Issue 44 (part 2) pg 30 – Revenue Certificates in Deeds

Cross References

From Section 79

Section 20 Assessment of duty by the Commissioners.
Schedule 1 Stamp Duties on Instruments

80 Reconstructions or amalgamations of companies

[FA1965 s31(1) to (3) and (5) to (8); FA1995 s144(2)]

[(1) (a) In this section—

"*acquiring company*" means, subject to paragraph (*b*), a company with limited liability;

"*shares*" includes stock and references to the undertaking of a target company include references to a part of the undertaking of a target company.

(b) In respect of instruments executed on or after 1 June 2005, references to "*acquiring company*", "*target company*" and "*company*" shall be construed as including a reference to a society registered under the Industrial and Provident Societies Act 1893.][1]

(2) Where [...][2] there exists a scheme for the bona fide reconstruction of any company or companies or the amalgamation of any companies and that, in connection with the scheme, there exist the following conditions, that is—

(a) a company with limited liability is to be registered, or a company has been established by Act of the Oireachtas, or the nominal share capital of a company has been increased;

(b) the company (in this section referred to as the "*acquiring company*") is to be registered or has been established or has increased its capital with a view to the acquisition of either—

(i) the undertaking of a particular existing company (in this section referred to as the "*target company*"), or

(ii) not less than 90 per cent of the issued share capital of a target company;

(c) the consideration for the acquisition (except such part of that consideration as consists in the transfer to or discharge by the acquiring company of liabilities of the target company) consists as to not less than 90 per cent of that consideration—

(i) where an undertaking is to be acquired, in the issue of shares in the acquiring company to the target company or to holders of shares in the target company, or

(ii) where shares are to be acquired, in the issue of shares in the acquiring company to the holders of shares in the target company in exchange for the shares held by them in the target company,

then, subject to this section, stamp duty under the following headings in *Schedule 1*—

(I) "CONVEYANCE or TRANSFER on sale of any stocks or marketable securities",

(II) "CONVEYANCE or TRANSFER on sale of a policy of insurance or a policy of life insurance where the risk to which the policy relates is located in the State", or

(III) "CONVEYANCE or TRANSFER on sale of any property other than stocks or marketable securities or a policy of insurance or a policy of life insurance",

shall not be chargeable on any instrument made for the purposes of or in connection with the transfer of the undertaking or shares, or on any instrument made for the purposes of or in connection with the assignment to the acquiring company of any debts, secured or unsecured, of the target company.

[(2A) (a) This subsection applies to any property, an instrument for the conveyance of which is chargeable to stamp duty under or by reference to the heading "CONVEYANCE or TRANSFER on sale of any property other than stocks or marketable securities or a policy of insurance or a policy of life insurance" in *Schedule 1*.

(b) Subsection (2) shall not apply to an instrument made for the purposes of or in connection with the transfer of an undertaking of a target company that includes any property to which this subsection applies, where a conveyance of that property has not been obtained by the target company prior to the date of the execution of the instrument.][3]

(3) [...][4]

(b) In the case of an instrument made for the purposes of or in connection with a transfer to a company within the meaning of the Companies Act, 1963, *subsection (2)* shall not apply unless the instrument is either—

(i) executed within a period of 12 months from the date of the registration of the acquiring company or the date of the resolution for the increase of the nominal share capital of the acquiring company, as the case may be, or

(ii) made for the purpose of effecting a conveyance or transfer in pursuance of an agreement which has been filed, or particulars of which have been filed, with the registrar of companies within that period of 12 months.

(4) This section shall not apply unless the scheme of reconstruction or amalgamation is effected for bona fide commercial reasons and does not form part of a scheme or arrangement of which the main purpose, or one of the main purposes, is avoidance of liability to stamp duty, income tax, corporation tax, capital gains tax or capital acquisitions tax.

(5) For the purposes of a claim for exemption under *subsection (2)*, a company which has, in connection with a scheme of reconstruction or amalgamation, issued any unissued share capital shall be treated as if it had increased its nominal share capital.

(6) A company shall not be deemed to be a target company within the meaning of this section unless it is provided by the memorandum of association of, or Act establishing, the acquiring company that one of the objects for which the company is formed is the acquisition of the undertaking of, or shares in, the target company, or unless it appears from the resolution, Act or other authority for the increase of the capital of the acquiring company that the increase is authorised for the purpose of acquiring the undertaking of, or shares in, the target company.

[...][5]

[...][6]

(8) If—

(a) in respect of any claim for exemption from duty under this section which has been allowed, it is subsequently found that [the exemption was not properly due][7], or that the conditions specified in *subsection (2)* are not fulfilled in the reconstruction or amalgamation as actually carried out,

(b) in respect of shares in the acquiring company which have been issued to the target company in consideration of the acquisition, the target company within a period of 2 years from the date, as the case may be, of the registration or establishment, or of the authority for the increase of the capital, of the acquiring company ceases, otherwise than in consequence of reconstruction, amalgamation or liquidation, to be the beneficial owner of the shares so issued to it, or

(c) in respect of any such exemption which has been allowed in connection with the acquisition by the acquiring company of shares in the target company, the acquiring company within a period of 2 years from the date of its registration or establishment or of the authority for the increase of its capital, as the case may be, ceases, otherwise than in consequence of reconstruction, amalgamation or liquidation, to be the beneficial owner of the shares so acquired,

then the exemption shall cease to be applicable and stamp duty shall be chargeable in respect of the conveyance or transfer as if *subsection (2)* had not been enacted together with [interest on the duty, [...][8], calculated in accordance with section 159D,][9] on which the duty is paid, in a case to which *paragraph (a)* applies, from the date of the conveyance or transfer or, in a case to which *paragraph (b)* applies, from the date the target company ceased to be the beneficial owner of the shares so issued to it or, in a case to which *paragraph (c)* applies, from the date the acquiring company ceased to be the beneficial owner of the shares so acquired.

(9) If in the case of any scheme of reconstruction or amalgamation the Commissioners are satisfied that at the proper time for making a claim for exemption from duty under *subsection (2)* there were in existence all the necessary conditions for such exemption other than the condition that not less than 90 per cent of the issued share capital of the target company would be acquired by the acquiring company, the Commissioners may—

(a) if it is proved to their satisfaction that not less than 90 per cent of the issued capital of the target company has under the scheme been acquired within a period of 6 months from—

(i) the last day of the period of one month after the first allotment of shares made for the purposes of the acquisition, or

(ii) the date on which an invitation was issued to the shareholders of the target company to accept shares in the acquiring company,

whichever first occurs,

and

(b) on production of the instruments on which the duty paid has been impressed,

repay such an amount of duty as would have been remitted if that condition had been originally fulfilled.

(10) This section shall apply notwithstanding—

(a) that the acquiring company referred to in this section is incorporated in another [Member State of the European Union or in an EEA State within the meaning of *section 80A*][10], or

(b) that the target company referred to in this section is incorporated outside the State,

but only where such acquiring company or target company incorporated outside the State corresponds, under the law of the place where it is incorporated, to an acquiring company or target company, as the case may be, within the meaning of this section and subject to any necessary modifications for the purpose of so corresponding, all the other provisions of this section are met.

Amendments

[1] Substituted by FA08 s116 with effect from 1 January 2008.

[2] Deleted by FA12 sched3(21)(a). In effect for all instruments that are executed on or after 7 July 2012 per S.I. No. 228 of 2012.

[3] Inserted by FA04 s68(1). This section has effect in relation to instruments executed on or after 20 February 2004.

[4] Deleted by FA12 sched3(21)(b). In effect for all instruments that are executed on or after 7 July 2012 per S.I. No. 228 of 2012.

[5] Deleted by FA13 s77(g).

[6] Deleted by FA12 sched3(21)(c). In effect for all instruments that are executed on or after 7 July 2012 per S.I. No. 228 of 2012.

[7] Substituted by FA12 sched3(21)(d). In effect for all instruments that are executed on or after 7 July 2012 per S.I. No. 228 of 2012.

[8] Deleted by F(No.2)A08 sched5(part5)(chap2)(7)(f).

[9] Substituted by FA05 sched5.

[10] Substituted by FA10 sched(4)(2)(c). Has effect as on and from 3 April 2010.

Note:

F(No.2)A08 sched5 (part5)(chap 2)(7)

As respects paragraph 7 of this Schedule subparagraphs (a) to (aa) (other than subparagraph (c)(i)(I)) of that paragraph have effect as on and from the passing of this Act and to the extent that Chapter 3A (being inserted into Part 47 of the Taxes Consolidation Act 1997 by Part 1 of this Schedule) applies to penalties incurred under the Stamp Duties Consolidation Act 1999 before the passing of this Act which on the passing of this Act have not been paid, it shall not apply to such penalties which are in the form of interest accrued under any provisions of the said Act.

Case Law

Patrick W Keane & Co v The Revenue Commissioners 2008 ITR 57 considered whether a transaction constituted a reconstruction or partition for the purpose of this section.

Baytrust Holdings Ltd v IRC 1971 3 All ER 76 considered the meaning of 'reconstruction' and 'undertaking'.

In Crane Fruehauf Ltd v IRC 1975 STC 51 an amalgamation was the coming together of two companies so that they were, after the transfer, owned by the same persons as before.

In E. Gomme Ltd v IRC 1964 3 All ER 497 the term undertaking was held to relate to the gross value of the undertaking.

Revenue Briefings

Tax Briefing

Tax Briefing June 2001 – Issue 44 (part 2) pg 30 – Revenue Certificates in Deeds

Cross References

From Section 80

Section 20 Assessment of duty by the Commissioners.
Section 80A Demutualisation of Assurance Companies.
Schedule 1 Stamp Duties on Instruments

80A Demutualisation of Assurance Companies

[(1) In this section—

"*acquiring company*" means a limited company which is incorporated in the State, in another Member State or in an EEA State;

"*assurance business*" has the meaning assigned to it by section 3 of the Insurance Act 1936;

"*assurance company*" means—

(a) an assurance company within the meaning of section 3 of the Insurance Act 1936, or

(b) a person that holds an authorisation within the meaning of the European Communities (Life Assurance) Framework Regulations 1994 (S.I. No. 360 of 1994);

"*demutualisation*" means an arrangement between an assurance company, being an assurance company which carries on a mutual life business, and its members under which—

(a) the assurance business or part of the business carried on by the assurance company is transferred to an acquiring company, and

(b) shares or the right to shares in the issuing company are issued or, as the case may be, granted to the members;

"*EEA Agreement*" means the Agreement on the European Economic Area signed at Oporto on 2 May 1992, as adjusted by the Protocol signed at Brussels on 17 March 1993;

"*EEA State*" means a state which is a contracting party to the EEA Agreement;

"*employee*", in relation to a company, includes any officer or director of the company and any other person taking part in the management of the affairs of the company;

"*issuing company*", in relation to a demutualisation, means an acquiring company or a parent company in relation to an acquiring company, including a company which becomes a parent company in relation to an acquiring company as part of the demutualisation;

"*member*", in relation to a reference to a member of an assurance company, or to a person who is entitled to be a member of an assurance company, includes a reference to a member of any particular class or description;

"*parent company*", in relation to an acquiring company, means a limited company incorporated in the State, in another Member State or in an EEA State, which owns directly or indirectly 100 per cent of the ordinary share capital of the acquiring company;

"*pensioner*", in relation to a company, means a person who is entitled, whether now or in the future, to a pension, lump sum, gratuity or other like benefit referable to the service of any person as an employee of the company;

"*shares*" includes stock.

(2) Stamp duty shall not be chargeable on any instrument made for the purposes of or in connection with a demutualisation where the conditions set out in subsection (3) are satisfied.

(3) The conditions referred to in subsection (2) are—

(a) shares in the issuing company must be offered to at least 90 per cent of the persons who immediately prior to the demutualisation are members of the assurance company, and

(b) all the shares in the issuing company which will be in issue immediately after the demutualisation, other than shares which are to be or have been issued pursuant to an offer to the public, must be offered to persons who, at the time of the offer, are—

(i) members of the assurance company,

(ii) persons who are entitled to become members of the assurance company, or

(iii) employees, former employees or pensioners of the assurance company or of a company which is a wholly-owned subsidiary of the assurance company.

(4) For the purposes of subsection (3)(*b*)(iii), a company is a wholly-owned subsidiary of another company (in this subsection referred to as the "*parent*") if it has no members other than the parent and the wholly-owned subsidiaries of the parent, or persons acting on behalf of the parent or its wholly-owned subsidiaries.

[...][1]

(6) This section shall not apply unless the demutualisation is carried out for bona fide commercial reasons and does not form part of a scheme or arrangement of which the main purpose, or one of the main purposes, is avoidance of liability to stamp duty, income tax, corporation tax, capital gains tax or capital acquisitions tax.

[...][2]

[...][3]

(8) Where, in respect of any claim for exemption from duty under this section which has been allowed, it is subsequently found that [the exemption was not properly due][4], or that the conditions set out in subsection (3) are not fulfilled in the demutualisation as actually carried out, then the exemption shall cease to be applicable and stamp duty shall be chargeable on the instrument as if subsection (2) had not been enacted together with interest on the duty, [...][5] calculated in accordance with section 159D, from the date of the instrument to the date on which the duty is paid.][6]

Amendments

[1] Deleted by FA12 sched3(22)(a). In effect for all instruments that are executed on or after 7 July 2012 per S.I. No. 228 of 2012.

[2] Deleted by FA13 s77(h).

[3] Deleted by FA12 sched3(22)(b). In effect for all instruments that are executed on or after 7 July 2012 per S.I. No. 228 of 2012.

[4] Substituted by FA12 sched3(22)(c). In effect for all instruments that are executed on or after 7 July 2012 per S.I. No. 228 of 2012.

[5] Deleted by F(No.2)A08 sched5(part5)(chap2)(7)(f).

[6] Inserted by FA06 s104(1). This section shall apply as respects instruments executed on or after 31 March 2006

Note:

F(No.2)A08 sched5 (part5)(chap 2)(7)

As respects paragraph 7 of this Schedule subparagraphs (a) to (aa) (other than subparagraph (c)(i)(I)) of that paragraph have effect as on and from the passing of this Act and to the extent that Chapter 3A (being inserted into Part 47 of the Taxes Consolidation Act 1997 by Part 1 of this Schedule) applies to penalties incurred under the Stamp Duties Consolidation Act 1999 before the passing of this Act which on the passing of this Act have not been paid, it shall not apply to such penalties which are in the form of interest accrued under any provisions of the said Act.

Cross References

From Section 80A

Section 20 Assessment of duty by the Commissioners.

To Section 80A

Section 80 Reconstructions or amalgamations of companies.

81 Young trained farmers

[FA1994 s112]

(1) In this section and *Schedule 2*—

"*an interest in land*" means an interest which is not subject to any power (whether or not contained in the instrument) on the exercise of which the land, or any part of or any interest in the land, may be revested in the person from whom it was conveyed or transferred or in any person on behalf of such person;

"*land*" means agricultural land and includes such farm buildings, farm houses and mansion houses (together with the lands occupied with such farm buildings, farm houses and mansion houses) as are of a character appropriate to the land;

"*young trained farmer*" means a person in respect of whom it is shown to the satisfaction of the Commissioners—

(a) that such person had not attained the age of 35 years on the date on which the instrument, as respect which relief is being claimed under this section, was executed, and

(b) (i) that such person is the holder of a qualification set out in *Schedule 2* and, in the case of a qualification set out in *subparagraph (c)*, *(d)*, *(e)*, *(f)* or *(g)* of *paragraph 3* or *paragraph 4* of that Schedule, is also the holder of a certificate issued by Teagasc certifying that such person has satisfactorily attended a course of training in farm management, the aggregate duration of which exceeded 80 hours, or

(ii) (I) that such person has satisfactorily attended full-time a course at a third-level institution in any discipline for a period of not less than 2 years' duration, and

(II) is the holder of a certificate issued by Teagasc certifying satisfactory attendance at a course of training in either or both agriculture and horticulture, the aggregate duration of which exceeded 180 hours,

or

(iii) if born before 1 January 1968 that such person is the holder of a certificate issued by Teagasc certifying that such person—

(I) has had farming as the principal occupation for a period of not less than 3 years, and

(II) has satisfactorily attended a course of training in either or both agriculture and horticulture, the aggregate duration of which exceeded 180 hours,

and notwithstanding *paragraphs (a)* and *(b)*, where Teagasc certifies that any other qualification corresponds to a qualification which is set out in *Schedule 2*, the Commissioners shall, for the purposes of this section, treat that other qualification as if it were the corresponding qualification so set out.

[(2) No stamp duty shall be chargeable under or by reference to the heading "CONVEYANCE or TRANSFER on sale of any property other than stocks or marketable securities or a policy of insurance or a policy of life insurance" in *Schedule 1* on any instrument to which this section applies.][1]

(3) This section applies to any instrument which operates as a conveyance or transfer (whether on sale or as a voluntary disposition inter vivos) of an interest in land to a young trained farmer where—

(a) the instrument contains a certificate that this section applies,

(b) a declaration made in writing by the young trained farmer, or each of them if there is more than one, is furnished to the Commissioners when the instrument is presented for stamping, confirming, to the satisfaction of the Commissioners, that it is the intention of such person, or each such person, for a period of not less than 5 years from the date of execution of the instrument to—

(i) spend not less than 50 per cent of that person's normal working time farming the land, and

(ii) retain ownership of the land,

and

(c) the identifying reference number, known as the Revenue and Social Insurance (RSI) Number, of the young trained farmer, or each of them if there is more than one, is furnished to the Commissioners when the instrument is presented for stamping.

(4) Notwithstanding *subsection (3),* this section shall apply where the property is conveyed or transferred into joint ownership where all the joint owners are young trained farmers or where any of the joint owners is a spouse of another joint owner who is a young trained farmer.

(5) Where this section would have applied to the instrument, except for the fact that a person to whom the land is being conveyed or transferred is not a young trained farmer on the date when the instrument was executed, by reason of not being the holder of one of the qualifications, or an equivalent qualification, specified in *Schedule 2* or, in the case of the requirement in *paragraph (b)(ii)(I)* of the definition of "*young*

trained farmer" in *subsection (1)*, not having attended full-time for the required 2 years' duration, but that such person had completed on that date at least one academic year of the prescribed course leading to an award of such qualification, or the course prescribed in *paragraph (b)(ii)(I)* of that definition, then—

(a) if such person becomes a holder of such qualification, or satisfactorily attends such course full-time for a period of 2 years, within a period of 3 years from the date of execution of the instrument, the Commissioners shall, on production of the stamped instrument to them within 6 months after the date when such person became the holder of such qualification, or completed the required 2 years' attendance on such course, and on furnishing satisfactory evidence of compliance with this subsection, the declaration and the Revenue and Social Insurance (RSI) Number, as provided for in *subsection (3)*, cancel and refund, without payment of interest on the duty, such duty as would not have been chargeable had this section applied to the instrument when it was first presented for stamping, and

(b) the period of 5 years provided for in *subsection (3)* in relation to the declaration to be made by such person, as it applies to normal working time, shall be reduced by the period of time that elapsed between the date of the instrument and the date on which such person became the holder of such qualification or completed the required 2 years' attendance on such course.

[(6) Subsection (2) shall not apply to an instrument unless it has, in accordance with *section 20*, been stamped with a particular stamp denoting that it is not chargeable with any duty or that it is duly stamped.][2]

[(7)

[(a) Where any person to whom land was conveyed or transferred by any instrument in respect of which relief from stamp duty under subsection (2) applied—

(i) disposes of such land, or part of such land (in this subsection referred to as a "*part disposal*"), within a period of 5 years from the date of execution of that instrument, and

(ii) does not fully expend the proceeds from such disposal, or as the case may be, such part disposal, in acquiring other land within a period of one year from the date of such disposal,

then, such person or, where there is more than one such person, each such person, jointly and severally, shall become liable to pay to the Commissioners [an amount (in this section referred to as a "*clawback*")][3] equal to an amount determined by the formula—

$$S \times \frac{N}{V}$$

where—

S is the amount of stamp duty which would have been charged on that instrument had relief under subsection (2) not applied,

V is the market value of all the land that was conveyed or transferred by the instrument immediately before the disposal, or as the case may be, the part disposal of the land, and

N is the amount of proceeds from the disposal, or as the case may be, the part disposal of the land that was not expended in acquiring other land.

(aa) [interest shall be payable on a [clawback][4] incurred under paragraph (*a*), calculated in accordance with section 159D,][5] from the date of disposal, or as the case may be, part disposal of the land to the date the [clawback][6] is remitted.

(ab) For the purposes of paragraph (*a*)—

(i) where a disposal of land is effected in whole or in part by way of a voluntary disposition inter vivos, an amount equal to the market value of the lands disposed of, at the date of the disposal, shall be deemed to be the proceeds from such disposal,

(ii) where any property is received by way of exchange, in whole or in part for a disposal, an amount equal to the market value of such property, at the date of the disposal, shall be deemed to be proceeds from such disposal, and

(iii) where subparagraph (ii) applies and property received by way of exchange is land or includes land, an amount equal to the market value of such land at the date of the disposal shall be deemed to have been expended in acquiring other land.

(ac) A person shall not be liable to a [clawback][7] under paragraph (*a*), if and to the extent that any [clawback][8] or, as the case may be, the aggregate of any [clawbacks][9], paid by that person under paragraph (*a*), exceeds the stamp duty which would have been charged on the instrument had relief under subsection (2) not applied.][10]

(b) Where any claim for relief from duty under this section has been allowed and it is subsequently found that a declaration made, or a certificate contained in the instrument, in accordance with subsection (3)—

(i) was untrue in any material particular which would have resulted in the relief afforded by this section not being granted, and

(ii) was made, or was included, knowing same to be untrue or in reckless disregard as to whether it was true or not,

then any person who made such a declaration, or where a false certificate has been included, the person or persons to whom the land is conveyed or transferred by the instrument, jointly and severally, shall be liable to pay to the Commissioners as a penalty an amount equal to 125 per cent of the duty which would have been charged on the instrument in the first instance had all the facts been truthfully declared and certified, together with [interest charged on that amount as may so become payable, calculated in accordance with section 159D,][11] from the date when the instrument was executed to the date the penalty is remitted.][12]

(8) Notwithstanding *subsection (7)*—

(a) where relief under this section was allowed in respect of any instrument, a disposal by a young trained farmer of part of the land to a spouse for the purpose of creating a joint tenancy in the land, or where the instrument conveyed or transferred the land to joint owners, a disposal by one joint owner to another of any part of the land, shall not be regarded as a disposal to which *subsection (7)* applies, but on such disposal, such part of the land shall be treated for the purposes of *subsection (7)* as if it had been conveyed or transferred immediately to the spouse or other joint owner by the instrument in respect of which relief from duty under this section was allowed in the first instance;

(b) a person shall not be liable to more than one penalty under *paragraph (b)* of *subsection (7)*;

(c) a person shall not be liable to a [clawback under *paragraph (a)*][13] of *subsection (7)* if and to the extent that such person has paid a penalty under *paragraph (b)* of *subsection (7)*, and

(d) a person shall not be liable to a [clawback under *paragraph (a)*][14] of *subsection (7)*, if and to the extent that such person has paid a penalty under *paragraph (a)* of *subsection (7)*.

[(9) This section shall apply as respects instruments executed before the date of the passing of the *Finance Act 2004*.][15]

Amendments

[1] Substituted by FA00 s126(1)(a). Shall apply and have effect in relation to instruments executed on or after 1 January 2000.

[2] Substituted by FA00 s126(1)(b). Shall apply and have effect in relation to instruments executed on or after 1 January 2000.

[3] Substituted by F(No.2)A08 sched5(part5)(chap2)(7)(g)(i)(I).

[4, 6] Substituted by F(No.2)A08 sched5(part5)(chap2)(7)(g)(i)(II).

[5, 11] Substituted by FA05 sched5.

[7, 8, 9] Substituted by F(No.2)A08 sched5(part5)(chap2)(7)(g)(i)(III).

[10] Substituted by FA05 s119(1). This section shall apply as respects disposals or part disposals of land effected on or after 3 February 2005.

[12] Substituted by FA00 s126(1)(c). Shall apply and have effect in relation to instruments executed on or after 1 January 2000.

[13, 14] Substituted by F(No.2)A08 sched5(part5)(chap2)(1)(g)(ii).

[15] Substituted by FA04 s69. The date of passing of FA04 was 25 March 2004.

Note:

F(No.2)A08 sched5 (part5)(chap 2)(7)

As respects paragraph 7 of this Schedule subparagraphs (a) to (aa) (other than subparagraph (c)(i)(I)) of that paragraph have effect as on and from the passing of this Act and to the extent that Chapter 3A (being inserted into Part 47 of the Taxes Consolidation Act 1997 by Part 1 of this Schedule) applies to penalties incurred under the Stamp Duties Consolidation Act 1999 before the passing of this Act which on the passing of this Act have not been paid, it shall not apply to such penalties which are in the form of interest accrued under any provisions of the said Act.

Revenue Briefings

Tax Briefing

Tax Briefing June 2001 – Issue 44 (part 2) pg 30 – Revenue Certificates in Deeds

eBrief

e-Brief No. 05/2009 – Stamp Duty: Late Stamping of Instruments

Cross References

From Section 81

Section 20 Assessment of duty by the Commissioners.

Schedule 1 Stamp Duties on Instruments

Schedule 2 Qualifications for Applying for Relief From Stamp Duty in Respect of Transfers to Young Trained Farmers

To Section 81

Section 81A Further relief from stamp duty in respect of transfers to young trained farmers.

Section 81AA Transfers to young trained farmers.

Schedule 2 Qualifications for Applying for Relief From Stamp Duty in Respect of Transfers to Young Trained Farmers

81A Further relief from stamp duty in respect of transfers to young trained farmers

[(1) In this section and *Schedule 2A*—

"*interest in land*" means an interest which is not subject to any power (whether or not contained in the instrument) on the exercise of which the land, or any part of or any interest in the land, may be revested in the person from whom it was conveyed or transferred or in any person on behalf of such person;

"*land*" means agricultural land and includes such farm buildings, farm houses and mansion houses (together with the lands occupied with such farm buildings, farm houses and mansion houses) as are of a character appropriate to the land;

"*Schedule 2A* qualification" means a qualification set out in *Schedule 2A*;

"*young trained farmer*" means a person in respect of whom it is shown to the satisfaction of the Commissioners that—

(a) the person had not attained the age of 35 years on the date on which the instrument, as respect which relief is being claimed under this section, was executed, and

(b) the conditions referred to in *subsection (2), (3) or (4)* are satisfied.

(2) The conditions required by this subsection are that the person, referred to in *paragraph (a)* of the definition of young trained farmer, is the holder of a *Schedule 2A* qualification, and—

(a) in the case of a qualification set out in *subparagraph (f)* of *paragraph 1*, or *subparagraph (h)* of *paragraph 2*, of that Schedule, is also the holder of a certificate awarded by the Further Education and Training Awards Council for achieving the minimum stipulated standard in assessments completed in a course of training approved by Teagasc—

(i) in either or both agriculture and horticulture, the aggregate duration of which exceeded 100 hours, and

(ii) in farm management, the aggregate duration of which exceeded 80 hours,

or

(b) in the case of a qualification set out in *subparagraph (b), (c)* or *(d)* of *paragraph 3* of that Schedule, is also the holder of a certificate awarded by the Further Education and Training Awards Council for achieving the minimum stipulated standard in assessments completed in a course of training, approved by Teagasc, in farm management, the aggregate duration of which exceeded 80 hours.

(3) The conditions required by this subsection are that the person, referred to in *paragraph (a)* of the definition of young trained farmer—

(a) has achieved the required standard for entry into the third year of a full-time course in any discipline of 3 or more years' duration at a third-level institution, and that has been confirmed by that institution, and

(b) is the holder of a certificate awarded by the Further Education and Training Awards Council for achieving a minimum stipulated standard in assessments completed in a course of training, approved by Teagasc—

(i) in either or both agriculture and horticulture, the aggregate duration of which exceeded 100 hours, and

(ii) in farm management, the aggregate duration of which exceeded 80 hours.

(4) The conditions required by this subsection are that the person, referred to in *paragraph (a)* of the definition of young trained farmer, is the holder of a letter of confirmation from Teagasc, confirming satisfactory completion of a course of training, approved by Teagasc, for persons, who in the opinion of Teagasc, are restricted in their learning capacity due to physical, sensory, mental health or intellectual disability.

(5) For the purposes of *subsection (2)*, where Teagasc certifies that—

(a) any other qualification corresponds to a *Schedule 2A* qualification, and

(b) that other qualification is deemed by the National Qualifications Authority of Ireland to be at least at a standard equivalent to that of the *Schedule 2A* qualification,

the Commissioners shall treat that other qualification as if it were a *Schedule 2A* qualification.

(6) No stamp duty shall be chargeable under or by reference to the heading "CONVEYANCE or TRANSFER on sale of any property other than stocks or marketable securities or a policy of insurance or a policy of life insurance" in *Schedule 1* on any instrument to which this section applies.

(7) This section applies to any instrument which operates as a conveyance or transfer (whether on sale or as a voluntary disposition inter vivos) of an interest in land to a young trained farmer where—

(a) the instrument contains a certificate that this section applies,

(b) a declaration made in writing by the young trained farmer, or each of them if there is more than one, is furnished to the Commissioners when the instrument is presented for stamping, confirming, to the satisfaction of the Commissioners, that it is the intention of such person, or each such person, for a period of not less than 5 years from the date of execution of the instrument to—

(i) spend not less than 50 per cent of that person's normal working time, farming the land, and

(ii) retain ownership of the land,

and

(c) the identifying reference number, known as the Personal Public Service (PPS) Number, of the young trained farmer, or each of them if there is more than one, is furnished to the Commissioners when the instrument is presented for stamping.

(8) Notwithstanding subsection (7), this section shall apply where the property is conveyed or transferred into joint ownership where all the joint owners are young trained farmers or where any of the joint owners is a spouse of another joint owner who is a young trained farmer.

(9) (a) For the purposes of this subsection, a person "achieves the standard" at any time where at that time the person—

(i) is the holder of a *Schedule 2A* qualification or a qualification treated, by virtue of subsection (5), as being a *Schedule 2A* qualification,

(ii) satisfies the conditions set out in subsection (3)(*a*), or

(iii) satisfies the conditions set out in subsection (4),

and whether a person has or has not achieved the standard shall be construed accordingly.

(b) This subsection applies to an instrument by means of which land is conveyed or transferred to a person (in this subsection referred to as the "*transferee*") who on the date the instrument was executed—

(i) was not a young trained farmer by reason only of the fact that the transferee on that date had not achieved the standard, and

(ii) had completed not less than one academic year of a course necessary to be taken to achieve the standard.

(c) Where within 3 years from the date of execution of an instrument to which this subsection refers, the transferee achieves the standard, the Commissioners shall, on production to them, within 6 months after the date on which the standard was achieved, of—

(i) the stamped instrument,

(ii) subject to *paragraph (d)*, the declaration referred to in *subsection (7)(b)*,

(iii) the Personal Public Service (PPS) Number referred to in *subsection (7)(c)*, and

(iv) satisfactory evidence of compliance with this subsection,

cancel and refund such duty as would not have been chargeable had this section applied to the instrument when it was first presented for stamping.

(d) For the purposes of *paragraph (c)*(ii), the period of 5 years referred to in *subsection (7)(b)* as it relates to the requirement that a person spend not less than 50 per cent of the person's normal working time farming land, shall be reduced by the period of time that elapsed between the date of the instrument and the date on which the transferee achieved the standard.

(10) *Subsection (6)* shall not apply to an instrument unless it has, in accordance with *section 20*, been stamped with a particular stamp denoting that it is not chargeable with any duty.

[(11) (a) Where any person to whom land was conveyed or transferred by any instrument in respect of which relief from stamp duty under subsection (6) applied—

(i) disposes of such land, or part of such land (in this subsection referred to as a "*part disposal*"), within a period of 5 years from the date of execution of that instrument, and

(ii) does not fully expend the proceeds from such disposal, or as the case may be, such part disposal, in acquiring other land within a period of one year from the date of such disposal,

then, such person or, where there is more than one such person, each such person, jointly and severally, shall become liable to pay to the Commissioners [an amount (in this section referred to as a "*clawback*")][1] equal to an amount determined by the formula—

$$S \times \frac{N}{V}$$

where—

S is the amount of stamp duty which would have been charged on that instrument had relief under subsection (6) not applied,

V is the market value of all the land that was conveyed or transferred by the instrument immediately before the disposal, or as the case may be, the part disposal of the land, and

N is the amount of proceeds from the disposal, or as the case may be, the part disposal of the land that was not expended in acquiring other land.

(aa) [interest shall be payable on a [clawback][2] incurred under *paragraph (a)*, calculated in accordance with *section 159D*,][3] from the date of disposal, or as the case may be, part disposal of the land to the date the [clawback][4] is remitted.

(ab) For the purposes of *paragraph (a)*—

(i) where a disposal of land is effected in whole or in part by way of a voluntary disposition inter vivos, an amount equal to the market value of the lands disposed of, at the date of the disposal, shall be deemed to be the proceeds from such disposal,

(ii) where any property is received by way of exchange, in whole or in part for a disposal, an amount equal to the market value of such property, at the date of the disposal, shall be deemed to be proceeds from such disposal, and

(iii) where *subparagraph (ii)* applies and property received by way of exchange is land or includes land, an amount equal to the market value of such land at the date of the disposal shall be deemed to have been expended in acquiring other land.

(ac) A person shall not be liable to a [clawback][5] under *paragraph (a)*, if and to the extent that any [clawback][6] or, as the case may be, the aggregate of any [clawbacks][7], paid by that person under *paragraph (a)*, exceeds the stamp duty which would have been charged on the instrument had relief under *subsection (6)* not applied.][8]

(b) Where any claim for relief from duty under this section has been allowed and it is subsequently found that a declaration made, or a certificate contained in the instrument, in accordance with *subsection (7)*—

(i) was untrue in any material particular which would have resulted in the relief afforded by this section not being granted, and

(ii) was made, or was included, knowing same to be untrue or in reckless disregard as to whether it was true or not,

then any person who made such a declaration, or where a false certificate has been included, the person or persons to whom the land is conveyed or transferred by the instrument, jointly and severally, shall be liable to pay to the Commissioners as a penalty an amount equal to 125 per cent of the duty which would have been charged on the instrument in the first instance had all the facts been truthfully declared and certified, together with [interest charged on that amount as may so become payable, calculated in accordance with *section 159D*,][9] from the date when the instrument was executed to the date the penalty is remitted.

(12) Notwithstanding *subsection (11)*—

(a) where relief under this section was allowed in respect of any instrument, a disposal by a young trained farmer of part of the land to a spouse for the purpose of creating a joint tenancy in the land, or where the instrument conveyed or transferred the land to joint owners, a disposal by one joint owner to another of any part of the land, shall not be regarded as a disposal to which *subsection (11)* applies, but on such disposal, such part of the land shall be treated for the purposes of *subsection (11)* as if it had been conveyed or transferred immediately to the spouse or other joint owner by the instrument in respect of which relief from duty under this section was allowed in the first instance,

(b) a person shall not be liable to more than one penalty under *paragraph (b)* of *subsection (11)*,

(c) a person shall not be liable to a [clawback under *paragraph (a)*][10] of *subsection (11)*, if and to the extent that such person has paid a penalty under *paragraph (b)* of *subsection (11)*, and

(d) a person shall not be liable to a [clawback under *paragraph (a)*][11] of *subsection (11)*, if and to the extent that such person has paid a penalty under *paragraph (a)* of *subsection (11)*.

(13) A person who, before the date of the passing of the *Finance Act 2004*, for the purposes of *section 81*—

(a) is the holder of a qualification set out in *Schedule 2* or a qualification certified by Teagasc as corresponding to a qualification set out in *Schedule 2*, and—

(i) a satisfactory attendance at a course of training in farm management, the aggregate duration of which exceeded 80 hours, is required, shall be deemed, for the purposes of this section, to be the holder of a qualification corresponding to that set out in *subparagraph (b)* of *paragraph 3* of *Schedule 2A*, or

(ii) a satisfactory attendance at a course of training is not required, shall be deemed, for the purposes of this section, to be the holder of a qualification corresponding to that set out in *subparagraph (a)* of *paragraph 2* of *Schedule 2A*,

(b) satisfies the requirements set out in *paragraph (b)(ii)(I)* of the definition of young trained farmer in *subsection (1)* of that section, shall be deemed for the purposes of this section, to have satisfied the requirements set out in *subsection (3)(a)*, and

(c) is the holder of a certificate issued by Teagasc certifying satisfactory attendance at a course of training—

(i) in farm management, the aggregate duration of which exceeded 80 hours, shall be deemed for the purposes of this section to be the holder of a certificate referred to in *subsection (2)(b)*, or

(ii) in either or both agriculture and horticulture, the aggregate duration of which exceeded 180 hours, shall be deemed for the purposes of this section to be the holder of a certificate referred to in *subsection (3)(b)*.

[(14) This section applies as respects instruments executed on or after 25 March 2004 and before the date of the passing of the Finance Act 2007.][12]][13]

Amendments

[1] Substituted by F(No.2)A08 sched5(part5)(chap2)(7)(h)(i)(I).

[2, 4] Substituted by F(No.2)A08 sched5(part5)(chap2)(7)(h)(i)(II).

[3, 9] Substituted by FA05 sched5.

[5, 6, 7] Substituted by F(No.2)A08 sched5(part5)(chap2)(7)(h)(i)(III).

[8] Substituted by FA05 s120(1). This section shall apply as respects disposals or part disposals of land effected on or after 3 February 2005.

[10, 11] Substituted by F(No.2)A08 sched5(part5)(chap2)(7)(h)(ii).

[12] Substituted by FA07 s102.

[13] Inserted by FA04 s70(a).

Note:

F(No.2)A08 sched5 (part5)(chap 2)(7)

As respects paragraph 7 of this Schedule subparagraphs (a) to (aa) (other than subparagraph (c)(i)(I)) of that paragraph have effect as on and from the passing of this Act and to the extent that Chapter 3A (being inserted into Part 47 of the Taxes Consolidation Act 1997 by Part 1 of this Schedule) applies to penalties incurred under the Stamp Duties Consolidation Act 1999 before the passing of this Act which on the passing of this Act have not been paid, it shall not apply to such penalties which are in the form of interest accrued under any provisions of the said Act.

Revenue Briefings

Tax Briefing

Tax Briefing November 2005 – Issue 61 – Tax Implications of The Single Payment Scheme

Revenue Information Notes

SD2B – Stamp Duty Exemption Transfers of Land to Young Trained Farmers

Cross References

From Section 81A

Section 20 Assessment of duty by the Commissioners.

Section 81 Young trained farmers.

Section 159D Calculation of interest on unpaid duty and other amounts.

Schedule 1 Stamp Duties on Instruments

Schedule 2 Qualifications for Applying for Relief From Stamp Duty in Respect of Transfers to Young Trained Farmers

Schedule 2A Qualifications for Applying for Relief From Stamp Duty in Respect of Transfers to Young Trained Farmers

To Section 81A

Section 81AA Transfers to young trained farmers.

Schedule 2A Qualifications for Applying for Relief From Stamp Duty in Respect of Transfers to Young Trained Farmers

81AA Transfers to young trained farmers

[(1) In this section and *Schedule 2B*—

"*interest in land*" means an interest which is not subject to any power (whether or not contained in the instrument) on the exercise of which the land, or any part of or any interest in the land, may be revested in the person from whom it was conveyed or transferred or in any person on behalf of such person;

"*land*" means agricultural land and includes such farm buildings, farm houses and mansion houses (together with the lands occupied with such farm buildings, farm houses and mansion houses) as are of a character appropriate to the land;

"*PPS Number*", in relation to a person, means the person"s Personal Public Service Number within the meaning of section 262 of the Social Welfare Consolidation Act 2005;

"*Schedule 2* qualification" means a qualification set out in *Schedule 2*;

"*Schedule 2A* qualification" means a qualification set out in *Schedule 2A*;

"*Schedule 2B* qualification" means a qualification set out in *Schedule 2B*;

"*young trained farmer*" means a person in respect of whom it is shown to the satisfaction of the Commissioners that—

(a) the person had not attained the age of 35 years on the date on which the instrument, in respect of which relief is being claimed under this section, was executed, and

(b) the conditions referred to in *subsection (2)*, *(3)*, *(4)* or *(5)* are satisfied;

"80 hours certificate" means a certificate awarded by the Further Education and Training Awards Council for achieving the minimum stipulated standard in assessments completed in a course of training, approved by Teagasc, in farm management, the aggregate duration of which exceeded 80 hours;

"180 hours certificate" means a certificate awarded by the Further Education and Training Awards Council for achieving the minimum stipulated standard in assessments completed in a course of training approved by Teagasc—

(a) in either or both agriculture and horticulture, the aggregate duration of which exceeded 100 hours, and

(b) in farm management, the aggregate duration of which exceeded 80 hours.

(2) The condition required by this subsection is that the person, referred to in *paragraph (a)* of the definition of young trained farmer, is the holder of a *Schedule 2B* qualification.

(3) The condition required by this subsection is that the person, referred to in *paragraph (a)* of the definition of young trained farmer, is the holder of a letter of confirmation from Teagasc, confirming satisfactory completion of a course of training, approved by Teagasc, for persons, who in the opinion of Teagasc, are restricted in their learning capacity due to physical, sensory or intellectual disability or to mental health.

(4) The conditions required by this subsection are that the person, referred to in *paragraph (a)* of the definition of young trained farmer, before 31 March 2008, is the holder of—

(a) (i) a qualification set out in *subparagraph (f)* of *paragraph 1*, or *subparagraph (h)* of *paragraph 2*, of *Schedule 2A*, and

(ii) a 180 hours certificate,

or

(b) (i) a qualification set out in *subparagraph (b)*, *(c)* or *(d)* of *paragraph 3* of *Schedule 2A*, and

(ii) an 80 hours certificate.

(5) The conditions required by this subsection are that the person, referred to in *paragraph (a)* of the definition of young trained farmer, before 31 March 2008—

(a) has achieved the required standard for entry into the third year of a full-time course in any discipline of 3 or more years" duration at a third-level institution, and that has been confirmed by the institution, and

(b) is the holder of a 180 hours certificate.

(6) For the purposes of *subsection (2)*, where Teagasc certifies that—

(a) any other qualification corresponds to a *Schedule 2B* qualification, and

(b) that other qualification is deemed by the [Qualifications and Quality Assurance Authority of Ireland][1] to be at least at a level equivalent to that of the *Schedule 2B* qualification,

the Commissioners shall treat that other qualification as if it were a *Schedule 2B* qualification.

(7) No stamp duty shall be chargeable under or by reference to the heading "CONVEYANCE or TRANSFER on sale of any property other than stocks or marketable securities or a policy of insurance or a policy of life insurance" in *Schedule 1* on any instrument to which this section applies.

[(8) This section applies to any instrument which operates as a conveyance or transfer (whether on sale or as a voluntary disposition inter vivos) of an interest in land to a young trained farmer where it is the intention of the young trained farmer, or each young trained farmer if there is more than one, for a period of 5 years from the date of execution of the instrument to—

(a) spend not less than 50 per cent of their normal working time farming the land, and

(b) retain ownership of the land.][2]

(9) Notwithstanding *subsection (8)*, this section shall apply where the property is conveyed or transferred into joint ownership where all the joint owners are young trained farmers or where any of the joint owners is a [spouse or civil partner][3] of another joint owner who is a young trained farmer.

[...][4]

(11) (a) For the purposes of this subsection, a person "achieves the standard" at any time where at that time the person—

(i) satisfies the conditions set out in *subsection (2)*, *(3)*, *(4)* or *(5)*, or

(ii) is the holder of a qualification treated, by virtue of *subsection (6)*, as being a *Schedule 2B* qualification,

and whether a person has or has not achieved the standard shall be construed accordingly.

(b) This subsection applies to an instrument by means of which land is conveyed or transferred to a person (in this subsection referred to as the "*transferee*") who on the date the instrument was executed was not a young trained farmer by reason only of the fact that the transferee on that date had not achieved the standard.

[(c) Where within 4 years from the date of execution of an instrument to which this subsection applies, the transferee achieves the standard, the Commissioners shall, where a claim for repayment is made to them by the transferee, or each of them if there is more than one, and where it is the intention of such person, or each such person, for a period of 5 years from the date on which the claim for repayment is made to the Commissioners to—

(i) spend not less than 50 per cent of that person's normal working time, farming the land, and

(ii) retain ownership of the land,

cancel and repay such duty as would have been chargeable had this section applied to the instrument when it was first presented for stamping.][5]

(12) (a) Where any person to whom land was conveyed or transferred by any instrument to which *subsection (7)* or *subsection (11)* applied—

(i) disposes of such land, or part of such land (in this subsection referred to as a "*part disposal*"), within a period of 5 years—

(I) in a case where *subsection (7)* applied, from the date of execution of that instrument, or

(II) in a case where *subsection (11)* applied, from the date the claim for repayment is made to the Commissioners,

and

(ii) does not fully expend the proceeds from such disposal or, as the case may be, such part disposal, in acquiring other land within a period of one year from the date of such disposal,

then, such person or, where there is more than one such person, each such person, jointly and severally, shall become liable to pay to the Commissioners [an amount (in this section referred to as a "*clawback*")][6] equal to an amount determined by the formula—

$$S \times \frac{N}{V}$$

where—

S is the amount of stamp duty that would have been charged on that instrument had *subsection (7)* not applied or, as the case may be, the amount of stamp duty that was charged on the instrument in the first instance and later repaid under *subsection (11)(c)*,

V is the market value, immediately before the disposal or, as the case may be, the part disposal, of all the land conveyed or transferred by the instrument, and

N is the amount of proceeds from the disposal or, as the case may be, the part disposal, that was not expended in acquiring other land.

(b) Interest shall be payable on a [clawback][7] incurred under *paragraph (a)*, calculated in accordance with section 159D, from the date of the disposal or, as the case may be, the part disposal, to the date the [clawback][8] is remitted.

(c) For the purposes of *paragraph (a)*—

(i) where a disposal of land is effected in whole or in part by way of a voluntary disposition inter vivos, an amount equal to the market value of the lands disposed of, at the date of the disposal, shall be deemed to be the proceeds from such disposal,

(ii) where any property is received by way of exchange, in whole or in part for a disposal, an amount equal to the market value of such property, at the date of the disposal, shall be deemed to be proceeds from such disposal, and

(iii) where subparagraph (ii) applies and property received by way of exchange is land or includes land, an amount equal to the market value of such land at the date of the disposal shall be deemed to have been expended in acquiring other land.

(d) A person shall not be liable to a [clawback][9] under *paragraph (a)*, if and to the extent that any [clawback][10] or, as the case may be, the aggregate of any [clawbacks][11], paid by that person under *paragraph (a)*, exceeds the stamp duty that would have been charged on the instrument had relief under *subsection (7)* not applied or, as the case may be, the stamp duty that was charged on the instrument in the first instance and later repaid under *subsection (11)(c)*.

(e) Where any claim for relief from duty under this section has been allowed and it is subsequently found that a declaration made, or a certificate contained in the instrument, in accordance with *subsection (8)*—

(i) was untrue in any material particular which would have resulted in the relief afforded by this section not being granted, and

(ii) was made, or was included, knowing same to be untrue or in reckless disregard as to whether it was true or not,

then any person who made such a declaration, or where a false certificate has been included, the person or persons to whom the land is conveyed or transferred by the instrument, jointly and severally, shall be liable to pay to the Commissioners as a penalty an amount equal to 125 per cent of the duty that would have been charged on the instrument in the first instance had all the facts been truthfully declared and certified, together with interest charged on that amount as may so become payable, calculated in accordance with section 159D, from the date when the instrument was executed to the date the penalty is remitted.

(f) Where any claim for relief from duty under this section has been allowed and it is subsequently found that a declaration made in accordance with *subsection (11)(c)(ii)*—

(i) was untrue in any material particular which would have resulted in the repayment of duty under *subsection (11)(c)* not being made, and

(ii) was made knowing same to be untrue or in reckless disregard as to whether it was true or not,

then any person who made such a declaration shall be liable to pay to the Commissioners, as a penalty, an amount equal to 125 per cent of the duty that was charged on the instrument in the first instance, together with interest charged on that amount calculated in accordance with section 159D, from the date the claim for repayment was made to the Commissioners to the date the penalty is remitted.

(13) Notwithstanding *subsection (12)*—

(a) where relief under *subsection (7)* was allowed in respect of any instrument or where *subsection (11)* applied to any instrument, a disposal by a young trained farmer of part of the land to a [spouse or civil partner][12] for the purpose of creating a joint tenancy in the land, or where the instrument conveyed or transferred the land to joint owners, a disposal by one joint owner to another of any part of the land, shall not be regarded as a disposal to which *subsection (12)* applies, but on such disposal, such part of the land shall be treated for the purposes of *subsection (12)*—

(i) in a case where *subsection (7)* applied, as if it had been conveyed or transferred immediately to the [spouse or civil partner][13] or other joint owner by the instrument in respect of which relief was allowed in the first instance, or

(ii) in a case where *subsection (11)* applied, as if it had been conveyed or transferred to the [spouse or civil partner][14] or other joint owner by the instrument to which *subsection (11)* applied, but at the date the claim for repayment is made to the Commissioners,

(b) a person shall not be liable to more than one penalty under *paragraph (e)* of *subsection (12)*,

(c) a person shall not be liable to a [an amount (in this section referred to as a "*clawback*")][15] of *subsection (12)*, if and to the extent that such person has paid a penalty under *paragraph (e)* or *(f)* of *subsection (12)*, and

(d) a person shall not be liable to a penalty under *paragraph (e)* or *(f)* of *subsection (12)*, if and to the extent that such person has paid a [an amount (in this section referred to as a "*clawback*")][16] of *subsection (12)*.

(14) A person who, before the date of the passing of the Finance Act 2004—

(a) is the holder of a *Schedule 2* qualification or a qualification certified by Teagasc as corresponding to a *Schedule 2* qualification and a satisfactory attendance at a course of training, approved by Teagasc, (in farm management, the aggregate duration of which exceeded 80 hours) is required for the purposes of *section 81*, shall be deemed, for the purposes of this section, to be the holder of a qualification corresponding to one of the qualifications set out in *subsection (4)(b)(i)*,

(b) is the holder of a *Schedule 2* qualification or a qualification certified by Teagasc as corresponding to a *Schedule 2* qualification and a satisfactory attendance at a course of training, approved by Teagasc, is not required for the purposes of *section 81*, shall be deemed, for the purposes of this section, to be the holder of a qualification corresponding to that set out in *subparagraph (b)* of *paragraph 1* of *Schedule 2B*,

(c) satisfies the requirements set out in *paragraph (b)(ii)(I)* of the definition of young trained farmer in *section 81(1)*, shall be deemed, for the purposes of this section, to have satisfied the conditions set out in *subsection (5)(a)*,

(d) is, for the purposes of *section 81*, the holder of a certificate issued by Teagasc certifying satisfactory attendance at a course of training, approved by Teagasc, in farm management, the aggregate duration of which exceeded 80 hours, shall be deemed, for the purposes of this section, to be the holder of an 80 hours certificate, or

(e) is, for the purposes of *section 81*, the holder of a certificate issued by Teagasc certifying satisfactory attendance at a course of training, approved by Teagasc, in either or both agriculture and horticulture, the aggregate duration of which exceeded 180 hours, shall be deemed, for the purposes of this section, to be the holder of a 180 hours certificate.

(15) A person who, before the date of the passing of the Finance Act 2007, is the holder of a *Schedule 2A* qualification or a qualification certified by Teagasc as corresponding to a *Schedule 2A* qualification, and is not required, for the purposes of section 81A, to be the holder of an 80 hours certificate or a 180 hours certificate, shall be deemed, for the purposes of this section, to be the holder of a qualification corresponding to that set out in *subparagraph (b)* of *paragraph 1* of *Schedule 2B*.

(16) This section applies as respects instruments executed on or after the date of the passing of the Finance Act 2007 and on or before [31 December 2018][17].][18]

Amendments

[1] Substituted by F(No.2)A13 s69(1)(a). Has effect in respect of certifications made by Teagasc on or after 6 November 2012.

[2] Substituted by FA12 sched3(23)(a). In effect for all instruments that are executed on or after 7 July 2012 per S.I. No. 228 of 2012.

[3, 12, 13, 14] Substituted by F(No.3)A11 sched2(3). Deemed to have come into operation in relation to stamp duty, as respects an instrument executed on or after 1 January 2011

[4] Deleted by FA12 sched3(23)(b). In effect for all instruments that are executed on or after 7 July 2012 per S.I. No. 228 of 2012.

[5] Deleted by FA12 sched3(23)(b). In effect for all instruments that are executed on or after 7 July 2012 per S.I. No. 228 of 2012.

[6] Substituted by F(No.2)A08 sched5(part5)(chap2)(7)(i)(i)(I).

[7, 8] Substituted by F(No.2)A08 sched5(part5)(chap2)(7)(i)(i)(II).

[9, 10, 11] Substituted by F(No.2)A08 sched5(part5)(chap2)(7)(i)(i)(III).

[15, 16] Substituted by F(No.2)A08 sched5(part5)(chap2)(7)(i)(ii).

[17] Substituted by FA15 s63.

[18] Inserted by FA07 s103(a). Deemed to have come into operation in relation to stamp duty, as respects an instrument executed on or after 1 January 2011.

Note:

F(No.2)A08 sched5 (part5)(chap 2)(7)

As respects paragraph 7 of this Schedule subparagraphs (a) to (aa) (other than subparagraph (c)(i)(I)) of that paragraph have effect as on and from the passing of this Act and to the extent that Chapter 3A (being inserted into Part 47 of the Taxes Consolidation Act 1997 by Part 1 of this Schedule) applies to penalties incurred under the Stamp Duties Consolidation Act 1999 before the passing of this Act which on the passing of this Act have not been paid, it shall not apply to such penalties which are in the form of interest accrued under any provisions of the said Act.

Revenue Briefings

Tax Briefing

Tax Briefing June 2000 – Issue 40 pg 32 – Features of Finance Act 2000 introduced at Committee Stage – Stamp Duty – Young Trained Farmers

eBrief

eBrief No. 01/2013 – Stamp Duty – Young Trained Farmer Relief – Commercial Woodlands Relief

Revenue Information Notes

SD2B – Stamp Duty Exemption Transfers of Land to Young Trained Farmers

SD10B – Revenue Certificates Required In Deeds (up to and including Finance Act 2011)

Cross References

From Section 81AA

Section 20 Assessment of duty by the Commissioners.

Section 81 Young trained farmers.

Section 81A Further relief from stamp duty in respect of transfers to young trained farmers.

Section 159D Calculation of interest on unpaid duty and other amounts.

Schedule 1 Stamp Duties on Instruments

Schedule 2 Qualifications for Applying for Relief From Stamp Duty in Respect of Transfers to Young Trained Farmers

Schedule 2A Qualifications for Applying for Relief From Stamp Duty in Respect of Transfers to Young Trained Farmers

Schedule 2B Qualifications for Applying for Relief from Stamp Duty in Respect of Transfers to Young Trained Farmers

To Section 81AA

Section 159A Time limits for claiming a repayment of stamp duty.

Schedule 2B Qualifications for Applying for Relief from Stamp Duty in Respect of Transfers to Young Trained Farmers

81B Farm consolidation relief

[(1) (a) In this section—

"*consolidation certificate*", in relation to an exchange of relevant land, means a certificate, issued for the purposes of this section by Teagasc to each farmer concerned in the exchange of relevant land, which identifies the lands concerned and the owners of such lands, and certifies that Teagasc is satisfied, on the basis of information available to Teagasc at the time of so certifying, that the exchange of relevant land complies, or will comply, with the conditions of consolidation set down in guidelines;

"*exchange of relevant land*" means an exchange under which an interest in relevant land is conveyed or transferred by a farmer to another farmer in exchange for receiving, by way of conveyance or transfer, an interest in relevant land from that other farmer; and includes an exchange where the relevant land is conveyed or transferred by or to joint owners where not all the joint owners are farmers;

"*farmer*" means a person who spends not less than 50 per cent of that person's normal working time farming;

"*farming*" includes the occupation of woodlands on a commercial basis;

"*guidelines*" and "*conditions of consolidation*" have, respectively, the meaning assigned to them by *paragraph (b)(i)*;

"*interest in relevant land*" means an interest which is not subject to any power (whether or not contained in the instrument or, as the case may be, instruments) on the exercise of which the relevant land, or any part of or any interest in the relevant land, may be revested in the person from whom it was conveyed or transferred or in any person on behalf of such person;

"*PPS number*" means a personal public service number within the meaning of *section 223* (as amended by section 12(1)(*a*) of the Social Welfare (Miscellaneous Provisions) Act 2002 (No. 8 of 2002)) of the Social Welfare (Consolidation) Act 1993;

"*relevant land*" means agricultural land, including lands suitable for occupation as woodlands on a commercial basis, in the State and such farm buildings together with the lands occupied with such farm buildings as are of a character appropriate to the relevant land but not including farm houses or mansion houses or the lands occupied with such farm houses and mansion houses unless such farm houses or mansion houses are derelict and unfit for human habitation;

"*valid consolidation certificate*", on any day, means a consolidation certificate which, as at that day, has not been withdrawn and which was issued within the period of one year ending on that day.

(b) For the purposes of this section—

(i) the Minister for Agriculture and Food with the consent of the Minister for Finance may make and publish guidelines, from time to time, setting out—

(I) how an application for a consolidation certificate, in relation to an exchange of relevant land, is to be made,

(II) the documentation required to accompany such an application,

(III) the conditions of consolidation, and

(IV) such other information as may be required in relation to such application,

(ii) where an application is made in that regard, Teagasc shall issue a consolidation certificate in respect of an exchange of relevant land where they are satisfied, on the basis of information available to Teagasc at that time, that an exchange of relevant land complies, or will comply, with the conditions of consolidation, and

(iii) Teagasc may, by notice in writing, withdraw any consolidation certificate already issued.

(2) This section applies to any instrument effecting an exchange of relevant land where—

(a) the instrument contains a certificate that this section applies,

(b) a consolidation certificate, in relation to the exchange of relevant land, which is a valid consolidation certificate on the date of execution of the instrument, is furnished to the Commissioners when the instrument is presented for stamping,

(c) a declaration of a kind referred to in subsection (3), is furnished to the Commissioners by each farmer who is a party to the instrument, when the instrument is presented for stamping,

(d) a declaration made in writing by each person, who is a party to the instrument, is furnished to the Commissioners, in such form as the Commissioners may specify, when the instrument is presented for stamping, declaring that it is the intention of each such person—

(i) to retain ownership of his or her interest in the relevant land conveyed or transferred to that person by such instrument, and

(ii) that the relevant land will be used for farming,

for a period of not less than 5 years from the date of execution of the instrument, and

(e) the PPS number of each person who is a party to the instrument is furnished to the Commissioners when the instrument is presented for stamping.

(3) The declaration referred to in subsection (2)(*c*) is a declaration made in writing by a farmer, in such form as the Commissioners may specify, which—

(a) is signed by the farmer, and

(b) declares that—

(i) the farmer will remain a farmer, and

(ii) the farmer will farm the relevant land, conveyed or transferred to the farmer by the instrument,

for a period of not less than 5 years from the date of execution of the instrument.

(4) Notwithstanding *section 37*—

(a) stamp duty shall not be chargeable on an instrument giving effect to an exchange of relevant land, to which this section applies, where the relevant lands exchanged are of equal value, and

(b) where the relevant lands exchanged are not of equal value, subject to subsection (5), stamp duty shall only be chargeable on the principal or only instrument giving effect to the exchange of relevant land as if it were a conveyance or transfer on sale of the relevant land which is of the greater value which was made—

(i) in consideration of a sum equal to the difference between the value of the relevant lands exchanged,

(ii) to the person or persons to whom the relevant land which is of the greater value is conveyed or transferred.

(5) Where relevant lands exchanged are not of equal value, the consideration paid or agreed to be paid for equality shall consist only of a payment in cash.

(6) Where subsection (4)(*b*) applies and there are several instruments for completing a title to relevant land the subject of an exchange of relevant land to which this section applies, the principal instrument is to be ascertained and the other instruments shall not be chargeable to stamp duty.

(7) Subsection (4) shall not apply to an instrument unless it has, in accordance with *section 20*, been stamped with a particular stamp denoting that it is duly stamped or, as the case may be, that it is not chargeable with any duty.

(8) For the purposes of subsection (7), where there are several instruments for completing a title to relevant land, the subject of an exchange of relevant land to which this section applies, all instruments shall, for the purposes of *section 20*, be presented to the Commissioners, at the same time.

(9) (a) Subject to *paragraph (b)*, where any person to whom relevant land was conveyed or transferred by any instrument in respect of which relief from duty under this section was allowed, disposes of such relevant land, or part of such relevant land, within a period of 5 years from the date of execution of the instrument, then such person or, where there is more than one such person, each such person, jointly and severally, shall become liable to pay to the Commissioners [an amount (in this section referred to as a "*clawback*")][1] equal to the amount of the difference between—

(i) the duty that would have been charged by virtue of *section 37* on the value of such relevant land (being all the relevant land, the subject of the exchange of relevant land, conveyed or transferred to that person), if such relevant land had been conveyed or transferred to that person or, where there is more than one such person, each such person, by an instrument to which this section had not applied, and

(ii) the duty, if any, which was charged by virtue of this section on the conveyance or transfer of such relevant land,

together with interest charged on that amount, calculated in accordance with section *section 159D*, from the date of disposal of the relevant land or, as the case may be, a part thereof, to the date the [clawback][2] is remitted.

(b) *Paragraph (a)* shall not apply to a disposal of relevant land—

(i) which is being compulsorily acquired, or

(ii) which is a disposal of relevant land under an exchange of relevant land effected by an instrument to which subsection (2) applies.

(c) Where any claim for relief from duty under this section has been allowed and it is subsequently found that a declaration referred to in *paragraph (c)* or *(d)* of *subsection (2)*—

(i) was untrue in any material particular which would have resulted in the relief afforded by this section not being granted, and

(ii) was made knowing same to be untrue or in reckless disregard as to whether it was true or not,

then the person or persons who made such a declaration, jointly and severally, shall become liable to pay to the Commissioners a penalty of an amount equal to the amount of the difference between—

(I) 125 per cent of the duty which would have been charged on the instrument or, as the case may be, the instruments, effecting the exchange of relevant land by virtue of *section 37* on the value of such relevant land conveyed or transferred to such person or persons, had all the facts been truthfully declared, and

(II) the amount of duty which was charged, if any,

together with interest charged on that amount, calculated in accordance with *section 159D*, from the date when the instrument was executed to the date the penalty is remitted.

(d) Where a consolidation certificate, purporting to be valid on the date of execution of an instrument effecting an exchange of relevant land, is furnished to the Commissioners when the instrument is presented for stamping and *subsection (2)* applied to the instrument and it subsequently transpires that the consolidation certificate was not a valid consolidation certificate on that date, the parties to the instrument, jointly and severally, shall become liable to pay to the Commissioners a penalty of an amount equal to the amount of the difference between—

(i) 125 per cent of the duty which would have been charged on the instrument or, as the case may be, the instruments, effecting the exchange of relevant land by virtue of *section 37* on the value of such relevant land conveyed or transferred to such person or persons, had *subsection (2)* not applied to the instrument, and

(ii) the amount of duty which was charged, if any,

together with interest charged on that amount, calculated in accordance with *section 159D*, from the date when the instrument was executed to the date the penalty is remitted.

(10) Notwithstanding subsection (9)—

(a) where relief under this section was allowed in respect of any instrument, a disposal by a farmer or other joint owner of part of the relevant land to a spouse for the purpose of creating a joint tenancy in the relevant land, or where the instrument conveyed or transferred the relevant land to joint owners, a disposal by one joint owner, to another joint owner (being a farmer) of any part of the relevant land, shall not be regarded as a disposal to which *subsection (9)* applies, but on such disposal, such part of the relevant land shall be treated for the purposes of *subsection (9)* as if it had been conveyed or transferred immediately to the spouse or other joint owner by the instrument in respect of which relief from duty under this section was allowed,

(b) a person shall not be liable, in respect of the same matter, to more than one [clawback or penalty under paragraph (*a*), (*c*) or (*d*), as the case may be,][3] of *subsection (9)*,

(c) a person shall not be liable, in respect of the same matter, to a [clawback under *paragraph (a)*][4] of *subsection (9)*, if and to the extent that such person has paid a penalty under *paragraph (c)* or *(d)* of *subsection (9)*,

(d) a person shall not be liable, in respect of the same matter, to a penalty under *paragraph (c)* of *subsection (9)*, if and to the extent that such person has paid a [clawback or penalty under paragraph (*a*) or (*d*), as the case may be,][5] of *subsection (9)*, and

(e) a person shall not be liable, in respect of the same matter, to a penalty under *paragraph (d)* of *subsection (9)*, if and to the extent that such person has paid a [clawback or penalty under paragraph (*a*) or (*c*), as the case may be,][6] of *subsection (9)*.

(11) This section shall not apply to any instrument effecting an exchange of relevant land where the party or, as the case may be, any of the parties to such instrument, is a company.

(12) This section shall apply as respects instruments executed on or after 1 July 2005 and on or before 30 June 2007.][7]

Amendments

[1, 2] Substituted by F(No.2)A08 sched5(part5)(chap2)(7)(j)(i).

[3] Substituted by F(No.2)A08 sched5(part5)(chap2)(7)(j)(ii)(I).

[4] Substituted by F(No.2)A08 sched5(part5)(chap2)(7)(j)(ii)(II).

[5] Substituted by F(No.2)A08 sched5(part5)(chap2)(7)(j)(ii)(III).

[6] Substituted by F(No.2)A08 sched5(part5)(chap2)(7)(j)(ii)(IV).

[7] Inserted by FA05 s121. This section shall apply as respects instruments executed on or after 1 July 2005 and on or before 30 June 2007.

Note:

F(No.2)A08 sched5 (part5)(chap 2)(7)

As respects paragraph 7 of this Schedule subparagraphs (a) to (aa) (other than subparagraph (c)(i)(I)) of that paragraph have effect as on and from the passing of this Act and to the extent that Chapter 3A (being inserted into Part 47 of the Taxes Consolidation Act 1997 by Part 1 of this Schedule) applies to penalties incurred under the Stamp Duties Consolidation Act 1999 before the passing of this Act which on the passing of this Act have not been paid, it shall not apply to such penalties which are in the form of interest accrued under any provisions of the said Act.

Revenue Briefings

eBrief

eBrief No. 43/2007 – Stamp Duty – Finance Act 2007 – Farm Consolidation Relief

Cross References

From Section 81B

Section 20 Assessment of duty by the Commissioners.
Section 37 Exchanges.
Section 159D Calculation of interest on unpaid duty and other amounts.
Section 223

81C Further farm consolidation relief

[(1) (a) In this section—

"*conditions of consolidation*" means the conditions of consolidation as set out in guidelines;

"*consolidation certificate*" means a certificate, issued for the purposes of this section by Teagasc to a farmer in relation to a sale and purchase of qualifying land both of which occur in the relevant period and within 18 months of each other, which identifies the lands concerned, the owners of such lands and certifies that Teagasc is satisfied, on the basis of information available to Teagasc at the time of so certifying, that the sale and purchase of qualifying land complies, or will comply, with the conditions of consolidation set down in guidelines;

"*farmer*" means a person who spends not less than 50 per cent of the person"s normal working time farming;

"*farming*" includes the occupation of woodlands on a commercial basis;

"*guidelines*" means guidelines made and published pursuant to *paragraph (b)(i)*;

"*interest in qualifying land*" means an interest in qualifying land which is not subject to any power (whether or not contained in the instrument) on the exercise of which the qualifying land, or any part of or any interest in the qualifying land, may be revested in the person from whom it was purchased or in any person on behalf of such person;

"*PPS Number*", in relation to a person, means the person"s Personal Public Service Number within the meaning of section 262 of the Social Welfare Consolidation Act 2005;

"*purchase of qualifying land*" means a conveyance or transfer (whether on sale or operating as a voluntary disposition inter vivos) of an interest in qualifying land to a farmer and includes a conveyance or transfer where the qualifying land is conveyed or transferred to joint owners where not all the joint owners are farmers; and the date of the purchase of qualifying land shall be the date on which the conveyance or transfer is executed;

"*qualifying land*" means relevant land in respect of which a consolidation certificate has been issued by Teagasc;

"*relevant land*" means agricultural land, including lands suitable for occupation as woodlands on a commercial basis, in the State and such farm buildings together with the lands occupied with such farm buildings as are of a character appropriate to the relevant land but not including farm houses or mansion houses or the lands occupied with such farm houses and mansion houses unless such farm houses or mansion houses are derelict and unfit for human habitation;

"*relevant period*" means the period commencing on 1 July 2007 and ending on 30 June 2009;

"*sale of qualifying land*" means a conveyance or transfer (whether on sale or operating as a voluntary disposition inter vivos) of an interest in qualifying land by a farmer and includes a conveyance or transfer where the qualifying land is conveyed or transferred by joint owners where not all the joint owners are farmers; and the date of the sale of qualifying land shall be the date on which the conveyance or transfer is executed;

"*valid consolidation certificate*" means a consolidation certificate which, on any day, has not been withdrawn as at that day.

(b) For the purposes of this section—

(i) the Minister for Agriculture and Food with the consent of the Minister for Finance may make and publish guidelines, from time to time setting out—

(I) how an application for a consolidation certificate is to be made,

(II) the documentation required to accompany such an application,

(III) the conditions of consolidation, and

(IV) such other information as may be required in relation to such application,

(ii) where an application is made in that regard, Teagasc shall issue a consolidation certificate in respect of a sale and purchase of relevant land, where they are satisfied, on the basis of information available to Teagasc at that time, that the sale and purchase of such lands complies, or will comply, with the conditions of consolidation, and

(iii) Teagasc may, by notice in writing, withdraw any consolidation certificate already issued.

(2) This section applies to a purchase of qualifying land by a farmer on any day (in this section referred to as the "*calculation day*") falling within the relevant period.

(3) Subject to *subsections (4)* and *(5)*, stamp duty shall be chargeable on the instrument giving effect to the purchase of qualifying land to which this section applies as if it were a purchase of qualifying land made in consideration of a sum determined by the formula—

$$(P - S)$$

where—

P is the aggregate of—

(a) the value of the qualifying land being purchased, and

(b) the value of all other qualifying land purchased by the farmer in the relevant period where the date of the purchase falls in the period of 18 months ending on the calculation day and where any such purchase was treated by virtue of this subsection as having been made in consideration of a lesser amount in consequence of a sale of qualifying land being made before the commencement of that 18 month period, that lesser amount shall be treated as the value of that purchase,

and

S is the aggregate of the value of all the qualifying land sold by the farmer in the relevant period where the date of the sale falls in the period of 18 months ending on the calculation day, to the extent that it has not given rise to a repayment of duty under *subsection (5)* in respect of a purchase of qualifying land made before the commencement of that 18 month period.

(4) Where an amount of duty has been paid in accordance with *subsection (3)* and is not repayable (in this subsection referred to as the "*relevant amount*") on a purchase of qualifying land by a farmer on a calculation day (in this subsection referred to as the "*first calculation day*"), the duty chargeable on a purchase of qualifying land by the farmer on a later calculation day, which falls within the period of 18 months commencing on the first calculation day, shall be reduced by the relevant amount.

(5) Where at any time in the period of 18 months commencing on a calculation day, qualifying land is sold by a farmer, that sale shall be treated as if it were a sale made on the calculation day and the duty chargeable, in accordance with *subsection (3)*, on the instrument giving effect to the purchase of qualifying land made on the calculation day shall be recomputed in accordance with *subsection (3)* and an amount equal to the difference between—

(a) the duty charged on the instrument prior to the recomputation, and

(b) the duty that is chargeable on the instrument after the recomputation,

shall, subject to compliance with the conditions set out in *subsection (6)*, be repaid by the Commissioners where a claim for repayment is made to them in that regard.

(6) A claim for relief under *subsection (3)* or a claim for relief by way of repayment under *subsection (5)*, made to the Commissioners under this section, shall be allowed on the production to them of—

(a) the instrument giving effect to the purchase of the qualifying land,

(b) a certified copy of the instrument giving effect to the sale of the qualifying land,

(c) a valid consolidation certificate in relation to the purchase and sale of the qualifying land in respect of which the claim for relief is being made,

(d) a declaration of a kind referred to in *subsection (7)*, made by each farmer who has purchased the qualifying land referred to in *paragraph (a)*,

(e) a declaration made in writing by each person, who has purchased the qualifying land referred to in *paragraph (a)*, in such form as the Commissioners may specify, declaring that it is the intention of such person—

(i) to retain ownership of his or her interest in the qualifying land, and

(ii) that the qualifying land will be used for farming,

for a period of not less than 5 years from the date on which the first claim for relief in respect of the qualifying land is made, and

(f) the PPS Number of each person who has purchased the qualifying land referred to in *paragraph (a)*.

(7) The declaration referred to in subsection (6)(*d*) is a declaration made in writing by a farmer, in such form as the Commissioners may specify, which—

(a) is signed by the farmer, and

(b) declares that the farmer—

(i) will remain a farmer, and

(ii) will farm the qualifying land referred to in *subsection (6)(a)*,

for a period of not less than 5 years from the date on which the first claim for relief in respect of the qualifying land is made.

(8) This section shall not apply to an instrument unless it has, in accordance with *section 20*, been stamped with a particular stamp denoting that it is duly stamped or, as the case may be, that it is not chargeable with any duty.

(9) (a) Subject to *paragraph (b)*, where any person who purchased qualifying land by any instrument in respect of which relief was allowed by the Commissioners, disposes of such qualifying land, or part of such qualifying land, within a period of 5 years from the date on which the first claim for relief in respect of the qualifying land is allowed, then such person or, where there is more than one such person, each such person, jointly and severally, shall become liable to pay to the Commissioners [an amount (in this section referred to as a "*clawback*")][1] equal to the amount of the difference between—

(i) the duty that would have been charged on the value of such qualifying land, if such qualifying land had been purchased by that person or, where there is more than one such person, each such person, by an instrument to which this section had not applied, and

(ii) the duty, if any, that was charged and is not repayable on the instrument concerned,

together with interest charged on that amount, calculated in accordance with *section 159D*, from the date of disposal of the qualifying land or, as the case may be, a part thereof, to the date the [clawback][2] is remitted.

(b) *Paragraph (a)* shall not apply to any disposal of qualifying land which is being compulsorily acquired but *subsection (5)* shall not apply to give relief, after that disposal, in respect of the duty already charged on the purchase of qualifying land.

(c) Where any claim for relief from duty under this section has been allowed and it is subsequently found that a declaration referred to in *paragraph (d)* or *(e)* of *subsection (6)*—

(i) was untrue in any material particular which would have resulted in the relief not being allowed, and

(ii) was made knowing same to be untrue or in reckless disregard as to whether it was true or not,

then the person or persons who made such a declaration, jointly and severally, shall become liable to pay to the Commissioners a penalty of an amount equal to the amount of the difference between—

(I) 125 per cent of the duty that would have been charged on the instrument had this section not applied due to all the facts not having been truthfully declared, and

(II) the duty, if any, that was charged and is not repayable on the instrument concerned,

together with interest charged on that amount, calculated in accordance with *section 159D*, from the date when the claim for relief was made to the Commissioners to the date the penalty is remitted.

(d) Where a consolidation certificate, purporting to be valid at the date when a claim for relief under this section is made to the Commissioners, is furnished to the Commissioners and it subsequently transpires that the consolidation certificate was not a valid consolidation certificate on that date, the parties to the instrument who have purchased the qualifying land, jointly and severally, shall become liable to pay to the Commissioners a penalty of an amount equal to the amount of the difference between—

(i) 125 per cent of the duty that would have been charged on the instrument had this section not applied to it, and

(ii) the duty, if any, that was charged and is not repayable on the instrument concerned,

together with interest charged on that amount, calculated in accordance with *section 159D*, from the date the claim for relief is made to the Commissioners to the date the penalty is remitted.

(10) Notwithstanding *subsection (9)*—

(a) where relief under this section was allowed in respect of any instrument, a disposal by a farmer or other joint owner of part of the qualifying land to a spouse for the purpose of creating a joint tenancy in the qualifying land, or where the instrument gave effect to the purchase of the qualifying land by joint owners, a disposal by one joint owner, to another joint owner (being a farmer) of any part of the qualifying land, shall not be regarded as a disposal to which *subsection (9)* applies, but on such disposal, such part of the qualifying land shall be treated for the purposes of *subsection (9)* as if it had been purchased immediately by the spouse or other joint owner by the instrument in respect of which relief was allowed,

(b) a person shall not be liable, in respect of the same matter, to more than one [clawback or penalty under paragraph *(a)*, *(c)* or *(d)*, as the case may be,][3] of *subsection (9)*,

(c) a person shall not be liable, in respect of the same matter, to a [clawback under *paragraph (a)*][4] of *subsection (9)*, if and to the extent that such person has paid a penalty under *paragraph (c)* or *(d)* of *subsection (9)*,

(d) a person shall not be liable, in respect of the same matter, to a penalty under *paragraph (c)* of *subsection (9)*, if and to the extent that such person has paid a [clawback or penalty under paragraph (*a*) or (*d*), as the case may be,][5] of *subsection (9)*, and

(e) a person shall not be liable, in respect of the same matter, to a penalty under *paragraph (d)* of *subsection (9)*, if and to the extent that such person has paid a [clawback or penalty under paragraph (*a*) or (*c*), as the case may be,][6] of *subsection (9)*.

(11) This section shall not apply to any instrument effecting a purchase of qualifying land where the purchaser of such land or, as the case may be, any of the purchasers, is a company.

(12) This section applies as respects instruments executed on or after 1 July 2007 and on or before [30 June 2011][7].][8]

Amendments

[1, 2] Substituted by F(No.2)A08 sched5(part5)(chap2)(7)(j)(i).

[3] Substituted by F(No.2)A08 sched5(part5)(chap2)(7)(j)(ii)(I).

[4] Substituted by F(No.2)A08 sched5(part5)(chap2)(7)(j)(ii)(II).

[5] Substituted by F(No.2)A08 sched5(part5)(chap2)(7)(j)(ii)(III).

[6] Substituted by F(No.2)A08 sched5(part5)(chap2)(7)(j)(ii)(IV).

[7] Substituted by F(No.2)A08 s85.

[8] Inserted by FA07 s104. By virtue of the Finance Act 2007 (Commencement of Section 104(1)) Order 2007 (SI 783/2007) this section came into operation on 3 December 2007.

Note:

F(No.2)A08 sched5 (part5)(chap 2)(7)

As respects paragraph 7 of this Schedule subparagraphs (a) to (aa) (other than subparagraph (c)(i)(I)) of that paragraph have effect as on and from the passing of this Act and to the extent that Chapter 3A (being inserted into Part 47 of the Taxes Consolidation Act 1997 by Part 1 of this Schedule) applies to penalties incurred under the Stamp Duties Consolidation Act 1999 before the passing of this Act which on the passing of this Act have not been paid, it shall not apply to such penalties which are in the form of interest accrued under any provisions of the said Act.

Revenue Briefings

eBrief

eBrief No. 43/2007 – Stamp Duty – Finance Act 2007 – Farm Consolidation Relief
eBrief No. 5/2008 – Stamp Duty – Farm Consolidation Relief

Revenue Information Notes

SD10A – Revenue Certificates Required In Deeds (for deeds prior to 8 December 2010)
SD 81C – Farm Consolidation Relief

Cross References

From Section 81C

Section 20 Assessment of duty by the Commissioners.
Section 159D Calculation of interest on unpaid duty and other amounts.

81D Relief for certain leases of farmland

[(1) In this section 'farming' includes the occupation of woodlands on a commercial basis.

(2) No stamp duty shall be chargeable under or by reference to the heading 'LEASE' in *Schedule 1* on any instrument to which this section applies.

(3) This section applies to an instrument which is a lease for a term not less than 6 years and not exceeding 35 years of any lands which are used exclusively for

farming carried on by the lessee on a commercial basis and with a view to the realisation of profits.

(4) For the purposes of this section the lessee shall, from the date on which the lease is executed, be a farmer who—

(a) is the holder of or, within a period of 4 years from the date of the lease, will be the holder of, a qualification set out in *Schedule 2, 2A* or *2B* to the Act, or

(b) spends not less than 50 per cent of that individual's normal working time farming land (including the leased land).

(5) If, at any time during the first 6 years of the period of the lease, any of the conditions of this section cease to be satisfied, *subsection (2)* shall not apply and the duty that would have been chargeable but for this section shall be chargeable and the lessee, or where there is more than one lessee, each such lessee, jointly and severally, shall be liable to pay to the Commissioners the amount of the duty together with interest calculated in accordance with *section 159D* from the date when any of those conditions cease to be satisfied to the date when the duty is remitted.

(6) *Subsection (5)* shall not apply where any of the conditions of this section are not complied with due to the death of the lessee or the permanent incapacity of the lessee, by reason of mental or physical infirmity, to continue to carry on farming.][1]

Amendments

[1] Inserted by FA14 s74. Comes into operation on such day as the Minister for Finance may appoint by order.

82 Charities

[FA1979 s50]

(1) Stamp duty shall not be chargeable on any conveyance, transfer or lease of land made, or agreed to be made, for charitable purposes in the State or Northern Ireland to a body of persons established for charitable purposes only or to the trustees of a trust so established.

[...][1]

Amendments

[1] Deleted by FA12 sched3(24). In effect for all instruments that are executed on or after 7 July 2012 per S.I. No. 228 of 2012.

Case Law

Four general categories of charitable purposes were established in the UK case of IT Comrs v Pemsel 1891 AC 531: 1. Relief of poverty, 2. Advancement of education, 3. Advancement of religion, 4. Other purposes beneficial to the community

Revenue Information Notes

CHY 1 – Applying for Relief from Tax on the Income and Property of Charities

Cross References

From Section 82

Section 20 Assessment of duty by the Commissioners.

To Section 82

Section 35 Deeds of enlargement.
Section 91 New dwellinghouses and apartments with floor area certificate.
Section 91A New dwellinghouses and apartments with floor area compliance certificate.
Section 92 New dwellinghouses and apartments with no floor area certificate.
Section 92B Residential property first time purchaser relief.

82A Approved bodies

[(1) In this section "*approved body*", "*designated securities*" and "*relevant donation*" have, respectively, the meanings assigned to them in section 848A (as amended by the *Finance Act 2006*) of the Taxes Consolidation Act 1997.

(2) Stamp duty shall not be chargeable on any instrument transferring designated securities, which are a relevant donation or part of a relevant donation, to an approved body.

[...][1]

Amendments

[1] Deleted by FA12 sched3(25). In effect for all instruments that are executed on or after 7 July 2012 per S.I. No. 228 of 2012.

Cross References

From Section 82A

Section 20 Assessment of duty by the Commissioners.

82B Approved sports bodies

[(1) In this section "*approved sports body*" means an "approved body of persons" within the meaning of section 235(1) of the Taxes Consolidation Act 1997.

(2) Stamp duty shall not be chargeable on any instrument operating as a conveyance, transfer or lease, of land to an approved sports body.

(3) Subsection (2) shall not apply to an instrument unless—

(a) the land conveyed, transferred or leased by the instrument will be used for the sole purpose of promoting athletic or amateur games or sports, and

[...][1]

(4) (a) Where an approved sports body to whom land was conveyed, transferred or leased by any instrument to which subsection (2) applied—

(i) disposes of such land, or part of such land (in this subsection referred to as a "*part disposal*"), and

(ii) does not fully apply the proceeds from such disposal or, as the case may be, such part disposal, to the sole purpose of promoting athletic or amateur games or sports,

then such approved sports body shall become liable to pay to the Commissioners [an amount (in this section referred to as a "*clawback*")][2] equal to an amount determined by the formula—

$$S \times \frac{N}{V}$$

where—

S is the amount of stamp duty that would have been charged on that instrument had subsection (2) not applied,

V is the market value, immediately before the disposal or the part disposal, of all the land conveyed, transferred or leased by the instrument, and

N is the amount of proceeds from the disposal or, as the case may be, the part disposal that has not been, or will not be, applied to the sole purpose of promoting athletic or amateur games or sports.

(b) For the purposes of paragraph (*a*)—

(i) where any property is received by way of exchange, in whole or in part for a disposal, and has been, or will be, applied to the sole purpose of promoting athletic or amateur games or sports, an amount equal to the market value of such property, at the date of the disposal, shall be deemed to be proceeds from such disposal which have been, or will be, applied to that same purpose, and

(ii) where a disposal of land is effected in whole or in part by way of a voluntary disposition inter vivos, an amount equal to the market value of the lands disposed of, at the date of the disposal, less the amount, if any, received as proceeds from the disposal, shall be deemed to be proceeds from the disposal which have not been, or will not be, applied to the sole purpose of promoting athletic or amateur games or sports.

(5) Where an approved sports body to whom land was conveyed, transferred or leased by any instrument to which subsection (2) applied, ceases, at any time, to use the land, beneficially owned by it, for the sole purpose of promoting athletic or amateur games or sports, the approved sports body shall become liable to pay to the Commissioners [an amount (in this section referred to as a "*clawback*")][3] equal to the amount of stamp duty which would have been charged on the instrument, in the first instance, had subsection (2) not applied.

(6) Interest shall be payable on a [clawback][4] incurred under subsection (4) or (5) calculated in accordance with section 159D, from the date of any disposal or cessation to the date the [clawback][5] is remitted.

(7) Notwithstanding subsections (4) and (5), the maximum [clawback][6] payable on any instrument shall not exceed the amount of duty which would have been charged on the instrument in the first instance had subsection (2) not applied.][7]

Amendments

[1] Deleted by FA13 sched2(2)(c). Deemed to have come into force and have taken effect as regards instruments first executed on or after 7 July 2012.

[2, 3] Substituted by F(No.2)A08 sched5(part5)(chap2)(7)(k)(i).

[4, 5] Substituted by F(No.2)A08 sched5(part5)(chap2)(7)(k)(ii).

[6] Substituted by F(No.2)A08 sched5(part5)(chap2)(7)(k)(iii).

[7] Inserted by FA07 s105(1). This section applies as respects instruments executed on or after 7 December 2006.

Note:

F(No.2)A08 sched5 (part5)(chap 2)(7)

As respects paragraph 7 of this Schedule subparagraphs (a) to (aa) (other than subparagraph (c)(i)(I)) of that paragraph have effect as on and from the passing of this Act and to the extent that Chapter 3A (being inserted into Part 47 of the Taxes Consolidation Act 1997 by Part 1 of this Schedule) applies to penalties incurred under the Stamp Duties Consolidation Act 1999 before the passing of this Act which on the passing of this Act have not been paid, it shall not apply to such penalties which are in the form of interest accrued under any provisions of the said Act.

Revenue Information Notes

SD10A – Revenue Certificates Required In Deeds (for deeds prior to 8 December 2010)
SD10B – Revenue Certificates Required In Deeds (up to and including Finance Act 2011)

Cross References

From Section 82B

Section 20 Assessment of duty by the Commissioners.
Section 159D Calculation of interest on unpaid duty and other amounts.

82C Pension schemes and charities

[(1) In this section—

'*Act of 1997*' means the Taxes Consolidation Act 1997;

'*charity*' means a body of persons or a trust established for charitable purposes only;

'*common contractual fund*' has the meaning given to it by *section 739I(1)(a)(i)* of the Act of 1997;

'*investment undertaking*' has the meaning given to it by *section 739B(1)* of the Act of 1997;

'*pension scheme*' means—

(a) a retirement benefits scheme, within the meaning of *section 771* of the Act of 1997, approved by the Commissioners for the purposes of Chapter 1 of *Part 30* of that Act,

(b) an annuity contract or a trust scheme or part of a trust scheme approved by the Commissioners under *section 784* of the Act of 1997,

(c) a PRSA contract, within the meaning of *section 787A* of the Act of 1997, in respect of a PRSA product, within the meaning of that section,

(d) an approved retirement fund within the meaning of *section 784A* of the Act of 1997,

(e) an approved minimum retirement fund within the meaning of *section 784C* of the Act of 1997, or

(f) a scheme within the meaning of *section 790B* of the Act of 1997;

'*specified fund*' means a common contractual fund, investment undertaking, unit linked life fund, or unit trust, all the issued units or shares of which are assets such that if those assets were disposed of by the unit holder or shareholder any gain accruing would be wholly exempt from capital gains tax (otherwise than by reason of residence);

'*unit linked life fund*' means a fund in which assets are held by an assurance company for the purposes of its new basis business;

'*unit trust*' means a unit trust to which *subsection (5)(a)(i)* of *section 731* of the Act of 1997 applies;

'assurance company' and 'new basis business' have the meanings given to them respectively by *section 730A* of the Act of 1997.

(2) Stamp duty shall not be chargeable on any instrument made for the purposes of a transfer of property—

(a) held by or for the benefit of a pension scheme or a charity, in circumstances where the property continues to be so held after the transfer has taken place,

(b) held by or for the benefit of a pension scheme or a charity to a specified fund, in circumstances where the specified fund issues units or shares to be held by or for the benefit of the pension scheme or the charity,

(c) held by a specified fund to or for the benefit of a pension scheme or charity, or

(d) held by a specified fund (in this paragraph referred to as a 'transferring fund') to another specified fund (in this paragraph referred to as a 'receiving fund') in circumstances where the receiving fund issues units or shares to—

(i) the transferring fund, or

(ii) the unit holders or shareholders in the transferring fund in respect of and in proportion to (or as nearly as they may be in proportion to) their holdings of units or shares in the transferring fund,

to be held by or for the benefit of the pension scheme or the charity.][1]

Amendments

[1] Inserted by FA12 s100(1)(b). Has effect in respect of instruments executed on or after 8 February 2012.

83 Instruments given by means of security to company by subsidiary [Deleted]

Deleted by FA07 s100(1)(c). This section applies to instruments executed on or after 7 December 2006.

83A Transfer of site to child

[(1) In this section—

["*site*", in relation to an instrument of conveyance, transfer or lease, means land comprising both—

(a) the area of land on which a dwelling house, referred to in *subsection (3)(c)*, is to be constructed, and

(b) an area of land for occupation and enjoyment with that dwelling house as its gardens or grounds which, exclusive of the area referred to in *paragraph (a)*, does not exceed 0.4047 hectare,

but does not include an area of land on which a building is situated which building at the date of execution of that instrument—

(i) was used or was suitable for use as a dwelling or for other purposes, or

(ii) was in the course of being constructed or adapted for use as a dwelling or for other purposes.][1]

(2) Stamp duty shall not be chargeable on any conveyance, transfer or lease of a site to which this section applies.

(3) This section applies to any instrument which operates as a conveyance, transfer or lease of a site and which contains a statement, in such form as the Commissioners may specify, certifying—

(a) that the person becoming entitled to the entire beneficial interest in the site is a child of the person or of each of the persons immediately theretofore entitled to the entire beneficial interest in the site,

(b) that at the date of the instrument the value of that site does not exceed [€500,000][2] and that the transaction thereby effected does not form part of a larger transaction or of a series of transactions whereby property with a value in excess of [€500,000][3] is conveyed, transferred or leased to that child,

(c) that the purpose of the conveyance, transfer or lease is to enable that child to construct a dwellinghouse on that site which will be occupied by that child as his or her only or main residence, and

(d) that the transaction thereby effected is the first and only conveyance, transfer or lease of a site for the benefit of that child from either or both of the parents of that child which contains the certificate specified in this section.

(4) *Subsection (2)* shall not apply to an instrument unless it has, in accordance with *section 20*, been stamped with a particular stamp denoting that it is not chargeable with any duty or that it is duly stamped.

(5) The furnishing of an incorrect statement within the meaning of *subsection (3)* shall be deemed to constitute the delivery of an incorrect statement for the purposes of section 1078 of the Taxes Consolidation Act, 1997.

[(6) This section shall not apply to an instrument executed on or after 8 December 2010.][4]][5]

Amendments

[1] Substituted by FA07 s106(1). This section applies as respects instruments executed on or after 1 February 2007.

[2, 3] Substituted by FA08 s117(1). Applies as respects instruments executed on or after 5 December 2007.

[4] Inserted by FA11 s63(1)(b). Shall not apply as respects any instrument executed before 1 July 2011 where—(a) the effect of the application of that subsection would be to increase the duty otherwise chargeable on the instrument, and (b) the instrument contains a statement, in such form as the Revenue Commissioners may specify, certifying that the instrument was executed solely in pursuance of a binding contract entered into before 8 December 2010.

[5] Inserted by FA01 s206(1). Applies and has effect in relation to instruments executed on or after 6 December 2000 subject to the substitution in subsection (3)(b) of "€254,000" for "£200,000", in each place where it occurs, for instruments executed on or after 1 January 2002.

Revenue Briefings

Tax Briefing

Tax Briefing June 2001 – Issue 44 (part 2) pg 30 – Revenue Certificates in Deeds

Revenue Information Notes

SD10A – Revenue Certificates Required In Deeds (for deeds prior to 8 December 2010)

Cross References

From Section 83A

Section 20 Assessment of duty by the Commissioners.

83B Certain family farm transfers

[(1) Stamp duty shall not be chargeable on any instrument operating as a conveyance or transfer of land, the subject of the disposal by the child referred to in paragraph (*d*) (inserted by the Finance Act 2007) of section 599(1) of the Taxes Consolidation Act 1997.

[...][1]][2]

Amendments

[1] Deleted by FA12 sched3(27). In effect for all instruments that are executed on or after 7 July 2012 per S.I. No. 228 of 2012.

[2] Inserted by FA07 s107(1). This section applies as respects instruments executed on or after 2 April 2007.

Revenue Information Notes

SD10A – Revenue Certificates Required In Deeds (for deeds prior to 8 December 2010)
SD10B – Revenue Certificates Required In Deeds (up to and including Finance Act 2011)

Cross References

From Section 83B

Section 20 Assessment of duty by the Commissioners.

83C Exchange of houses

[(1) In this section—

"*excess land*" means an area of land other than land referred to in the definition of "*house*";

"*house*" means a building or part of a building, used or suitable for use as a dwelling, and includes an area of land for occupation and enjoyment with the dwelling as its gardens or grounds which, exclusive of the area of the land on which the dwelling is constructed, does not exceed 0.4047 hectare;

"*house builder*" means a person who has constructed a new house and includes a person who is connected, within the meaning of section 10 of the Taxes Consolidation Act 1997, with the first-mentioned person as part of an arrangement in connection with the construction or disposal of the house;

"*new house*" means a house that immediately prior to a conveyance, transfer or lease of the house by the house builder has not previously been occupied or sold;

"*old house*" means a house that, immediately prior to a conveyance or transfer of the house by an individual, has been occupied by the individual or any other individual.

(2) This section applies to an instrument which operates as a conveyance or transfer of an old house by an individual (whether alone or with other individuals) to a house builder where—

(a) the instrument contains a certificate that this section applies,

(b) either or both the house builder and any other person conveys, transfers or leases a new house to the individual (whether alone or with other individuals), and

(c) the conveyance or transfer of the old house is entered into in consideration of the conveyance, transfer or lease of the new house (in this section referred to as an "*exchange of houses*").

(3) Notwithstanding section 37, stamp duty shall not be chargeable on an instrument to which this section applies in so far as the instrument effects the conveyance or transfer of an old house by an individual (whether alone or with other individuals) to a house builder.

(4) Where subsection (3) applies and the old house and the new house are not of equal value, any consideration paid or agreed to be paid for equality shall consist only of a payment in cash.

(5) Where excess land is conveyed or transferred by an individual to a house builder by an instrument to which this section applies, the instrument, in so far as it conveys or transfers excess land, shall be chargeable to stamp duty, in respect of the excess land, as if it were a conveyance or transfer on sale of the excess land with the substitution of the value of the excess land thereby conveyed or transferred for the amount or value of the consideration for the sale.

(6) Subsection (3) shall not apply to an instrument unless it has, in accordance with section 20, been stamped with a particular stamp denoting that it is duly stamped or, as the case may be, that it is not chargeable with any duty.

(7) For the purposes of subsection (6), where any exchange of houses is effected by more than one instrument, the instruments shall, for the purposes of section 20, be presented to the Commissioners at the same time.

(8) (a) Where relief from stamp duty arises under this section, on the first occurrence of either of the events specified in paragraph (*c*), the house builder shall become liable to pay the Commissioners an amount (in this subsection referred to as a "*clawback*") equal to the amount of the duty that would have been charged on the instrument by virtue of section 37, in respect of the conveyance or transfer of the old house to the house builder, together with interest charged on that amount, calculated in accordance with section 159D, from the date of the first occurrence of either of the said events to the date the clawback is paid.

(b) Where relief from stamp duty arises under this section and it is subsequently found that the certificate, referred to in subsection (2)(*a*), contained in the instrument—

(i) was untrue in any material particular which would have resulted in the relief afforded by this section not applying, and

(ii) was included knowing same to be untrue or in reckless disregard as to whether it was true or not,

then, where a false certificate has been included in the instrument, the house builder shall be liable to pay to the Commissioners a penalty in an amount equal to 125 per cent of the duty that would have been charged on the instrument by virtue of section 37, in respect of the conveyance or transfer of the old house to the house builder, had all the facts been truthfully certified, together with interest charged on that amount, calculated in accordance with section 159D, from the date the instrument was executed to the date the penalty is paid.

(c) The events referred to in paragraph (*a*) are that—

(i) the old house, or part of the old house, is conveyed or transferred by the house builder to another person, or

(ii) the old house is not conveyed or transferred by the house builder to another person on or before 31 December 2010.

(9) Notwithstanding subsection (8)—

(a) a house builder shall not be liable to a clawback under paragraph (*a*) of subsection (8) if and to the extent that the house builder has paid a penalty under paragraph (*b*) of the said subsection,

(b) a house builder shall not be liable to a penalty under paragraph (*b*) of subsection (8) if and to the extent that the house builder has paid a clawback under paragraph (*a*) of the said subsection.

(10) This section applies as respects instruments executed on or after 7 May 2009 and on or before 31 December 2010.][1]

Amendments

[1] Inserted by FA09 s24.

Revenue Briefings

eBrief

eBrief No. 31/2009 – Stamp Duty – Property 'trade-in' scheme

Cross References

From Section 83C

Section 10 Adhesive stamps.

CHAPTER 2

Other Instruments

84 Repayment of stamp duty on certain transfers of shares

[FA1986 s98(1)(*b*) and (2)]

(1) In this section "*approved scheme*", "*participant*", "*the release date*" and "*shares*" have the same meanings, respectively, as in section 509 of the Taxes Consolidation Act, 1997.

(2) Where, in relation to an instrument, it is shown to the satisfaction of the Commissioners that the instrument gives effect, on or after the release date, to the transfer of shares by, or on behalf of, a person who is, or had become, entitled to those shares as a participant in an approved scheme, the Commissioners shall repay such an amount of the stamp duty as was paid, by reference to the heading "CONVEYANCE or TRANSFER on sale of any stocks or marketable securities" in *Schedule 1*, on the instrument in respect of those shares.

Cross References

From Section 84

Schedule 1 Stamp Duties on Instruments

85 Certain loan capital and securities

[FA1993 s106]

(1) In this section "*loan capital*" means any debenture stock, bonds or funded debt, by whatever name known, or any capital raised which is borrowed or has the character of borrowed money, whether in the form of stock or in any other form.

[(1A) For the purposes of *subsection (2)(d)* "*enhanced equipment trust certificate*" means loan capital issued by a company to raise finance of acquire, develop or lease aircraft.][1]

(2) Stamp duty shall not be chargeable on—

(a) the issue, whether in bearer form or otherwise, of—

(i) any Government loan within the meaning assigned by section 134(10) of the Finance Act, 1990, or

[(ii) any other loan capital;][2]

(b) the transfer of loan capital of a company or other body corporate which—

(i) does not carry a right of conversion into stocks or marketable securities (other than loan capital) of a company having a register in the State or into loan capital having such a right,

(ii) does not carry rights of the same kind as shares in the capital of a company, including rights such as voting rights, a share in the profits or a share in the surplus on liquidation,

[…][3]

(iv) is issued for a price which is not less than 90 per cent of its nominal value, and

[(v) does not carry a right to a sum in respect of repayment or interest which is related to certain movements in an index or indices (based wholly or partly and directly or indirectly on stocks or marketable securities) specified in any instrument or other document relating to the loan capital,][4]

[…][5]

(c) the issue or transfer of securities issued by a qualifying company within the meaning of section 110 of the Taxes Consolidation Act, 1997, where the money raised by such securities is used in the course of its [business, and][6]

[(d) the issue, transfer or redemption of an enhanced equipment trust certificate.][7]

Amendments

[1] Inserted by FA13 s80(a).

[2] Substituted by FA07 s100(1)(d). This section applies to instruments executed on or after 7 December 2006.

[3] Deleted by FA08 s118(1)(a). This section applies to transfers of loan capital made on or after 13 March 2008.

[4] Substituted by FA08 s118(1)(b). This section applies to transfers of loan capital made on or after 13 March 2008.

[5] Deleted by FA13 s80(b).

[6] Substituted by FA13 s80(b).

[7] Inserted by FA13 s80(b).

85A Certain investment certificates

[Stamp duty shall not be chargeable on the issue, transfer or redemption of an investment certificate within the meaning of section 267N (inserted by the Finance Act 2010) of the Taxes Consolidation Act 1997.][1]

Amendments

[1] Inserted by FA10 s(137). Has effect as on and from 3 April 2010.

86 Certain loan stock

[FA1970 s44(1) and (2)]

Stamp duty shall not be chargeable on transfers of any loan stock—

(a) of a company registered or established in the State or a Board established by or under an Act of the Oireachtas or the Oireachtas of Saorstát Éireann the payment of the interest on which is guaranteed by the Minister, or

(b) of the Electricity Supply Board, Radio Telefís Éireann, [...][1], [...][2] [or Bord Gáis Éireann][3] to which *paragraph (a)* does not apply.

Amendments

[1] Repealed by ICCBA00 (Commencement) (Sections 5 and 7) Order 2001 (SI 46/2001) as respects loan stock issued after 12 February 2001.

[2] Deleted by FA00 s127(1)(b). Has effect in relation to transfers of loan stock executed where the loan stock was issued on or after 10 February 2000.

[3] Substituted by FA01 s207(1). Has effect as respects instruments executed on or after 15 February 2001 but only in relation to loan stock issued on or after 15 February 2001.

Cross References

To Section 86

Schedule 4 Consequential Amendments

86A Enterprise securities market

[(1) Stamp duty shall not be chargeable on any conveyance or transfer of stocks or marketable securities admitted to the Enterprise Securities Market operated by the Irish Stock Exchange Limited.

(2) *Subsection (1)* shall not apply to any conveyance or transfer of stocks or marketable securities where the admission of the stocks or marketable securities to the Enterprise Securities Market has been

cancelled by the Irish Stock Exchange Limited.][1]

Amendments

[1] Inserted by F(No.2)A13 s70(1). Comes into operation on such day as the Minister for Finance may by order appoint.

87 Stock borrowing

[FA1995 s150]

(1) In this section—

"*collateral stock*", in relation to a stock borrowing, means stock which is transferred to the lender by means of security for the performance of the undertaking referred to in *paragraph (b)* of the definition of "*stock borrowing*";

"*equivalent stock*" means stock of an identical type, nominal value, description and amount as was so obtained from the lender or where, since the date of the stock borrowing, such stock has been paid or has been converted, subdivided, consolidated, redeemed, made the subject of a takeover, call on partly paid stock, capitalisation issue, rights issue, distribution or other similar event, then "*equivalent stock*" means—

(a) in the case of conversion, subdivision or consolidation, the stock into which the borrowed stock has been converted, subdivided or consolidated,

(b) in the case of redemption, a sum of money equivalent to the proceeds of the redemption,

(c) in the case of takeover, a sum of money or stock, being the consideration or alternative consideration which the lender has directed the stock borrower to accept,

(d) in the case of a call on partly paid stock, the paid-up stock but only where the lender shall have paid to the stock borrower the sum due,

(e) in the case of a capitalisation issue, the borrowed stock together with the stock allotted by means of a bonus on that borrowed stock,

(f) in the case of a rights issue, the borrowed stock together with the stock allotted on that borrowed stock, which the lender has directed the borrower to take up but only where the lender shall have paid to the stock borrower all and any sum due in respect of the stock allotted,

(g) in the event that a distribution is made in respect of the borrowed stock in the form of stock or a certificate which may at a future date be exchanged for stock or where an option is exercised to take a distribution in the form of stock or a certificate which may at a future date be exchanged for stock, the borrowed stock together with stock or a certificate equivalent to those allotted, and

(h) in the case of any event similar to any of the foregoing, the borrowed stock together with or replaced by a sum of money or stock equivalent to that received in respect of such borrowed stock resulting from such events;

[...][1]

[...][2]

["*stock borrowing*" means a transaction in which a person other than an individual (in this section referred to as the "*stock borrower*")—

(a) obtains stock from another person other than an individual (in this section referred to as the "*lender*"), and

(b) gives an undertaking to provide to the lender, not later than [12 months][3] after the date on which the said stock borrower obtained the stock referred to in paragraph (a), equivalent stock;][4]

"*stock return*", in relation to a stock borrowing, means a transaction or transactions in which, in respect of such stock borrowing, the undertaking referred to in *paragraph (b)* of the definition of "*stock borrowing*" is carried out within the period referred to in that paragraph.

(2) Stamp duty shall not be chargeable—

(a) on a stock borrowing or on a stock return, or

(b) on the transfer of collateral stock to the lender.

(3) If and to the extent that the stock borrower does not return or cause to be returned to the lender before the expiration of the period of [12 months][5] from the date of the stock borrowing equivalent stock the stock borrower shall pay to the Commissioners within 14 days after the expiration of that period the amount of ad valorem duty which would have been chargeable on the stock so obtained if this section had not been enacted and if any stock borrower fails to duly pay any sum which that borrower is liable to pay under this subsection, that sum, together with [interest on that sum, calculated in accordance with *section 159D*,][6] after the expiration of that period of [12 months][7] to the date of [payment of that sum and, by means of a penalty,][8][...][9] a sum equal to 1 per cent of the duty for each day the duty remains unpaid[...][10].

(4) Every stock borrower shall maintain[, for a period of 3 years from the date of the stock borrowing,][11] separate records of each stock borrowing and any stock return made in respect of that stock borrowing and such records shall include, in respect of each stock borrowing, the following:

[...][12]

(b) the name and address of the lender;

(c) the type, nominal value, description and amount of stock borrowed from the lender;

(d) the date on which the stock was transferred from the lender to the stock borrower;

(e) the date on which equivalent stock should be returned to the lender;

(f) the type, nominal value, description and amount of the stock returned to the lender and the date of the stock return;

(g) where *paragraph (a), (b), (c), (d), (e), (f), (g)* or *(h)* of the definition of "*equivalent stock*" in *subsection (1)* applies, full details of that equivalent stock.

Amendments

[1,2] Deleted by FA00 s128(1)(a)(i). Shall apply to stock borrowing transactions entered into on or after 6 April 1999.

[3] Substituted by FA05 s122(1)(a). This section applies to stock borrowing transactions entered into on or after 25 March 2005

[4] Substituted by FA00 s128(1)(a)(ii). Shall apply to stock borrowing transactions entered into on or after 6 April 1999.

[5,7] Substituted by FA05 s122(1)(b). This section applies to stock borrowing transactions entered into on or after 25 March 2005

[6] Substituted by FA05 sched5.

[8] Substituted by FA09 s30(3)(a). This section is deemed to have come into force and have taken effect as on and from 24 December 2008.

[9] Deleted by F(No.2)A08 sched5(part5)(chap2)(7)(l).

[10] Deleted by F(No.2)A08 sched4(part1). Applies as respects any tax that becomes due and payable on or after 1 March 2009.

[11] Inserted by FA00 s128(1)(c)(i). Shall apply to stock borrowing transactions entered into on or after 10 February 2000.

[12] Deleted by FA00 s128(1)(c)(ii). Shall apply to stock borrowing transactions entered into on or after 10 February 2000.

Note:

F(No.2)A08 sched5 (part5)(chap 2)(7)

As respects paragraph 7 of this Schedule subparagraphs (a) to (aa) (other than subparagraph (c)(i)(I)) of that paragraph have effect as on and from the passing of this Act and to the extent that Chapter 3A (being inserted into Part 47 of the Taxes Consolidation Act 1997 by Part 1 of this Schedule) applies to penalties incurred under the Stamp Duties Consolidation Act 1999 before the passing of this Act which on the passing of this Act have not been paid, it shall not apply to such penalties which are in the form of interest accrued under any provisions of the said Act.

Revenue Briefings

eBrief

eBrief No. 56/2012 – Tax Treatment of Stocklending/Sale and Repurchase (repo) Transactions

Cross References

From Section 87

Section 159D Calculation of interest on unpaid duty and other amounts.

To Section 87

Section 87A Stock repo

87A Stock repo

[(1) In this section—

"*equivalent stock*" has the meaning assigned to it by *section 87* subject to references—

(a) to "*obtained from the lender*" being read as "*transferred to the repo buyer*",

(b) to "*stock borrowing*" being read as "*stock transfer*",

(c) to "*lender*" being read as "*repo seller*",

(d) to "*stock borrower*" being read as "*repo buyer*",

(e) to "*borrowed stock*" being read as "*stock transferred*", and

(f) to "*borrower*" being read as "*repo buyer*";

"*repurchase agreement*" means an agreement between a person other than an individual (in this section referred to as the "*repo seller*") and another person other than an individual (in this section referred to as the "*repo buyer*") whereby the repo seller agrees to sell stock to the repo buyer on terms that the repo seller will repurchase, and the repo buyer will resell, equivalent stock not later than [12 months][1] after the date of the stock transfer;

"*stock return*" means a transaction or transactions whereby a repo buyer conveys equivalent stock to a repo seller in pursuance of a repurchase agreement and within the [12 month time limit][2] referred to in the repurchase agreement;

"*stock transfer*" means a transaction whereby a repo seller conveys stock to a repo buyer in pursuance of a repurchase agreement.

(2) Stamp duty shall not be chargeable on a stock transfer or on a stock return.

(3) If and to the extent that the repo seller does not repurchase or cause to be repurchased from the repo buyer before the expiration of the period of [12 months][3] from the date of the stock transfer equivalent stock the repo buyer shall pay to the Revenue Commissioners within 14 days after the expiration of that period the amount of ad valorem duty which would have been chargeable on the stock so transferred if this section had not been enacted.

(4) If any repo buyer fails to duly pay any sum which that repo buyer is liable to pay under *subsection (3)*, that sum, together with—

(a) [interest on that sum, calculated in accordance with section 159D,][4] after the expiration of the period of [12 months][5] referred to in *subsection (3)* to the date of payment of that sum, and

(b) [...][6] [by means of a penalty, a sum equal to 1 per cent][7] of the duty for each day the duty remains unpaid,

[...][8].

(5) Every repo buyer shall maintain, for a period of 3 years from the date of the stock transfer, separate records of each stock transfer and any stock return made in respect of that stock transfer and such records shall include, in respect of each stock transfer, the following:

(a) the name and address of the repo seller;

(b) the type, nominal value, description and amount of the stock transferred by the repo seller;

(c) the date on which the stock was transferred to the repo buyer;

(d) the date on which equivalent stock should be repurchased by the repo seller;

(e) the type, nominal value, description and amount of the stock returned by the repo buyer to the repo seller and the date of such return;

(f) where *paragraph (a)*, *(b)*, *(c)*, *(d)*, *(e)*, *(f)*, *(g)* or *(h)* of the definition of "*equivalent stock*" applies, full details of that equivalent stock.][9]

Amendments

[1] Substituted by FA05 s123(1)(a)(i). This section applies to stock transfers executed on or after 25 March 2005

[2] Substituted by FA05 s123(1)(a)(ii). This section applies to stock transfers executed on or after 25 March 2005

[3] Substituted by FA05 s123(1)(b). This section applies to stock transfers executed on or after 25 March 2005

[4] Substituted by FA05 sched5.

[5] Substituted by FA05 s123(1)(c). This section applies to stock transfers executed on or after 25 March 2005

[6] Deleted by F(No.2)A08 sched5(part5)(chap2)(7)(m).

[7] Substituted by FA09 s30(3)(b). This section is deemed to have come into force and have taken effect as on and from 24 December 2008.

[8] Deleted by F(No.2)A08 sched4(part1). Applies as respects any tax that becomes due and payable on or after 1 March 2009.

[9] Inserted by FA00 s129(1). subsections (1) and (2) of section 87A, apply to a stock transfer and a stock return in respect of such stock transfer each of which are executed on or after 6 April 1999, subsections (3), (4) and (5) of section 87A, apply to a stock transfer and a stock return in respect of such stock transfer each of which are executed on or after 10 February 2000.

Note:

F(No.2)A08 sched5 (part5)(chap 2)(7)

As respects paragraph 7 of this Schedule subparagraphs (a) to (aa) (other than subparagraph (c)(i)(I)) of that paragraph have effect as on and from the passing of this Act and to the extent that Chapter 3A (being inserted into Part 47 of the Taxes Consolidation Act 1997 by Part 1 of this Schedule) applies to penalties incurred under the Stamp Duties Consolidation Act 1999 before the passing of this Act which on the passing of this Act have not been paid, it shall not apply to such penalties which are in the form of interest accrued under any provisions of the said Act.

Revenue Briefings

eBrief

eBrief No. 56/2012 – Tax Treatment of Stocklending/Sale and Repurchase (repo) Transactions

Cross References

From Section 87A

Section 87 Stock borrowing.

87B Merger of companies

[(1) In this section—

'*cross-border merger*' has the same meaning as in Regulation 2(1) of the European Communities (Cross-Border Mergers) Regulations 2008 (S.I. No. 157 of 2008);

'*merger*' has the same meaning as in Regulation 4 of the European Communities (Mergers and Divisions of Companies) Regulations 1987 (S.I. No. 137of1987);

'*SE*' means a European public limited-liability company (*Societas Europaea* or SE) as provided for by the SE Regulation;

'*SE merger*' means the formation of an SE by merger of 2 or more companies in accordance with *Article 2(1)* and *subparagraph (a)* or *(b)* of *Article 17(2)* of the SE Regulation;

'*SE Regulation*' means Council Regulation (EC) No. 2157/2001 of 8 October 2001* on the Statute for a European company (SE).

*OJ No. L294, 10.11.2001, p.1

(2) Stamp duty shall not be chargeable on an instrument made for the purposes of the transfer of assets pursuant to a merger, a cross-border merger or an SE merger.][1]

Amendments

[1] Inserted by FA12 s99.

88 Certain stocks and marketable securities

[FA1992 s206]

(1) (a) In *subparagraph (ii)* of *paragraph (b)*—

"*collective investment scheme*" means a scheme which is an arrangement made for the purpose, or having the effect, solely or mainly, of providing facilities for the participation by the public or other investors, as beneficiaries, in profits or income arising from the acquisition, holding, management or disposal of securities or any other property;

"*units*" includes shares and any other instruments granting an entitlement to shares in the investments or income of, or receive a distribution from, a collective investment scheme.

(b) Subject to *subsection (2)*, stamp duty shall not be chargeable on any conveyance or transfer of—

[(i) units in an investment undertaking within the meaning of *section 739B* of the Taxes Consolidation Act 1997,][1]

[(ia) units in a common contractual fund within the meaning of *section 739I* of the Taxes Consolidation Act 1997,

(ib) units in an investment limited partnership within the meaning of *section 739J* of the Taxes Consolidation Act 1997,][2]

(ii) units in a collective investment scheme which is incorporated or otherwise formed under the law of a territory outside the State,

(iii) units of a unit trust to which subsection [(5) or (6)][3] of section 731 of the Taxes Consolidation Act, 1997, relates, or

(iv) stocks or marketable securities of a [company or other body corporate][4] which is not registered in the State.

(2) *Paragraph (b)* of *subsection (1)* shall not apply where the conveyance or transfer of units (being units within the meaning of *subparagraph (ii)* of *paragraph (b)* of *subsection (1)*) or stocks or marketable securities (being stocks or marketable securities within the meaning of *subparagraph (iv)* of *paragraph (b)* of *subsection (1)*), as the case may be, relates to—

(a) any immovable property situated in the State or any right over or interest in such property, or [(b) any stocks or marketable securities of a company which is registered in the State, other than a company which is—

(i) an investment undertaking within the meaning of *section 739B* of the Taxes Consolidation Act 1997, or

(ii) a qualifying company within the meaning of *section 110* of the Taxes Consolidation Act 1997.][5]

Amendments

[1] Substituted by FA13 s81(a).

[2] Inserted by FA13 s81(b).

[3] Substituted by FA12 s100(1)(c).

[4] Substituted by FA12 s100(1)(d).

[5] Substituted by FA13 s81(c).

Cross References

To Section 88

Section 75 Relief for intermediaries.

88A Reorganisation of undertakings for collective investment

[Stamp duty shall not be chargeable on any conveyance or transfer of assets in respect of which no chargeable gain accrues by virtue of section 739A (inserted by the Finance Act, 2000) of the Taxes Consolidation Act, 1997.][1]

Amendments

[1] Inserted by FA00 s130(1). This section shall apply and have effect in relation to a conveyance or transfer executed on or after 23 March 2000

88B Funds: reorganisation

[(1) In this section—

"*domestic fund*" means an investment undertaking within the meaning of section 739B of the Taxes Consolidation Act 1997 other than an investment undertaking referred to in section 739I(1)(a)(ii) of that Act;

"*foreign fund*" means an arrangement which takes effect by virtue of the law of a territory outside the State, being an arrangement made for the purpose, or having the effect, solely or mainly, of providing facilities for the participation by the public or other investors, as beneficiaries, in profits or income arising from the acquisition, holding, management or disposal of securities or any other property;

"*units*", in relation to a domestic fund or, as the case may be, a foreign fund, includes shares and any other instruments granting an entitlement to shares in the investments or income of, or to receive a distribution from, a domestic fund or, as the case may be, a foreign fund.

[(2) Stamp duty shall not be chargeable on any instrument made for the purposes of or in connection with any arrangement between a foreign fund and a domestic fund, being an arrangement entered into for the purposes of or in connection with a scheme of reconstruction or amalgamation under which—

(a) the foreign fund transfers assets to the domestic fund and the domestic fund—

(i) issues units to persons who hold units in the foreign fund in respect of and in proportion to (or as nearly as may be in proportion to) their holdings of units in the foreign fund, or

(ii) issues units directly to the foreign fund,

or

(b) the domestic fund transfers assets to the foreign fund and the foreign fund—

(i) issues units to persons who hold units in the domestic fund in respect of and in proportion to (or as nearly as may be in proportion to) their holdings of units in the domestic fund, or

(ii) issues units directly to the domestic fund.][1]][2]

Amendments

[1] Substituted by FA12 s100(1)(e).

[2] Inserted by FA06 S107(1). This section applies as respects instruments executed on or after 31 March 2006.

88C Reconstructions or amalgamations of certain common contractual funds

[Stamp duty shall not be chargeable on any instrument made for the purposes of or in connection with a scheme for the reconstruction or amalgamation of a common contractual fund to which *subsection (3)* (inserted by the *Finance Act 2006*) of section 739H of the Taxes Consolidation Act 1997 applies.][1]

Amendments

[1] Inserted by FA06 s107(1). This section applies as respects instruments executed on or after 31 March 2006

88D Reconstructions or amalgamations of certain investment undertakings

[(1) Subject to subsection (2), stamp duty shall not be chargeable on an instrument made for the purposes of or in connection with a scheme for the reconstruction or amalgamation of an investment undertaking to which subsections (1), (1A) and (1B) (inserted by the *Finance Act 2008*) and (2) of section 739H of the Taxes Consolidation Act 1997 apply.

(2) Subsection (1) shall not apply to an instrument made for the purposes of or in connection with a scheme for the reconstruction or amalgamation of a common contractual fund within the meaning of section 739I(1)(*a*)(ii) of the Taxes Consolidation Act 1997.][1]

Amendments

[1] Inserted by FA08 s119(1). This section applies as respects instruments executed on or after 13 March 2008.

88E Transfer of assets within unit trusts

[(1) In this section—

"*investment undertaking*" means—

(a) an investment undertaking to which *paragraph (a)* of the definition of "*investment undertaking*" in section 739B(1) of the Taxes Consolidation Act 1997 relates, and

(b) an investment undertaking that is a "*unit trust*";

"*relevant Regulations*" has the same meaning as in section 739B(1) of the Taxes Consolidation Act 1997;

"*unit trust*" has the same meaning as in relevant Regulations.

(2) Stamp duty shall not be chargeable on any instrument made for the purposes of the transfer of assets within an investment undertaking.][1]

Amendments

[1] Inserted by FA10 s(138)(b). Has effect as on and from 3 April 2010.

88F Reconstruction or amalgamation of offshore funds

[Stamp duty shall not be chargable on any instrument made for the purposes of or in connection with—

(a) a scheme of reconstruction or amalgamation of an offshore fund to which *section 747F* of the Taxes Consolidation Act 1997 refers, or

(b) an exchange referred to in *paragraph (b)* of *section 747E(1A)* of the Taxes Consolidation Act 1997.][1]

Amendments

[1] Inserted by FA12 s100(1)(f).

88G Amalgamation of unit trusts

[Stamp duty shall not be chargeable on any instrument made for the pur poses of or in connection with a scheme of amalgamation to which *section 739D(8C)* of the Taxes Consolidation Act 1997 refers.][1]

Amendments

[1] Inserted by FA12 s100(1)(g).

89 Foreign Government securities

[(1) In this section—

"*foreign local authority*" means an authority, corresponding in substance to a local authority for the purposes of the Local Government Act 2001, which is established outside the State and whose functions are carried on primarily outside the State;

"*foreign local government*" means any local or regional government in any jurisdiction outside the State.

(2) Stamp duty shall not be chargeable on any conveyance or transfer of stocks or other securities of the government of any territory outside the State, of a foreign local government or of a foreign local authority.][1]

Amendments

[1] Substituted by FA03 s138(1). This section has effect in relation to instruments executed on or after 6 February 2003.

90 Certain financial services instruments

[FA1992 s207]

(1) In this section—

"*American depositary receipt*" means an instrument—

(a) which acknowledges—

(i) that a depositary or a nominee acting on such depositary's behalf, holds stocks or marketable securities, and

(ii) that the holder of the instrument has rights in or in relation to such stocks or marketable securities including the right to receive such stocks or marketable securities from the depositary or such depositary's nominee,

and

(b) which—

(i) is dealt in on a recognised stock exchange which is situated in the United States of America or Canada, or

(ii) represents stocks or marketable securities which are so dealt in;

"*commodities*" means tangible assets (other than currency, securities, debts or other assets of a financial nature) which are dealt in on a recognised commodity exchange;

"*debt factoring agreement*" means an agreement for the sale, or a transfer on sale, of a debt or part of a debt where such sale occurs in the ordinary course of the business of the vendor or the purchaser;

"*depositary*" means a person who holds stocks or marketable securities in trust for or on behalf of holders of depositary receipts and who maintains a register of ownership of such depositary receipts;

"*financial futures agreement*" means a forward agreement which is for the time being dealt in on a recognised futures exchange or a recognised stock exchange;

"*forward agreement*" means—

(a) an agreement under which a party to the agreement agrees—

(i) to buy or sell commodities, currency, stocks or marketable securities, or

(ii) to pay or receive a sum of money, whether or not such money is actually paid or received,

at a specified date or within a specified or determinable period of time and pursuant to which the price or currency exchange rate concerned or, in the case of a sum of money, the interest (if any) payable, or expressed to be payable, on such sum of money is determined or determinable at the time of the execution of the agreement, or

(b) an agreement conferring the right to receive certain payments and imposing the liability to make certain payments, the receipt and making of the payments being dependent on and related to certain movements in a specified stock exchange index or specified stock exchange indices;

"*option agreement*" means an agreement under which a right is conferred on a party to the agreement to do, at the party's discretion, either or both of the following, that is—

(a) to buy from or sell to or buy from and sell to another party to the agreement—

(i) specified stocks, marketable securities, commodities or currency,

(ii) an agreement conferring the right to receive certain payments and imposing the liability to make certain payments, the receipt and making of the payments being dependent on and related to certain movements in a specified stock exchange index or specified stock exchange indices,

on or before a specified date at a price that is determined or determinable at the time of the execution of the agreement,

(b) to borrow money from or lend money to another party to the agreement for or within a specified period in consideration of the payment of interest by the party by whom the money is borrowed or to whom it is lent to the other party concerned at a rate that is determined or determinable at the time of the execution of the agreement;

"*swap agreement*" means an agreement under which the parties to the agreement exchange payments or repayments of money in respect of which such parties have obligations or rights and which are denominated in a specified currency or are subject to the payment of a specified rate of interest or relate to the price of specified commodities, stocks or marketable securities, for payments or repayments of the same kind which are denominated in another specified currency or are subject to the payment of a specified different rate of interest or relate to the price of other specified commodities, stocks or marketable securities.

(2) Stamp duty shall not be chargeable on any of the following instruments:

(a) a debt factoring agreement;

(b) a swap agreement;

(c) a forward agreement;

(d) a financial futures agreement;

(e) an option agreement;

(f) a combination of any 2 or more of the instruments specified in *paragraphs (a)* to *(e)*;

(g) a transfer of, or an agreement to transfer—

(i) any instrument specified in *paragraphs (a)* to *(e)*, or a combination of any 2 or more such instruments,

(ii) [a lease or an interest in a lease][1] other than a lease to which any heading in *Schedule 1* applies, or

(iii) an American depositary receipt.

(3) *Subsection (2)* shall not apply if the instrument, other than an instrument which is a transfer of, or an agreement to transfer, an American depositary receipt relates to—

(a) immovable property situated in the State or any right over or interest in such property, or

[(b) any stocks or marketable securities of a company which is registered in the State, other than a company which is—

(i) an investment undertaking within the meaning of *section 739B* of the Taxes Consolidation Act 1997, or

(ii) a qualifying company within the meaning of *section 110* of the Taxes Consolidation Act 1997.][2]

(4) Notwithstanding that, in respect of any particular provision it contains, an instrument is exempt from stamp duty under this section, if the instrument is liable to stamp duty in respect of any other provision it contains under any heading in *Schedule 1*, the instrument shall be chargeable with the latter stamp duty.

Amendments

[1] Substituted by FA12 s100(1)(h).

[2] Substituted by FA13 s81(d).

Cross References

From Section 90
Schedule 1 Stamp Duties on Instruments

90A Greenhouse gas emissions allowance

[[(1) In this section '*greenhouse gas emissions allowance*' means carbon offsets within the meaning of *section 110(1)* of the Taxes Consolidation Act 1997.][1]

(2) Subject to subsection (3), stamp duty shall not be chargeable under or by reference to any heading in Schedule 1 on an instrument for the sale, transfer or other disposition of a greenhouse gas emissions allowance.

(3) Where stamp duty is chargeable on an instrument under or by reference to any heading in Schedule 1 and part of the property concerned consists of a greenhouse gas emissions allowance—

(a) the consideration in respect of which stamp duty would otherwise be chargeable shall be apportioned, on such basis as is just and reasonable, as between the part of the property which consists of a greenhouse gas emissions allowance and the part which does not, and

(b) the instrument shall be chargeable only in respect of the consideration attributable to such of the property as is not a greenhouse gas emissions allowance.

[...][2]

(5) Where part of the property referred to in subsection (1) of section 45 consists of a greenhouse gas emissions allowance, that subsection shall have effect as if the words "in such manner as is just and reasonable" were substituted for "in such manner, as the parties think fit".

(6) Where part of the property referred to in subsection (3) of section 45 consists of a greenhouse gas emissions allowance and both or, as the case may be, all the relevant persons are connected with one another, that subsection shall have effect as if the words, "the consideration shall be apportioned in such manner as is just and reasonable, so that a distinct consideration for each separate part or parcel is set forth in the conveyance relating to such separate part or parcel, and such conveyance shall be charged with ad valorem duty in respect of such distinct consideration" were substituted for "for distinct parts of the consideration, then the conveyance of each separate part or parcel shall be charged with ad valorem duty in respect of the distinct part of the consideration specified in the conveyance".

(7) For the purposes of subsection (6), a person is a relevant person if that person is a person by or for whom the property is contracted to be purchased and the question of whether persons are connected with one another shall be construed in accordance with section 10 of the Taxes Consolidation Act 1997 and as if the reference to the Capital Gains Tax Acts in the definition of "*relative*" in that section was replaced by a reference to the Stamp Duties Consolidation Act 1999.

(8) Where subsection (5) or (6) applies, and the consideration is apportioned in a manner that is not just and reasonable, the conveyance relating to the separate part or parcel of property shall be chargeable with ad valorem duty as if the value of that separate part or parcel of property were substituted for the distinct consideration set forth in that conveyance.][3]

Amendments

[1] Substituted by FA12 s101.

[2] Deleted by FA12 s97(1)(a). Applies as respects instruments executed on or after 7 December 2011. Does not apply as respects any instrument executed before 1 July 2012 where—

(a) the effect of the application of that subsection would be to increase the duty otherwise chargeable on the instrument, and

(b) the instrument contains a statement in such form as the Revenue Commissioners may specify, certifying that the instrument was executed solely in pursuance of a binding contract entered into before 7 December 2011.

[3] Inserted by FA08 s120(1). Applies as respects instruments executed on or after 5 December 2007.

Cross References

From Section 90A

Schedule

Section 45 Directions as to apportionment of consideration.

Schedule 1 Stamp Duties on Instruments

91 New dwellinghouses and apartments with floor area certificate

[FA1969 s49(1) and (2B)]

(1) Subject to *subsection (2)*, an instrument giving effect to the purchase of a dwellinghouse or apartment on the erection of that dwellinghouse or apartment shall be exempt from all stamp duties.

(2) (a) In this subsection, "*floor area certificate*" means a certificate issued by the Minister for the Environment and Local Government certifying that that Minister is satisfied, on the basis of the information available to that Minister at the time of so certifying, that the total floor area of that dwellinghouse or apartment measured in the manner referred to in section 4(2)(*b*) of the Housing (Miscellaneous Provisions) Act, 1979, does not or will not exceed the maximum total floor area standing specified in regulations under that section 4(2)(*b*) and is not or will not be less than the minimum total floor area standing so specified.

(b) *Subsection (1)* shall have effect in relation to an instrument only if the instrument contains a statement, in such form as the Commissioners may specify, certifying that—

(i) the instrument gives effect to the purchase of a dwellinghouse or apartment on the erection of that dwellinghouse or apartment,

(ii) until the expiration of the period of 5 years commencing on the date of the execution of the instrument or the subsequent sale (other than a sale the contract for which, if it were a written conveyance, would not, apart from *section 82*, be charged with full ad valorem duty or a sale to a company under the control of the vendor or of any person entitled to a beneficial interest in the dwellinghouse or apartment immediately prior to the sale or to a company which would, in relation to a notional gift of shares in that company taken, immediately prior to the sale, by any person so entitled, be under the control of the donee or successor within the meaning of [section 27 of the Capital Acquisitions Tax Consolidation Act 2003][1], irrespective of the shares the subject matter of the notional gift) of the dwellinghouse or apartment concerned, whichever event first occurs, that dwellinghouse or apartment will be occupied as the only or principal place of residence of the purchaser, or if there be more than one purchaser, of any one or more of the purchasers or of some other person in right of the purchaser or, if there be more than one purchaser, of some other person in right of any one or more of the purchasers and that [no person—][2]

[(I) other than a person who, while in such occupation, derives rent or payment in the nature of rent in consideration for the provision, on or after 6 April 2001, of furnished residential accommodation in part of the dwellinghouse or apartment concerned, or

(II) other than by virtue of a title prior to that of the purchaser,

will derive any rent or payment in the nature of rent for the use of that dwellinghouse or apartment, or of any part of it, during that period, and][3]

(iii) on the date of execution of the instrument there exists a valid floor area certificate in respect of that dwellinghouse or apartment.

(c) Where, in relation to an instrument which is exempted from stamp duty by virtue of *subsection (1)* and at any time during the period referred to in *paragraph (b)(ii)*, [some person, other than a person referred to in clause (I) or (II) of subsection (2)(*b*)(ii)][4], derives any rent or payment in the nature of rent for the use of the dwellinghouse or apartment concerned, or of any part of it, the purchaser, or where there be more than one purchaser, each such purchaser, shall—

(i) jointly and severally become liable to pay to the Commissioners [an amount (in this section referred to as a "*clawback*")][5] equal to the amount of the duty which would have been charged in the first instance if the dwellinghouse or apartment had been conveyed or transferred or leased by an instrument to which this section had not applied together with [interest charged on that amount, calculated in accordance with *section 159D*,][6] from the date when the rent or payment is first received to the date [the clawback][7] is remitted, and

(ii) the person who receives the rent or payment shall, within 6 months after the date of the payment, notify the payment to the Commissioners on a form provided, or approved of, by them for the purposes of this section, unless that person is already aware that the Commissioners have already received such a notification from another source.

(d) The furnishing of an incorrect statement within the meaning of *paragraph (b)* shall be deemed to constitute the delivery of an incorrect statement for the purposes of section 1078 of the Taxes Consolidation Act, 1997.

[(2A) Notwithstanding subsection (2)(*b*), subsection (2)(*c*) shall not apply to an instrument to which subsection (1) applied to the extent that any rent or payment in the nature of rent, for the use of the dwellinghouse or apartment or any part of the dwellinghouse or apartment, is derived—

(a) on or after 5 December 2007, and

(b) after the expiration of a period of 2 years which commences on the date of the execution of the instrument concerned.][8]

[(3) This section shall apply as respects instruments executed before 1 April 2004.][9]

Amendments

[1] Substituted by CATCA03 sched3 and s119.

[2, 3] Substituted by FA01 s208(1)(a)(i). Applies and has effect in relation to instruments executed on or after 6 December 2000.

[4] Substituted by FA01 s208(1)(a)(ii). Applies and has effect in relation to instruments executed on or after 6 December 2000.

[5] Substituted by F(No.2)A08 sched5(part5)(chap2)(7)(n)(i).

[6] Substituted by FA05 sched5.

[7] Substituted by F(No.2)A08 sched5(part5)(chap2)(7)(n)(ii).

[8] Inserted by FA08 s122(1)(a). This section is deemed to have applied as on and from 5 December 2007.

[9] Inserted by FA04 s71.

Note:

F(No.2)A08 sched5 (part5)(chap 2)(7)

As respects paragraph 7 of this Schedule subparagraphs (a) to (aa) (other than subparagraph (c)(i)(I)) of that paragraph have effect as on and from the passing of this Act and to the extent that Chapter 3A (being inserted into Part 47 of the Taxes Consolidation Act 1997 by Part 1 of this Schedule) applies to penalties incurred under the Stamp Duties Consolidation Act 1999 before the passing of this Act which on the passing of this Act have not been paid, it shall not apply to such penalties which are in the form of interest accrued under any provisions of the said Act.

Revenue Briefings

Tax Briefing

Tax Briefing April 2009 – Issue 71 – Stamp Duty Audit: Owner/Occupier Relief
Tax Briefing September 2009 – Issue 73 – 'Rent-to-Buy' (and similar) Schemes
Tax Briefing June 2001 – Issue 44 (part 2) pg 30 – Revenue Certificates in Deeds

Cross References

From Section 91

Section 82 Charities.
Section 159D Calculation of interest on unpaid duty and other amounts.

To Section 91

Section 91A New dwellinghouses and apartments with floor area compliance certificate.
Section 92 New dwellinghouses and apartments with no floor area certificate.

91A New dwellinghouses and apartments with floor area compliance certificate

[(1) (a) In this section—

"floor area compliance certificate", in respect of a dwellinghouse or apartment, means a certificate issued by the Minister for the Environment, Heritage and Local Government certifying that that Minister is satisfied, on the basis of the information available to that Minister at the time of so certifying, that—

(i) the total floor area of the dwellinghouse or apartment—

(I) does not, or will not, exceed 125 square metres, and

(II) is not, or will not, be less than 38 square metres,

and

(ii) the dwellinghouse or apartment complies or will comply with such conditions, if any, as may be set down in regulations made by that Minister from time to time for the purposes of this section;

"*valid floor area compliance certificate*" means a floor area compliance certificate which has not been withdrawn.

(b) For the purposes of this section the Minister for the Environment, Heritage and Local Government—

(i) may make regulations from time to time—

(I) specifying the manner in which the total floor area of a dwellinghouse or apartment is to be measured, and

(II) setting down conditions in relation to standards of construction of dwellinghouses and apartments and the provision of water, sewerage and other services therein,

(ii) may issue a floor area compliance certificate in respect of a dwellinghouse or apartment to a person where that Minister is satisfied, on the basis of information provided to that Minister by the person, or by a person on behalf of the person, that the person is registered for value-added tax and is the holder of a current certificate of authorisation within the meaning of section 530(1) of the Taxes Consolidation Act 1997 or a current tax clearance certificate within the meaning of section 1094(1) or section 1095(1) of the Taxes Consolidation Act 1997,

(iii) may, by notice in writing, withdraw any such certificate already issued, and

(iv) may not issue a floor area compliance certificate in respect of a dwellinghouse or apartment unless any person authorised in writing by that Minister for the purposes of this section is permitted to inspect the dwellinghouse or apartment at all reasonable times on production, if so requested by a person affected, of his or her authorisation.

(2) For the purposes of this section, the Commissioners or any person authorised by the Commissioners on their behalf, may, by notice in writing, request the Minister for the Environment, Heritage and Local Government to provide them, or any person so authorised, with the information, referred to in *paragraph (b)(ii)* of *subsection (1)*, which was supplied by a person in support of the person's application for a floor area compliance certificate.

(3) Subject to *subsection (4)*, an instrument giving effect to the purchase of a dwellinghouse or apartment on the erection of that dwellinghouse or apartment shall be exempt from all stamp duties.

(4) *Subsection (3)* shall have effect in relation to an instrument only if the instrument contains a statement, in such form as the Commissioners may specify, certifying that—

(a) the instrument gives effect to the purchase of a dwellinghouse or apartment on the erection of that dwellinghouse or apartment,

(b) until the expiration of the period of [2 years][1] commencing on the date of the execution of the instrument or the subsequent sale of the dwellinghouse or apartment concerned, whichever event first occurs, that dwellinghouse or apartment will be occupied as the only or principal place of residence of the purchaser, or if there be more than one purchaser, of any one or more of the purchasers or of some other person in right of the purchaser or, if there be more than one purchaser, of some other person in right of any one or more of the purchasers and that no person—

(i) other than a person who, while in such occupation, derives rent or payment in the nature of rent in consideration for the provision, on or after 1 April 2004, of furnished residential accommodation in part of the dwellinghouse or apartment concerned, or

(ii) other than by virtue of a title prior to that of the purchaser,

will derive any rent or payment in the nature of rent for the use of that dwellinghouse or apartment, or of any part of it, during that period, and

(c) on the date of execution of the instrument there exists a valid floor area compliance certificate in respect of that dwellinghouse or apartment.

(5) In *subsection (4)(b)*, the reference to the subsequent sale does not include a reference to a sale the contract for which, if it were a written conveyance, would not, apart from *section 82*, be charged with full ad valorem duty or a sale to a company under the control of the vendor or of any person entitled to a beneficial interest in the dwellinghouse or apartment immediately prior to the sale or to a company which would, in relation to a notional gift of shares in that company taken, immediately prior to the sale, by any person so entitled, be under the control of the donee or successor within the meaning of section 27 of the Capital Acquisitions Tax Consolidation Act 2003, irrespective of the shares the subject matter of the notional gift.

(6) Where, in relation to an instrument which is exempted from stamp duty by virtue of *subsection (3)* and at any time during the period referred to in *subsection (4)(b)*, some person, other than a person referred to in *subparagraph (i)* or *(ii)* of *subsection (4)(b)*, derives any rent or payment in the nature of rent for the use of the dwellinghouse or apartment concerned, or of any part of it, then the purchaser, or where there be more than one purchaser, each such purchaser, shall—

(a) jointly and severally become liable to pay to the Commissioners [an amount (in this section referred to as a "*clawback*")][2] equal to the amount of the duty which would have been charged in the first instance if the dwellinghouse or apartment had been conveyed or transferred or leased by an instrument to which this section had not applied together with [interest charged on that amount, calculated in accordance with *section 159D*,][3] from the date when the rent or payment is first received to the date [the clawback][4] is remitted, and

(b) the person who receives the rent or payment shall, within 6 months after the date of the payment, notify the payment to the Commissioners on a form provided, or approved of, by them for the purposes of this section, unless that person is already aware that the Commissioners have already received such a notification from another source.

[(6A) Notwithstanding *subsection (4)*, *subsection (6)* shall not apply to an instrument, being an instrument executed before 5 December 2007, to which *subsection (3)* applied to the extent that any rent or payment in the nature of rent, for the use of the dwellinghouse or apartment or any part of the dwellinghouse or apartment, is derived—

(a) on or after 5 December 2007, and

(b) after the expiration of a period of 2 years which commences on the date of the execution of the instrument concerned.][5]

(7) Where a valid floor area certificate, within the meaning of *section 91*, has issued in respect of a dwellinghouse or apartment, that certificate shall be deemed to be a valid floor area compliance certificate within the meaning of this section, where an exemption from stamp duty is claimed under this section in respect of the dwellinghouse or apartment concerned.

(8) The furnishing of an incorrect statement within the meaning of *subsection (4)* shall be deemed to constitute the delivery of an incorrect statement for the purposes of section 1078 of the Taxes Consolidation Act 1997.

(9) Every regulation made under this section shall be laid before Dáil Éireann as soon as may be after it is made and, if a resolution annulling the regulation is passed by Dáil Éireann within the next 21 days on which Dáil Éireann has sat after the regulation is laid before it, the regulation shall be annulled accordingly, but without prejudice to the validity of anything previously done thereunder.][6]

[(10) This section shall not apply to an instrument executed on or after 8 December 2010.][7]

Amendments

[1] Substituted by FA08 s122(1)(b)(i). Applies as respects instruments executed on or after 5 December 2007.

[2] Substituted by F(No.2)A08 sched5(part5)(chap2)(7)(n)(i).

[3] Substituted by FA05 sched5.

[4] Substituted by F(No.2)A08 sched5(part5)(chap2)(7)(n)(ii).

[5] Inserted by FA08 s122(1)(b)(ii). This section is deemed to have applied as on and from 5 December 2007.

[6] Inserted by FA04 s72(1). This section applies as respects instruments executed on or after 1 April 2004.

[7] Inserted by FA11 s63(1)(c). Shall not apply as respects any instrument executed before 1 July 2011 where—(a) the effect of the application of that subsection would be to increase the duty otherwise chargeable on the instrument, and (b) the instrument contains a statement, in such form as the Revenue Commissioners may specify, certifying that the instrument was executed solely in pursuance of a binding contract entered into before 8 December 2010.

Note:

F(No.2)A08 sched5 (part5)(chap 2)(7)

As respects paragraph 7 of this Schedule subparagraphs (a) to (aa) (other than subparagraph (c)(i)(I)) of that paragraph have effect as on and from the passing of this Act and to the extent that Chapter 3A (being inserted into Part 47 of the Taxes Consolidation Act 1997 by Part 1 of this Schedule) applies to penalties incurred under the Stamp Duties Consolidation Act 1999 before the passing of this Act which on the passing of this Act have not been paid, it shall not apply to such penalties which are in the form of interest accrued under any provisions of the said Act.

Revenue Briefings

Tax Briefing

Tax Briefing June 2001 – Issue 44 (part 2) pg 30 – Revenue Certificates in Deeds
Tax Briefing April 2009 – Issue 71 – Stamp Duty Audit: Owner/Occupier Relief
Tax Briefing September 2009 – Issue 73 – 'Rent-to-Buy' (and similar) Schemes

Revenue Information Notes

SD10A – Revenue Certificates Required In Deeds (for deeds prior to 8 December 2010)

Cross References

From Section 91A

Section 82 Charities.
Section 91 New dwellinghouses and apartments with floor area certificate.
Section 159D Calculation of interest on unpaid duty and other amounts.

To Section 91A

Section 92 New dwellinghouses and apartments with no floor area certificate.
Section 92B Residential property first time purchaser relief.

92 New dwellinghouses and apartments with no floor area certificate

[F(No. 2)A1998 s14; FA1997 s123 and s124]

(1) (a) Where, in relation to an instrument to which this subsection applies—

(i) the instrument is one to which *section 29* applies, that section shall apply to that instrument as if—

(I) the following subsection were substituted for *subsection (2)* of that section:

"(2) Notwithstanding *section 43*, where, in connection with, or as part of any arrangement involving, a sale of any land, a dwellinghouse or apartment has been built, or is in the course of being built, or is to be built, on that land, any instrument whereby such sale is effected shall be chargeable to stamp duty under the heading "CONVEYANCE or TRANSFER on sale of any property other than stocks or marketable securities or a policy of insurance or a policy of life insurance" in *Schedule 1*, as if the property concerned were residential property on an amount which is the greater of—

(a) any consideration paid in respect of the sale of that land, and

(b) 25 per cent of the aggregate of the consideration at *paragraph (a)* and the consideration paid, or to be paid, in respect of the building of the dwellinghouse or apartment on that land.";

(II) the following paragraphs were inserted into *subsection (3)* of that section:

"(b) This subsection does not apply where the dwellinghouse or apartment concerned was occupied by any person, other than in connection with the building of that dwellinghouse or apartment, at any time prior to the agreement for sale of the land.

(c) The amount on which stamp duty is chargeable by virtue of this section shall be deemed to be the amount or value of the consideration for the sale in respect of which that duty is chargeable.";

and

(III) "such aggregate consideration" were substituted for "the aggregate consideration which is chargeable under *subsection (2)*" in *paragraph (a)* of *subsection (4)* of that section;

(ii) the instrument is one to which *section 53* applies, that section shall apply to that instrument as if—

(I) the following subsection were substituted for *subsection (2)* of that section:

"(2) Notwithstanding *subsection (2)* of *section 52*, where, in connection with, or as part of any arrangement involving, a lease of any land, a dwellinghouse or apartment has been built, or is in the course of being built, or is to be built, on that land, any instrument whereby such lease is effected shall be chargeable to stamp duty under *subparagraph (a)* of *paragraph (3)* of the heading "*LEASE*" in *Schedule 1*, as if the property concerned were residential property on an amount which is the greater of—

(a) any consideration (other than rent) paid in respect of the lease of that land, and

(b) 25 per cent of the aggregate of the consideration at *paragraph (a)* and the consideration paid, or to be paid, in respect of the building of the dwellinghouse or apartment on that land.";

(II) the following paragraphs were inserted into *subsection (3)* of that section:

"(b) This subsection does not apply where the dwellinghouse or apartment concerned was occupied by any person, other than in connection with the building of that dwellinghouse or apartment, at any time prior to the agreement for lease of the land.

(c) The amount on which stamp duty is chargeable by virtue of this section shall be deemed to be the amount or value of the consideration for the lease in respect of which that duty is chargeable.";

and

(III) "such aggregate consideration" were substituted for "the aggregate consideration which is chargeable under *subsection (2)*" in *paragraph (a)* of *subsection (4)* of that section;

and

(iii) the instrument gives effect to the purchase of a dwellinghouse or apartment on the erection of that dwellinghouse or apartment and [*sections 29*, *53*, *91* and *91A*][1] do not apply, the consideration (other than rent) for the sale shall for the purposes of ad valorem duty be treated as being reduced by 75 per cent.

(b) This subsection applies to an instrument which contains a statement, in such form as the Commissioners may specify, certifying that—

[(i) the instrument—

(I) is one to which *section 29* or *53*, applies and that *sections 91* and *91A* do not apply, or

(II) gives effect to the purchase of a dwellinghouse or apartment on the erection of that dwellinghouse or apartment and that *sections 29*, *53*, *91* and *91A* do not apply,

(ia) on the date of execution of the instrument there exists a certificate, signed by such person or class of persons as may be set down in regulations made by the Minister for the Environment, Heritage and Local Government from time to time for the purposes of this section, stating that the total floor area of the dwellinghouse or apartment does or will exceed 125 square metres, and][2]

(ii) until the expiration of the period of [2 years][3] commencing on the date of the execution of the instrument or the subsequent sale (other than a sale the contract for which, if it were a written conveyance, would not, apart from *section 82*, be charged with full ad valorem duty or a sale to a company under the control of the vendor or of any person entitled to a beneficial interest in the dwellinghouse or apartment immediately prior to the sale or to a company which would, in relation to a notional gift of shares in that company taken, immediately prior to the sale, by any person so entitled, be under the control of the donee or successor within the meaning of [section 27 of the Capital Acquisitions Tax Consolidation Act 2003][4], irrespective of the shares the subject matter of the notional gift) of the dwellinghouse or apartment concerned, whichever event first occurs, that dwellinghouse or apartment will be occupied as the only or principal place of residence of the purchaser, or if there be more than one purchaser, of any one or more of the purchasers or of some other person in right of the purchaser or, if there be more than one purchaser, of some other person in right of any one or more of the purchasers and that [no person—][5]

[(I) other than a person who, while in such occupation, derives rent or payment in the nature of rent in consideration for the provision, on or after 6 April 2001, of furnished residential accommodation in part of the dwellinghouse or apartment concerned, or

(II) other than by virtue of a title prior to that of the purchaser,

will derive any rent or payment in the nature of rent for the use of that dwellinghouse or apartment, or of any part of it, during that period.][6]

(2) Where *subsection (1)* applies to an instrument and at any time during the period referred to in *paragraph (b)(ii)* of that subsection, [some person, other than a person referred to in clause (I) or (II) of *subsection (1)(b)(ii)*][7], derives any rent or payment in the nature of rent for the use of the dwellinghouse or apartment concerned, or of any part of it, the purchaser, or where there be more than one purchaser, each such purchaser, shall—

(a) jointly and severally become liable to pay to the Commissioners [an amount (in this section referred to as a "*clawback*")][8] equal to the difference between the amount of the duty which would have been charged in the first instance if the dwellinghouse or apartment had been conveyed or transferred or leased by an instrument to which *subsection (1)* had not applied and the amount of duty which was actually charged together with [interest charged on that amount, calculated in accordance with *section 159D*,][9] from the date when the rent or payment is first received to the date [the clawback][10] is remitted, and

(b) the person who receives the rent or payment shall, within 6 months after the date of the payment, notify the payment to the Commissioners on a form provided, or approved of, by them for the purposes of this section, unless that person is already aware that the Commissioners have already received such a notification from another source.

[(2A) Notwithstanding *subsection (1)(b)*, subsection (2) shall not apply to an instrument, being an instrument executed before 5 December 2007, to which *subsection (1) (a)* applied to the extent that any rent or payment in the nature of rent, for the use of the dwellinghouse or apartment or any part of the dwellinghouse or apartment, is derived—

(a) on or after 5 December 2007, and

(b) after the expiration of a period of 2 years which commences on the date of the execution of the instrument concerned.][11]

[(3) The furnishing of an incorrect statement within the meaning of *subsection (1) (b)* shall be deemed to constitute the delivery of an incorrect statement for the purposes of section 1078 of the Taxes Consolidation Act 1997.

(4) For the purposes of this section, the Minister for the Environment, Heritage and Local Government may make regulations from time to time—

(a) specifying the manner in which the total floor area of a dwellinghouse or apartment is to be measured, and

(b) specifying the person or class of persons who may sign a certificate referred to in *subsection(1) (b)*(i*a*).

(5) Every regulation made under this section shall be laid before Dáil Éireann as soon as may be after it is made and, if a resolution annulling the regulation is passed by Dáil Éireann within the next 21 days on which Dáil Éireann has sat after the regulation is laid before it, the regulation shall be annulled accordingly, but without prejudice to the validity of anything previously done thereunder.][12]

[(6) This section shall not apply to an instrument executed on or after 8 December 2010.][13]

Amendments

[1] Substituted by FA04 s73(1)(a). This section applies as respects instruments executed on or after 1 July 2004 other than instruments executed on or after 1 July 2004 solely in pursuance of binding contracts entered into before 1 April 2004.

[2] Substituted by FA04 s73(1)(b). This section applies as respects instruments executed on or after 1 July 2004 other than instruments executed on or after 1 July 2004 solely in pursuance of binding contracts entered into before 1 April 2004.

[3] Substituted by FA08 s122(1)(c)(i). Applies as respects instruments executed on or after 5 December 2007.

[4] Substituted by CATCA03 sched3 and s119.

[5, 6] Substituted by FA01 s208(1)(b)(i). Applies and has effect in relation to instruments executed on or after 6 December 2000.

[7] Substituted by FA01 s208(1)(b)(ii). Shall apply and have effect in relation to instruments executed on or after 6 December 2000.

[8] Substituted by F(No.2)A08 sched5(part5)(chap2)(7)(n)(i).

[9] Substituted by FA05 sched5.

[10] Substituted by F(No.2)A08 sched5(part5)(chap2)(7)(n)(ii).

[11] Inserted by FA08 s122(1)(c)(ii). This section is deemed to have applied as on and from 5 December 2007.

[12] Inserted by FA04 s73(1)(c). This section applies as respects instruments executed on or after 1 July 2004 other than instruments executed on or after 1 July 2004 solely in pursuance of binding contracts entered into before 1 April 2004.

[13] Inserted by FA11 s63(1)(d). Shall not apply as respects any instrument executed before 1 July 2011 where— (a) the effect of the application of that subsection would be to increase the duty otherwise chargeable on the instrument, and (b) the instrument contains a statement, in such form as the Revenue Commissioners

may specify, certifying that the instrument was executed solely in pursuance of a binding contract entered into before 8 December 2010.

Note:

F(No.2)A08 sched5 (part5)(chap 2)(7)

As respects paragraph 7 of this Schedule subparagraphs (a) to (aa) (other than subparagraph (c)(i)(I)) of that paragraph have effect as on and from the passing of this Act and to the extent that Chapter 3A (being inserted into Part 47 of the Taxes Consolidation Act 1997 by Part 1 of this Schedule) applies to penalties incurred under the Stamp Duties Consolidation Act 1999 before the passing of this Act which on the passing of this Act have not been paid, it shall not apply to such penalties which are in the form of interest accrued under any provisions of the said Act.

Revenue Briefings

Tax Briefing

Tax Briefing June 2001 – Issue 44 (part 2) pg 30 – Revenue Certificates in Deeds
Tax Briefing April 2009 – Issue 71 – Stamp Duty Audit: Owner/Occupier Relief
Tax Briefing September 2009 – Issue 73 – 'Rent-to-Buy' (and similar) Schemes

Revenue Information Notes

SD10A – Revenue Certificates Required In Deeds (for deeds prior to 8 December 2010)

Cross References

From Section 92

Section 29 Conveyance on sale combined with building agreement for dwellinghouse or apartment.
Section 43 Further consideration in respect of substantial improvements not chargeable.
Section 52 Charging of duty on leases, etc.
Section 53 Lease combined with building agreement for dwellinghouse or apartment.
Section 82 Charities.
Section 91 New dwellinghouses and apartments with floor area certificate.
Section 91A New dwellinghouses and apartments with floor area compliance certificate.
Section 159D Calculation of interest on unpaid duty and other amounts.
Schedule 1 Stamp Duties on Instruments

To Section 92

Section 92A Residential property owner occupier relief.
Section 92B Residential property first time purchaser relief.

92A Residential property owner occupier relief

[(1) The amount of stamp duty chargeable under or by reference to *paragraphs (1)* to *(6)* of the Heading "CONVEYANCE or TRANSFER on sale of any property other than stocks or marketable securities or a policy of insurance or a policy of life insurance" or *clauses (i)* to *(vi)* of *paragraph (3)(a)* of the Heading "LEASE", as the case may be, in *Schedule 1* on any instrument to which this section applies shall be reduced, where *paragraph (1)* or *clause (i)* applies, to nil, and where—

(a) *paragraph (2)* or *clause (ii)* applies, to an amount equal to three-ninths,

(b) *paragraph (3)* or *clause (iii)* applies, to an amount equal to four-ninths,

(c) *paragraph (4)* or *clause (iv)* applies, to an amount equal to five-ninths,

(d) *paragraph (5)* or *clause (v)* applies, to an amount equal to six-ninths,

(e) *paragraph (6)* or *clause (vi)* applies, to an amount equal to seven and one half-ninths,

of the amount which would otherwise have been chargeable but where the amount so obtained is a fraction of £1 that amount shall be rounded up to the nearest £.

(2) This section shall apply to—

(a) any instrument to which *section 92* applies, or

(b) any instrument, other than one to which *section 92* applies, which contains a statement, in such form as the Commissioners may specify, certifying that—

(i) the instrument gives effect to the purchase of a dwellinghouse or apartment, and

(ii) [no person —][1]

[(I) other than a person who, while in such occupation, derives rent or payment in the nature of rent in consideration for the provision, on or after 6 April 2001, of furnished residential accommodation in part of the dwellinghouse or apartment concerned, or

(II) other than by virtue of a title prior to that of the purchaser,

will derive any rent or payment in the nature of rent for the use of that dwellinghouse or apartment, or of any part of it, during that period.][2]

(3) Where *subsection (1)* applies to an instrument and at any time during the period referred to in *section 92(1)(b)(ii)* or in *subsection (2)(b)(ii)* of this section, [some person, other than a person referred to in *clause (I)* or *(II)* of *subsection (2)(b)(ii)*][3], derives any rent or payment in the nature of rent for the use of the dwellinghouse or apartment concerned, or of any part of it, the purchaser, or where there be more than one purchaser, each such purchaser, shall—

(a) jointly and severally become liable to pay to the Commissioners a penalty equal to the difference between the amount of the duty which would have been charged in the first instance if the dwellinghouse or apartment had been conveyed or transferred or leased by an instrument to which *subsection (1)* had not applied and the amount of duty which was actually charged together with [interest charged on that amount, calculated in accordance with *section 159D*,][4] from the date when the rent or payment is first received to the date the penalty is remitted, and

(b) the person who receives the rent or payment shall, within 6 months after the date of the payment, notify the payment to the Commissioners on a form provided, or approved of, by them for the purposes of this section, unless that person is already aware that the Commissioners have already received such a notification from another source.

(4) Where the instrument is one to which this section and *section 92* applies—

(a) the reference in *subsection (3)* to the amount of duty which would have been charged in the first instance shall be construed as a reference to the duty which would have been charged had the relief under *section 92* continued to apply, and

(b) the reference to the amount of duty which was actually charged in *subsection (2)(a)* of *section 92* shall be construed as a reference to the duty which would have been charged had the relief under this section been denied,

and the penalty referred to in *subsection (3)* shall be in addition to any penalty payable under *section 92*.

(5) Notwithstanding *subsection (2)*, *subsection (1)* shall not apply unless the consideration for the sale or lease concerned which is attributable to residential property is wholly attributable to residential property which would otherwise qualify for relief under this section or where the sale or lease concerned forms part of a larger transaction or of a series of transactions unless the aggregate consideration for

that larger transaction or series of transactions which is attributable to residential property is wholly attributable to residential property which would otherwise qualify for relief under this section.

(6) Notwithstanding *subsection (2)*, this section shall not apply to an instrument to which *section 92B* applies.

[(7) Notwithstanding *subsection (2)*, *subsection (3)* shall not apply to an instrument to which *subsection (1)* applied and which was executed before 6 December 2001 to the extent that any rent or payment in the nature of rent is derived on or after 6 December 2001, for the use of the dwellinghouse or apartment or any part of the dwellinghouse or apartment.

(8) This section shall not apply to an instrument executed on or after 6 December 2001.][5]][6]

Amendments

[1, 2] Substituted by FA01 s208(1)(c)(i). Shall apply and have effect in relation to instruments executed on or after 6 December 2000.

[3] Substituted by FA01 s208(1)(c)(ii) in relation to instruments executed on or after 6 December 2000.

[4] Substituted by FA05 sched5.

[5] Inserted by FA02 s113(1)(a). This section is deemed to have applied as on and from 6 December 2001.

[6] Inserted by F(No.2)A00 s4.

Revenue Briefings

Tax Briefing

Tax Briefing June 2001 – Issue 44 (part 2) pg 30 – Revenue Certificates in Deeds
Tax Briefing April 2009 – Issue 71 – Stamp Duty Audit: Owner/Occupier Relief
Tax Briefing September 2009 – Issue 73 – 'Rent-to-Buy' (and similar) Schemes

Cross References

From Section 92A

Section 92 New dwellinghouses and apartments with no floor area certificate.
Section 92B Residential property first time purchaser relief.
Section 159D Calculation of interest on unpaid duty and other amounts.

92B Residential property first time purchaser relief

[(1) [In this section—][1] "first time purchaser"[, in relation to a purchaser,][2]means—

(a) a person, or

(b) as respects instruments executed on or after 27 June 2000, a person, being an individual,

who, at the time of the execution of the instrument to which this section applies, has not, either individually or jointly with any other person or persons, previously purchased (other than the purchase of a leasehold interest by way of grant or assignment for any term not exceeding one year), or previously built—

(i) directly or indirectly on his or her own behalf, or

(ii) as respects instruments executed on or after 27 June 2000, in a fiduciary capacity,

another dwellinghouse or apartment or a part of another dwellinghouse or apartment and for the purposes of this definition—

(I) any dwellinghouse or apartment taken under a conveyance or transfer operating as a voluntary disposition within the meaning of *section 30* of the Principal Act shall be deemed to have been taken by way of purchase where that conveyance or transfer was executed on or after 22 June 2000, and

(II) any part of a dwellinghouse or apartment taken under a conveyance or transfer operating as a voluntary disposition within the meaning of *section 30* of the Principal Act shall be deemed to have been taken by way of purchase where that conveyance or transfer was executed on or after [27 June 2000;][3]

["*purchaser*" means an individual who purchases a dwellinghouse or apartment or an interest in a dwellinghouse or apartment, where the consideration for the purchase required to be paid by the individual is derived from the individual's own means, which may be or may include consideration derived from—

(a) an unconditional gift, or

(b) a bona fide loan evidenced in writing,

made to the individual for the purposes of the purchase concerned.][4]

[(1A) For the purposes of the definition of "*purchaser*"—

(a) a gift shall be deemed not to be an unconditional gift where the donor of the gift concerned—

(i) is not a party to the instrument giving effect to the purchase of the dwellinghouse or apartment or the interest in the dwellinghouse or apartment, and

(ii) (I) intends to occupy or does occupy the dwellinghouse or apartment with the purchaser as the only or principal place of residence of each of them, or

(II) as part of an understanding or agreement can have—

(A) the dwellinghouse or apartment or the interest in the dwellinghouse or apartment, or

(B) a part of the dwellinghouse or apartment or a part of the interest in the dwellinghouse or apartment,

transferred to that donor at some time after the date of execution of the instrument concerned,

and

(b) where some or all of the consideration, required to be paid by the purchaser for the purchase of the dwellinghouse or apartment or the interest in the dwellinghouse or apartment, is derived from a loan, and where the individual making the loan—

(i) is not a party to the instrument giving effect to the purchase of the dwellinghouse or apartment or the interest in the dwellinghouse or apartment, and

(ii) (I) intends to occupy or does occupy the dwellinghouse or apartment with the purchaser as the only or principal place of residence of each of them, or

(II) as part of an understanding or agreement can have—

(A) the dwellinghouse or apartment or the interest in the dwellinghouse or apartment, or

(B) a part of the dwellinghouse or apartment or a part of the interest in the dwellinghouse or apartment, transferred to the individual who made the loan at some time after the date of execution of the instrument concerned,

then such loan shall not be regarded as a bona fide loan.

(1B) *Subsection (1A)* shall not apply to a purchaser, where the donor of the gift, or the individual making the loan, to the purchaser is a parent of the purchaser.][5]

[(2) Stamp duty shall not be chargeable under or by reference to [*paragraphs (2)* to *(4)*][6] of the Heading "CONVEYANCE or TRANSFER on sale of any property other than stocks or marketable securities or a policy of insurance or a policy of life insurance" or [clauses (ii) to (iv)][7] of *paragraph (3)(a)* of the Heading "LEASE", as the case may be, in Schedule 1 on any instrument to which this section applies.][8]

(3) This section shall apply to—

(a) any instrument to which *section 92* applies and which contains a statement, in such form as the Commissioners may specify, certifying that the purchaser, or where there is more than one purchaser, each and every one of the purchasers, is a [first time purchaser][9]

(b) [any instrument, to which neither *section 92* nor *subsection (3A)* applies, which contains a statement, in such form as the Commissioners may specify, certifying that *subsection (3A)* does not apply,][10] that the purchaser, or where there is more than one purchaser, each and every one of the purchasers, is a first time purchaser, and that—

(i) the instrument gives effect to the purchase of a dwellinghouse or apartment, and

(ii) until the expiration of the period of [2 years][11] commencing on the date of the execution of the instrument or the subsequent sale (other than a sale the contract for which, if it were a written conveyance, would not, apart from *section 82*, be charged with full ad valorem duty or a sale to a company under the control of the vendor or of any person entitled to a beneficial interest in the dwellinghouse or apartment immediately prior to the sale or to a company which would, in relation to a notional gift of shares in that company taken, immediately prior to the sale, by any person so entitled, be under the control of the donee or successor within the meaning of [section 27 of the Capital Acquisitions Tax Consolidation Act 2003][12], irrespective of the shares the subject matter of the notional gift) of the dwellinghouse or apartment concerned, whichever event first occurs, that dwellinghouse or apartment will be occupied as the only or principal place of residence of the purchaser, or if there be more than one purchaser, of any one or more of the purchasers or of some other person in right of the purchaser or, if there be more than one purchaser, of some other person in right of any one or more of the purchasers and [no person—][13]

[(I) other than a person who, while in such occupation, derives rent or payment in the nature of rent in consideration for the provision, on or after 6 April 2001, of furnished residential accommodation in part of the dwellinghouse or apartment concerned, or

(II) other than by virtue of a title prior to that of the purchaser,

will derive any rent or payment in the nature of rent for the use of that dwellinghouse or apartment, or of any part of it, [during that period, and][14]][15]

[(c) any instrument, executed on or after 31 March 2007 and on or before the date of the passing of the *Finance (No. 2) Act 2007*, that does not contain such a statement as is referred to in *paragraph* (*a*) or (*b*)—

(i) where—

(I) *section 92* applies to that instrument, and

(II) the purchaser has complied with, and has undertaken to continue to be bound by, the conditions, liabilities and obligations under *section 92* and has satisfied, or, as the case may be, undertaken to be bound by, the conditions (including the condition set out in such a statement as is referred to in *paragraph* (*a*) notwithstanding that the said instrument does not contain such a statement), liabilities and obligations referred to in this section,

or

(ii) where—

(I) had that instrument contained a statement such as is referred to in *paragraph* (*b*), such statement would have been true and correct, and

(II) the purchaser has satisfied, or, as the case may be, undertaken to be bound by, the conditions (including the conditions set out in such a statement as is referred to in *paragraph* (*b*) notwithstanding that the said instrument does not contain such a statement), liabilities and obligations referred to in this section.][16]

[(3A) This subsection applies to an instrument—

(a) which gives effect to the purchase of a dwelling-house or apartment on the erection of the dwellinghouse or apartment, or

(b) to which *section 29* or *53* applies,

where the total floor area of that dwellinghouse or apartment—

(i) does not, or will not, exceed 125 square metres, and

(ii) is not, or will not, be less than 38 square metres,

as measured in the manner specified in regulations made by the Minister for the Environment, Heritage and Local Government for the purposes of *section 91A*.][17]

(4) Where *subsection (2)* applies to an instrument and at any time during the period referred to in *section 92(1)(b)(ii)* or in *subsection (3)(b)(ii)* of this section, [some person, other than a person referred to in clause (I) or (II) of *subsection (3)(b)(ii)*][18], derives any rent or payment in the nature of rent for the use of the dwellinghouse or apartment concerned, or of any part of it, the purchaser, or where there be more than one purchaser, each such purchaser, shall—

(a) jointly and severally become liable to pay to the Commissioners [an amount (in this section referred to as a "*clawback*")][19] equal to [...][20] the amount of the duty which would have been charged in the first instance if the dwellinghouse or apartment had been conveyed or transferred or leased by an instrument to which *subsection (2)* had not applied [...][21] together with [interest charged on that amount, calculated in accordance with *section 159D*,][22] from the date when the rent or payment is first received to the date [the clawback][23] is remitted, and

(b) the person who receives the rent or payment shall, within 6 months after the date of the payment, notify the payment to the Commissioners on a form provided, or approved of, by them for the purposes of this section, unless that person is already aware that the Commissioners have already received such a notification from another source.

[(4A) Notwithstanding *subsection (3)*, *subsection (4)* shall not apply to an instrument, being an instrument executed before 5 December 2007, to which *subsection (2)* applied to the extent that any rent or payment in the nature of rent, for the use of the dwellinghouse or apartment or any part of the dwellinghouse or apartment, is derived—

(a) on or after 5 December 2007, and

(b) after the expiration of a period of 2 years which commences on the date of the execution of the instrument concerned.][24]

(5) Where the instrument is one to which this section and *section 92* applies—

(a) the reference in *subsection (4)* to the amount of duty which would have been charged in the first instance shall be construed as a reference to the duty which would have been charged had the relief under *section 92* continued to apply, and

(b) the reference to the amount of duty which was actually charged in *subsection (2)(a)* of *section 92* shall be construed as a reference to the duty which would have been charged had the relief under this section been denied,

and the [clawback][25] referred to in *subsection (4)* shall be in addition to any [clawback][26] payable under *section 92*.

(6) Notwithstanding *subsection (3)*, *subsection (2)* shall not apply to an instrument which gives effect to a sale or lease of more than one unit of residential property or where the sale or lease concerned forms part of a larger transaction or of a series of transactions comprising more than one unit of residential property.

(7) Notwithstanding *subsection (1)*, a trustee of a trust to which section 189A of the Taxes Consolidation Act, 1997, applies shall be deemed to be a first time purchaser for the purposes of the definition in *subsection (1)*, in respect of a conveyance or transfer including a conveyance or transfer operating as a voluntary disposition within the meaning of *section 30* of the Principal Act, to that trustee of that trust, of a dwellinghouse or apartment or a part of a dwellinghouse or apartment, subject to—

(a) where there is only one beneficiary of that trust, this subsection applying to one such conveyance or transfer only, being the first such conveyance or transfer executed on or after the date of the establishment of that trust, and

(b) where there is more than one beneficiary of that trust, this subsection applying to as many conveyances or transfers, executed on or after the date of the establishment of that trust, as there are beneficiaries of that trust for whose benefit any such conveyance or transfer is made.

[(7A) (a) In this subsection—

"*incapacitated individual*" means an individual who is permanently incapacitated by reason of mental infirmity, but is capable of residing on his or her own with appropriate care;

"*qualifying dwellinghouse*" means a dwellinghouse or apartment or part of a dwellinghouse or apartment, which will be occupied by the incapacitated individual as his or her principal place of residence, and will not be occupied by either parent of the incapacitated individual or by a trustee as his or her principal place of residence;

"*trustee*" means a trustee of a trust in respect of which it is shown to the satisfaction of the Commissioners, that—

(i) the trust has been established exclusively for the benefit of an incapacitated individual, and

(ii) the trust funds are applied for the benefit of that individual at the discretion of the trustees of the trust.

(b) Notwithstanding *subsection (1)*, where a parent of an incapacitated individual or a trustee purchases a qualifying dwellinghouse, the parent or the trustee, as the case may be, shall be deemed to be a first time purchaser, for the purposes of the definition in *subsection (1)*, in respect of a conveyance or transfer of the qualifying dwellinghouse executed on or after 1 January 2010, including a conveyance or transfer operating as a voluntary disposition within the meaning of *section 30*, to that parent or trustee.

(c) This subsection shall apply to only one such conveyance or transfer referred to in *paragraph (b)*, being the first such conveyance or transfer executed by the parent or by the trustee, as the case may be.][27]

[(8) (a) (i) Notwithstanding *subsection (1)*, a spouse to a marriage (in this subsection referred to as a "*claimant*"), the subject of a decree of divorce, a decree of judicial separation, a decree of nullity or a deed of separation (in this subsection referred to as a "*decree*"), shall be deemed to be a first time purchaser for the purposes of the definition in *subsection (1)*, in respect of the first conveyance or transfer, including a conveyance or transfer operating as a voluntary disposition within the meaning of *section 30*, to the claimant, of a dwelling house, after the date of the decree, where the conditions set out in *subparagraph (ii)* are satisfied.

(ii) The conditions required by this subparagraph are that—

(I) immediately prior to the date of the decree, the claimant is not beneficially entitled to an interest in any dwelling house other than the dwelling house referred to in clause (II),

(II) the dwelling house, most recently acquired prior to the date of the decree, which was the only or main residence of the claimant and his or her spouse at some time prior to the date of the decree, did not cease to be occupied, at the date of the decree, by the spouse of the claimant as his or her only or main residence and the spouse was beneficially entitled to an interest in the dwelling house on that date or acquired such an interest after that date by virtue or in consequence of, the decree, and

(III) at the date of execution of the instrument, giving effect to the conveyance or transfer, the claimant is not beneficially entitled to an interest in the dwelling house referred to in clause (II).

(aa) (i) Where, by reason only of the fact that the first conveyance or transfer (referred to in *paragraph (a)(i)*) of a dwelling house was executed on or before the date of the decree, and as a consequence the claimant cannot satisfy the conditions set out in clauses (I) and (III) of *paragraph (a)(ii)*, the claimant shall be deemed to be a first time purchaser for the purposes of the definition in *subsection (1)*, where the first conveyance or transfer is executed in the period of 6 months ending on the date of the decree and the conditions set out in *subparagraph (ii)* are satisfied.

(ii) The conditions required by this subparagraph are that—

(I) the first conveyance or transfer was made in anticipation of the decree, and

(II) immediately before the date of the decree, the claimant was not beneficially entitled to an interest in any dwelling house other than the dwelling house referred to in *subparagraph (i)* and the dwelling house referred to in clause (II) of *paragraph (a)(ii)*.

(iii) Where by virtue of *subparagraph (i)* a claimant is deemed to be a first time purchaser in respect of a first conveyance or transfer, the Commissioners, on a claim being made to them on that behalf and on the conditions set out in *subparagraph (iv)* being satisfied, shall cancel and repay such duty or part of such duty as would not have been chargeable had *paragraph (a)* applied to the conveyance or transfer when it was first presented for stamping.

(iv) The conditions required by this subparagraph are that the claimant, when making a claim for repayment, shall produce to the Commissioners—

(I) the stamped instrument,

(II) a copy of the decree,

(III) a declaration made in writing by the claimant, in such form as the Commissioners may specify, confirming to the satisfaction of the Commissioners that—

(A) the conveyance or transfer was made in connection with the decree,

(B) immediately before the date of the decree, the claimant was not beneficially entitled to an interest in any dwelling house other than the dwelling house referred to in *subparagraph (i)* and the dwelling house referred to in clause (II) of *paragraph (a)(ii)*,

(C) the dwelling house referred to in clause (II) of *paragraph (a)(ii)* did not cease to be occupied, at the date of the decree, by the spouse of the claimant as his or her only or main residence and the spouse was beneficially entitled to an interest in the dwelling house on that date or acquired such an interest after that date by virtue or in consequence of the decree,

(D) at the time of making the claim for repayment, the claimant was not beneficially entitled to an interest in the dwelling house referred to in clause (II) of *paragraph (a)(ii)*,

[(E) since the date of execution of the conveyance or transfer, the conditions referred to in *subsection (3)(b)(ii)* or *(4A)*, as the case may be, or the conditions referred to in *subsection (1)(b)(ii)* or *(2A)* of *section 92*, as the case may be, have been complied with and will be complied with for the remainder of the 2 year period referred to in the subsection that applies to the conveyance or transfer concerned,][28]

(F) the conveyance or transfer is one to which *subsection (3A)* does not apply, and

(G) where the dwelling house was conveyed or transferred to the claimant and another person, that the other person was a first time purchaser within the meaning of *subsection (1)*, immediately prior to the date of execution of the conveyance or transfer concerned,

(IV) the PPS Number of the claimant and any other person to whom the dwelling house was conveyed or transferred, and

(V) such other evidence that the Commissioners may require for the purposes of this subparagraph.

(v) *Subsection (4)* shall apply to a conveyance or transfer to which *subparagraph (ii)* applies as it applies to an instrument to which *subsection (2)* applies, with any necessary modifications.][29]

(b) In this subsection—

"*decree of divorce*" means a decree under section 5 of the Family Law (Divorce) Act, 1996, or any decree to like effect that was granted under the law of a country or jurisdiction other than the State and is recognised in the State;

"*decree of judicial separation*" means a decree under section 3 of the Judicial Separation and Family Law Reform Act, 1989, or any decree to like effect that was granted under the law of a country or jurisdiction other than the State and is recognised in [the State;][30]

["*decree of nullity*" means a decree granted by the High Court declaring a marriage to be null and void or any decree to like effect that was granted under the law of a country or judisdiction other than the State and is recognised [in the State;][31]][32]

["*deed of separation*" means a deed of separation executed by both spouses to a marriage and the date of a deed of separation is the date on which such deed is executed by both spouses to the marriage;

"*dwelling house*" means a dwelling house or apartment or a part of a dwelling house or apartment;

"*PPS Number*", in relation to a person, means the person's Personal Public Service Number within the meaning of section 262 of the Social Welfare Consolidation Act 2005.][33]

[(9) Where, by virtue of the amendment of this section by the Finance (No. 2) Act 2007, an instrument is one in respect of which stamp duty is not chargeable under or by reference to any of the paragraphs or, as the case may be, clauses referred to in subsection (2), the Commissioners, on a claim being made to them in that behalf and on the conditions set out in subsection (10) being satisfied, shall cancel and repay such duty paid as would not have been charged had this section been so amended before the instrument was executed.

(10) The conditions required by this subsection are that the purchaser (in this subsection referred to as the "*claimant*"), when making a claim for repayment, shall produce to the Commissioners—

(a) the stamped instrument,

(b) a declaration made in writing by the claimant, in such form as the Commissioners may specify, confirming to the satisfaction of the Commissioners that—

(i) where the instrument is one to which this section applies by virtue of *paragraph* (*a*) or (*b*) of *subsection (3)*, the claimant has complied with the conditions, liabilities and obligations under either or both this section and *section 92*, as the case may be, and has undertaken to continue to be bound by those conditions, liabilities and obligations,

(ii) where the instrument is one to which *subsection (3)(c)(i)* applies, the claimant has complied with, and has undertaken to continue to be bound by, the conditions, liabilities and obligations under *section 92* and has satisfied, or, as the case may be, undertaken to be bound by, the conditions (including the condition set out in such a statement as is referred to in *paragraph* (*a*) of that subsection notwithstanding that the said instrument does not contain such a statement), liabilities and obligations referred to in this section, or

(iii) where the instrument is one to which *subsection (3)(c)(ii)* applies, the claimant has satisfied, or, as the case may be, undertaken to be bound by, the conditions (including the conditions set out in such a statement as is referred to in *paragraph* (*b*) of that subsection notwithstanding that the said instrument does not contain such a statement), liabilities and obligations referred to in this section,

and

(c) such information as the Commissioners may reasonably require for the purposes of this subsection.

(11) A reference in *subsection (3)(c)* or *subsection (10)* to the purchaser, shall be construed as including a reference, where there is more than one purchaser, to each and every one of the purchasers.][34]

[(12) This section shall not apply to an instrument executed on or after 8 December 2010.][35]][36]

Amendments

[1] Substituted by FA08 s122(1)(d)(i)(I). Applies as respects instruments executed on or after 31 January 2008.

[2] Inserted by FA08 s122(1)(d)(i)(II)(A). Applies as respects instruments executed on or after 31 January 2008.

[3] Substituted by FA08 s122(1)(d)(i)(II)(B). Applies as respects instruments executed on or after 31 January 2008.

[4] Inserted by FA08 s122(1)(d)(i)(III). Applies as respects instruments executed on or after 31 January 2008.

[5] Inserted by FA08 s122(1)(d)(ii). Applies as respects instruments executed on or after 31 January 2008.

[6, 7] Substituted by FA08 s122(1)(d)(iii). Applies as respects instruments executed on or after 5 November 2007.

[8] Substituted by F(No.2)A07 s1(a). This section applies as respects instruments executed on or after 31 March 2007.

[9, 14, 16] Substituted by F(No.2)A07 s1(b). This section applies as respects instruments executed on or after 31 March 2007.

[10, 17] Substituted by FA05 s126(1)(b). Applies as respects instruments executed on or after 1 March 2005.

[11] Substituted by FA08 s122(1)(d)(iv). Applies as respects instruments executed on or after 5 December 2007.

[12] Substituted by CATCA03 sched3 and s119.

[13, 15] Substituted by FA01 s208(1)(d)(i). Shall apply and have effect in relation to instruments executed on or after 6 December 2000.

[18] Substituted by FA01 s208(1)(d)(ii). Shall apply and have effect in relation to instruments executed on or after 6 December 2000.

[19] Substituted by F(No.2)A08 sched5(part5)(chap2)(7)(n)(i).

[20, 21] Substituted by F(No.2)A07 s1(c). This section applies as respects instruments executed on or after 31 March 2007.

[22] Substituted by FA05 sched5.

[23] Substituted by F(No.2)A08 sched5(part5)(chap2)(7)(n)(ii).

[24] Inserted by FA08 s122(1)(d)(v). This section is deemed to have applied as on and from 5 December 2007.

[25, 26] Substituted by F(No.2)A08 sched5(part5)(chap2)(7)(o).

[27] Inserted by FA11 s63(1)(e). Shall not apply as respects any instrument executed before 1 July 2011 where—(a) the effect of the application of that subsection would be to increase the duty otherwise chargeable on the instrument, and (b) the instrument contains a statement, in such form as the Revenue Commissioners may specify, certifying that the instrument was executed solely in pursuance of a binding contract entered into before 8 December 2010.

[28] Substituted by F(No.2)A08 sched6(2)(b). Has effect as on and from 24 December 2008.

[29] Substituted by FA07 s108(1)(a). This section applies as respects instruments executed on or after 1 February 2007.

[30] Substituted by FA01 s208(1)(d)(vi). Paragraph (d)(iii), (v) and (vi) of subsection (1) shall apply and have effect in relation to instruments executed on or after 15 June 2000.

[31] Substituted by FA07 s108(1)(b)(i). This section applies as respects instruments executed on or after 1 February 2007.

[32] Inserted by FA01 s208(1)(d)(vi). Paragraph (d)(iii), (v) and (vi) of subsection (1) shall apply and have effect in relation to instruments executed on or after 15 June 2000.

[33] Inserted by FA07 s108(1)(b)(ii). This section applies as respects instruments executed on or after 1 February 2007.

[34] Substituted by F(No.2)A07 s1(d). This section applies as respects instruments executed on or after 31 March 2007.

[35] Inserted by FA11 s63(1)(f). Shall not apply as respects any instrument executed before 1 July 2011 where – (a) the effect of the application of that subsection would be to increase the duty otherwise chargeable on the instrument, and (b) the instrument contains a statement, in such form as the Revenue Commissioners may specify, certifying that the instrument was executed solely in pursuance of a binding contract entered into before 8 December 2010.

[36] Inserted by FA00No2 s4.

Note:

F(No.2)A08 sched5 (part5)(chap 2)(7)

As respects paragraph 7 of this Schedule subparagraphs (a) to (aa) (other than subparagraph (c)(i)(I)) of that paragraph have effect as on and from the passing of this Act and to the extent that Chapter 3A (being inserted into Part 47 of the Taxes Consolidation Act 1997 by Part 1 of this Schedule) applies to penalties incurred under the Stamp Duties Consolidation Act 1999 before the passing of this Act which on the passing of this Act have not been paid, it shall not apply to such penalties which are in the form of interest accrued under any provisions of the said Act.

Revenue Briefings

Tax Briefing

Tax Briefing April 2009 – Issue 71 – Stamp Duty Audit: Owner/Occupier Relief
Tax Briefing September 2009 – Issue 73 – 'Rent-to-Buy' (and similar) Schemes

Cross References

From Section 92B

Section 29 Conveyance on sale combined with building agreement for dwellinghouse or apartment.
Section 30 Voluntary dispositions inter vivos chargeable as conveyances or transfers on sale.
Section 53 Lease combined with building agreement for dwellinghouse or apartment.
Section 82 Charities.
Section 91A New dwellinghouses and apartments with floor area compliance certificate.
Section 92 New dwellinghouses and apartments with no floor area certificate.
Section 159D Calculation of interest on unpaid duty and other amounts.

To Section 92B

Section 92A Residential property owner occupier relief.

92C Residential property investor relief [Deleted]

Deleted by FA02 s113(1)(c). Has effect in relation to instruments executed on or after 6 December 2001.

93 Houses acquired from industrial and provident societies

[FA1969 s49(3)]

Stamp duty shall not be chargeable on a conveyance, transfer or lease of a house by a society registered under the Industrial and Provident Societies Acts, 1893 to 1978, and made, in accordance with a scheme for the provision of houses for its members, to a member or to such member and the [spouse or civil partner][1] of the member.

Amendments

[1] Substituted by F(No.3)A11 sched2(4). Deemed to have come into operation in relation to stamp duty, as respects an instrument executed on or after 1 January 2011

93A Approved voluntary body

[(1) Stamp duty shall not be chargeable on any conveyance, transfer or lease of land to a voluntary body, approved by the Minister for the Environment and Local Government under section 6 of the Housing (Miscellaneous Provisions) Act, 1992, for the purposes of the Housing Acts, 1966 to 1998.][1]

Amendments

[1] Inserted by FA01 s210(1). Applies and has effect in relation to instruments executed on or after 15 February 2001.

94 Purchase of land from Land Commission

[FA1967 s20]

(1) In this section "*qualified person*" has the same meaning as in section 5 of the Land Act, 1965, and "*advance*" means an advance under that section.

(2) Stamp duty shall not be chargeable on an instrument giving effect to the purchase of land by a qualified person, being an instrument either—

(a) which contains a charge on the land in favour of the Irish Land Commission for repayment of an advance, or

(b) on which there is endorsed an order made by the Irish Land Commission charging the land with an advance.

95 Commercial woodlands

[FA1990 s120]

(1) In this section "*trees*" means woodlands managed on a commercial basis and with a view to the realisation of profits.

(2) This section applies to an instrument, being a conveyance or transfer on sale of land, or a lease of land, where [...][1] trees are growing on a substantial part of such land.

(3) Stamp duty shall not be chargeable on any instrument to which this section applies, in respect of such part of the consideration for the sale or lease as represents the value of trees growing on the land.

Amendments

[1] Deleted by FA12 sched3(28). In effect for all instruments that are executed on or after 7 July 2012 per S.I. No. 228 of 2012.

Revenue Briefings

Tax Briefing

Tax Briefing June 2001 – Issue 44 (part 2) pg 30 – Revenue Certificates in Deeds

eBrief

eBrief No. 01/2013 – Stamp Duty – Young Trained Farmer Relief – Commercial Woodlands Relief

Revenue Information Notes

SD10A – Revenue Certificates Required In Deeds (for deeds prior to 8 December 2010)
SD10B – Revenue Certificates Required In Deeds (up to and including Finance Act 2011)

96 Transfers between spouses

[FA1990 s114]

(1) Subject to *subsection (2)*, stamp duty shall not be chargeable on any instrument, other than a conveyance or transfer referred to in *subsection (1), (2), (3)* or *(4)* of *section 46* or *subsection (1)(b)* of *section 73* whereby any property is transferred [by a spouse or spouses of a marriage to either spouse or to both spouses of that marriage, or by a civil partner or the civil partners in a civil partnership to either civil partner or both civil partners in that civil partnership.][1]

(2) *Subsection (1)* shall not apply to an instrument whereby any property or any part of, or beneficial interest in, any property is transferred to a person other than a [spouse or civil partner][2] referred to in that subsection.

[...][3]

Amendments

[1] Substituted by F(No.3)A11 sched2(5). Deemed to have come into operation in relation to stamp duty, as respects an instrument executed on or after 1 January 2011

[2] Substituted by F(No.3)A11 sched2(6). Deemed to have come into operation in relation to stamp duty, as respects an instrument executed on or after 1 January 2011

[3] Deleted by FA12 sched3(29). In effect for all instruments that are executed on or after 7 July 2012 per S.I. No. 228 of 2012.

Revenue Briefings

Tax Briefing

Tax Briefing June 2001 – Issue 44 (part 2) pg 30 – Revenue Certificates in Deeds

Cross References

From Section 96

Section 30 Voluntary dispositions inter vivos chargeable as conveyances or transfers on sale.

Section 46 Directions as to sub-sales.
Section 73 Exemptions.

97 Certain transfers following the dissolution of a marriage

[FA1997 s127(1) to (3)]

(1) Subject to *subsection (2)*, stamp duty shall not be chargeable on an instrument by which property is transferred pursuant to an order to which this subsection applies by [either or both of the spouses or the civil partners who were parties to the marriage or the civil partnership concerned, as the case may be,][1] to either or both of them.

(2) (a) *Subsection (1)* applies—

(i) to a relief order, within the meaning of section 23 of the Family Law Act, 1995, made following the dissolution of a marriage, [...][2]

(ii) to an order under Part III of the [Family Law (Divorce) Act 1996 or Part 12 of the Civil Partnership and Certain Rights and Obligations of Cohabitants Act 2010, or][3] .

[(iii) to an order or other determination to like effect, which is analogous to an order referred to in subparagraph (i) or (ii), of a court under the law of another territory made under or in consequence of the dissolution of [a marriage or a civil partnership][4], being a dissolution that is entitled to be recognised as valid in the State.][5]

(b) *Subsection (1)* does not apply in relation to an instrument referred to in that subsection by which any part of or beneficial interest in the property concerned is transferred to a person other than the [spouses or civil partners][6] concerned.

[...][7]

Amendments

[1] Substituted by F(No.3)A11 sched2(7). Deemed to have come into operation in relation to stamp duty, as respects an instrument executed on or after 1 January 2011

[2] Deleted by FA00 s131(1)(a). This section shall apply to an order or other determination to like effect where the order or the determination is made on or after 10 February 2000.

[3] Substituted by F(No.3)A11 sched2(8). Deemed to have come into operation in relation to stamp duty, as respects an instrument executed on or after 1 January 2011

[4] Substituted by F(No.3)A11 sched2(9). Deemed to have come into operation in relation to stamp duty, as respects an instrument executed on or after 1 January 2011

[5] Inserted by FA00 s131(1)(c). This section shall apply to an order or other determination to like effect where the order or the determination is made on or after 10 February 2000.

[6] Substituted by F(No.3)A11 sched2(10). Deemed to have come into operation in relation to stamp duty, as respects an instrument executed on or after 1 January 2011

[7] Deleted by FA12 sched3(30). In effect for all instruments that are executed on or after 7 July 2012 per S.I. No. 228 of 2012.

Cross References

From Section 97

Section 30 Voluntary dispositions inter vivos chargeable as conveyances or transfers on sale.

97A Certain transfers by cohabitants

[(1) Stamp duty shall not be chargeable on an instrument executed on or after 1 January 2011 by which property is transferred pursuant to an order under section 174 of the Civil Partnership and Certain Rights and Obligations of Cohabitants Act 2010 by a cohabitant (within the meaning of that Act) to his or her cohabitant.

(2) *Subsection (1)* does not apply in relation to an instrument referred to in that subsection by which any part of or beneficial interest in the property concerned is transferred to a person other than the cohabitants concerned.

[...][1]][2]

Amendments

[1] Deleted by FA12 sched3(31). In effect for all instruments that are executed on or after 7 July 2012 per SI No. 228 of 2012.

[2] Inserted by F(No.3) A11 sched2(11). Deemed to have come into operation in relation to stamp duty, as respects an instrument on or after 1 January 2011.

98 Foreign immovable property

[FA1992 s209]

(1) Stamp duty shall not be chargeable on any instrument which is a conveyance, transfer, assignment, lease or licence of any immovable property situated outside the State.

(2) *Subsection (1)* shall not apply if the instrument relates to—

- (a) any immovable property situated in the State, or any right over or interest in such property, or
- [(b) the stocks or marketable securities of a company, other than a company which is an investment undertaking within the meaning of *section 739B* of the Taxes Consolidation Act 1997, which is registered in the State.][1]

Amendments

[1] Substituted by FA12 s100(1)(i).

99 Dublin Docklands Development Authority

[(1) In this section "*wholly-owned subsidiary*" has the meaning assigned to it by section 9 of the Taxes Consolidation Act, 1997 (as amended by the *Finance Act, 2001*).

(2) Stamp Duty shall not be chargeable on any instrument under which any land, easement, way-leave, water right or any right over or in respect of the land or water is acquired by the Dublin Docklands Development Authority or any of its wholly-owned subsidiaries.][1]

Amendments

[1] Substituted by FA01 s205.

99A Courts Service

[Stamp duty shall not be chargeable on any instrument under which any land, easement, way-leave, water right or any right over or in respect of the land or water is acquired by the Courts Service.][1]

Amendments

[1] Inserted by FA06 s108(1). This section applies as respects instruments executed on or after 31 March 2006.

99B Sport Ireland

[Stamp duty shall not be chargeable on any instrument under which any land, easement, way-leave, water right or any right over or in respect of the land or water is acquired by Sport Ireland.][1]

Amendments

[1] Inserted by SIA15 s28.

100 Temple Bar Properties Limited

[FA1992 s216(1) to (3)]

(1) Stamp duty shall not be chargeable on any instrument under which any land, or any interest in land, easement, way-leave, water right or any other right is acquired in the Temple Bar area, that is, "*the area*" as described in the First Schedule in the Temple Bar Area Renewal and Development Act, 1991, by Temple Bar Properties Limited, or any subsidiary of Temple Bar Properties Limited.

(2) For the purposes of *subsection (1)*, a company shall be deemed to be a subsidiary of Temple Bar Properties Limited if—

(a) Temple Bar Properties Limited—

(i) is a member of the company and controls the composition of at least half of the company's board of directors,

(ii) holds at least half in nominal value of the company's equity share capital, or

(iii) holds at least half in nominal value of the company's shares carrying voting rights (other than voting rights which arise only in specified circumstances),

or

(b) the company is a subsidiary of any company which is a subsidiary of Temple Bar Properties Limited.

101 Intellectual property

[[(1) In this section '*intellectual property*' means a specified intangible asset within the meaning of *section 291A(1)* of the Taxes Consolidation Act 1997.][1]

(2) Subject to subsection (3), stamp duty shall not be chargeable under or by reference to any heading in *Schedule 1* on an instrument for the sale, transfer or other disposition of intellectual property.

(3) Where stamp duty is chargeable on an instrument under or by reference to any heading in *Schedule 1* and part of the property concerned consists of intellectual property—

(a) the consideration in respect of which stamp duty would otherwise be chargeable shall be apportioned, on such basis as is just and reasonable, as between the part of the property which consists of intellectual property and the part which does not, and

(b) the instrument shall be chargeable only in respect of the consideration attributable to such of the property as is not intellectual property.

[. . .][2]

(5) Where part of the property referred to in subsection (1) of *section 45* consists of intellectual property, that subsection shall have effect as if the words "in such manner as is just and reasonable" were substituted for "in such manner, as the parties think fit".

(6) Where part of the property referred to in subsection (3) of *section 45* consists of intellectual property and both or, as the case may be, all the relevant persons are connected with one another, that subsection shall have effect as if the words ", the consideration shall be apportioned in such manner as is just and reasonable, so that a distinct consideration for each separate part or parcel is set forth in the conveyance relating to such separate part or parcel, and such conveyance shall be charged with ad valorem duty in respect of such distinct consideration." were substituted for "for distinct parts of the consideration, then the conveyance of each separate part or parcel shall be charged with ad valorem duty in respect of the distinct part of the consideration specified in the conveyance.".

(7) For the purposes of subsection (6), a person is a relevant person if that person is a person by or for whom the property is contracted to be purchased and the question of whether persons are connected with one another shall be construed in accordance with section 10 of the Taxes Consolidation Act 1997 and as if the reference to the Capital Gains Tax Acts in the definition of relative in that section was replaced by a reference to the *Stamp Duties Consolidation Act 1999.*

(8) Where subsection (5) or (6) applies, and the consideration is apportioned in a manner that is not just and reasonable, the conveyance relating to the separate part or parcel of property shall be chargeable with ad valorem duty as if the value of that separate part or parcel of property were substituted for the distinct consideration set forth in that conveyance.][3]

Amendments

[1] Substituted by FA12 s102.

[2] Deleted by FA12 s97(1)(b). Applies as respects instruments executed on or after 7 December 2011. Does not apply as respects any instrument executed before 1 July 2012 where—

(a) the effect of the application of that subsection would be to increase the duty otherwise chargeable on the instrument, and

(b) the instrument contains a statement, in such form as the Revenue commissioners may specify, certifying that the instrument was executed solely in pursuance of a binding contract entered into before 7 December 2011.

[3] Substituted by FA04 s74(1). With effect from 1 April 2004 per SI 140 of 2004.

Cross References

From Section 101

Section 45 Directions as to apportionment of consideration.
Schedule 1 Stamp Duties on Instruments

101A Single farm payment entitlement

[(1) In this section "*payment entitlement*" has the same meaning as it has for the purposes of [Regulation (EU) No. 1307/2013 of the European Parliament and of the Council of 17 December 2013*]][1]

* OJ No. L347, 20.12.2013, p.608

(2) Subject to subsection (3), stamp duty shall not be chargeable under or by reference to any heading in *Schedule 1* on an instrument for the sale, transfer or other disposition of a payment entitlement.

(3) Where stamp duty is chargeable on an instrument under or by reference to any heading in *Schedule 1* and part of the property concerned consists of a payment entitlement—

(a) the consideration in respect of which stamp duty would otherwise be chargeable shall be apportioned, on such basis as is just and reasonable, as between the part of the property which consists of a payment entitlement and the part which does not, and

(b) the instrument shall be chargeable only in respect of the consideration attributable to such of the property as is not a payment entitlement.

[. . .][2]

(5) Where part of the property referred to in *subsection (1)* of *section 45* consists of a payment entitlement, that subsection shall have effect as if the words "in such manner as is just and reasonable" were substituted for "in such manner, as the parties think fit".

(6) Where part of the property referred to in *subsection (3)* of *section 45* consists of a payment entitlement and both or, as the case may be, all the relevant persons are connected with one another, that subsection shall have effect as if the words ", the consideration shall be apportioned in such manner as is just and reasonable, so that a distinct consideration for each separate part or parcel is set forth in the conveyance relating to such separate part or parcel, and such conveyance shall be charged with ad valorem duty in respect of such distinct consideration." were substituted for "for distinct parts of the consideration, then the conveyance of each separate part or parcel shall be charged with ad valorem duty in respect of the distinct part of the consideration specified in the conveyance.".

(7) For the purposes of *subsection (6)*, a person is a relevant person if that person is a person by or for whom the property is contracted to be purchased and the question of whether persons are connected with one another shall be construed in accordance with section 10 of the Taxes Consolidation Act 1997 and as if the reference to the Capital Gains Tax Acts in the definition of "*relative*" in that section was replaced by a reference to the Stamp Duties Consolidation Act 1999.

(8) Where *subsection (5)* or *(6)* applies, and the consideration is apportioned in a manner that is not just and reasonable, the conveyance relating to the separate part or parcel of property shall be chargeable with ad valorem duty as if the value of that separate part or parcel of property were substituted for the distinct consideration set forth in that conveyance.][3]

Amendments

[1] Substituted by FA14 sched3(2). Has effect as respects instruments executed on or after 1 January 2015.

[2] Deleted by FA12 s97(1)(c). Applies as respects instruments executed on or after 7 December 2011. Does not apply as respects any instrument executed before 1 July 2012 where—

(a) the effect of the application of that subsection would be to increase the duty otherwise chargeable on the instrument, and

(b) the instrument contains a statement, in such form as the Revenue Commissioners may specify, certifying that the instrument was executed solely in pursuance of a binding contract entered into before 7 December 2011.

[3] Inserted by FA06 s109(1). This section applies as respects instruments executed on or after 1 January 2005.

Revenue Briefings

Tax Briefing

Tax Briefing November 2005 – Issue 61 – Tax Implications of The Single Payment Scheme
Tax Briefing December 2006 – Issue 65 – Single Farm Payment – Finance Act 2006 Amendments

Cross References

From Section 101A

Section 45 Directions as to apportionment of consideration.
Schedule 1 Stamp Duties on Instruments

102 The Alfred Beit Foundation

[FA1977 s48]

Stamp duty shall not be chargeable or payable on any conveyance, transfer or letting made by Alfred Lane Beit and Clementine Mabel Beit, or either of them, to The Alfred Beit Foundation, which was incorporated under the Companies Act, 1963, on 23 March 1976.

103 Shared ownership leases

[FA1993 s101(1), (2)(*b*) and (3)]

(1) In this section—

"*appropriate person*" means any one of the following, namely—

(a) a person who holds a licence granted by the Central Bank of Ireland under section 9 of the Central Bank Act, 1971, or under section 10 of the Trustee Savings Banks Act, 1989,

[...][1]

[...][2]

(d) a building society which has been incorporated under the Building Societies Act, 1989, or which is deemed by virtue of section 124(2) of that Act to be so incorporated,

(e) the holder of an authorisation for the purposes of the European Communities (Non-Life Insurance) Regulations, 1976 (S.I. No. 115 of 1976), as amended by the European Communities (Non-Life Insurance) (Amendment) Regulations, 1991 (S.I. No. 142 of 1991),

(f) the holder of an authorisation granted under the European Communities (Life Assurance) Regulations, 1984 (S.I. No. 57 of 1984),

(g) a body approved of by the Minister for the Environment and Local Government for the purposes of section 6 of the Housing (Miscellaneous Provisions) Act, 1992,

(h) the National Building Agency Limited,

(i) a company within the meaning of section 2 of the Companies Act, 1963, which the Minister for the Environment and Local Government has certified to the satisfaction of the Commissioners to be a company incorporated with the principal object of providing assistance on a non-profit making basis with a view to enabling persons to acquire housing for themselves,

(j) a society registered under the Industrial and Provident Societies Acts, 1893 to 1978, in respect of which the Minister for the Environment and Local Government has certified to the satisfaction of the Commissioners to be a society established with the principal object of providing assistance on a non-profit making basis with a view to enabling persons to acquire housing for themselves;

"*shared ownership lease*" has the same meaning as in section 2 of the Housing (Miscellaneous Provisions) Act, 1992.

(2) Subject to *subsection (3)*, stamp duty shall not be chargeable on—

(a) a shared ownership lease, or

(b) an instrument whereby the lessee of a shared ownership lease exercises the right referred to in section 2(1)(*c*) of the Housing (Miscellaneous Provisions) Act, 1992, other than such a lease or instrument where such lease was granted on the erection of a house which at that time exceeded the maximum floor area then standing specified in regulations made under section 4(2)(*b*) of the Housing (Miscellaneous Provisions) Act, 1979.

(3) *Subsection (2)* shall apply where the shared ownership lease concerned has been granted by an appropriate person.

Amendments

[1] Repealed by ACCBA01 s12(1). With effect from 28 February 2002 per SI 69 of 2002.

[2] Repealed by ICCBA00 s7(1). With effect from 12 February 2001 per SI 46 of 2001.

104 Licences and leases granted under Petroleum and Other Minerals Development Act, 1960, etc.

[FA1991 s93]

Stamp duty shall not be chargeable on—

(a) a licence granted under section 8, 9 or 19 of the Petroleum and Other Minerals Development Act, 1960,

(b) a lease granted under section 13 of that Act, or

(c) an instrument for the sale, assignment or transfer of any such licence or lease or any right or interest in any such licence or lease.

105 Securitisation agreements

[FA1996 s117(1) and (2)]

(1) In this section "*designated body*" and "*housing authority*" have the same meanings, respectively, as in section 1(1) of the Securitisation (Proceeds of Certain Mortgages) Act, 1995.

(2) Stamp duty shall not be chargeable on—

[...][1]

(b) the transfer of securities issued by a designated body.

Amendments

[1] Deleted by FA07 s100(1)(e). This section applies to instruments executed on or after 7 December 2006.

106 Housing Finance Agency

[FA1989 s66(1) and (2)]

Stamp duty shall not be chargeable on any agreement or other instrument made for the purposes of, or in connection with, securing the advancement of moneys to housing authorities (within the meaning of the Housing Act, 1966) by the Housing Finance Agency p.l.c.

Cross References

To Section 106

Section 123A Debit cards.

106A National Building Agency Limited

[(1) Stamp duty shall not be chargeable on any conveyance, transfer or lease of land to the National Building Agency Limited for the purposes of the Housing Acts, 1966 to 1998.][1]

Amendments

[1] Inserted by FA01 s211(1). Applies and has effect in relation to instruments executed on or after 26 January 2001.

106B Housing authorities and Affordable Homes Partnership

[(1) In this section "*housing authority*" means—

(a) a housing authority, within the meaning of the Housing Acts 1966 to 2009, in connection with any of its functions under those Acts, or

(b) the Affordable Homes Partnership established under article 4(1) of the Affordable Homes Partnership (Establishment) Order 2005 (S.I. No. 383 of 2005) in connection with the services specified in article 4(2) of that Order, as amended by the Affordable Homes Partnership (Establishment) Order 2005 (Amendment) Order 2007 (S.I. No. 293 of 2007).

(2) Stamp duty shall not be chargeable on any instrument giving effect to the conveyance, transfer or lease of a house, building or land to a housing authority.

(3) Stamp duty on any instrument giving effect to the conveyance, transfer or lease of a house, building or land by a housing authority chargeable, as specified in Schedule 1, shall not exceed €100.][1]

Amendments

[1] Substituted by FA11 s(64)(1). Applies to an instrument executed on or after 1 April 2011.

106C Grangegorman Development Agency

[Stamp duty shall not be chargeable on any conveyance, transfer or lease of land to the Grangegorman Development Agency in connection with its functions.][1]

Amendments

[1] Inserted by FA12 s103.

107 Certain mortgages of stock [Deleted]

Deleted by FA07 s100(1)(c). This section applies to instruments executed on or after 7 December 2006.

108 National Treasury Management Agency, etc. [Deleted]

Deleted by FA14 s73(b).

108A National Development Finance Agency, etc. [Repealed]

Repealed by NTMA(A)A14 part5(1).

108AA Strategic Banking Corporation of Ireland

[(1) Stamp duty shall not be chargeable under or by reference to any heading in *Schedule 1* on an instrument for the sale, transfer, lease or other disposition of any property, asset or documentation to the Strategic Banking Corporation of Ireland or to a subsidiary wholly owned by it or a subsidiary wholly owned by any such subsidiary.

(2) For the purposes of *subsection (1)*, whether a subsidiary is wholly owned shall be construed in accordance with *section 9 (1)(d)* of the Taxes Consolidation Act 1997.][1]

Amendments

[1] Inserted by SBCoIA14 part7(2). Does not apply in circumstances where the Minister does not hold all of the shares in the SBCI.

108B National Asset Management Agency

[(1) In this section:

"*acquired bank asset*", "*bank asset*" and "*participating institution*" have, respectively, the meanings given by section 4(1) of the Act of 2009;

"*Act of 2009*" means the National Asset Management Agency Act 2009;

"*NAMA*" means the National Asset Management Agency;

"*NAMA-subsidiary*", in relation to an instrument referred to in *subsection (3)*, means a body corporate which at the time of execution of the instrument is associated with NAMA in accordance with the provisions of section 79.

(2) (a) Where NAMA directly owns any part of the ordinary share capital, within the meaning of section 79, of another body corporate (in this subsection referred to as the "*first body corporate*"), then NAMA shall be deemed to be associated with the first body corporate in accordance with the provisions of section 79.

(b) Where the first body corporate is associated, directly or indirectly, with another body corporate (referred to in this paragraph as the "*second body corporate*") in accordance with the provisions of section 79, then NAMA shall be deemed to be associated with the second body corporate in accordance with the provisions of section 79.

(3) Stamp duty shall not be chargeable under or by reference to any Heading in Schedule 1 on an instrument—

(a) for the sale, transfer, lease or other disposition of any property, asset or documentation to NAMA or a NAMA-subsidiary by NAMA, a NAMA-subsidiary or a participating institution,

(b) for the transfer, to a NAMA-subsidiary or a participating institution, of securities issued in accordance with the Act of 2009 for the purposes of section 47(2)(b), 48(2)(b) or 49 of that Act,

(c) for the transfer to a NAMA-subsidiary by NAMA or a NAMA-subsidiary of securities issued in accordance with the Act of 2009 for the purposes of section 47(2)(a) or 48(2)(a) of that Act,

(d) for the transfer to a participating institution of a bank asset, security or other property by NAMA or a NAMA-subsidiary in connection with section 125 of the [Act of 2009,][1]

(e) for the transfer or other disposition to NAMA or a NAMA-subsidiary of any property in settlement or part settlement of an [acquired bank asset,][2]

[(f) for the sale, transfer, lease or other disposition of any property, asset or documentation to NAMA or a NAMA group entity (within the meaning of the *Irish Bank Resolution Corporation Act 2013*)by—

(i) the Central Bank of Ireland,

(ii) IBRC (within the meaning of the *Irish Bank Resolution Corporation Act 2013*),

(iii) a subsidiary or subsidiary undertaking (both within the meaning of the *Irish Bank Resolution Corporation Act 2013*) of IBRC, or

(iv) a special liquidator appointed under *section 7* of the *Irish Bank Resolution Corporation Act 2013*,

or

(g) for the transfer to the Central Bank of Ireland of securities issued under *section 48* of the Act of 2009 for the purpose specified in *subsection (2)(b)* of that section.][3]

(4) *Section 12(2)* shall not apply to an instrument to which *subsection (3)* applies.

(5) This section applies as respects instruments executed on or after the establishment day (within the meaning of section 4 of the Act of 2009).][4]

Amendments

[1] Substituted by IBRCA13 s22(a).

[2] Substituted by IBRCA13 s22(b).

[3] Inserted by IBRCA13 s22(c).

[4] Inserted by National Asset Management Agency Act 2009 Sched 3 part 9. This section applies as respects instruments executed on or after the establishment day (within the meaning of section 4 of the Act of 2009). "Establishment Day" 21 December 2009 as per SI 547/2009.

108C Ireland Strategic Investment Fund

[Stamp duty shall not be chargeable under or by reference to any Heading in *Schedule 1* on an instrument for the sale, transfer, lease or other disposition of any property, asset or documentation to a Fund investment vehicle (within the meaning of *section 37* of the *National Treasury Management Agency (Amendment) Act 2014*) of which the Minister is the sole beneficial owner.][1]

Amendments

[1] Inserted by NTMA(A)A14 part5(2).

109 Certain instruments made in anticipation of a formal insurance policy

[FA1982 s94(4)(*b*)(i)]

Stamp duty shall not be chargeable on—

(a) cover notes, slips and other instruments usually made in anticipation of the issue of a formal policy, not being instruments relating to life insurance,

(b) instruments embodying alterations of the terms or conditions of any policy of insurance other than life insurance,

and an instrument exempted by virtue of *paragraph (a)* shall not be taken for the purposes of this Act to be a policy of insurance.

110 Certain health insurance contracts

[FA1997 s129(1)]

Stamp duty shall not be chargeable on a health insurance contract (being a health insurance contract within the meaning of section 2 of the Health Insurance Act, 1994).

110A Certain policies of insurance

[(1) This section shall apply to a policy of insurance, being insurance of a class specified in Part A of Annex I to the European Communities (Life Assurance) Framework Regulations, 1994 (S.I. No. 360 of 1994), which—

(a) provides for periodic payments to an individual in the event of loss or diminution of income in consequence of ill health, or

(b) provides for the payment of an amount or amounts to an individual in consequence of ill health, disability, accident or hospitalisation.

(2) Stamp duty shall not be chargeable under or by reference to the Heading "POLICY OF INSURANCE other than Life Insurance where the risk to which the policy relates is located in the State." in Schedule 1 on any policy of insurance to which this section applies.][1]

Amendments

[1] Inserted by FA01 s212(1). Applies and has effect in relation to instruments executed on or after 1 January 2001.

Cross References

From Section 110A

Schedule 1 Stamp Duties on Instruments

111 Oireachtas funds

[FA1958 s59]

Stamp duty shall not be chargeable on any instrument where the amount of such duty chargeable on the instrument, but for this section, would be payable solely out of moneys provided by the Oireachtas.

112 Certificates of indebtedness, etc.

[FA1943 s15]

(1) In this section "*certificate of indebtedness*" means a document, whether sealed with the official seal of the Minister or signed by the Minister or by one of his or her officers authorised in that behalf by the Minister, whereby the Minister or any such officer so authorised certifies (either expressly or impliedly) the amount of the indebtedness of the State or of a public fund of the State in respect of moneys or securities or both moneys and securities borrowed from a particular person by the Minister in exercise of a power conferred on him or her by statute.

(2) Neither a certificate of indebtedness nor any agreement, receipt, bill of exchange, [...][1], [...][2] or other instrument embodied or contained in a certificate of indebtedness and relating to the transaction to which such certificate relates shall be liable to any stamp duty.

Amendments

[1] Deleted by FA07 s101(1)(h). This section applies to instruments drawn, made or executed on or after 2 April 2007.

[2] Deleted by FA07 s100(1)(f). This section applies to instruments executed on or after 7 December 2006.

113 Miscellaneous instruments

[SA1891 First Sch.]

Stamp duty shall not be chargeable on any of the following instruments:

(a) instruments transferring shares [or any other interest][1] in—

[(i) stocks, funds or securities of the Government, Oireachtas, the Minister or any other Minister of the Government,][2]

(ii) any stock or other form of security to which section 39 of the Taxes Consolidation Act, 1997, applies,

(iii) any stock or other form of security to which section 40 of the Taxes Consolidation Act, 1997, applies,

(iv) stocks or funds of the Government or Parliament of the late United Kingdom of Great Britain and Ireland which are registered in the books of the Bank of Ireland in Dublin;

(b) instruments for the sale, transfer, or other disposition, either absolutely [...][3] or otherwise, of any ship or vessel or aircraft, or any part, interest, share, or property of or in any ship or vessel or aircraft;

(c) testaments and testamentary instruments;

(d) bonds given to sheriffs or other persons on the replevy of any goods or chattels, and assignments of such bonds;

(e) instruments made by, to, or with the Commissioners of Public Works in Ireland.

Amendments

[1] Inserted by FA14 s75(a).

[2] Substituted by FA14 s75(b).

[3] Deleted by FA07 s100(1)(g). This section applies to instruments executed on or after 7 December 2006.

PART 8

Companies Capital Duty

114 Interpretation (Part 8)

[FA1973 s67]

(1) In this Part, except where the context otherwise requires—

"*capital company*" means one of the following, namely—

(a) a company incorporated with limited liability, or a limited partnership formed under the law of the State or a company or partnership which is incorporated or formed in any other Member State and which, under the law of that State, corresponds to any such company or partnership,

(b) any other company, firm, association or legal person the shares in whose capital or assets can be dealt in on a stock exchange,

(c) any other company, firm, association or legal person operating for profit whose members have the right to dispose of their shares to third parties without prior authorisation and are responsible for the debts of the company, firm, association or legal person only to the extent of their shares;

"*Member State*" means a Member State of the European Community;

"*registrar*" means the registrar of companies within the meaning of the Companies Act, 1963;

"*stamp duty*" means the stamp duty imposed by *section 116*;

"*statement*" means the statement required to be delivered under *section 117(1)*;

"*third country*" means a State which is not a Member State;

"*transaction*" means a transaction to which *section 116(1)* applies.

(2) In this Part, except where the context otherwise requires, reference to stamp duty paid means stamp duty paid to the Commissioners.

Cross References

From Section 114

Section 116 Charge of stamp duty.

Section 117 Statement to be charged with stamp duty.

To Section 114

Schedule 4 Consequential Amendments

115 Restriction of application (Part 8)

[FA1973 s67A, s67B and s67C]

(1) This Part shall not apply to—

(a) any undertaking for collective investment in transferable securities (UCITS) to which Council Directive 85/611/EEC of 20 December, 1985 (OJ No. L375, 31/12/85), and any Directive amending that Council Directive, relates,

(b) any investment company to which Part XIII of the Companies Act, 1990, relates, or

(c) any investment limited partnership within the meaning of section 3 of the Investment Limited Partnerships Act, 1994.

116 Charge of stamp duty

[FA1973 s68]

(1) This section applies to the following transactions:

(a) the formation of a capital company;

(b) the conversion into a capital company of a company, firm, association or legal person which is not a capital company;

(c) an increase in the capital of a capital company by the contribution of assets of any kind other than an increase in capital through capitalisation of profits or of reserves, whether temporary or permanent reserves, but including the conversion of loan stock of a capital company into share capital;

(d) an increase in the assets of a capital company by the contribution of assets of any kind in consideration, not of shares in the capital or assets of the company, but of rights of the same kind as those of members of the company such as voting rights, a share in the profits or a share in the surplus on liquidation;

(e) the transfer from a third country to the State of the effective centre of management of a capital company whose registered office is in a third country;

(f) the transfer from a third country to the State of the registered office of a capital company whose effective centre of management is in a third country;

(g) the transfer from a Member State to the State of the effective centre of management of a capital company which is not considered to be a capital company in the other Member State;

(h) the transfer from a Member State to the State of the registered office of a capital company whose effective centre of management is in a third country and which is not considered to be a capital company in the Member State from which the registered office is being transferred.

(2) Stamp duty shall be charged on the statement required to be delivered under this Part where, at the date of a transaction, or as a result of the transaction—

(a) the effective centre of management of the capital company is in the State, or

(b) if the effective centre of management of the capital company is in a third country, the registered office of the capital company is in the State,

and the provisions of this Act shall, subject to the provisions of this Part, apply in relation to this duty as if it were imposed by *section 2*.

Cross References

From Section 116

Section 2 Charging of, liability for, and recovery of stamp duty.

To Section 116

Section 114 Interpretation (Part 8).
Section 118 Amount on which stamp duty chargeable.
Section 120A Relief in respect of certain payments of stamp duty.
Section 160 Repeals.
Schedule 4 Consequential Amendments

117 Statement to be charged with stamp duty

[FA1973 s69]

(1) [Where any transaction takes place before 7 December 2005,][1] a statement of the assets, liabilities and expenses referred to in *section 118* shall be delivered to the registrar—

(a) in the case of the formation of a capital company which is to be incorporated under the Companies Act, 1963, or formed under the Limited Partnerships Act, 1907, before the incorporation or registration of that capital company or partnership, and

(b) in any other case, within 30 days after the date of the transaction,

and the statement shall be charged with stamp duty at the rate of [0.5 per cent][2] of the amount determined in accordance with *section 118* but where the calculation results in an amount which is not a multiple of [€1][3] [the amount so calculated shall, if less than €1, be rounded up to €1 and, if more than €1, be rounded down to the nearest €][4].

(2) Notwithstanding *subsection (1)*, in the case referred to in *paragraph (a)* of *subsection (1)*—

[…][5]

(b) *if there is difficulty in ascertaining the exact amount in respect of which stamp duty is chargeable, the statement shall be charged in the first instance with stamp duty at the rate specified in subsection (1)* in respect of such amount as the Commissioners consider appropriate and, if afterwards—

(i) it is established that too little duty has been paid, the additional duty shall be payable and be treated as duty in arrear, and

(ii) it is established that too much duty has been paid, the excess shall be repaid by the Commissioners with interest at the rate of [0.0161 per cent per day or part of a day][6].

(3) Simple interest shall be payable […][7] on so much of the stamp duty charged on the statement required to be delivered under *subsection (1)(b)* as remains unpaid after the expiration of one month from the date of the transaction which gave rise to the charge for duty, and such [interest shall be payable, calculated in accordance with section 159D, until the day on which the duty is paid][8] and it shall be chargeable and recoverable in the same manner as if it were part of the duty.

(4) [interest shall be chargeable on the additional duty payable under subsection (2)(*b*)(i) and shall be calculated in accordance with section 159D,][9] from the date of the transaction which gave rise to the charge for duty until the date of payment of the duty.

(5) The registrar shall not incorporate a capital company which is to be incorporated under the Companies Act, 1963, or register a capital company which is to be formed under the Limited Partnerships Act, 1907, until the statement referred to in *subsection (1)* in relation to the company is duly stamped or in the case of a capital company specified in *section 120* the statement has, in accordance with the provisions of *section 20*, been stamped with a particular stamp denoting that it is not chargeable with stamp duty.

Amendments

[1] Substituted by FA06 s110(a).

[2] Substituted by FA05 s127(1)(a)(i). Applies as respects transactions effected on or after 2 December 2004

[3] Substituted by FA01 sched5.

[4] Substituted by FA05 s127(1)(a)(ii). Applies as respects transactions effected on or after 3 February 2005.

[5] Deleted by FA05 s127(1)(b). Applies as respects transactions effected on or after 3 February 2005.

[6] Substituted by FA02 s129(6)(d).

[7] Deleted by F(No.2)A08 sched5(part5)(chap2)(7)(q).

[8, 9] Substituted by FA05 sched5.

Note:

F(No.2)A08 sched5 (part5)(chap 2)(7)

As respects paragraph 7 of this Schedule subparagraphs (a) to (aa) (other than subparagraph (c)(i)(I)) of that paragraph have effect as on and from the passing of this Act and to the extent that Chapter 3A (being inserted into Part 47 of the Taxes Consolidation Act 1997 by Part 1 of this Schedule) applies to penalties incurred under the Stamp Duties Consolidation Act 1999 before the passing of this Act which on the passing of this Act have not been paid, it shall not apply to such penalties which are in the form of interest accrued under any provisions of the said Act.

Cross References

From Section 117

Section 20 Assessment of duty by the Commissioners.
Section 118 Amount on which stamp duty chargeable.
Section 120 Exemption for certain companies.

To Section 117

Section 114 Interpretation (Part 8).
Section 119 Reconstructions or amalgamations of capital companies.
Section 159C Time limits for making enquiries etc. and assessments by the Commissioners.
Schedule 4 Consequential Amendments

118 Amount on which stamp duty chargeable

[FA1973 s70]

(1) Stamp duty shall be charged—

(a) in the case of a transaction specified in *paragraph (a), (c)* or *(d)* of *section 116(1)*, in respect of the amount of the actual value, at the date of the transaction, of the assets of any kind contributed or to be contributed in connection with the transaction by the members of the capital company concerned after the deduction of the liabilities attaching to such assets and assumed by the capital company and of the expenses incurred by the capital company in connection with such contribution;

(b) in the case of a transaction specified in *paragraph (b), (e), (f), (g)* or *(h)* of *section 116(1)*, in respect of the amount of the actual value, at the date of the transaction, of the assets of any kind of the capital company concerned after the deduction of its liabilities on that date and of the expenses incurred by the company in connection with the transaction.

(2) Notwithstanding *subsection (1)*—

(a) *the amount in respect of which stamp duty is charged shall not be less than the nominal value of the shares (if any) in the company concerned allotted to the members of the capital company in connection with the transaction or belonging to the members of the capital company immediately after the transaction;*

(b) *in arriving at the amount of the actual value in respect of which the duty is charged, there shall be excluded the amount of any assets referred to in subsection (1)* contributed in connection with the transaction by a member with unlimited liability or the share of such a member in the assets of the company.

Cross References

From Section 118

Section 116 Charge of stamp duty.

To Section 118

Section 117 Statement to be charged with stamp duty.

Section 120A Relief in respect of certain payments of stamp duty.
Section 121 Appeals in certain cases.

119 Reconstructions or amalgamations of capital companies

[FA1973 s72]

(1) If, in the case of a transaction, a capital company or a capital company which is in the process of being formed (in this section referred to as the "*acquiring company*") acquires either—

(a) the undertaking or part of the undertaking of another capital company (in this section referred to as the "*target company*"), or

(b) share capital of another capital company to an extent that, after that transaction, but not necessarily as a result of that transaction, the acquiring company owns at least 75 per cent of the issued share capital of that other company (in this section referred to as the "*target company*"),

then, subject to this section, stamp duty on the statement delivered in accordance with *section 117(1)* shall be charged at the rate of zero per cent (in this section referred to as the "*reduced rate*").

(2) Notwithstanding *subsection (1)*, where the percentage referred to in *paragraph (b)* of *subsection (1)* is reached by means of 2 or more transactions, the reduced rate shall apply only to the transaction whereby this percentage is achieved and to any transaction subsequent to the achievement and retention of that percentage.

(3) *Subsection (1)* of this section shall apply only where the consideration for the acquisition (except such part of the consideration as consists of the transfer to or discharge by the acquiring company of liabilities of the target company) consists—

(a) where the undertaking or part of the undertaking of the target company is acquired, of the issue of shares in the acquiring company to the target company or to holders of shares in the target company, or

(b) where shares of the target company are acquired, of the issue of shares in the acquiring company to the holders of shares in the target company in exchange for shares held by them in the target company,

with or without a payment in cash, but where there is a payment in cash that payment shall not exceed 10 per cent of the nominal value of the shares in the acquiring company which are comprised in the consideration.

(4) The statement, which by virtue of this section is charged at the reduced rate, shall become chargeable with stamp duty at the rate specified in *section 117* if the acquiring company does not retain, for a period of 5 years from the date of the transaction in respect of which stamp duty at the reduced rate was charged, at least 75 per cent of the issued share capital of the target company and all the shares which it held following that transaction, including the shares acquired whether by means of a transaction or otherwise before that transaction and held at the time of the transaction.

[(5) Notwithstanding *subsection (4)*, the reduced rate shall continue to apply if the transfer, as a result of which the shares in question were not held for a period of 5 years, was—

(a) a transfer forming part of a transaction, taking place before 7 December 2005, which would of itself qualify for the reduced rate pursuant to *subsection (1)*,

(b) a transfer forming part of a transaction, taking place on or after 7 December 2005, which would of itself so qualify had the transaction taken place before 7 December 2005, or

(c) a transfer in the course of a liquidation of the acquiring company.][1]

(6) Where, by reason of *subsection (4)*, stamp duty becomes chargeable at the rate specified in *section 117* when the acquiring company concerned within a period of 5 years from the date of any transaction in respect of which stamp duty was charged at the reduced rate—

(a) ceases to retain at least 75 per cent of the issued share capital of the target company concerned, or

(b) disposes of any of the shares of the target company which it held after the transaction to which the reduced rate was applied,

then the statement which was delivered to the registrar pursuant to *section 117(1)* in relation to the transaction in respect of which stamp duty was charged at the reduced rate shall be charged with stamp duty at the rate which would have been charged in the first instance if *subsection (1)* had not applied to the transaction and the statement thus charged shall have applied to it this Part except that, for the purposes of *subsections (3)* and *(4)* of *section 117*, the date of the transaction shall be the date on which the event specified in *paragraph (a)* or *(b)*, as the case may be, occurred.

(7) This section shall apply only where the effective centre of management or the registered office of the target company concerned is in a Member State.

(8) For the purposes of this section, a company, partnership, firm, association or legal person that is considered to be a capital company in another Member State shall be deemed to be a target company notwithstanding that it is not considered to be a capital company.

Amendments

[1] Substituted by FA06 s110(b).

Cross References

From Section 119

Section 117 Statement to be charged with stamp duty.

120 Exemption for certain companies

[FA1973 s73]

Stamp duty shall not be charged in the case of a transaction that is effected by—

(a) a capital company which is formed for the purpose of and carries on exclusively the business of supplying a public service such as public transport or port facilities, or supplying water, gas or electricity, and not less than 50 per cent of the issued capital of which is owned by the State or a local authority, or

(b) a capital company whose objects are exclusively cultural, charitable or educational.

Cross References

To Section 120

Section 117 Statement to be charged with stamp duty.

120A Relief in respect of certain payments of stamp duty

[The statement required to be delivered pursuant to this Part in respect of a transaction specified in *section 116(1)(c)* shall, in any case where, within the period of 4 years immediately before the date of the transaction and on or after 4 August 1973, there has been a reduction in the issued capital of the capital company concerned as a result of losses sustained by the company, be charged at the rate of zero per cent in respect of so much of the amount determined in accordance with *section 118* as corresponds to the reduction in issued capital or to so much of the reduction in issued capital to which the rate of zero per cent had not been applied in respect of an earlier transaction occurring since the reduction in capital.][1]

Amendments

[1] Inserted by FA00 s132(1). This section shall apply and have effect in relation to transactions executed on or after 15 December 1999.

Cross References

From Section 120A

Section 116 Charge of stamp duty.

Section 118 Amount on which stamp duty chargeable.

121 Appeals in certain cases

[FA1973 s74]

A person who is dissatisfied with a decision of the Commissioners under this Part on the amount of the actual value of any assets referred to in *section 118* may—

(a) in the case of land, appeal against the decision in the manner prescribed by section 33 of the Finance (1909-10) Act, 1910, and so much of Part I of that Act as relates to appeals shall, with any necessary modifications, apply to an appeal under this section as if the appeal were an appeal under that section,

(b) in the case of assets other than land, appeal against the decision to the Appeal Commissioners (within the meaning of section 850 of the Taxes Consolidation Act, 1997) and the provisions of Chapter 1 of Part 40 (Appeals) of the Taxes Consolidation Act, 1997, shall, with any necessary modifications, apply as they apply for the purpose of income tax.

Cross References

From Section 121

Section 118 Amount on which stamp duty chargeable.

122 Recovery of stamp duty and furnishing of information

[FA1973 s75]

(1) Stamp duty and the interest on such duty shall be recoverable from the capital company concerned and, in any case where the capital company is not a body corporate, shall be recoverable from the members of the capital company jointly and severally.

(2) All statements used for the purpose of this Part shall be in such form and contain such particulars as may be required by the Commissioners and every person accountable for stamp duty shall, if so required by the Commissioners, verify such particulars and deliver to them such evidence as they may require relating to any transaction or to any company concerned in any such transaction.

PART 9

Levies

123 Cash cards

[FA1992 s203]

(1) In this section—

["*accounting period*" has the same meaning as it has for the purposes of section 27 of the Taxes Consolidation Act 1997, but where such accounting period commences after 31 December 2004 and ends after 31 December 2005, it shall be deemed, for the purposes of this section, to be an accounting period ending on 31 December 2005;][1]

["*bank*" includes—

(a) a person who holds a licence granted under section 9 of the Central Bank Act 1971, and

(b) a credit institution (within the meaning of the European Communities (Licensing and Supervision of Credit Institutions) Regulations 1992 (S.I. No. 395 of 1992)) and a financial institution within that meaning;][2]

"*building society*" means a building society which stands incorporated, or deemed by section 124(2) of the Building Societies Act, 1989, to be incorporated, under that Act and includes a company registered under section 106 of that Act;

["*card account*" means an account maintained by a promoter to which amounts of cash obtained by a person by means of a cash card are charged or to which amounts in respect of goods, services or cash obtained by a person by means of a combined card are charged;][3]

["*cash card*" means a card, not being a combined card, issued by a promoter to a person having an address in the State by means of which cash may be obtained by the person from an automated teller machine;][4]

["*combined card*" means a cash card which also contains the functions of a debit card within the meaning assigned to it by *section 123A*;][5]

["*due date*", in relation to an accounting period, means—

(a) in the case of any year prior to the year 2005, the date of the end of the accounting period ending in that year, and

(b) in the case of the year 2005, the date of the end of the accounting period or each of them, if there is more than one, ending in that year;][6]

"*promoter*" means a bank or a building society.

[(2) A promoter shall, in each year, within one month of the due date, in relation to each accounting period, deliver to the Commissioners a statement in writing showing the number of cash cards and combined cards issued at any time by the promoter and which are valid at any time during the accounting period.][7]

(3) Notwithstanding *subsection (2)*—

(a) if the [cash card or combined card][8] is not used at any time during any accounting period referred to in *subsection (2)*,

(b) if the [cash card or combined card][9] is issued in respect of a card account—

(i) which is a deposit account, and

(ii) the average of the daily positive balances in the account does not exceed [€12.70][10] in any accounting period referred to in *subsection (2)*, or [(c) if the cash card is a replacement for a cash card, or a combined card is a replacement for a combined card, which is already included in the relevant statement,][11]

then it shall not be included in the statement relating to such period.

[(4) Subject to subsection (4A), there shall be charged on every statement delivered in pursuance of subsection (2)—

(a) a stamp duty at the rate of €10 or, where the statement is in respect of an accounting period deemed under this section to end on 31 December 2005, a rate calculated by multiplying one-twelfth of €10 by the number of months in the accounting period, in respect of each cash card, and

(b) a stamp duty at the rate of €20 or, where the statement is in respect of an accounting period deemed under this section to end on 31 December 2005, a rate calculated by multiplying one-twelfth of €20 by the number of months in the accounting period, in respect of each combined card,

included in the number of cash cards and combined cards shown in the statement.

(4A) Notwithstanding subsection (4)—

(a) in a case to which subsection (4)(*a*) applies, the rate calculated by multiplying one-twelfth of €10 by the number of months in an accounting period shall be—

(i) €2.50, where there are 3 months in the accounting period, and

(ii) €7.50, where there are 9 months in the accounting period,

and

(b) in a case to which subsection (4)(*b*) applies, the rate calculated by multiplying one-twelfth of €20 by the number of months in an accounting period shall be—

(i) €5, where there are 3 months in the accounting period, and

(ii) €15, where there are 9 months in the accounting period.][12]

(5) The duty charged by *subsection (4)* on a statement delivered by a promoter pursuant to *subsection (2)* shall be paid by the promoter on delivery of the statement.

(6) There shall be furnished to the Commissioners by a promoter such particulars as the Commissioners may deem necessary in relation to any statement required by this section to be delivered by the promoter.

(7) In the case of failure by a promoter to deliver any statement required by *subsection (2)* within the time provided for in that subsection or of failure to pay the duty chargeable on any such statement on the delivery of the statement, the promoter shall be liable to pay, [...][13] in addition to the duty, [interest on the duty, calculated in accordance with section 159D,][14] from the date to which the statement relates (in this subsection referred to as the "*due date*") to the date on which the duty is paid and also, by means of [penalty][15], a sum of [€380][16] for each day the duty remains unpaid after the expiration of one month from the due date [...][17].

(8) The delivery of any statement required by *subsection (2)* may be enforced by the Commissioners under section 47 of the Succession Duty Act, 1853, in all respects as if such statement were such account as is mentioned in that section and the failure to deliver such statement were such default as is mentioned in that section.

(9) A promoter shall be entitled to charge to the card account the amount of stamp duty payable in respect of the [cash card or combined card][18] by virtue of this section and may apply the terms and conditions governing that account to interest on that amount.

(10) An account, charge card, company charge card or supplementary card within the meaning, in each case, assigned to it by *section 124* and which attracts the payment of the stamp duty payable by virtue of that section shall not attract the payment of the stamp duty payable by virtue of this section.

(11) Where a promoter changes its accounting period and, as a result, stamp duty under this section would not be chargeable or payable in a year (in this section referred to as "*the relevant year*"), then the following provisions shall apply:

(a) duty shall be chargeable and payable in the relevant year as if the accounting period had not been changed,

(b) duty shall also be chargeable and payable within one month of the date of the end of the accounting period ending in the relevant year, and

(c) the duty chargeable and payable by virtue of *paragraph (b)* shall, subject to *subsection (3)*, be chargeable and payable in respect of [cash cards and combined cards][19] issued at any time by the promoter and which are valid at any time during the period from the due date as determined by *paragraph (a)* to the due date as determined by *paragraph (b)*.

[(12) This section does not apply to any statement that falls to be delivered by a promoter in respect of a due date falling after 31 December 2005.][20]

Amendments

[1] Substituted by FA05 s128(1)(a)(i)(I).

[2] Substituted by FA05 s128(1)(a)(i)(II).

[3, 4] Substituted by FA03 s140(1)(a)(i)(II). Has effect as respects cash cards and combined cards valid at any time after 4 December 2002 which are included in any statement which falls to be delivered by a promoter after that date.

[5] Inserted by FA03 s140(1)(a)(i)(III). Has effect as respects cash cards and combined cards valid at any time after 4 December 2002 which are included in any statement which falls to be delivered by a promoter after that date.

[6] Substituted by FA05 s128(1)(a)(i)(III).

[7] Substituted by FA05 s128(1)(a)(ii).

[8, 9, 18] Substituted by FA03 s140(1)(a)(iii). Has effect as respects cash cards and combined cards valid at any time after 4 December 2002 which are included in any statement which falls to be delivered by a promoter after that date.

[10, 16] Substituted by FA01 sched5.

[11] Substituted by FA03 s140(1)(a)(iv). Has effect as respects cash cards and combined cards valid at any time after 4 December 2002 which are included in any statement which falls to be delivered by a promoter after that date.

[12] Substituted by FA05 s128(1)(a)(iii).

[13] Deleted by F(No.2)A08 sched5(part5)(chap2)(7)(r)(i).

[14] Substituted by FA05 sched5.

[15] Substituted by F(No.2)A08 sched5(part5)(chap2)(7)(r)(ii).

[17] Deleted by FA08No.2 sched4(part1). Applies as respects any tax that becomes due and payable on or after 1 March 2009.

[19] Substituted by FA03 s140(1)(a)(ii). Has effect as respects cash cards and combined cards valid at any time after 4 December 2002 which are included in any statement which falls to be delivered by a promoter after that date.

[20] Inserted by FA05 s128(1)(a)(iv).

Note:

F(No.2)A08 sched5 (part5)(chap 2)(7)

As respects paragraph 7 of this Schedule subparagraphs (a) to (aa) (other than subparagraph (c)(i)(I)) of that paragraph have effect as on and from the passing of this Act and to the extent that Chapter 3A (being inserted into Part 47 of the Taxes Consolidation Act 1997 by Part 1 of this Schedule) applies to penalties incurred under the Stamp Duties Consolidation Act 1999 before the passing of this Act which on the passing of this Act have not been paid, it shall not apply to such penalties which are in the form of interest accrued under any provisions of the said Act.

Cross References

From Section 123

Section 123A Debit cards.
Section 124 Credit cards and charge cards.

To Section 123

Section 123A Debit cards.
Section 126B Assessment of duty charged on statements.
Section 159C Time limits for making enquiries etc. and assessments by the Commissioners.
Section 160 Repeals.

123A Debit cards

[(1) In this section—

["*accounting period*" has the same meaning as it has for the purposes of section 27 of the Taxes Consolidation Act 1997, but where such accounting period commences after 31 December 2004 and ends after 31 December 2005, it shall be deemed, for the purposes of this section, to be an accounting period ending on 31 December 2005;][1]

["*bank*" includes—

(a) a person who holds a licence granted under section 9 of the Central Bank Act 1971, and

(b) a credit institution (within the meaning of the European Communities (Licensing and Supervision of Credit Institutions) Regulations 1992 (S.I. No. 395 of 1992)) and a financial institution within that meaning;][2]

"*building society*" means a building society which stands incorporated, or deemed by section 124(2) of the Building Societies Act 1989, to be incorporated, under that Act and includes a company registered under *section 106* of that Act;

"*card account*" means an account maintained by a promoter to which, amongst other possible amounts, amounts in respect of goods, services or cash obtained by a person by means of a debit card, within the meaning of this section, are charged;

"*debit card*" means a card, not being a combined card within the meaning assigned to it by *section 123*, issued by a promoter to a person having an address in the State by means of which goods, services or cash may be obtained by the person and amounts in respect of the goods, services or cash may be charged to the card account;

["*due date*", in relation to an accounting period, means—

(a) in the case of the year 2002, the date of the end of the accounting period ending in that year, where that date is on or after 5 December 2002,

(b) in the case of the year 2003 and 2004, the date of the end of the accounting period ending in that year, and

(c) in the case of the year 2005, the date of the end of the accounting period, or each of them if there is more than one, ending in that year;][3]

"*promoter*" means a bank or a building society.

[(2) A promoter shall, within 2 months of the due date, in relation to each accounting period falling in the year 2002 and, within one month of the due date falling in each of the years 2003, 2004 and 2005, deliver to the Commissioners a statement in writing showing the number of debit cards issued at any time by the promoter and which are valid—

(a) in the case of the year 2002, at any time during the period from 5 December 2002 to the due date,

(b) in the case of the year 2003, at any time during the accounting period ending in that year but not before 5 December 2002 where that date falls within the accounting period, and

(c) in the case of the year 2004 and 2005, at any time during the accounting period.][4]

(3) Notwithstanding *subsection (2)*—

(a) if the debit card is not used at any time during any period referred to in *paragraph (a)*, *(b)* or *(c)* of *subsection (2)*,

(b) if the debit card is issued in respect of a card account—

(i) which is a deposit account, and

(ii) the average of the daily positive balances in the account does not exceed €12.70 in any of the periods referred to in *paragraph (a)*, *(b)* or *(c)* of *subsection (2)*,

or

(c) if the debit card is a replacement for a debit card which is already included in the relevant statement,

then it shall not be included in the statement relating to such period.

[(4) Subject to *subsection (4A)*, there shall be charged on every statement delivered in pursuance of *subsection (2)* a stamp duty at the rate of €10 or, where the statement is in respect of an accounting period deemed under this section to end on 31 December 2005, a rate calculated by multiplying one-twelfth of €10 by the number of months in the accounting period, in respect of each debit card included in the number of cards shown in the statement.

(4A) Notwithstanding *subsection (4)*, the rate calculated by multiplying one-twelfth of €10 by the number of months in an accounting period shall be—

(a) €2.50, where there are 3 months in the accounting period, and

(b) €7.50, where there are 9 months in the accounting period.][5]

(5) The duty charged by *subsection (4)* on a statement delivered by a promoter pursuant to *subsection (2)* shall be paid by the promoter on delivery of the statement.

(6) There shall be furnished to the Commissioners by a promoter such particulars as the Commissioners may deem necessary in relation to any statement required by this section to be delivered by the promoter.

(7) In the case of failure by a promoter to deliver any statement required by *subsection (2)* within the time provided for in that subsection or of failure to pay the duty chargeable on any such statement on the delivery of the statement, the promoter shall be liable to pay, [...][6] in addition to the duty, [interest on the duty, calculated in accordance with section 159D,][7] from the date to which the statement relates (in this subsection referred to as the "*due date*") to the date on which the duty is paid and also, by means of [penalty][8], a sum of €380 for each day the duty remains unpaid after the expiration of one month from the due date [...][9].

(8) The delivery of any statement required by *subsection (2)* may be enforced by the Commissioners under section 47 of the Succession Duty Act 1853 in all respects as if such statement were such account as is mentioned in that section and the failure to deliver such statement were such default as is mentioned in that section.

(9) A promoter shall be entitled to charge to the card account the amount of stamp duty payable in respect of the debit card by virtue of this section and may apply the terms and conditions governing that account to interest on that amount.

(10) An account, charge card, company charge card or supplementary card within the meaning, in each case, assigned to it by *section 124* and which attracts the payment of the stamp duty payable by virtue of that section shall not attract the payment of the stamp duty payable by virtue of this section.

(11) Where a promoter changes its accounting period and, as a result, stamp duty under this section would not be chargeable or payable in a year (in this section referred to as the "*relevant year*"), then the following provisions shall apply:

(a) duty shall be chargeable and payable in the relevant year as if the accounting period had not been changed,

(b) duty shall also be chargeable and payable within one month of the date of the end of the accounting period ending in the relevant year, and

(c) the duty chargeable and payable by virtue of *paragraph (b)* shall, subject to *subsection (3)*, be chargeable and payable in respect of debit cards issued at any time by the promoter and which are valid at any time during the period from the due date as determined by *paragraph (a)* to the due date as determined by *paragraph (b)*.

[(12) This section does not apply to any statement that falls to be delivered by a promoter in respect of a due date falling after 31 December 2005.][10]][11]

Amendments

[1] Substituted by FA05 s128(1)(b)(i)(I).

[2] Substituted by FA05 s128(1)(b)(i)(II).

[3] Substituted by FA05 s128(1)(b)(i)(III).

[4] Substituted by FA05 s128(1)(b)(ii).

[5] Substituted by FA05 s128(1)(b)(iii).

[6] Deleted by F(No.2)A08 sched5(part5)(chap2)(7)(r)(i).

[7] Substituted by FA05 sched5.

[8] Substituted by F(No.2)A08 sched5(part5)(chap2)(7)(r)(ii).

[9] Deleted by F(No.2)A08 sched4(part1). Applies as respects any tax that becomes due and payable on or after 1 March 2009.

[10] Inserted by FA05 s128(1)(b)(iv).

[11] Inserted by FA03 s140(1)(b). Has effect as respects any statement which falls to be delivered by a promoter on or after 5 December 2002.

Note:

F(No.2)A08 sched5 (part5)(chap 2)(7)

As respects paragraph 7 of this Schedule subparagraphs (a) to (aa) (other than subparagraph (c)(i)(I)) of that paragraph have effect as on and from the passing of this Act and to the extent that Chapter 3A (being inserted into Part 47 of the Taxes Consolidation Act 1997 by Part 1 of this Schedule) applies to penalties incurred under the Stamp Duties Consolidation Act 1999 before the passing of this Act which on the passing of this Act have not been paid, it shall not apply to such penalties which are in the form of interest accrued under any provisions of the said Act.

Cross References

From Section 123A

Section 106 Housing Finance Agency.
Section 123 Cash cards.
Section 124 Credit cards and charge cards.

To Section 123A

Section 123 Cash cards.

Section 126B Assessment of duty charged on statements.

123B Cash, combined and debit cards

[(1) In this section—

["*account holder*", in relation to a basic payment account, means the person in whose name the account is held;][1]

[…][2]

["*basic payment account*" means a card account—

(a) which is issued only to an account holder who in the period of financial exclusion—

(i) did not hold a card account, or

(ii) held a card account but no account holder initiated transactions occurred on that account in the period of financial exclusion,

(b) where, in respect of every 2 consecutive quarters, all amounts paid into the card account, other than amounts paid to the account holder by electronic funds transfer under the Social Welfare Acts, do not exceed €4,500 (in this section referred to as the 'threshold amount') in each quarter, and

(c) which is a standard bank account with [one of the following][3]:

(i) Allied Irish Banks plc;

(ii) the Governor and Company of the Bank of Ireland;

(iii) Permanent TSB plc;][4]

[…][5]

["*card account*" means an account maintained by a promoter to which—

(a) amounts of cash obtained by a person by means of a cash card are charged, or

(b) amounts in respect of goods, services or cash obtained by a person by means of a combined card or debit card are charged;][6]

"*cash card*" means a card, not being a combined card, issued by a promoter to a person having an address in the State, by means of which cash may be obtained by the person from an automated teller machine;

["*cash transaction*" means a transaction by means of which a person obtains cash from an automated teller machine situated in the State by means of a cash card or a combined card;][7]

["*chargeable period*" means the year 2008 and each subsequent year;][8]

["*combined card*" means a card, issued by a promoter to a person having an address in the State, which contains 2 functions being the function of a cash card and the function of a debit card;][9]

["*credit institution*" has the same meaning as it has in the European Union (Capital Requirements) Regulations 2014 (S.I. No. 158 of 2014);

"*credit union*" has the same meaning as it has in the Credit Union Acts 1997 to 2012;][10]

"*debit card*" means a card, not being a combined card, issued by a promoter to a person having an address in the State, by means of which goods, services or cash may be obtained by the person and amounts in respect of the goods, services or cash may be charged to the card account;

["*financial institution*" has the same meaning as it has in the European Union (Capital Requirements) Regulations 2014;][11]

["*period of financial exclusion*" means the period of 3 years immediately preceding the date of an application to open a basic payment account;][12]

"*promoter*" [means a credit institution or a financial institution other than a credit union or An Post and any of its subsidiaries][13]

["*quarter*" means a period of 3 consecutive months or any commensurate period by reference to which a promoter in the course of its business calculates all amounts paid [into a card account.][14]][15]

[(1B) Where the promoter has served notice of the termination of the basic payment account, the account shall not cease to be a basic payment account until the expiry of 2 months from the date of service of the notice.][16]

[(2) A promoter shall, within one month of the end of each year, commencing with the year 2016, deliver to the Commissioners a statement in writing showing—

(a) the number of cash cards and combined cards issued at any time by the promoter that are valid on 31 December in the year,

(b) the number of cash transactions completed in the year using a card valid on 31 December in the year in respect of each type of card,

(c) the number of cash cards to which the monetary cap referred to in *subsection (4)* has been applied,

(d) the number of combined cards, both functions of which were used in the year, to which the monetary cap referred to in *subsection (4)* has been applied, and

(e) the number of combined cards, only the cash card function of which was used in the year, to which the monetary cap referred to in *subsection (4)* has been applied.][17]

[(2A) For the purposes of *subsection (2)*, a cash card or a combined card shall be valid on 31 December of a particular year where—

(a) the card has not expired or been cancelled before that date, and

(b) on that date, the address of the person to whom the card was issued is in the State.

(2B) A promoter shall, within one month of the end of each year, commencing with the year 2016, deliver to the Commissioners a statement in writing showing the number of each type of card to which the monetary cap referred to in *subsection (4)* has not been applied, together with the number of cash transactions in the year in respect of those cards.

(2C) Where a cash card or combined card issued by a promoter in respect of a card account and valid on 31 December in a particular year (in this subsection referred to as the 'final card') has been issued following the cancellation or expiry in that year of another card of the same type issued by the promoter in respect of the card account (in this subsection referred to as a 'previous card'), each such previous card shall be taken to be the final card for the purposes of this section.][18]

[(3) Notwithstanding *subsection (2)*—

(a) if the cash card or combined card is not used at any time during a year,

(b) if the cash card or combined card is issued in respect of a card account—

(i) which is a deposit account, and

(ii) the average of the daily positive balances in the account does not exceed €12.70 during that year, or

(c) if the cash card or combined card is issued in respect of a basic payment account,

then it shall not be included in the statement relating to that year.][19]

[(4) Stamp duty shall be charged on every statement delivered in pursuance of *subsection (2)* at the rate of €0.12 for each cash transaction included in the statement, but the amount charged in respect of—

(a) any individual combined card, both functions of which were used in the year, shall not exceed €5,

(b) any individual combined card, only the cash card function of which was used in the year, shall not exceed €2.50, and

(c) any individual cash card, shall not exceed €2.50.][20]

included in the number of cards shown in the statement.][14]

(5) The duty charged by *subsection (4)* on a statement delivered by a promoter pursuant to subsection (2)[, less any preliminary duty charged on a statement required to be delivered in accordance with section 123C in respect of the same chargeable period,][21] shall be paid by the promoter on delivery of the statement.

(6) There shall be furnished to the Commissioners by a promoter such particulars as the Commissioners may deem necessary in relation to any statement required by this section to be delivered by the promoter.

(7) In the case of failure by a promoter to pay any duty required to be paid in accordance with this section, the promoter shall be liable to pay, [...][22], in addition to the duty, interest on that duty, calculated in accordance with section *159D*, for the period commencing on the date the duty was so required to be paid and ending on the date the duty was paid and also, by means of a [penalty][23], a sum of €380 for each day in that period [...][24].

(8) The delivery of any statement required by *subsection (2)* may be enforced by the Commissioners under section 47 of the Succession Duty Act 1853 in all respects as if such statement were such account as is mentioned in that section and the failure to deliver such statement were such default as is mentioned in that section.

(9) A promoter shall be entitled to charge to the card account the amount of stamp duty payable in respect [of a cash card or combined card][25] by virtue of this section and may apply the terms and conditions governing that account to interest on that amount.

(10) An account, charge card, company charge card or supplementary card within the meaning, in each case, assigned to it by *section 124* and which attracts the payment of the stamp duty payable by virtue of that section shall not attract the payment of the stamp duty payable by virtue of this section.][26]

[(11) The Minister, following a review of this section, for the purposes of ensuring that the conditions governing the opening of a basic payment account are such that the section achieves its intended purpose may by order vary—

(a) the duration of the period of financial exclusion, and

(b) the threshold amount, subject to a maximum variation of 20 per cent.

(12) Every order made by the Minister under *subsection (11)* shall be laid before Dáil Éireann as soon as may be after it is made and, if a resolution annulling the order is passed by Dáil Éireann within the next 21 days on which Dáil Éireann

has sat after the order is laid before it, the order shall be annulled accordingly, but without prejudice to the validity of anything previously done under the order.][27]

Amendments

[1] Substituted by FA13 s82(a).

[2, 5] Deleted by FA15 s64(1)(a)(i). Effective from 1 January 2016.

[3] Substituted by FA15 s64(1)(a)(iv). Effective from 1 January 2016.

[4] Substituted by FA13 s82(b).

[6] Substituted by FA15 s64(1)(a)(iii). Effective from 1 January 2016.

[7, 10, 11] Inserted by FA15 s64(1)(a)(ii). Effective from 1 January 2016.

[8] Inserted by FA08 s123(1)(a)(i). Has effect as respects any statement that falls to be delivered by a bank or building society after 31 December 2008.

[9] Substituted by FA06 s111(1)(a). This section shall have effect as respects any statement which falls to be delivered by a promoter after 31 December 2006.

[12, 15] Inserted by FA13 s82(c).

[13] Substituted by FA15 s64(1)(a)(v). Effective from 1 January 2016.

[14] Substituted by FA15 s64(1)(a)(vi). Effective from 1 January 2016.

[16] Inserted by FA13 s82(d).

[17] Substituted by FA15 s64(1)(b). Effective from 1 January 2016.

[18] Inserted by FA15 s64(1)(c). Effective from 1 January 2016.

[19] Substituted by FA15 s64(1)(d). Effective from 1 January 2016.

[20] Substituted by FA15 s64(1)(e). Effective from 1 January 2016.

[21] Inserted by FA08 s123(1)(a)(iii). Has effect as respects any statement that falls to be delivered by a bank or building society after 31 December 2008.

[22] Deleted by F(No.2)A08 sched5(part5)(chap2)(7)(s)(i).

[23] Substituted by F(No.2)A08 sched5(part5)(chap2)(7)(s)(ii).

[24] Deleted by F(No.2)A08 sched4(part1). Applies as respects any tax that becomes due and payable on or after 1 March 2009.

[25] Substituted by FA15 s64(1)(f). Effective from 1 January 2016.

[26] Inserted by FA05 s128(1)(c).

[27] Inserted by FA13 s82(f).

Note:

F(No.2)A08 sched5 (part5)(chap 2)(7)

As respects paragraph 7 of this Schedule subparagraphs (a) to (aa) (other than subparagraph (c)(i)(I)) of that paragraph have effect as on and from the passing of this Act and to the extent that Chapter 3A (being inserted into Part 47 of the Taxes Consolidation Act 1997 by Part 1 of this Schedule) applies to penalties incurred under the Stamp Duties Consolidation Act 1999 before the passing of this Act which on the passing of this Act have not been paid, it shall not apply to such penalties which are in the form of interest accrued under any provisions of the said Act.

The amendments made by FA15 s64 do not apply in respect of the year 2015.

Cross References

From Section 123B

Section 47 Principal instrument, how to be ascertained.
Section 123C Preliminary duty: cash, combined and debit cards.
Section 124 Credit cards and charge cards.
Section 159D Calculation of interest on unpaid duty and other amounts.

To Section 123B

Section 123C Preliminary duty: cash, combined and debit cards.
Section 126B Assessment of duty charged on statements.

123C Preliminary duty: cash, combined and debit cards

[(1) In this section—

"*accountable person*" means a bank or building society within the meaning of section 123B;

"*base period*", in relation to a due date, means the year ending immediately before the due date in respect of which a statement is required to be delivered to the Commissioners under section 123B;

"*chargeable period*", in relation to a due date, means the year ending immediately after the due date in respect of which a statement is required to be delivered to the Commissioners under section 123B;

"*due date*" means—

(a) in respect of the year 2008, 15 December in that year, and

(b) in respect of any year subsequent to the year 2008, 15 December in that year;

"preliminary duty', in relation to a chargeable period ending immediately after a due date, means an amount determined by the formula—

$$A \times B$$

where—

A is an amount equal to the stamp duty charged on a specified statement in respect of the base period ending immediately prior to the due date, and

[B is—

(a) 40 per cent where the base period is 2007, or

(b) 80 per cent where the base period is a subsequent year;][1]

"*specified statement*" means a statement within the meaning of section 123B.

(2) This section applies to an accountable person who is required to deliver to the Commissioners a specified statement in respect of a base period.

(3) An accountable person shall in the year 2008 and each subsequent year, not later than the due date in respect of that year, deliver to the Commissioners a statement in writing showing the stamp duty charged on the specified statement for that person in respect of the base period.

(4) Where at any time in a period commencing after the expiration of a base period and ending immediately before the due date relating to the base period—

(a) an accountable person ceased to carry on a business in the course of which the person was required to deliver a specified statement for the base period, and

(b) another person (in this subsection referred to as the "*successor person*") acquires the whole, or substantially the whole, of the business,

then the successor person shall deliver a statement on the due date in accordance with subsection (3) as if the successor person was the accountable person.

(5) There shall be charged on any statement delivered in accordance with subsection (3) a stamp duty equal to the amount of the preliminary duty.

(6) The stamp duty charged by subsection (5) on a statement delivered by an accountable person pursuant to subsection (3) shall be paid by the person upon delivery of the statement.

(7) There shall be furnished to the Commissioners by an accountable person such particulars as the Commissioners may require in relation to any statement required by this section to be delivered by the person.

(8) In the case of failure by an accountable person—

(a) to deliver any statement required to be delivered by that person under subsection (3), or

(b) to pay the duty charged on any such statement,

on or before the due date in respect of the year concerned, the person shall, from the due date concerned until the day on which the stamp duty is paid, be liable to pay, [...][2], in addition to the stamp duty, interest on the stamp duty, calculated in accordance with section 159D and also from 15 December of the year in which the statement is to be delivered in accordance with subsection (3), by way of a further penalty, a sum of €380 for each day the duty remains unpaid [...][3].

(9) The delivery of any statement required by subsection (3) may be enforced by the Commissioners under section 47 of the Succession Duty Act 1853 in all respects as if such statement were such account as is mentioned in that section and the failure to deliver such statement were such default as is mentioned in that section.

(10) Where—

(a) the preliminary duty charged on a statement has been paid in whole or in part by an accountable person in respect of a due date, and

(b) the duty charged on a specified statement in respect of the chargeable period ending immediately after the due date is an amount which is less than the preliminary duty charged in respect of the due date,

then the preliminary duty paid, to the extent that it exceeds the duty charged on the specified statement concerned, shall be repaid.

(11) Where at any time in a period commencing after a due date and ending before the expiration of the chargeable period ending immediately after the due date—

(a) the person (in this subsection referred to as the "*predecessor person*") ceased to carry on a business in the course of which the person was required to deliver to the Commissioners a statement under this section in respect of the due date,

(b) the person delivered the statement and paid the stamp duty charged on such statement, and

(c) another person (in this subsection referred to as the "*successor person*") acquires the whole, or substantially the whole, of the business,

then the successor person shall be entitled to deduct the stamp duty charged on the statement delivered by the predecessor person in respect of that due date from the duty charged on the specified statement in respect of the chargeable period ending immediately after the due date which the successor person is required to deliver in respect of the business acquired.

(12) The stamp duty and any [interest or penalty][4] payable under this section shall not be allowed as a deduction for the purposes of the computation of any tax or duty payable by the accountable person which is under the care and management of the Commissioners.][5]

Amendments

[1] Substituted by FA08No.2 s86(1)(b).

[2] Deleted by F(No.2)A08 sched5(part5)(chap2)(7)(t)(i).

[3] Deleted by F(No.2)A08 sched4(part1). Applies as respects any tax that becomes due and payable on or after 1 March 2009.

[4] Substituted by F(No.2)A08 sched5(part5)(chap2)(7)(u).

[5] Inserted by FA08 s123(1)(c).

Note:

F(No.2)A08 sched5 (part5)(chap 2)(7)

As respects paragraph 7 of this Schedule subparagraphs (a) to (aa) (other than subparagraph (c)(i)(I)) of that paragraph have effect as on and from the passing of this Act and to the extent that Chapter 3A (being inserted into Part 47 of the Taxes Consolidation Act 1997 by Part 1 of this Schedule) applies to penalties incurred under the Stamp Duties Consolidation Act 1999 before the passing of this Act which on the passing of this Act have not been paid, it shall not apply to such penalties which are in the form of interest accrued under any provisions of the said Act.

Cross References

From Section 123C

Section 123B Cash, combined and debit cards.

Section 159D Calculation of interest on unpaid duty and other amounts.

To Section 123C

Section 123B Cash, combined and debit cards.

Section 126B Assessment of duty charged on statements.

124 Credit cards and charge cards

[F(No. 2)A1981 s17]

(1) (a) In this subsection—

"*account*" means an account maintained by a bank to which amounts in respect of goods, services or cash obtained by an individual by means of a credit card are charged;

["*account holder*" means the person in whose name an account is maintained by a bank;

["*bank*" means a credit institution or a financial institution other than a credit union or An Post and any of its subsidiaries;][1]][2]

["*chargeable period*" means the 12 month period ending on 1 April 2009 and each subsequent 12 month period;][3]

"*credit card*" means a card issued by a bank to an individual having an address in the State by means of which goods, services and cash may be obtained by the individual and amounts in respect of the goods, services and cash may be charged [to the account;][4]

["*credit institution*" has the same meaning as it has in the European Union (Capital Requirements) Regulations 2014 (S.I. No. 158 of 2014);

"*credit union*" has the same meaning as it has in the Credit Union Acts 1997 to 2012;

"*financial institution*" has the same meaning as it has in the European Union (Capital Requirements) Regulations 2014;][5]

["*letter of closure*", in relation to an account, means a letter, in such form as the Commissioners may specify, issued during a relevant period by a bank to an account holder in respect of an account which has been closed during the relevant period confirming that the account holder has, during the relevant period, accounted for the amount of stamp duty—

(i) which the bank is required to pay in respect of the account for the relevant period, or

(ii) which another bank (not being a branch of the same bank) is required to pay for the relevant period in respect of another account which has been closed during the relevant period;

"*relevant period*" means a 12 month period ending on 1 April in any year commencing with the 12 month period ending on 1 April 2006;

"*replacement account*" means an account that is opened and maintained by a bank in the name of an account holder during a relevant period—

(i) where an account in the name of the account holder was, during the relevant period, previously closed by the bank, or

(ii) where the account holder has furnished to the bank during the relevant period a letter of closure issued by another bank (not being a branch of the same bank) in relation to an account in the name of the account holder which was closed during the relevant period.][6]

[(b) A bank shall, within 3 months of the end of each relevant period, deliver to the Commissioners a statement in writing showing in respect of accounts maintained by the bank at any time during the relevant period—

(i) the number of accounts that are replacement accounts, and

(ii) the number of accounts that are not replacement accounts.][7]

(c) There shall be charged on every statement delivered in pursuance of *paragraph (b)* a stamp duty at the rate of [€30][8] in respect of each account included in the number of accounts shown in the statement.

[(d) Notwithstanding *paragraph (c)*, where a bank maintains a replacement account at any time during a relevant period, the bank shall be exempt from stamp duty on that replacement account.

(e) A bank shall not issue a letter of closure during a relevant period in respect of an account that has been closed during the relevant period where—

(i) the account holder has not accounted for the amount of stamp duty which the bank is required to pay in respect of the account for the relevant period, or

(ii) the bank is not in possession of a letter of closure, in respect of another account closed during the relevant period, received from the account holder during the relevant period.

(f) Where a bank treats an account as a replacement account by virtue of the account holder furnishing a letter of closure, the bank shall not, by virtue of that letter, treat any other account as a replacement account.

(g) A bank shall not issue more than one original letter of closure in respect of an account and may only issue a duplicate letter of closure to an account holder to whom an original letter of closure issued where the bank is satisfied that the original letter of closure has been lost or destroyed and where such letter states that it is a duplicate of an original letter of closure.][9]

(2) (a) In this subsection—

"*account*" means an account maintained by a promoter to which amounts in respect of goods, services or cash obtained by an individual by means of a charge card are charged;

["*account holder*" means the person in whose name an account is maintained by a promoter;][10]

["*chargeable period*" means the 12 month period ending on 1 April 2009 and each subsequent 12 month period;][11]

"*charge card*" means a card (other than a card known as "*an in-house card*") issued by a person (in this section referred to as "*a promoter*") to an individual having an address in the State by means of which goods, services or cash may be obtained by the individual and amounts in respect of the goods, services or cash may be charged to the account;

["*charge card*", in relation to an account, means a charge card used to obtain goods, services or cash, amounts in respect of which are charged to the account;][12]

"*company charge card*" means—

(i) a charge card issued by a promoter to a person (other than an individual) having an address in the State which, if it were issued to an individual, would be regarded as a charge card, or

(ii) a charge card issued by a promoter to an employee, nominee or agent of such a person in such person "s capacity as such employee, nominee or agent;

["*letter of closure*", in relation to an account, means a letter, in such form as the Commissioners may specify, issued during a relevant period by a promoter to an account holder in respect of an account which has been closed during the relevant period—

(i) confirming that the account holder has, during the relevant period, accounted for the amount of stamp duty which the promoter is required to pay in respect of charge cards, in relation to the account, for the relevant period and stating the number of cards in respect of which the promoter is so liable to pay, and

(ii) confirming, where it is the case, that the account holder has, during the relevant period, accounted for the amount of stamp duty which another promoter (not being a branch of the same promoter) is required to pay for the relevant period in respect of charge cards in relation to another account which has been closed during the relevant period and stating the number of cards in respect of which that other promoter is so liable to pay;

"*relevant period*" means a 12 month period ending on 1 April in any year commencing with the 12 month period ending on 1 April 2006;

"*replacement account*" means an account that is opened and maintained by a promoter in the name of an account holder during a relevant period—

(i) where an account (in this section referred to as an "*original account*") in the name of the account holder was, in the relevant period, previously closed by the promoter, or

(ii) where the account holder has furnished, during the relevant period, a letter of closure issued by another promoter (not being a branch of the same promoter) in relation to an account in the name of the account holder which was closed during the relevant period;

"*replacement card*" means a charge card in relation to a replacement account.][13]

[...][14]

"*supplementary card*" means a company charge card which is issued by a promoter to a person (other than an individual) and is additional to another company charge card issued by the promoter to that person.

[(b) A promoter shall, within 3 months of the end of each relevant period, deliver to the Commissioners a statement in writing showing in respect of the charge cards issued or renewed by the promoter and expressed to be valid at any time during the relevant period—

(i) the number of cards that are replacement cards, and

(ii) the number of cards that are not replacement cards.][15]

(c) There shall be charged on every statement delivered in accordance with *paragraph (b)* a stamp duty at the rate of [€30][16] in respect of each charge card, company charge card and supplementary card included in the number of cards shown in the statement.][17]

[(d) Notwithstanding *paragraph (c)*, stamp duty shall only be chargeable on replacement cards in relation to a replacement account maintained by a promoter at any time during a relevant period—

(i) where the replacement account replaces an account maintained by the same promoter, to the extent that the number of such charge cards, in relation to the account, exceeds the number of charge cards in relation to the original account, or

(ii) where the replacement account replaces an account maintained by another promoter, to the extent that the number of such charge cards, in relation to the account, exceeds the aggregate number of charge cards stated in the letter of closure in relation to that other account.

(e) A promoter shall not issue a letter of closure during a relevant period in respect of an account that has been closed during the relevant period where the account holder has not accounted for the amount of stamp duty which the promoter is required to pay in respect of the charge cards to which the account relates, for the relevant period.

(f) Where a promoter treats an account as a replacement account by virtue of the account holder furnishing a letter of closure, the promoter shall not, by virtue of that letter, treat any other account as a replacement account.

(g) A promoter shall not issue more than one original letter of closure in respect of an account and may only issue a duplicate letter of closure to an account holder to whom the original letter of closure issued where the promoter is satisfied that the original letter of closure has been lost or destroyed and where such duplicate letter states that it is a duplicate of an original letter of closure.][18]

(3) There shall be furnished to the Commissioners by a bank or a promoter, as the case may be, such particulars as the Commissioners may deem necessary in relation to any statement required by this section to be delivered by the bank or promoter.

(4) (a) The duty charged by *subsection (1)(c)* on a statement delivered by a bank pursuant to *subsection (1)(b)*[, less any preliminary duty charged on a statement required to be delivered in accordance with section 124A in respect of the same chargeable period,][19] shall be paid by the bank on delivery of the statement.

(b) The duty charged by *subsection (2)(c)* on a statement delivered by a promoter pursuant to *subsection (2)(b)*[, less any preliminary duty charged on a statement required to be delivered in accordance with section 124A in respect of the same chargeable period,][20] shall be paid by the promoter on delivery of the statement.

(5) (a) In this subsection "*due date*" means—

(i) in relation to a statement required to be delivered pursuant to *subsection (1)(b)*, the [1 April][21] in the year in which the statement is required by that subsection to be delivered to the Commissioners, and

(ii) in relation to a statement required to be delivered pursuant to *subsection (2)(b)*, [the [1 April][22] in the year in which][23] the statement is required by that subsection to be delivered to the Commissioners.

(b) In the case of failure by a bank or promoter, as the case may be, to deliver any statement required by *subsection (1)* or *(2)* within the time specified in those subsections or of failure to pay the duty [required to be paid in accordance with this section][24], the bank or promoter, as the case may be, shall be liable to pay, [...][25] in addition to the duty, [interest on the duty, calculated in accordance with section 159D,][26] from the due date until the day on which the duty is paid and also, by means of [penalty][27], a sum of [€380][28] for each day the duty remains unpaid after the expiration of 3 months from the due date [...][29].

[(5A) A bank or a promoter is required to retain any original letter of closure or any duplicate of such letter received from an account holder for a period of 4 years from the date of receipt of such letter.

(5B) A letter of closure, in relation to an account, shall only be issued to one person in whose name the account is maintained notwithstanding that there is more than one such person.][30]

(6) The delivery of any statement required by *subsection (1)* or *(2)* may be enforced by the Commissioners under section 47 of the Succession Duty Act, 1853, in all respects as if such statement were such account as is mentioned in that section and the failure to deliver such statement were such default as is mentioned in that section.

(7) A bank or a promoter, as the case may be, shall be entitled to charge to the relevant account the amount of the stamp duty payable under this section by reference to that account or by reference to the charge card, company charge card or supplementary card to which the account relates [at the end of the relevant period or at the time when the account maintained by the bank or promoter in the name of the account holder is closed where that occurs during the relevant period][31] and may apply the terms and conditions governing that account to interest on that amount.

Amendments

[1] Substituted by FA15 s65(a). Effective from 1 January 2016.

[2] Inserted by FA05 s128(1)(d)(i)(I)(A). Has effect as respects accounts maintained by a bank or, as the case may be, a promoter after 1 April 2005.

[3] Inserted by FA08 s123(1)(b)(i). Has effect as respects any statement that falls to be delivered by a bank or promoter after 1 April 2009.

[4] Substituted by FA05 s128(1)(d)(i)(I)(B). Has effect as respects accounts maintained by a bank or, as the case may be, a promoter after 1 April 2005.

[5] Inserted by FA15 s65(b). Effective from 1 January 2016.

[6] Inserted by FA05 s128(1)(d)(i)(I)(C). Has effect as respects accounts maintained by a bank or, as the case may be, a promoter after 1 April 2005.

[7] Substituted by FA05 s128(1)(d)(i)(II). Has effect as respects accounts maintained by a bank or, as the case may be, a promoter after 1 April 2005.

[8] Substituted by FA08 s123(1)(b)(ii). Has effect as respects any statement that falls to be delivered by a bank or promoter after 1 April 2008.

[9] Inserted by FA05 s128(1)(d)(i)(III). Has effect as respects accounts maintained by a bank or, as the case may be, a promoter after 1 April 2005.

[10] Inserted by FA05 s128(1)(d)(ii)(I)(A). Has effect as respects accounts maintained by a bank or, as the case may be, a promoter after 1 April 2005.

[11] Inserted by FA08 s123(1)(b)(iii)(I). Has effect as respects any statement that falls to be delivered by a bank or promoter after 1 April 2009.

[12] Inserted by FA05 s128(1)(d)(ii)(I)(B). Has effect as respects accounts maintained by a bank or, as the case may be, a promoter after 1 April 2005.

[13] Inserted by FA05 s128(1)(d)(ii)(I)(C). Has effect as respects accounts maintained by a bank or, as the case may be, a promoter after 1 April 2005.

[14] Deleted by FA03 s140(1)(c)(iii)(II)(A). Has effect as respects any statement which falls to be delivered by a promoter in respect of a due date falling after 1 April 2003.

[15] Substituted by FA05 s128(1)(d)(ii)(II). Has effect as respects accounts maintained by a bank or, as the case may be, a promoter after 1 April 2005.

[16] Substituted by FA08 s123(1)(b)(iii)(II). Has effect as respects any statement that falls to be delivered by a bank or promoter after 1 April 2008.

[17] Substituted by FA03 s140(1)(c)(iii)(II)(B). Has effect as respects any statement which falls to be delivered by a promoter in respect of a due date falling after 1 April 2003.

[18] Inserted by FA05 s128(1)(d)(ii)(III). Has effect as respects accounts maintained by a bank or, as the case may be, a promoter after 1 April 2005.

[19, 20] Inserted by FA08 s123(1)(b)(iv). Has effect as respects any statement that falls to be delivered by a bank or promoter after 1 April 2009.

[21, 22] Substituted by FA05 s128(1)(d)(iii). Has effect as respects accounts maintained by a bank or, as the case may be, a promoter after 1 April 2005.

[23] Substituted by FA03 s140(1)(c)(iv). Has effect as respects any statement which falls to be delivered by a promoter in respect of a due date falling after 1 April 2003.

[24] Substituted by FA08 s123(1)(b)(v). Has effect as respects any statement that falls to be delivered by a bank or promoter after 1 April 2009.

[25] Deleted by F(No.2)A08 sched5(part5)(chap2)(7)(r)(i).

[26] Substituted by FA05 sched5.

[27] Substituted by F(No.2)A08 sched5(part5)(chap2)(7)(r)(ii).

[28] Substituted by FA01 sched5.

[29] Deleted by F(No.2)A08 sched4(part1). Applies as respects any tax that becomes due and payable on or after 1 March 2009.

[30] Inserted by FA05 s128(1)(d)(iv). Has effect as respects accounts maintained by a bank or, as the case may be, a promoter after 1 April 2005.

[31] Inserted by FA08 s123(1)(b)(vi). Has effect as respects any statement that falls to be delivered by a bank or promoter after 1 April 2009.

Note:

F(No.2)A08 sched5 (part5)(chap 2)(7)

As respects paragraph 7 of this Schedule subparagraphs (a) to (aa) (other than subparagraph (c)(i)(I)) of that paragraph have effect as on and from the passing of this Act and to the extent that Chapter 3A (being inserted into Part 47 of the Taxes Consolidation Act 1997 by Part 1 of this Schedule) applies to penalties incurred under the Stamp Duties Consolidation Act 1999 before the passing of this Act which on the passing of this Act have not been paid, it shall not apply to such penalties which are in the form of interest accrued under any provisions of the said Act.

Cross References

From Section 124

Section 124A Preliminary duty: credit and charge cards.

To Section 124

Section 123 Cash cards.

Section 123A Debit cards.
Section 123B Cash, combined and debit cards.
Section 124A Preliminary duty: credit and charge cards.
Section 126B Assessment of duty charged on statements.
Section 160 Repeals.

124A Preliminary duty: credit and charge cards

[(1) In this section—

"*accountable person*" means a bank or promoter within the meaning of section 124;

"*base period*", in relation to a due date, means the 12 month period ending on 1 April immediately before the due date in respect of which a statement is required to be delivered to the Commissioners under section 124;

"*chargeable period*", in relation to a due date, means the 12 month period ending on 1 April immediately after the due date commencing with the 12 month period ending on 1 April 2009 and each subsequent 12 month period in respect of which a statement is required to be delivered to the Commissioners under section 124;

"*due date*" means—

(a) in respect of the 12 month period ending on 1 April 2009, 15 December 2008, and

(b) in respect of each subsequent 12 month period, 15 December in the preceding year;

"*preliminary duty*", in relation to a chargeable period ending immediately after a due date, means an amount determined by the formula—

$$A \times B$$

where—

A is an amount equal to the stamp duty charged on a specified statement in respect of the base period ending immediately prior to the due date, and

B is 80 per cent;

"*specified statement*" means a statement within the meaning of subsection (1) or, as the case may be, subsection (2) of section 124.

(2) This section applies to an accountable person who is required to deliver to the Commissioners a specified statement in respect of a base period.

(3) An accountable person shall in the year 2008 and each subsequent year, not later than the due date in respect of that year, deliver to the Commissioners a statement in writing showing the stamp duty charged on the specified statement for that person in respect of the base period.

(4) Where at any time in a period commencing after the expiration of a base period and ending immediately before the due date relating to the base period—

(a) an accountable person ceased to carry on a business in the course of which the person was required to deliver a specified statement for the base period, and

(b) another person (in this subsection referred to as the "*successor person*") acquires the whole, or substantially the whole, of the business,

then the successor person shall deliver a statement on the due date in accordance with subsection (3) as if the successor person was the accountable person.

(5) There shall be charged on any statement delivered in accordance with subsection (3) a stamp duty equal to the amount of the preliminary duty.

(6) The stamp duty charged by subsection (5) on a statement delivered by an accountable person pursuant to subsection (3) shall be paid by the person upon delivery of the statement.

(7) There shall be furnished to the Commissioners by an accountable person such particulars as the Commissioners may require in relation to any statement required by this section to be delivered by the person.

(8) In the case of failure by an accountable person—

(a) to deliver any statement required to be delivered by that person under subsection (3), or

(b) to pay the duty charged on any such statement,

on or before the due date in respect of the year concerned, the person shall, from the due date concerned until the day on which the stamp duty is paid, be liable to pay, by way of penalty, in addition to the stamp duty, interest on the stamp duty, calculated in accordance with section 159D and also from 15 December of the year in which the statement is to be delivered in accordance with subsection (3), by way of a [penalty][1], a sum of €380 for each day the duty remains unpaid [...][2].

(9) The delivery of any statement required by subsection (3) may be enforced by the Commissioners under section 47 of the Succession Duty Act 1853 in all respects as if such statement were such account as is mentioned in that section and the failure to deliver such statement were such default as is mentioned in that section.

(10) Where—

(a) the preliminary duty charged on a statement has been paid in whole or in part by an accountable person in respect of a due date, and

(b) the duty charged on a specified statement in respect of the chargeable period ending immediately after the due date is an amount which is less than the preliminary duty charged in respect of the due date,

then the preliminary duty paid, to the extent that it exceeds the duty charged on the specified statement concerned, shall be repaid.

(11) Where at any time in a period commencing after a due date and ending before the expiration of the chargeable period ending immediately after the due date—

(a) the person (in this subsection referred to as the "*predecessor person*") ceased to carry on a business in the course of which the person was required to deliver to the Commissioners a statement under this section in respect of the due date,

(b) the person delivered the statement and paid the stamp duty charged on such statement, and

(c) another person (in this subsection referred to as the "*successor person*") acquires the whole, or substantially the whole, of the business,

then the successor person shall be entitled to deduct the stamp duty charged on the statement delivered by the predecessor person in respect of that due date from the duty charged on the specified statement in respect of the chargeable period ending immediately after the due date which the successor person is required to deliver in respect of the business acquired.

(12) The stamp duty and any [interest or penalty][3] payable under this section shall not be allowed as a deduction for the purposes of the computation of any tax or duty payable by the accountable person which is under the care and management of the Commissioners.][4]

Amendments

[1] Substituted by F(No.2)A08 sched5(part5)(chap2)(7)(t)(ii).

[3] Substituted by F(No.2)A08 sched5(part5)(chap2)(7)(u).

[4] Inserted by FA08 s123(1)(d).

Note:

F(No.2)A08 sched5 (part5)(chap 2)(7)

As respects paragraph 7 of this Schedule subparagraphs (a) to (aa) (other than subparagraph (c)(i)(I)) of that paragraph have effect as on and from the passing of this Act and to the extent that Chapter 3A (being inserted into Part 47 of the Taxes Consolidation Act 1997 by Part 1 of this Schedule) applies to penalties incurred under the Stamp Duties Consolidation Act 1999 before the passing of this Act which on the passing of this Act have not been paid, it shall not apply to such penalties which are in the form of interest accrued under any provisions of the said Act.

Cross References

From Section 124A

Section 124 Credit cards and charge cards.
Section 159D Calculation of interest on unpaid duty and other amounts.

To Section 124A

Section 124 Credit cards and charge cards.
Section 126B Assessment of duty charged on statements.

124B Certain premiums of life assurance

[(1) In this section—

["*assessable amount*", in relation to a quarter, means the gross amount received by an insurer by means of premiums in that quarter for policies of life insurance referred to in classes I, II, III, IV, V and VI of Annex I to the Directive to the extent that the risks to which those policies of life insurance relate are located in the State (being risks deemed to be located in the State by virtue of *section 61*) but excluding amounts received in respect of pension business which shall be construed in accordance with subsections (2) and (3) of section 706 of the Taxes Consolidation Act 1997 and excluding amounts received in the course of or by means of reinsurance;][1]

"*Directive*" means Directive 2002/83/EC of the European Parliament and of the Council of 5 November 2002* concerning life assurance;

*OJ No. L345, 19 December 2002, p.1.

["*due date*" means, in respect of the quarter ending on—

(a) 31 March in any year, 25 April in the same year,

(b) 30 June in any year, 25 July in the same year,

(c) 30 September in any year, 25 October in the same year, and

(d) 31 December in any year, 25 January in the following year;][2]

"*insurer*" means—

(a) a person who is the holder of an assurance licence under the Insurance Act 1936,

(b) the holder of an authorisation within the meaning of the European Communities (Life Assurance) Framework Regulations 1994 (S.I. No. 360 of 1994), or

[(c) the holder of an official authorisation to undertake insurance in Iceland, Liechtenstein or Norway, pursuant to the EEA Agreement, within the meaning of the Agreement on the European Economic Area signed at

Oporto on 2 May 1992, as adjusted by all subsequent agreements to that Agreement, who is carrying on business of life assurance in the State;][3]

"*life assurance*" means insurance of a class referred to in Annex I to the Directive;

"*premium*" has the same meaning as in the Insurance Act 1936;

"*quarter*", in relation to a year, means a period of 3 months ending on 31 March, 30 June, 30 September or 31 December.

(2) An insurer shall, in each year, not later than the due date for each quarter, commencing with the quarter ending on 30 September 2009, deliver to the Commissioners a statement in writing showing the assessable amount for the insurer in respect of that quarter.

(3) There shall be charged on every statement delivered pursuant to subsection (2) a stamp duty of an amount equal to 1 per cent of the assessable amount shown in the statement.

(4) The duty charged by subsection (3) on a statement delivered by an insurer pursuant to subsection (2) shall be paid by the insurer to the Commissioners on delivery of the statement.

(5) There shall be furnished to the Commissioners by an insurer such particulars as the Commissioners may deem necessary in relation to any statement required by this section to be delivered by the insurer.

(6) In the case of failure by an insurer—

(a) to deliver not later than the due date any statement required to be delivered by the insurer pursuant to subsection (2), or

(b) to pay the stamp duty chargeable on any such statement on delivery of the statement,

the insurer shall—

(i) from that due date until the day on which the stamp duty is paid, be liable to pay, in addition to the stamp duty, interest on the stamp duty calculated in accordance with section 159D, and

(ii) from that due date, be liable to pay a penalty of €380 for each day the stamp duty remains unpaid.

(7) Where during any quarter but before the due date—

(a) an insurer ceases to carry on a business in the course of which the insurer is required to deliver a statement (in this subsection referred to as the "*first-mentioned statement*") pursuant to subsection (2) (including any case where the insurer is so required by virtue of the prior operation of this subsection) but has not done so before that cesser, and

(b) another person (in this subsection referred to as the "*successor*") acquires the whole, or substantially the whole, of the business,

then—

(i) the insurer is not required to deliver the first-mentioned statement, and

(ii) the successor shall—

(I) where the successor is, apart from this subsection, required to deliver a statement (in this subsection referred to as the "*second-mentioned statement*") pursuant to subsection (2) (including any case where the successor is so required by virtue of the prior operation of this subsection) in respect of the same quarter but has not done so before that acquisition, include in that second-mentioned statement the assessable amount that would have been required to have been shown in the first-mentioned statement had the insurer not ceased to carry on the business concerned,

(II) where subparagraph (I) does not apply, deliver the first-mentioned statement as if the successor were the insurer.

(8) The delivery of any statement required by subsection (2) may be enforced by the Commissioners under section 47 of the Succession Duty Act 1853 in all respects as if such statement were such account as is mentioned in that section and the failure to deliver such statement were such default as is mentioned in that section.][4]

Amendments

[1] Substituted by FA10 s(139)(1)(a). Has effect from 1 January 2010.

[2] Substituted by FA10 s(139)(1)(b). Has effect in respect of all statements to be delivered to the Commissioners after 31 December 2009.

[3] Substituted by FA10 s(139)(1)(c). Has effect from 1 January 2010.

[4] Inserted by FA09 s26(1)(a). Applies as respects so much of the assessable amount as is comprised of premiums received on or after 1 August 2009 in respect of contracts of insurance whenever entered into by an insurer.

Cross References

From Section 124B

Section 61 Location of insurance risk for stamp duty purposes.
Section 159D Calculation of interest on unpaid duty and other amounts.

To Section 124B

Section 126B Assessment of duty charged on statements.

125 Certain premiums of insurance

[FA1982 s92(1) to (7)]

(1) In this section—

"*assessable amount*", in relation to a quarter, means the gross amount received by an insurer by means of premiums (including, in the case of an insurer who is a leading insurer (within the meaning of the European Communities (Co-insurance) Regulations, 1983 (S.I. No. 65 of 1983)), the amount received by means of overall premiums (within the above meaning)) in that quarter in respect of policies of insurance to the extent that the risks to which those policies relate are located in the State (being risks deemed to be located in the State by virtue of *section 61*), but without having regard to an excluded amount;

"*excluded amount*" means—

(a) an amount received in the course or by means of re-insurance;

(b) a premium received in respect of business in the following classes of the Annex to First Council Directive 73/239/EEC of 24 July 1973 (OJ No. L228, 16/8/1973), namely, 4, 5, 6, 7, 11 and 12, in classes 1 and 10 in so far as they relate to the insurance of passengers in marine and aviation vehicles and carriers liability insurance, respectively, and in class 14 in so far as it relates to export credit;

(c) a premium received in respect of business in classes I, II, III, IV, V, VI, VII, VIII and IX of the Annex to First Council Directive 79/267/EEC of 5 March 1979 (OJ No. L63, 13/3/1979);

(d) a premium received in respect of health insurance business (being health insurance business within the meaning of section 2 of the Health Insurance Act, 1994);

[(e) a premium received in respect of a contract of insurance, the sole purpose of which is to provide for the making of payments for the reimbursement or discharge in whole or in part of fees or charges in respect of the provision of dental services, other than those involving surgical procedures carried out in a hospital by way of hospital in-patient services within the meaning of section 2(1) of the Health Insurance Act 1994;][1]

"*insurer*" means a person who is the holder of an assurance licence under the Insurance Act, 1936, or is the holder of an authorisation within the meaning of the European Communities (Non-Life Insurance) Framework Regulations, 1994 (S.I. No. 359 of 1994), or who carries on the business of insurance in compliance with the Assurance Companies Act, 1909;

"*premium*" has the same meaning as in the Insurance Act, 1936;

"*quarter*" means a period of 3 months ending on the 31st day of March, the 30th day of June, the 30th day of September or the 31st day of December.

(2) An insurer shall, in each year, within [25 days][2] from the end of each quarter, deliver to the Commissioners a statement in writing showing the assessable amount for that insurer in respect of that quarter.

(3) There shall be charged on every statement delivered in pursuance of *subsection (2)* a stamp duty of an amount equal to [3 per cent][3] of the assessable amount shown in the statement.

(4) The duty charged by *subsection (3)* on a statement delivered by an insurer pursuant to *subsection (2)* shall be paid by the insurer on delivery of the statement.

(5) There shall be furnished to the Commissioners by an insurer such particulars as the Commissioners may deem necessary in relation to any statement required by this section to be delivered by the insurer.

(6) In the case of failure by an insurer to deliver any statement required by *subsection (2)* within the time specified in that subsection or of failure by an insurer to pay any duty chargeable on any such statement on the delivery of that statement, the insurer shall be liable to pay,[...][4] in addition to the duty, [interest on the duty, calculated in accordance with section 159D,][5] from the expiration of the quarter to which the statement relates until the day on which the duty is paid.

(7) The delivery of any statement required by *subsection (2)* may be enforced by the Commissioners under section 47 of the Succession Duty Act, 1853, in all respects as if such statement were such account as is mentioned in that section and the failure to deliver such statement were such default as is mentioned in that section.

Amendments

[1] Inserted by FA04 s75(1). This section applies as respects contracts of insurance entered into on or after the date of the passing of the Finance Act 2004.

[2] Substituted by FA12 s105(1).

[3] Substituted by FA09 s26(1)(b). Applies as respects so much of the assessable amount as is comprised of premiums received on or after 1 June 2009 in respect of offers of insurance or notices of renewal of insurance issued by an insurer on or after 8 April 2009.

[4] Deleted by F(No.2)A08 sched5(part5)(chap2)(7)(v).

[5] Substituted by FA05 sched5.

Note:

F(No.2)A08 sched5 (part5)(chap 2)(7)

As respects paragraph 7 of this Schedule subparagraphs (a) to (aa) (other than subparagraph (c)(i)(I)) of that paragraph have effect as on and from the passing of this Act and to the extent that Chapter 3A (being inserted into Part 47 of the Taxes Consolidation Act 1997 by Part 1 of this Schedule) applies to penalties incurred under the Stamp Duties Consolidation Act 1999 before the passing of this Act which on the passing of this Act have not been paid, it shall not apply to such penalties which are in the form of interest accrued under any provisions of the said Act.

Cross References

From Section 125
Section 61 Location of insurance risk for stamp duty purposes.

To Section 125
Section 126B Assessment of duty charged on statements.
Section 160 Repeals.

125A Levy on authorised insurers

[(1) In this section—

["*accounting period*" means a period of 3 consecutive months beginning on 1 January, 1 April, 1 July or 1 October;][1]

["*advanced cover*" and "*non-advanced cover*", in relation to a relevant contract, have the same meanings respectively as in *section 6A* of the Health Insurance Act 1994;][2]

'*authorised insurer*' means any undertaking (not being a restricted membership undertaking) entered in The Register of Health Benefits Undertakings, lawfully carrying on such business of medical insurance referred to in the definition of 'relevant contract' but, in relation to an individual, also means any under taking (not being a restricted membership undertaking) authorised pursuant to Council Directive No. 73/239/EEC of 24 July 1973*, Council Directive No. 88/357/EEC of 22 June 1988†, and Council Directive No. 92/49/EEC of 18 June 1992‡, where such a contract was effected with the individual when the individual was not resident in the State but was resident in another Member State of the European Communities;

*OJ No. L228, 16.08.1973, p.3

†OJ No. L172, 04.07.1988, p.1

‡OJ No. L228, 11.08.1992, p.1

["*due date*", in relation to an accounting period, means the 21st day of the second next month following the end of that accounting period;][3]

[…][4]

'*excluded contract of insurance*' means—

(a) a contract of insurance which comes within the meaning of *paragraph (d)* of the definition of '*health insurance contract*' in *section 2(1)* of the Health Insurance Act 1994, or

(b) a contract of insurance relating solely to charges for public hospital in-patient services made under the Health (In-Patient Charges) Regulations 1987 (S.I. No. 116 of 1987);

'*in-patient indemnity payment*' has the same meaning as in *section 2(1)* of the Health Insurance Act 1994;

'*insured person*', in relation to a relevant contract, means an individual, the spouse or civil partner of the individual, or the children or other dependents of the individual or of the spouse or civil partner of the individual, in respect of whom the relevant contract provides specifically, whether in conjunction with other benefits or not, for the reimbursement or discharge, in whole or in part, of actual health expenses (within the meaning of *section 469* of the Taxes Consolidation Act 1997);

'*relevant contract*' means a contract of insurance (not being an excluded contract of insurance) which provides for the making of in-patient indemnity payments under the contract and which, in relation to an individual, the spouse or civil partner of the individual, or the children or other dependents of the individual or of the spouse or civil partner of the individual, provides specifically, whether in conjunction with other benefits or not, for the reimbursement or discharge, in whole or in part, of actual health expenses (within the meaning of *section 469* of the Taxes Consolidation Act 1997), being a contract of medical insurance;

'*restricted membership undertaking*' has the same meaning as in *section 2(1)* of the Health Insurance Act 1994;

["*specified rate*" means—

(a) in respect of relevant contracts renewed or entered into on or after 1 January 2014 and on or before 28 February 2014—

(i) €100.00 in respect of an insured person aged less than 18 years insured under a relevant contract which provides for non-advanced cover,

(ii) €120.00 in respect of an insured person aged less than 18 years insured under a relevant contract which provides for advanced cover,

(iii) €290.00 in respect of an insured person aged 18 years or over insured under a relevant contract which provides for non-advanced cover, and

(iv) €350.00 in respect of an insured person aged 18 years or over insured under a relevant contract which provides for advanced cover,

and

(b) in respect of relevant contracts renewed or entered into on or after 1 March 2014—

(i) €100.00 in respect of an insured person aged less than 18 years insured under a relevant contract which provides for non-advanced cover,

(ii) €135.00 in respect of an insured person aged less than 18 years insured under a relevant contract which provides for advanced cover,

(iii) €290.00 in respect of an insured person aged 18 years or over insured under a relevant contract which provides for non-advanced cover, and

(iv) €399.00 in respect of an insured person aged 18 years or over insured under a relevant contract which provides for advanced cover.][5]

[...][6]

[(2) Subject to *subsections (7)*, *(10)* and *(11)*, an authorised insurer shall, in respect of each subsequent accounting period and not later than the due date, deliver to the Commissioners a statement in writing showing the number of insured persons—

(a) aged less than 18 years on the first day of the accounting period insured under a relevant contract which provides for non-advanced cover,

(b) aged less than 18 years on the first day of the accounting period insured under a relevant contract which provides for advanced cover,

(c) aged 18 years or over on the first day of the accounting period insured under a relevant contract which provides for non-advanced cover, and

(d) aged 18 years or over on the first day of the accounting period insured under a relevant contract which provides for advanced cover,

in respect of whom a relevant contract between the authorised insurer and the insured person, being the individual referred to in the definition of "*insured person*" in *subsection (1)*, is renewed, or entered into, during the accounting period concerned.][7]

[...][8]

(3) There shall be charged on every statement delivered by an authorised insurer pursuant to [*subsection (2)* [...][9]][10] a stamp duty in respect of each insured person at the specified rate.

(4) The duty charged by *subsection (3)* on a statement delivered by an authorised insurer pursuant to [*subsection (2)* [...][11]][12] shall be paid by the authorised insurer on delivery of the statement.

(5) There shall be furnished to the Commissioners by an authorised insurer such particulars as the Commissioners may deem necessary in relation to any statement required by this section to be delivered by the authorised insurer.

(6) In the case of failure by an authorised insurer in respect of an accounting period—

(a) to deliver not later than the due date any statement required by [*subsection (2)* [...][13]][14] to be delivered by the authorised insurer, or

(b) to pay the stamp duty chargeable on any such statement on the delivery of the statement,

the authorised insurer shall—

(i) from that due date until the day on which the stamp duty is paid, be liable to pay, in addition to the duty, interest on the stamp duty calculated in accordance with *section 159D*, and

(ii) from that due date, be liable to pay a penalty of €380 for each day the duty remains unpaid.

(7) Where during any accounting period but before the due date—

(a) an authorised insurer ceases to carry on a business in the course of which the insurer is required to deliver a statement (in this subsection referred to as the '*first-mentioned statement*') pursuant to [*subsection (2)* [...][15]][16] (including any case where the authorised insurer is so required by virtue of the prior operation of this subsection) but has not done so before that cesser, and

(b) another person (in this subsection referred to as the '*successor*') acquires the whole, or substantially the whole, of the business,

then—

(i) the authorised insurer is not required to deliver the first-mentioned statement, and

(ii) the successor shall—

(I) if the successor is, apart from this subsection, required to deliver a statement (in this subsection referred to as the 'second-mentioned statement') pursuant to [*subsection (2)* [...][17]][18] (including any case where the successor is so required by virtue of the prior operation of this subsection) in respect of the same accounting period but has not done so before that acquisition, include in that second-mentioned statement the number of insured persons that would have been required to have been shown in the first-mentioned statement had the authorised insurer not ceased to carry on the business concerned,

(II) if *subparagraph (I)* is not applicable, deliver the first-mentioned statement as if the successor were the authorised insurer.

(8) The delivery of any statement required by [*subsection (2)* [...][19]][20] may be enforced by the Commissioners under *section 47* of the Succession Duty Act 1853 in all respects as if such statement were such account as is mentioned in that section and the failure to deliver such statement were such default as is mentioned in that section.

(9) The stamp duty, interest and any penalty payable under this section shall not be allowed as a deduction for the purposes of the computation of any tax or duty payable by the authorised insurer which is under the care and management of the Commissioners.

(10) Where an insured person, being the individual referred to in the definition of '*insured person*', shows to the satisfaction of an authorised insurer (in this subsection referred to as the '*second authorised insurer*') that another authorised insurer (in this subsection referred to as the '*first authorised insurer*') with whom that individual renewed, or entered into, a relevant contract during an accounting period, was required to include that insured person in a statement to be delivered pursuant to [*subsection (2)* [...][21]][22] to the Commissioners in respect of the same accounting period, then the second authorised insurer, with whom the individual entered into a later relevant contract during the same accounting period, may exclude such insured person from the statement to be delivered pursuant to [*subsection (2)* [...][23]][24] to the Commissioners by the second authorised insurer in respect of the same accounting period.

(11) Where an insured person, being an insured person under a relevant contract who is not the individual referred to in the definition of '*insured person*' in relation to the relevant contract concerned, shows to the satisfaction of an authorised insurer (in this subsection referred to as the '*second authorised insurer*') that another authorised insurer (in this subsection referred to as the '*first authorised insurer*') with whom that person was an insured person named on a relevant contract renewed, or entered into, by an individual referred to in the definition of '*insured person*' during an accounting period, was required to include that insured person in a statement to be delivered pursuant to [*subsection (2)* [...][25]][26] to the Commissioners for the same accounting period, then the second authorised insurer, with whom the insured person entered into a relevant contract during the same accounting period, may exclude such insured person from the statement to be delivered pursuant to [*subsection (2)* [...][27]][28] to the Commissioners by the second authorised insurer in respect of the same accounting period.

(12) Where—

(a) a relevant contract is renewed or entered into by an individual referred to in the definition of '*insured person*' during an accounting period (in this subsection referred to as the '*initial accounting period*'), and

(b) the relevant contract is for a period of more than 12 months,

then, without prejudice to the treatment to be accorded to the relevant contract and the initial accounting period by [*subsection (2)* […][29]][30], the relevant contract shall be deemed, for the purposes of this section, to be renewed during—

[(i) the accounting period in which the second 12 months, or lesser period, of the relevant contract commences, and

(ii) each further accounting period in which any subsequent 12 months, or lesser period, of the relevant contract commences.][31]][32]

Amendments

[1] Substituted by HI(A)A13 s12(1)(a)(i). Comes into operation on 1 January 2014.

[2] Inserted by FA13 s83(d).

[3] Substituted by HI(A)A13 s12(1)(a)(ii). Comes into operation on 1 January 2014..

[4, 6] Deleted by HI(A)A13 s12(1)(a)(iii). Comes into operation on 1 January 2014.

[5] Substituted by HI(A)A13 s12(1)(a)(iv). Comes into operation on 1 January 2014.

[7] Substituted by HI(A)A13 s12(1)(b). Comes into operation on 1 January 2014.

[8] Deleted by HI(A)A13 s12(1)(c). Comes into operation on 1 January 2014.

[9, 11, 13, 15, 17, 19, 21, 23, 25, 27, 29] Deleted by HI(A)A13 s12(1)(d). Comes into operation on 1 January 2014.

[10, 12, 14, 16, 18, 20, 22, 24, 26, 28, 30] Substituted by FA13 s83(g).

[31] Substituted by FA13 s83(h).

[32] Substituted by FA12 s105(5). Does not apply to any accounting period ending before 1 January 2013 and section 125A, as it applies immediately before that date, continues to apply to any duty payable in respect of any such accounting period.

Revenue Briefings

eBrief

eBrief No. 020/2015 – Levy on Authorised Insurers – Health Insurance (Amendment) Act 2014 changes

Cross References

From Section 125A

Section 126B Assessment of duty charged on statements.
Section 159D

125B Levy on pension schemes

[(1) In this section—

"*Act of 1997*" means the Taxes Consolidation Act 1997;

"*administrator*", in relation to a scheme, means the trustees or other persons having the management of the assets of the scheme, and in particular, but without prejudice to the generality of the foregoing, references to the administrator of a scheme include—

(a) an administrator, within the meaning of section 770(1) of the Act of 1997,

(b) a person mentioned in section 784 or 785 of the Act of 1997, lawfully carrying on the business of granting annuities on human life, including the person mentioned in section 784(4A)(ii) of that Act, and

(c) a PRSA administrator, within the meaning of section 787A(1) of the Act of 1997;

"*assets*" means all property, including investments, deposits, debts and contracts of assurance, held for the purposes of a scheme, other than excluded assets;

"*chargeable amount*", in relation to a chargeable person and any assets, means the aggregate market value of the assets (other than an asset that is land, in which case the market value of the land shall be taken as not including the amount of any outstanding borrowings used to acquire the land)—

(a) on 30 June for the year 2011, 2012, [2013, 2014 or 2015][1], as the case may be, or

(b) where the assets are not contracts of assurance and are held for the purposes of a scheme of a kind described in paragraph (a) of the definition of "scheme" that is a defined benefit scheme or a one member scheme and the chargeable person so decides, and where accounts are prepared to an appropriate accounting standard, on the last day of the accounting period of the scheme ended in the period of 12 months immediately preceding 30 June of the year 2011, 2012, [2013, 2014 or 2015][2], as the case may be,

and in respect of which the chargeable person is the administrator or insurer on the date concerned;

"*chargeable person*", in relation to the assets of a scheme, means—

(a) where the assets are not contracts of assurance, the administrator in relation to the scheme, and

(b) where the assets are contracts of assurance, the insurer in relation to such a contract,

and, where the context admits, includes a successor within the meaning of subsection (9);

"*contract of assurance*" means—

(a) any contract of a type described in section 706(3) of the Act of 1997, and

(b) any other policy or contract of assurance made by an insurer with a person or persons having the management of a scheme of a kind described in paragraph (a) of the definition of "scheme", other than a one member scheme;

"*defined benefit scheme*" has the meaning assigned to it in section 2(1) of the Pensions Act 1990;

"*due date*" means 25 September of the year 2011, 2012, [2013, 2014 or 2015][3], as the case may be;

"*excluded assets*", in relation to a scheme of a kind described in paragraph (a) of the definition of "scheme", means assets representing the liabilities of the scheme which are attributable to the provision of relevant benefits (within the meaning of section 770 of the Act of 1997) in respect of any member of such a scheme—

(a) whose employment in relation to the scheme at the date the chargeable amount for the year concerned is determined—

(i) is and always was, or

(ii) where the employment has ceased before that date, whose employment always had been,

exercised wholly outside the State and who, at that date, was not in receipt of such benefits, and

(b) whose employment in relation to the scheme was wholly exercised outside the State and who at the date the chargeable amount for the year concerned is determined was in receipt of such benefits;

"*insurer*" means an insurance undertaking within the meaning of the European Communities (Life Assurance) Framework Regulations 1994 (S.I. No. 360 of 1994);

"*market value*" shall be construed in accordance with section 548 of the Act of 1997;

"*member*", in relation to a scheme of a kind described in paragraph (a) of the definition of "scheme", means any person admitted to membership under the rules of the scheme;

"*one member scheme*" means a scheme of a kind described in paragraph (a) of the definition of "scheme" in respect of which approval of the scheme by the Commissioners requires the person or persons having the management of the scheme to deliver annual scheme accounts to the Commissioners;

"*pension fund*", in relation to an insurer, shall be construed in accordance with subsection (2) of section 706 of the Act of 1997 and as if the business referred to in paragraph (a) of that subsection includes policies of assurance referred to in paragraph (b) of the definition of "contract of assurance";

"*scheme*" means—

(a) a retirement benefits scheme, within the meaning of section 771 of the Act of 1997—

[(i) approved by the Commissioners for the purposes of *Chapter 1* of *Part 30* of that Act, or

(ii) approved by the Commissioners under any other enactment (including an enactment that is repealed) and in respect of which the provisions of *Chapter 1* of *Part 30* of the Act of 1997 were applied,][4]

other than a scheme where—

(I) the trustees have passed a resolution to wind up the scheme, and

(II) the employer is insolvent for the purposes of the Protection of Employees (Employers' Insolvency) Act 1984,

(b) an annuity contract or a trust scheme or part of a trust scheme approved by the Commissioners under section 784 or 785 of the Act of 1997 or, as the case may be, under both of those sections of that Act, other than an annuity contract or trust scheme or part of a trust scheme so approved in respect of which a lump sum, to which paragraph (b) of section 784(2) of the Act of 1997 applies, has been paid to the individual entitled to an annuity under the contract, trust scheme or part of a trust scheme, as the case may be, or

(c) a PRSA contract, within the meaning of section 787A of the Act of 1997, in respect of a PRSA product, within the meaning of that section, other than a PRSA contract in respect of which a lump sum, to which paragraph (a) of section 787G(3) of the Act of 1997 applies, has been paid or made available to the PRSA contributor;

"*valuation date*" means the appropriate date as determined for the purposes of paragraph (a) or (b) of the definition of "chargeable amount".

(2) A chargeable person shall in respect of the due date in each of the years 2011, 2012, [2013, 2014 and 2015][5], and not later than the due date concerned, deliver to

the Commissioners a statement, in such electronic format as the Commissioners may specify, showing the chargeable amount for that year in respect of the chargeable person.

[(3) A stamp duty of an amount equal to—

(a) 0.6 per cent of the chargeable amount for each of the years 2011, 2012 and 2013,

(b) 0.75 per cent of the chargeable amount for the year 2014, and

(c) 0.15 per cent of the chargeable amount for the year 2015,

shall be charged on every statement delivered by a chargeable person pursuant to *subsection (2)*.][6]

(4) The duty charged under subsection (3) on a statement delivered by a chargeable person pursuant to subsection (2) shall be paid, by such electronic means as the Commissioners may specify, by the charge able person on delivery of the statement.

(5) (a) A chargeable person who, in relation to the assets of a scheme, being a scheme approved by the Commissioners, is liable to pay the duty charged under subsection (3) on a statement delivered by the chargeable person pursuant to subsection (2) shall, for the purposes of payment of the duty, be entitled to dispose of or appropriate such assets of the scheme as are required to meet the amount of the duty so pay able and the scheme shall not cease to be a scheme approved by the Commissioners as a consequence of any such disposal or appropriation by the chargeable person.

(b) Where in pursuance of this section a chargeable person who, in relation to the assets of a scheme, being a scheme approved by the Commissioners, is not a trustee of the scheme, pays the duty charged under subsection (3) by the disposal or appropriation of such assets of the scheme as are required to meet the amount of duty so payable, then the trustees shall allow such disposal or appropriation and the chargeable person shall be acquitted and discharged of any such disposal or appropriation as if the amount of duty had not been so paid, and the scheme shall not cease to be a scheme approved by the Commissioners as a consequence of any such disposal or appropriation by the chargeable person.

(6) Where in pursuance of this section a chargeable person disposes of or appropriates an asset of a scheme in accordance with subsection (5)(a), then no action shall lie against the chargeable person in any court by reason of such disposal or appropriation.

(7) (a) Where, in relation to the assets of a scheme, being a scheme approved by the Commissioners, the chargeable person is not a trustee of the scheme, then the chargeable person and the trustees of the scheme shall each be liable for the payment of the duty charged under subsection (3) on a statement delivered to the Commissioners by the chargeable person pursuant to subsection (2) and their liability shall be joint and several.

(b) Where, in relation to the assets of a scheme, being a scheme approved by the Commissioners, that is a one member scheme, the chargeable person is a trustee of that scheme but is not a member of that scheme, then the chargeable person and a trustee who is a member of that scheme shall each be liable for the payment of the duty charged under subsection (3) on a statement delivered to the Commissioners by the chargeable person pursuant to subsection (2) and their liability shall be joint and several.

(8) In the case of failure by a chargeable person—

(a) to deliver not later than the due date any statement required to be delivered by the chargeable person pursuant to subsection (2), or

(b) to pay the duty chargeable on any such statement on delivery of the statement,

the chargeable person shall—

(i) from that due date until the day on which the duty is paid, be liable to pay, in addition to the duty, interest on the duty calculated in accordance with *section 159D*, and

(ii) from that due date, be liable to pay a penalty of €380 for each day the duty remains unpaid.

(9) Where before a due date—

(a) a chargeable person ceases to carry on a business in the course of which the chargeable person is required to deliver a statement (in this subsection referred to as the "first-mentioned statement") pursuant to subsection (2) (including any case where the chargeable person is so required by virtue of the prior operation of this subsection) but has not done so before that cesser, and

(b) another person (in this subsection referred to as the "successor") acquires the whole, or substantially the whole, of the business,

then—

(i) the chargeable person is not required to deliver the first-mentioned statement, and

(ii) the successor shall—

(I) where the successor is, apart from this subsection, required to deliver a statement (in this subsection referred to as the "second mentioned statement") pursuant to subsection (2) (including any case where the successor is so required by virtue of the prior operation of this subsection) in respect of the same due date but has not done so before that acquisition, include in that second-mentioned statement the chargeable amount for the year concerned that would have been required to have been shown in the first-mentioned statement had the chargeable person not ceased to carry on the business concerned,

(II) where subparagraph (I) does not apply, deliver the first-mentioned statement as if the successor were the chargeable person.

(10) The delivery of any statement required by subsection (2) may be enforced by the Commissioners under section 47 of the Succession Duty Act 1853 in all respects as if such statement were such account as is mentioned in that section and the failure to deliver such statement were such default as is mentioned in that section.

(11) The duty charged by this section shall not be allowed as a deduction or as a credit for the purpose of the computation or charge of any tax or duty under the care and management of the Commissioners.

(12) Notwithstanding any provision of any enactment (including this Act), or any rule of law, or anything contained in the rules of a scheme, being a scheme approved by the Commissioners, or the terms and conditions of any contract, being a contract approved by the Commissioners, if under this section—

(a) a chargeable person who is an insurer pays an amount to the Commissioners in respect of the duty in relation to a contract of assurance, the amount shall be deemed to be a necessary disbursement from the pension fund of the insurer and the insurer may adjust accordingly any current or prospective benefits or guarantees under the contract, and any such adjustment of benefits or guarantees by the insurer shall not result in the contract ceasing to be a contract approved by the Commissioners, and

(b) a chargeable person who is an administrator pays an amount to the Commissioners in respect of the duty in relation to the assets of a scheme, or where an amount in respect of the duty in relation to the assets of a scheme has been paid to the Commissioners by any other chargeable person, the aggregate of the amount of duty paid by the administrator and the other chargeable person shall be deemed to be a necessary disbursement from those assets, and the benefits payable currently or prospectively to any member under the scheme may accordingly be adjusted by the trustees, but the diminution in value of those benefits shall not exceed the amount disbursed from the assets attributable at the valuation date to the scheme's liabilities in respect of that member, and any such adjustment of benefits by the trustees shall not result in the scheme ceasing to be a scheme approved by the Commissioners.

(13) For the purposes of subsections (5) and (12), the Commissioners may, where they consider it appropriate, review any such disposal or appropriation of an asset as is referred to in subsection (5), or any such adjustment of benefits as is referred to in subsection (12), to ensure that any such disposal, appropriation or adjustment, as the case may be, is in keeping with the requirements of this section, and for the purposes of subsection (12) the Commissioners may consult with such other persons as, in their opinion, may be of assistance to them.][7]

Amendments

[1, 2] Substituted by F(No.2)A13 s71(a)(i).

[3] Substituted by F(No.2)A13 s71(a)(ii).

[4] Substituted by FA12 s105(3).

[5] Substituted by F(No.2)A13 s71(b).

[6] Substituted by F(No.2)A13 s71(c).

[7] Inserted by F(No.2)A11 s4(1)(a).

Revenue Briefings

Tax Briefing

Issue Number 04 – 2011 Finance (No.2) Act 2011 – Levy on Pension Schemes

eBrief

eBrief No. 39/2011 – Levy on Pension Schemes

126 Certain statements of interest

[FA1986 s94(1) to (8)]

(1) (a) In this section—

"*corporation tax*" means the corporation tax charged by the Taxes Consolidation Act, 1997;

"*Corporation Tax Acts*" has the same meaning as in section 1 of the Taxes Consolidation Act, 1997;

"*relevant interest*" means any interest or other distribution which—

(i) is received by a company (in this section referred to as "*the lender*") which is within the charge to corporation tax,

(ii) is payable out of the assets of another company (in this subsection referred to as "*the borrower*") which is resident in the State for the purposes of corporation tax, in respect of a security of the borrower which is a security falling within subparagraph (ii), (iii)(I) or (v) of section 130(2)(*d*) of the Taxes Consolidation Act, 1997, and

(iii) is a distribution for the purposes of the Corporation Tax Acts;

"*relevant period*" means any period of 6 months ending on the 31st day of January or the 31st day of July.

(b) For the purposes of this section, any amount which, in a relevant period, is debited to a borrower's account with a lender in respect of relevant interest shall be treated as an amount received by the lender in that relevant period.

(2) A lender shall, within 30 days from the end of each relevant period, deliver to the Commissioners a statement in writing showing the amount of the relevant interest for that lender in respect of that relevant period.

(3) There shall be charged on every statement delivered in pursuance of *subsection (2)* a stamp duty of an amount equal to 12 per cent of the amount of the relevant interest shown in the statement.

(4) Notwithstanding *subsection (3)*, in a case where the amount of the relevant interest received by a lender in respect of a security referred to in *subsection (1)* is an amount which is less than what would have been received by that lender had the security yielded simple interest at the rate of 6 per cent per annum throughout the period for which the relevant interest was payable, the stamp duty charged on the statement on the amount of the relevant interest for that security shall be an amount equal to 8 per cent of the amount received.

(5) The duty charged by *subsection (3)* on a statement delivered by a lender pursuant to *subsection (2)* shall be paid by the lender on delivery of the statement.

(6) There shall be furnished to the Commissioners by a lender such particulars as the Commissioners may deem necessary in relation to any statement required by this section to be delivered by a lender.

(7) In the case of failure by a lender to deliver any statement required by *subsection (2)* within the time specified in that subsection or of failure by a lender to pay any duty chargeable on any such statement on the delivery of such statement, the lender shall be liable to pay,[...][1] in addition to the duty, interest on the duty at the rate of 2.5 per cent for each month or part of a month from the expiration of the relevant period to which the statement relates until the date on which the duty is paid.

(8) The delivery of any statement required by *subsection (2)* may be enforced by the Commissioners under section 47 of the Succession Duty Act, 1853, in all respects as if such statement were such account as is mentioned in that section and the failure to deliver such statement were such default as is mentioned in that section.

(9) The stamp duty charged by this section shall not be allowed as a deduction for the purposes of the computation of any tax or duty under the care and management of the Commissioners payable by the lender.

Amendments

[1] Deleted by F(No.2)A08 sched5(part5)(chap2)(7)(w).

Note:

F(No.2)A08 sched5 (part5)(chap 2)(7)

As respects paragraph 7 of this Schedule subparagraphs (a) to (aa) (other than subparagraph (c)(i)(I)) of that paragraph have effect as on and from the passing of this Act and to the extent that Chapter 3A (being inserted into Part 47 of the Taxes Consolidation Act 1997 by Part 1 of this Schedule) applies to penalties incurred under the Stamp Duties Consolidation Act 1999 before the passing of this Act which on the passing of this Act have not been paid, it shall not apply to such penalties which are in the form of interest accrued under any provisions of the said Act.

Cross References

To Section 126

Section 159D Calculation of interest on unpaid duty and other amounts.
Section 160 Repeals.
Schedule 4 Consequential Amendments

126A Levy on certain financial institutions

[(1) (a) In this section—

"*appropriate tax*" has the meaning assigned to it by section 256 of the Taxes Consolidation Act 1997;

"*assessable amount*", in relation to a relevant person, means the relevant retention tax in relation to the person;

"*average relevant deposits*", in relation to a company, means an amount specified in a notice given by the Central Bank to a company for the purposes of this section, being an amount equal to the average of the end-month amounts of non-Government deposits of Irish residents for each of the calendar months in the year 2001;

"*company*" has the same meaning as in section 4 of the Taxes Consolidation Act 1997;

"*non-Government deposits of Irish residents*", in relation to a company, means the amount specified as non-Government deposits of Irish residents in a return made by the company before 4 December 2002 to the Central Bank of Ireland in accordance with section 18 of the Central Bank Act 1971 (as amended by section 37 of the Central Bank Act 1989 and section 8 of the Central Bank Act 1998);

"*due date*" means—

(i) in respect of the year 2003, 20 October 2003,

(ii) in respect of the year 2004, 20 October 2004, and

(iii) in respect of the year 2005, 20 October 2005;

"*group assessable amount*", in relation to a year, means the aggregate of the assessable amounts in relation to companies which, at the due date for the year, are members of the group;

"*group relevant deposits*" for any year in relation to a group of companies, means the aggregate of the amounts of average relevant deposits in relation to companies which, on the due date for the year, are members of the group;

"*group stamp duty*", in relation to a group of companies, means the aggregate of the amounts of stamp duty which would, if *subsection (7)* were deleted, be payable under *subsection (6)* by companies which, on the due date for the year, are members of the group;

"*relevant person*" means a person who was obliged to pay—

(i) appropriate tax under section 258(3), or

(ii) an amount on account of appropriate tax under section 258(4) or 259(4),

of the Taxes Consolidation Act 1997 in the year 2001;

"*relevant retention tax*", in relation to a relevant person, means an amount determined by the formula—

$$A + B — C$$

where—

A is an amount equal to the aggregate of—

(i) appropriate tax paid by the person in the year 2001 under section 258(3) of the Taxes Consolidation Act 1997, and

(ii) the amount paid by the person in the year 2001 on account of appropriate tax under section 258(4) or 259(4) of that Act,

B is the aggregate of any amounts of appropriate tax, or any amounts on account of appropriate tax, paid by the person after the year 2001 which, in accordance with section 258 or 259 of that Act, should have been paid by the person in the year 2001, and

C is the aggregate of any amounts of appropriate tax paid by the person in the year 2001 which—

(i) are included in A, and

(ii) were agreed by the person and an officer of the Commissioners at or before the time of payment as being tax which, in accordance with the said section 258, should have been paid before the year 2001;

"*year 2001*" means the period of 12 months ending on 31 December 2001.

(b) For the purposes of this section—

(i) 2 companies shall be deemed to be members of a group if one company is a 51 per cent subsidiary (within the meaning of section 9 of the Taxes Consolidation Act 1997) of the other company or both companies are 51 per cent subsidiaries of a third company, and

(ii) a company and all its 51 per cent subsidiaries shall form a group and, where that company is a member of a group as being itself a 51 per cent subsidiary, that group shall comprise all its 51 per cent subsidiaries and the first-mentioned group shall be deemed not to be a group; but a company which is not a member of a group shall be treated as if it were a member of a group which consists of that company, and accordingly references to group assessable amount, group relevant deposits and group stamp duty shall be construed as if they were respectively references to assessable amount, relevant deposits and stamp duty of that company.

(2) A relevant person shall for each of the years 2003, 2004 and 2005, not later than the due date in respect of that year, deliver to the Commissioners a statement in writing showing—

(a) the assessable amount for that person, and

(b) any amount which has been apportioned to the person in accordance with *subsection (7)*.

(3) Where at any time in a period commencing on 1 January 2001 and ending immediately before a due date—

(a) a relevant person ceased to carry on a business in the course of which the person was obliged to pay any amount under section 258 or 259 of the Taxes Consolidation Act 1997, and

(b) another person (in this section referred to as the "*successor person*") acquired the whole, or substantially the whole, of the business,

the relevant person shall not be required to deliver a statement on the due date in accordance with *subsection (2)* but the successor person shall—

(i) where the successor person is, apart from this subsection, required to deliver a statement on the due date in accordance with *subsection (2)*, increase the assessable amount in that statement by the assessable amount in relation to the relevant person, and

(ii) in any other case, deliver a statement on the due date in accordance with *subsection (2)* as if the successor person were the relevant person.

(4) Where at any time in a period commencing at the time at which a successor person acquired the whole, or substantially the whole, of a business from the relevant person referred to in *subsection (3)* such that that subsection applies to the successor person and ending immediately before a due date—

(a) the successor person ceased to carry on the business so acquired, and

(b) another person (in this section referred to as the "*next successor person*") acquired the whole, or substantially the whole, of the business,

the successor person shall not be required to deliver a statement on the due date in accordance with *subsection (3)* but the next successor person shall—

(i) where the next successor person is, apart from this subsection, required to deliver a statement on the due date in accordance with *subsection (2)*, increase the assessable amount in that statement by the assessable amount in relation to the relevant person, and

(ii) in any other case, deliver a statement on the due date in accordance with *subsection (2)* as if the next successor person were the relevant person.

(5) Where at any time in a period commencing at the time at which a next successor person acquired the whole, or substantially the whole, of a business such that that person was required—

(a) to increase an assessable amount by an assessable amount in relation to a relevant person, or

(b) to deliver a statement as if the next successor person were a relevant person,

and ending immediately before a due date—

(i) the next successor person ceased to carry on the business so acquired, and

(ii) another person (in this section referred to as the "*further successor person*") acquired the whole, or substantially the whole, of the business,

the next successor person shall not be required to deliver a statement on the due date in accordance with *subsection (4)* but the further successor person shall—

(I) where the further successor person is, apart from this subsection, required to deliver a statement on the due date in accordance with *subsection (2)*, increase the assessable amount in that statement by the assessable amount in relation to the relevant person, and

(II) in any other case, deliver a statement on the due date in accordance with *subsection (2)* as if the further successor person were the relevant person,

and so on for further successions.

(6) Subject to *subsection (7)*, there shall be charged on any statement delivered in accordance with *subsection (2)* a stamp duty of an amount equal to 50 per cent of the assessable amount.

(7) (a) Where, as respects a group of companies, the group stamp duty for a year exceeds an amount equal to 0.15 per cent of the group relevant deposits for the year, so much of the excess as bears to that amount the same proportion as the assessable amount for the year in relation to a company which is a member of the group bears to the group assessable amount for that year shall be apportioned to the company; but the companies which are members of the group may, by giving notice in writing to the Commissioners by the due date for that year, elect to have the excess apportioned in such manner as is specified in the notice.

(b) Where an amount (in this paragraph referred to as the "*apportioned amount*") has been apportioned to a company under *paragraph (a)*, the amount to be charged under *subsection (6)* shall be reduced by the apportioned amount.

(8) The stamp duty charged by *subsection (6)* upon a statement delivered by a relevant person in accordance with *subsection (2)* shall be paid by that person upon delivery of the statement.

(9) There shall be furnished to the Commissioners by a relevant person such particulars as the Commissioners may require in relation to any statement required by this section to be delivered by the person.

(10) In the case of failure by a relevant person—

(a) to deliver any statement required to be delivered by that person under *subsection (2)*, or

(b) to pay the stamp duty chargeable on any such statement,

on or before the due date in respect of the year concerned, the person shall, from the due date concerned until the day on which the stamp duty is paid, be liable to pay, by way of penalty, in addition to the stamp duty, [interest on the stamp duty, calculated in accordance with section 159D][1] and also from 20 October of the year in which the statement is to be delivered in accordance with *subsection (2)*, by way of penalty, a sum equal to 1 per cent of the stamp duty for each day the stamp duty remains unpaid and each penalty shall be recoverable in the same manner as if the penalty were part of the stamp duty.

(11) The delivery of any statement required by *subsection (2)* may be enforced by the Commissioners under section 47 of the Succession Duty Act 1853, in all respects as if such statement were such account as is mentioned in that section and the failure to deliver such statement were such default as is mentioned in that section.

(12) The stamp duty and any penalty due under *subsection (10)* charged by this section shall not be allowed as a deduction for the purposes of the computation of any tax or duty payable by the relevant person which is under the care and management of the Commissioners.][2]

Amendments

[1] Substituted by FA05 sched5.

[2] Inserted by FA03 s141.

126AA Further levy on certain financial institutions

[(1) In this section—

"*appropriate tax*" has the meaning assigned to it by *section 256* of the Taxes Consolidation Act 1997;

"*assessable amount*", in relation to a relevant person, means the relevant retention tax in relation to the person;

"*relevant business*" means the business of a relevant person of taking and holding relevant deposits (within the meaning of section 256 of the Taxes Consolidation Act 1997) in respect of which the person was obliged to pay any amount under *section 258* or *259* of the Taxes Consolidation Act 1997;

"*due date*" means—

(a) in respect of the year 2014, 20 October 2014,

(b) in respect of the year 2015, 20 October 2015, and

(c) in respect of the year 2016, 20 October 2016;

"*relevant person*" means—

(a) a person who, in the year 2011, was a holder of a licence granted under *section 9* of the Central Bank Act 1971 or held a licence or other similar authorisation under the law of any other Member State of the European Communities which corresponds to a licence granted under that section, or

(b) a person who, in the year 2011, was a building society within the meaning of the Building Societies Act 1989 or a society established in accordance with the law of any other Member State of the European Communities which corresponds to that Act,

and the person—

(i) was obliged, in the year 2011, to pay—

(I) appropriate tax under *section 258(3)* of the Taxes Consolidation Act 1997, or

(II) an amount on account of appropriate tax under *section 258(4)* or *259(4)* of that Act,

and

(ii) is carrying on a trade or business in the State (whether including a relevant business or not),

but a person shall not be regarded as a relevant person where the relevant retention tax in relation to the person in the year 2011 did not exceed €100,000;

"*relevant retention tax*", in relation to a relevant person, means an amount determined by the formula—

$$A + B - C$$

where—

A is an amount equal to the aggregate of—

(a) appropriatetax paid by the person in the year 2011 under *section 258(3)* of the Taxes Consolidation Act 1997, and

(b) the amount paid by the person in the year 2011 on account of appropriate tax under *section 258(4)* or *259(4)* of that Act,

B is the aggregate of any amounts of appropriate tax, or any amounts on account of appropriate tax, paid by the person after the year 2011 which, in accordance with *section 258* or *259* of that Act, should have been paid by the person in the year 2011, and

C is the aggregate of any amounts of appropriate tax paid by the person in the year 2011 which—

(a) are included in A, and

(b) were agreed by the person and an officer of the Commissioners at or before the time of payment as being tax which, in accordance with the said *section 258*, should have been paid before the year 2011;

"*year 2011*" means the period of 12 months ending on 31 December 2011.

(2) A relevant person shall for each of the years 2014, 2015 and 2016, not later than the due date in respect of that year, deliver to the Commissioners a statement in writing showing the assessable amount for that person.

(3) Where at any time in a period commencing on 1 January 2011 and ending immediately before a due date—

(a) a relevant person ceased to carry on a relevant business, and

(b) another person (in this section referred to as the 'successor person') acquired the whole, or substantially the whole, of the relevant business,

the relevant person shall not be required to deliver a statement on the due date in accordance with *subsection (2)* but the successor person shall—

(i) where the successor person is, apart from this subsection, required to deliver a statement on the due date in accordance with *subsection (2)*, increase the assessable amount in that statement by the assessable amount in relation to the relevant person, and

(ii) in any other case, deliver a statement on the due date in accordance with *subsection (2)* as if the successor person were the relevant person.

(4) Where at any time in a period commencing at the time at which a successor person acquired the whole, or substantially the whole, of a relevant business from the relevant person referred to in *subsection (3)* such that that subsection applies to the successor person and ending immediately before a due date—

(a) the successor person ceased to carry on the relevant business so acquired, and

(b) another person (in this section referred to as the 'next successor person') acquired the whole, or substantially the whole, of the relevant business,

the successor person shall not be required to deliver a statement on the due date in accordance with *subsection (3)* but the next successor person shall—

(i) where the next successor person is, apart from this subsection, required to deliver a statement on the due date in accordance with *subsection (2)*, increase the assessable amount in that statement by the assessable amount in relation to the relevant person, and

(ii) in any other case, deliver a statement on the due date in accordance with *subsection (2)* as if the next successor person were the relevant person.

(5) Where at any time in a period commencing at the time at which a next successor person acquired the whole, or substantially the whole, of a relevant business such that that person was required—

(a) to increase an assessable amount by an assessable amount in relation to a relevant person, or

(b) to deliver a statement as if the next successor person were a relevant person,

and ending immediately before a due date—

(i) the next successor person ceased to carry on the relevant business so acquired, and

(ii) another person (in this section referred to as the 'further successor person') acquired the whole, or substantially the whole, of the relevant business,

the next successor person shall not be required to deliver a statement on the due date in accordance with *subsection (4)* but the further successor person shall—

(I) where the further successor person is, apart from this subsection, required to deliver a statement on the due date in accordance with *subsection (2)*, increase the assessable amount in that statement by the assessable amount in relation to the relevant person, and

(II) in any other case, deliver a statement on the due date in accordance with *subsection (2)* as if the further successor person were the relevant person,

and so on for further successions.

(6) There shall be charged on any statement delivered in accordance with *subsection (2)* a stamp duty of an amount equal to 35 per cent of the assessable amount.

(7) The stamp duty charged by *subsection (6)* upon a statement delivered by a relevant person in accordance with *subsection (2)* shall be paid by that person upon delivery of the statement.

(8) There shall be furnished to the Commissioners by a relevant person such particulars as the Commissioners may require in relation to any statement required by this section to be delivered by the person.

(9) In the case of failure by a relevant person—

(a) to deliver any statement required to be delivered by that person under *subsection (2)*, or

(b) to pay the stamp duty chargeable on any such statement,

on or before the due date in respect of the year concerned, the person shall, from the due date concerned until the day on which the stamp duty is paid, be liable to pay, in addition to the stamp duty, interest on the stamp duty, calculated in accordance with *section 159D* and also from 20 October of the year in which the statement is to be delivered in accordance with *subsection (2)*, by way of penalty, a sum of €380 for each day the stamp duty remains unpaid.

(10) The delivery ofany statement required by *subsection (2)* may be enforced by the Commissioners under section 47 of the Succession Duty Act 1853, in all respects as if such statement were such account as is mentioned in that section and the failure to deliver such statement were such default as is mentioned in that section.

(11) The stamp duty, interest on the stamp duty and any penalty due under *subsection (9)* charged by this section shall not be allowed as a deduction for the purposes of the computation of any tax or duty payable by the relevant person which is under the care and management of the Commissioners.][1]

Amendments

[1] Inserted by F(No.2)A13 s72.

126B Assessment of duty charged on statements

[(1) In this section—

"*relevant person*" means—

(a) a bank or building society within the meaning of section 123, 123A or 123B,

(b) an accountable person within the meaning of section 123C (inserted by the *Finance Act 2008*) or 124A (inserted by the *Finance Act 2008*),

[(c) a bank or promoter within the meaning of section 124,

[(d) an insurer within the meaning of *section 124B*,

(e) an insurer within the meaning of *section 125*,

(f) an authorised insurer within the meaning of *section 125A*, [...][1]

(g) a chargeable person within the meaning of [*section 125B*, or][2]][3]][4]

[(h) a relevant person within the meaning of *section 126AA*;][5]

"*Appeal Commissioners*" has the meaning assigned to it by section 850 of the Taxes Consolidation Act 1997;

["*specified section*" means section 123, 123A, 123B, 123C, 124, 124A, [124B, [125, [125A, 125B or 126AA][6, 7]][8].][9]

(2) Where, at any time, it appears to the Commissioners, that a relevant person—

(a) has failed to deliver a statement, or

(b) has not delivered a full and proper statement,

required to be delivered under a specified section, the Commissioners may make an assessment on the relevant person of the amount which, to the best of their judgment, is the amount of stamp duty which would have been charged on the statement if it had been delivered and if it were full and proper.

(3) The Commissioners may serve notice in writing of the assessment of stamp duty on any relevant person.

(4) Subject to subsection (5), where an assessment is made on a relevant person under subsection (2), the relevant person shall be liable—

(a) where the relevant person has failed to deliver a statement, for the payment of the stamp duty assessed, and any [interest and penalty][10] in relation to the duty as if the duty was charged on the statement, unless on delivery of the statement to them, the Commissioners make another assessment to be substituted for such assessment, or

(b) where the relevant person has not delivered a full and proper statement, for payment of the stamp duty assessed, and any [interest and penalty][11] relating to the duty as if the duty was charged on the statement,

[...][12]

(5) A relevant person who is dissatisfied with an assessment of the Commissioners made on the person under subsection (2) may, on payment of the duty in conformity with the assessment, appeal to the Appeal Commissioners against the assessment by giving notice in writing to the Commissioners within 30 days of the date of the assessment, and the appeal shall be heard and determined by the Appeal Commissioners whose determination shall be final and conclusive unless the appeal is required to be reheard by a judge of the Circuit Court or a case is required to be stated in relation to it for the opinion of the High Court on a point of law.

(6) Subject to this section, Chapter 1 of Part 40 (Appeals) of the Taxes Consolidation Act 1997, shall, with any necessary modifications, apply as it applies for the purpose of income tax.

(7) If at any time it appears that for any reason an assessment is incorrect the Commissioners shall make such other assessment as they consider appropriate, which assessment shall be substituted for the first-mentioned assessment.

(8) If at any time it appears that for any reason the assessment was an underassessment the Commissioners shall make such additional assessment as they consider appropriate.

(9) Where an assessment referred to in this section becomes final and conclusive, the assessment shall have the same force and effect as if it were an assessment in respect of which no notice of appeal had been given, and subsection (4) shall apply accordingly.

[...][13]][14]

Amendments

[1] Deleted by FA14 s76(a)(i).

[2] Substituted by FA14 s76(a)(ii).

[3] Substituted by FA12 s105(4)(a).

[4] Substituted by F(No.2) A11 s4(1)(b)(i).

[5] Inserted by FA14 s76(a)(iii).

[6] Substituted by FA12 s105(4)(b).

[7] Substituted by FA14 s76(b).

[8] Substituted by F(No.2)A11 s4(1)(b)(ii).

[9] Substituted by FA09 s26(1)(c)

[10, 11] Substituted by F(No.2)A08 sched5(part5)(chap2)(7)(x).

[12, 13] Deleted by F(No.2)A08 sched4(part1). Applies as respects any tax that becomes due and payable on or after 1 March 2009.

[14] Inserted by FA08 s124 with effect from 1 January 2008.

Note:

F(No.2)A08 sched5 (part5)(chap 2)(7)

As respects paragraph 7 of this Schedule subparagraphs (a) to (aa) (other than subparagraph (c)(i)(I)) of that paragraph have effect as on and from the passing of this Act and to the extent that Chapter 3A (being inserted into Part 47 of the Taxes Consolidation Act 1997 by Part 1 of this Schedule) applies to penalties incurred under the Stamp Duties Consolidation Act 1999 before the passing of this Act which on the passing of this Act have not been paid, it shall not apply to such penalties which are in the form of interest accrued under any provisions of the said Act.

Cross References

From Section 126B

Section 123 Cash cards.
Section 123A Debit cards.
Section 123B Cash, combined and debit cards.
Section 123C Preliminary duty: cash, combined and debit cards.
Section 124 Credit cards and charge cards.
Section 124A Preliminary duty: credit and charge cards.
Section 124B Certain premiums of life assurance.
Section 125 Certain premiums of insurance.
Section 125B Levy on pension schemes.

To Section 126B

Section 5 Agreement as to payment of stamp duty on instruments.
Section 125A Levy on authorised insurers.

PART 10

Enforcement

127 Terms on which instruments not duly stamped may be received in evidence

[SA1891 s14]

(1) On the production of an instrument chargeable with any duty as evidence in any court of civil judicature in any part of the State, or before any arbitrator or referee, notice shall be taken by the judge, arbitrator, or referee of any omission or insufficiency of the stamp on the instrument, and if the instrument is one which may legally be stamped after execution, it may, on payment to the officer of the court whose duty it is to read the instrument, or to the arbitrator or referee, of the amount of the unpaid [duty, including any surcharge incurred under *section 14A(3)*, and interest][1] payable on stamping the same, be received in evidence, saving all just exceptions on other grounds.

(2) The officer, or arbitrator, or referee receiving the [duty, including any surcharge incurred under *section 14A(3)*, and interest][2] shall give a receipt for the same, and make an entry in a book kept for that purpose of the payment and of the amount of the payment, and shall communicate to the Commissioners the name or title of the proceeding in which, and of the party from whom, the officer, or arbitrator, or referee, as the case may be, received the [duty, including any surcharge incurred under *section 14A(3)*, and interest][3], and the date and description of the instrument, and shall pay over to such person as the Commissioners may appoint the money received by such officer, arbitrator or referee, [as the case may be, for the duty, including any surcharge incurred under *section 14A(3)*, and interest][4] [...][5].

[(3) On production to the Commissioners of any instrument on which any duty, including any surcharge incurred under *section 14A(3)*, and interest has been paid under subsection (1), together with the receipt, and an electronic return or a paper return has been delivered to the Commissioners, the Commissioners shall treat the duty, including any surcharge incurred under *section 14A(3)*, and interest as paid in the e-stamping system.][6]

(4) Except as provided for in this section, an instrument executed in any part of the State, or relating, wherever executed, to any property situated, or to any matter or thing done or to be done, in any part of the State, shall not, except in criminal proceedings or in civil proceedings by the Commissioners to recover stamp duty, be given in evidence, or be available for any purpose, unless it is not chargeable with duty or it is duly stamped in accordance with the law in force at the time when it was first executed.

[(5) For the purposes of *subsection (4)*, an instrument that has been stamped by means of the e-stamping system is deemed to have been duly stamped notwithstanding any objection relating to duty.][7]

Amendments

[1] Substituted by FA12 sched3(32)(a). In effect for all instruments that are executed on or after 7 July 2012 per SI No. 228 of 2012.

[2, 3] Substituted by FA12 sched3(32)(b). In effect for all instruments that are executed on or after 7 July 2012 per SI No. 228 of 2012.

[4] Substituted by FA13 sched2(2)(d).

[5] Deleted by FA12 sched3(32)(b). In effect for all instruments that are executed on or after 7 July 2012 per SI No. 228 of 2012.

[6] Substituted by FA12 sched3(32)(c). In effect for all instruments that are executed on or after 7 July 2012 per SI No. 228 of 2012.

[7] Inserted by FA12 sched3(32)(d). In effect for all instruments that are executed on or after 7 July 2012 per SI No. 228 of 2012.

Case Law

Evidence cannot include an unstamped document. Sun Alliance Insurance Ltd v IRC 1972 Ch 133

Cross References

To Section 127

Section 12 Particulars delivered stamps.
Section 27 Stamping of certain foreign bills of exchange.
Section 30 Voluntary dispositions inter vivos chargeable as conveyances or transfers on sale.
Section 71 Application and adaptation of other Parts of this Act.

128 Rolls, books, etc., to be open to inspection

[SA1891 s16]

(1) In this section "*document*" includes—

(a) any instrument, roll, book or record,

(b) any record of an entry in a document, and

(c) any information stored, maintained or preserved by means of any mechanical or electronic device, whether or not stored, maintained or preserved in a legible form.

(2) Subject to *subsection (3)*, any person who is a party to any instrument, or who has in his or her custody or under his or her control any document, the inspection of which may tend to secure any duty, or to prove or lead to the discovery of any fraud, negligence, or omission in relation to any duty shall, within 14 days of a request by means of a notice in writing from the Commissioners—

(a) provide such information as the Commissioners deem necessary, and

(b) permit any person authorised by the Commissioners, to inspect any such document and to take such notes, extracts, prints, printouts and copies as such person may deem necessary,

and in case of refusal to so provide or permit by the first-mentioned person, that refusal shall be deemed to constitute a failure by that person to comply with subparagraph (iv) of paragraph (*g*) of subsection (2) of section 1078 of the Taxes Consolidation Act, 1997, and if the refusal continues after conviction such person shall be guilty of a further offence on every day on which the refusal continues and for each such offence such person shall be liable to a fine not exceeding [€125][1].

(3) It shall be a good defence in a prosecution for an offence under *subsection (2)* for the accused to show that the accused is required or entitled by law to refuse the request of the Commissioners.

Amendments

[1] Substituted by FA01 sched5.

Cross References

To Section 128

Schedule 4 Consequential Amendments

128A Obligation to retain records

[(1) In this section—

'*records*' includes books, accounts, documents and any other data maintained manually or by any electronic, photographic or other process, relating to—

(a) a liability to stamp duty, and

(b) a relief or any exemption claimed under any provision of this Act.

(2) Every accountable person shall retain, or cause to be retained on his or her behalf, records of the type referred to in *subsection (1)* as are required to enable—

(a) a true return or statement to be made for the purposes of this Act, and

(b) a claim to a relief or an exemption under any provision of this Act to be substantiated.

(3) Any records required to be retained by virtue of this section shall be retained—

(a) in its written form, or

(b) subject to *section 887(2)* of the Taxes Consolidation Act 1997, by means of any electronic, photographic or other process.

(4) Records retained for the purposes of *subsections (2)* and *(3)* shall be retained by the person required to retain the records for a period of 6 years commencing on the later of—

(a) the date an electronic return or a paper return was delivered to the Commissioners, or

(b) the date that the duty was paid to the Commissioners.

(5) Any person who fails to comply with *subsection (2)*, *(3)*or*(4)* in respectof the retention of any records relating to a liability to stamp duty, or a relief or an exemption, is liable to a penalty of €3,000.]

Amendments

[1] Inserted by FA12 sched3(33). In effect for all instruments that are executed on or after 7 July 2012 per SI No. 228 of 2012.

128B Power of inspection

[(1) In this section—

'*authorised officer*' means an officer of the Revenue Commissioners authorised by them in writing to exercise the powers conferred by this section;

'*employee*' means an employee who by virtue of his or her employment is in a position to, or to procure—

(a) the production of the books, records or other documents,

(b) the furnishing of information, explanations and particulars, and

(c) the giving of all assistance, to an authorised officer, as may be required under *subsection (3)*;

'*records*' has the same meaning as in *section 128A*;

'*relevant person*' means an accountable person and, where records are retained on his or her behalf, a person who retains the records;

'*return*' means an electronic return or a paper return.

(2) An authorised officer may at all reasonable times enter any premises or place of business of a relevant person for the purpose of auditing a return.

(3) An authorised officer may require a relevant person or an employee of the relevant person to produce records or other documents and to furnish information, explanations and particulars and to give all assistance, which the authorised officer reasonably requires for the purposes of his or her audit under *subsection (2)*.

(4) An authorised officer may take extracts from or copies of all or any part of the records or other documents or other material made available to him or her or require that copies of records or other documents be made available to him or her, in exercising or performing his or her powers or duties under this section.

(5) An authorised officer when exercising or performing his or her powers or duties under this section shall, on request, produce his or her authorisation for the purposes of this section.

(6) An employee of a relevant person who fails to comply with the requirements of the authorised officer in the exercise or performance of the authorised officer's powers or duties under this section shall be liable to a penalty of €1,265.

(7) A relevant person who fails to comply with the requirements of the authorised officer in the exercise or performance of the authorised officer's powers or duties under this section shall be liable to a penalty of €19,045 and if that failure continues a further penalty of €2,535 for each day on which the failure continues.][1]

Amendments

[1] Inserted by FA12 sched3(33). In effect for all instruments that are executed on or after 7 July 2012 per SI No. 228 of 2012.

129 Penalty for enrolling, etc., instrument not duly stamped, etc.

[SA1891 s17 and s41]

(1) If any person whose office it is to enrol, register, or enter in or on any rolls, books, or records any instrument chargeable with duty, enrols, registers, or enters any such instrument not being duly stamped, such person shall incur a penalty of [€630][1].

(2) A bill of sale which is chargeable to stamp duty shall not be registered under any Act for the time being in force relating to the registration of bills of sale unless the original, duly stamped, is produced to the proper officer.

Amendments

[1] Substituted by FA01 sched5.

Cross References

To Section 129

Section 71 Application and adaptation of other Parts of this Act.

130 Assignment of policy of life insurance to be stamped before payment of money assured

[SA1891 s118; FA 1924 s38(1)]

(1) No assignment of a policy of life insurance which is chargeable to stamp duty shall confer on the assignee named in that assignment, the assignee's executors, administrators, or assigns, any right to sue for the moneys assured or secured by the policy, or to give a valid discharge for the moneys, or any part of the moneys, unless the assignment is duly stamped, and no payment shall be made to any person claiming under any such assignment unless the same is duly stamped.

(2) If any payment is made in contravention of this section, the stamp duty not paid on the assignment, together with the [interest and penalty][1] payable on stamping the same, shall be a debt due to the Minister for the benefit of the Central Fund from the person by whom the payment is made and shall be payable to the Commissioners and may (without prejudice to any other mode of recovery of the duty or of the [interest and penalty][2] payable on stamping) be sued for and recovered by action, or other appropriate proceeding, at the suit of the Attorney General in any court of competent jurisdiction.

Amendments

[1, 2] Substituted by F(No.2)A08 sched5(part5)(chap2)(7)(z).

Note:

F(No.2)A08 sched5 (part5)(chap 2)(7)

As respects paragraph 7 of this Schedule subparagraphs (a) to (aa) (other than subparagraph (c)(i)(I)) of that paragraph have effect as on and from the passing of this Act and to the extent that Chapter 3A (being inserted into Part 47 of the Taxes Consolidation Act 1997 by Part 1 of this Schedule) applies to penalties incurred under the Stamp Duties Consolidation Act 1999 before the passing of this Act which on the passing of this Act have not been paid, it shall not apply to such penalties which are in the form of interest accrued under any provisions of the said Act.

131 Conditions and agreements as to stamp duty void [Deleted]

Deleted by FA13 s77(i).

132 Application of section 962 of Taxes Consolidation Act, 1997 [Deleted]

Deleted by F(No.2)A08 sched4(part1). Applies as respects any tax that becomes due and payable on or after 1 March 2009.

133 Application of certain provisions relating to penalties under Taxes Consolidation Act, 1997

[FA1991 s109(1)]

Sections 987(4), 1061, 1062, 1063, 1064, […][1] 1066 and 1068 of the Taxes Consolidation Act, 1997, shall, with any necessary modifications, apply to a fine or penalty under—

(a) this Act, or

(b) any other enactment providing for fines or penalties in relation to stamp duty,

as if the fine or penalty were a penalty under the Income Tax Acts, and section 22 of the Inland Revenue Regulation Act, 1890, shall not apply in a case to which any of those sections of the Taxes Consolidation Act, 1997, apply by virtue of this section.

Amendments

[1] Deleted by F(No.2)A13 s78(4).

134 Evidence in proceedings for recovery of stamp duty, etc. [Deleted]

Deleted by F(No.2)A08 sched4(part1). Applies as respects any tax that becomes due and payable on or after 1 March 2009.

134A Penalties

[(1) In this section—

"*carelessly*" means failure to take reasonable care;

"*liability to duty*" means a liability to the amount of the difference specified in subsection (7), (8) or (9) arising from any matter referred to in subsections (2) and (4);

"*instruction*", "*relevant system*" and "*system-member*" have each the same meaning as they have, respectively, in section 68(2);

['*person*' means—

(a) for the purposes of *subsections (2)(b)* and *(4)(b)*, a system-member,

(b) for the purposes of *subsections (2)(c)* and *(4)(c)*, an accountable person where an electronic return or a paper return is caused to be delivered, or is delivered, to the Commissioners, and

(c) for the purposes of *subsection (2)(d)*, an accountable person where an electronic return or a paper return, which is required to be delivered, is not delivered to the Commissioners;][1]

"*prompted qualifying disclosure*", in relation to a person, means a qualifying disclosure that has been made to the Commissioners or to a Revenue officer in the period between—

(a) the date on which the person is notified by a Revenue officer of the date on which an investigation or inquiry into any matter occasioning a liability to duty of that person will start, and

(b) the date that the investigation or inquiry starts;

"*qualifying disclosure*", in relation to a person, means—

(a) in relation to a penalty referred to in subsection (3), a disclosure that the Commissioners are satisfied is a disclosure of complete information in relation to, and full particulars of, all matters occasioning a liability to duty that gives rise to a penalty referred to in subsection (3), and full particulars of all matters occasioning any liability to tax that gives rise to a penalty referred to in section 1077E(4) of the Taxes Consolidation Act 1997, section 116(4) of the Value-Added Tax Consolidation Act 2010 and the application of section 1077E(4) of the Taxes Consolidation Act 1997 to the Capital Acquisitions Tax Consolidation Act 2003, and

(b) in relation to a penalty referred to in subsection (5), a disclosure that the Commissioners are satisfied is a disclosure of complete information in relation to, and full particulars of, all matters occasioning a liability to duty that gives rise to a penalty referred to in subsection (5),

made in writing to the Commissioners or to a Revenue officer and signed by or on behalf of that person and that is accompanied by—

(i) a declaration, to the best of that person's knowledge, information and belief, made in writing that all matters contained in the disclosure are correct and complete, and

(ii) a payment of the tax and duty payable in respect of any matter contained in the disclosure and the interest on late payment of that tax and duty;

"*Revenue officer*" means an officer of the Commissioners;

"*unprompted qualifying disclosure*", in relation to a person, means a qualifying disclosure that the Revenue Commissioners are satisfied has been voluntarily furnished to them—

(a) before an investigation or inquiry had been started by them or by a Revenue officer into any matter occasioning a liability to duty of that person, or

(b) where the person is notified by a Revenue officer of the date on which an investigation or inquiry into any matter occasioning a liability to duty of that person will start, before that notification.

(2) Where any person deliberately—

(a) executes any instrument in which all the facts and circumstances affecting the liability of such instrument to duty, or the amount of the duty with which such instrument is chargeable, are not fully and truly set forth in the instrument or in any statement to which section 8(2) relates,

(b) enters or causes to be entered an incorrect instruction in a relevant system and such incorrect instruction gives rise to an underpayment of stamp duty, or results in a claim for exemption from duty to which there is no entitlement, [...][2]

(c) causes an incorrect electronic return or a paper return to be delivered, or delivers an incorrect electronic return or a paper return, to the Commissioners which does not reflect all the facts and circumstances affecting the liability of such instrument to duty or the amount of the duty with which such instrument is chargeable that are required by the Commissioners to be disclosed on [such return, or][3]

[(d) fails to deliver or cause to be delivered an electronic return or a paper return which is required to be delivered to the Commissioners,][4]

then that person shall incur a penalty of €1,265 and a further penalty.

(3) The further penalty referred to—

(a) in subsection (2) in relation to paragraph (*a*) of that subsection, shall be the amount specified in subsection (7),

(b) in subsection (2) in relation to paragraph (*b*) of that subsection, shall be the amount specified in subsection (8), [...][5]

(c) in subsection (2) in relation to paragraph (*c*) of that subsection, shall be the amount specified in [subsection (9), and][6]

[(d) in *subsection (2)* in relation to *paragraph (d)* of that subsection, shall be the amount specified in *subsection (9A)*,][7]

reduced, where the person who incurred the penalty co-operated fully with any investigation or inquiry started by the Commissioners or by a Revenue officer into any matter occasioning a liability to duty of that person, to—

(i) 75 per cent of that amount where paragraph (ii) or (iii) does not apply,

(ii) 50 per cent of that amount where a prompted qualifying disclosure has been made by the person, or

(iii) 10 per cent of that amount where an unprompted qualifying disclosure has been made by the person.

(4) Where any person carelessly but not deliberately—

(a) executes any instrument in which all the facts and circumstances affecting the liability of such instrument to duty, or the amount of the duty with which such instrument is chargeable, are not fully and truly set forth in the instrument or in any statement to which section 8(2) relates,

(b) enters or causes to be entered an incorrect instruction in a relevant system and such incorrect instruction gives rise to an underpayment of duty, or results in a claim for exemption from duty to which there is no entitlement, [...][8]

(c) causes an incorrect electronic return or a paper return to be delivered, or delivers an incorrect electronic return or a paper return, to the Commissioners which does not reflect all the facts and circumstances affecting the liability of such instrument to duty or the amount of the duty with which such instrument is chargeable that are required by the Commissioners to be disclosed on [such return, or][9] [(d) fails to deliver or cause to be delivered an electronic return or a paper return which is required to be delivered to the Commissioners,][10]

then that person shall incur a penalty of €1,265 and a further penalty.

(5) (a) The further penalty referred to—

(i) in subsection (4) in relation to paragraph (*a*) of that subsection, shall be the amount specified in subsection (7),

(ii) in subsection (4) in relation to paragraph (*b*) of that subsection, shall be the amount specified in subsection (8), and

(iii) in subsection (4) in relation to paragraph (*c*) of that subsection, shall be the amount specified in subsection (9),

reduced to 40 per cent where the excess referred to in subparagraph (I) of paragraph (*b*) applies and to 20 per cent in other cases.

(b) Where the person who incurred the penalty co-operated fully with any investigation or inquiry started by the Commissioners or by a Revenue officer into any matter occasioning a liability to duty of that person the further penalty referred to—

(i) in subsection (4) in relation to paragraph (*a*) of that subsection, shall be the amount specified in subsection (7),

(ii) in subsection (4) in relation to paragraph (*b*) of that subsection, shall be the amount specified in subsection (8), and

(iii) in subsection (4) in relation to paragraph (*c*) of that subsection, shall be the amount specified in subsection (9),

reduced—

(I) where the amount of the difference referred to in subsection (7), (8) or (9), as the case may be, exceeds 15 per cent of the amount referred to in subsection (7)(*b*), (8)(*b*) or (9)(*b*), as the case may be, to—

(A) 30 per cent of the amount of the difference (in clauses (B) and (C) referred to as "*that amount*") where clause (B) or (C) does not apply,

(B) 20 per cent of that amount where a prompted qualifying disclosure has been made by that person, or

(C) 5 per cent of that amount where an unprompted qualifying disclosure has been made by that person,

or

(II) where the amount of the difference referred to in subsection (7), (8) or (9), as the case may be, does not exceed 15 per cent of the amount referred to in subsection (7)(*b*), (8)(*b*) or (9)(*b*), as the case may be, to—

(A) 15 per cent of the amount of the difference (in clauses (B) and (C) referred to as "*that amount*") where clause (B) or (C) does not apply,

(B) 10 per cent of that amount where a prompted qualifying disclosure has been made by that person, or

(C) 3 per cent of that amount where an unprompted qualifying disclosure has been made by that person.

[(5A) (a) The further penalty referred to in *subsection (4)* in relation to *paragraph (d)* of that subsection, shall be the amount specified in *subsection (9A)* reduced to 40 per cent.

(b) Where the person who incurred the penalty co-operated fully with any investigation or enquiry started by the Commissioners or by a Revenue officer into any matter occasioning a liability to duty of that person, the further penalty referred to in *subsection (4)* in relation to *paragraph (d)* of that subsection, shall be the amount specified in *subsection (9A)* reduced to—

(i) 30 per cent of that amount where *subparagraph (ii)* or *(iii)* does not apply,

(ii) 20 per cent of that amount where a prompted qualifying disclosure has been made by that person, or

(iii) 5 per cent of that amount where an unprompted qualifying disclosure has been made by that person.][11]

(6) Where any person neither deliberately nor carelessly—

(a) executes an instrument and it comes to that person's notice that the instrument or any statement to which section 8(2) relates does not fully and truly set forth all the facts and circumstances,

(b) enters or causes to be entered an instruction in a relevant system and it comes to that person's notice that the instruction was an incorrect instruction, [...][12]

(c) causes to be delivered or delivers an electronic return or a paper return and it comes to that person's notice that the electronic return or paper return does not reflect all the facts and circumstances that are required by the Commissioners to be disclosed on [such return, or][13]

[(d) fails to deliver or cause to be delivered an electronic return or a paper return which is required to be delivered to the Commissioners,][14]

then, unless the error is remedied without unreasonable delay, the person shall be treated for the purposes of this section as having acted deliberately.

(7) The amount referred to in [subsection (3)(*a*) and paragraphs (*a*)(i) and (*b*)(i) of subsection (5)][15] shall be the amount of the difference between—

(a) the amount of duty payable in respect of the instrument based on the facts and circumstances set forth and delivered, and

(b) the amount of the duty which would have been the amount so payable if the instrument and any accompanying statement had fully and truly set forth all the facts and circumstances referred to in subsections (1) and (2) of section 8.

(8) The amount referred to in [subsection (3)(*b*) and paragraphs (*a*)(ii) and (*b*)(ii) of subsection (5)][16] shall be the amount of the difference between—

(a) the duty so paid (if any), and

(b) the duty which would have been payable if the instruction had been entered correctly.

(9) The amount referred to in [subsection (3)(*c*) and paragraphs (*a*)(iii) and (*b*)(iii) of subsection (5)][17] shall be the amount of the difference between—

(a) the amount of duty payable in respect of the instrument based on the facts and circumstances disclosed on such return, and

(b) the amount of duty that would have been the amount so payable if all the facts and circumstances affecting the liability of such instrument to duty or the amount of the duty with which such instrument is chargeable, that are required to be disclosed on such return by the Commissioners, had been disclosed to them.

[(9A) The amount referred to in *subsection (3)(d)* and in *subsection (5A)* is the amount of duty that would have been payable if a return had been delivered.][18]

(10) Where a second qualifying disclosure is made by a person within 5 years of such person's first qualifying disclosure, then as regards matters pertaining to the second disclosure—

(a) in relation to subsection (3)—

(i) paragraph (ii) shall apply as if "75 per cent" were substituted for "50 per cent", and

(ii) paragraph (iii) shall apply as if "55 per cent" were substituted for "10 per cent", and

(b) in relation to subparagraph (I) of subsection (5)(*b*)—

(i) clause (B) shall apply as if "30 per cent" were substituted for "20 per cent", and

(ii) clause (C) shall apply as if "20 per cent" were substituted for "5 per cent".

(11) Where a third or subsequent qualifying disclosure is made by a person within 5 years of such person's second qualifying disclosure, then as regards matters pertaining to the third or subsequent disclosure, as the case may be—

(a) the further penalty referred to in paragraphs (*a*), (*b*) and (*c*) of subsection (3) shall not be reduced, and

(b) the reduction referred to in sub-paragraph (I) of subsection (5)(*b*) shall not apply.

(12) A disclosure, in relation to a person, shall not be a qualifying disclosure where—

(a) before the disclosure is made, a Revenue officer had started an inquiry or an investigation into any matter contained in that disclosure and had contacted or notified the person, or a person representing the person, in this regard, or

(b) matters contained in the disclosure are matters—

(i) that have become known or are about to become known, to the Commissioners through their own investigations or through an investigation conducted by a statutory body or agency,

(ii) that are within the scope of an inquiry being carried out wholly or partly in public, or

(iii) to which the person who made the disclosure is linked, or about to be linked, publicly.][19]

Amendments

[1] Substituted by FA12 sched3(34)(a). In effect for all instruments that are executed on or after 7 July 2012 per SI No. 228 of 2012.

[2] Deleted by FA12 sched3(34)(b). In effect for all instruments that are executed on or after 7 July 2012 per SI No. 228 of 2012.

[3] Substituted by FA12 sched3(34)(b). In effect for all instruments that are executed on or after 7 July 2012 per SI No. 228 of 2012.

[4] Inserted by FA12 sched3(34)(b). In effect for all instruments that are executed on or after 7 July 2012 per SI No. 228 of 2012.

[5] Deleted by FA12 sched3(34)(c). In effect for all instruments that are executed on or after 7 July 2012 per SI No. 228 of 2012.

[6] Substituted by FA12 sched3(34)(c). In effect for all instruments that are executed on or after 7 July 2012 per SI No. 228 of 2012.

[7] Inserted by FA12 sched3(34)(c). In effect for all instruments that are executed on or after 7 July 2012 per SI No. 228 of 2012.

[8] Deleted by FA12 sched3(34)(d). In effect for all instruments that are executed on or after 7 July 2012 per SI No. 228 of 2012.

[9] Substituted by FA12 sched3(34)(d). In effect for all instruments that are executed on or after 7 July 2012 per SI No. 228 of 2012.

[10] Inserted by FA12 sched3(34)(d). In effect for all instruments that are executed on or after 7 July 2012 per SI No. 228 of 2012.

[11] Inserted by FA12 sched3(34)(e). In effect for all instruments that are executed on or after 7 July 2012 per SI No. 228 of 2012.

[12] Deleted by FA12 sched3(34)(f). In effect for all instruments that are executed on or after 7 July 2012 per SI No. 228 of 2012.

[13] Substituted by FA12 sched3(34)(f). In effect for all instruments that are executed on or after 7 July 2012 per SI No. 228 of 2012.

[14] Inserted by FA12 sched3(34)(f). In effect for all instruments that are executed on or after 7 July 2012 per SI No. 228 of 2012.

[15] Substituted by FA09 s30(3)(c)(i). Has effect as respects penalties incurred on or after 3 June 2009.

[16] Substituted by FA09 s30(3)(c)(ii). Has effect as respects penalties incurred on or after 3 June 2009.

[17] Substituted by FA09 s30(3)(c)(iii). Has effect as on and from 24 December 2008.

[18] Inserted by FA12 sched3(34)(g). In effect for all instruments that are executed on or after 7 July 2012 per SI No. 228 of 2012.

[19] Inserted by F(No.2)A08 sched5(part5)(chap1)(5)(d). Has effect as respects penalties incurred on or after 24 December 2008.

Revenue Information Notes

Code of Practice for Revenue Audit and other compliance interventions 2014

Cross References

From Section 134A

Section 8 Facts and circumstances affecting duty to be set forth in instruments, etc.
Section 68 Interpretation (Part 6).

To Section 134A

Section 8 Facts and circumstances affecting duty to be set forth in instruments, etc.
Section 16 Surcharges to apply when apportionment is not just and reasonable.
Section 76 Obligations of system-members.

PART 11

Management Provisions

CHAPTER 1

Interpretation, Application and Care and Management

135 Interpretation (Part 11)

[SDMA1891 s27 (part); Par.16(1) I.R.(Adap.)O 1923]

In this Part—

"*duty*" means any stamp duty for the time being chargeable by law;

"*office of the Commissioners*" means an office of the Commissioners where stamps are provided;

"*officer*" means officer of the Commissioners;

"*stamp*" is a stamp provided or to be provided by a Government Department.

Cross References

To Section 135

Schedule 4 Consequential Amendments

136 Application (Part 11)

[SDMA1891 s1 (part)]

This Part shall apply to all duties and to all fees which are for the time being directed to be collected or received by means of stamps.

137 Stamp duties under care and management of the Commissioners

[SDMA1891 s1 (part)]

All duties for the time being chargeable by law as stamp duties shall be under the care and management of the Commissioners.

137A Information exchange with Property Registration Authority

[(1) In this section "*Authority*" means An tÚdarás Clárúcháin Maoine or, in the English language, the Property Registration Authority.

(2) The Authority shall, at such intervals as are specified by the Revenue Commissioners, supply to the Revenue Commissioners such information in the Authority's possession as may be required for the performance of the functions of the Revenue Commissioners under this Act.

(3) Notwithstanding any obligation to maintain secrecy or any other restriction on the disclosure or production of information obtained by or furnished to the Commissioners, the Commissioners shall, at such intervals as are specified by the Authority, supply to the Authority such information in the Commissioners' possession which may be required by the Authority when considering stamp duty in relation to documents presented for registration.][1]

Amendments

[1] Inserted by FA10 s(135). Has effect as on and from 3 April 2010.

137B Information exchange with Property Services Regulatory Authority

[(1) In this section "*Authority*" means An tUdarás Rialála Seirbhísí Maoine or, in the English language, the Property Services Regulatory Authority.

(2) Notwithstanding any obligation to maintain secrecy or any other restriction on the disclosure or production of information obtained by or furnished to the Commissioners, the Commissioners shall, at such intervals as are specified by the Authority on or after the establishment day within the meaning of *section 2(1)* of the *Property Services (Regulation) Act 2011*, supply to the Authority, such information in the Commissioners' e-stamping system (including information which was in that system before that establishment day) as may be required by the Authority for the performance of the functions of the Authority.][1]

Amendments

[1] Inserted by PS(R) A11 s9.

137C Provision of information to Commissioner of Valuation

[(1) In this section "*Commissioner of Valuation*" means a Commissioner appointed under *section 9(5)* of the Valuation Act 2001.

(2) Notwithstanding any obligation to maintain secrecy or any other restriction on the disclosure or production of information obtained by or furnished to the Commissioners, the Commissioners shall, at such intervals as are specified by the Commissioner of Valuation, supply to the Commissioner of Valuation such information in the Commissioners' e-stamping system as may be required by the Commissioner of Valuation for the performance of the functions of the Commissioner of Valuation.][1]

Amendments

[1] Inserted by PS(R) A11 s9.

CHAPTER 2

Mode of Recovering Money Received for Duty

138 Moneys received for duty and not appropriated to be recoverable in High Court [Deleted]

Deleted by F(No.2)A08 sched4(part1). Applies as respects any tax that becomes due and payable on or after 1 March 2009.

CHAPTER 3

Offences

139 Certain offences in relation to dies and stamps provided by the Commissioners to be offences

[SDMA1891 s13(3) to (9)]

Every person who does, or causes or procures to be done, or knowingly aids, abets, or assists in doing, any of the acts following, that is—

(a) fraudulently prints or makes an impression on any material from a genuine die;

(b) fraudulently cuts, tears, or in any way removes from any material any stamp, with intent that any use should be made of such stamp or of any part of such stamp;

(c) fraudulently mutilates any stamp, with intent that any use should be made of any part of such stamp;

(d) fraudulently fixes or places on any material or on any stamp, any stamp or part of a stamp which, whether fraudulently or not, has been cut, torn, or in any way removed from any other material, or out of or from any other stamp;

(e) fraudulently erases or otherwise either really or apparently removes from any stamped material any name, sum, date, or other matter or thing written on the stamped material, with the intent that any use should be made of the stamp on such material;

(f) knowingly sells or exposes for sale or utters or uses any stamp which has been fraudulently printed or impressed from a genuine die;

(g) knowingly, and without lawful excuse (the proof of which shall lie on the person accused) has in such person's possession any stamp which has been fraudulently printed or impressed from a genuine die, or any stamp or part of a stamp which has been fraudulently cut, torn, or otherwise removed from any material, or any stamp which has been fraudulently mutilated, or any stamped material out of which any name, sum, date, or other matter or thing has been fraudulently erased or otherwise either really or apparently removed,

shall be guilty of an offence and section 1078 (which relates to revenue offences) of the Taxes Consolidation Act, 1997, shall for the purposes of such offence be construed in all respects as if such offence were an offence under subsection (2) of that section.

Cross References

To Section 139

Section 140 Proceedings for detection of forged dies, etc.
Schedule 4 Consequential Amendments

140 Proceedings for detection of forged dies, etc.

[SDMA1891 s16]

On information given before a judge of the District Court on oath that there is just cause to suspect any person of being guilty of any of the offences specified in *section 139*, such judge may, by a warrant under his or her hand, cause every house, room, shop, building, or place belonging to or occupied by the suspected person, or where such person is suspected of being or having been in any way engaged or concerned in the commission of any such offence, or of secreting any machinery, implements, or utensils applicable to the commission of any such offence, to be searched, and if on such search any of those several matters and things are found, the same may be seized and carried away, and shall afterwards be delivered over to the Commissioners.

Cross References

From Section 140

Section 139 Certain offences in relation to dies and stamps provided by the Commissioners to be offences.

To Section 140

Schedule 4 Consequential Amendments

141 Proceedings for detection of stamps stolen or obtained fraudulently

[SDMA1891 s17]

(1) Any judge of the District Court having jurisdiction in the place where any stamps are known or supposed to be concealed or deposited, may, on reasonable suspicion that the same have been stolen or fraudulently obtained, issue a warrant for the seizure of the stamps, and for apprehending and bringing before such judge or any other judge of the District Court within the same jurisdiction the person in whose possession or custody the stamps may be found, to be dealt with according to law.

(2) If the person does not satisfactorily account for the possession of the stamps or it does not appear that the same were purchased by such person at an office of the Commissioners, or from some person duly appointed to sell and distribute stamps or duly licensed to deal in stamps, the stamps shall be forfeited, and shall be delivered over to the Commissioners.

(3) Notwithstanding *subsections (1)* and *(2)*, if at any time within 6 months after the delivery of the stamps under *subsection (2)* any person makes out to the satisfaction of the Commissioners that any stamps so forfeited were stolen or otherwise fraudulently obtained from such person, and that the same were purchased by such person at an office of the Commissioners, or from some person duly appointed to sell and distribute stamps, or duly licensed to deal in stamps, such stamps may be delivered up to such person.

Cross References

To Section 141

Schedule 4 Consequential Amendments

142 Licensed person in possession of forged stamps to be presumed guilty until contrary is shown

[SDMA1891 s18]

(1) If any forged stamps are found in the possession of any person appointed to sell and distribute stamps, or being or having been licensed to deal in stamps, that person shall be deemed and taken, unless the contrary is satisfactorily proved, to have had the same in his or her possession knowing them to be forged, and with intent to sell, use, or utter them, and shall be liable to the punishment imposed by law on a person selling, using, uttering, or having in possession forged stamps knowing the same to be forged.

(2) If the Commissioners have cause to suspect any such person of having in such person's possession any forged stamps, they may by warrant under their hands authorise any person to enter between the hours of 9 a.m. and 7 p.m. into any house, room, shop, or building of or belonging to the suspected person, and if on demand of admittance, and notice of the warrant, the door of the house, room, shop, or building, or any inner door of such house, room, shop, or building is not opened, the authorised person may break open the same and search for and seize any stamps that may be found in the house, room, shop or building or in the custody or possession of the suspected person.

(3) All members of the Garda Síochána are required, on request by any person authorised pursuant to *subsection (2),* to aid and assist in the execution of the warrant.

(4) Any person who—

(a) refuses to permit any such search or seizure to be made in accordance with *subsection (2)*, or

(b) assaults, opposes, molests, or obstructs any person so authorised in the due execution of the powers conferred by this section or any person acting to aid or assist a person so authorised,

and any member of the Garda Síochána who on a request under *subsection (3)* refuses or neglects to aid and assist any person so authorised in the due execution of such person's powers shall incur a penalty of [€1,265][1].

Amendments

[1] Substituted by FA01 sched5.

Cross References

To Section 142

Schedule 4 Consequential Amendments

143 Mode of proceeding when stamps are seized

[SDMA1891 s19]

Where stamps are seized under a warrant, the person authorised by the warrant shall, if required, give to the person in whose custody or possession the stamps are found an acknowledgement of the number, particulars, and amount of the stamps, and permit the stamps to be marked before the removal of those stamps.

144 Defacement of adhesive stamps

[SDMA1891 s20]

(1) Every person who by any writing in any manner defaces any adhesive stamp before it is used shall incur a penalty of [€630][1].

(2) Notwithstanding *subsection (1)*, any person may with the express sanction of the Commissioners, and in conformity with the conditions which they may prescribe, write on or otherwise appropriate an adhesive stamp before it is used for the purpose of identification of such stamp.

Amendments

[1] Substituted by FA01 sched5.

Cross References

To Section 144

Schedule 4 Consequential Amendments

145 Penalty for frauds in relation to duties

[SDMA1891 s21]

Any person who practises or is concerned in any fraudulent act, contrivance, or device, not specially provided for by law, with intent to defraud the State of any duty shall be guilty of an offence and section 1078 (which relates to revenue offences) of the Taxes Consolidation Act, 1997, shall for the purposes of such offence be construed in all respects as if such offence were an offence under subsection (2) of that section.

CHAPTER 4

Sale of Stamps

146 Power to grant licences to deal in stamps

[SDMA1891 s3]

(1) The Commissioners may, in their discretion, grant a licence to any person to deal in stamps at any place to be named in the licence.

(2) The licence shall specify the full name and place of abode of the person to whom the same is granted, and a description of every house, shop, or place, in or at which such person is authorised to deal in stamps.

(3) Every person to whom a licence is granted shall give security in the sum of [€1,265][1] in such manner and form as the Commissioners shall prescribe, and, if by bond, the bond shall be exempt from stamp duty.

(4) One licence and one bond only shall be required for any number of persons in partnership, and the licence may at any time be revoked by the Commissioners.

(5) Every person licensed to deal in stamps shall cause to be visibly and legibly painted and shall keep so painted in letters of not less than one inch in length on some conspicuous place on the outside of the front of every house, shop, or place in or at which such person is licensed to deal in stamps, such person's full name, together with the words "*Licensed to sell stamps*", and for every neglect or omission so to do shall incur a penalty of [€1,265][2].

Amendments

[1, 2] Substituted by FA01 sched5.

147 Penalty for unauthorised dealing in stamps, etc.

[SDMA1891 s4]

(1) If any person who is not duly appointed to sell and distribute stamps deals in any manner in stamps, without being licensed so to do, or at any house, shop, or place not specified in such person's licence such person shall be guilty of an offence and section 1078 (which relates to revenue offences) of the Taxes Consolidation Act, 1997, shall for the purposes of such offence be construed in all respects as if such offence were an offence under subsection (2) of that section.

(2) If any person who is not duly appointed to sell and distribute stamps, or duly licensed to deal in stamps, has, or puts on such person's premises either in the inside or on the outside of the premises, or on any board or any material exposed to public view, and whether the same be affixed to such person's premises or not, any letters importing or intending to import that such person deals in stamps, or is licensed so to do, such person shall incur a penalty of [€1,265][1].

Amendments

[1] Substituted by FA01 sched5.

Cross References

To Section 147

Schedule 4 Consequential Amendments

148 Provisions as to determination of a licence

[SDMA1891 s5]

(1) If the licence of any person to deal in stamps expires or is revoked, or if any person licensed to deal in stamps dies or becomes bankrupt, and any such person at the expiration or revocation of his or her licence, or at the time of his or her death or bankruptcy, has in his or her possession any stamps, such person, or such person's executor or administrator, or the receiver or trustee or official assignee under such person's bankruptcy, may, within 6 months after the expiration or revocation of the licence, or after the death or bankruptcy, as the case may be, bring or send the stamps to an office of the Commissioners.

(2) The Commissioners may in any such case pay to the person bringing or sending stamps the amount of the duty on the stamps, deducting from such amount the proper discount, if proof to their satisfaction is furnished that the same were actually in the possession of the person, whose licence has expired or been revoked, or so dying or becoming bankrupt, for the purpose of sale, at the time of the expiration or revocation of the licence, or of his or her death or bankruptcy, and that the stamps were purchased or procured by that person at an office of the Commissioners, or from some person duly appointed to sell and distribute stamps, or duly licensed to deal in stamps.

149 Penalty for hawking stamps

[SDMA1891 s6]

(1) If any person, whether licensed to deal in stamps or not, hawks or carries about for sale or exchange, any stamps, the following shall apply:

   (a) such person shall, in addition to any other fine or penalty to which he or she may be liable, be guilty of an offence and section 1078 (which relates to revenue offences) of the Taxes Consolidation Act, 1997, shall for the purposes of such offence be construed in all respects as if such offence were an offence under subsection (2) of that section;

   (b) all stamps which are found in the possession of the offender shall be forfeited, and shall be delivered to the Commissioners, to be disposed of as they think fit.

(2) Any person may arrest a person found committing an offence under this section, and take that person before a judge of the District Court having jurisdiction where the offence is committed, who shall hear and determine the matter.

Cross References

To Section 149

Schedule 4 Consequential Amendments

150 Discount

[SDMA1891 s8]

On the sale of stamps such discount shall be allowed to the purchasers of the stamps as the Minister directs.

CHAPTER 5

Allowance for Spoiled or Misused Stamps

151 Allowance for spoiled stamps

[SDMA1891 s9]

(1) Subject to such regulations as the Commissioners may think proper to make, and to the production of such evidence by statutory declaration or otherwise as the Commissioners may require, allowance shall be made by the Commissioners for stamps in any of the following cases:

(a) the stamp on any material inadvertently and undesignedly spoiled, obliterated, or by any means rendered unfit for the purpose intended, before the material bears the signature of any person or any instrument written on the material is executed by any party;

(b) any adhesive stamp which has been inadvertently and undesignedly spoiled or rendered unfit for use and has not in the opinion of the Commissioners been affixed to any material;

(c) any adhesive stamp representing a fee capable of being collected by means of such stamp which has been affixed to material where a certificate from the proper officer is produced to the effect that the stamp should be allowed;

(d) the stamp on any bill of exchange signed by or on behalf of the drawer which has not been accepted or made use of in any manner or delivered out of such drawer's hands for any purpose other than by means of tender for acceptance;

[...][1]

[(f) the stamp on any bill of exchange which from any omission or error has been spoiled or rendered useless, although the same, being a bill of exchange, may have been accepted or endorsed, where another completed and duly stamped bill of exchange is produced identical in every particular, except in the correction of the error or omission, with the spoiled bill;][2]

(g) the stamp used for any of the following instruments, that is—

(i) an instrument executed by any party to the instrument, but afterwards found to be absolutely void from the beginning,

(ii) an instrument executed by any party to the instrument, but afterwards found unfit, by reason of any error or mistake in the instrument, for the purpose originally intended,

(iii) an instrument executed by any party to the instrument which has not been made use of for any purpose, and which by reason of the inability or refusal of some necessary party to sign the same or to complete the transaction according to the instrument, is incomplete and insufficient for the purpose for which it was intended,

(iv) an instrument executed by any party to the instrument, which by reason of the refusal of any person to act under the same, or for want of enrolment or registration within the time required by law, fails of the intended purpose or becomes void, or

(v) an instrument executed by any party to the instrument which is inadvertently and undesignedly spoiled, and in lieu of which another instrument made between the same parties and for the same purpose is executed and duly stamped, or which becomes useless in consequence of the transaction intended to be effected by the instrument being effected by some other instrument duly stamped.

(2) Notwithstanding *subsection (1)*, allowance shall not be made by the Commissioners for spoiled stamps unless—

[(a) the application for relief is made within the period of 4 years after the stamp has been spoiled or become useless or, in the case of an executed instrument, within the period of 4 years from the date the instrument was stamped by the Commissioners,][3]

(b) in the case of an executed instrument no legal proceeding has been commenced in which the instrument could or would have been given or offered in evidence, and that the instrument is given up to be cancelled,

(c) in the case of an executed instrument the instrument has not achieved the purpose for which it was intended being the purpose of registering title to the property being conveyed or transferred by that instrument.

Amendments

[1] Deleted by FA07 s101(1)(i)(i). This section applies to instruments drawn, made or executed on or after 2 April 2007.

[2] Substituted by FA07 s101(1)(i)(ii). This section applies to instruments drawn, made or executed on or after 2 April 2007.

[3] Substituted by FA12 sched3(35). In effect for all instruments that are executed on or after 7 July 2012 per SI No. 228 of 2012.

152 Allowance for misused stamps

[When any person has inadvertently used, for an instrument liable to duty, a stamp of greater value than was necessary, or has inadvertently used a stamp for an instrument not liable to any duty, the Commissioners may, on application made within the period of 4 years from the date the instrument was stamped by the Commissioners, and on the instrument, if liable to duty, being stamped with the proper duty, cancel or allow as spoiled the stamp so misused.][1]

Amendments

[1] Substituted by FA12 sched3(36). In effect for all instruments that are executed on or after 7 July 2012 per SI No. 228 of 2012.

153 Allowance, how to be made

[SDMA1891 s11]

In any case in which allowance is made for spoiled or misused stamps the Commissioners may give in lieu of the allowance other stamps of the same denomination and value, or if required, and they think proper, stamps of any other denomination to the same amount in value, or in their discretion, the same value in money, deducting from the value of the stamps the discount allowed on the purchase of stamps of the like description.

154 Stamps not wanted may be repurchased by the Commissioners

[SDMA1891 s12]

When any person is possessed of a stamp which has not been spoiled or rendered unfit or useless for the purpose intended, but for which such person has no immediate use, the Commissioners may, if they think fit, repay to such person the value of the stamp in money, deducting the proper discount, on such person's delivering up the stamp to be cancelled, and proving to their satisfaction that it was purchased by such person at an office of the Commissioners, or from some person duly appointed to sell and distribute stamps or duly licensed to deal in stamps, within the period of [4 years from the date the stamp was purchased][1] and with a bona fide intention to use it.

Amendments

[1] Substituted by FA12 sched3(37). In effect for all instruments that are executed on or after 7 July 2012 per SI No. 228 of 2012.

155 Allowance for lost instruments

[SDMA1891 s12A]

(1) Where an instrument which was executed and duly stamped has been accidentally lost (in this section referred to as the "*lost instrument*") the Commissioners may—

(a) on application made by the person by whom it was first or alone executed,

(b) on the giving of an undertaking by that person to deliver up the lost instrument to them to be cancelled if it is subsequently found, and

(c) on satisfactory proof of the payment of the duty,

give other stamps of the same value in money but the stamps so given shall only be used for the purpose of stamping another instrument made between the same persons and for the same purpose.

(2) For the purposes of this section the Commissioners may require the delivery to them, in such form as they may specify, of a statutory declaration by any person who was concerned with the delivery of the lost instrument to them for stamping.

CHAPTER 6

Miscellaneous

156 Discontinuance of dies

[SDMA1891 s22; RA1898 s10(1) and (2)]

(1) Whenever the Commissioners determine to discontinue the use of any die, and provide a new die to be used in lieu of the discontinued die, and give public notice of their determination in the Iris Oifigiúil then from and after any day to be stated in the notice (such day not being within one month after the same is so published) the new die shall be the only lawful die for denoting the duty chargeable in any case in which the discontinued die would have been used and every instrument first executed by any person, or bearing date after the day so stated, and stamped with the discontinued die, shall be deemed to be not duly stamped.

(2) Whenever the Commissioners give public notice in the Iris Oifigiúil that the use of any die has been discontinued, then, whether a new die has been provided or

not, from and after any day to be stated in the notice (that day not being within one month after the notice is so published), that die shall not be a lawful die for denoting the payment of duty, and every instrument first executed by any person, or bearing date, after the day so stated in the notice, and stamped with duty denoted by the discontinued die, shall be deemed to be not duly stamped.

(3) (a) If any instrument stamped with a discontinued die, and first executed after the day so stated at any place outside the State, is brought to the Commissioners within 14 days after it has been received in the State, then on proof of the facts to the satisfaction of the Commissioners the stamp on that instrument shall be cancelled, and the instrument shall be stamped with the same amount of duty by means of a lawful die without the payment of any [interest or penalty][1].

(b) All persons having in their possession any material stamped with the discontinued die, and which by reason of the providing of such new die has been rendered useless, may at any time within 6 months after the day stated in the notice send the same to an office of the Commissioners, and the Commissioners may on receipt of that material cause the stamp on such material to be cancelled, and the same material, or, if the Commissioners think fit, any other material, to be stamped with a lawful die in lieu of and to an equal amount with the stamp so cancelled.

Amendments

[1] Substituted by F(No.2)A08 sched5(part5)(chap2)(7)(aa).

Note:

F(No.2)A08 sched5 (part5)(chap 2)(7)

As respects paragraph 7 of this Schedule subparagraphs (a) to (aa) (other than subparagraph (c)(i)(I)) of that paragraph have effect as on and from the passing of this Act and to the extent that Chapter 3A (being inserted into Part 47 of the Taxes Consolidation Act 1997 by Part 1 of this Schedule) applies to penalties incurred under the Stamp Duties Consolidation Act 1999 before the passing of this Act which on the passing of this Act have not been paid, it shall not apply to such penalties which are in the form of interest accrued under any provisions of the said Act.

157 Declarations, affidavits and oaths, how to be made

[SDMA1891 s24; RA1898 s7(6)]

Any statutory declaration, affidavit or oath to be made in pursuance of or for the purposes of this or any other Act for the time being in force relating to duties may be made before any of the Commissioners, or any officer or person authorised by them in that behalf, or before any commissioner for oaths or any peace commissioner or notary public in any part of the State, or at any place outside the State, before any person duly authorised to administer oaths there.

Cross References

To Section 157

Schedule 4 Consequential Amendments

158 Mode of granting licences

[SDMA1891 s25]

Any licence or certificate to be granted by the Commissioners under this Part or any other Act for the time being in force relating to duties may be granted by such officer or person, as the Commissioners may authorise in that behalf.

158A Delegation

[Anything required to be done by the Commissioners under this Act, other than the making of regulations or an authorisation under this section, may be done by such officer or officers, or class of officer or officers, of the Commissioners as the Commissioners authorise in writing in that behalf and different officers or classes of officers may be authorised for different purposes.][1]

Amendments

[1] Inserted by FA12 sched3(38). In effect for all instruments that are executed on or after 7 July 2012 per SI No. 228 of 2012.

159 Recovery of penalties, etc [Deleted]

Deleted by F(No.2)A08 sched4(part1). Applies as respects any tax that becomes due and payable on or after 1 March 2009.

CHAPTER 7

Time Limit for Repayment of Stamp Duty, Interest on Repayment and Time Limits for Enquiries and Assessments

159A Time limits for claiming a repayment of stamp duty

[(1) Without prejudice to any other provision of this Act containing a shorter time limit for the making of a claim for repayment, no stamp duty shall be repaid to a person in respect of a valid claim (within the meaning of *section 159B*), unless that valid claim is made within the period of 4 years from, as the case may be, the date the instrument was stamped by the Commissioners, [the date the statement of liability was delivered to the Commissioners, the date the operator-instruction referred to in section 69 was made or the date the person achieves the standard within the meaning of *section 81AA(11)(a)*.][1]

(2) *Subsection (1)* shall not apply to a repayment claim in respect of stamp duty arising on or before the date of the passing of the Finance Act 2003, where a valid claim is made on or before 31 December 2004.][2]

Amendments

[1] Substituted by FA07 s111.

[2] Inserted by FA03 s142(1). With effect from 31 October 2003 per SI 514 of 2003.

Cross References

From Section 159A

Section 69 Operator-instruction deemed to be an instrument of conveyance or transfer.
Section 81AA Transfers to young trained farmers.
Section 159B Interest on repayments of stamp duty.

159B Interest on repayments of stamp duty

[(1) In this section—

"*relevant date*", in relation to a repayment of stamp duty, means:

(a) the date which is [93 days][1] after the date on which a valid claim in respect of the repayment is made to the Commissioners, or

(b) where the repayment is due to a mistaken assumption in the operation of stamp duty on the part of the Commissioners, the date which is the date of the payment of stamp duty, interest, a surcharge or a penalty, as the case may be, which has given rise to that repayment.

"*relevant document*" means—

(a) an instrument stamped by the Commissioners, or a statement of liability delivered to the Commissioners under any provision of this Act, or

(b) an operator-instruction entered in a relevant system under *section 69*.

"*repayment*" means a repayment of stamp duty including a repayment of—

(a) any interest charged,

(b) any surcharge imposed,

(c) any penalty incurred,

under any provision of this Act in relation to stamp duty.

(2) No interest shall be payable in respect of a repayment claim made under any other provision of this Act unless such interest falls to be paid under this section.

(3) Subject to the provisions of this section, where a person is entitled to a repayment in respect of a relevant document, to which this section applies, the amount of the repayment shall, subject to a valid claim in respect of the repayment being made to the Commissioners and subject to [*section 960H(4)*][2] of the Taxes Consolidation Act 1997, carry simple interest at the rate of 0.011 per cent, or such other rate (if any) prescribed by the Minister by order under *subsection (8)*, for each day or part of a day for the period commencing on the relevant date and ending on the date upon which the repayment is made.

(4) A claim for repayment under this section shall only be treated as a valid claim when—

(a) it has been made in accordance with the provisions of the law (if any) relating to stamp duty under which such claim is made,

and

(b) all information which the Commissioners may reasonably require to enable them determine if and to what extent a repayment is due, has been furnished to them.

(5) Interest shall not be payable under this section if it amounts to €10 or less.

[(6) Except as provided for by this Act or *section 941* of the Taxes Consolidation Act 1997 as it applies for the purposes of stamp duties, the Commissioners shall not repay an amount of duty paid to them or pay interest in respect of an amount of duty paid to them.][3]

(7) Income tax shall not be deductible on any payment of interest under this section and such interest shall not be reckoned in computing income for the purposes of the Tax Acts.

(8) (a) The Minister may, from time to time, make an order prescribing a rate for the purposes of *subsection (3)*.

(b) Every order made by the Minister under *paragraph (a)* shall be laid before Dáil Éireann as soon as may be after it is made and, if a resolution annulling the order is passed by Dáil Éireann within the next 21 days on which Dáil Éireann has sat after the order is laid before it, the order shall be annulled accordingly, but without prejudice to the validity of anything previously done under it.

(9) The Commissioners may make regulations as they deem necessary in relation to the operation of this section.][4]

Amendments

[1] Substituted by FA07 s121(5).

[2] Substituted by FA13 sched2(2)(e).

[3] Substituted by FA12 s128(2). Shall apply as respects any tax (within the meaning of section 865B (inserted by subsection (1)(d))) paid or remitted to the Revenue Commissioners or the Collector-General, as the case may be, whether before, on or 31 March 2012.

[4] Inserted by FA03 s142(1). With effect from 1 November 2003 per SI 514 of 2003.

Cross References

From Section 159B
Section 69 Operator-instruction deemed to be an instrument of conveyance or transfer.

To Section 159B
Section 159A Time limits for claiming a repayment of stamp duty.

159C Time limits for making enquiries etc. and assessments by the Commissioners

[(1) In this section—

["*neglect*", in connection with or in relation to a relevant instrument, means—

(a) subject to *paragraph (b)*, in the case of an instrument or a specified statement, a failure to disclose in the instrument, or as the case may be, in the specified statement, all the facts and circumstances affecting the liability to duty of such instrument or specified statement,

(b) in the case of an instrument to which *section 8(2)* applies, as between both the instrument and the statement referred to in that section, a failure to disclose all the facts and circumstances affecting the liability to duty of such instrument, or

(c) in the case of an instruction of the type referred to in *section 76*, a failure to enter a correct instruction in a relevant system within the meaning of *section 68*;][1]

"*relevant instrument*" means—

(a) an instrument stamped by the Commissioners or a [specified statement delivered to the Commissioners][2], or

(b) an instruction of the type referred to in *section 76*;

"*relevant period*", in relation to a relevant instrument, means the period of 4 years commencing on the date the instrument was stamped by the Commissioners, or the date the statement was delivered to the Commissioners, or the date the instruction [was made;][3]

["*specified statement*" means—

(a) an account delivered to the Commissioners under *section 5*,

(b) a statement that is required to be delivered to the registrar under *section 117(1)(b)*, or

(c) a statement that is required to be delivered to the Commissioners under *Part 9*.][4]

(2) The making of enquiries or the taking of other action by the Commissioners for the purpose of satisfying themselves as to the correctness or otherwise of the charge arising, either directly or indirectly, to stamp duty in respect of a relevant instrument may not be initiated after the expiry of the relevant period.

(3) Notwithstanding any other provision in any other section of this Act, an assessment made in connection with or in relation to any relevant instrument may not be made after the expiry of the relevant period.

(4) The time limit referred to in *subsections (2)* and *(3)* shall not apply where the Commissioners have reasonable grounds for believing that any form of fraud or neglect has been committed by or on behalf of any person in connection with or in relation to any relevant instrument which is the subject of any enquiries, action or assessment.][5]

Amendments

[1] Substituted by FA05 s129(1)(a). This section is effective from 3 February 2005.

[2] Substituted by FA05 s129(1)(b). This section is effective from 3 February 2005.

[3] Substituted by FA05 s129(1)(c). This section is effective from 3 February 2005.

[4] Inserted by FA05 s129(1)(d). This section is effective from 3 February 2005.

[5] Inserted by FA03 s142(1). With effect from 1 January 2005 per SI 514 of 2003.

Cross References

From Section 159C

Section 5 Agreement as to payment of stamp duty on instruments.
Section 8 Facts and circumstances affecting duty to be set forth in instruments, etc.
Section 68 Interpretation (Part 6).
Section 76 Obligations of system-members.
Section 117 Statement to be charged with stamp duty.
Section 123 Cash cards.

CHAPTER 8

Calculation of Interest on Unpaid Duty and Other Amounts

159D Calculation of interest on unpaid duty and other amounts

[(1) In this section—

"*period of delay*", in relation to any unpaid duty or other amount referred to in a specified provision, means the period referred to in the specified provision in respect of which period interest is chargeable, charged, payable or recoverable, as the case may be, in accordance with that provision;

["*relevant period*", in relation to a period of delay which falls into more than one of the periods specified in column (1) of the Table to subsection (2), means any part of the period of delay which falls into, or is the same as, a period specified in that column;][1]

"*specified provision*" means any section of this Act other than *section 126(7)* which provides for interest to be charged, chargeable, payable or recoverable, as the case may be, in respect of any unpaid duty or other amount due and payable under that section.

[(2) The amount of interest charged, chargeable, payable or recoverable in respect of any unpaid duty or other amount due and payable or recoverable under a specified provision—

(a) where one of the periods specified in column (1) of the Table to this subsection includes or is the same as the period of delay, shall be the amount determined by the formula—

$$A \times D \times P$$

where—

A is the duty or other amount due and payable under the specified provision which remains unpaid,

D is the number of days (including part of a day) forming the period of delay, and

P is the appropriate percentage in column (2) of the Table to this subsection opposite the period specified in column (1) of the said Table within which the period of delay falls or which is the same as the period of delay,

and

(b) where a continuous period formed by more than one period specified in column (1) of the Table to this subsection, but not (as in subsection (*a*)) only one such period, includes or is the same as the period of delay, shall be the aggregate of the amounts due in respect of each relevant period which forms part of the period of delay, and the amount due in respect of each such relevant period shall be determined by the formula—

$$A \times D \times P$$

where—

A is the duty or other amount due and payable under the specified provision which remains unpaid,

D is the number of days (including part of a day) forming the relevant period, and

P is the appropriate percentage in column (2) of the Table to this subsection opposite the period specified in column (1) of the said Table within which the period of delay falls or which is the same as the relevant period.

Table

(Period) (1)	(Percentage) (2)
From 1 April 2005 to 30 June 2009	0.0273%
From 1 July 2009 to the date of payment	0.0219%][2]][3]

Amendments

[1] Inserted by FA09 s29(2)(a). Applies as respects any unpaid tax or duty, as the case may be, that has not been paid before 1 July 2009 regardless of whether that tax or duty became due and payable before, on or after that date.

[2] Substituted by FA09 s29(2)(b). Applies as respects any unpaid tax or duty, as the case may be, that has not been paid before 1 July 2009 regardless of whether that tax or duty became due and payable before, on or after that date.

[3] Inserted by FA05 s145(3). Applies as respects interest to be charged, chargeable, payable or recoverable, as the case may be, for any day or part of a day on or after 1 April 2005 in respect of any unpaid stamp duty or other amount due under the Stamp Duties Consolidation Act 1999 which is due to be paid whether before, on or after 1 April 2005.

Cross References

From Section 159D

Section 126 Certain statements of interest.

To Section 159D

Section 81A Further relief from stamp duty in respect of transfers to young trained farmers.

Section 81B Farm consolidation relief.
Section 81C Further farm consolidation relief.
Section 81AA Transfers to young trained farmers.
Section 82B Approved sports bodies
Section 87 Stock borrowing.
Section 91 New dwellinghouses and apartments with floor area certificate.
Section 91A New dwellinghouses and apartments with floor area compliance certificate.
Section 92 New dwellinghouses and apartments with no floor area certificate.
Section 92A Residential property owner occupier relief.
Section 92B Residential property first time purchaser relief.
Section 123B Cash, combined and debit cards.
Section 123C Preliminary duty: cash, combined and debit cards.
Section 124A Preliminary duty: credit and charge cards.
Section 124B Certain premiums of life assurance.

PART 12

Repeals, etc.

160 Repeals

(1) Subject to *subsection (2)*, each enactment mentioned in *column (2)* of *Schedule 3* (which in this Act are collectively referred to as "*the repealed enactments*") is hereby repealed or revoked to the extent specified opposite that mentioned in *column (3)* of that Schedule.

(2) This Act shall not apply in relation to stamp duty on—

(a) instruments specified in *Schedule 1* which were executed before the date of the passing of this Act,

(b) transactions, within the meaning of *section 116*, taking place before the date of the passing of this Act,

(c) statements, within the meaning of *sections 123(2), 124(1)(b), 124(2)(b), 124(2)(d)(i), 125(2)* and *126(2)*, which would fall to be delivered under the repealed enactments before the date of the passing of this Act,

and the repealed enactments shall continue to apply in relation to stamp duty on the—

(i) instruments mentioned in *paragraph (a)*,

(ii) transactions mentioned in *paragraph (b)*, and

(iii) statements mentioned in *paragraph (c)*,

to the same extent that they would have applied if this Act had not been enacted.

(3) Notwithstanding *subsection (1)*, any provision of the repealed enactments which imposes a fine, forfeiture, penalty or punishment for any act or omission shall, in relation to any act or omission which took place or began before the date of the passing of this Act, continue to apply in substitution for the provision of this Act to which it corresponds.

(4) Anything done under or in connection with the provisions of the repealed enactments which correspond to the provisions of this Act shall be deemed to have been done under or in connection with the provisions of this Act to which those provisions of the repealed enactments correspond; but nothing in this subsection shall affect the operation of *subsections (3)* and *(4)* of *section 163*.

Cross References

From Section 160

Section 116 Charge of stamp duty.
Section 123 Cash cards.
Section 124 Credit cards and charge cards.
Section 125 Certain premiums of insurance.
Section 126 Certain statements of interest.
Section 163 Continuity and construction of certain references to old and new law.
Schedule 1 Stamp Duties on Instruments
Schedule 3 Enactments Repealed or Revoked

To Section 160

Schedule 3 Enactments Repealed or Revoked

161 Saving for enactments not repealed

This Act (other than *subsections (2)* to *(4)* of *section 163*) shall apply subject to so much of any Act as contains provisions relating to or affecting stamp duties as—

(a) is not repealed by this Act, and

(b) would have operated in relation to stamp duties if this Act had not been substituted for the repealed enactments.

Cross References

From Section 161

Section 163 Continuity and construction of certain references to old and new law.

162 Consequential amendments to other enactments

Schedule 4, which provides for amendments to other enactments consequential on the passing of this Act, shall apply for the purposes of this Act.

Cross References

From Section 162

Schedule 4 Consequential Amendments

To Section 162

Schedule 4 Consequential Amendments

163 Continuity and construction of certain references to old and new law

(1) The Commissioners shall have all the jurisdictions, powers and duties in relation to stamp duties and fees collected by means of stamps under this Act which they had before the passing of this Act.

(2) The continuity of the operation of the law relating to stamp duties and fees collected by means of stamps shall not be affected by the substitution of this Act for the repealed enactments.

(3) Any reference, whether express or implied, in any enactment or document (including this Act and any Act amended by this Act)—

(a) to any provision of this Act, or

(b) to things done or to be done under or for the purposes of any provisions of this Act,

shall, if and in so far as the nature of the reference permits, be construed as including, in relation to the times, years or periods, circumstances or purposes in relation to which the corresponding provision in the repealed enactments applied or had applied, a reference to, or, as the case may be, to things done or to be done under or for the purposes of, that corresponding provision.

(4) Any reference, whether express or implied, in any enactment or document (including the repealed enactments and enactments passed and documents made after the passing of this Act)—

(a) to any provision of the repealed enactments, or

(b) to things done or to be done under or for the purposes of any provisions of the repealed enactments,

shall, if and in so far as the nature of the reference permits, be construed as including, in relation to the times, years or periods, circumstances or purposes in relation to which the corresponding provision of this Act applies, a reference to, or, as the case may be, to things done or to be done under or for the purposes of, that corresponding provision.

Cross References

To Section 163

Section 160 Repeals.

Section 161 Saving for enactments not repealed.

164 Short title

This Act may be cited as the *Stamp Duties Consolidation Act, 1999.*

SCHEDULE 1

Stamp Duties on Instruments

Section 2

[SA1891 First Sch.; FA 1899 s5(1)]

Heading *Duty*

[...][1]

[...][2]

AGREEMENT for a Lease, or for any letting.

See LEASE.

AGREEMENT for sale of property.

See CONVEYANCE or TRANSFER on sale.

ANNUITY.

Conveyance in consideration of.

See CONVEYANCE or TRANSFER on sale.

Purchase of.

See CONVEYANCE or TRANSFER on sale.

[...][3]

[...][4]

ASSIGNMENT.

[...][5]

[...][6]

On a sale or otherwise.

See CONVEYANCE or TRANSFER.

ASSURANCE.

See POLICY.

[BILL OF EXCHANGE.

Where drawn on an account in the State [€0.50][7].

Exemptions

(1) Draft or order drawn by any banker in the State on any other banker in the State, not payable to bearer or to order, and used solely for the purpose of settling or clearing any account between such bankers.

(2) Letter written by a banker in the State to any other banker in the State, directing the payment of any sum of money, the same not being payable to bearer or to order, and such letter not being sent or delivered to the person to whom payment is to be made or to any person on such person's behalf.

(3) Draft or order drawn by the Accountant of the Courts of Justice.

(4) Coupon or warrant for interest attached to and issued with any security, or with an agreement or memorandum for the renewal or extension of time for payment of a security.

(5) Coupon for interest on a marketable security being one of a set of coupons whether issued with the security or subsequently issued in a sheet.

(6) Direct debits and standing orders.

(7) Bill drawn on or on behalf of the Minister for Finance by which payment in respect of prize bonds is effected.][8]

BILL OF SALE.

Absolute.

See CONVEYANCE or TRANSFER on sale.

[...][9]

[...][10]

BOND in relation to any annuity on the original creation and sale of that annuity.

See CONVEYANCE or TRANSFER on sale.

[...][11]

[...][12]

CHEQUE.

See BILL OF EXCHANGE.

CONTRACT.

See AGREEMENT.

CONVEYANCE or TRANSFER on sale of any stocks or marketable securities

[(1) Where the amount or value of the consideration for the sale which is attributable to stocks or marketable securities does not exceed €1,000 and the instrument[...][13] does not form part of a larger transaction or of a series of transactions in respect of which the amount or value, or the aggregate amount or value, of the consideration which is attributable to stocks or marketable securities exceeds €1,000:	
for the consideration which is attributable to stocks or marketable securities	Exempt.
(2) Where *paragraph (1)* does not apply: for the consideration which is attributable to stocks or marketable securities	1 per cent of the consideration but where the calculation results in an amount which is not a multiple of €1 the amount so calculated shall [...][14] if more than €1, be rounded down to the nearest €.][15]

Exemption.

Foreign loan security issued by or on behalf of a company or body of persons corporate or unincorporate formed or established in the State. For the purposes of this exemption a "*foreign loan security*" means a security issued outside the State in respect of a loan which is expressed in a currency other than the currency of the State and is neither offered for subscription in the State nor offered for subscription with a view to an offer for sale in the State of securities in respect of the loan.

CONVEYANCE or TRANSFER on sale of a policy of insurance or a policy of life insurance where the risk to which the policy relates is located in the State	0.1 per cent of the consideration but where the calculation results in an amount which is not a multiple of [€1][16] the amount so calculated shall be rounded [down to the nearest €][17].

CONVEYANCE or TRANSFER on sale of any property other than stocks or marketable securities or a policy of insurance or a policy of life assurance.

[(1) Where the amount or value of the consideration for the sale is wholly or partly attributable to residential property and [...][18]	
[...][19]	
[...][20] the transaction effected by that instrument does not form part of a larger transaction or of a series of transactions in respect of which, had there been a larger transaction or a series of transactions, the amount or value, or the aggregate amount or value, of the consideration (other than the consideration for the sale concerned which is wholly or partly attributable to residential property) would have been wholly or partly attributable to residential property:	1 per cent of the first €1,000,000 of the consideration and 2 per cent of the balance of the consideration thereafter but where the calculation results in an amount which is not a multiple of €1 the amount so calculated shall be rounded down to the nearest €.
for the consideration which is attributable to residential property	
(2) Where *paragraph (1)* does not apply and the amount or value of the consideration for the sale is wholly or partly attributable to residential property and [...][21]	

[...][22]

[...][23] the transaction effected by that instrument forms part of a larger transaction or of a series of transactions in respect of which the amount or value, or the aggregate amount or value, of the consideration which is attributable to residential property is an amount equal to Y

where—

Y is the amount or value, or the aggregate amount or value, of the consideration in respect of the larger transaction or of the series of transactions which is attributable to residential property:

for the consideration which is attributable to residential property	Stamp duty of an amount determined by the formula— $$\frac{A \times B}{C}$$ where— A is the amount of stamp duty that would have been chargeable under *paragraph (1)* on the amount or value, or the aggregate amount or value, of the consideration in respect of the larger transaction or of the series of transactions which is attributable to residential property had *paragraph 1* applied to such consideration, B is the amount or value of the consideration for the sale concerned which is attributable to residential property, and C is the amount or value, or the aggregate amount or value, of the consideration in respect of the larger transaction or of the series of transactions which is attributable to residential property, but where the calculation results in an amount which is not a multiple of €1 the amount so calculated shall be rounded down to the nearest €.
[...][24]	
(4) Where the amount or value of the consideration for the sale is wholly or partly attributable to property which is not residential property	2 per cent of the consideration which is attributable to property which is not residential property but where the calculation results in an amount which is not a multiple of €1 the amount so calculated shall be rounded down to the nearest €.

(5) Where *paragraph (4)* applies in the case of a conveyance or transfer on sale or in the case of a conveyance or transfer operating as a voluntary disposition inter vivos [of property that is land][25]—

[(a) the instrument is executed—

(i) on or after 1 January 2015 and before 1 January 2016, or

(ii) on or after 1 January 2016 and before 1 January 2018 and the individual by whom the property is being conveyed or transferred has not, at the date of the conveyance or transfer, attained the age of 67 years,

(aa) the individual to whom the property is being conveyed or transferred is an individual—

(i) who, from the date of conveyance or transfer and for a period of not less than 6 years thereafter—

(I) farms the land, or

(II) leases it for a period of not less than 6 years to an individual who farms the land,

and

(ii) who, in a case where *subclause (I)* applies—

(I) is the holder of or, within a period of 4 years from the date of transfer or conveyance, will be the holder of, a qualification set out in *Schedule 2, 2A* or *2B* to the Act, or

(II) spends not less than 50 per cent of that individual's normal working time farming land (including the land conveyed or transferred),

(ab) in a case where *subparagraph (aa)(i)(II)* applies, the individual to whom the land is leased—

(i) is the holder of or, within a period of 4 years from the date of transfer or conveyance, will be the holder of, a qualification set out in *Schedule 2, 2A* or *2B* to the Act, or

(ii) spends not less than 50 per cent of that individual's normal working time farming land (including the land conveyed or transferred),

(ac) the land is farmed on a commercial basis and with a view to the realisation of profits from that land, and][26]

(b) [...][27] the person becoming entitled to the entire beneficial interest in the property (or, where more than one person becomes entitled to a beneficial interest in the property, each of them) is related to the person or each of the persons immediately theretofore entitled to the entire beneficial interest in the property in one or other of the following ways, that is, as a lineal descendant, parent, grandparent, step-parent, husband or wife, brother or sister of a parent or brother or sister, or lineal descendant of a parent, husband or wife or brother or sister, or is, as respects the person or each of the persons immediately theretofore entitled, his or her civil partner, the civil partner of either of his or her parents or a lineal descendant of his or her civil partner

a duty of an amount equal to one-half of the ad valorem stamp duty which, but for the provisions of this paragraph, would be chargeable under this heading but where the calculation results in an amount which is not a multiple of €1 the amount so calculated shall be rounded down to the nearest €.][28]

[(5A) Where any of the conditions in *paragraph (5)* are not complied with, at the time of the conveyance or transfer or subsequently, *paragraph (5)* shall not apply, any additional duty shall be chargeable by reference to the rate of duty in *paragraph (4)* and the provisions of this Act, in relation to the delivering of returns, the charging of interest and (where appropriate) the incurring of a penalty shall apply from the date on which compliance with any such condition ceases.][29]

[...][30]

[...][31]

COUNTERPART.

See DUPLICATE.

[...][32]

COVENANT in relation to any annuity on the original creation and sale of that annuity.

See CONVEYANCE or TRANSFER on sale.

[...][33]

[...][34]

DRAFT for money.

See BILL OF EXCHANGE.

DUPLICATE or COUNTERPART of any instrument chargeable with any duty.

Where such duty does not amount to [€12.50][35]	The same duty as the original instrument.
In any other case	[€12.50][36].

[...][37]

[EXCHANGE — instruments effecting.

In the case specified in *section 37* , see that section.][38]

Exemption.

Instrument which contains a statement certifying exchange which is not an exchange which is specified in *section 37* .

[...][39]

INSURANCE.

See POLICY.

LEASE.

(1) For any indefinite term or any term not exceeding 35 years of any dwellinghouse, part of a dwellinghouse, or apartment at a rent not exceeding [€30,000][40] per annum	Exempt.
(2) For any definite term less than a year of any lands, tenements or heritable subjects	The same duty as a lease for a year at the rent reserved for the definite term.

(3) For any other definite term or for any indefinite term of any lands, tenements, or heritable subjects—

[(a) where the consideration, or any part of the consideration (other than rent), moving either to the lessor or to any other person, consists of any money, stock or security, and

(i) the amount or value of such consideration for the lease is wholly or partly attributable to residential property and the [...][41]

[...][42]

[...][43] the transaction effected by that instrument does not form part of a larger transaction or of a series of transactions in respect of which, had there been a larger transaction or a series of transactions, the amount or value, or the aggregate amount or value, of the consideration (other than the consideration for the lease concerned which is wholly or partly attributable to residential property and other than rent) would have been wholly or partly attributable to residential property:

for the consideration which is attributable to residential property	1 per cent of the first €1,000,000 of the consideration and 2 per cent of the balance of the consideration thereafter but where the calculation results in an amount which is not a multiple of €1 the amount so calculated shall be rounded down to the nearest €.
(ii) the amount or value of such consideration for the lease is wholly or partly attributable to residential property and [...][44] [...][45] [...][46] the transaction effected by that instrument forms part of a larger transaction or of a series of transactions in respect of which the amount or value, or the aggregate amount or value, of the consideration (other than rent) which is attributable to residential property is an amount equal to Y where— Y is the amount or value, or the aggregate amount or value, of the consideration (other than rent)in respect of the larger transaction or of the series of transactions which is attributable to residential property, and clause (i) does not apply:	
for the consideration which is attributable to residential property	Stamp duty of an amount determined by the formula— $$\frac{A \times B}{C}$$ where— A is the amount of stamp duty that would have been chargeable under clause (i) on the amount or value, or the aggregate amount or value, of the consideration (other than rent) in respect of the larger transaction or of the series of transactions which is attributable to residential property had clause (i) applied to such consideration, B is the amount or value of the consideration (other than rent) for the lease concerned which is attributable to residential property, and C is the amount or value, or the aggregate amount or value, of the consideration (other than rent) in respect of the larger transaction or of the series of transactions which is attributable to residential property, but where the calculation results in an amount which is not a multiple of €1 the amount so calculated shall be rounded down to the nearest €.

[...][47]

(b) where the consideration, or any part of the consideration (other than rent), moving either to the lessor or to any other person, consists of any money, stock or security, and the amount or value of such consideration is wholly or partly attributable to property which is not residential property	2 per cent of the consideration which is attributable to property which is not residential property but where the calculation results in an amount which is not a multiple of €1 the amount so calculated shall be rounded down to the nearest €.][48]
(c) where the consideration or any part of the consideration is any rent, in respect of such consideration, whether reserved as a yearly rent or otherwise:	
(i) if the term does not exceed 35 years or is indefinite	1 per cent of the average annual rent but where the calculation results in an amount which is not a multiple of [€1][49] the amount so calculated shall be rounded [down to the nearest €][50].
(ii) if the term exceeds 35 years but does not exceed 100 years	6 per cent of the average annual rent but where the calculation results in an amount which is not a multiple of [€1][51] the amount so calculated shall be rounded [down to the nearest €][52].
(iii) if the term exceeds 100 years	12 per cent of the average annual rent but where the calculation results in an amount which is not a multiple of [€1][53] the amount so calculated shall be rounded [down to the nearest €][54].
(4) Lease made subsequently to, and in conformity with, an agreement duly stamped under the provisions of [*section 50* or *50A*][55]	[€12.50][56].
(5) Of any other kind not already described under this heading which relates to immovable property situated in the State or to any right over or interest in such property	[€12.50][57].

[...][58]

[...][59]

[...][60]

ORDER for the payment of money.

See BILL OF EXCHANGE.

PARTITION or DIVISION — instruments effecting.

In the case specified in *section 38*, see that section.

[...][61]

POLICY OF INSURANCE other than Life Insurance where the risk to which the policy relates is located in the State.

Where there is one premium only and the amount of that premium equals or exceeds [€20][62] or, where there is more than one premium and the total amount payable in respect of that premium in any period of 12 months equals or exceeds [€20][63]	[€1][64].

[...][65]

[RELEASE or RENUNCIATION of any property, or of any right or interest in any property.

On a sale.

See CONVEYANCE or TRANSFER on sale.

Exemption.

Instrument which contains a statement certifying that the instrument is a release or renunciation of property, or of a right or interest in property, which is not a release or renunciation on a sale.][66]

SHARE WARRANT issued under the provisions of the Companies Act, 1963, and **STOCK CERTIFICATE to bearer,** and any instrument to bearer issued by or on behalf of any company or body of persons formed or established in the State and having a like effect as such a share warrant or such a stock certificate to bearer, expressed in the currency of the State

A duty of an amount equal to 3 times the amount of the ad valorem stamp duty which would be chargeable on a deed transferring the share or shares or stock specified in the warrant or certificate or instrument having a like effect as such a warrant or certificate if the consideration for the transfer were the nominal value of such share or shares or stock.

[SURRENDER of any property, or of any right or interest in any property.

On a sale.

See CONVEYANCE or TRANSFER on sale.

Exemption.

Instrument which contains a statement certifying that the instrument is a surrender of property, or of a right or interest in property, not being a surrender on a sale.][67]

TRANSFER.

See CONVEYANCE or TRANSFER.

Amendments

[1, 2] Deleted by FA07 s100(1)(h)(i)(I). This section applies to instruments executed on or after 7 December 2006.

[3, 4] Deleted by FA07 s100(1)(h)(ii). This section applies to instruments executed on or after 7 December 2006.

[5, 6] Deleted by FA07 s100(1)(h)(iii). This section applies to instruments executed on or after 7 December 2006.

[7] Substituted by F(No.2)A08 s87(1)(a). Applies as respects bills of exchange drawn on or after 15 October 2008.

[8] Substituted by FA07 s101(1)(j)(i). This section applies to instruments drawn, made or executed on or after 2 April 2007.

[9, 10] Deleted by FA07 s100(1)(h)(iv). This section applies to instruments executed on or after 7 December 2006.

[11] Deleted by FA07 s100(1)(h)(i)(II). This section applies to instruments executed on or after 7 December 2006.

[12] Deleted by FA07 s100(1)(h)(i)(III). This section applies to instruments executed on or after 7 December 2006.

[13] Deleted by FA12 sched3(39)(a)(i). In effect for all instruments that are executed on or after 7 July 2012 per SI No. 228 of 2012.

[14] Deleted by FA12 sched3(39)(a)(ii). In effect for all instruments that are executed on or after 7 July 2012 per SI No. 228 of 2012.

[15] Substituted by F(No.2)A08 s87(1)(b). Applies as respects instruments executed on or after 24 December 2008.

[16, 17, 35, 36, 49, 50, 51, 52, 53, 54, 56, 57, 62, 63, 64] Substituted by FA01 sched5.

[18, 19, 20] Deleted by FA12 sched3(39)(b)(i). In effect for all instruments that are executed on or after 7 July 2012 per SI No. 228 of 2012.

[21, 22, 23] Deleted by FA12 sched3(39)(b)(ii). In effect for all instruments that are executed on or after 7 July 2012 per SI No. 228 of 2012.

[24] Deleted by FA12 sched3(39)(b)(iii). In effect for all instruments that are executed on or after 7 July 2012 per SI No. 228 of 2012.

[25] Inserted by FA14 s77(1)(a)(i). Comes into operation on 1 January 2015.

[26] Substituted by FA14 s77(1)(a)(ii). Comes into operation on 1 January 2015.

[27] Deleted by FA14 s77(1)(a)(iii). Comes into operation on 1 January 2015.

[28] Substituted by FA12 sched2(1). Applies as respects instruments executed on or after 7 December 2011.

[29] Inserted by FA14 s77(1)(b). Comes into operation on 1 January 2015.

[30] Deleted by FA07 s100(1)(h)(i)(IV). This section applies to instruments executed on or after 7 December 2006.

[31] Deleted by FA07 s101(1)(j)(iii)(I). This section applies to instruments drawn, made or executed on or after 2 April 2007.

[32] Deleted by FA07 s100(1)(h)(i)(V). This section applies to instruments executed on or after 7 December 2006.

[33] Deleted by FA07 s100(1)(h)(i)(VI). This section applies to instruments executed on or after 7 December 2006.

[34] Deleted by FA07 s100(1)(h)(i)(VII). This section applies to instruments executed on or after 7 December 2006.

[37] Deleted by FA07 s100(1)(h)(i)(VIII). This section applies to instruments executed on or after 7 December 2006.

[38] Substituted by FA07 s101(1)(j)(ii). This section applies to instruments drawn, made or executed on or after 2 April 2007.

[39] Deleted by FA07 s100(1)(h)(i)(IX). This section applies to instruments executed on or after 7 December 2006.

[40] Substituted by FA08 s125(1)(c). Applies as respects instruments executed on or after 13 March 2008.

[41, 42, 43] Deleted by FA12 sched3(39)(c)(i). In effect for all instruments that are executed on or after 7 July 2012 per SI No. 228 of 2012.

[44, 45, 46] Deleted by FA12 sched3(39)(c)(ii). In effect for all instruments that are executed on or after 7 July 2012 per SI No. 228 of 2012.

[47] Deleted by FA12 sched3(39)(c)(iii). In effect for all instruments that are executed on or after 7 July 2012 per SI No. 228 of 2012.

[48] Substituted by FA12 sched2(2). Applies as respects instruments executed on or after 7 December 2011. Does not apply as respects any instrument executed before 1 July 2012 where—

(a) the effect of the application of that subsection would be to increase the duty otherwise chargeable on the instrument, and

(b) the instrument contains a statement in such form as the Revenue Commissioners may specify, certifying that the instrument was executed solely in pursuance of a binding contract entered into before 7 December 2011.

[55] Substituted by FA13 s78(1)(d). Applies as respects instruments executed on or after 13 February 2013 other than instruments executed solely in pursuance of a binding contract or agreement entered into before 13 February 2013.

[58] Deleted by FA07 s101(1)(j)(iii)(II). This section applies to instruments drawn, made or executed on or after 2 April 2007.

[59] Deleted by FA07 s100(1)(h)(i)(X). This section applies to instruments executed on or after 7 December 2006.

[60] Deleted by FA07 s100(1)(h)(i)(XI). This section applies to instruments executed on or after 7 December 2006.

[61] Deleted by FA01 s213(1)(c). Applies and has effect in relation to instruments executed and policies of life insurance varied on or after 1 January 2001.

[65] Deleted by FA07 s101(1)(j)(iii)(III). This section applies to instruments drawn, made or executed on or after 2 April 2007.

[66] Substituted by FA07 s101(1)(j)(iv). This section applies to instruments drawn, made or executed on or after 2 April 2007.

[67] Substituted by FA07 s101(1)(j)(v). This section applies to instruments drawn, made or executed on or after 2 April 2007.

Revenue Briefings

Tax Briefing

Tax Briefing June 2001 – Issue 44 (part 2) pg 30 – Revenue Certificates in Deeds

Revenue Information Notes

SD10A – Revenue Certificates Required In Deeds (for deeds prior to 8 December 2010)
SD10B – Revenue Certificates Required In Deeds (up to and including Finance Act 2011)

Cross References

From Schedule 1

Section 2 Charging of, liability for, and recovery of stamp duty.
Section 37 Exchanges.
Section 38 Partitions or divisions.
Section 50 Agreements for not more than 35 years charged as leases.
Section 50A Agreements for more than 35 years charged as leases.

To Schedule 1

Section 1 Interpretation.
Section 2 Charging of, liability for, and recovery of stamp duty.
Section 3 Variation of certain rates of duty by order.
Section 5 Agreement as to payment of stamp duty on instruments.
Section 17 Furnishing of an incorrect certificate.
Section 29 Conveyance on sale combined with building agreement for dwellinghouse or apartment.
Section 37 Exchanges.
Section 45A Aggregation of transactions.
Section 46 Directions as to sub-sales.
Section 48 Stamp duty and value-added tax.
Section 53 Lease combined with building agreement for dwellinghouse or apartment.
Section 54 Leases deemed to operate as voluntary dispositions inter vivos.
Section 56 Stamp duty and value-added tax.
Section 62 Limitation of stamp duty on certain instruments relating to 2 or more distinct matters.
Section 63 Letters of renunciation.
Section 70 Rate of duty.
Section 73 Exemptions.
Section 79 Conveyances and transfers of property between certain bodies corporate.
Section 80 Reconstructions or amalgamations of companies.
Section 81 Young trained farmers.
Section 81A Further relief from stamp duty in respect of transfers to young trained farmers.
Section 81AA Transfers to young trained farmers.
Section 84 Repayment of stamp duty on certain transfers of shares.
Section 90 Certain financial services instruments.
Section 90A Greenhouse gas emissions allowance.
Section 92 New dwellinghouses and apartments with no floor area certificate.
Section 101 Intellectual property.
Section 101A Single farm payment entitlement.
Section 110A Certain policies of insurance.
Section 160 Repeals.

SCHEDULE 2

Qualifications for Applying for Relief from Stamp Duty in Respect of Transfers to Young Trained Farmers

Section 81

[FA1994 s112 and Sch.6]

1. Qualifications awarded by Teagasc:
   - (a) Certificate in Farming;
   - (b) Diploma in Commercial Horticulture;
   - (c) Diploma in Amenity Horticulture;
   - (d) Diploma in Pig Production;
   - (e) Diploma in Poultry Production.
2. Qualifications awarded by the Farm Apprenticeship Board:
   - (a) Certificate in Farm Management;
   - (b) Certificate in Farm Husbandry;
   - (c) Trainee Farmer Certificate.
3. Qualifications awarded by a third-level institution:
   - (a) Degree in Agricultural Science awarded by the National University of Ireland through University College Dublin, National University of Ireland, Dublin;
   - (b) Degree in Horticultural Science awarded by the National University of Ireland through University College Dublin, National University of Ireland, Dublin;
   - (c) Degree in Veterinary Science awarded by the National University of Ireland through University College Dublin, National University of Ireland, Dublin;
   - (d) Degree in Rural Science awarded by the National University of Ireland through University College Cork — National University of Ireland, Cork or by the University of Limerick;
   - (e) Diploma in Rural Science awarded by the National University of Ireland through University College Cork — National University of Ireland, Cork;
   - (f) Degree in Dairy Science awarded by the National University of Ireland through University College Cork — National University of Ireland, Cork;
   - (g) Diploma in Dairy Science awarded by the National University of Ireland through University College Cork — National University of Ireland, Cork.
4. Certificates awarded by the National Council for Educational Awards:
   - (a) National Certificate in Agricultural Science studied through Kildalton Agricultural College and Waterford Institute of Technology;
   - (b) National Certificate in Business Studies (Agri-business) studied through the Franciscan Brothers Agricultural College, Mountbellew, and Galway-Mayo Institute of Technology.

Cross References

From Schedule 2

Section 81 Young trained farmers.

To Schedule 2

Section 81 Young trained farmers.
Section 81A Further relief from stamp duty in respect of transfers to young trained farmers.
Section 81AA Transfers to young trained farmers.

SCHEDULE 2A

Qualifications for Applying for Relief from Stamp Duty in Respect of Transfers to Young Trained Farmers

[Section 81A

1. Qualifications awarded by the Further Education and Training Awards Council:
   (a) Vocational Certificate in Agriculture — Level 3;
   (b) Advanced Certificate in Agriculture;
   (c) Vocational Certificate in Horticulture — Level 3;
   (d) Vocational Certificate in Horse Breeding and Training — Level 3;
   (e) Vocational Certificate in Forestry — Level 3;
   (f) Awards other than those referred to in *subparagraphs (a)* to *(e)* of this paragraph which are at a standard equivalent to the standard of an award under *subparagraph (a)* of this paragraph.
2. Qualifications awarded by the Higher Education and Training Awards Council:
   (a) National Certificate in Agriculture;
   (b) National Diploma in Agriculture;
   (c) National Certificate in Science in Agricultural Science;
   (d) National Certificate in Business Studies in Agri-Business;
   (e) National Certificate in Technology in Agricultural Mechanisation;
   (f) National Diploma in Horticulture;
   (g) National Certificate in Business Studies in Equine Studies;
   (h) National Certificate or Diploma awards other than those referred to in *subparagraphs (a)* to *(g)* of this paragraph.
3. Qualifications awarded by other third-level institutions:
   (a) Primary degrees awarded by the faculties of General Agriculture and Veterinary Medicine at University College Dublin;
   (b) Bachelor of Science (Education) in Biological Sciences awarded by the University of Limerick;
   (c) Bachelor of Science in Equine Science awarded by the University of Limerick;
   (d) Diploma or Certificate in Science (Equine Science) awarded by the University of Limerick.][1]

Amendments

[1] Inserted by FA04 s70(b).

Cross References

From Schedule 2A

Section 81A Further relief from stamp duty in respect of transfers to young trained farmers.

To Schedule 2A

Section 81A Further relief from stamp duty in respect of transfers to young trained farmers.
Section 81AA Transfers to young trained farmers.

SCHEDULE 2B

Qualifications for Applying for Relief from Stamp Duty in Respect of Transfers to Young Trained Farmers

[Section 81AA

[1. Qualifications awarded by the [Qualifications and Quality Assurance Authority of Ireland][1]:

(a) Level 6 Advanced Certificate in Farming;

(b) Level 6 Advanced Certificate in Agriculture;

(c) Level 6 Advanced Certificate in Dairy Herd Management;

(d) Level 6 Advanced Certificate in Drystock Management;

(e) Level 6 Advanced Certificate in Agricultural Mechanisation;

(f) Level 6 Advanced Certificate in Farm Management;

(g) Level 6 Advanced Certificate in Machinery and Crop Management;

(h) Level 6 Advanced Certificate in Horticulture;

(i) Level 6 Advanced Certificate in Forestry;

(j) Level 6 Advanced Certificate in Stud Management;

[(*k*) Level 6 Advanced Certificate in Horsemanship;

(*l*) Level 6 Specific Purpose Certificate in Farm Administration.][2]

2. Qualifications awarded by the [Qualifications and Quality Assurance Authority of Ireland][3]:

(a) Higher Certificate in Agriculture;

(b) Bachelor of Science in Agriculture;

(c) Higher Certificate in Agricultural Science;

(d) Bachelor of Science in Agricultural Science;

(e) Bachelor of Science (Honours) in Land Management, Agriculture;

(f) Bachelor of Science (Honours) in Land Management, Horticulture;

(g) Bachelor of Science (Honours) in Land Management, Forestry;

(h) Higher Certificate in Engineering in Agricultural Mechanisation;

(i) Bachelor of Business in Rural Enterprise and Agri-Business;

(j) Bachelor of Science in Agriculture and Environmental Management;

(k) Bachelor of Science in Horticulture;

(l) Bachelor of Arts (Honours) in Horticultural Management;

(m) Bachelor of Science in Forestry;

(n) Higher Certificate in Business in Equine Studies;

(o) Bachelor of Business in Equine [Studies;][4].

[(p) Higher Certificate in Science Applied Agriculture;

(q) Bachelor of Science (Honours) in Sustainable Agriculture.][5]

3. Qualifications awarded by other third-level institutions:

(a) Bachelor of Agricultural Science — Animal Crop Production awarded by University College Dublin;

[(aa) Bachelor of Agricultural Science — Agri-Environmental Science awarded by University College Dublin;][6]

(b) Bachelor of Agricultural Science — Animal Science awarded by University College Dublin;

[(ba) Bachelor of Agricultural Science – Animal Science Equine awarded by University College Dublin;

(bb) Bachelor of Agricultural Science – Dairy Business awarded by University College Dublin;][7]

(c) Bachelor of Agricultural Science — Food and Agribusiness Management awarded by University College Dublin;

(d) Bachelor of Agricultural Science — Forestry awarded by University College Dublin;

(e) Bachelor of Agricultural Science — Horticulture, Landscape and Sportsturf Management awarded by University College Dublin;

(f) Bachelor of Veterinary Medicine awarded by University College Dublin;

(g) Bachelor of Science in Equine Science awarded by the University of Limerick;

(h) Diploma in Equine Science awarded by the [University of Limerick;][8]][9]

[(i) Bachelor of Science (Honours) in Agriculture awarded by the Dundalk Institute of Technology.][10]

Amendments

[1] Substituted by F(No.2)A13 s69(1)(b)(i). Has effect in respect of qualifications awarded on or after 6 November 2012.

[2] Substituted by FA12 s106.

[3] Substituted by F(No.2)A13 s69(1)(b)(ii). Has effect in respect of qualifications awarded on or after 6 November 2012.

[4] Substituted by F(No.2)A13 s69(1)(b)(iii).

[5] Substituted by FA14 s78.

[6] Inserted by FA10 s(141). Has effect as on and from 3 April 2010.

[7] Inserted by F(No.2)A13 s69(1)(b)(iv).

[8] Substituted by FA15 s62(a). Takes effect from 21 December 2015.

[9] Inserted by FA07 s103(b).

[10] Inserted by FA15 s62(b). Takes effect from 21 December 2015.

Revenue Information Notes

SD2B – Stamp Duty Exemption Transfers of Land to Young Trained Farmers

Cross References

From Schedule 2B

Section 81AA Transfers to young trained farmers.

To Schedule 2B

Section 81AA Transfers to young trained farmers.

SCHEDULE 3

Enactments Repealed or Revoked

Section 160

PART 1

Acts Repealed

Session and Chapter or Year and Number (1)	Short Title (2)	Extent of Repeal (3)
54 & 55 Vict., c.38.	Stamp Duties Management Act, 1891.	The whole Act, in so far as it is unrepealed.
54 & 55 Vict., c.39.	Stamp Act, 1891.	The whole Act, in so far as it is unrepealed.
57 & 58 Vict., c.30.	Finance Act, 1894.	Section 39.
58 Vict., c.16.	Finance Act, 1895.	Section 16 and the Schedule.
60 & 61 Vict., c.24.	Finance Act, 1897.	Section 8.
61 & 62 Vict., c.10.	Finance Act, 1898.	Sections 5 and 6.
61 & 62 Vict., c.46.	Revenue Act, 1898.	Sections 7, 10 and 13.
62 & 63 Vict., c.9.	Finance Act, 1899.	Sections 5, 6 and 14.
63 Vict., c.7.	Finance Act, 1900.	Section 10.
3 Edw. 7, c.46.	Revenue Act, 1903.	Section 9.
9 Edw. 7, c.43.	Revenue Act, 1909.	Sections 7 and 8.
10 Edw. 7, c.8.	Finance (1909-10) Act, 1910.	Sections 4 and 74.
10 & 11 Geo. 5, c.18.	Finance Act, 1920.	Sections 37 and 43.
12 & 13 Geo. 5, c.17.	Finance Act, 1922.	Sections 46 and 47.
No. 27 of 1924.	Finance Act, 1924.	Section 38, in so far as it relates to stamp duties.
No. 35 of 1926.	Finance Act, 1926.	Section 39, in so far as it relates to stamp duties.
No. 5 of 1929.	Finance (Customs and Stamp Duties) Act, 1929.	Section 5.
No. 32 of 1929.	Finance Act, 1929.	Section 36.
No. 31 of 1931.	Finance Act, 1931.	Section 32.
No. 20 of 1932.	Finance Act, 1932.	Section 50.
No. 15 of 1933.	Finance Act, 1933.	Sections 40, 41 and 43.
No. 31 of 1934.	Finance Act, 1934.	Section 34.
No. 7 of 1935.	Finance (Miscellaneous Provisions) Act, 1935.	Section 6 and Part II of the Schedule.
No. 31 of 1936.	Finance Act, 1936.	Section 25.
No. 14 of 1942.	Finance Act, 1942.	Section 21.
No. 16 of 1943.	Finance Act, 1943.	Sections 14 to 16.
No. 13 of 1949.	Finance Act, 1949.	Section 24.
No. 14 of 1952.	Finance Act, 1952.	Section 19.
No. 22 of 1954.	Finance Act, 1954.	Section 23.

Session and Chapter or Year and Number (1)	Short Title (2)	Extent of Repeal (3)
No. 36 of 1954.	Solicitors Act, 1954.	Section 72.
No. 13 of 1955.	Finance Act, 1955.	Section 16.
No. 25 of 1958.	Finance Act, 1958.	Sections 59 and 60.
No. 18 of 1959.	Finance Act, 1959.	Sections 75(4) and 76.
No. 19 of 1960.	Finance Act, 1960.	Section 36.
No. 23 of 1961.	Finance Act, 1961.	Sections 29 and 30.
No. 15 of 1962.	Finance Act, 1962.	Sections 17 and 18.
No. 23 of 1963.	Finance Act, 1963.	Sections 40, 41 and 43.
No. 22 of 1965.	Finance Act, 1965.	Section 31.
No. 17 of 1967.	Finance Act, 1967.	Section 20.
No. 21 of 1969.	Finance Act, 1969.	Sections 49 and 50.
No. 14 of 1970.	Finance Act, 1970.	Sections 40 to 47 and the First Schedule.
No. 23 of 1971.	Finance Act, 1971.	Sections 43 and 44.
No. 19 of 1972.	Finance Act, 1972.	Section 35.
No. 22 of 1972.	Value-Added Tax Act, 1972.	Section 38(4).
No. 19 of 1973.	Finance Act, 1973.	Sections 62 to 75 and section 92(6).
No. 27 of 1974.	Finance Act, 1974.	Sections 81 to 83.
No. 6 of 1975.	Finance Act, 1975.	Sections 48 and 49 and the Fourth Schedule.
No. 16 of 1976.	Finance Act, 1976.	Sections 47 and 48.
No. 18 of 1977.	Finance Act, 1977.	Sections 47 and 48.
No. 21 of 1978.	Finance Act, 1978.	Sections 31 to 35.
No. 11 of 1979.	Finance Act, 1979.	Sections 50 to 53 and section 56.
No. 14 of 1980.	Finance Act, 1980.	Sections 85 to 87.
No. 16 of 1981.	Finance Act, 1981.	Sections 47 to 50.
No. 28 of 1981.	Finance (No. 2) Act, 1981.	Sections 16 and 17.
No. 14 of 1982.	Finance Act, 1982.	Sections 91 to 96 and the Fourth Schedule.
No. 15 of 1983.	Finance Act, 1983.	Sections 90 to 93.
No. 24 of 1983.	Postal and Telecommunications Services Act, 1983.	Section 5(4)(*c*).
No. 9 of 1984.	Finance Act, 1984.	Sections 97 to 103.
No. 10 of 1985.	Finance Act, 1985.	Sections 55 to 57.
No. 13 of 1986.	Finance Act, 1986.	Sections 92 to 99 and section 101.
No. 10 of 1987.	Finance Act, 1987.	Sections 48 and 49.
No. 12 of 1988.	Finance Act, 1988.	Sections 64 and 65.
No. 10 of 1989.	Finance Act, 1989.	Sections 64, 66, 67, 68, 71 and 72.
No. 10 of 1990.	Finance Act, 1990.	Sections 108 to 116, sections 118 and 120 and the Ninth Schedule.
No. 13 of 1991.	Finance Act, 1991.	Sections 88 to 106, sections 108 to 111 and the Fifth Schedule.
No. 9 of 1992.	Finance Act, 1992.	Sections 199 to 211, section 213, sections 215 to 217 and the Seventh Schedule.
No. 28 of 1992.	Finance (No. 2) Act, 1992.	Section 28.

Session and Chapter or Year and Number (1)	Short Title (2)	Extent of Repeal (3)
No. 13 of 1993.	Finance Act, 1993.	Sections 100 to 106.
No. 13 of 1994.	Finance Act, 1994.	Sections 102 to 109, sections 111, 112 and 161(4) and the Sixth Schedule.
No. 8 of 1995.	Finance Act, 1995.	Sections 142 to 150.
No. 9 of 1996.	Finance Act, 1996.	Sections 101 to 111, sections 113 to 119 and the Fourth Schedule.
No. 25 of 1996.	Disclosure of Certain Information for Taxation and Other Purposes Act, 1996.	Section 7.
No. 31 of 1996.	Criminal Assets Bureau Act, 1996.	Section 24(3).
No. 22 of 1997.	Finance Act, 1997.	Sections 115 to 130 and the Eighth Schedule.
No. 3 of 1998.	Finance Act, 1998.	Sections 118 to 125 and Schedule 8.
No. 15 of 1998.	Finance (No. 2) Act, 1998.	Sections 5 to 14 and the Schedule.
No. 2 of 1999.	Finance Act, 1999.	Sections 140 to 197 and Schedules 5 and 6.

PART 2

Statutory Instrument Revoked

Year and Number	Citation	Extent of Revocation
No. 4 of 1923.	Inland Revenue (Adaptation of Taxing Acts) Order, 1923.	Paragraphs 16 and 17.

Cross References

From Schedule 3
Section 160 Repeals.

To Schedule 3
Section 160 Repeals.

SCHEDULE 4

Consequential Amendments

Section 162.

In the enactments specified in *column (1)* of the following Table for the words set out or referred to in *column (2)* there shall be substituted the words set out in the corresponding entry in *column (3)*.

Enactment amended (1)	Words to be replaced (2)	Words to be substituted (3)
Forgery Act, 1913:		
section 8(2)(*b*)	Stamp Duties Management Act, 1891 (as amended by the Finance Act, 1989)	*Part 11* of the *Stamp Duties Consolidation Act, 1999*
section 18(1A)	Stamp Duties Management Act, 1891 (as amended by the Finance Act, 1989)	*Part 11* of the *Stamp Duties Consolidation Act, 1999*
Electricity (Supply) Act, 1927, section 95	section fifty-nine of the Stamp Act, 1891	*section 31* of the *Stamp Duties Consolidation Act, 1999*
Statute of Limitations, 1957, section 60	Stamp Act, 1891	*Stamp Duties Consolidation Act, 1999*
Companies Act, 1963:		
section 58(2)	Stamp Act, 1891	*Stamp Duties Consolidation Act, 1999*
section 58(2)	section 12	*section 20*
Stock Transfer Act, 1963:		
section 4(3)	section 74 of the Finance (1909-10) Act, 1910	*section 30* of the *Stamp Duties Consolidation Act, 1999*
section 4(4)	subsection (4) or (5) of section 58 of the Stamp Act, 1891	*subsection (1)* or *(2)* of *section 46* of the *Stamp Duties Consolidation Act, 1999*
Finance Act, 1980, section 78(6)	Stamp Duties Management Act, 1891	*Part 11* of the *Stamp Duties Consolidation Act, 1999*
Housing Finance Agency Act, 1981, section 16	section 44 of the Finance Act, 1970	*section 86* of the *Stamp Duties Consolidation Act, 1999*
	said section 44	that *section 86*
Postal and Telecommunications Services Act, 1983:		
section 5(4)(*b*)	Stamp Act, 1891	*Stamp Duties Consolidation Act, 1999*
section 69(2)	sections 4, 6, 13 and 16 to 20 of the Stamp Duties Management Act, 1891	*sections 139* to *144* and *147* and *149* of the *Stamp Duties Consolidation Act, 1999*
section 69(3)	section 16 or 17 of the Stamp Duties Management Act, 1891	*section 140* or *141* of the *Stamp Duties Consolidation Act, 1999*
section 69(5)	section 9 of the Stamp Act, 1891	*section 10(5)* of the *Stamp Duties Consolidation Act, 1999*
section 69(8)	section 18(2) of the Stamp Duties Management Act, 1891	*section 142(2)* of the *Stamp Duties Consolidation Act, 1999*
Finance Act, 1989:		
section 48(1)	Stamp Duties Management Act, 1891	*Part 11* of the *Stamp Duties Consolidation Act, 1999*
section 48(3)	Stamp Duties Management Act, 1891	*Part 11* of the *Stamp Duties Consolidation Act, 1999*

Enactment amended (1)	Words to be replaced (2)	Words to be substituted (3)
Building Societies Act, 1989, section 118(2)	sections 67 to 75 of the Finance Act, 1973	*Part 8* of the *Stamp Duties Consolidation Act, 1999*
Trustee Savings Banks Act, 1989, section 64	sections 67 to 75 of the Finance Act, 1973	*Part 8* of the *Stamp Duties Consolidation Act, 1999*
Companies Act, 1990, section 208, paragraph (*c*)	section 68 of the Finance Act, 1973	*section 116* of the *Stamp Duties Consolidation Act, 1999*
	section 69 of the Finance Act, 1973	*section 117* of the *Stamp Duties Consolidation Act, 1999*
Solicitors (Amendment) Act, 1994, section 72(1)	section 24 of the Stamp Duties Management Act, 1891	*section 157* of the *Stamp Duties Consolidation Act, 1999*
Stamp Duty (Particulars to be Delivered) Regulations, 1995 (S.I. No. 144 of 1995)	section 107 of the Finance Act, 1994 (No. 13 of 1994)	*section 12* of the *Stamp Duties Consolidation Act, 1999*
Taxes Consolidation Act, 1997:		
section 487(1)(*a*) in paragraph (iii)(II) of the definition of "*accounting profit*"	section 94 of the Finance Act, 1986	*section 126* of the *Stamp Duties Consolidation Act, 1999*
section 905(2)(*c*)(iii)	section 16 of the Stamp Act, 1891	*section 128* of the *Stamp Duties Consolidation Act, 1999*
section 1002(1)(*a*), in the definition of "*the Acts*"	Stamp Act, 1891	*Stamp Duties Consolidation Act, 1999*
section 1089(1)	section 15 of the Stamp Act, 1891, and subsections (2) and (3) of section 69 of the Finance Act, 1973	*section 14* and *subsections (3)* and *(4)* of *section 117* of the *Stamp Duties Consolidation Act, 1999*

Cross References

From Schedule 4

Section 10 Adhesive stamps.
Section 12 Particulars delivered stamps.
Section 14 Penalty on stamping instruments after execution.
Section 20 Assessment of duty by the Commissioners.
Section 30 Voluntary dispositions inter vivos chargeable as conveyances or transfers on sale.
Section 31 Certain contracts to be chargeable as conveyances on sale.
Section 46 Directions as to sub-sales.
Section 86 Certain loan stock.
Section 114 Interpretation (Part 8).
Section 116 Charge of stamp duty.
Section 117 Statement to be charged with stamp duty.
Section 126 Certain statements of interest.
Section 128 Rolls, books, etc., to be open to inspection.
Section 135 Interpretation (Part 11).
Section 139 Certain offences in relation to dies and stamps provided by the Commissioners to be offences.
Section 140 Proceedings for detection of forged dies, etc.
Section 141 Proceedings for detection of stamps stolen or obtained fraudulently.
Section 142 Licensed person in possession of forged stamps to be presumed guilty until contrary is shown.
Section 144 Defacement of adhesive stamps.
Section 147 Penalty for unauthorised dealing in stamps, etc.
Section 149 Penalty for hawking stamps.
Section 157 Declarations, affidavits and oaths, how to be made.
Section 162 Consequential amendments to other enactments.

To Schedule 4

Section 162 Consequential amendments to other enactments.

TABLE OF CASES

Stamp Duties Consolidation Act, 1999

All references to sections or schedules in Stamp Duties Consolidation Act, 1999

ABBREVIATIONS

AC = Law Reports Appeal Cases
ALL ER = All England Law Reports
CH = Chancery
ITR = Irish Tax Reports
IR = Irish Reports
KB = King's Bench
QB = Queen's Bench
STC = Simon's Tax Cases

Case	Case Reference	Section
Baytrust Holdings Ltd v IRC	1971 3 All ER 76	s80
Brooklands Selangor Holdings Ltd v IRC	1970 1 All ER 76	s79
Byrne v Revenue Commissioners	1935 IR 644	s152
Canada Safeway Ltd v IRC	1972 1 All ER 666	s79
Central and District Properties Ltd v IRC	1996 2 All ER 433	s79
Cherry Court v Revenue Commissioners	1995 V ITR 180	s1
Corey v IRC	1965 2 All ER 45	s31
Crane Fruehauf Ltd v IRC	1975 STC 51	s80
E. Gomme Ltd v IRC	1964 3 All ER 497	s80
Faber v IRC	1936 1 All ER 617	s2
Fitch Lovell Ltd v IRC	1962 3 All ER 685	s1
Fleetwood-Hesketh v IRC	1936 1 KB 351	s1
IRC v Maples	1908 AC 22	s2
IT Comrs v Pemsel	1891 AC 531	s82
Littlewoods Mail Order Stores Ltd v IRC	1961 Ch 210, 1961 1 All ER 195, 1961 2 WLR 25, 1961 TR 321	s1
National Westminster Bank plc v IRC	1994 3 All ER 1	s79
Patrick W Keane & Co v The Revenue Commissioners	2008 ITR 57	s80
Re Deane (Deceased)	1936 IR 556	s2
Re Ferguson (Deceased)	1935 IR 21	s2

Case	Case Reference	Section
Revenue Commissioners v Glenkerrin Homes Ltd	2007 ITR 119	s1
Sun Alliance Insurance Ltd v IRC	1972 Ch 133	s127
Terence Byrne v The Revenue Commissioners	1934 V ITR 560	s152
Viek Investments Ltd v Revenue Commissioners	1991 IV ITR 367	s1
Waterford Glass (Group Services) Ltd v Revenue Commissioners	1989 IV ITR 187	s1
Western Abyssinian Mining Syndicate Ltd v IRC	1935 14 ATC 286	s1
Wimpey (George) & Co Ltd v IRC	1974 2 All ER 602	s1

SUBJECT INDEX

Stamp Duties Consolidation Act 1999

D

E

F

N

O

S

T